STRANGERS IN PARADISE

POCKET BOOK COLLECTION

art and story by

TERRY MOORE

3

publisher • Robyn Moore
colorist • Brian Miller

Visit the Strangers In Paradise website at
www.strangersinparadise.com

Published by
Abstract Studio, Inc.
P. O. Box 271487
Houston, TX 77277

ISBN: 1-892597-30-6

This book collects the complete works of Strangers in Paradise
Volume III, issues #18 – #24, #26 – #32, #34 – #38

Printed in Canada

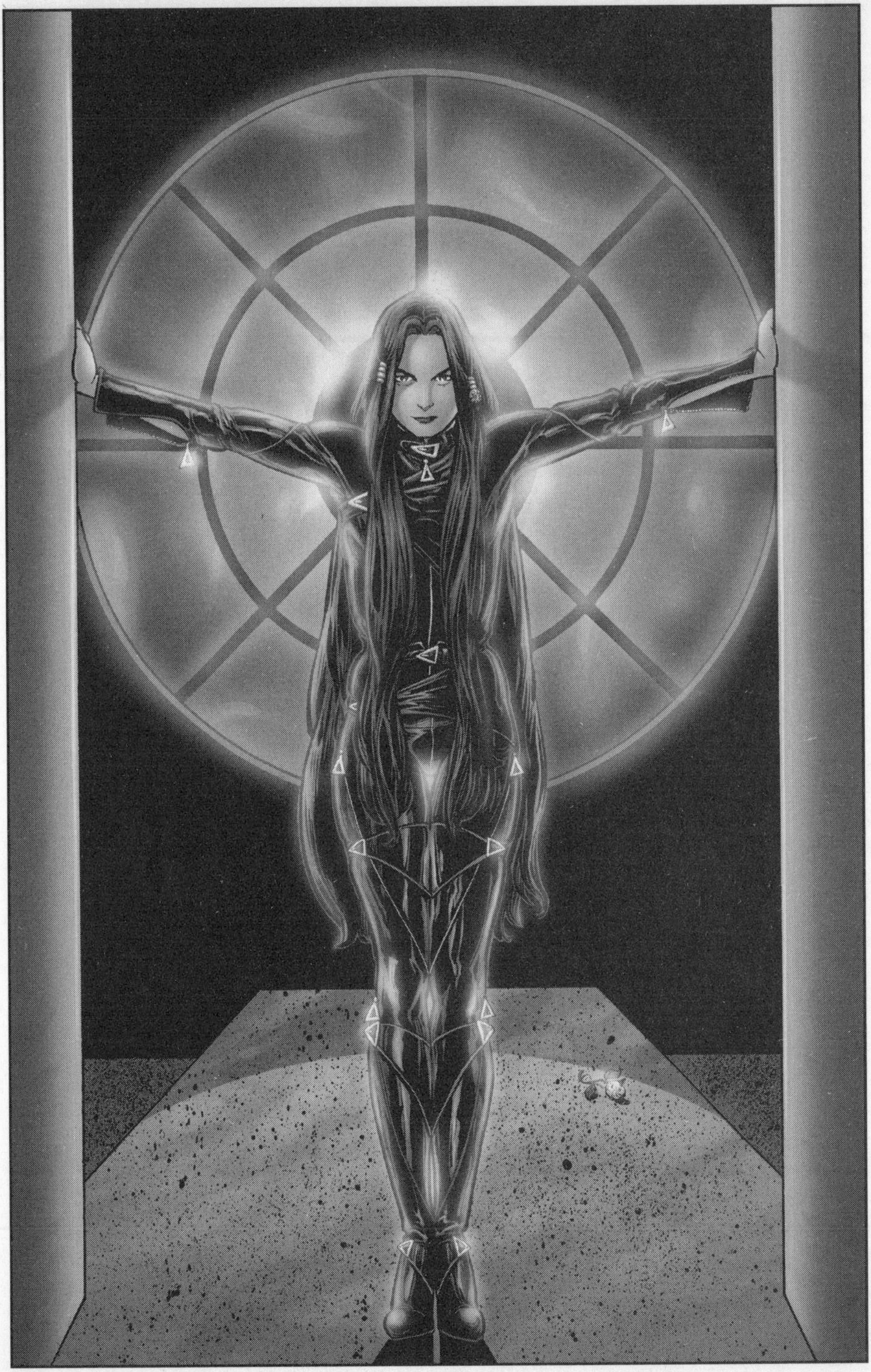

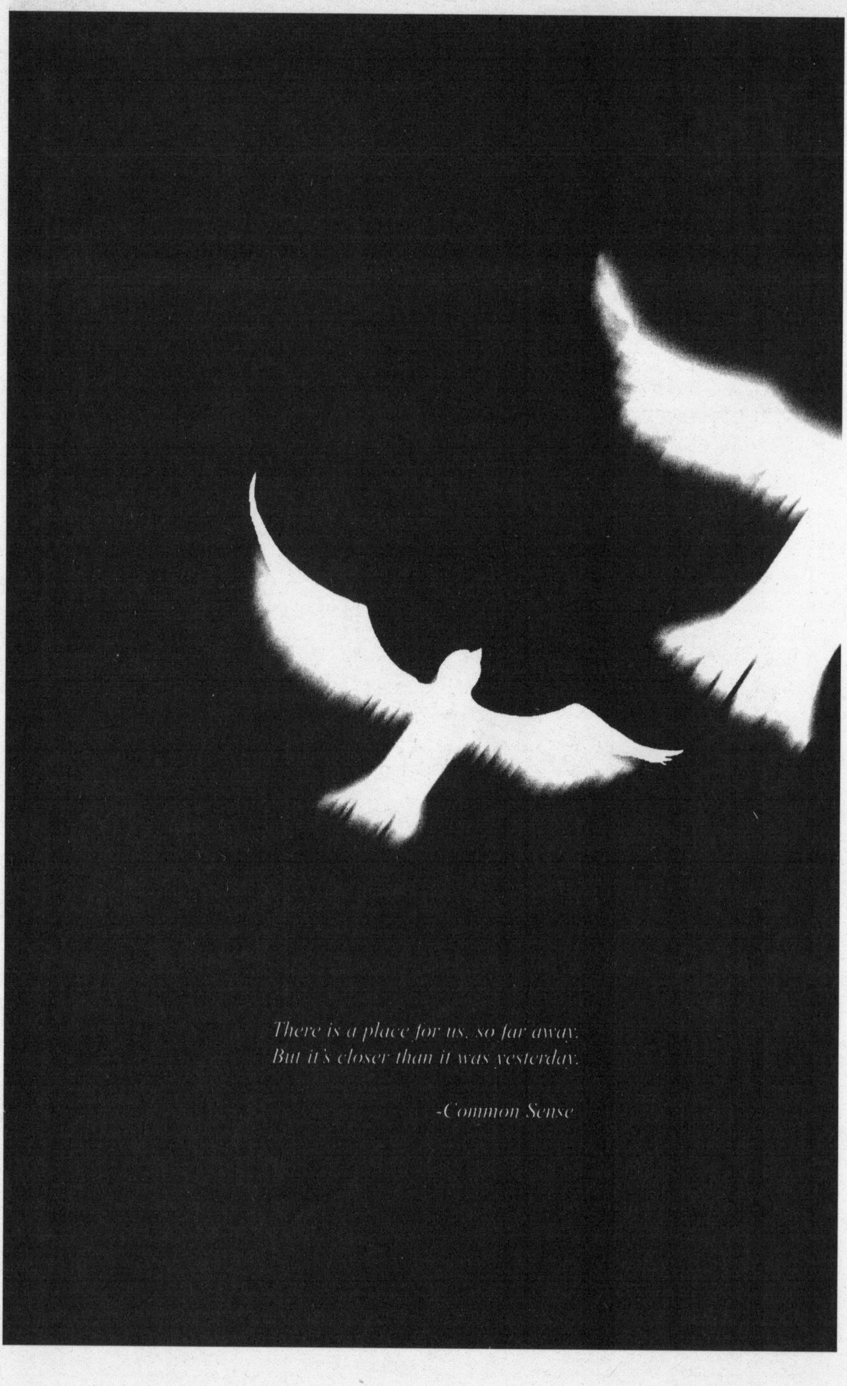
There is a place for us, so far away.
But it's closer than it was yesterday.
-Common Sense

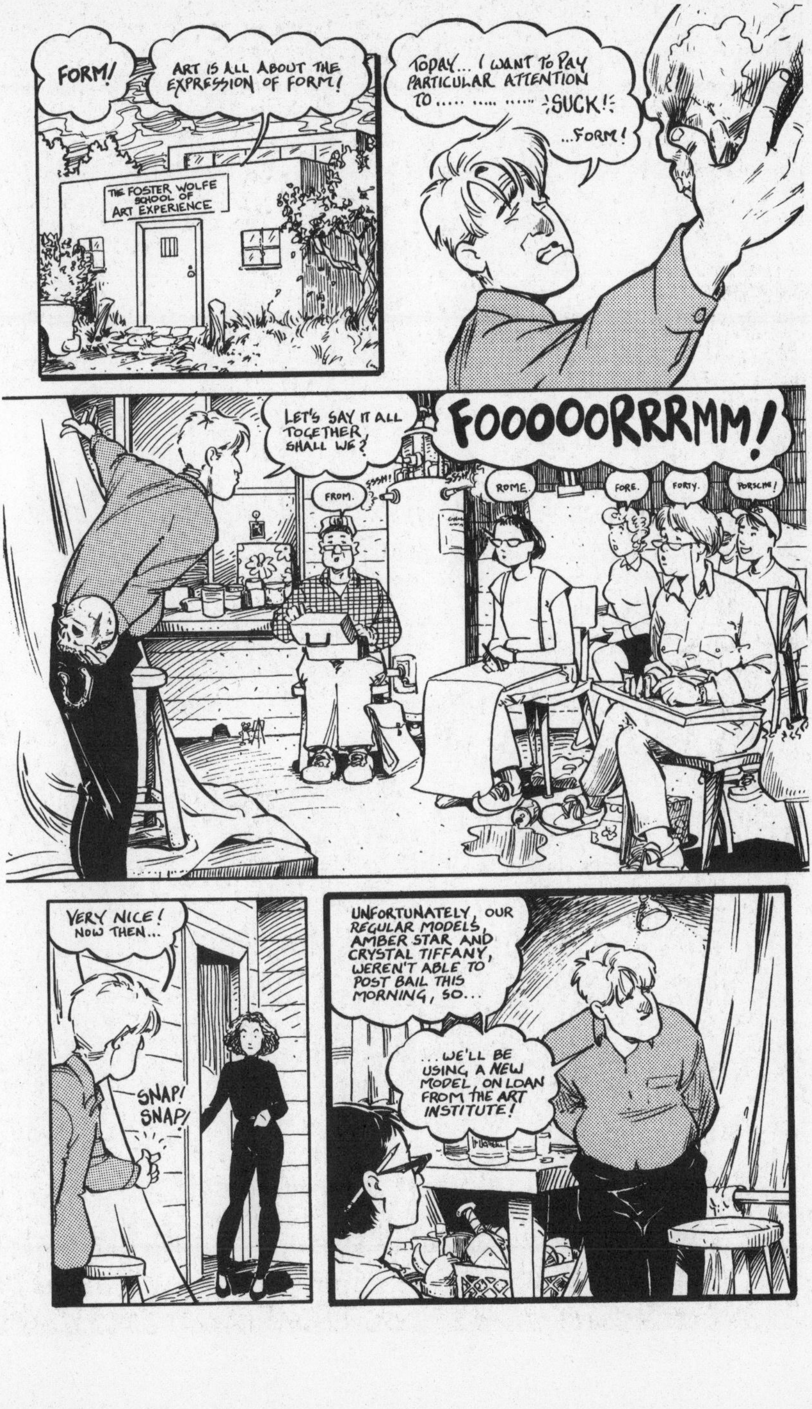
FORM!
ART IS ALL ABOUT THE EXPRESSION OF FORM!
THE FOSTER WOLFE SCHOOL OF ART EXPERIENCE
TODAY... I WANT TO PAY PARTICULAR ATTENTION TO..... .... SUCK!
...FORM!
LET'S SAY IT ALL TOGETHER, SHALL WE?
FOOOOORRRMM!
FROM.
SSSH!
SSSH!
ROME.
FORE.
FORTY.
PORSCHE!
VERY NICE! NOW THEN...
SNAP! SNAP!
UNFORTUNATELY, OUR REGULAR MODELS, AMBER STAR AND CRYSTAL TIFFANY, WEREN'T ABLE TO POST BAIL THIS MORNING, SO...
...WE'LL BE USING A NEW MODEL, ON LOAN FROM THE ART INSTITUTE!

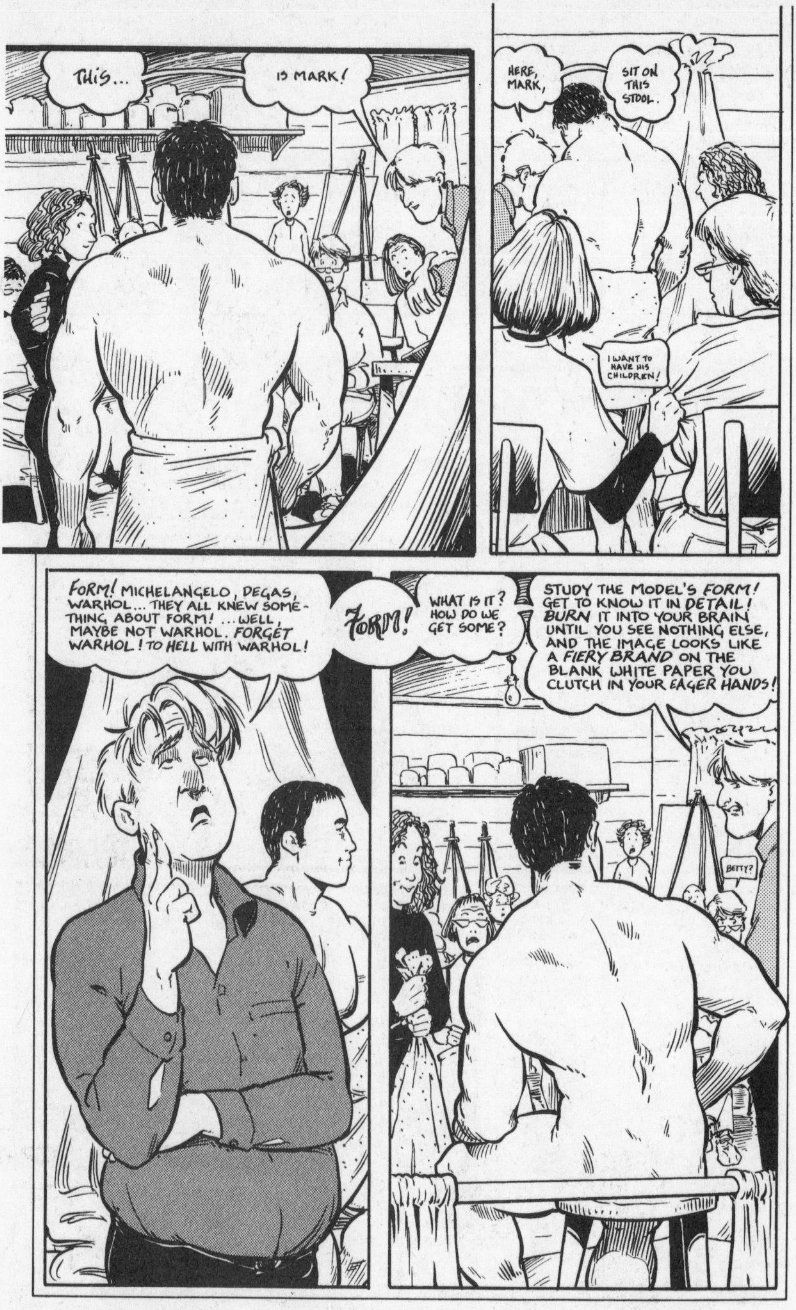
THIS...
IS MARK!
HERE, MARK,
SIT ON THIS STOOL.
I WANT TO HAVE HIS CHILDREN!
FORM! MICHELANGELO, DEGAS, WARHOL... THEY ALL KNEW SOMETHING ABOUT FORM! ...WELL, MAYBE NOT WARHOL. FORGET WARHOL! TO HELL WITH WARHOL!
FORM!
WHAT IS IT? HOW DO WE GET SOME?
STUDY THE MODEL'S FORM! GET TO KNOW IT IN DETAIL! BURN IT INTO YOUR BRAIN UNTIL YOU SEE NOTHING ELSE, AND THE IMAGE LOOKS LIKE A FIERY BRAND ON THE BLANK WHITE PAPER YOU CLUTCH IN YOUR EAGER HANDS!
BETTY?

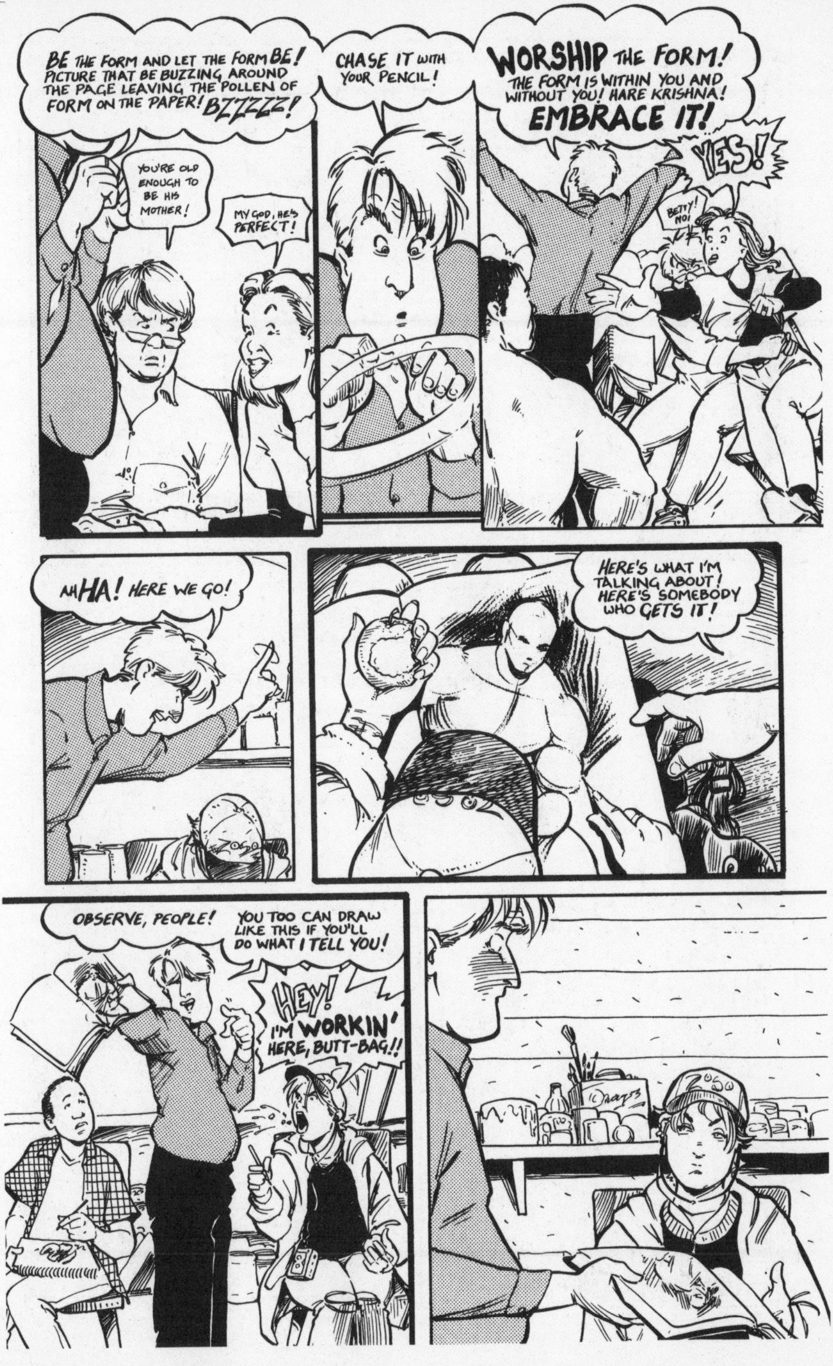
BE THE FORM AND LET THE FORM BE! PICTURE THAT BE BUZZING AROUND THE PAGE LEAVING THE POLLEN OF FORM ON THE PAPER! BZZZZZ!
YOU'RE OLD ENOUGH TO BE HIS MOTHER!
MY GOD, HE'S PERFECT!
CHASE IT WITH YOUR PENCIL!
WORSHIP THE FORM! THE FORM IS WITHIN YOU AND WITHOUT YOU! HARE KRISHNA! EMBRACE IT!
YES!
BETTY! NO!
AHHA! HERE WE GO!
HERE'S WHAT I'M TALKING ABOUT! HERE'S SOMEBODY WHO GETS IT!
OBSERVE, PEOPLE!
YOU TOO CAN DRAW LIKE THIS IF YOU'LL DO WHAT I TELL YOU!
HEY! I'M WORKIN' HERE, BUTT-BAG!!

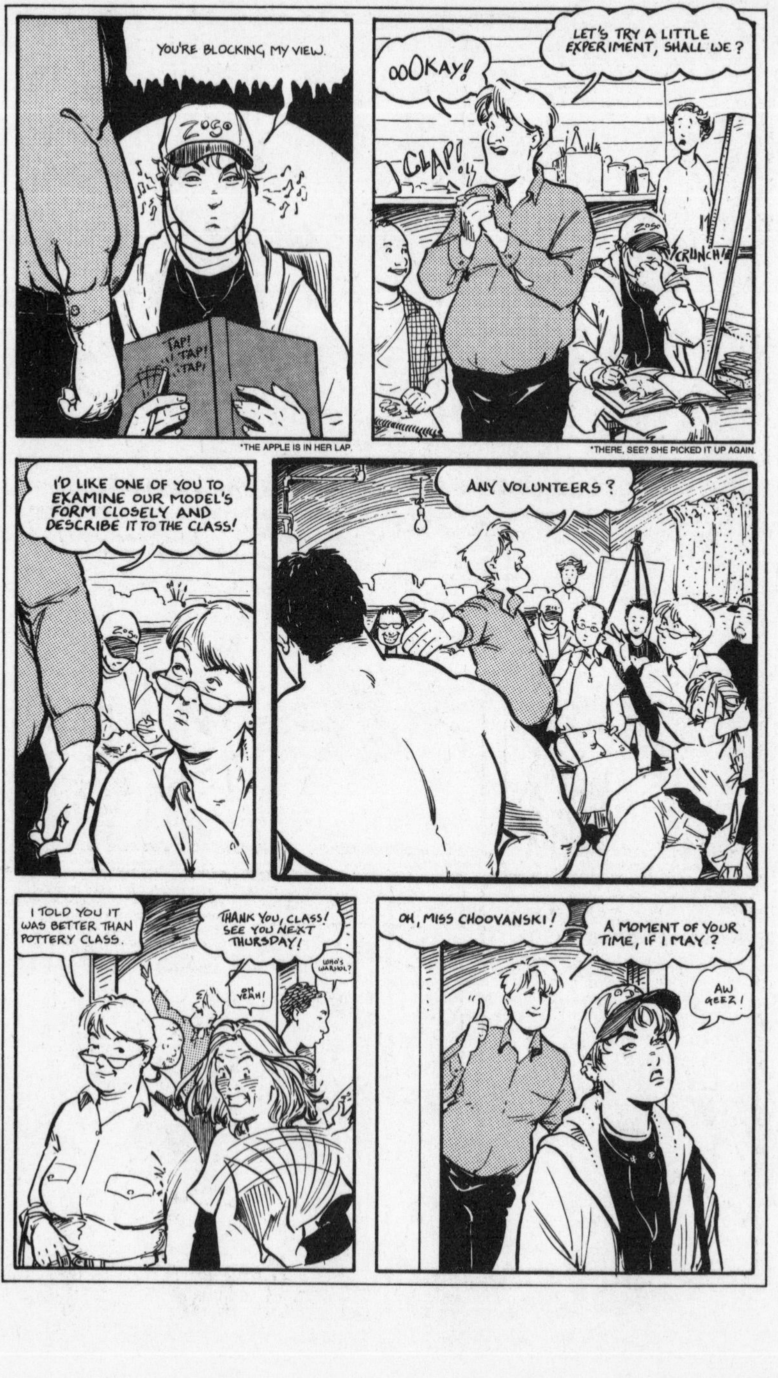

YOU'RE BLOCKING MY VIEW.
TAP! TAP! TAP!
*THE APPLE IS IN HER LAP.
LET'S TRY A LITTLE EXPERIMENT, SHALL WE?
OOOKAY!
CLAP!
CRUNCH!
*THERE, SEE? SHE PICKED IT UP AGAIN.
I'D LIKE ONE OF YOU TO EXAMINE OUR MODEL'S FORM CLOSELY AND DESCRIBE IT TO THE CLASS!
ANY VOLUNTEERS?
I TOLD YOU IT WAS BETTER THAN POTTERY CLASS.
THANK YOU, CLASS! SEE YOU NEXT THURSDAY!
OH YEAH!
WHO'S WARHOL?
OH, MISS CHOOVANSKI!
A MOMENT OF YOUR TIME, IF I MAY?
AW GEEZ!

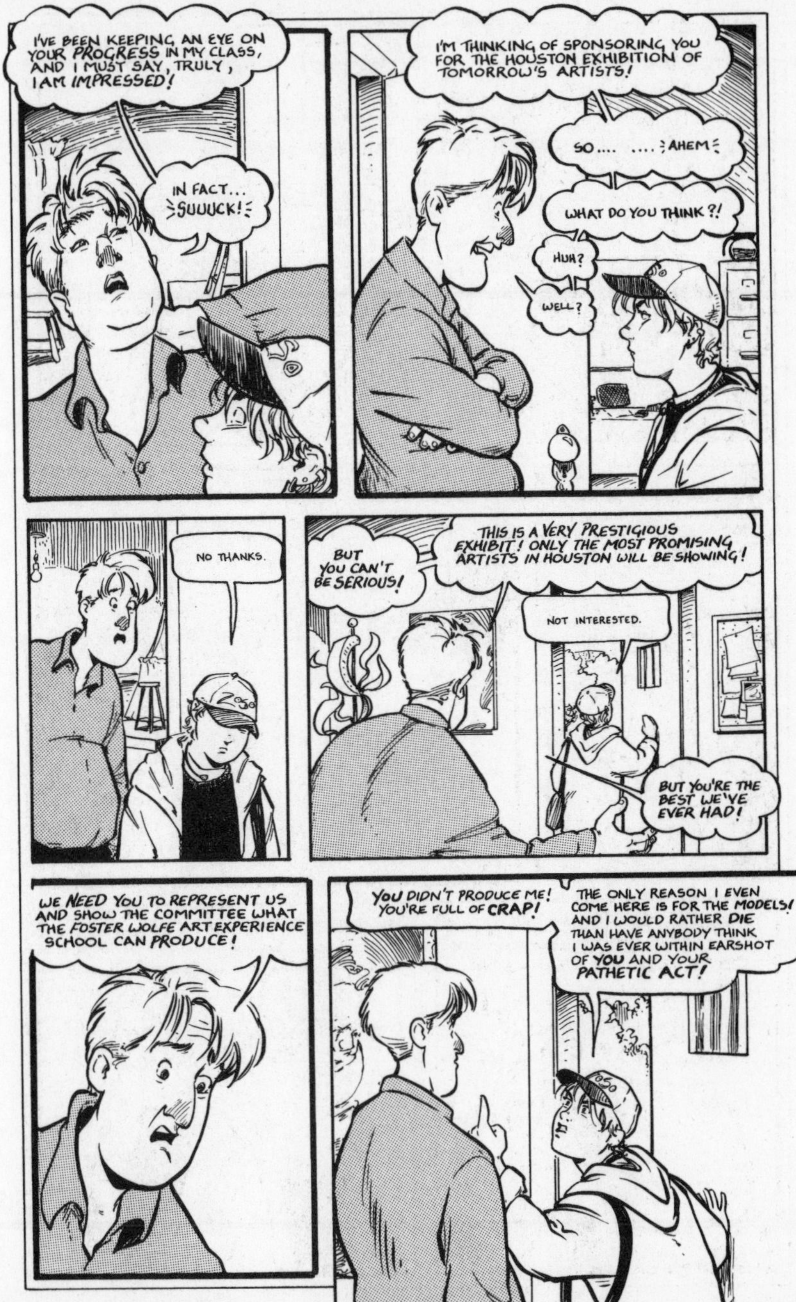
I'VE BEEN KEEPING AN EYE ON YOUR PROGRESS IN MY CLASS, AND I MUST SAY, TRULY, I AM IMPRESSED!
IN FACT... SUUUCK!
I'M THINKING OF SPONSORING YOU FOR THE HOUSTON EXHIBITION OF TOMORROW'S ARTISTS!
SO.... ....AHEM
WHAT DO YOU THINK?!
HUH?
WELL?
NO THANKS.
BUT YOU CAN'T BE SERIOUS!
THIS IS A VERY PRESTIGIOUS EXHIBIT! ONLY THE MOST PROMISING ARTISTS IN HOUSTON WILL BE SHOWING!
NOT INTERESTED.
BUT YOU'RE THE BEST WE'VE EVER HAD!
WE NEED YOU TO REPRESENT US AND SHOW THE COMMITTEE WHAT THE FOSTER WOLFE ART EXPERIENCE SCHOOL CAN PRODUCE!
YOU DIDN'T PRODUCE ME! YOU'RE FULL OF CRAP!
THE ONLY REASON I EVEN COME HERE IS FOR THE MODELS! AND I WOULD RATHER DIE THAN HAVE ANYBODY THINK I WAS EVER WITHIN EARSHOT OF YOU AND YOUR PATHETIC ACT!

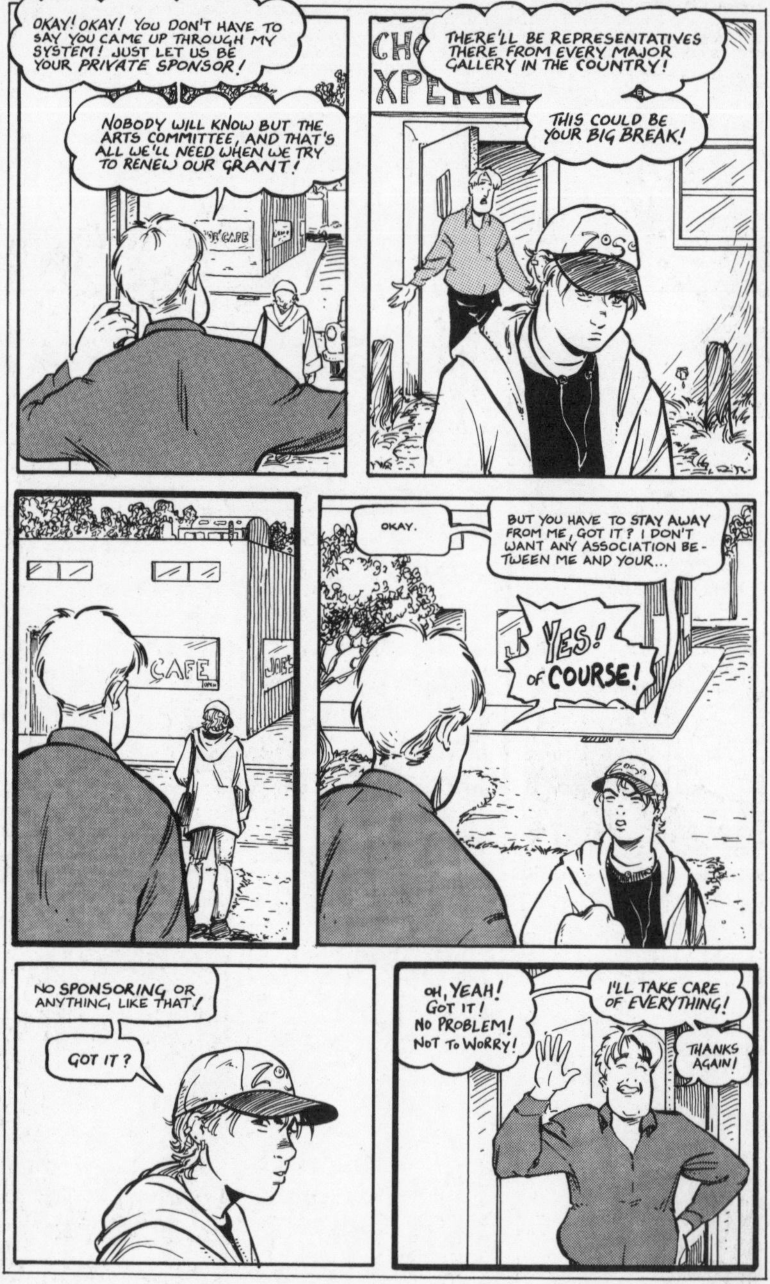
OKAY! OKAY! YOU DON'T HAVE TO SAY YOU CAME UP THROUGH MY SYSTEM! JUST LET US BE YOUR PRIVATE SPONSOR!
NOBODY WILL KNOW BUT THE ARTS COMMITTEE, AND THAT'S ALL WE'LL NEED WHEN WE TRY TO RENEW OUR GRANT!
THERE'LL BE REPRESENTATIVES THERE FROM EVERY MAJOR GALLERY IN THE COUNTRY!
THIS COULD BE YOUR BIG BREAK!
OKAY.
BUT YOU HAVE TO STAY AWAY FROM ME, GOT IT? I DON'T WANT ANY ASSOCIATION BE-TWEEN ME AND YOUR...
YES! OF COURSE!
NO SPONSORING OR ANYTHING LIKE THAT!
GOT IT?
OH, YEAH! GOT IT! NO PROBLEM! NOT TO WORRY!
I'LL TAKE CARE OF EVERYTHING!
THANKS AGAIN!

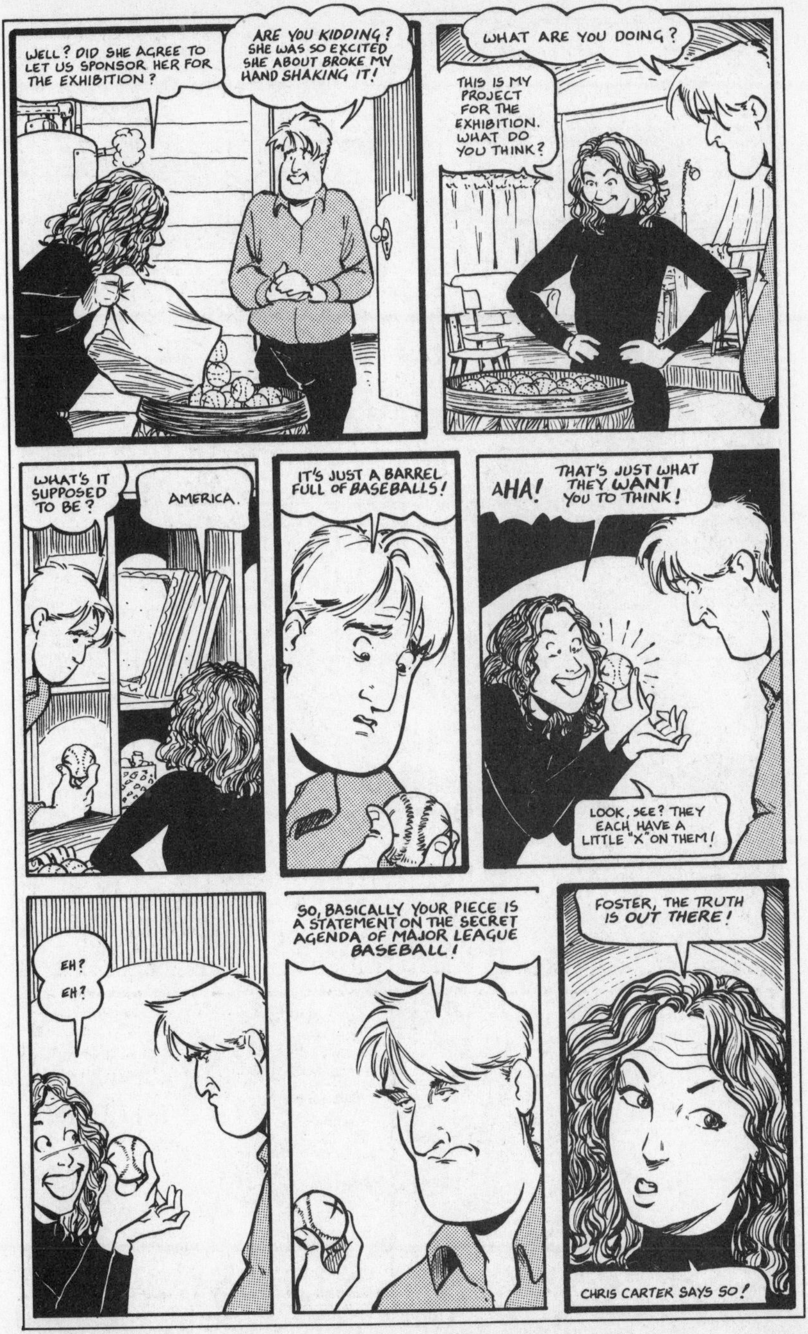
WELL? DID SHE AGREE TO LET US SPONSOR HER FOR THE EXHIBITION?
ARE YOU KIDDING? SHE WAS SO EXCITED SHE ABOUT BROKE MY HAND SHAKING IT!
WHAT ARE YOU DOING?
THIS IS MY PROJECT FOR THE EXHIBITION. WHAT DO YOU THINK?
WHAT'S IT SUPPOSED TO BE?
AMERICA.
IT'S JUST A BARREL FULL OF BASEBALLS!
AHA!
THAT'S JUST WHAT THEY WANT YOU TO THINK!
LOOK, SEE? THEY EACH HAVE A LITTLE "X" ON THEM!
EH?
EH?
SO, BASICALLY YOUR PIECE IS A STATEMENT ON THE SECRET AGENDA OF MAJOR LEAGUE BASEBALL!
FOSTER, THE TRUTH IS OUT THERE!
CHRIS CARTER SAYS SO!

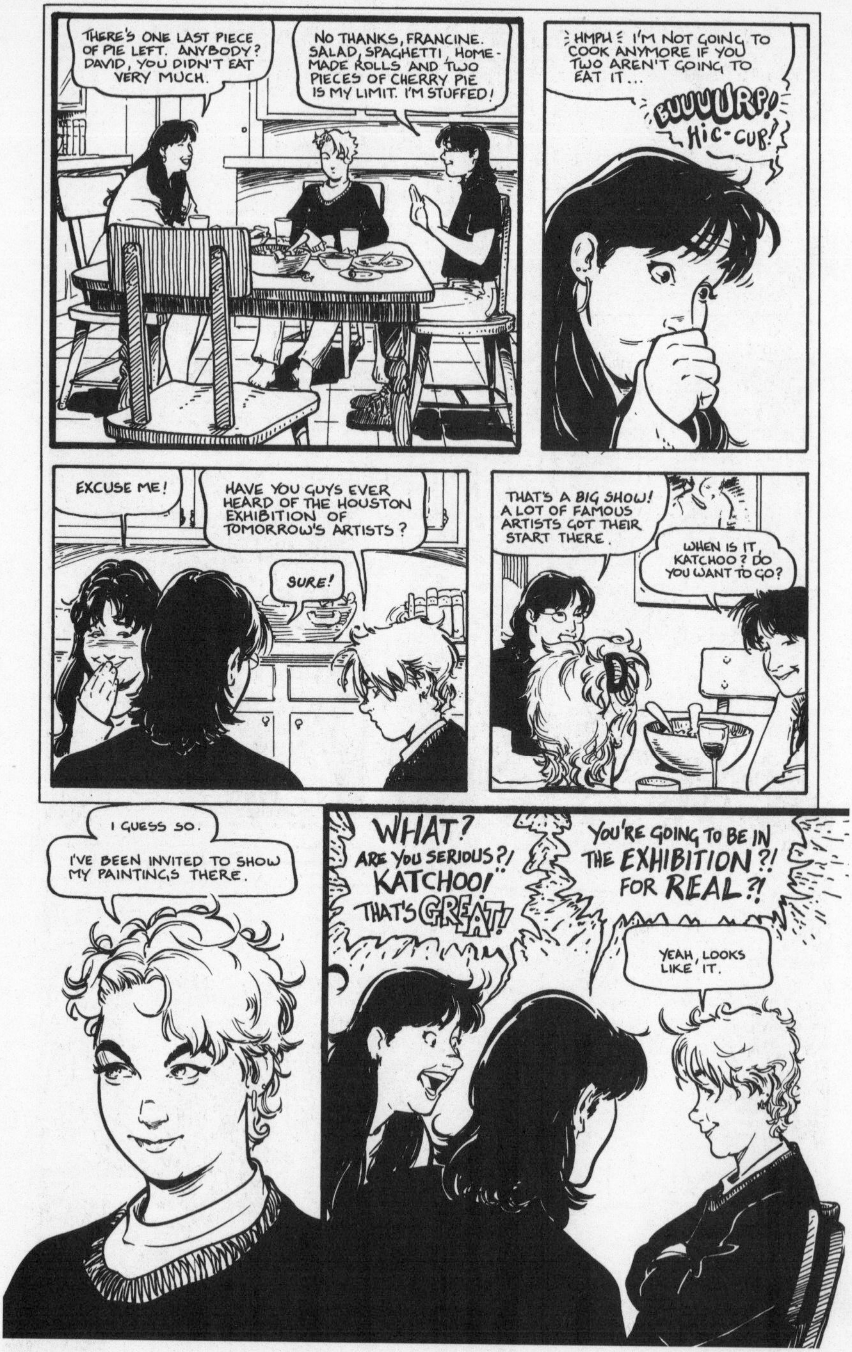
THERE'S ONE LAST PIECE OF PIE LEFT. ANYBODY? DAVID, YOU DIDN'T EAT VERY MUCH.
NO THANKS, FRANCINE. SALAD, SPAGHETTI, HOME-MADE ROLLS AND TWO PIECES OF CHERRY PIE IS MY LIMIT. I'M STUFFED!
HMPH I'M NOT GOING TO COOK ANYMORE IF YOU TWO AREN'T GOING TO EAT IT...
BUUUURP!
HIC-CUP!
EXCUSE ME!
HAVE YOU GUYS EVER HEARD OF THE HOUSTON EXHIBITION OF TOMORROW'S ARTISTS?
SURE!
THAT'S A BIG SHOW! A LOT OF FAMOUS ARTISTS GOT THEIR START THERE.
WHEN IS IT, KATCHOO? DO YOU WANT TO GO?
I GUESS SO.
I'VE BEEN INVITED TO SHOW MY PAINTINGS THERE.
WHAT? ARE YOU SERIOUS?! KATCHOO! THAT'S GREAT!
YOU'RE GOING TO BE IN THE EXHIBITION?! FOR REAL?!
YEAH, LOOKS LIKE IT.

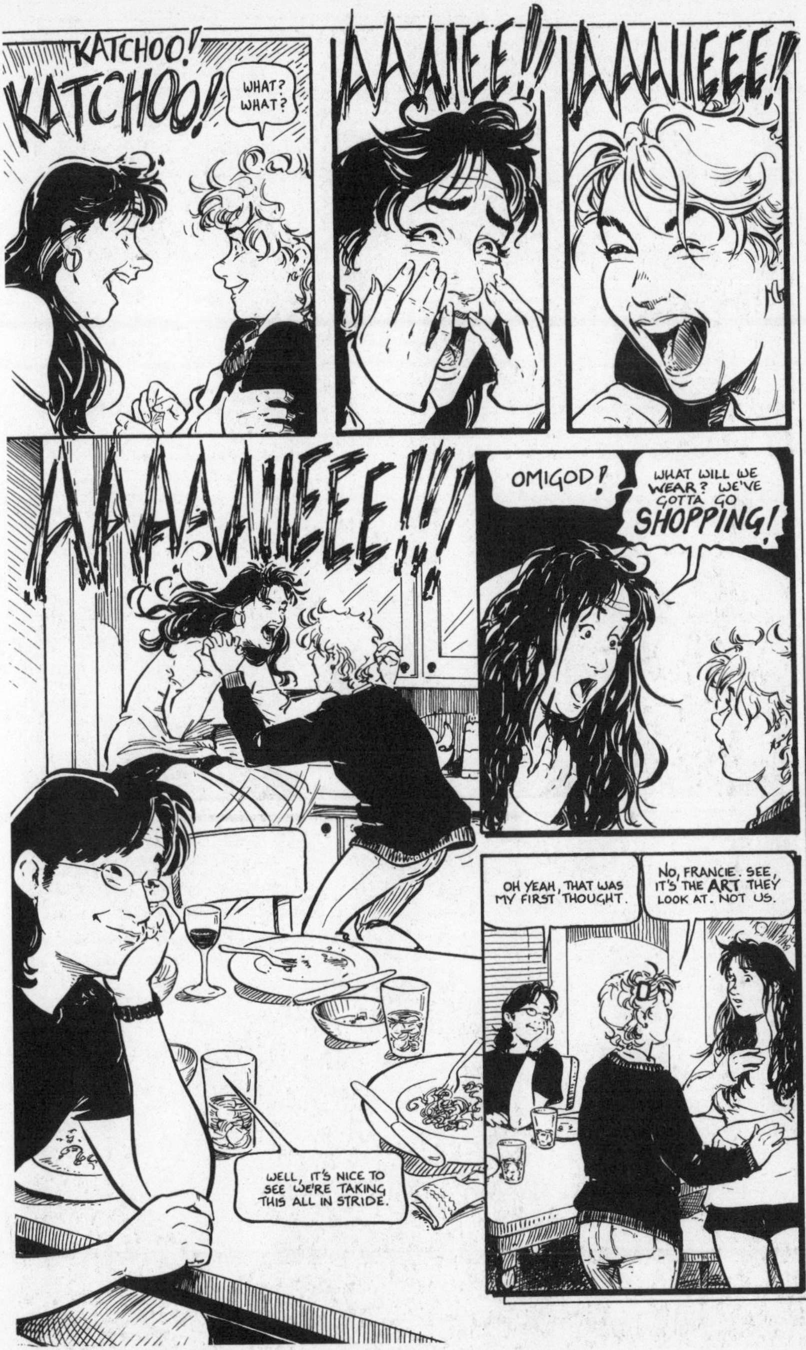
KATCHOO!
KATCHOO!
WHAT? WHAT?
AAAIEE!!
AAAIIEEE!
AAAAAIIEEE!!!
OMIGOD!
WHAT WILL WE WEAR? WE'VE GOTTA GO SHOPPING!
WELL, IT'S NICE TO SEE WE'RE TAKING THIS ALL IN STRIDE.
OH YEAH, THAT WAS MY FIRST THOUGHT.
NO, FRANCIE. SEE, IT'S THE ART THEY LOOK AT. NOT US.

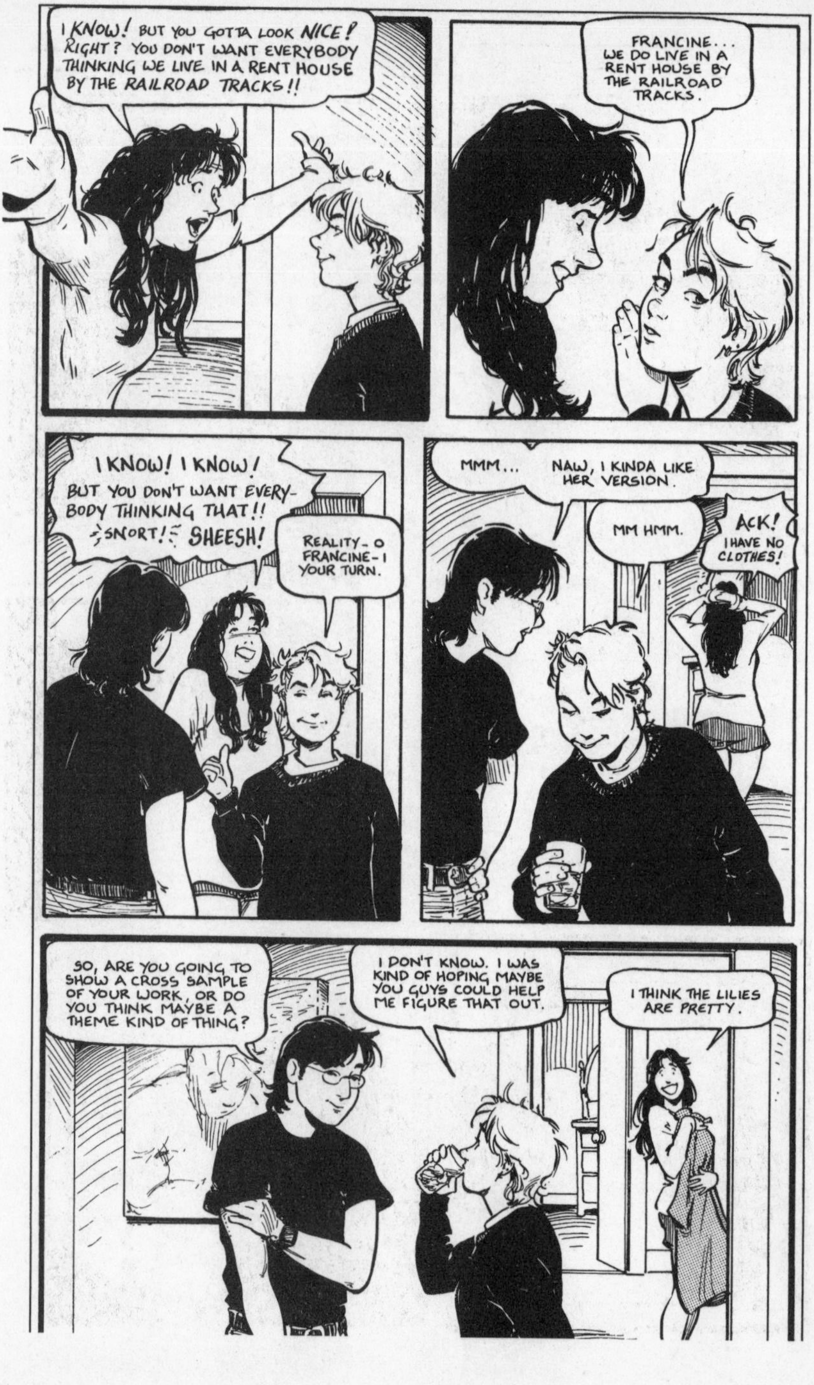
I KNOW! BUT YOU GOTTA LOOK NICE! RIGHT? YOU DON'T WANT EVERYBODY THINKING WE LIVE IN A RENT HOUSE BY THE RAILROAD TRACKS!!
FRANCINE... WE DO LIVE IN A RENT HOUSE BY THE RAILROAD TRACKS.
I KNOW! I KNOW! BUT YOU DON'T WANT EVERYBODY THINKING THAT!! SNORT! SHEESH!
REALITY-O FRANCINE-I YOUR TURN.
MMM...
NAW, I KINDA LIKE HER VERSION.
MM HMM.
ACK! I HAVE NO CLOTHES!
SO, ARE YOU GOING TO SHOW A CROSS SAMPLE OF YOUR WORK, OR DO YOU THINK MAYBE A THEME KIND OF THING?
I DON'T KNOW. I WAS KIND OF HOPING MAYBE YOU GUYS COULD HELP ME FIGURE THAT OUT.
I THINK THE LILIES ARE PRETTY.

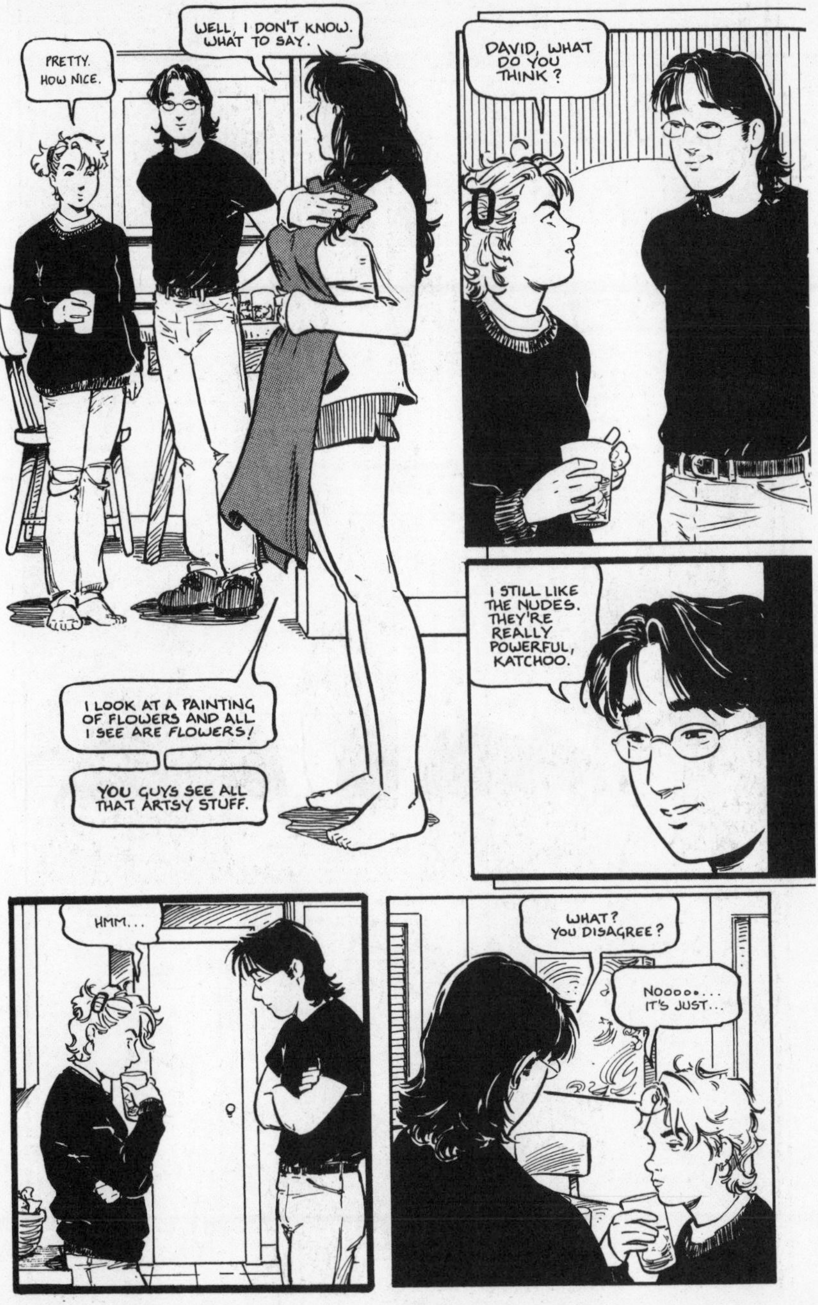
PRETTY. HOW NICE.
WELL, I DON'T KNOW. WHAT TO SAY.
I LOOK AT A PAINTING OF FLOWERS AND ALL I SEE ARE FLOWERS!
YOU GUYS SEE ALL THAT ARTSY STUFF.
DAVID, WHAT DO YOU THINK?
I STILL LIKE THE NUDES. THEY'RE REALLY POWERFUL, KATCHOO.
HMM...
WHAT? YOU DISAGREE?
Noooo.... IT'S JUST...

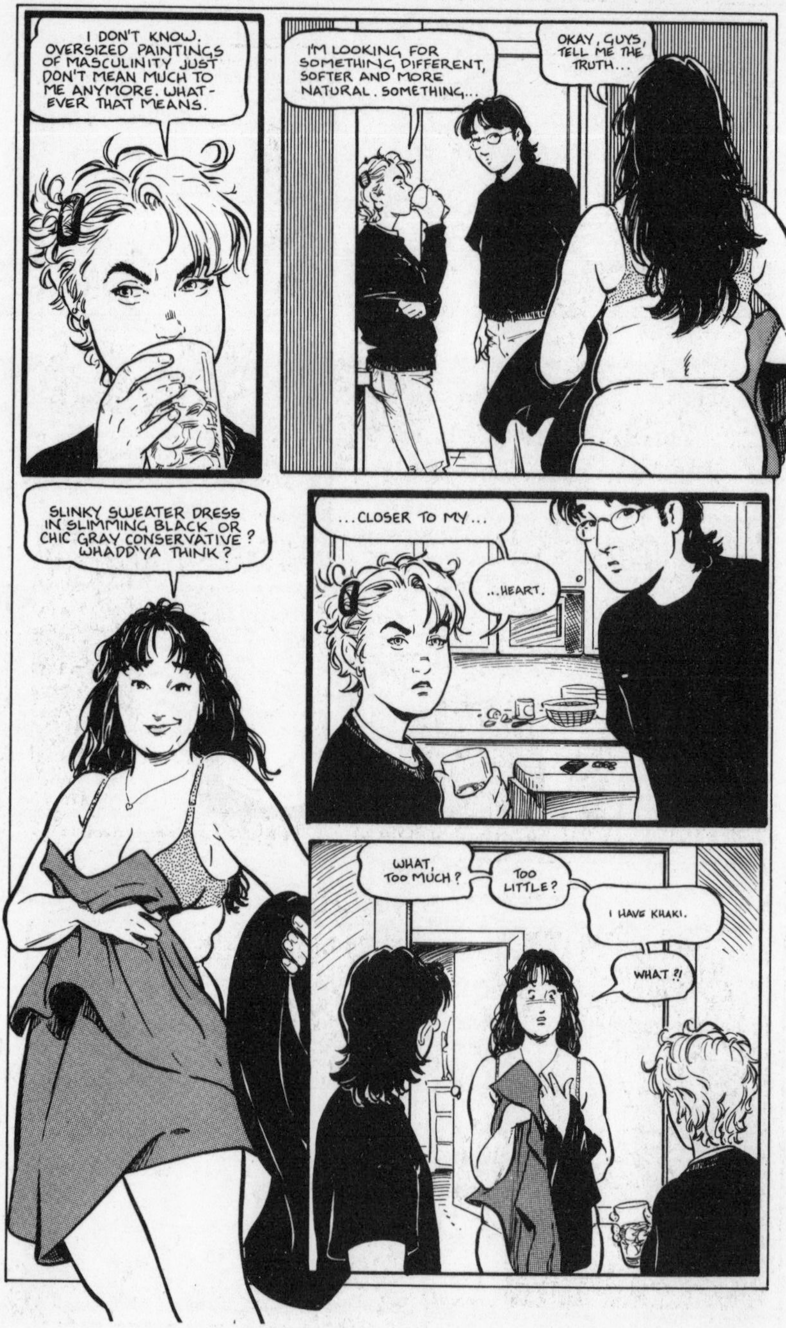
I DON'T KNOW. OVERSIZED PAINTINGS OF MASCULINITY JUST DON'T MEAN MUCH TO ME ANYMORE. WHAT-EVER THAT MEANS.
I'M LOOKING FOR SOMETHING DIFFERENT, SOFTER AND MORE NATURAL. SOMETHING...
OKAY, GUYS, TELL ME THE TRUTH...
SLINKY SWEATER DRESS IN SLIMMING BLACK OR CHIC GRAY CONSERVATIVE? WHADD'YA THINK?
...CLOSER TO MY...
...HEART.
WHAT, TOO MUCH?
TOO LITTLE?
I HAVE KHAKI.
WHAT?!

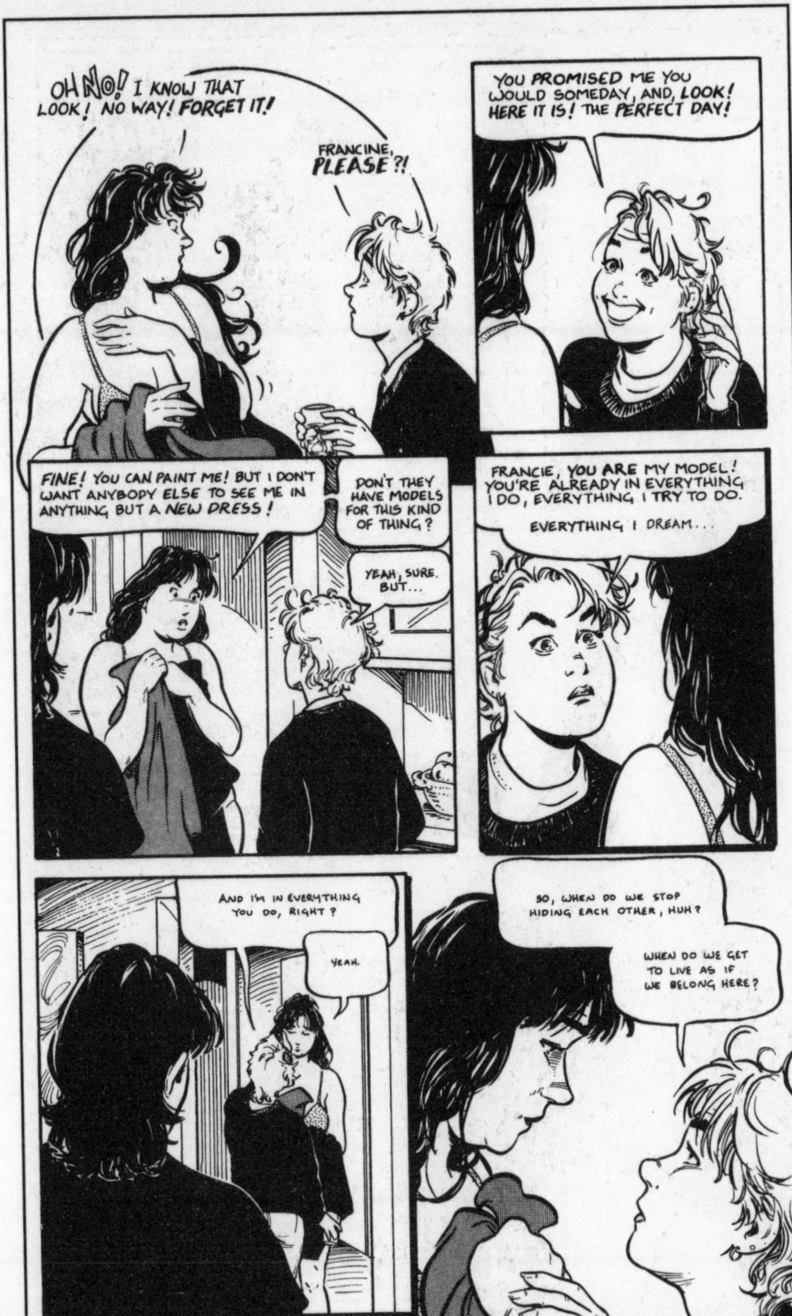
OH NO! I KNOW THAT LOOK! NO WAY! FORGET IT!
FRANCINE, PLEASE?!
YOU PROMISED ME YOU WOULD SOMEDAY, AND, LOOK! HERE IT IS! THE PERFECT DAY!
FINE! YOU CAN PAINT ME! BUT I DON'T WANT ANYBODY ELSE TO SEE ME IN ANYTHING BUT A NEW DRESS!
DON'T THEY HAVE MODELS FOR THIS KIND OF THING?
YEAH, SURE. BUT...
FRANCIE, YOU ARE MY MODEL! YOU'RE ALREADY IN EVERYTHING I DO, EVERYTHING I TRY TO DO.
EVERYTHING I DREAM...
AND I'M IN EVERYTHING YOU DO, RIGHT?
YEAH.
SO, WHEN DO WE STOP HIDING EACH OTHER, HUH?
WHEN DO WE GET TO LIVE AS IF WE BELONG HERE?

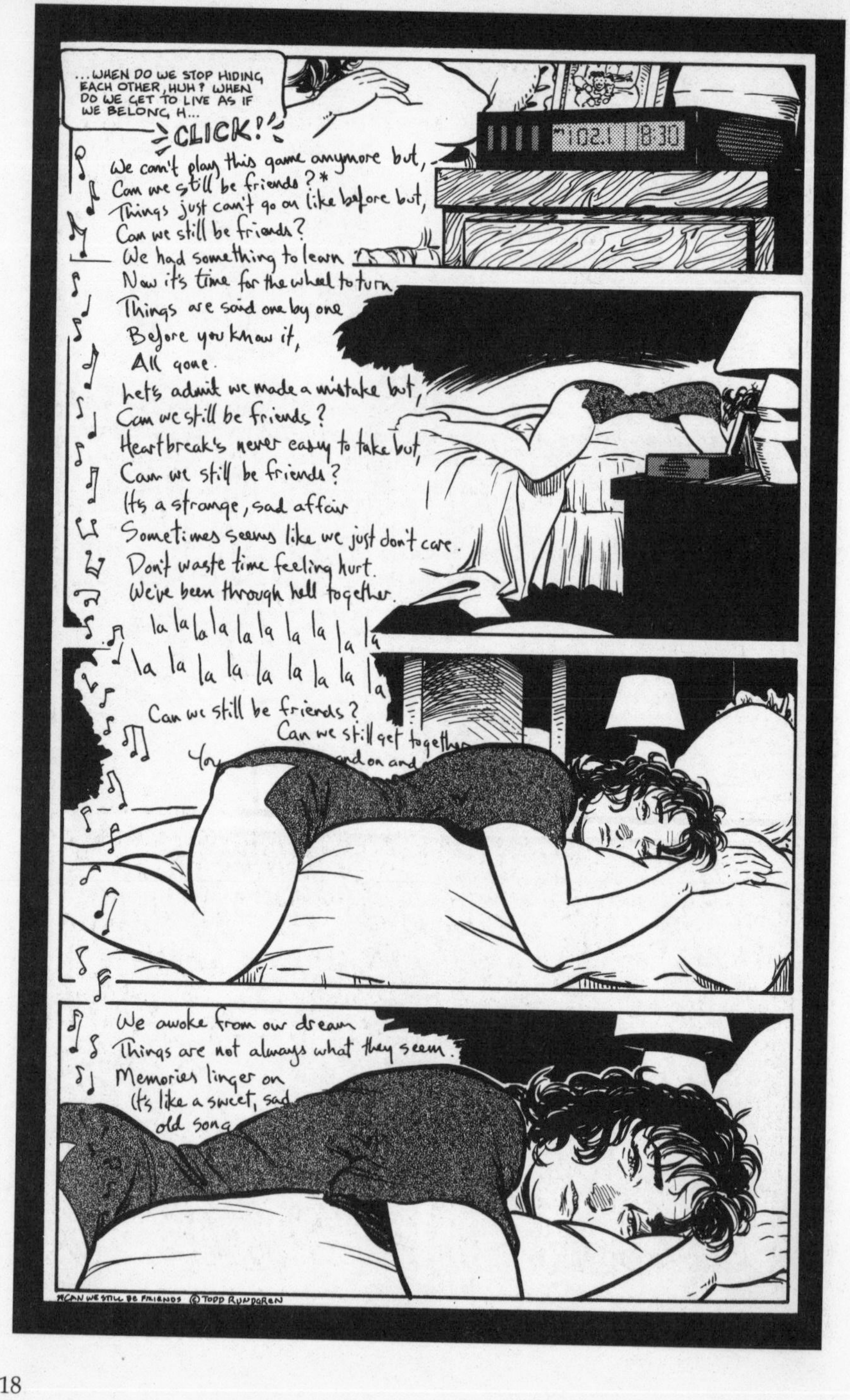
...WHEN DO WE STOP HIDING EACH OTHER, HUH? WHEN DO WE GET TO LIVE AS IF WE BELONG H...
CLICK!
7102.1 1830
We can't play this game anymore but,
Can we still be friends?*
Things just can't go on like before but,
Can we still be friends?
We had something to learn
Now it's time for the wheel to turn
Things are said one by one
Before you know it,
All gone.
Let's admit we made a mistake but,
Can we still be friends?
Heartbreak's never easy to take but,
Can we still be friends?
It's a strange, sad affair
Sometimes seems like we just don't care.
Don't waste time feeling hurt.
We've been through hell together.
la la la la la la la la la la
la la la la la la la la la la
Can we still be friends?
Can we still get together
and on and
We awoke from our dream
Things are not always what they seem.
Memories linger on
It's like a sweet, sad old song
*CAN WE STILL BE FRIENDS © TODD RUNDGREN

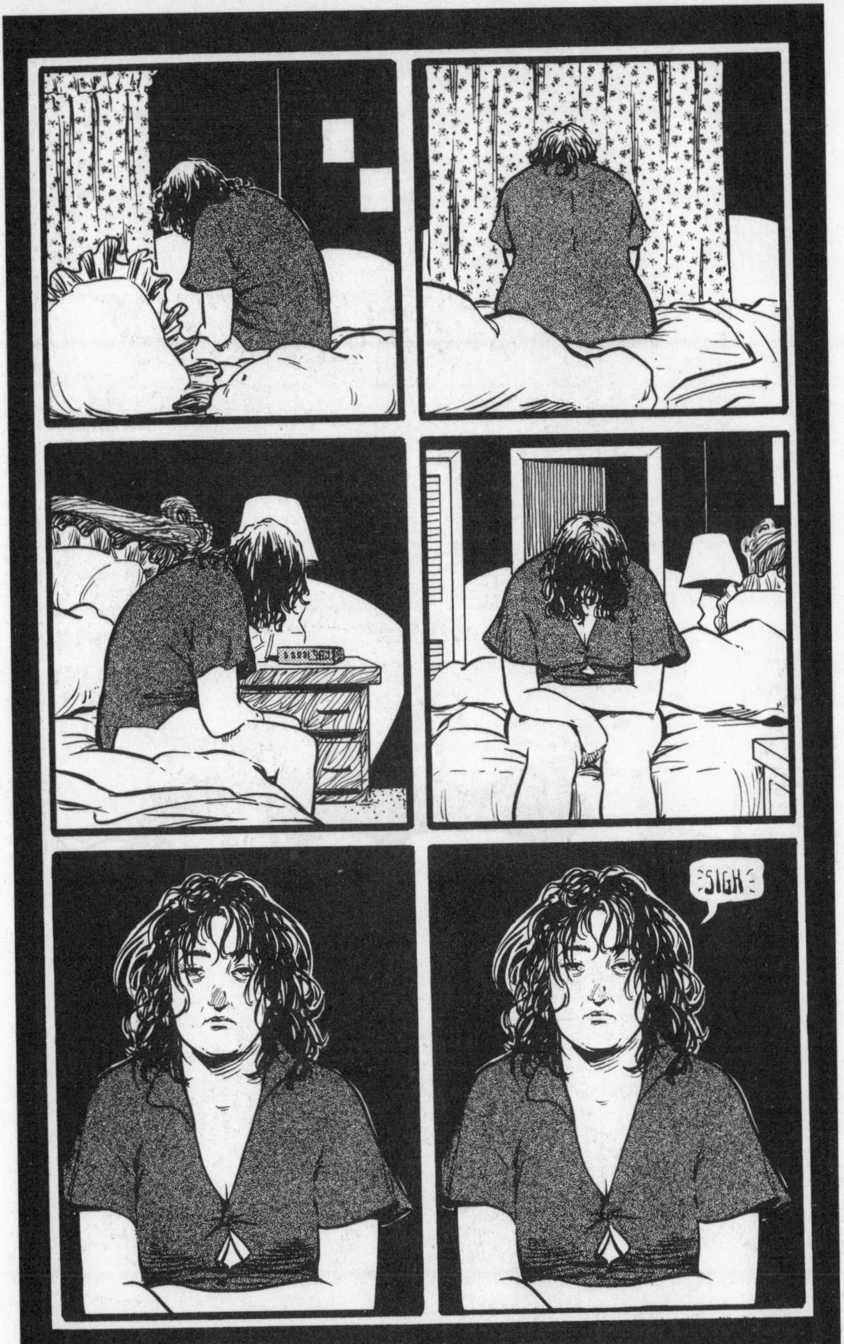
SIGH

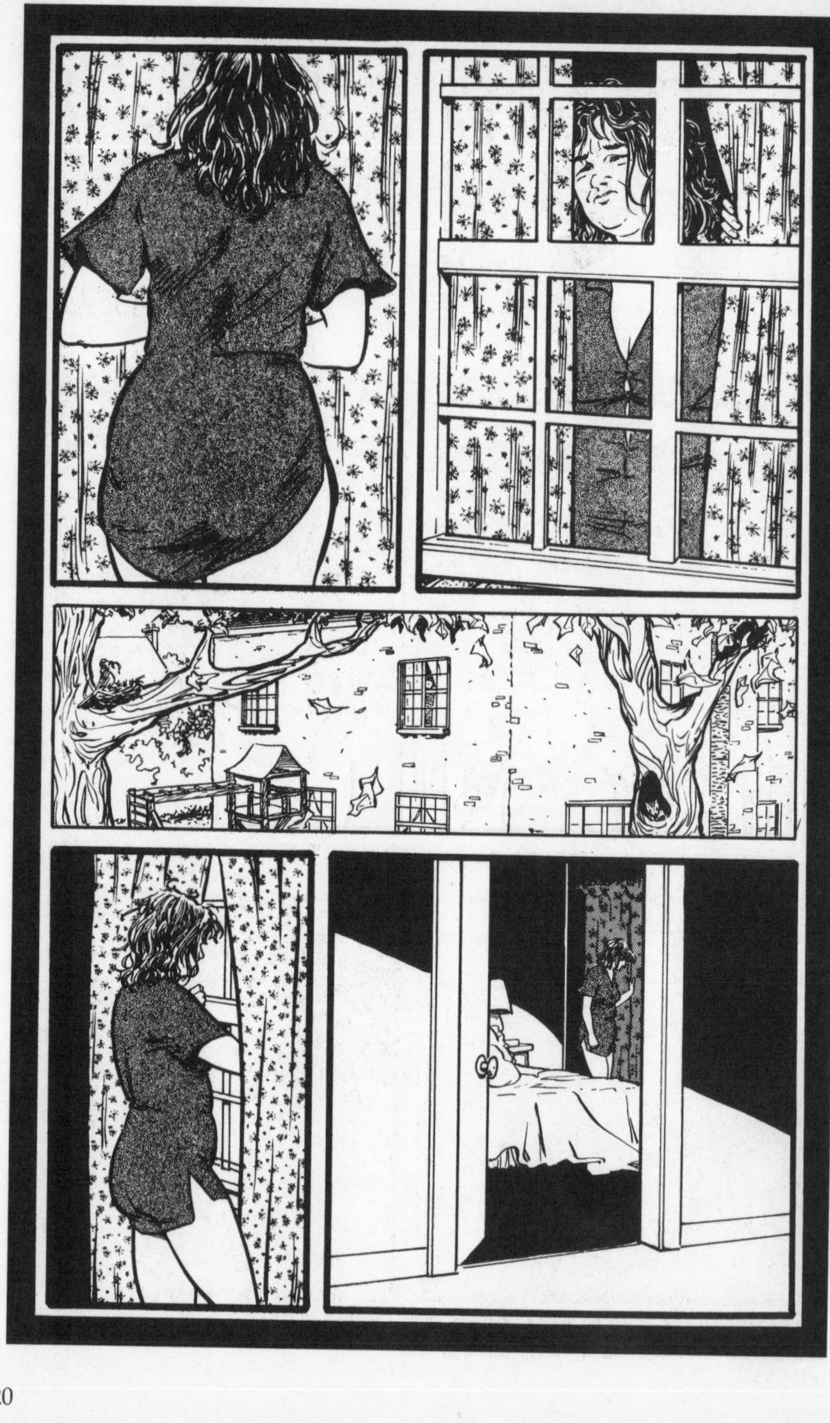

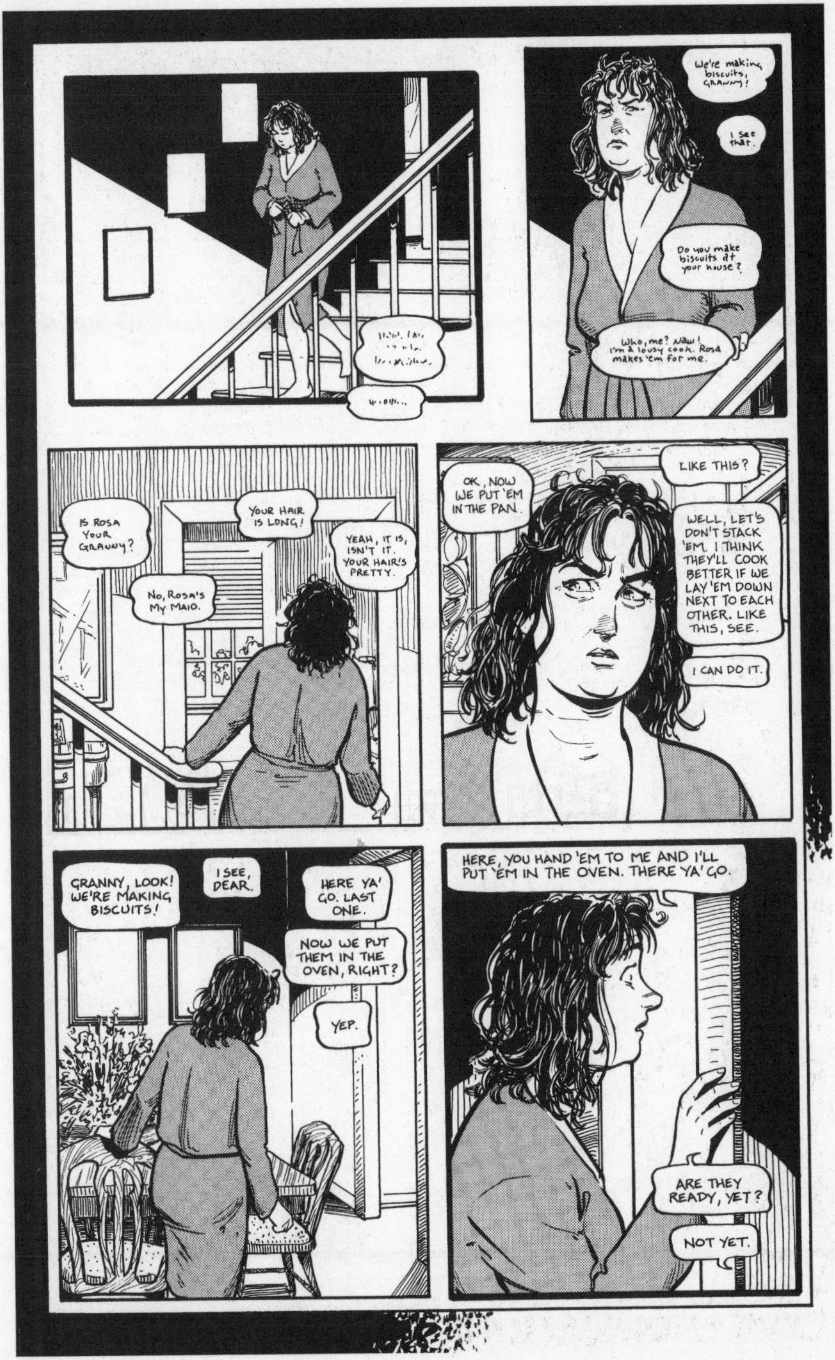
We're making biscuits, GRANNY!
I see that.
Do you make biscuits at your house?
Who, me? Naw! I'm a lousy cook. Rosa makes 'em for me.
IS ROSA YOUR GRANNY?
YOUR HAIR IS LONG!
YEAH, IT IS, ISN'T IT. YOUR HAIR'S PRETTY.
NO, ROSA'S MY MAID.
OK, NOW WE PUT 'EM IN THE PAN.
LIKE THIS?
WELL, LET'S DON'T STACK 'EM. I THINK THEY'LL COOK BETTER IF WE LAY 'EM DOWN NEXT TO EACH OTHER. LIKE THIS, SEE.
I CAN DO IT.
GRANNY, LOOK! WE'RE MAKING BISCUITS!
I SEE, DEAR.
HERE YA' GO. LAST ONE.
NOW WE PUT THEM IN THE OVEN, RIGHT?
YEP.
HERE, YOU HAND 'EM TO ME AND I'LL PUT 'EM IN THE OVEN. THERE YA' GO.
ARE THEY READY, YET?
NOT YET.

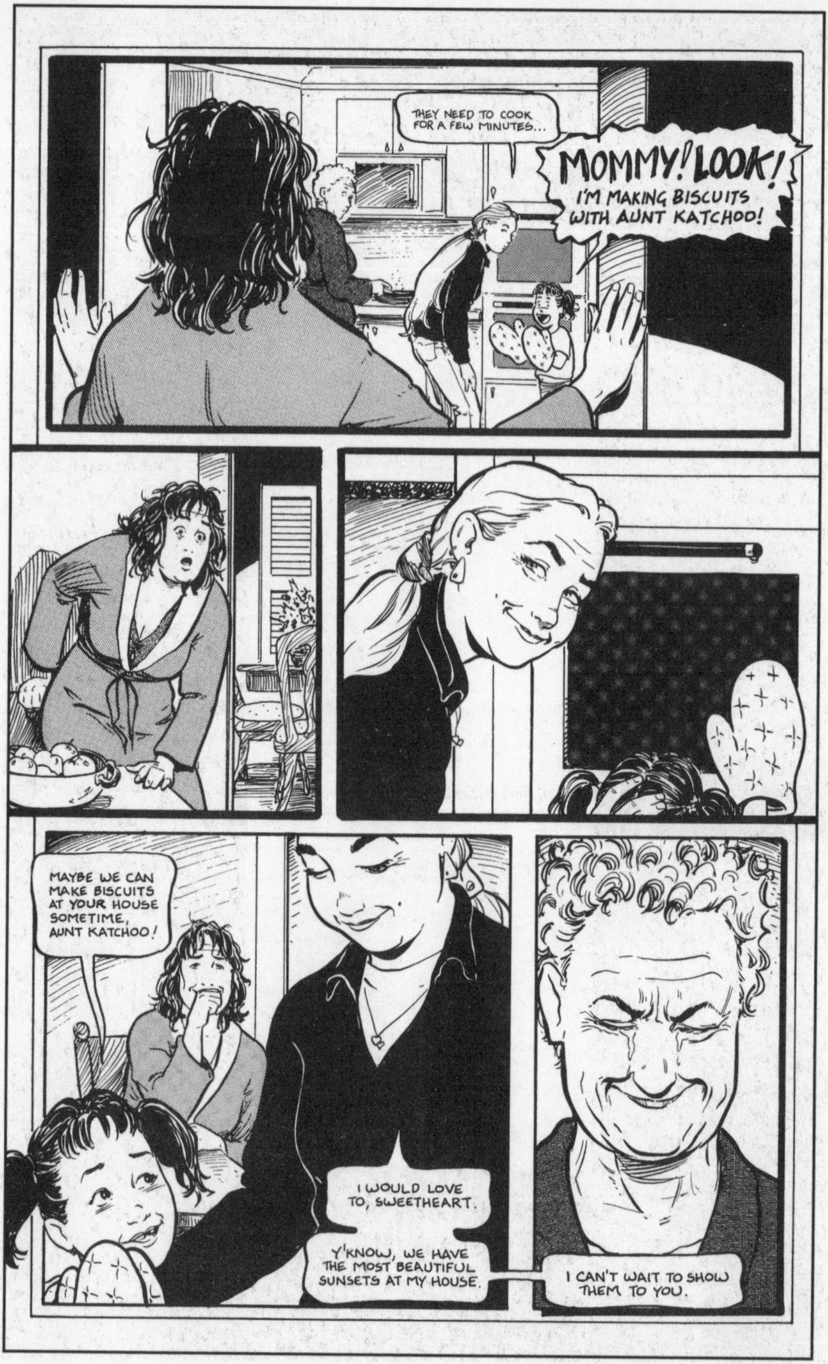
THEY NEED TO COOK FOR A FEW MINUTES...
MOMMY! LOOK! I'M MAKING BISCUITS WITH AUNT KATCHOO!
MAYBE WE CAN MAKE BISCUITS AT YOUR HOUSE SOMETIME, AUNT KATCHOO!
I WOULD LOVE TO, SWEETHEART.
Y'KNOW, WE HAVE THE MOST BEAUTIFUL SUNSETS AT MY HOUSE.
I CAN'T WAIT TO SHOW THEM TO YOU.

So softly and tenderly, I pull you
to my heart.
> You never thought
> to cover up.

But something's wrong, I feel
so rushed.
> The air you breathe,
> it's not enough.

Now whatever will ever become
of me?
> Elegant waste and chivalry.

Will I dream my life along?
> Or wake to find your
> timing gone.

Will I dream of wonderous things?
> Things that only God
> has seen.

Or will I grow to love this world?
> And only see the
> man machine.

Yet, here I stand, against the wall.
> Afraid to breathe.
> Afraid you'll fall.

That's when you come and hold me
tight. Tell me. . .
> Everything will be alright.

So softly and tenderly I pull you to
my heart.
> You never thought to cover up.

But something's wrong, I feel so
rushed.
> The air we breathe. . .

It's not enough.

WHEN I WAS THIRTEEN I WATCHED A CLASSMATE DIE ON THE CONCRETE BESIDE A SCHOOL BUS. IN THE NOISE AND PLAY OF PUSHING CHILDREN THE LITTLE BOY HAD BEEN THRUST BEFORE THE APPROACHING BUS AND RUN OVER. WAITING FOR THE AMBULANCE, WE STOOD AROUND HIM LIKE A WALL OF LIFE AND WATCHED HIM DIE.

AT FIRST HE GROANED AND COULDN'T MOVE, HIS EYES SHUT TIGHT. BUT AS THE CROWD RECALLED THE HORRIFIC MOMENT AGAIN AND AGAIN FROM VARIOUS POINTS OF VIEW, THE BOY GREW SILENT. HE OPENED HIS EYES AND LOOKED BEYOND OUR SILHOUETTES TO WATCH THE SUN WITH A PEACEFUL CALM. THEN I REALIZED HE NO LONGER SAW THE SKY OR FELT THE AUTUMN BREEZE, NOR DID HE FEEL ANY PAIN OR HEAR THE SOUND OF TEACHERS CRYING.

I DON'T KNOW WHAT FABRIC LIES BENEATH THE LIFE WE LIVE, BUT ON THE OTHER SIDE OF OUR MORTAL PAIN IS A PLACE OF SANCTUARY. I KNOW BECAUSE I STOOD BESIDE A LITTLE BOY AND WATCHED HIM FIND IT ONCE.

YEARS LATER, I HELD EMMA'S HAND UNTIL SHE FOUND SANCTUARY IN THE SNOW FALLING OUTSIDE HER WINDOW. THEN I FOUND IT IN THE BACKSEAT OF A SPEEDING POLICE CAR, UNDER FRANCINE'S TEARS.

I GUESS THAT'S WHY I CAME BACK. THERE'S SOMETHING MORE IMPORTANT THAN THE WORK WE DO AND THE ROLES WE PLAY. THERE'S SOMETHING MORE THAN HOW WE MOVE OR WHERE. THERE'S SOMETHING ABOUT WHO WE TOUCH AND WHY, AND IT MATTERS MORE THAN WE CAN UNDERSTAND OR PERHAPS REMEMBER.

SO, IT DOESN'T MATTER WHAT HAPPENED OR WHAT WAS SAID THAT AWFUL SUMMER TEN YEARS BEFORE, IF FRANCINE NEEDS ME I'LL BE HERE FOR HER, TO HOLD HER HAND AND LET HER KNOW SHE'S NOT ALONE. I OWE HER THAT MUCH, DON'T YOU SEE? IN HER EYES I FOUND SANCTUARY. AND NOW, WHEN LIFE IS SHADOWS IN THE SUN, FRANCINE LOOKS FOR IT, TOO. BUT ISN'T IT IRONIC SHE LOOKS TO ME FOR SOMETHING I SAW IN HER ALL ALONG?

I DON'T KNOW, MAYBE SANCTUARY ISN'T REALLY FOUND IN THE SUN OR SNOW OR A LOVED ONE'S TEARS. MAYBE, WHEN THE MOMENT'S RIGHT THESE THINGS MERELY CATCH A REFLECTION OF OUR OWN SOUL AND REMIND US OF WHO WE REALLY ARE AND THAT HOME IS NEVER ALL THAT FAR AWAY — JUST BEYOND THE SILHOUETTES THAT DARK THE SUN.

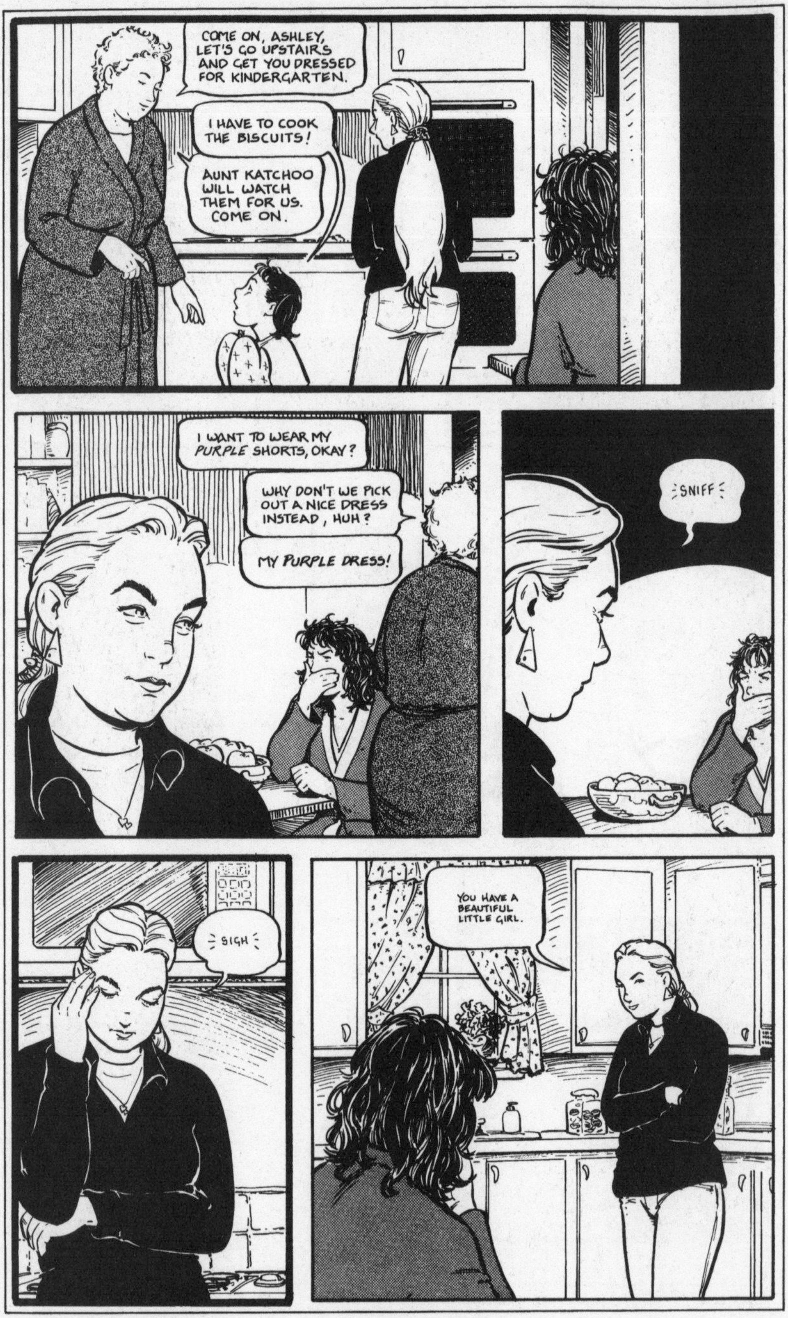
COME ON, ASHLEY, LET'S GO UPSTAIRS AND GET YOU DRESSED FOR KINDERGARTEN.
I HAVE TO COOK THE BISCUITS!
AUNT KATCHOO WILL WATCH THEM FOR US. COME ON.
I WANT TO WEAR MY PURPLE SHORTS, OKAY?
WHY DON'T WE PICK OUT A NICE DRESS INSTEAD, HUH?
MY PURPLE DRESS!
SNIFF
SIGH
YOU HAVE A BEAUTIFUL LITTLE GIRL.

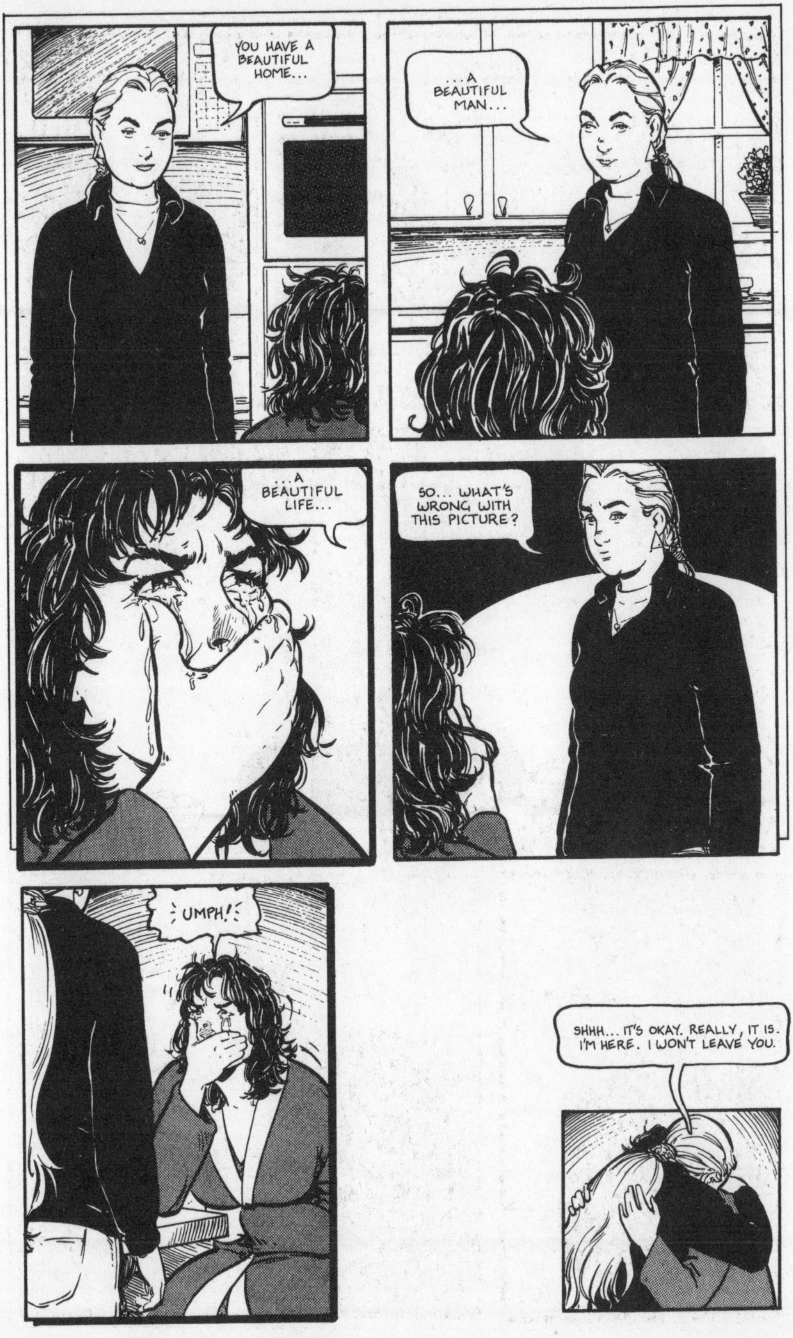
YOU HAVE A BEAUTIFUL HOME...
...A BEAUTIFUL MAN...
...A BEAUTIFUL LIFE...
SO... WHAT'S WRONG WITH THIS PICTURE?
UMPH!
SHHH... IT'S OKAY. REALLY, IT IS. I'M HERE. I WON'T LEAVE YOU.

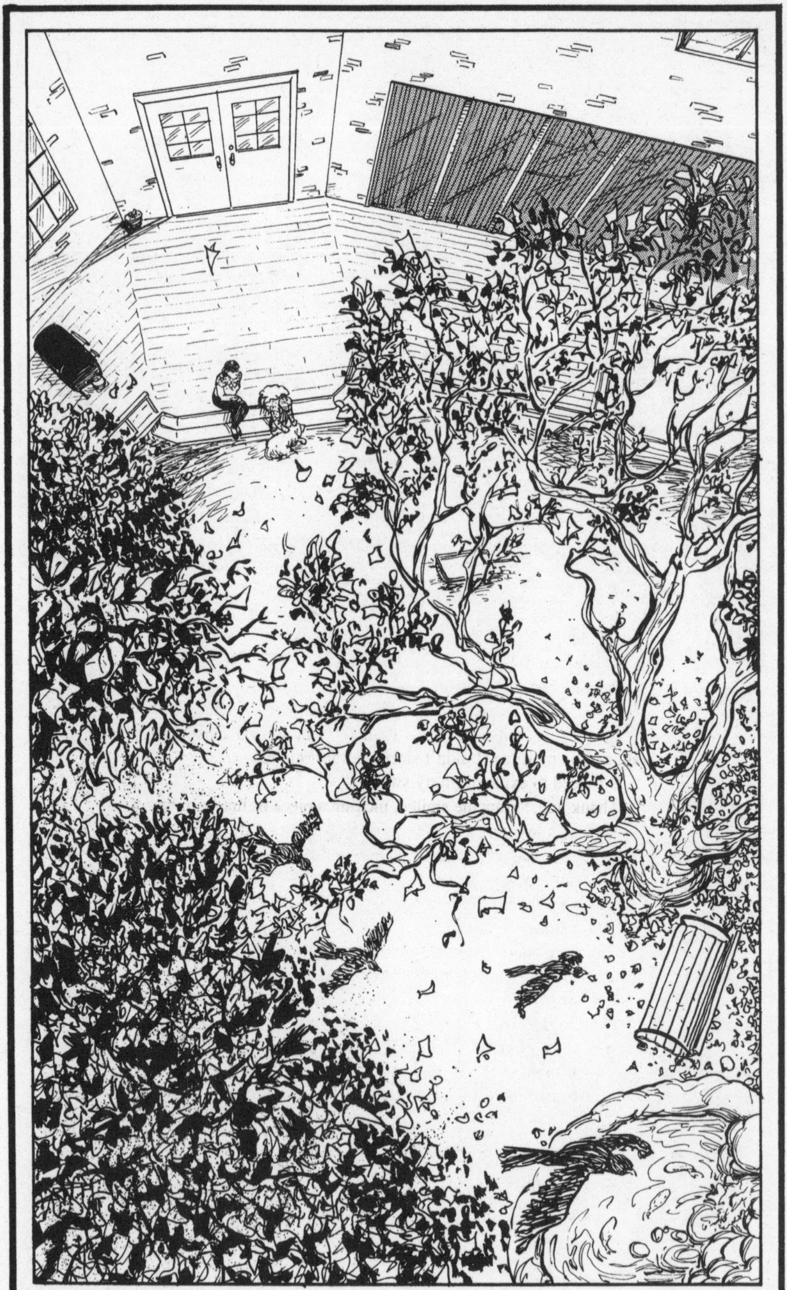

Katchoo pulled the rubber ball from Mikey's mouth and tossed
it into the yard again, sending the golden retriever scampering
through the autumn leaves in pursuit. It was a rare day in
Houston, cool and crisp. Finally, the sky had lost its summer pale
and recovered a brilliant blue. Katchoo was used to the beauty,
she saw it every day in the mountains. But she had lived in
Houston once and she understood the novelty of a pretty day for
the locals.

The back door opened and Francine stepped out onto the deck
that Brad built the year they moved in. She sat down beside
Katchoo and raised a hand to shade her eyes from the sunlight.
They exchanged smiles. Katchoo noted with sadness that her
friend looked too old for her age. Despite the fact that she had
spent the last hour bathing, shampooing, putting on makeup and
a fashionable outfit, nothing could hide the lines of heartbreak on
Francine's face. Her eyes, once chocolate brown and glimmering,
looked dull and tired to Katchoo earlier this morning. Only now,
as she smiled, did they begin to show signs of life.

"Feeling better?" Katchoo asked.

"Oh yeah. It's amazing what a shower and clean clothes will
do for you, isn't it?" Francine replied. "I'm sorry I looked so
ragged this morning. I didn't sleep well last night."

"No need to explain. Pretty sweater."

"Thank you," Francine smiled, picking a piece of lint from her
chest. Katchoo noted the cascade of wrinkles this produced
around Francine's jaw. "I got this in Santa Fe."

"Oh really? When were you in Santa Fe?"

"Brad and I went skiing there last Christmas."

"Did you stay in town?"

"Yeah, we stayed right by the plaza, downtown. One of those
beautiful old places, you know? Very elegant, with all this south-
western charm. They served tea in the lobby every afternoon."

"Oh, the Hotel St. Francis?" said Katchoo.

"Yes. that's the one. And at night we walked along this street
lined with candles. . ."

"Yeah, Canyon Road. They line the walls and houses with lumi-

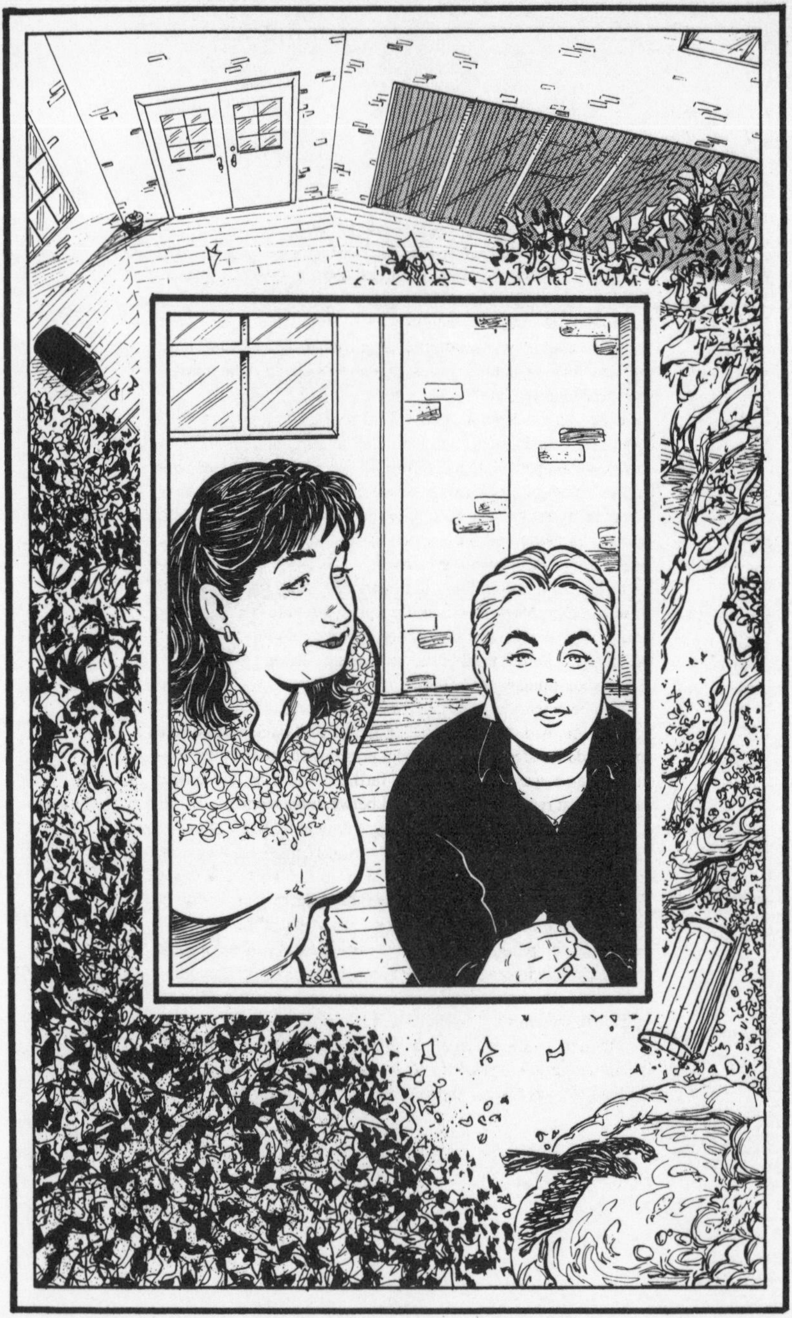

narias for the holidays. It's beautiful, isn't it?"

"Yes! You've been there?" Francine asked.

"I live just north of Santa Fe, about forty five minutes away, in the mountains," Katchoo smiled.

Francine's eyebrows shot up in surprise. "I didn't know that!" she exclaimed. "To think I was so close! All this time I thought you were living in Hawaii."

"I was. I lived there six years. But I sold the house and moved about four years ago."

Mikey bumped Katchoo's hands with the ball, demanding another round of the game. Katchoo dutifully pried the slippery wet prize from the dog's mouth and tossed it across the yard into the bushes along the back fence. Mikey disappeared into the landscape, his tail waving goodbye.

"I lived in New York for awhile after that," Katchoo continued. "Had a nice little apartment on the upper east side. Then I took a trip to New Mexico and found this place in the mountains and I thought, this is it, y'know? This is where I belong."

Francine smiled at the concept.

"I've been there ever since," Katchoo sighed.

Mikey returned, happy and out of breath. He laid down in a bare spot beside the steps and watched the yard with satisfaction, confident that it was safe from any further attacks by the rubber nemesis that remained incarcerated between his teeth.

Francine realized she was staring at Katchoo. She blinked and looked away. The neighbors cat sat perched on the fence nearby, watching snowbirds gather in the trees. Watching and waiting. Francine had spent countless afternoons on these steps watching the world spin beneath the sun. Then, just when it had felt like it was going to spin out of control. . , instinctively, she turned to make sure Katchoo was still there.

Katchoo stroked Mikey's coat, lulling him to sleep. All was right with the world.

"I thought I saw you a couple of days ago," Francine said softly, "In the gazebo behind the Ridley Hotel."

"Really? I was there. I had to come to town last weekend to take

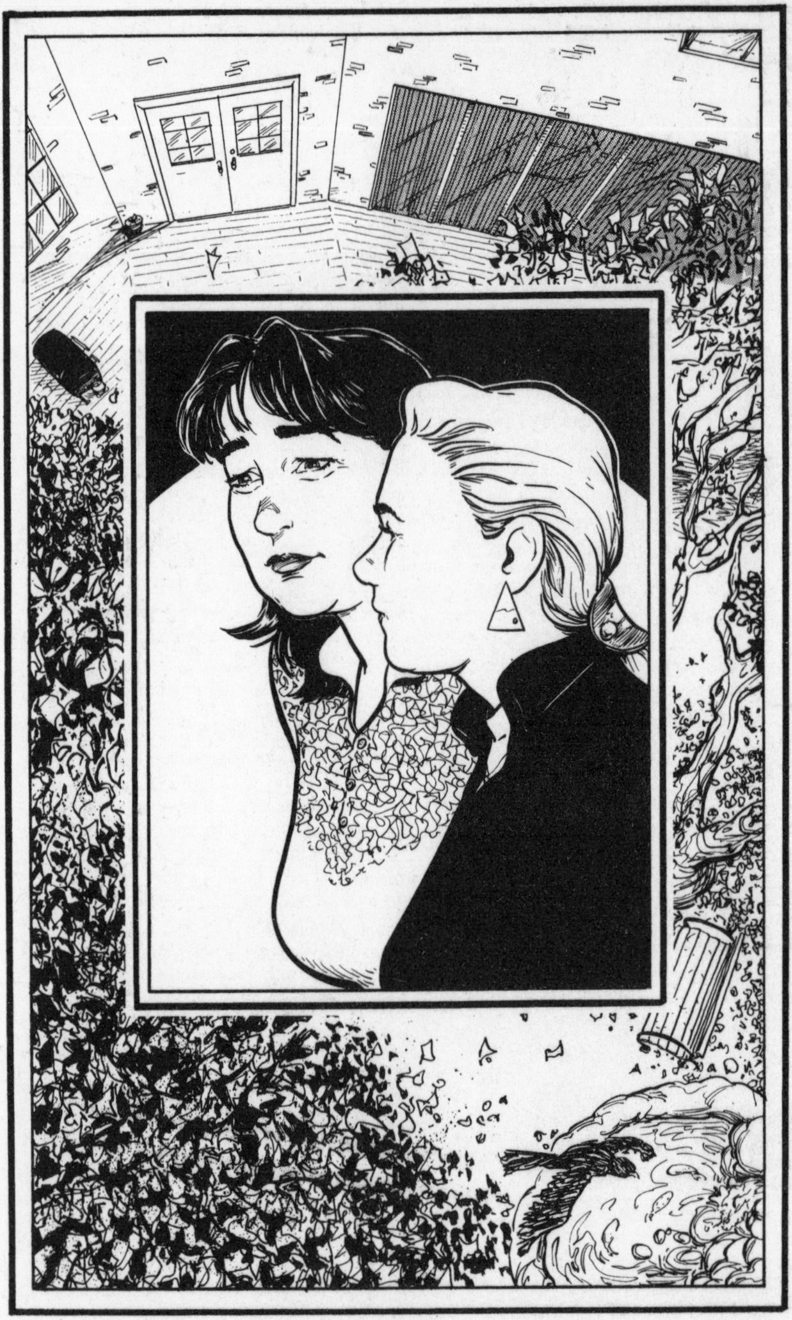

care of some business. Why didn't you say something?"

"I was going to, but I got held up, and then you were gone."

"It must have been when I was checking out. I went to look at the lake before I caught a cab."

"I was beginning to wonder if I just imagined it. You know, wishful thinking."

"No," Katchoo said, her smile dropping slightly. "My mother died last week. I had to come take care of the arrangements and all that."

"Oh, Katchoo, I'm so sorry!"

"It's okay, really. We weren't that close, y'know. I paid for her care, but that's about it. She made her choice a long time ago."

They sat in silence for awhile, watching a squirrel pick through dinner in the grass. Finally, Francine asked the question that had been on her mind all morning.

"So, after all this time, going on what, ten years. . .?"

"Ten years, two months, three weeks and a day," Katchoo replied.

Francine smiled, "Ooookay. So, after ten years, two months, three weeks. . ."

"And a day."

"And a day. After all that, I find you in my kitchen. How did I get so lucky all of a sudden?"

"Your mother called me," replied Katchoo with a wry smile.

"My *mother?*"

"Can you believe it?" Katchoo giggled, "I've been giving her my numbers all these years, y'know, in case of emergency."

Francine shook her head in wonder, "She never said a word."

"I thought she was just throwing 'em away."

Francine looked at Katchoo in amazement, allowing this new bit of information to soak in. All the time she had felt so isolated, so impossibly out of contact, Katchoo had been just a phone call away. A call her mother finally made for her.

"I've missed you, Katina," Francine said.

"I've missed you too, Francie," Katchoo smiled. The time seemed right. Katchoo cleared her throat nervously. "Listen,

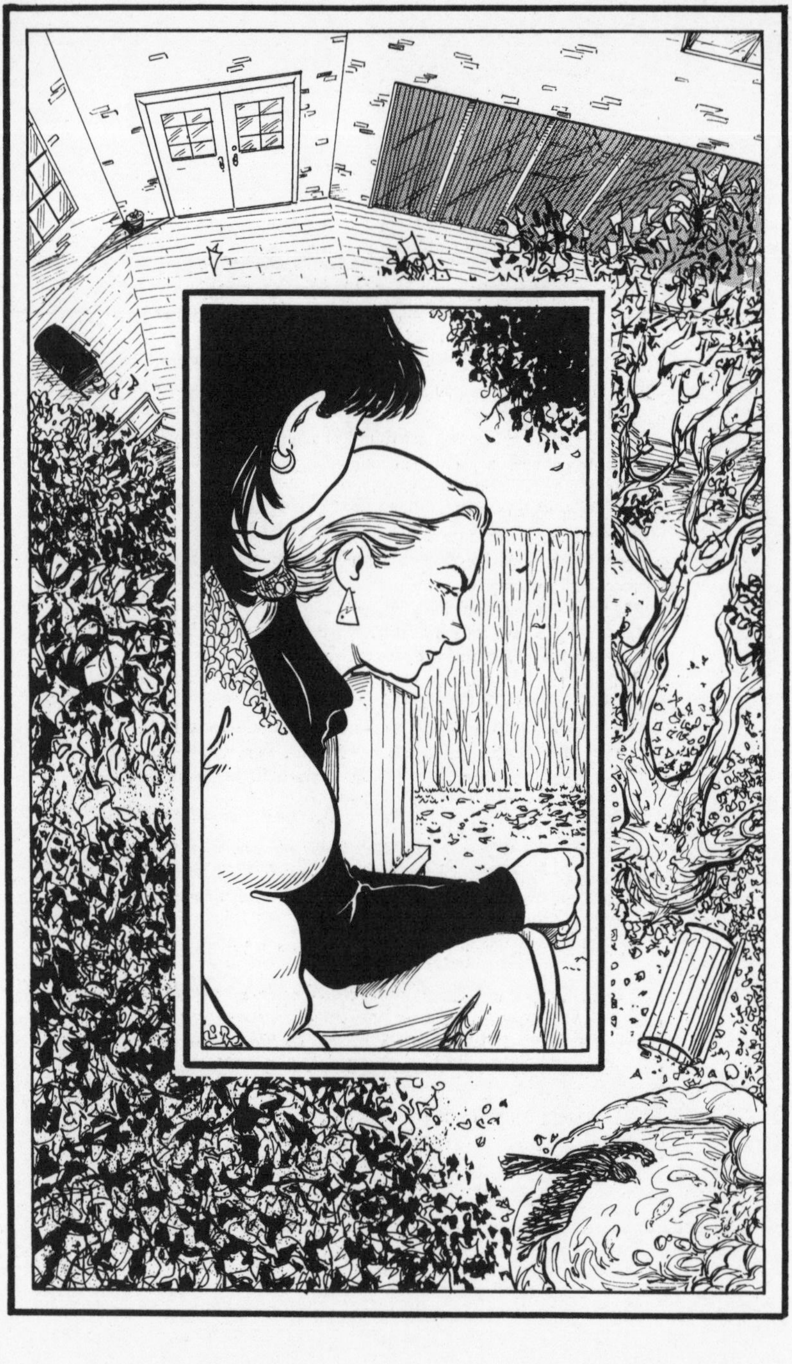

Francine. . ."

"You haven't said a word about David!" Francine interrupted. "How is he? Did you two go to Hawaii and get married like you said you would? You know, I've always tried to picture you guys living there in your beach house with these great tans and all."

Katchoo picked up a twig and pulled at the fragile buds hanging on the stem.

"It's a lot easier to picture you two in Santa Fe, though. David's always been a jean-jacket kind of guy, know what I mean? Gosh, I can't wait to see him! Oh god, can you imagine, the three of us back together again?"

Katchoo picked at the twig in silence, methodically stripping the outer bark. Francine frowned. She saw the muscles in Katchoo's jaw tighten.

"I'm sorry, did I say something wrong?"

Katchoo sighed and looked as if she were about to reply but thought better of it, avoiding eye contact.

"Katchoo, David is alright, isn't he? You guys did get married and all that, right? I mean, I just assumed. . ."

"Yeah, we were married. We had the ceremony on the cliffs near Hana. We lived in the house there," Katchoo sighed. "That was the happiest time of my life. I thought I was going to spend the rest of my life there, in Hawaii. . . with David."

"What happened?"

Katchoo took a deep breath and let it out slowly. She felt her eyes burning and swore harshly to herself. Control. Control. Francine waited. She wanted an answer now. Katchoo could feel her watching. Eyes down, her thoughts raced.

"Katchoo?" Francine whispered, the color draining from her face.

Katchoo dropped the last bit of twig onto the miniature pyramid of twig bits between her boots. Everything had been so perfect once, the three of them against the world. Then one day they woke up and it was gone. Just gone. Like a singer losing his voice or an actor losing his timing. Nothing gold can stay, someone once wrote, and Katchoo knew the day it slipped away.

MY FOOT'S ASLEEP.

YOU'RE WHINING AGAIN.

I CAN'T FEEL MY FOOT. IS IT STILL THERE? CAN YOU SEE IT? IT'S NOT BLUE OR ANYTHING, IS IT?

FRANCINE, I SWEAR YOU'RE SO HIGH MAINTENANCE! ALL YOU HAVE TO DO IS SIT THERE. LOOK AT ME, I HAVE TO STAND AND MOVE MY ARM.

HOW MUCH LONGER?

WE JUST STARTED! I HAVEN'T EVEN FINISHED THE CHARCOAL SKETCH.

DID YOU HEAR THAT? WAS THAT THE DOOR?

WOULD YOU RELAX? GAH! NOBODY'S GOING TO WALK IN ON US. DAVID'S AT SCHOOL, THE FRONT DOOR'S LOCKED, THE BACK DOOR'S LOCKED. . .

I WISH I HADN'T EATEN BREAKFAST. I LOOK FAT, DON'T I?

YOU DON'T LOOK FAT. YOU LOOK MARVELOUS. SIMPLY MARVELOUS.

SHUT UP.

I WILL IF YOU WILL.

ALRIGHT, FINE.

FINE.

FINE.

ALRIGHT THEN.

STOP IT, I'LL LOSE MY POSE.

OKAY, WAIT. WAIT. I JUST NEED TO GET YOUR FACE HERE. HOLD STILL, JUST. . .

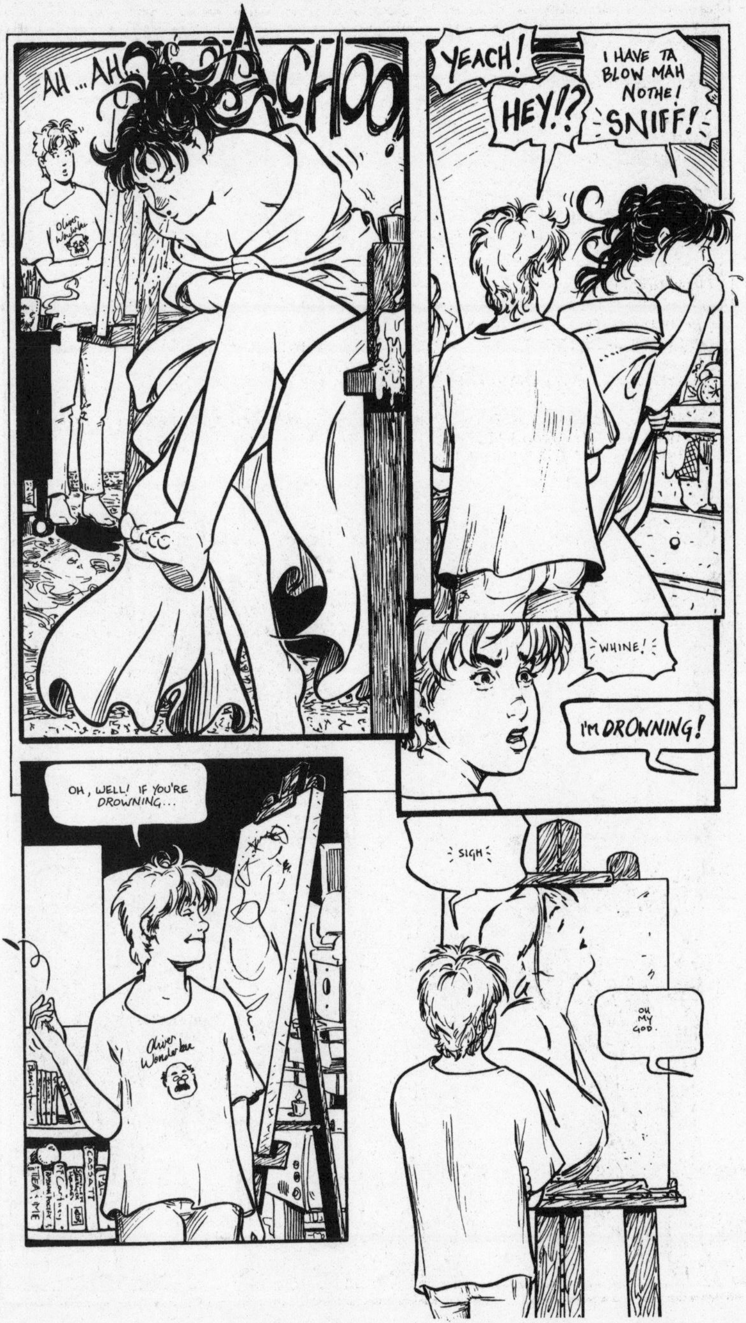
AH...AH...
ACHOO!
YEACH!
HEY!?
I HAVE TA BLOW MAH NOTHE!
SNIFF!
WHINE!
I'M DROWNING!
OH, WELL! IF YOU'RE DROWNING...
SIGH
OH MY GOD.

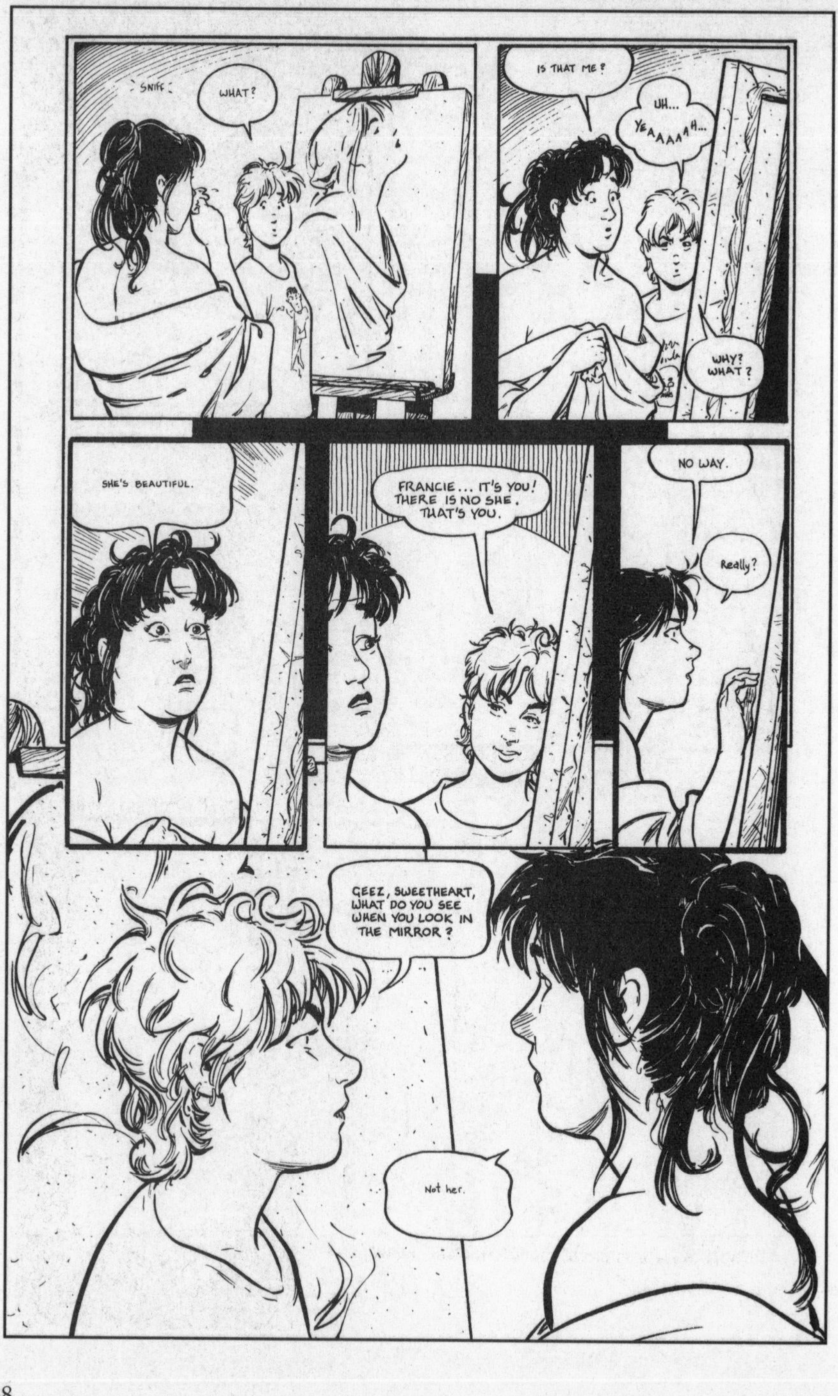
SNIFF
WHAT?
IS THAT ME?
UH... YEAAAAAAH...
WHY? WHAT?
SHE'S BEAUTIFUL.
FRANCIE... IT'S YOU! THERE IS NO SHE. THAT'S YOU.
NO WAY.
Really?
GEEZ, SWEETHEART, WHAT DO YOU SEE WHEN YOU LOOK IN THE MIRROR?
Not her.

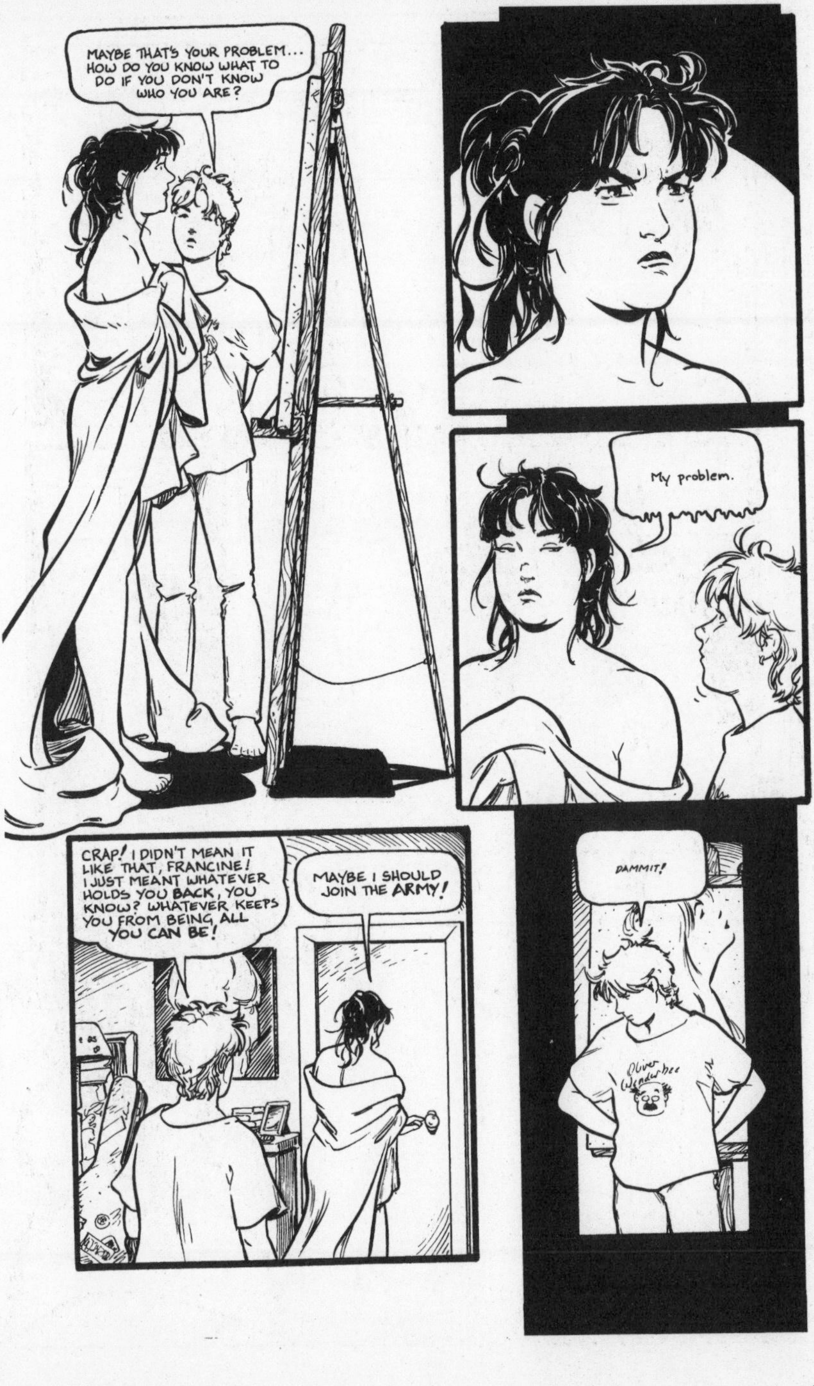
MAYBE THAT'S YOUR PROBLEM... HOW DO YOU KNOW WHAT TO DO IF YOU DON'T KNOW WHO YOU ARE?
My problem.
CRAP! I DIDN'T MEAN IT LIKE THAT, FRANCINE! I JUST MEANT WHATEVER HOLDS YOU BACK, YOU KNOW? WHATEVER KEEPS YOU FROM BEING ALL YOU CAN BE!
MAYBE I SHOULD JOIN THE ARMY!
DAMMIT!
Oliver Wenderbee

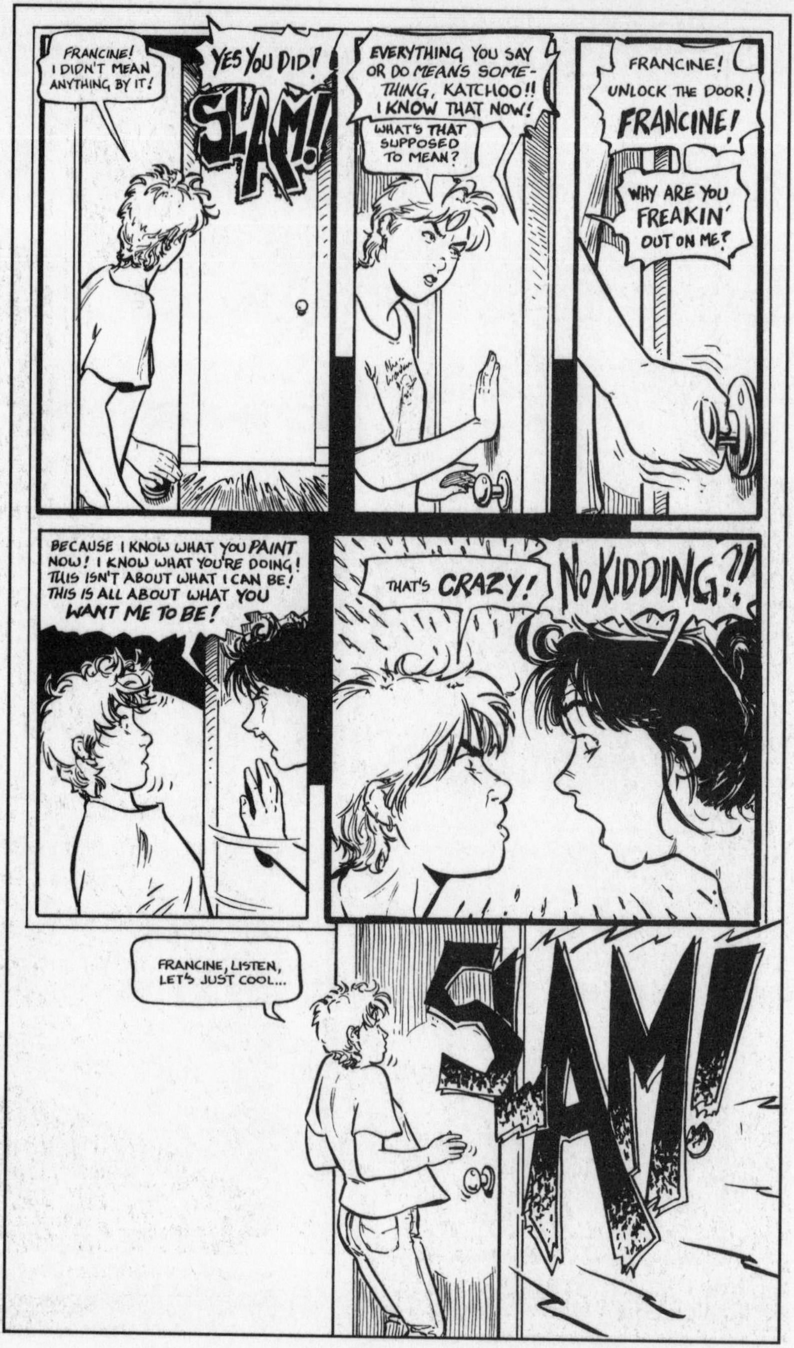
FRANCINE! I DIDN'T MEAN ANYTHING BY IT!
YES YOU DID!
SLAM!!
EVERYTHING YOU SAY OR DO MEANS SOMETHING, KATCHOO!! I KNOW THAT NOW!
WHAT'S THAT SUPPOSED TO MEAN?
FRANCINE! UNLOCK THE DOOR! FRANCINE!
WHY ARE YOU FREAKIN' OUT ON ME?
BECAUSE I KNOW WHAT YOU PAINT NOW! I KNOW WHAT YOU'RE DOING! THIS ISN'T ABOUT WHAT I CAN BE! THIS IS ALL ABOUT WHAT YOU WANT ME TO BE!
THAT'S CRAZY!
NO KIDDING?!!
FRANCINE, LISTEN, LET'S JUST COOL...
SLAM!

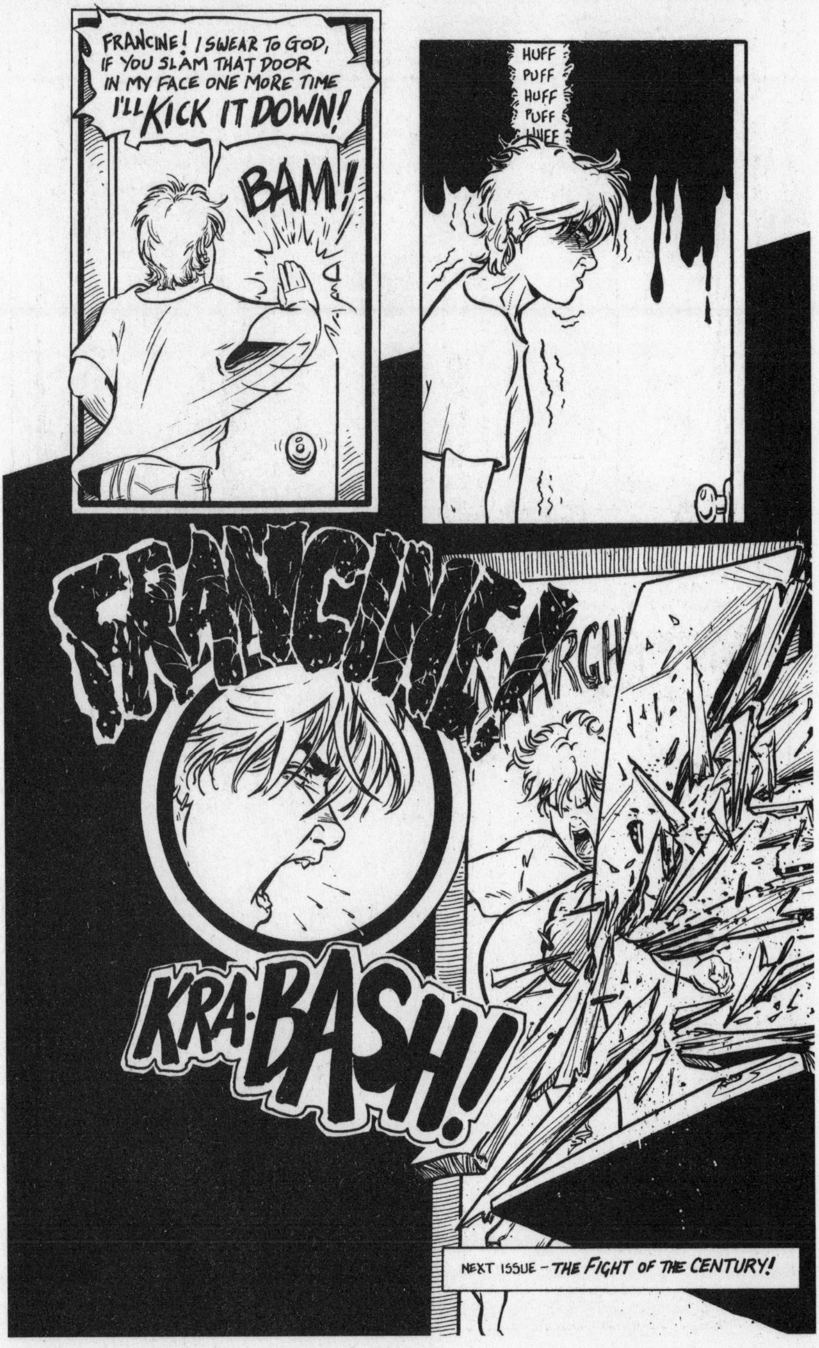
FRANCINE! I SWEAR TO GOD, IF YOU SLAM THAT DOOR IN MY FACE ONE MORE TIME I'LL KICK IT DOWN!
BAM!
HUFF
PUFF
HUFF
PUFF
FRANCINE!
ARGH
KRA-BASH!
NEXT ISSUE – THE FIGHT OF THE CENTURY!

Talk to me and justify it.
Let me see, don't try to hide it;
Talk to me and justify it,
Let me see, I won't be denied.
Talk to me and justify it.
Let me see, don't try to hide it;
Talk to me and justify it,
Let me see, I won't be denied.

In your life I will call you to sea,
The Winter Queen sings low.
Winter years come.

See the hearts winter claims
In frozen war.
You can't get warm.
Winter years come.

Talk to me and justify it.
Let me see, don't try to hide it;
Talk to me and justify it,
Let me see, I won't be denied.
Talk to me and justify it.
Let me see, don't try to hide it;
Talk to me and justify it,
Let me see, I won't be denied.
Talk to me and justify it.
Let me see, don't try to hide it;
Talk to me and justify it,
Let me see, I won't be denied.
Talk to me and justify it.

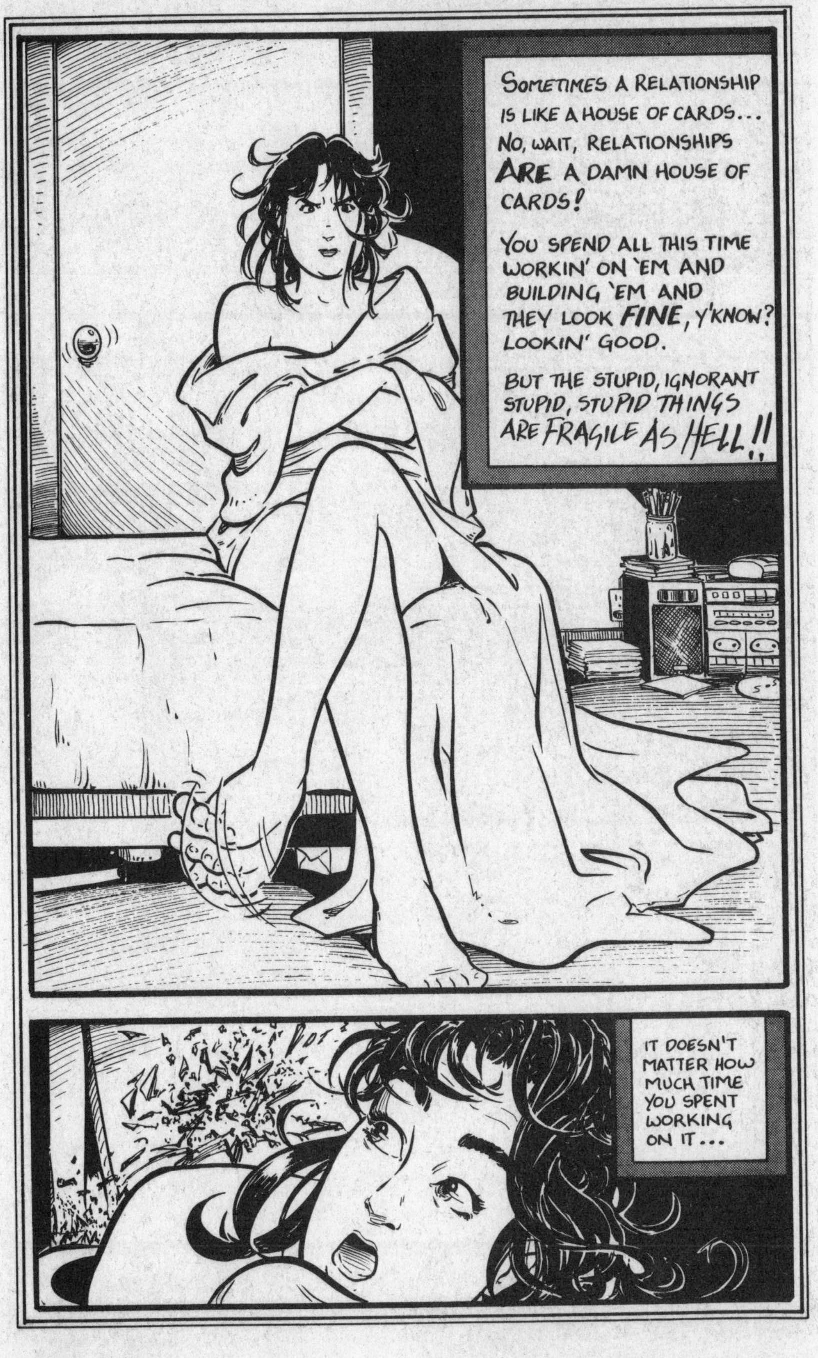
SOMETIMES A RELATIONSHIP IS LIKE A HOUSE OF CARDS... NO, WAIT, RELATIONSHIPS ARE A DAMN HOUSE OF CARDS!
YOU SPEND ALL THIS TIME WORKIN' ON 'EM AND BUILDING 'EM AND THEY LOOK FINE, Y'KNOW? LOOKIN' GOOD.
BUT THE STUPID, IGNORANT STUPID, STUPID THINGS ARE FRAGILE AS HELL!!
IT DOESN'T MATTER HOW MUCH TIME YOU SPENT WORKING ON IT...

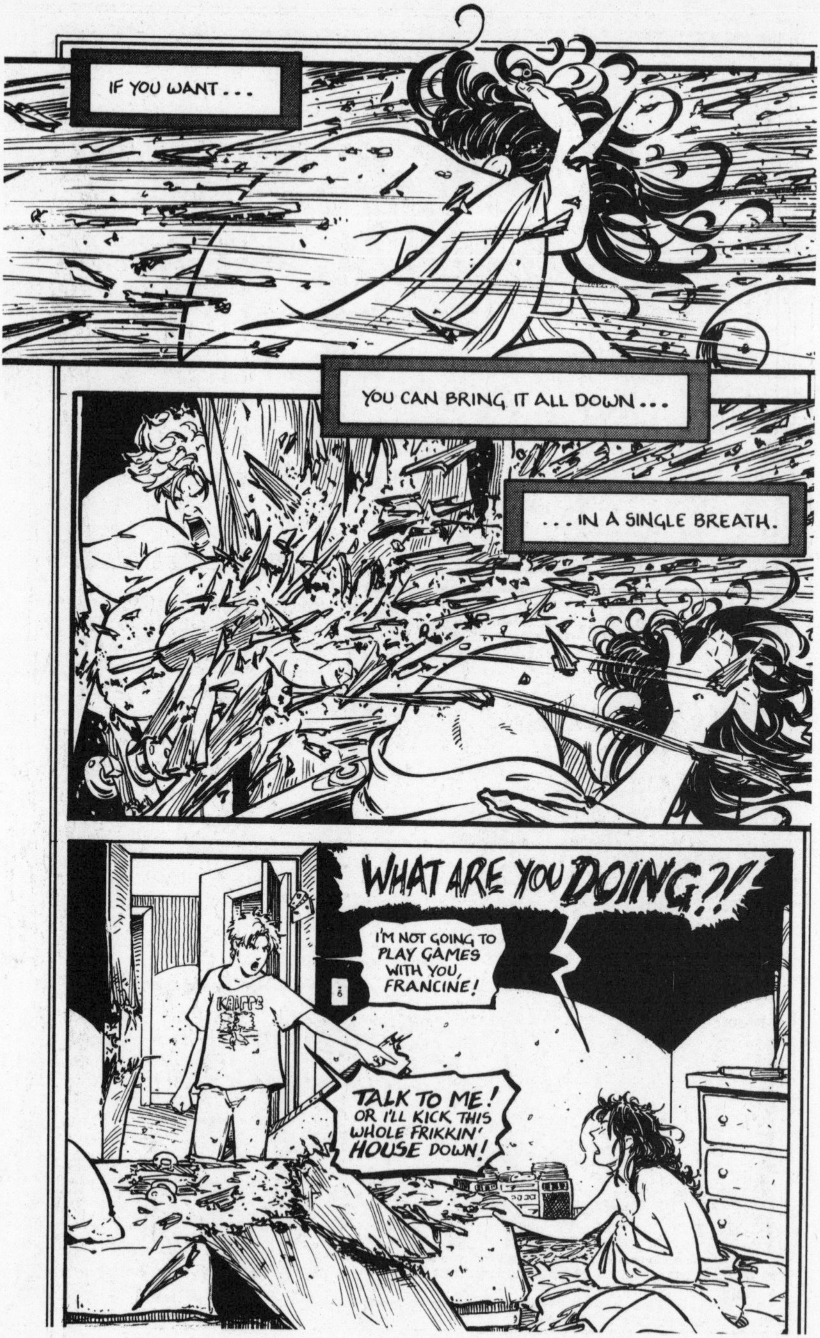

IF YOU WANT . . .
YOU CAN BRING IT ALL DOWN . . .
. . . IN A SINGLE BREATH.
WHAT ARE YOU DOING?!
I'M NOT GOING TO PLAY GAMES WITH YOU, FRANCINE!
TALK TO ME! OR I'LL KICK THIS WHOLE FRIKKIN' HOUSE DOWN!

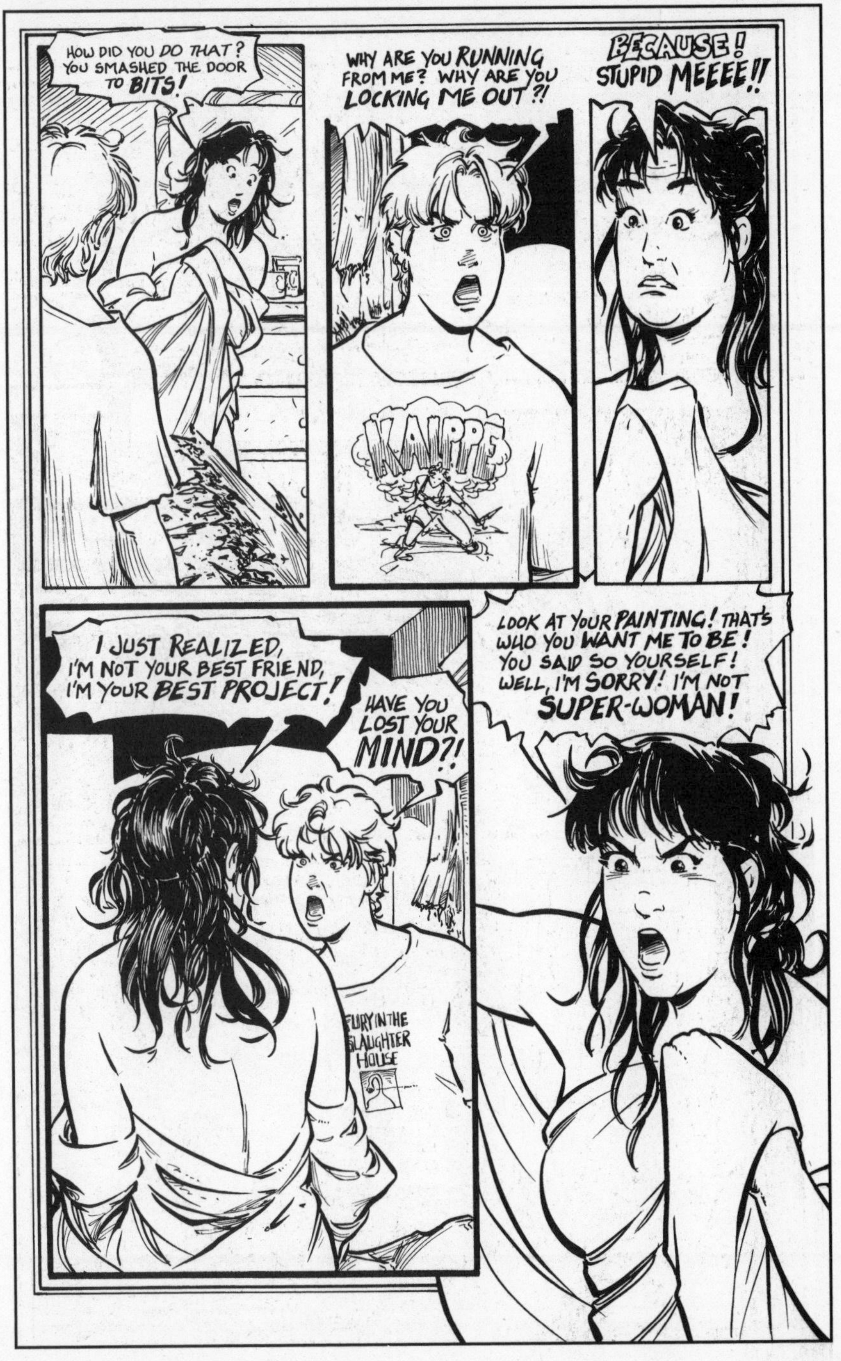
HOW DID YOU DO THAT? YOU SMASHED THE DOOR TO BITS!
WHY ARE YOU RUNNING FROM ME? WHY ARE YOU LOCKING ME OUT?!
BECAUSE! STUPID MEEEE!!
I JUST REALIZED, I'M NOT YOUR BEST FRIEND, I'M YOUR BEST PROJECT!
HAVE YOU LOST YOUR MIND?!
LOOK AT YOUR PAINTING! THAT'S WHO YOU WANT ME TO BE! YOU SAID SO YOURSELF! WELL, I'M SORRY! I'M NOT SUPER-WOMAN!
KAIPPE
FURY IN THE SLAUGHTER HOUSE

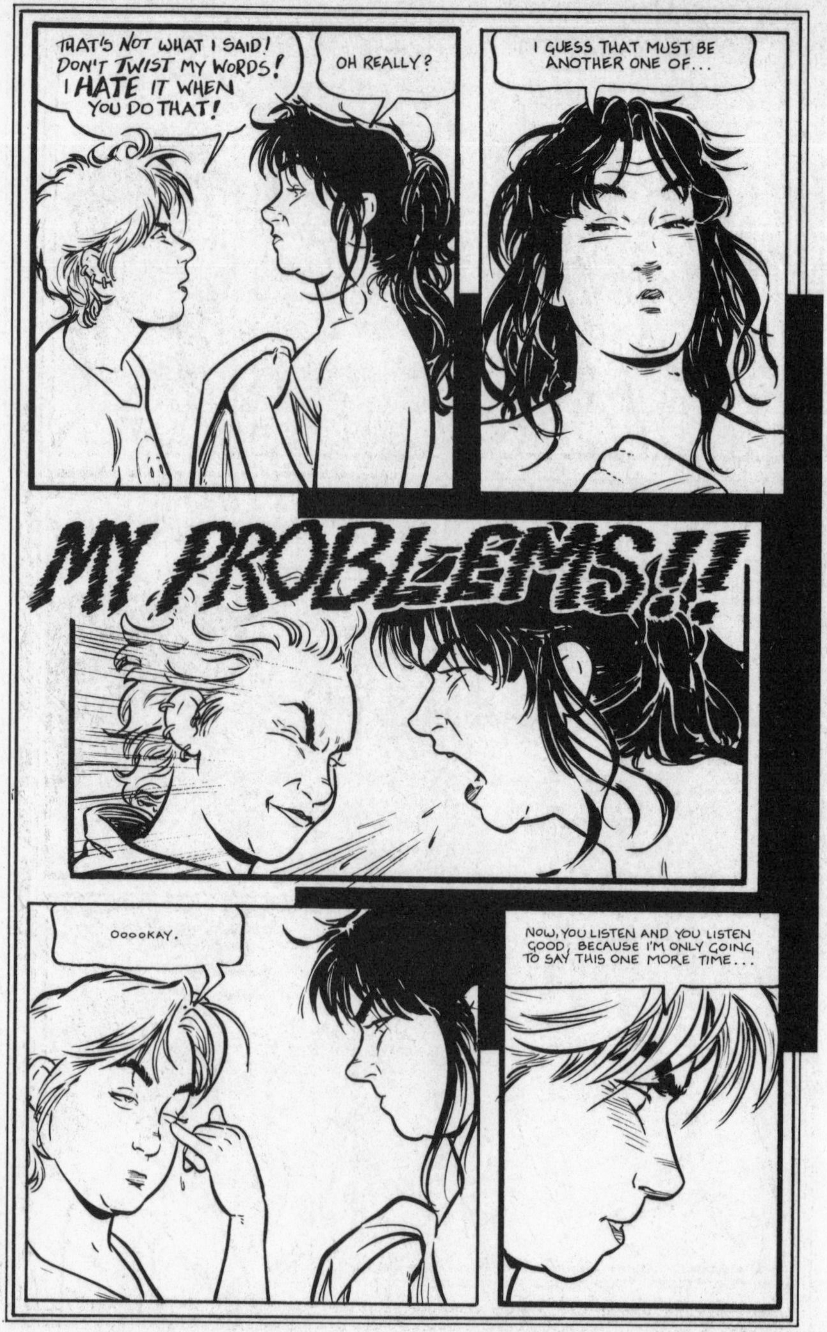

THAT'S NOT WHAT I SAID! DON'T TWIST MY WORDS! I HATE IT WHEN YOU DO THAT!
OH REALLY?
I GUESS THAT MUST BE ANOTHER ONE OF...
MY PROBLEMS!!
OOOOKAY.
NOW, YOU LISTEN AND YOU LISTEN GOOD, BECAUSE I'M ONLY GOING TO SAY THIS ONE MORE TIME...

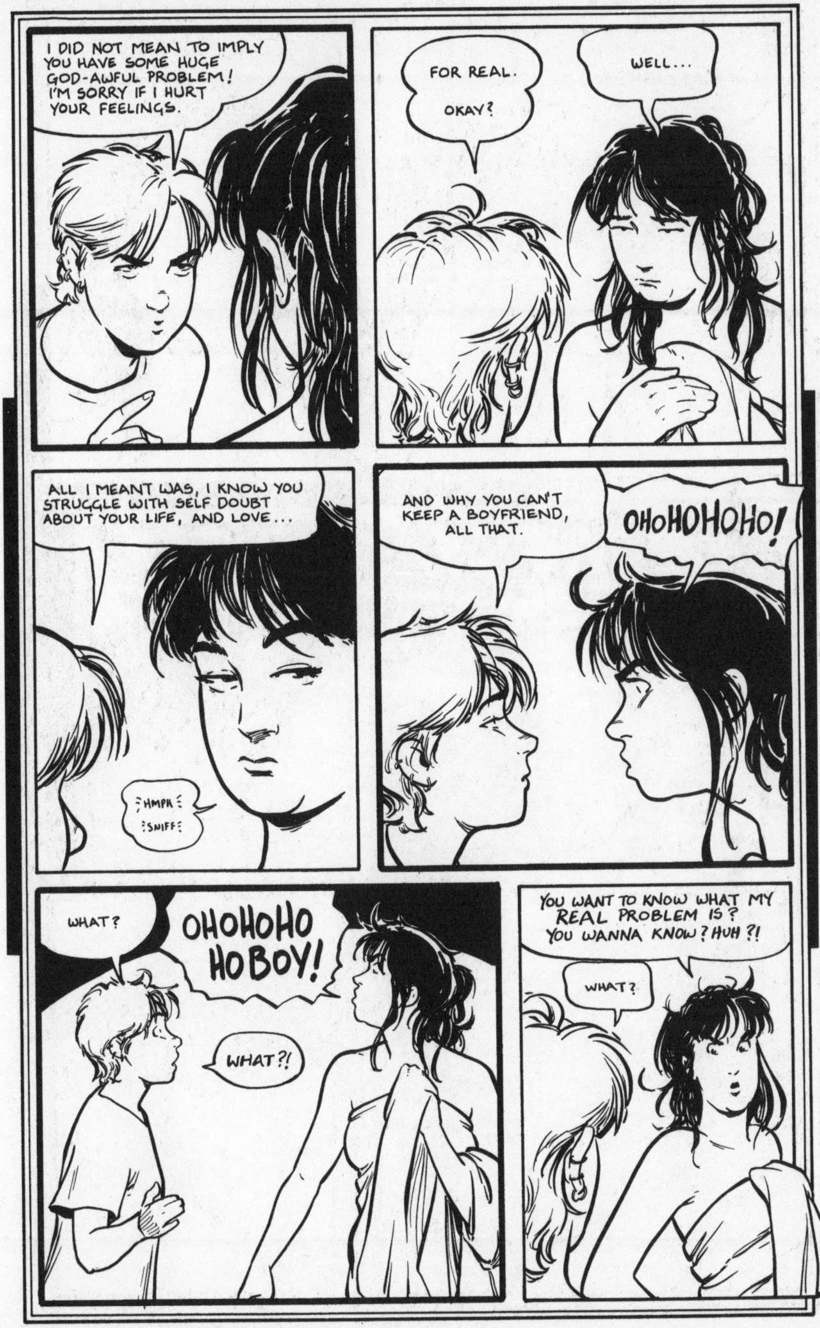
I DID NOT MEAN TO IMPLY YOU HAVE SOME HUGE GOD-AWFUL PROBLEM! I'M SORRY IF I HURT YOUR FEELINGS.
FOR REAL.
OKAY?
WELL...
ALL I MEANT WAS, I KNOW YOU STRUGGLE WITH SELF DOUBT ABOUT YOUR LIFE, AND LOVE...
HMPH
SNIFF
AND WHY YOU CAN'T KEEP A BOYFRIEND, ALL THAT.
OHOHOHOHO!
WHAT?
OHOHOHO HOBOY!
WHAT?!
YOU WANT TO KNOW WHAT MY REAL PROBLEM IS? YOU WANNA KNOW? HUH?!
WHAT?

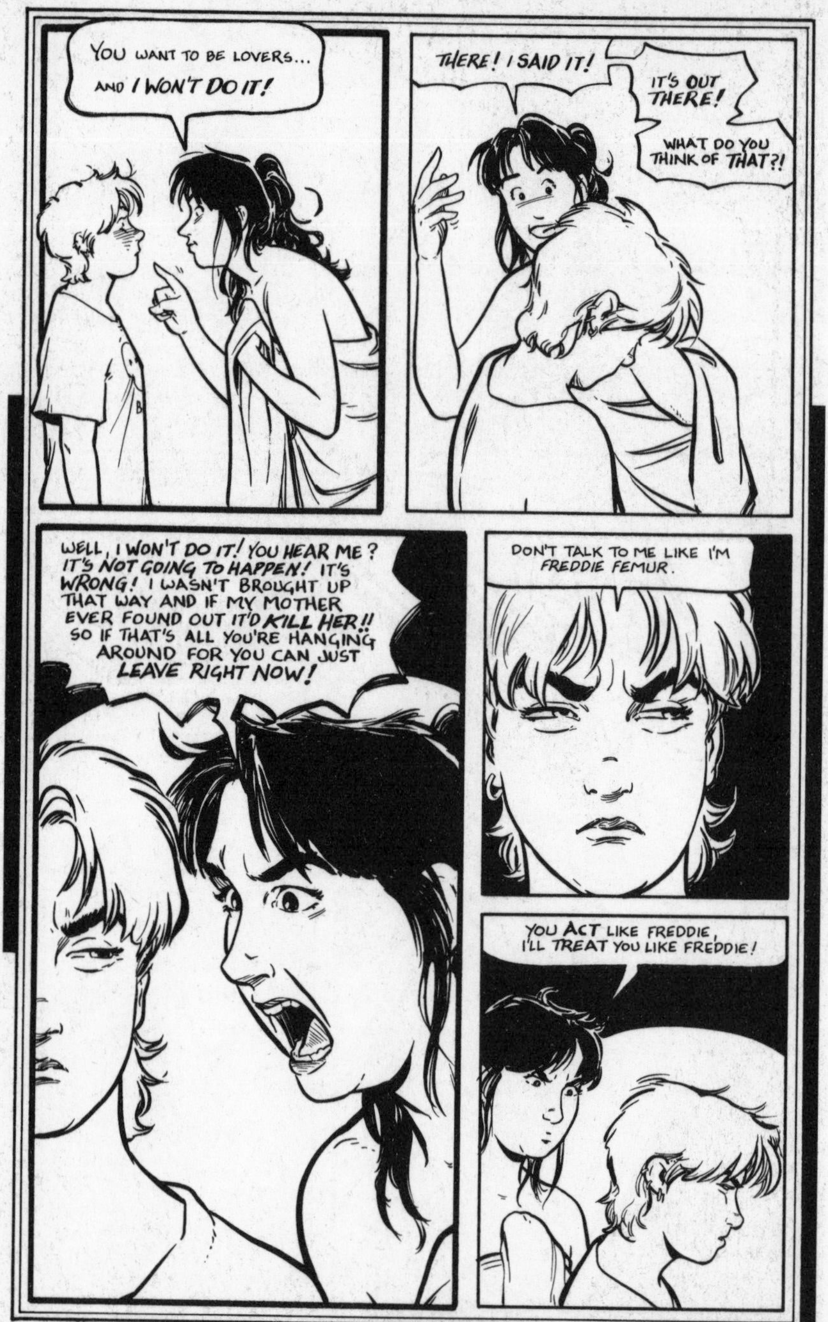

YOU WANT TO BE LOVERS... AND I WON'T DO IT!
THERE! I SAID IT!
IT'S OUT THERE!
WHAT DO YOU THINK OF THAT?!
WELL, I WON'T DO IT! YOU HEAR ME? IT'S NOT GOING TO HAPPEN! IT'S WRONG! I WASN'T BROUGHT UP THAT WAY AND IF MY MOTHER EVER FOUND OUT IT'D KILL HER!! SO IF THAT'S ALL YOU'RE HANGING AROUND FOR YOU CAN JUST LEAVE RIGHT NOW!
DON'T TALK TO ME LIKE I'M FREDDIE FEMUR.
YOU ACT LIKE FREDDIE, I'LL TREAT YOU LIKE FREDDIE!

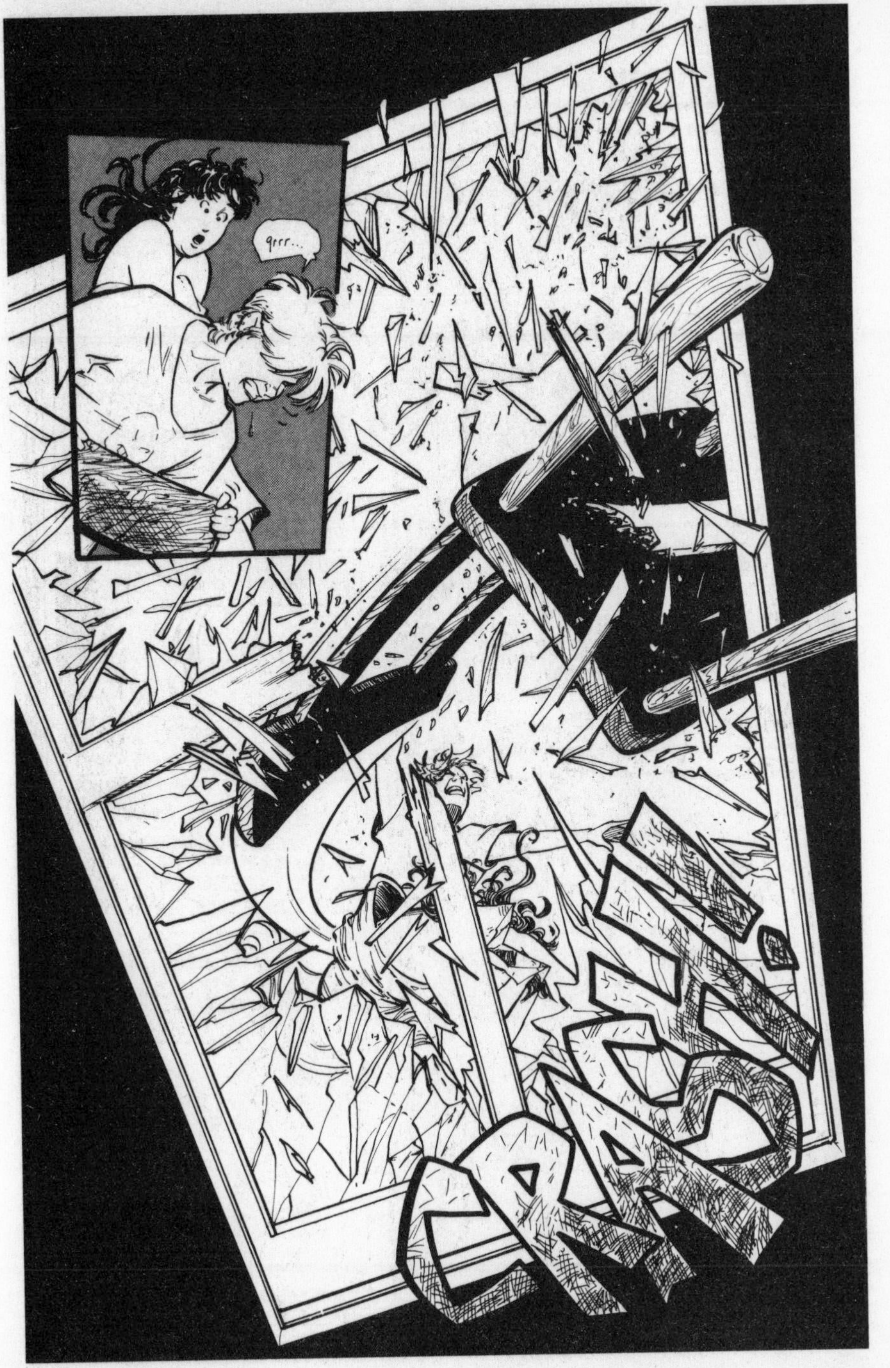
grrr...
CRASH!!

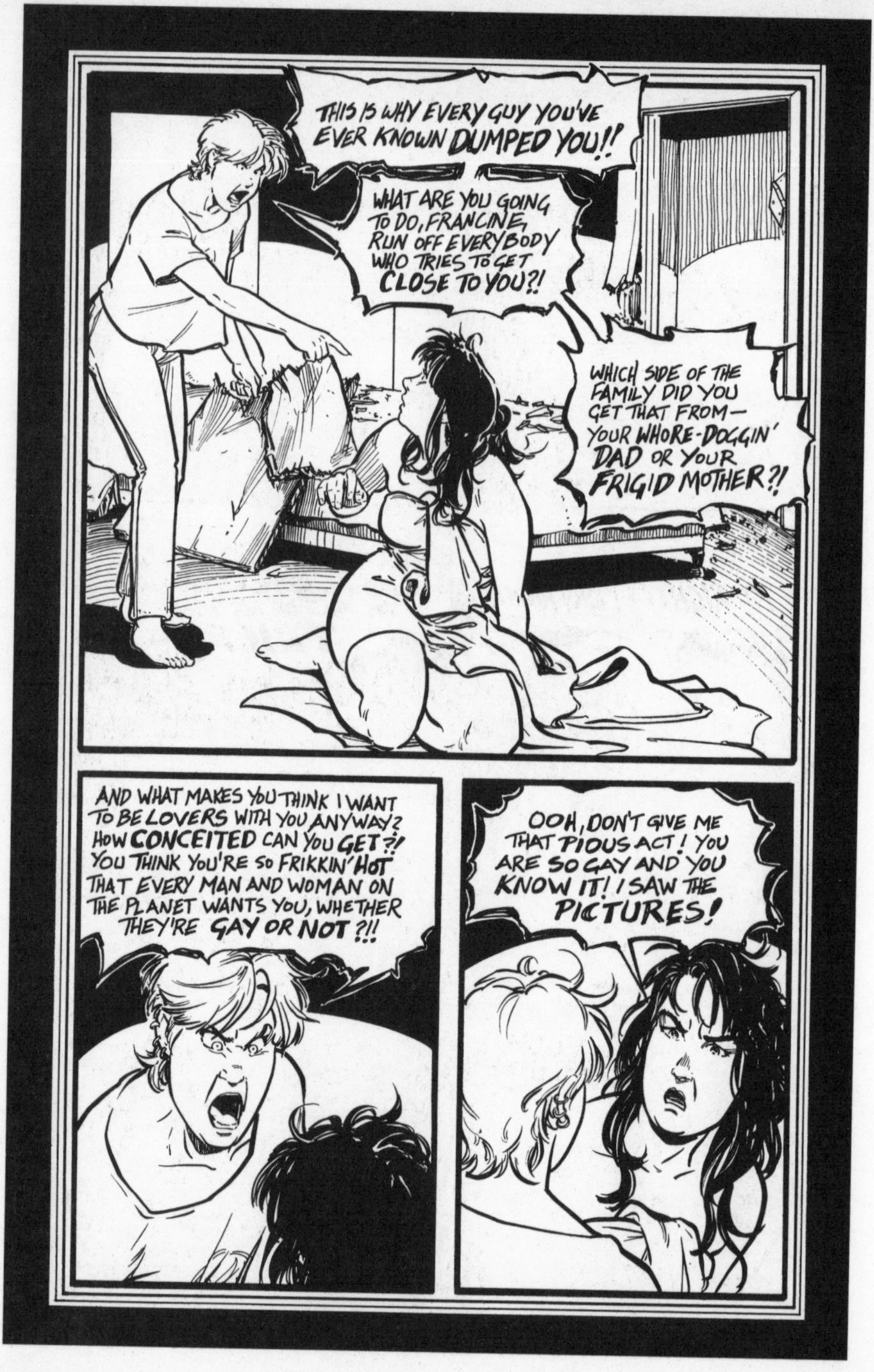
THIS IS WHY EVERY GUY YOU'VE EVER KNOWN DUMPED YOU!!
WHAT ARE YOU GOING TO DO, FRANCINE, RUN OFF EVERYBODY WHO TRIES TO GET CLOSE TO YOU?!
WHICH SIDE OF THE FAMILY DID YOU GET THAT FROM— YOUR WHORE-DOGGIN' DAD OR YOUR FRIGID MOTHER?!
AND WHAT MAKES YOU THINK I WANT TO BE LOVERS WITH YOU ANYWAY? HOW CONCEITED CAN YOU GET?! YOU THINK YOU'RE SO FRIKKIN' HOT THAT EVERY MAN AND WOMAN ON THE PLANET WANTS YOU, WHETHER THEY'RE GAY OR NOT?!!
OOH, DON'T GIVE ME THAT PIOUS ACT! YOU ARE SO GAY AND YOU KNOW IT! I SAW THE PICTURES!

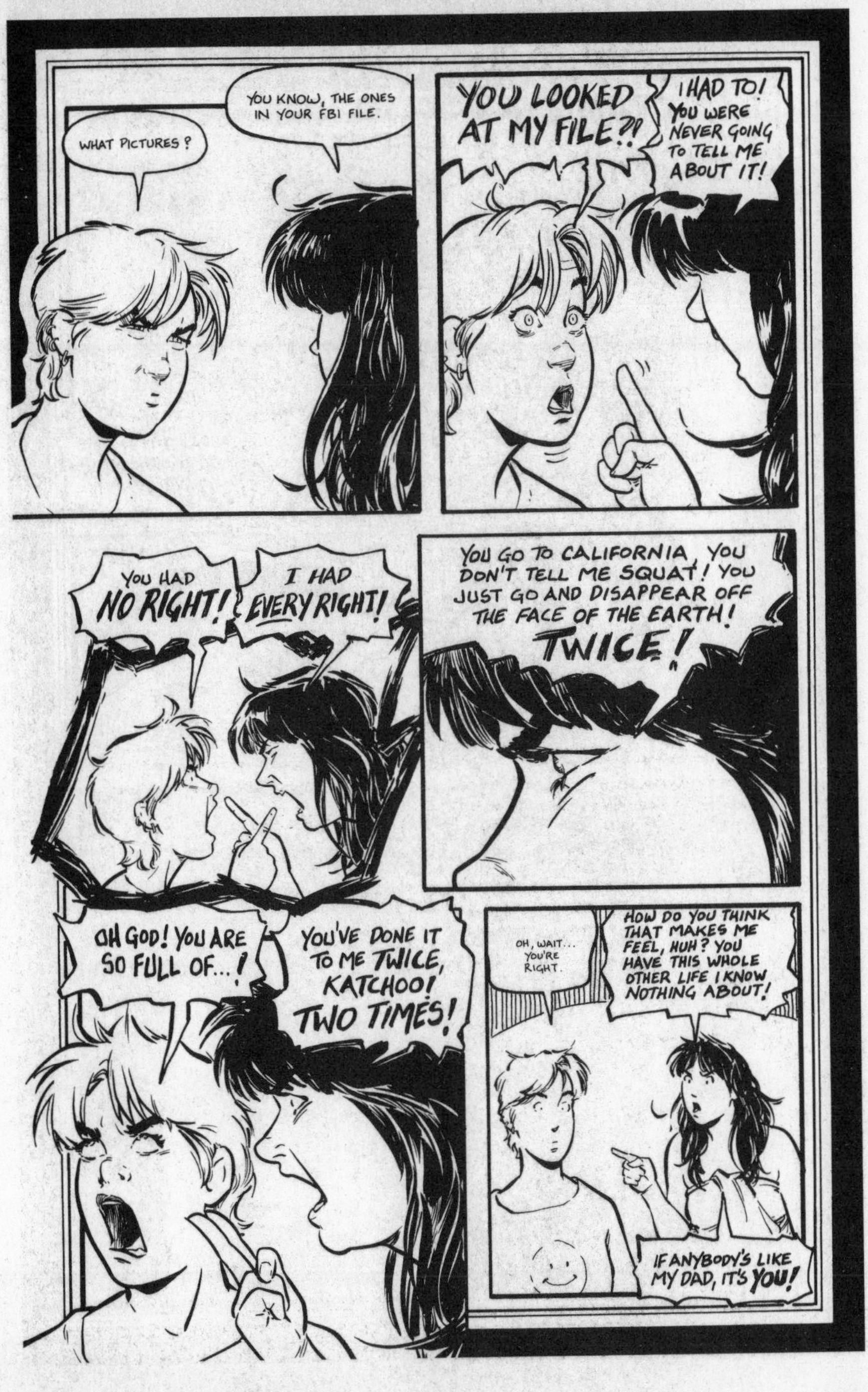
WHAT PICTURES ?
YOU KNOW, THE ONES IN YOUR FBI FILE.
YOU LOOKED AT MY FILE?!
I HAD TO! YOU WERE NEVER GOING TO TELL ME ABOUT IT!
YOU HAD NO RIGHT!
I HAD EVERY RIGHT!
YOU GO TO CALIFORNIA, YOU DON'T TELL ME SQUAT! YOU JUST GO AND DISAPPEAR OFF THE FACE OF THE EARTH! TWICE!
OH GOD! YOU ARE SO FULL OF...!
YOU'VE DONE IT TO ME TWICE, KATCHOO! TWO TIMES!
OH, WAIT... YOU'RE RIGHT.
HOW DO YOU THINK THAT MAKES ME FEEL, HUH? YOU HAVE THIS WHOLE OTHER LIFE I KNOW NOTHING ABOUT!
IF ANYBODY'S LIKE MY DAD, IT'S YOU!

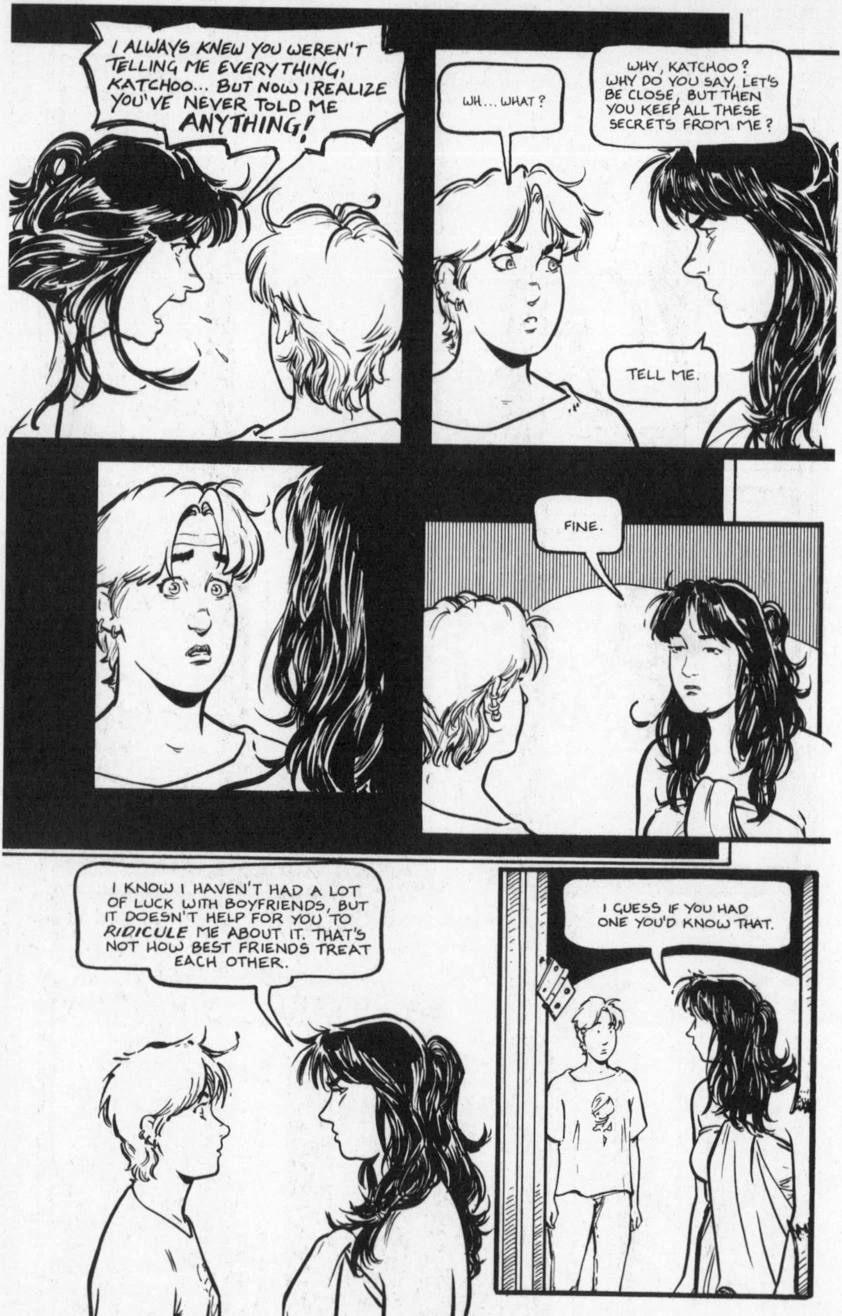
I ALWAYS KNEW YOU WEREN'T TELLING ME EVERYTHING, KATCHOO... BUT NOW I REALIZE YOU'VE NEVER TOLD ME ANYTHING!
WH... WHAT?
WHY, KATCHOO? WHY DO YOU SAY, LET'S BE CLOSE, BUT THEN YOU KEEP ALL THESE SECRETS FROM ME?
TELL ME.
FINE.
I KNOW I HAVEN'T HAD A LOT OF LUCK WITH BOYFRIENDS, BUT IT DOESN'T HELP FOR YOU TO RIDICULE ME ABOUT IT. THAT'S NOT HOW BEST FRIENDS TREAT EACH OTHER.
I GUESS IF YOU HAD ONE YOU'D KNOW THAT.

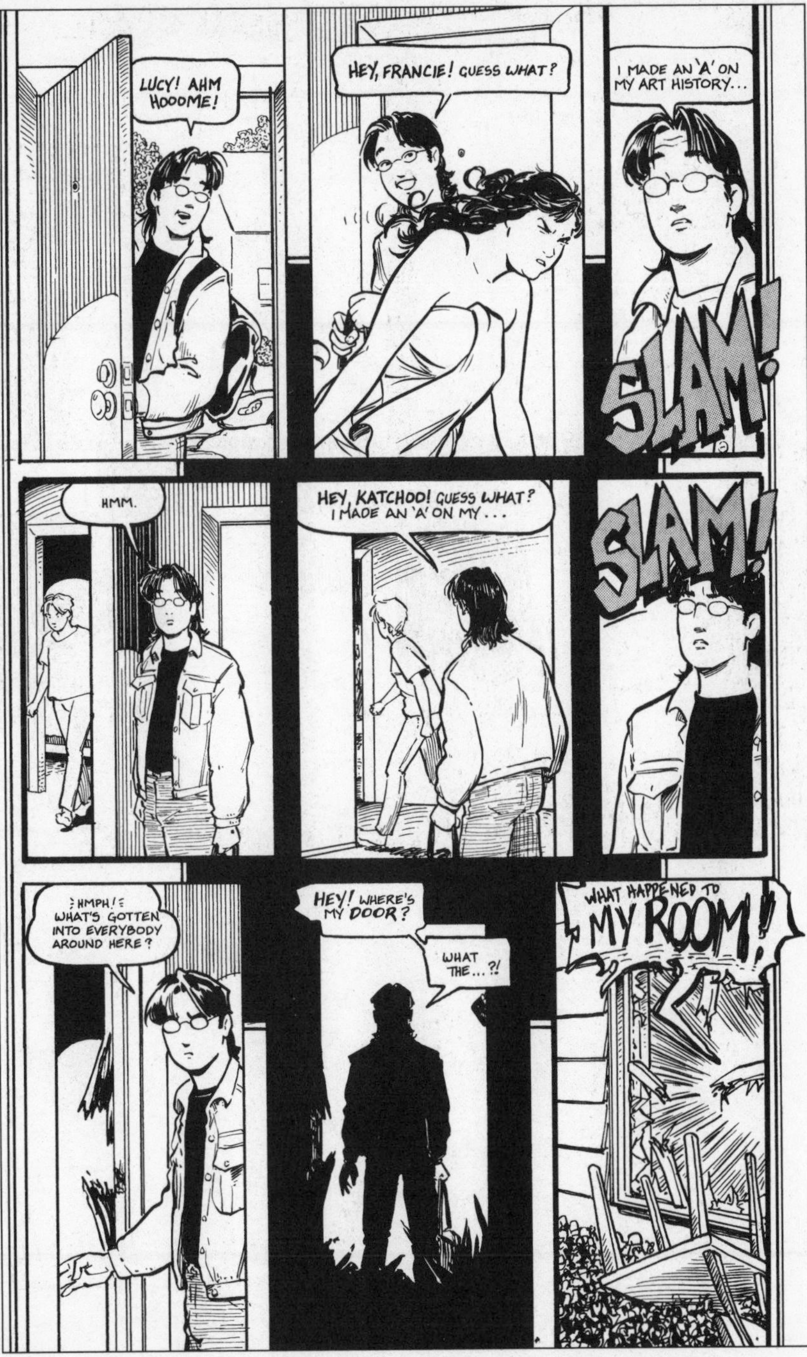
LUCY! AHM HOOOME!
HEY, FRANCIE! GUESS WHAT?
I MADE AN 'A' ON MY ART HISTORY...
SLAM!
HMM.
HEY, KATCHOO! GUESS WHAT? I MADE AN 'A' ON MY...
SLAM!
HMPH! WHAT'S GOTTEN INTO EVERYBODY AROUND HERE?
HEY! WHERE'S MY DOOR?
WHAT THE...?!
WHAT HAPPENED TO MY ROOM!

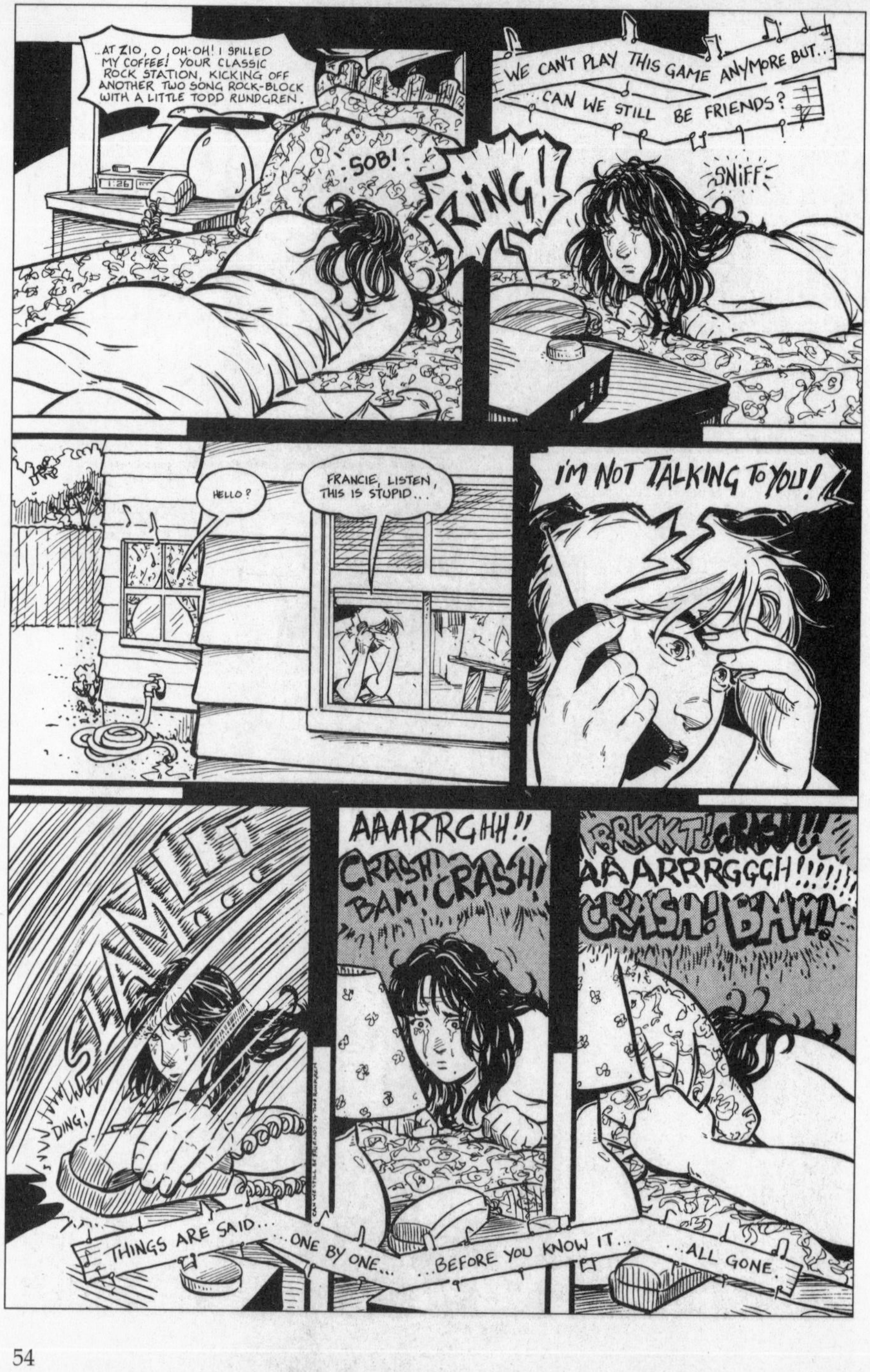
..AT ZIO, O, OH-OH! I SPILLED MY COFFEE! YOUR CLASSIC ROCK STATION, KICKING OFF ANOTHER TWO SONG ROCK-BLOCK WITH A LITTLE TODD RUNDGREN.
SOB!
WE CAN'T PLAY THIS GAME ANYMORE BUT...
...CAN WE STILL BE FRIENDS?
RING!
SNIFF
HELLO?
FRANCIE, LISTEN, THIS IS STUPID...
I'M NOT TALKING TO YOU!
SLAM!!...
DING!
AAARRGHH!!
CRASH! BAM! CRASH!
BRKKT! CRASH!!
AAARRRGGGH!!!!
CRASH! BAM!
THINGS ARE SAID...
...ONE BY ONE...
...BEFORE YOU KNOW IT...
...ALL GONE.

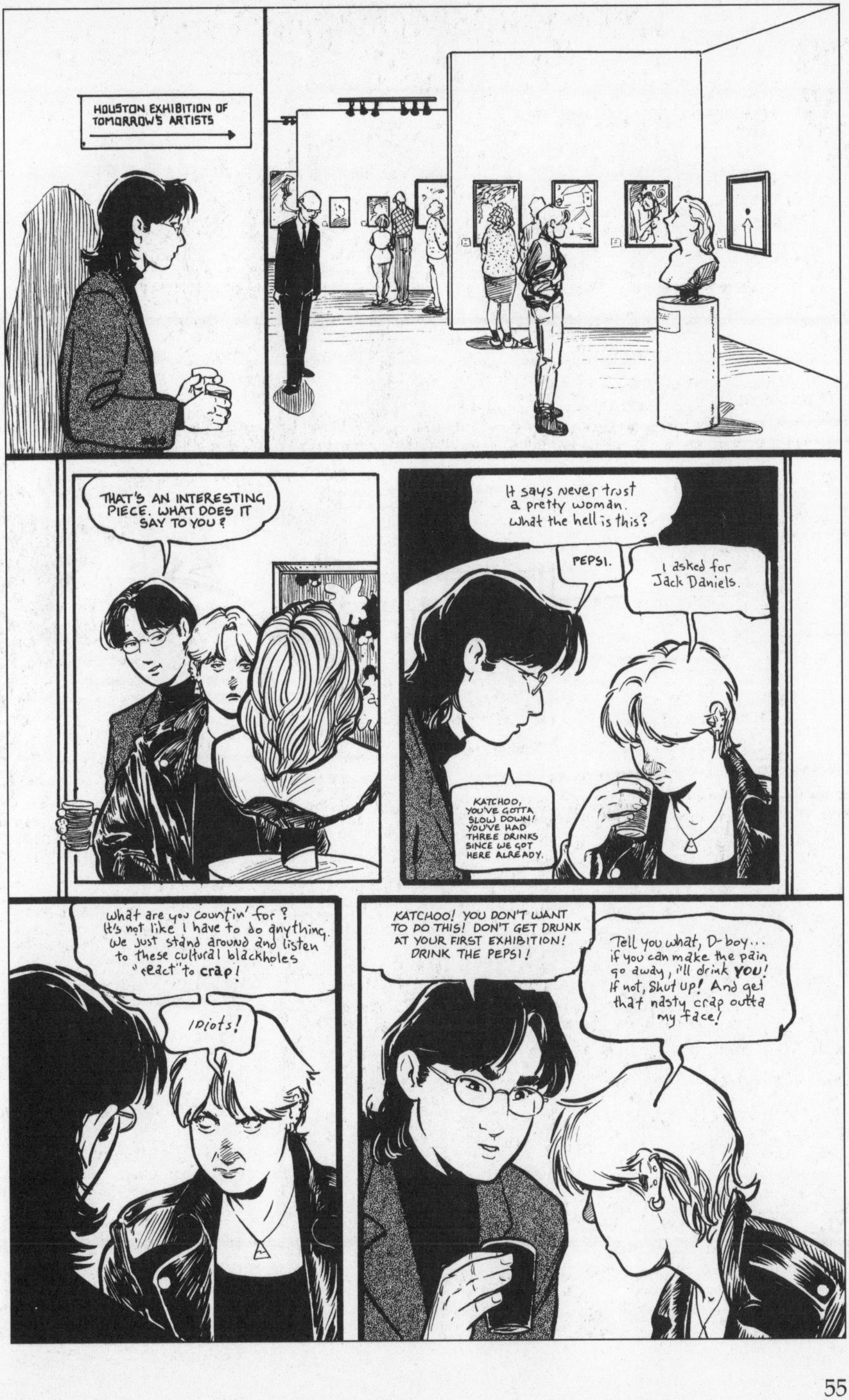

HOUSTON EXHIBITION OF TOMORROW'S ARTISTS
THAT'S AN INTERESTING PIECE. WHAT DOES IT SAY TO YOU?
It says never trust a pretty woman. What the hell is this?
PEPSI.
I asked for Jack Daniels.
KATCHOO, YOU'VE GOTTA SLOW DOWN! YOU'VE HAD THREE DRINKS SINCE WE GOT HERE ALREADY.
What are you countin' for? It's not like I have to do anything. We just stand around and listen to these cultural blackholes "react" to crap!
Idiots!
KATCHOO! YOU DON'T WANT TO DO THIS! DON'T GET DRUNK AT YOUR FIRST EXHIBITION! DRINK THE PEPSI!
Tell you what, D-boy... if you can make the pain go away, I'll drink YOU! If not, Shut up! And get that nasty crap outta my face!

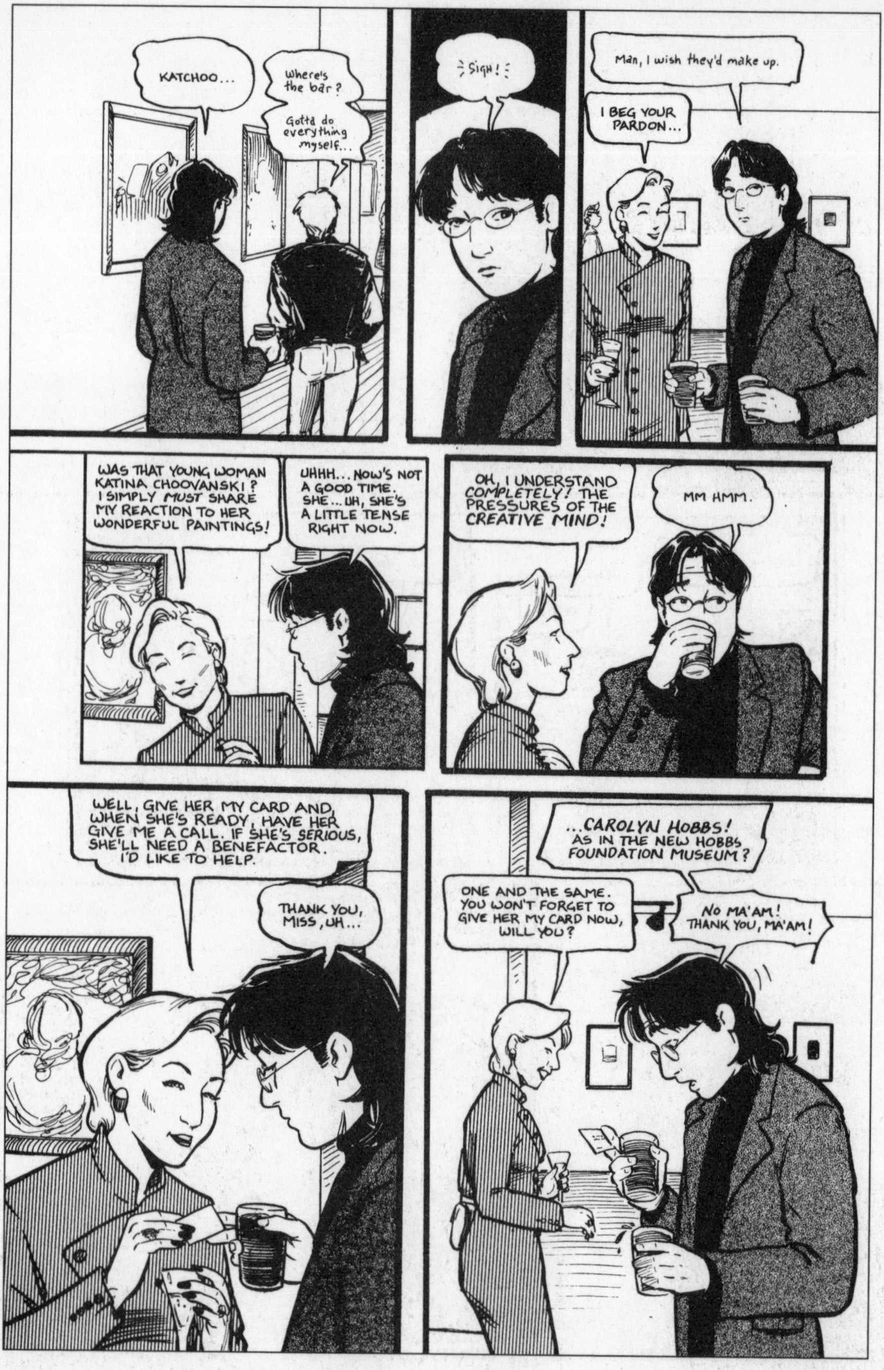
KATCHOO...
Where's the bar?
Gotta do everything myself...
SIGH!
Man, I wish they'd make up.
I BEG YOUR PARDON...
WAS THAT YOUNG WOMAN KATINA CHOOVANSKI? I SIMPLY MUST SHARE MY REACTION TO HER WONDERFUL PAINTINGS!
UHHH... NOW'S NOT A GOOD TIME. SHE... UH, SHE'S A LITTLE TENSE RIGHT NOW.
OH, I UNDERSTAND COMPLETELY! THE PRESSURES OF THE CREATIVE MIND!
MM HMM.
WELL, GIVE HER MY CARD AND, WHEN SHE'S READY, HAVE HER GIVE ME A CALL. IF SHE'S SERIOUS, SHE'LL NEED A BENEFACTOR. I'D LIKE TO HELP.
THANK YOU, MISS, UH...
...CAROLYN HOBBS! AS IN THE NEW HOBBS FOUNDATION MUSEUM?
ONE AND THE SAME. YOU WON'T FORGET TO GIVE HER MY CARD NOW, WILL YOU?
NO MA'AM! THANK YOU, MA'AM!

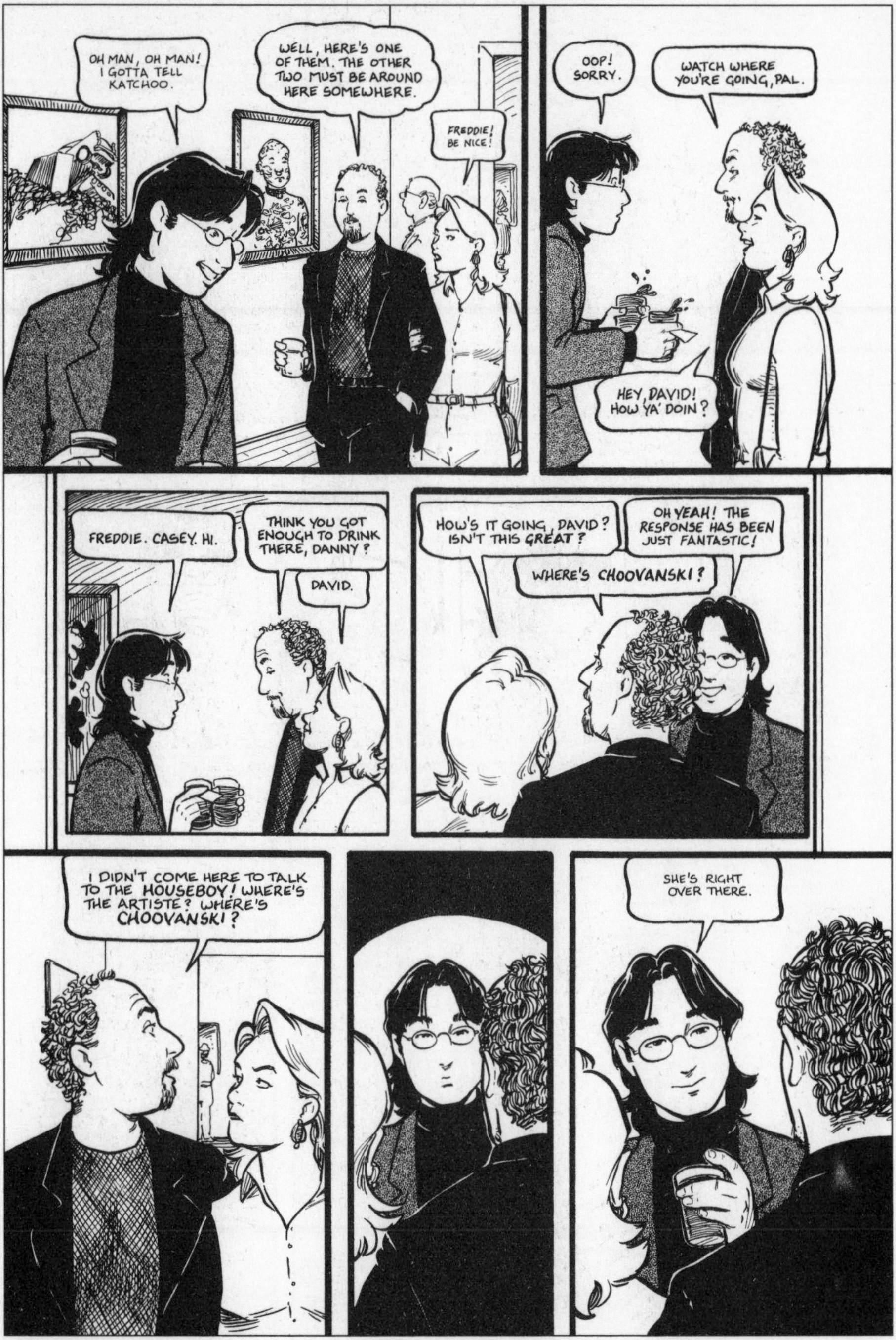
OH MAN, OH MAN! I GOTTA TELL KATCHOO.
WELL, HERE'S ONE OF THEM. THE OTHER TWO MUST BE AROUND HERE SOMEWHERE.
FREDDIE! BE NICE!
OOP! SORRY.
WATCH WHERE YOU'RE GOING, PAL.
HEY, DAVID! HOW YA' DOIN?
FREDDIE. CASEY. HI.
THINK YOU GOT ENOUGH TO DRINK THERE, DANNY?
DAVID.
HOW'S IT GOING, DAVID? ISN'T THIS GREAT?
OH YEAH! THE RESPONSE HAS BEEN JUST FANTASTIC!
WHERE'S CHOOVANSKI?
I DIDN'T COME HERE TO TALK TO THE HOUSEBOY! WHERE'S THE ARTISTE? WHERE'S CHOOVANSKI?
SHE'S RIGHT OVER THERE.

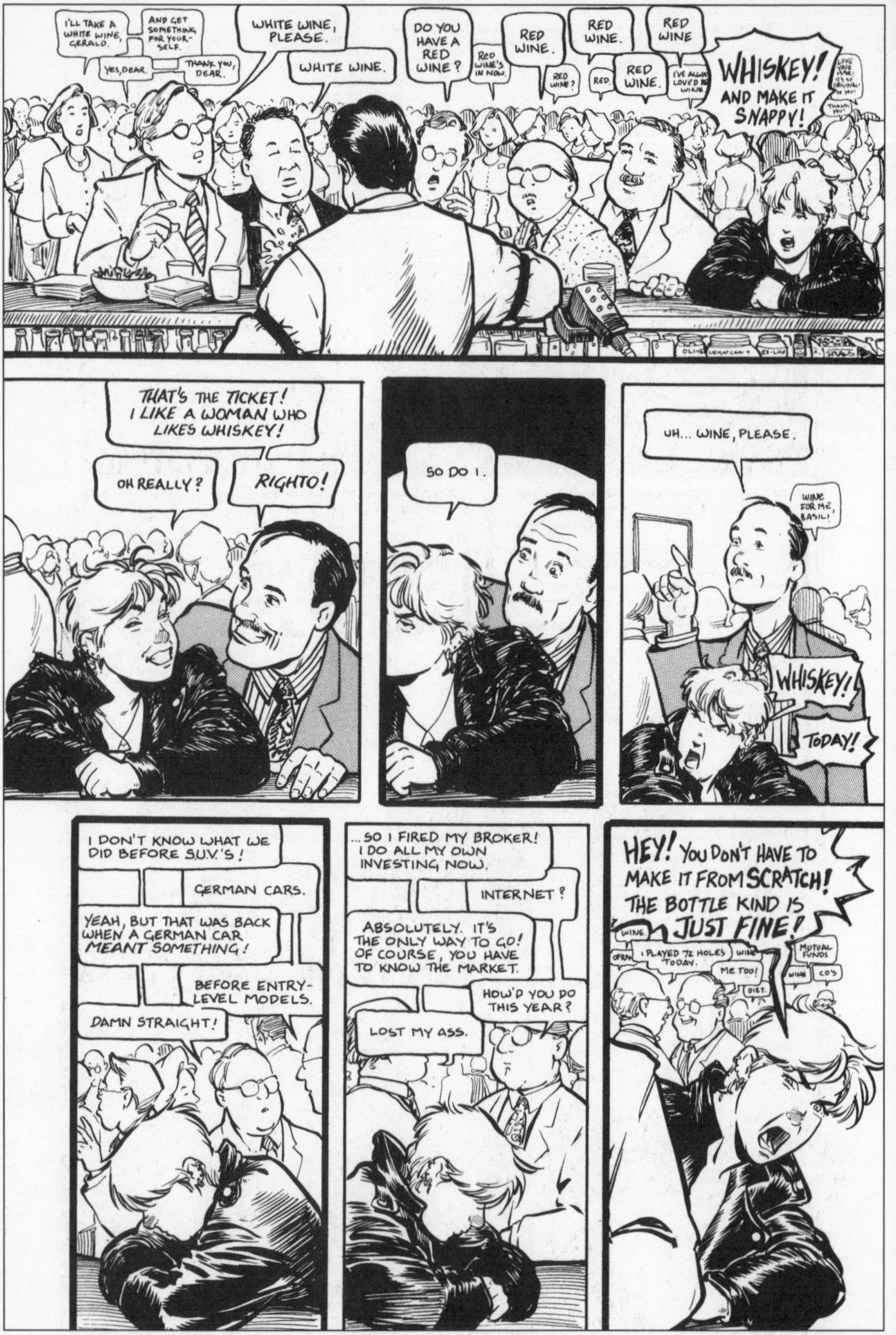
I'LL TAKE A WHITE WINE, GERALD.
AND GET SOMETHING FOR YOURSELF.
YES, DEAR.
THANK YOU, DEAR.
WHITE WINE, PLEASE.
WHITE WINE.
DO YOU HAVE A RED WINE?
RED WINE'S IN NOW.
RED WINE.
RED WINE?
RED WINE.
RED.
RED WINE.
RED WINE
WHISKEY! AND MAKE IT SNAPPY!
THANK YOU!
THAT'S THE TICKET! I LIKE A WOMAN WHO LIKES WHISKEY!
OH REALLY?
RIGHTO!
SO DO I.
UH... WINE, PLEASE.
WINE FOR ME, BASIL!
WHISKEY!
TODAY!
I DON'T KNOW WHAT WE DID BEFORE S.U.V.'S!
GERMAN CARS.
YEAH, BUT THAT WAS BACK WHEN A GERMAN CAR MEANT SOMETHING!
BEFORE ENTRY-LEVEL MODELS.
DAMN STRAIGHT!
...SO I FIRED MY BROKER! I DO ALL MY OWN INVESTING NOW.
INTERNET?
ABSOLUTELY. IT'S THE ONLY WAY TO GO! OF COURSE, YOU HAVE TO KNOW THE MARKET.
HOW'D YOU DO THIS YEAR?
LOST MY ASS.
HEY! YOU DON'T HAVE TO MAKE IT FROM SCRATCH! THE BOTTLE KIND IS JUST FINE!
WINE.
I PLAYED 72 HOLES TODAY.
ME TOO!
DIET.
MUTUAL FUNDS
CD'S

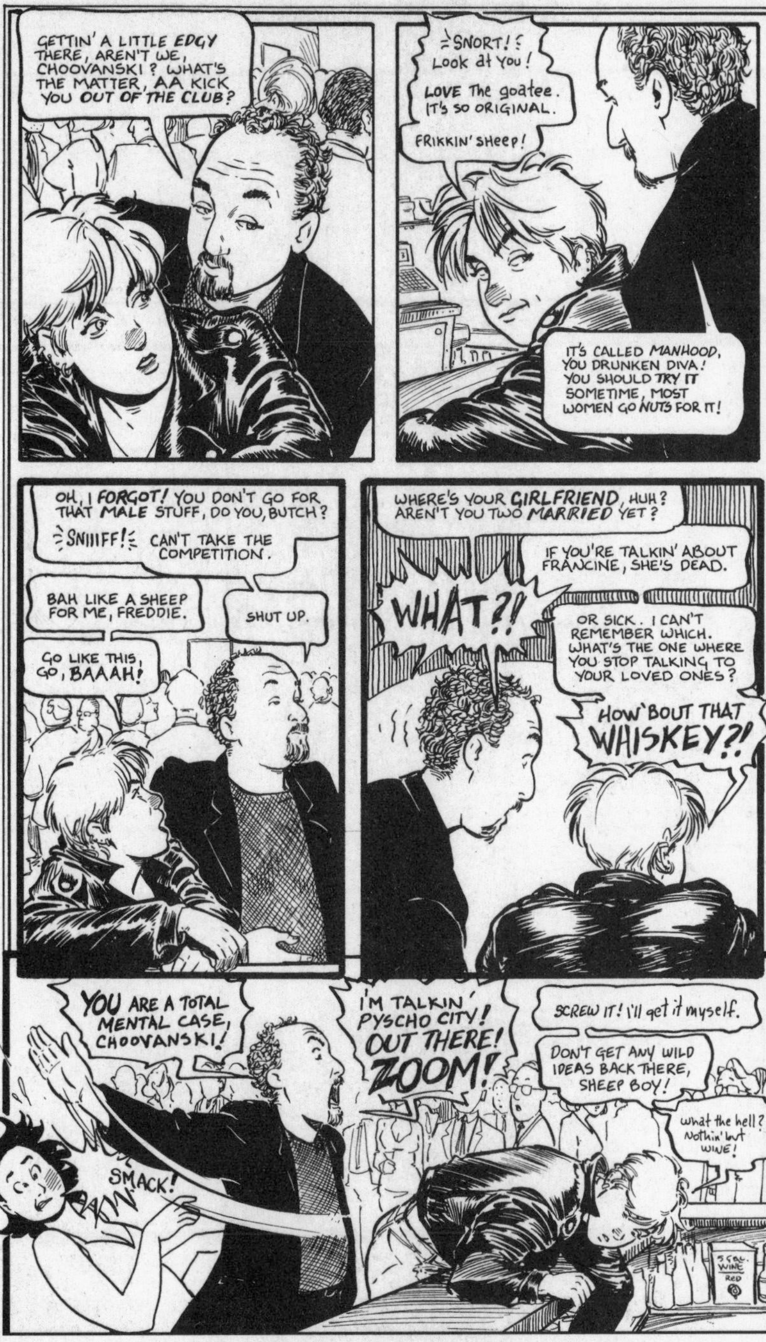
GETTIN' A LITTLE EDGY THERE, AREN'T WE, CHOOVANSKI? WHAT'S THE MATTER, AA KICK YOU OUT OF THE CLUB?
SNORT! Look at You!
LOVE The goatee. It's so ORIGINAL.
FRIKKIN' SHEEP!
IT'S CALLED MANHOOD, YOU DRUNKEN DIVA! YOU SHOULD TRY IT SOMETIME, MOST WOMEN GO NUTS FOR IT!
OH, I FORGOT! YOU DON'T GO FOR THAT MALE STUFF, DO YOU, BUTCH?
SNIIIFF! CAN'T TAKE THE COMPETITION.
BAH LIKE A SHEEP FOR ME, FREDDIE.
SHUT UP.
GO LIKE THIS, GO, BAAAH!
WHERE'S YOUR GIRLFRIEND, HUH? AREN'T YOU TWO MARRIED YET?
IF YOU'RE TALKIN' ABOUT FRANCINE, SHE'S DEAD.
WHAT?!
OR SICK. I CAN'T REMEMBER WHICH. WHAT'S THE ONE WHERE YOU STOP TALKING TO YOUR LOVED ONES?
HOW'BOUT THAT WHISKEY?!
YOU ARE A TOTAL MENTAL CASE, CHOOVANSKI!
I'M TALKIN' PYSCHO CITY! OUT THERE! ZOOM!
SCREW IT! I'll get it myself.
DON'T GET ANY WILD IDEAS BACK THERE, SHEEP BOY!
what the hell? Nothin' but WINE!
SMACK!

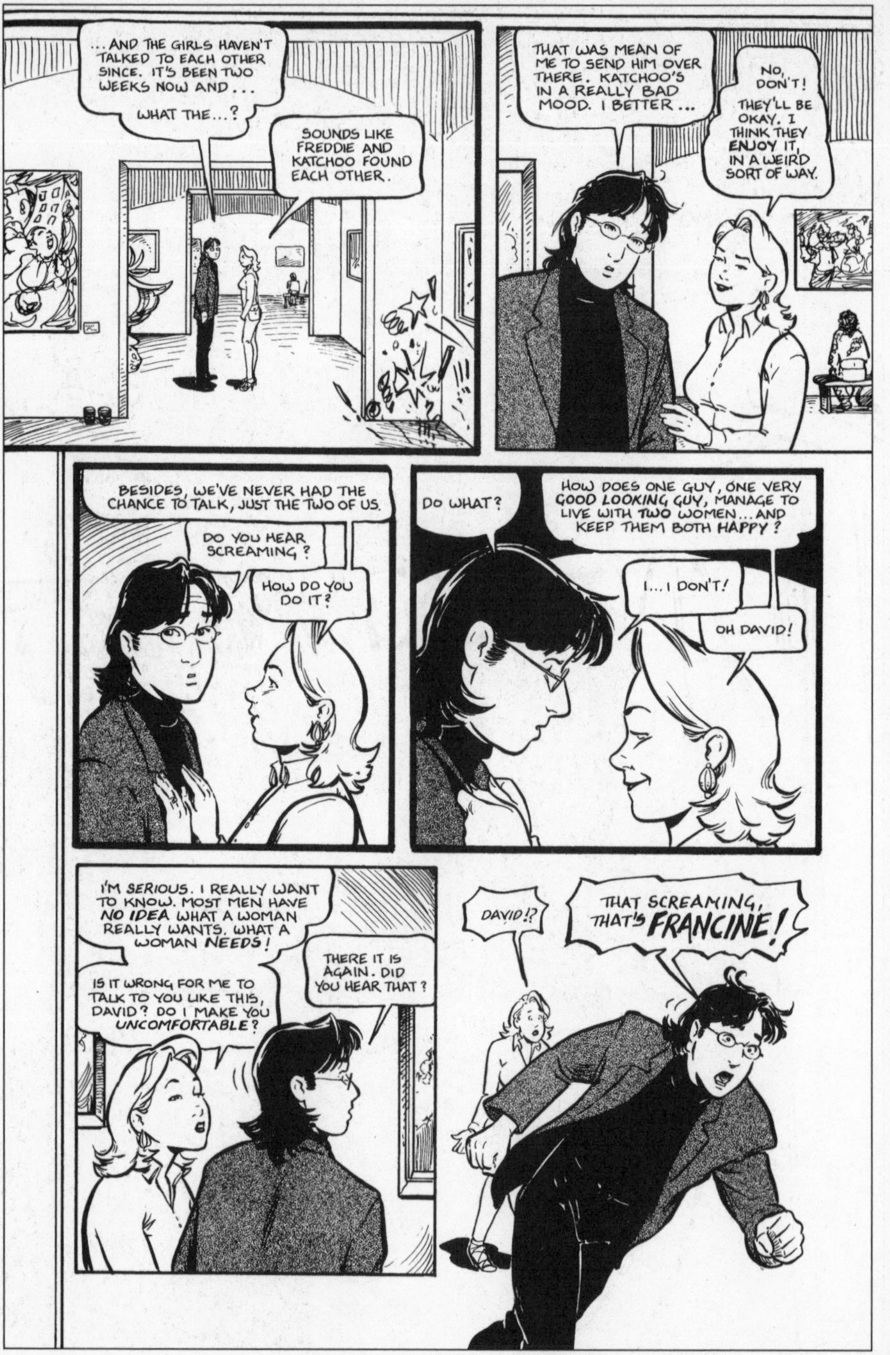

... AND THE GIRLS HAVEN'T TALKED TO EACH OTHER SINCE. IT'S BEEN TWO WEEKS NOW AND ...
WHAT THE...?
SOUNDS LIKE FREDDIE AND KATCHOO FOUND EACH OTHER.
THAT WAS MEAN OF ME TO SEND HIM OVER THERE. KATCHOO'S IN A REALLY BAD MOOD. I BETTER ...
NO, DON'T!
THEY'LL BE OKAY. I THINK THEY ENJOY IT, IN A WEIRD SORT OF WAY.
BESIDES, WE'VE NEVER HAD THE CHANCE TO TALK, JUST THE TWO OF US.
DO YOU HEAR SCREAMING?
HOW DO YOU DO IT?
DO WHAT?
HOW DOES ONE GUY, ONE VERY GOOD LOOKING GUY, MANAGE TO LIVE WITH TWO WOMEN... AND KEEP THEM BOTH HAPPY?
I... I DON'T!
OH DAVID!
I'M SERIOUS. I REALLY WANT TO KNOW. MOST MEN HAVE NO IDEA WHAT A WOMAN REALLY WANTS. WHAT A WOMAN NEEDS!
IS IT WRONG FOR ME TO TALK TO YOU LIKE THIS, DAVID? DO I MAKE YOU UNCOMFORTABLE?
THERE IT IS AGAIN. DID YOU HEAR THAT?
DAVID!?
THAT SCREAMING, THAT'S FRANCINE!

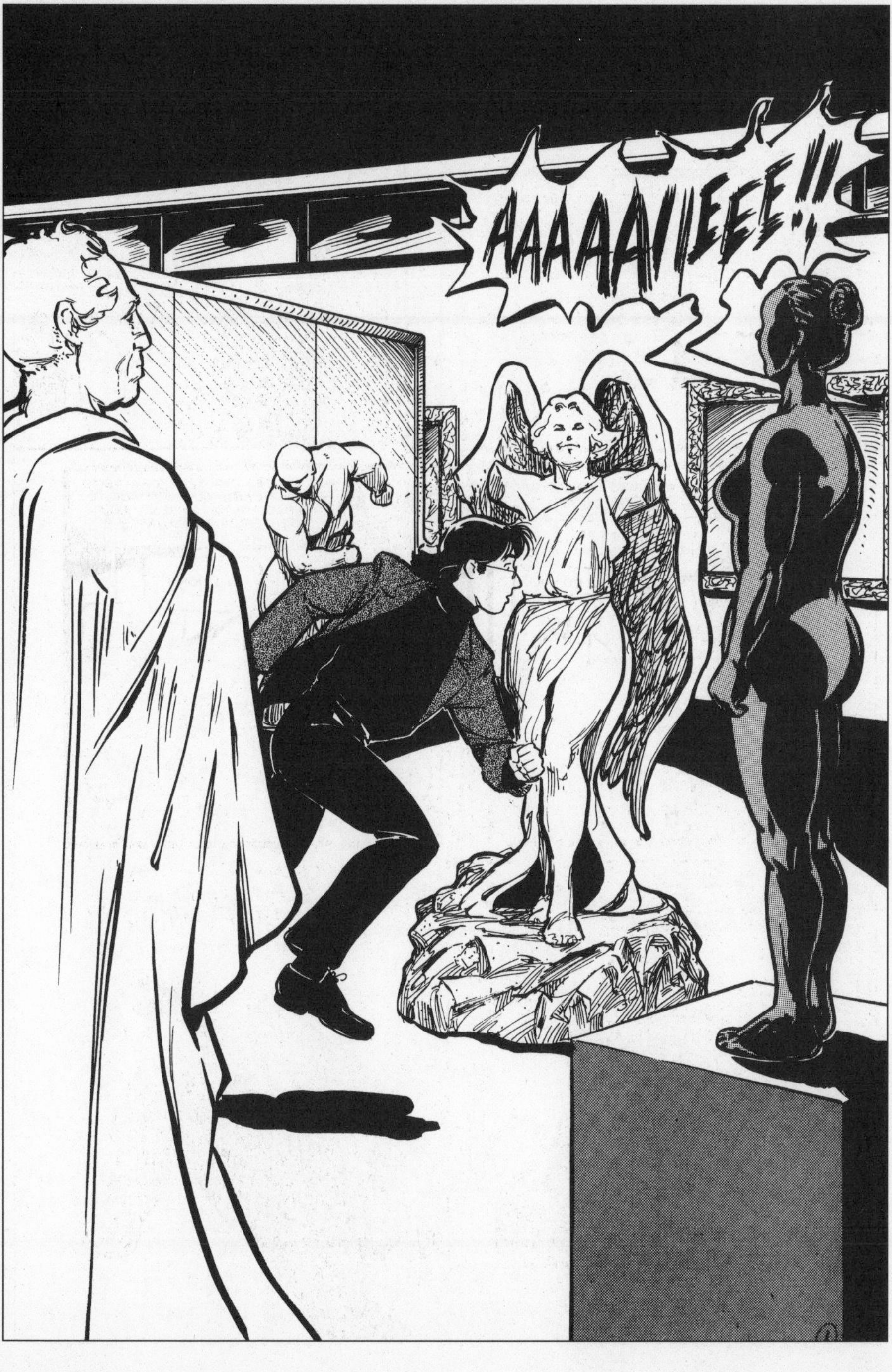
AAAAAIIEEE!!

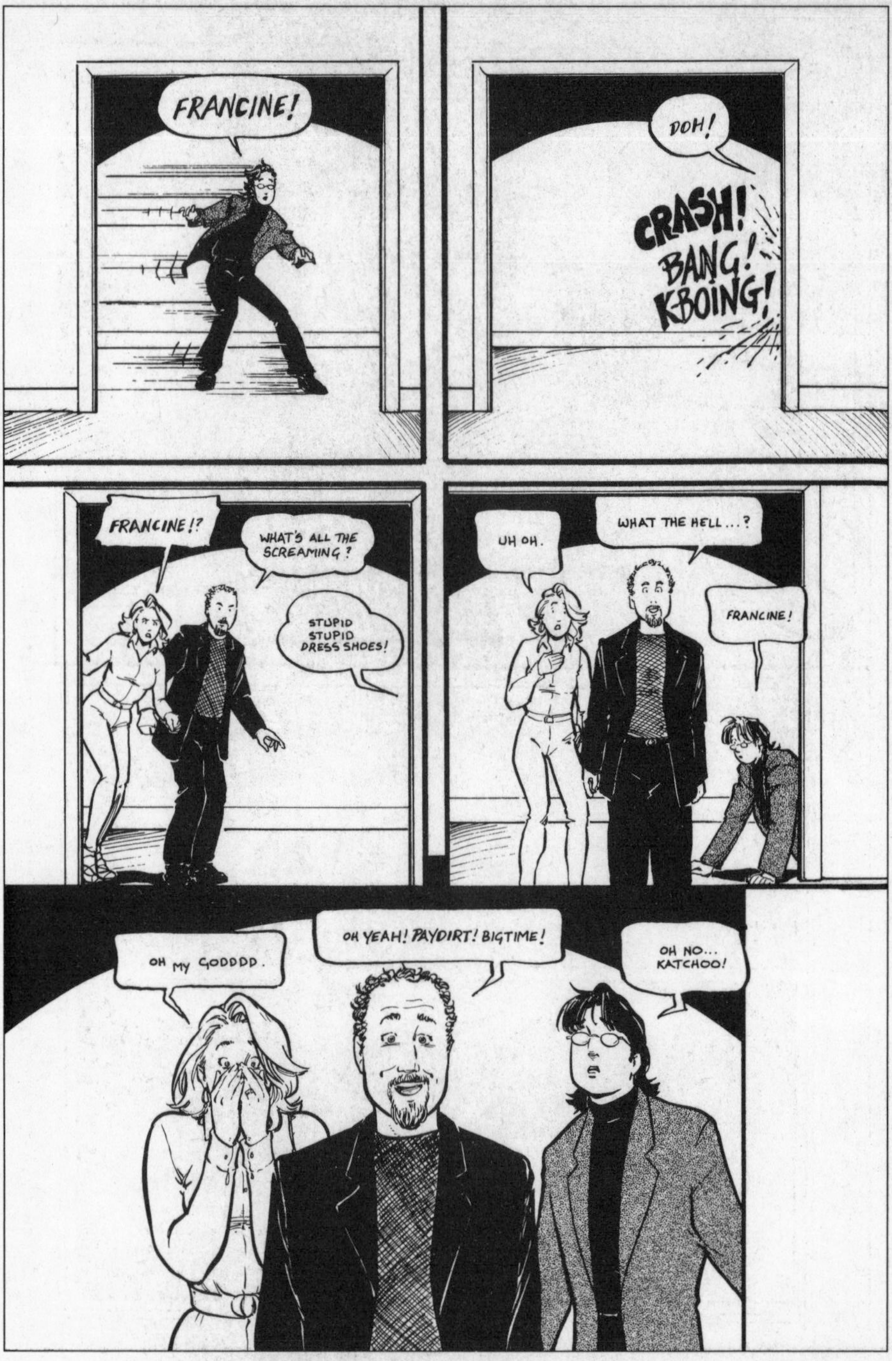
FRANCINE!
DOH!
CRASH! BANG! K-BOING!
FRANCINE!?
WHAT'S ALL THE SCREAMING?
STUPID STUPID DRESS SHOES!
UH OH.
WHAT THE HELL...?
FRANCINE!
OH MY GODDDD.
OH YEAH! PAYDIRT! BIGTIME!
OH NO... KATCHOO!

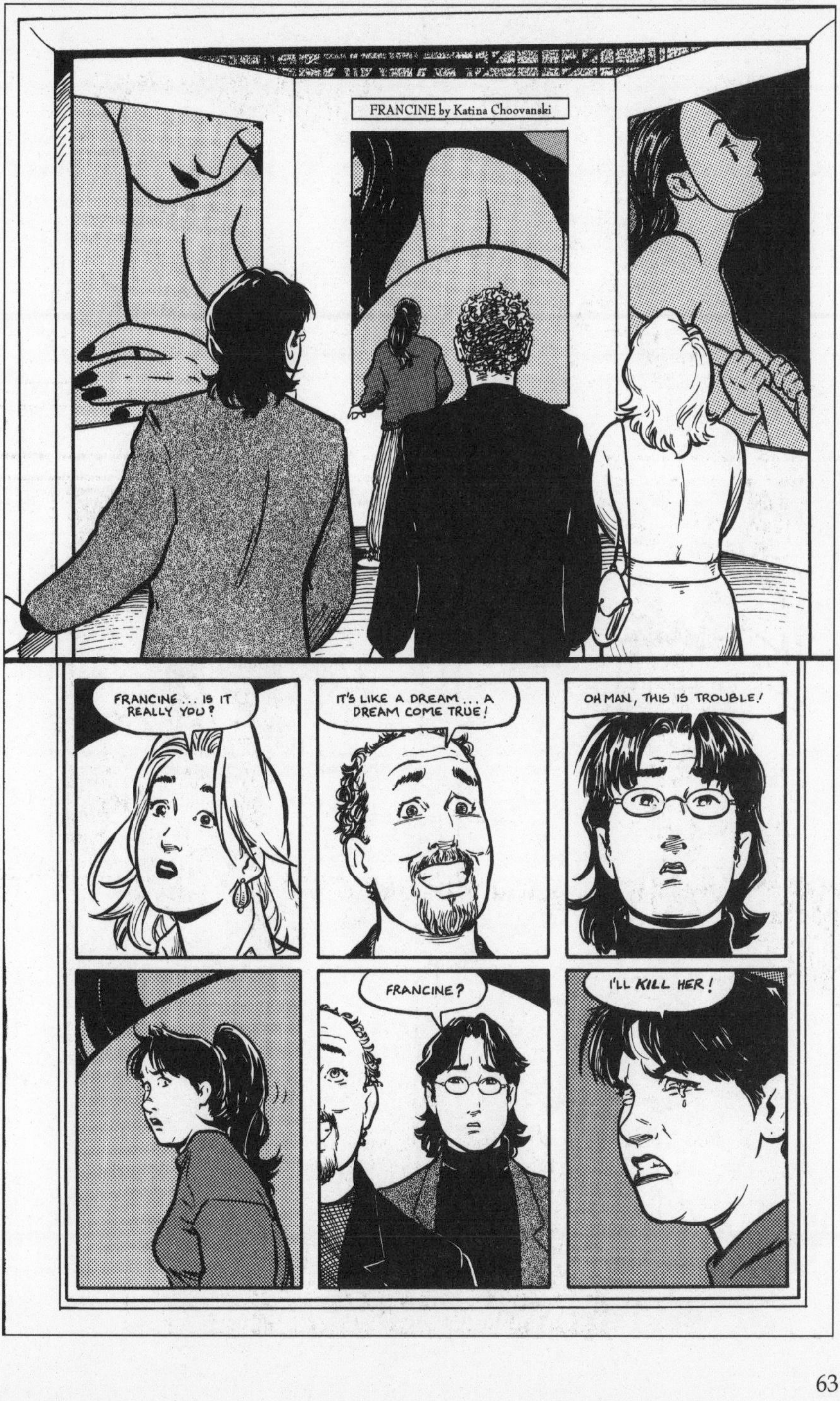
FRANCINE by Katina Choovanski
FRANCINE ... IS IT REALLY YOU?
IT'S LIKE A DREAM ... A DREAM COME TRUE!
OH MAN, THIS IS TROUBLE!
FRANCINE?
I'LL KILL HER!

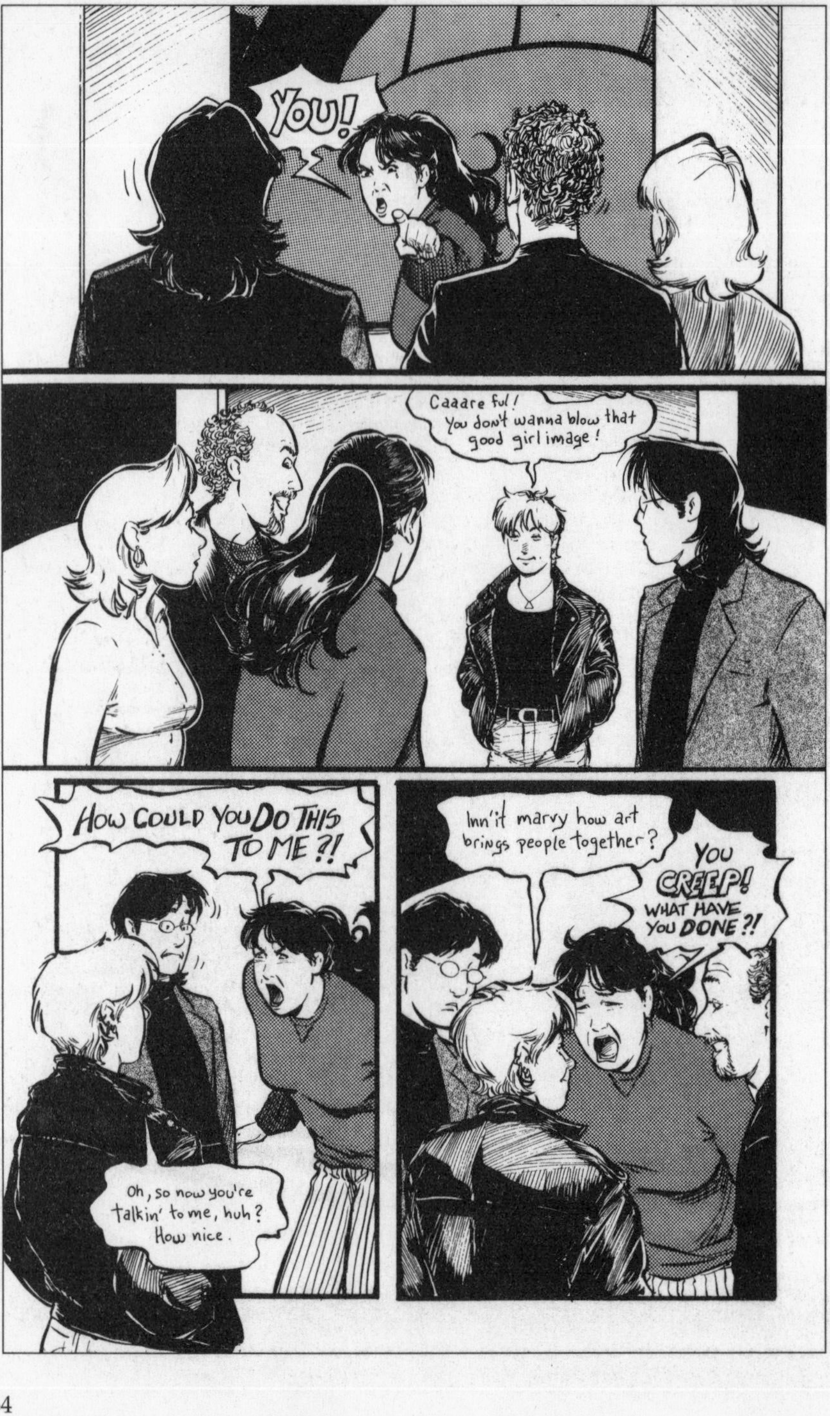
YOU!
Caaare ful! You don't wanna blow that good girl image!
HOW COULD YOU DO THIS TO ME?!
Oh, so now you're talkin' to me, huh? How nice.
Inn'it marvy how art brings people together?
YOU CREEP! WHAT HAVE YOU DONE?!

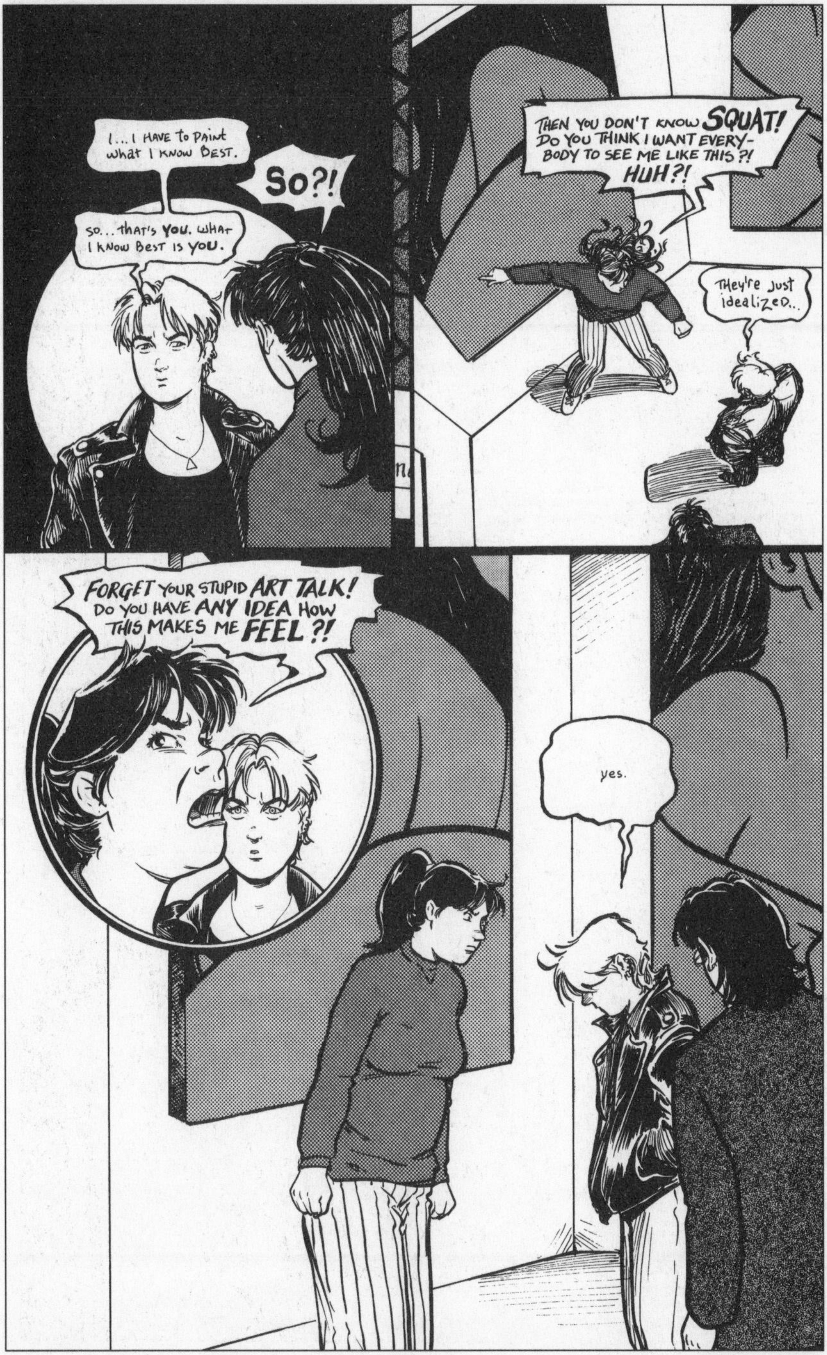
I... I HAVE TO PAINT what I KNOW BEST.
SO?!
SO... THAT'S YOU. WHAT I KNOW BEST IS YOU.
THEN YOU DON'T KNOW SQUAT! DO YOU THINK I WANT EVERY-BODY TO SEE ME LIKE THIS?! HUH?!
THEY'RE JUST idealized..
FORGET YOUR STUPID ART TALK! DO YOU HAVE ANY IDEA HOW THIS MAKES ME FEEL?!
yes.

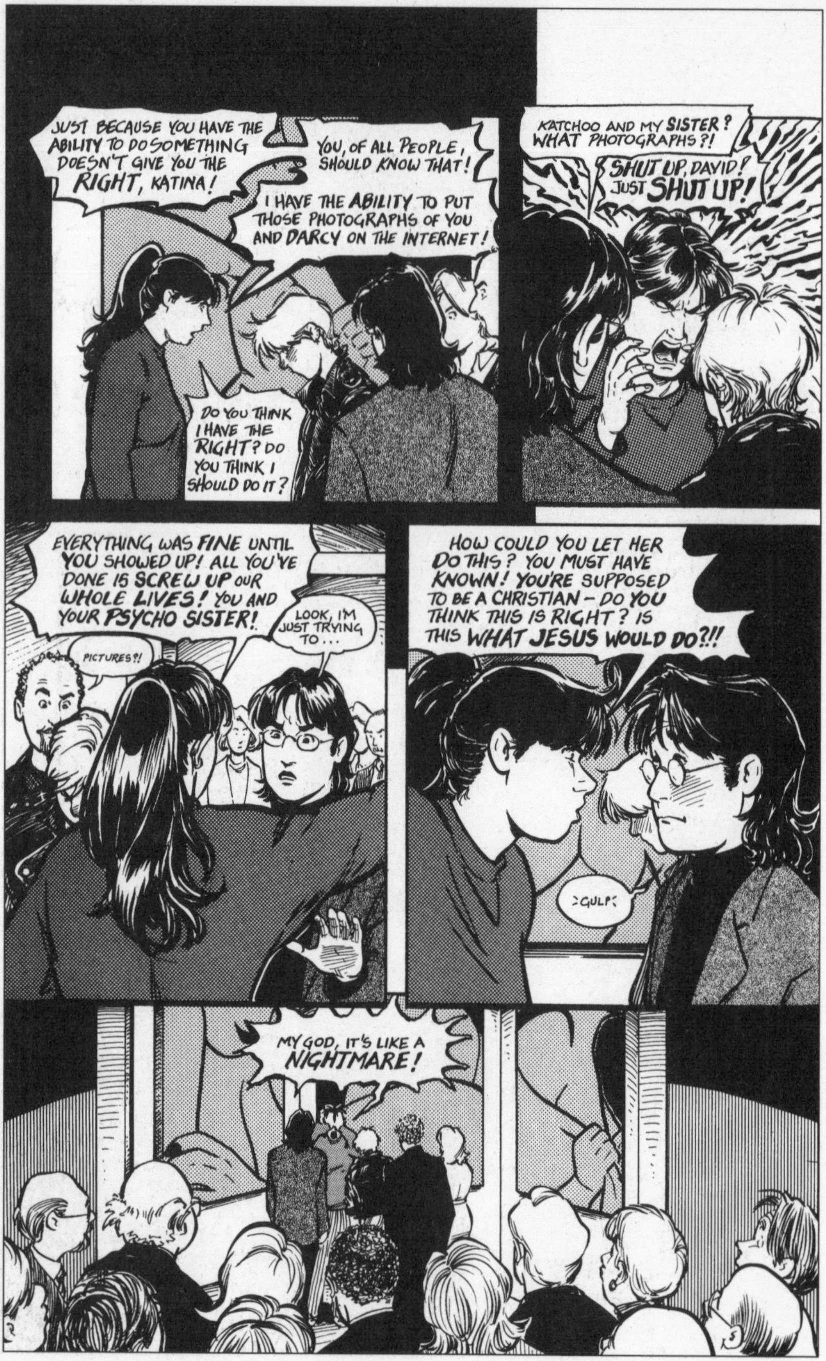
JUST BECAUSE YOU HAVE THE ABILITY TO DO SOMETHING DOESN'T GIVE YOU THE RIGHT, KATINA!
YOU, OF ALL PEOPLE, SHOULD KNOW THAT!
I HAVE THE ABILITY TO PUT THOSE PHOTOGRAPHS OF YOU AND DARCY ON THE INTERNET!
DO YOU THINK I HAVE THE RIGHT? DO YOU THINK I SHOULD DO IT?
KATCHOO AND MY SISTER? WHAT PHOTOGRAPHS?!
SHUT UP, DAVID! JUST SHUT UP!
EVERYTHING WAS FINE UNTIL YOU SHOWED UP! ALL YOU'VE DONE IS SCREW UP OUR WHOLE LIVES! YOU AND YOUR PSYCHO SISTER!
PICTURES?!
LOOK, I'M JUST TRYING TO...
HOW COULD YOU LET HER DO THIS? YOU MUST HAVE KNOWN! YOU'RE SUPPOSED TO BE A CHRISTIAN - DO YOU THINK THIS IS RIGHT? IS THIS WHAT JESUS WOULD DO?!!
>GULP<
MY GOD, IT'S LIKE A NIGHTMARE!

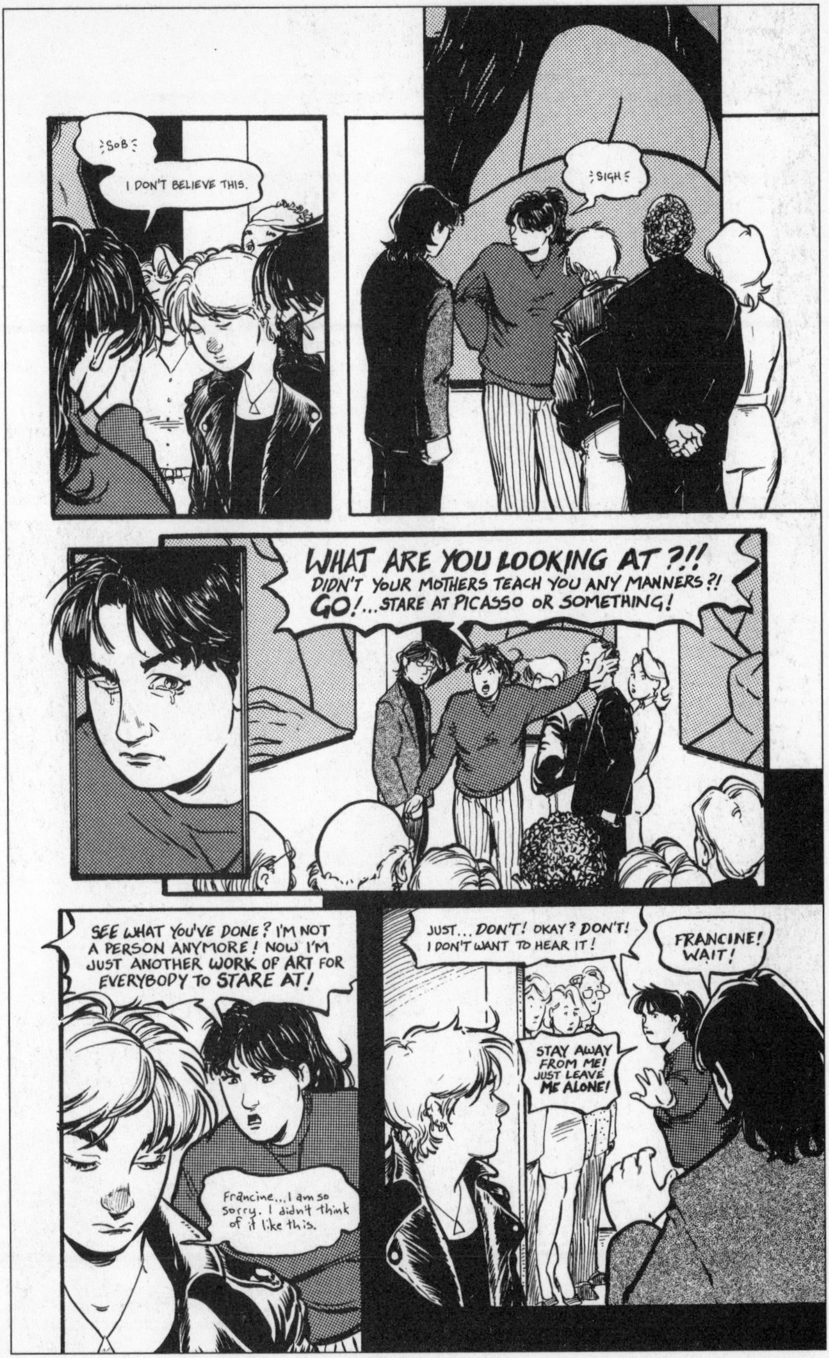
SOB
I DON'T BELIEVE THIS.
SIGH
WHAT ARE YOU LOOKING AT ?!! DIDN'T YOUR MOTHERS TEACH YOU ANY MANNERS ?! GO!... STARE AT PICASSO OR SOMETHING!
SEE WHAT YOU'VE DONE? I'M NOT A PERSON ANYMORE! NOW I'M JUST ANOTHER WORK OF ART FOR EVERYBODY TO STARE AT!
Francine... I am so sorry. I didn't think of it like this.
JUST... DON'T! OKAY? DON'T! I DON'T WANT TO HEAR IT!
FRANCINE! WAIT!
STAY AWAY FROM ME! JUST LEAVE ME ALONE!

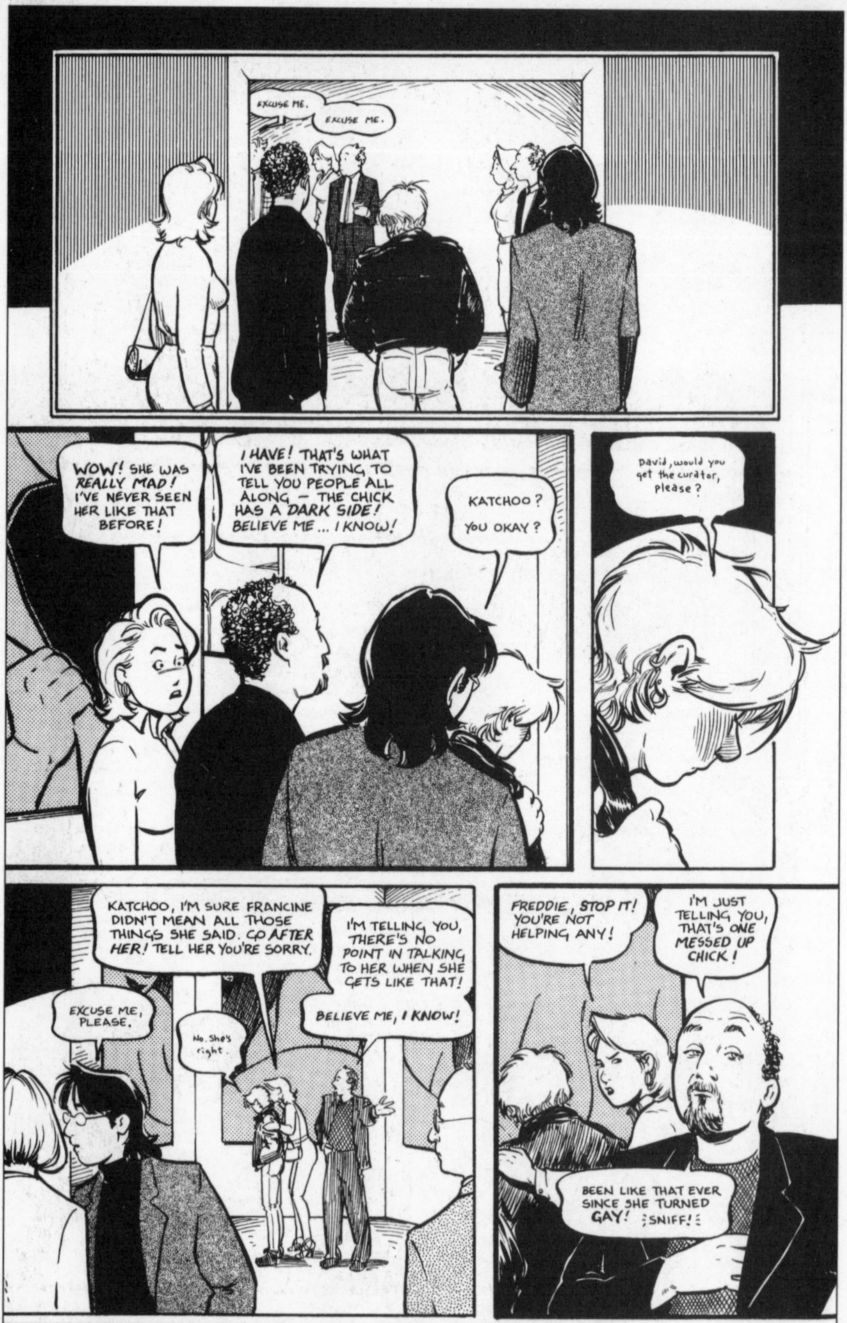

EXCUSE ME.
EXCUSE ME.
WOW! SHE WAS REALLY MAD! I'VE NEVER SEEN HER LIKE THAT BEFORE!
I HAVE! THAT'S WHAT I'VE BEEN TRYING TO TELL YOU PEOPLE ALL ALONG — THE CHICK HAS A DARK SIDE! BELIEVE ME ... I KNOW!
KATCHOO? YOU OKAY?
David, would you get the curator, please?
KATCHOO, I'M SURE FRANCINE DIDN'T MEAN ALL THOSE THINGS SHE SAID. GO AFTER HER! TELL HER YOU'RE SORRY.
I'M TELLING YOU, THERE'S NO POINT IN TALKING TO HER WHEN SHE GETS LIKE THAT!
BELIEVE ME, I KNOW!
EXCUSE ME, PLEASE.
No. She's right.
FREDDIE, STOP IT! YOU'RE NOT HELPING ANY!
I'M JUST TELLING YOU, THAT'S ONE MESSED UP CHICK!
BEEN LIKE THAT EVER SINCE SHE TURNED GAY! ;SNIFF!

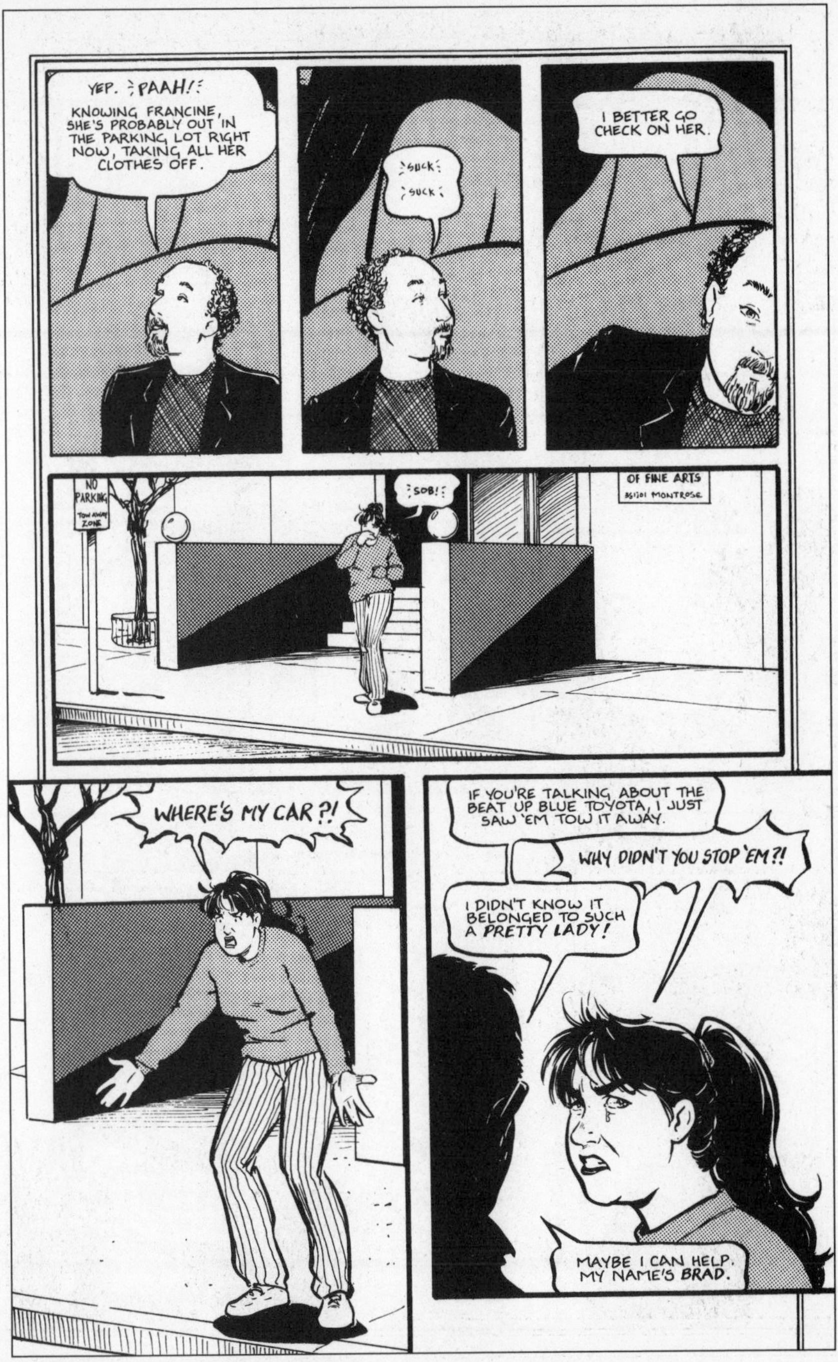
YEP. PAAH!
KNOWING FRANCINE, SHE'S PROBABLY OUT IN THE PARKING LOT RIGHT NOW, TAKING ALL HER CLOTHES OFF.
SUCK
SUCK
I BETTER GO CHECK ON HER.
NO PARKING
TOW AWAY ZONE
SOB!
OF FINE ARTS
MONTROSE
WHERE'S MY CAR?!
IF YOU'RE TALKING ABOUT THE BEAT UP BLUE TOYOTA, I JUST SAW 'EM TOW IT AWAY.
WHY DIDN'T YOU STOP 'EM?!
I DIDN'T KNOW IT BELONGED TO SUCH A PRETTY LADY!
MAYBE I CAN HELP. MY NAME'S BRAD.

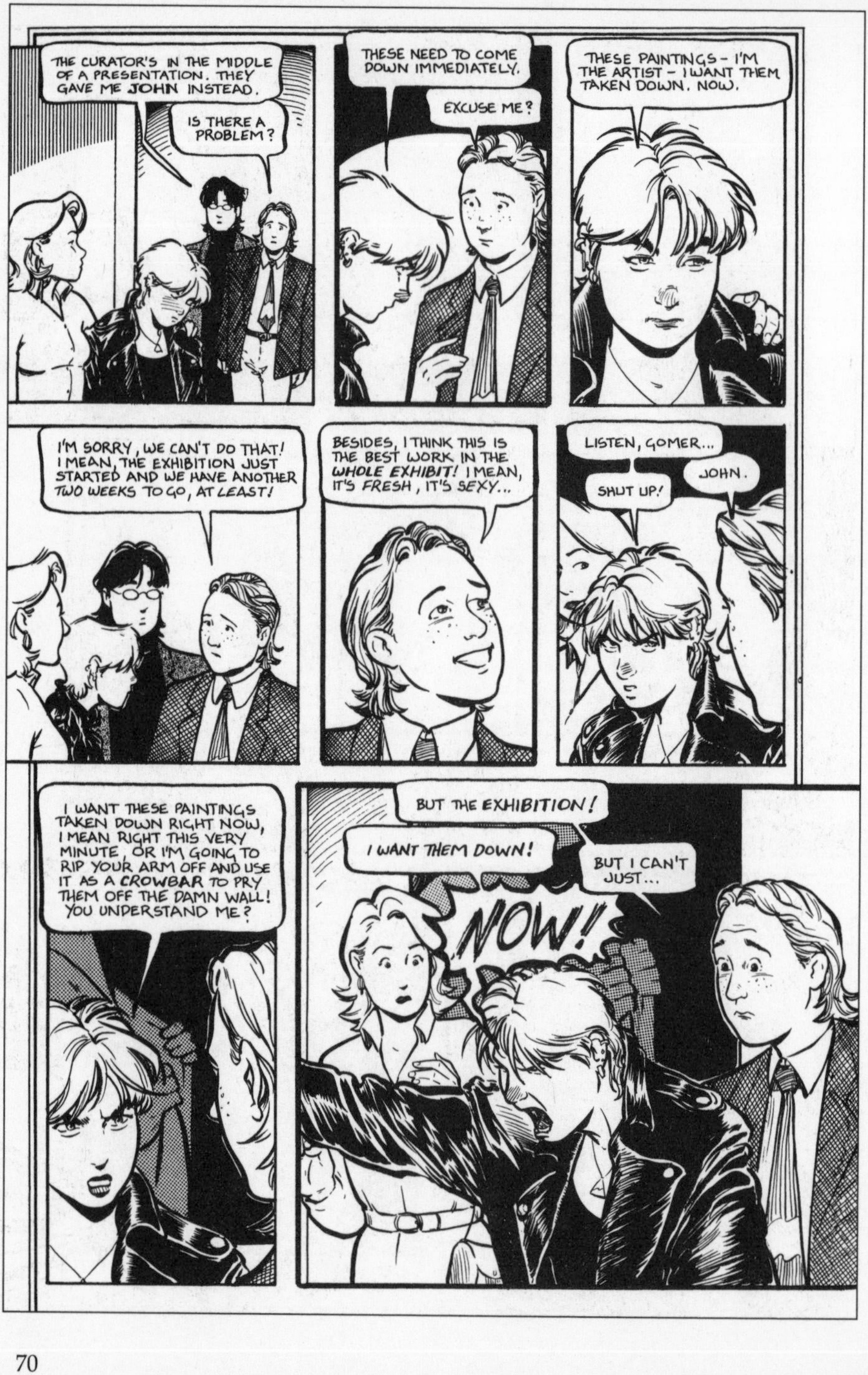
THE CURATOR'S IN THE MIDDLE OF A PRESENTATION. THEY GAVE ME JOHN INSTEAD.
IS THERE A PROBLEM?
THESE NEED TO COME DOWN IMMEDIATELY.
EXCUSE ME?
THESE PAINTINGS - I'M THE ARTIST - I WANT THEM TAKEN DOWN. NOW.
I'M SORRY, WE CAN'T DO THAT! I MEAN, THE EXHIBITION JUST STARTED AND WE HAVE ANOTHER TWO WEEKS TO GO, AT LEAST!
BESIDES, I THINK THIS IS THE BEST WORK IN THE WHOLE EXHIBIT! I MEAN, IT'S FRESH, IT'S SEXY...
LISTEN, GOMER...
JOHN.
SHUT UP!
I WANT THESE PAINTINGS TAKEN DOWN RIGHT NOW, I MEAN RIGHT THIS VERY MINUTE, OR I'M GOING TO RIP YOUR ARM OFF AND USE IT AS A CROWBAR TO PRY THEM OFF THE DAMN WALL! YOU UNDERSTAND ME?
BUT THE EXHIBITION!
I WANT THEM DOWN!
BUT I CAN'T JUST...
NOW!

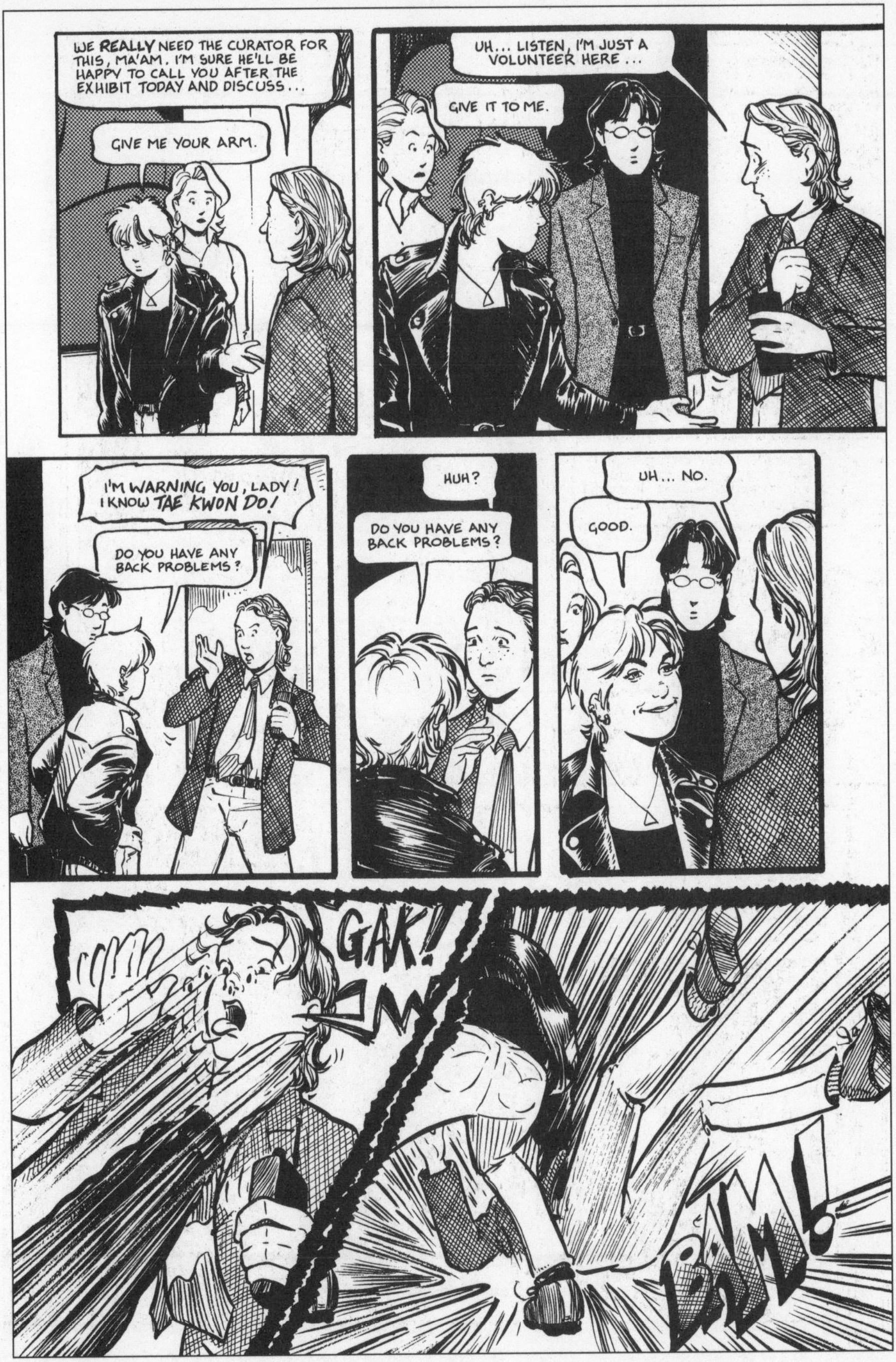
WE REALLY NEED THE CURATOR FOR THIS, MA'AM. I'M SURE HE'LL BE HAPPY TO CALL YOU AFTER THE EXHIBIT TODAY AND DISCUSS...
GIVE ME YOUR ARM.
UH... LISTEN, I'M JUST A VOLUNTEER HERE...
GIVE IT TO ME.
I'M WARNING YOU, LADY! I KNOW TAE KWON DO!
DO YOU HAVE ANY BACK PROBLEMS?
HUH?
DO YOU HAVE ANY BACK PROBLEMS?
UH... NO.
GOOD.
GAK!
BAM!

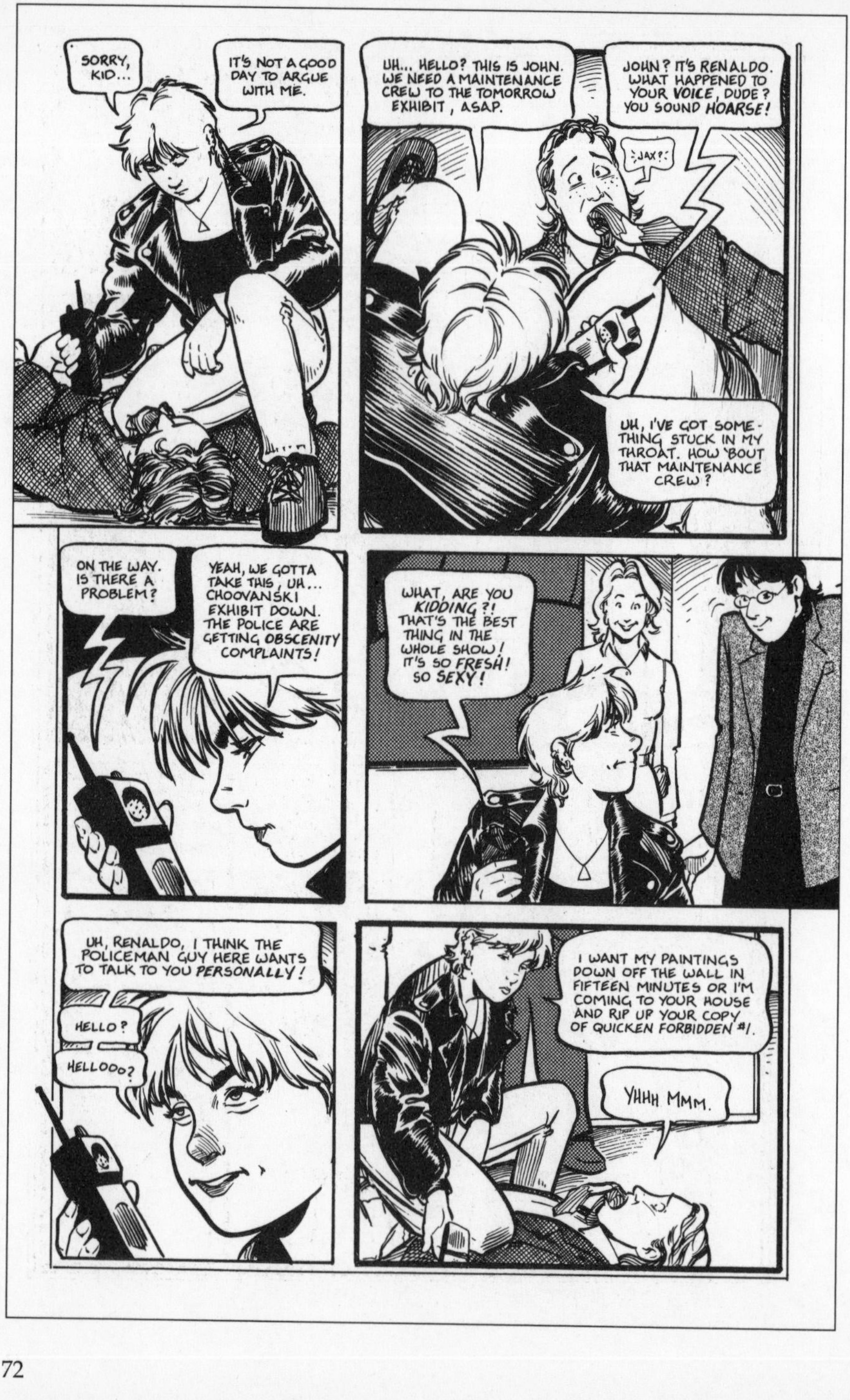
SORRY, KID...
IT'S NOT A GOOD DAY TO ARGUE WITH ME.
UH... HELLO? THIS IS JOHN. WE NEED A MAINTENANCE CREW TO THE TOMORROW EXHIBIT, ASAP.
JOHN? IT'S RENALDO. WHAT HAPPENED TO YOUR VOICE, DUDE? YOU SOUND HOARSE!
JAX?
UH, I'VE GOT SOMETHING STUCK IN MY THROAT. HOW 'BOUT THAT MAINTENANCE CREW?
ON THE WAY. IS THERE A PROBLEM?
YEAH, WE GOTTA TAKE THIS, UH... CHOOVANSKI EXHIBIT DOWN. THE POLICE ARE GETTING OBSCENITY COMPLAINTS!
WHAT, ARE YOU KIDDING?! THAT'S THE BEST THING IN THE WHOLE SHOW! IT'S SO FRESH! SO SEXY!
UH, RENALDO, I THINK THE POLICEMAN GUY HERE WANTS TO TALK TO YOU PERSONALLY!
HELLO?
HELLOoo?
I WANT MY PAINTINGS DOWN OFF THE WALL IN FIFTEEN MINUTES OR I'M COMING TO YOUR HOUSE AND RIP UP YOUR COPY OF QUICKEN FORBIDDEN #1.
YHHH MMM.

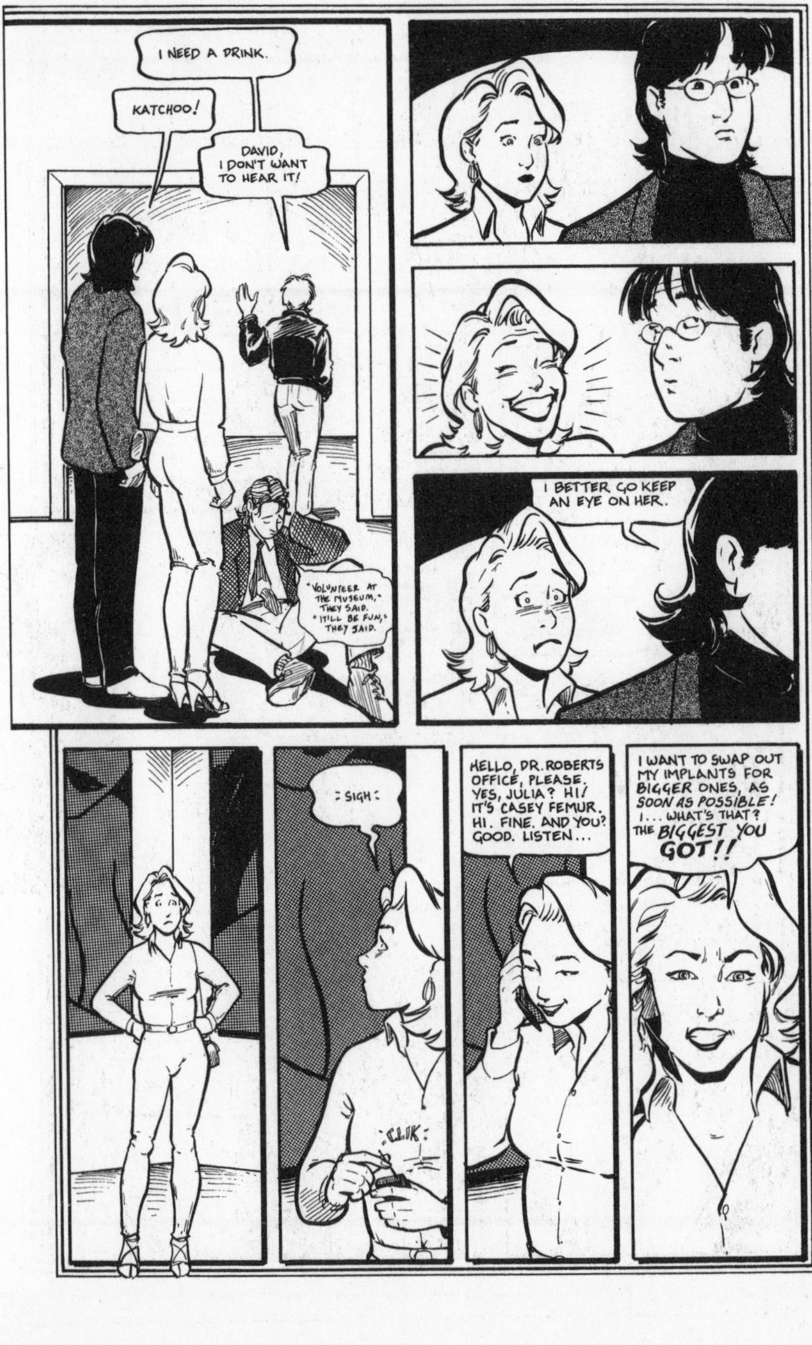
I NEED A DRINK.
KATCHOO!
DAVID, I DON'T WANT TO HEAR IT!
"VOLUNTEER AT THE MUSEUM," THEY SAID. "IT'LL BE FUN," THEY SAID.
I BETTER GO KEEP AN EYE ON HER.
: SIGH :
: CLIK :
HELLO, DR. ROBERTS OFFICE, PLEASE. YES, JULIA? HI! IT'S CASEY FEMUR. HI. FINE. AND YOU? GOOD. LISTEN...
I WANT TO SWAP OUT MY IMPLANTS FOR BIGGER ONES, AS SOON AS POSSIBLE! I... WHAT'S THAT? THE BIGGEST YOU GOT!!

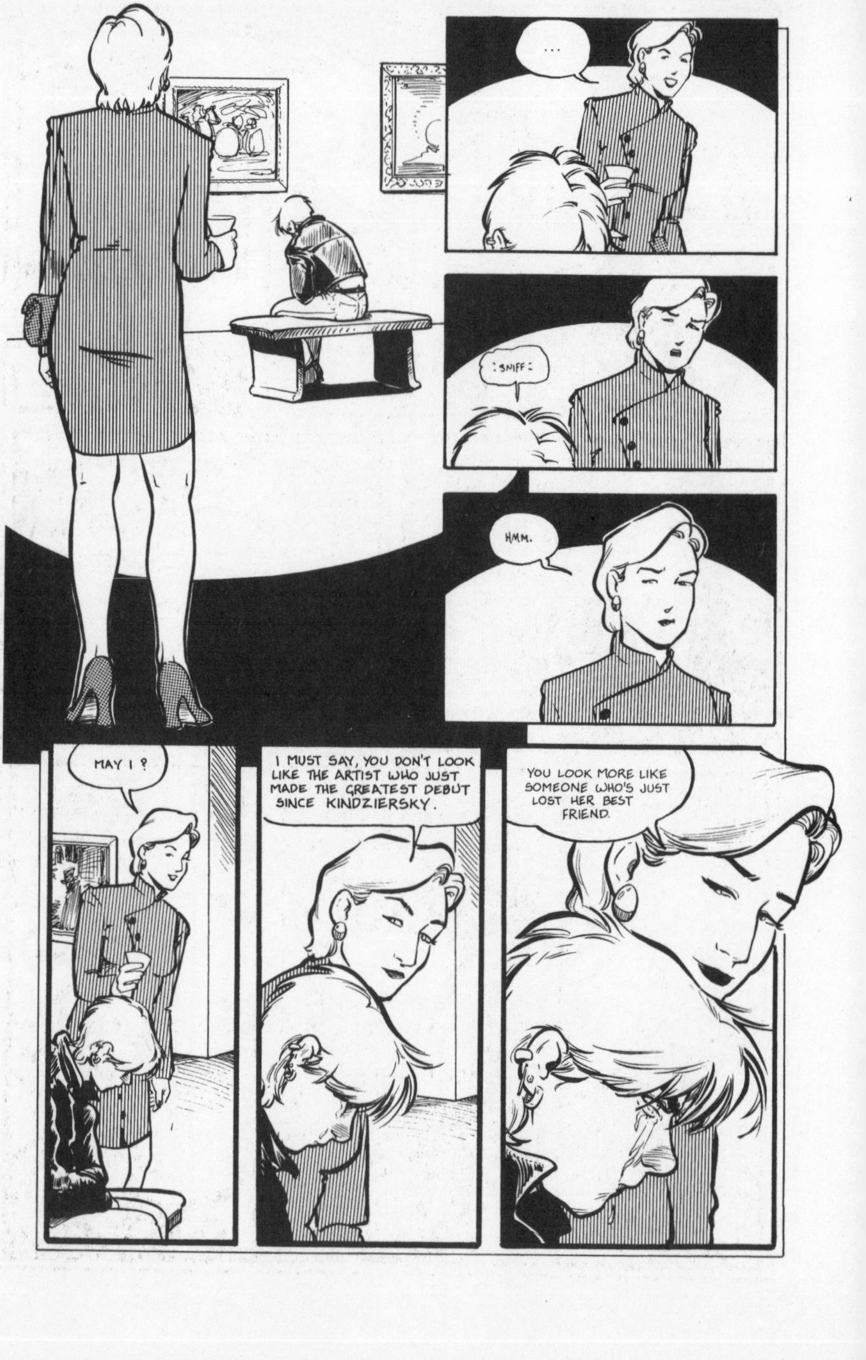
...
: SNIFF :
HMM.
MAY I ?
I MUST SAY, YOU DON'T LOOK LIKE THE ARTIST WHO JUST MADE THE GREATEST DEBUT SINCE KINDZIERSKY.
YOU LOOK MORE LIKE SOMEONE WHO'S JUST LOST HER BEST FRIEND.

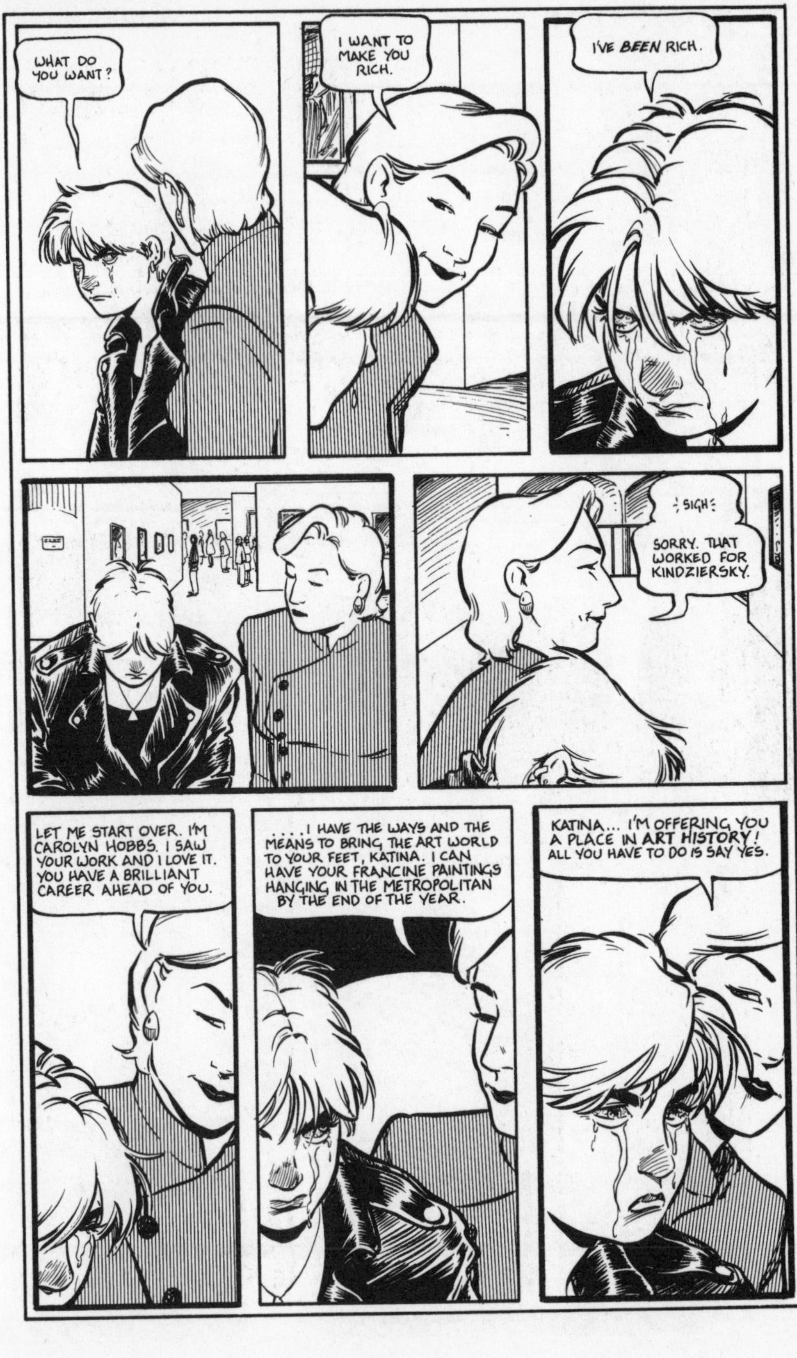
WHAT DO YOU WANT?
I WANT TO MAKE YOU RICH.
I'VE BEEN RICH.
SIGH
SORRY. THAT WORKED FOR KINDZIERSKY.
LET ME START OVER. I'M CAROLYN HOBBS. I SAW YOUR WORK AND I LOVE IT. YOU HAVE A BRILLIANT CAREER AHEAD OF YOU.
....I HAVE THE WAYS AND THE MEANS TO BRING THE ART WORLD TO YOUR FEET, KATINA. I CAN HAVE YOUR FRANCINE PAINTINGS HANGING IN THE METROPOLITAN BY THE END OF THE YEAR.
KATINA... I'M OFFERING YOU A PLACE IN ART HISTORY! ALL YOU HAVE TO DO IS SAY YES.

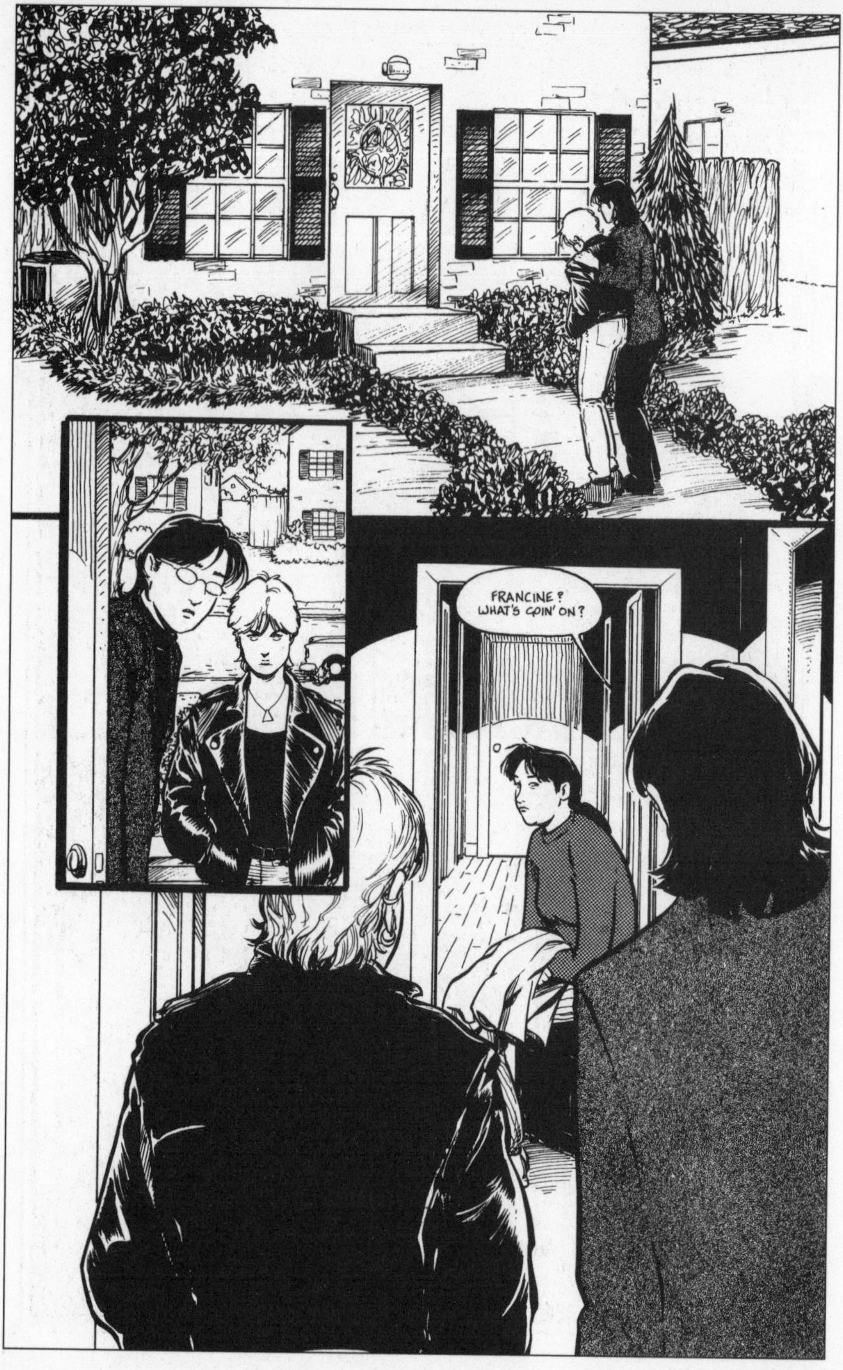
FRANCINE?
WHAT'S GOIN' ON?

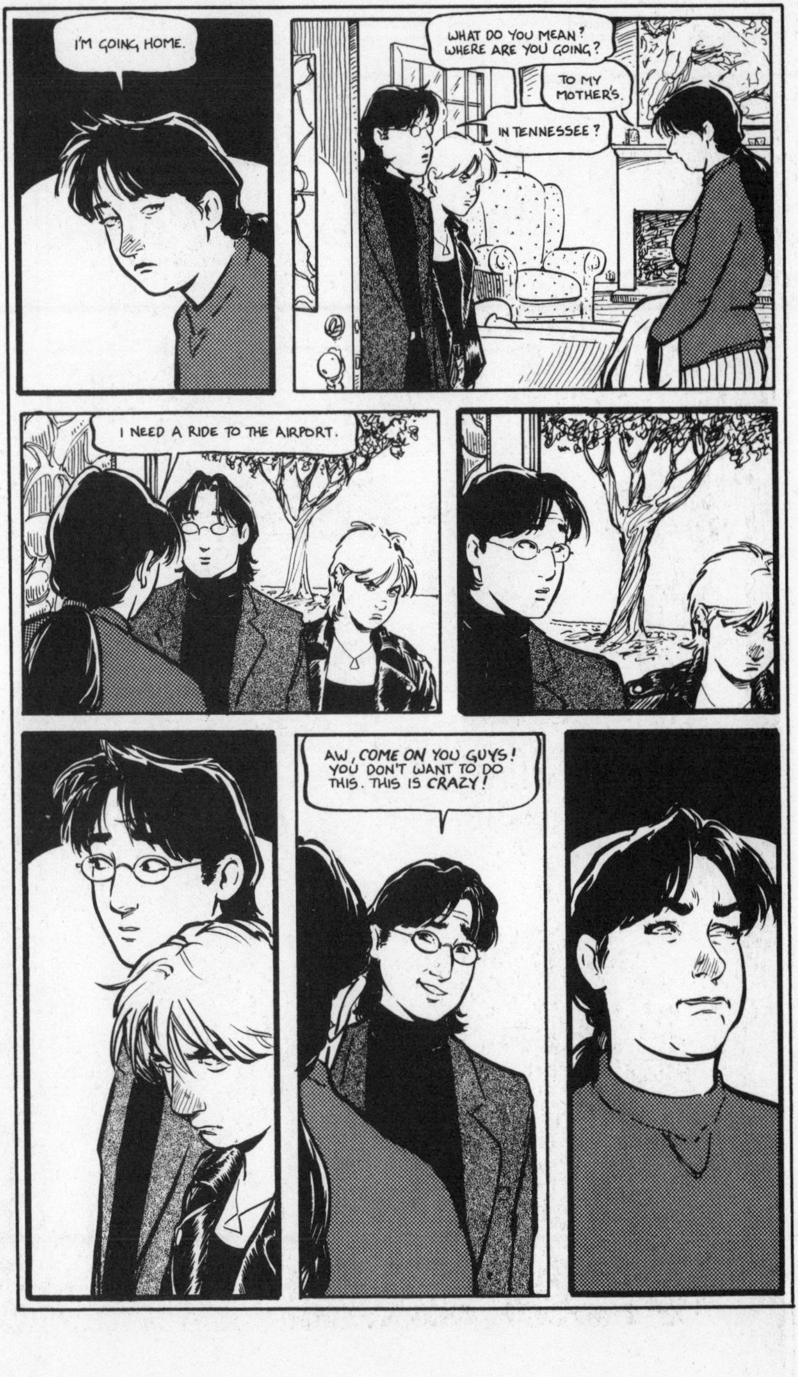
I'M GOING HOME.
WHAT DO YOU MEAN? WHERE ARE YOU GOING?
TO MY MOTHER'S.
IN TENNESSEE?
I NEED A RIDE TO THE AIRPORT.
AW, COME ON YOU GUYS! YOU DON'T WANT TO DO THIS. THIS IS CRAZY!

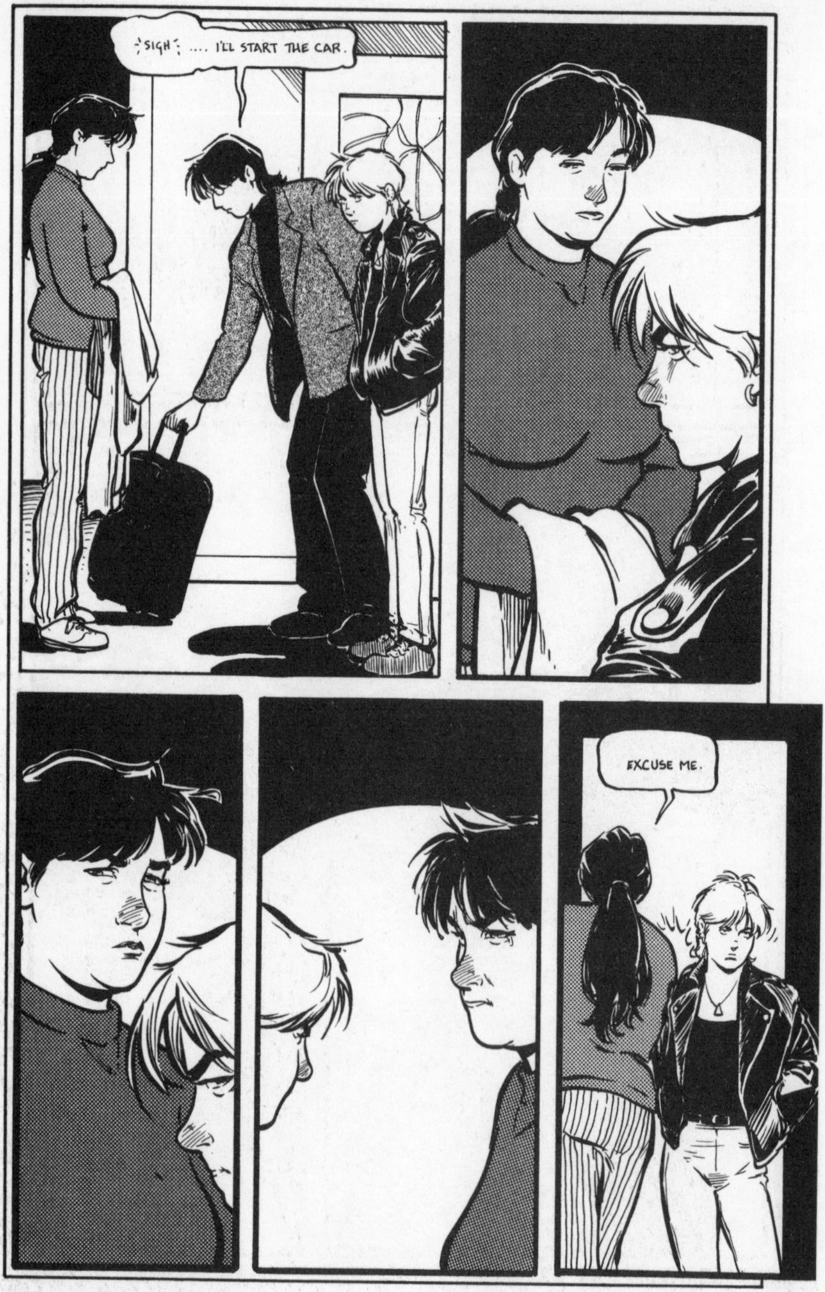

SIGH .... I'LL START THE CAR.
EXCUSE ME.

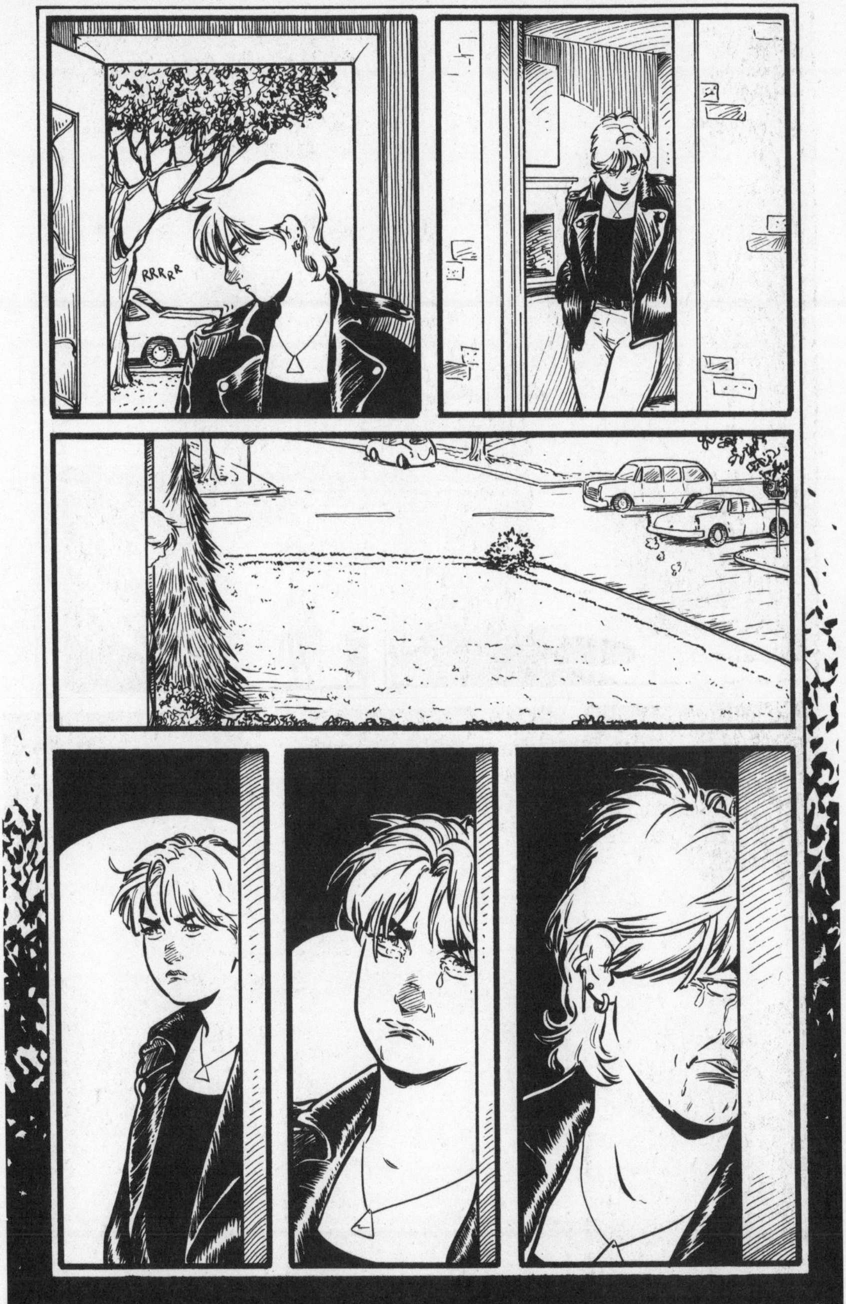
RRRRR

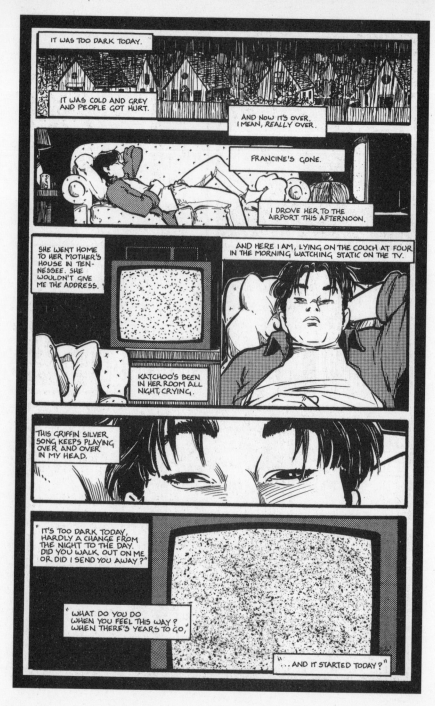

IT WAS TOO DARK TODAY.

IT WAS COLD AND GREY AND PEOPLE GOT HURT.

AND NOW IT'S OVER. I MEAN, REALLY OVER.

FRANCINE'S GONE.

I DROVE HER TO THE AIRPORT THIS AFTERNOON.

SHE WENT HOME TO HER MOTHER'S HOUSE IN TENNESSEE. SHE WOULDN'T GIVE ME THE ADDRESS.

AND HERE I AM, LYING ON THE COUCH AT FOUR IN THE MORNING WATCHING STATIC ON THE TV.

KATCHOO'S BEEN IN HER ROOM ALL NIGHT, CRYING.

THIS GRIFFIN SILVER SONG KEEPS PLAYING OVER AND OVER IN MY HEAD.

"IT'S TOO DARK TODAY, HARDLY A CHANGE FROM THE NIGHT TO THE DAY. DID YOU WALK OUT ON ME OR DID I SEND YOU AWAY?"

"WHAT DO YOU DO WHEN YOU FEEL THIS WAY? WHEN THERE'S YEARS TO GO,"

"...AND IT STARTED TODAY?"

80

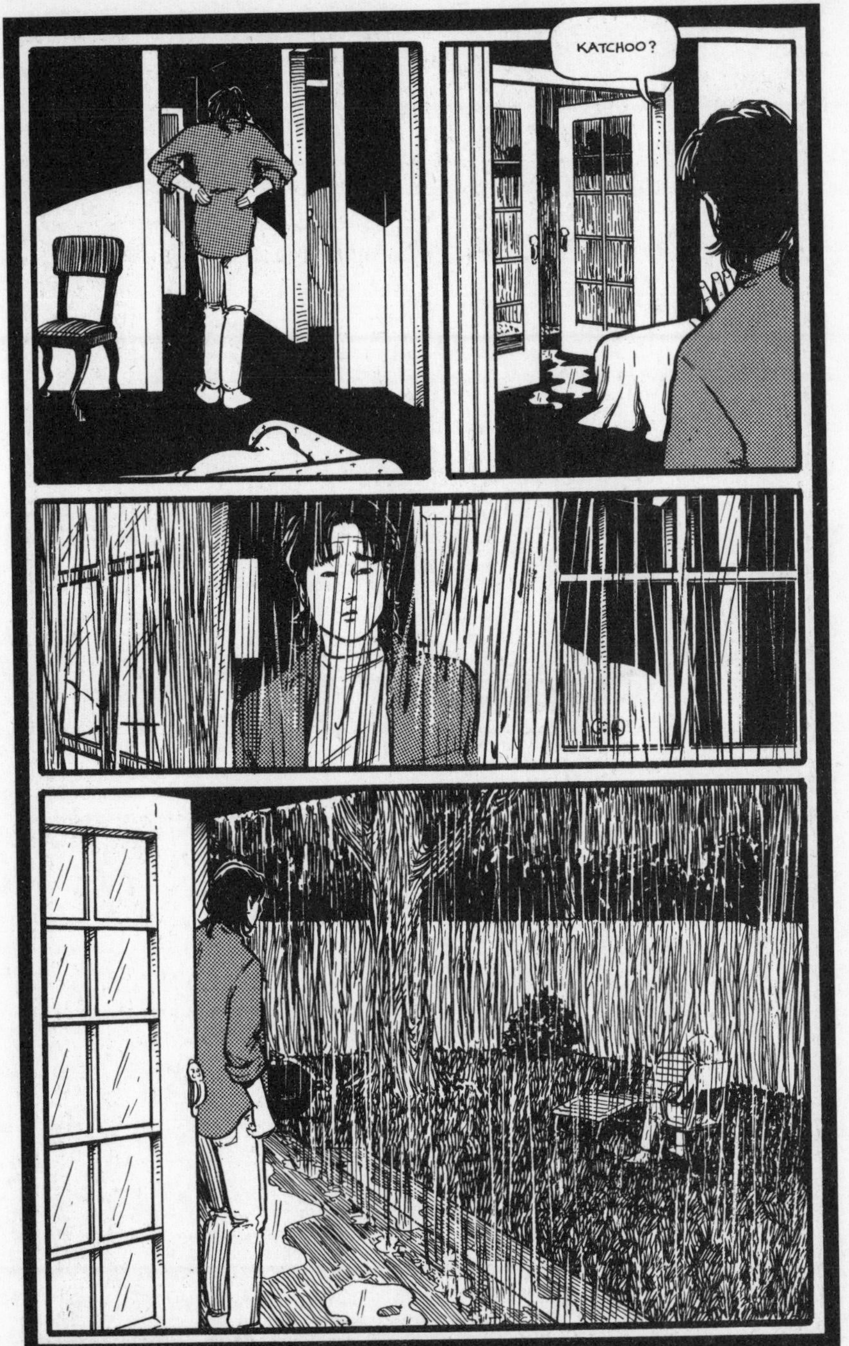
KATCHOO?

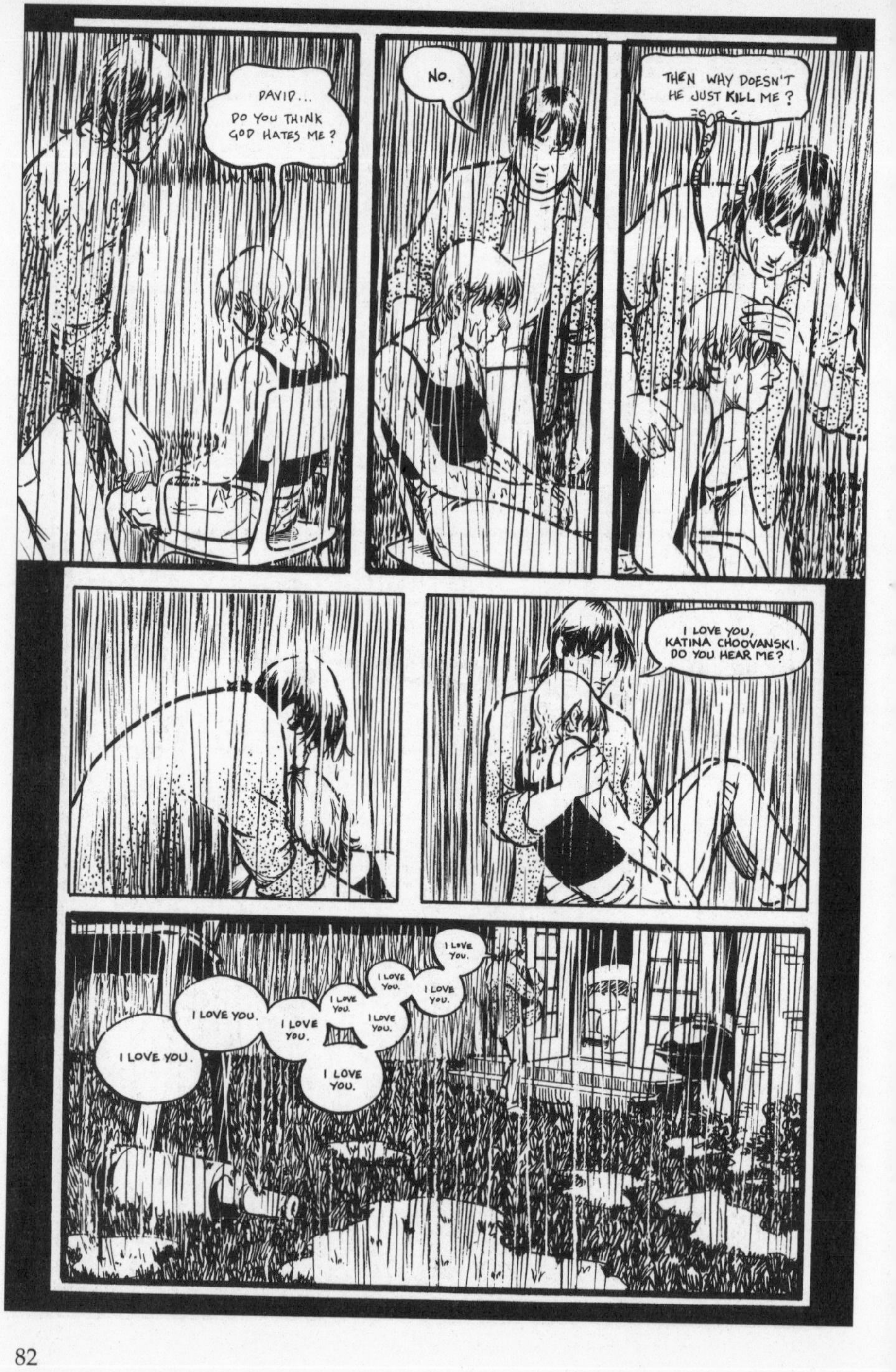
DAVID...
DO YOU THINK GOD HATES ME?
NO.
THEN WHY DOESN'T HE JUST KILL ME?
I LOVE YOU, KATINA CHOOVANSKI. DO YOU HEAR ME?
I LOVE YOU.
I LOVE YOU.
I LOVE YOU.
I LOVE YOU.
I LOVE YOU.
I LOVE YOU.
I LOVE YOU.
I LOVE YOU.
I LOVE YOU.

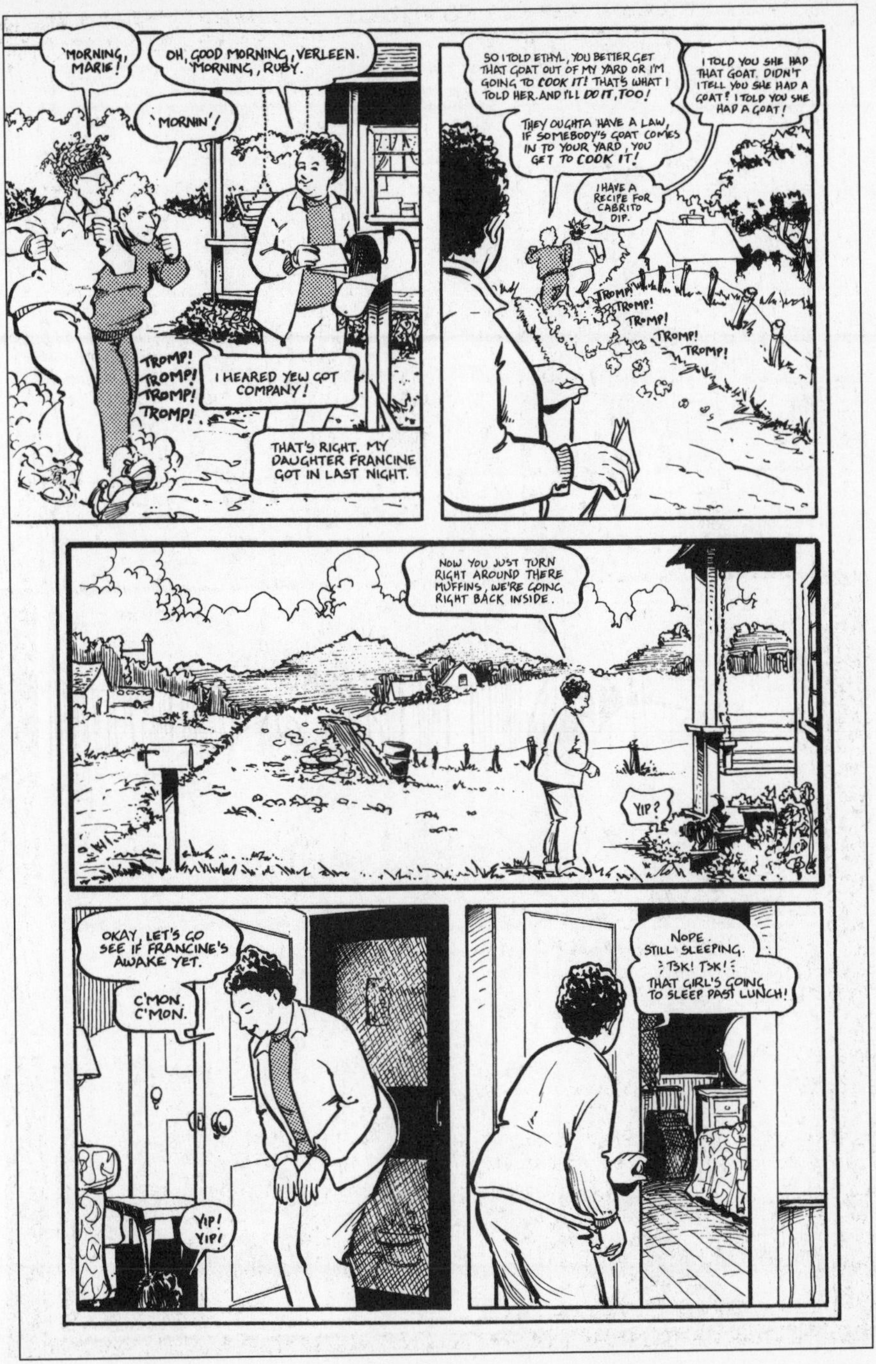

'MORNING, MARIE!
OH, GOOD MORNING, VERLEEN. 'MORNING, RUBY.
'MORNIN'!
TROMP! TROMP! TROMP! TROMP!
I HEARED YEW GOT COMPANY!
THAT'S RIGHT. MY DAUGHTER FRANCINE GOT IN LAST NIGHT.
SO I TOLD ETHYL, YOU BETTER GET THAT GOAT OUT OF MY YARD OR I'M GOING TO COOK IT! THAT'S WHAT I TOLD HER. AND I'LL DO IT, TOO!
I TOLD YOU SHE HAD THAT GOAT. DIDN'T I TELL YOU SHE HAD A GOAT! I TOLD YOU SHE HAD A GOAT!
THEY OUGHTA HAVE A LAW, IF SOMEBODY'S GOAT COMES IN TO YOUR YARD, YOU GET TO COOK IT!
I HAVE A RECIPE FOR CABRITO DIP.
TROMP! TROMP! TROMP! TROMP! TROMP!
NOW YOU JUST TURN RIGHT AROUND THERE MUFFINS, WE'RE GOING RIGHT BACK INSIDE.
YIP?
OKAY, LET'S GO SEE IF FRANCINE'S AWAKE YET.
C'MON. C'MON.
YIP! YIP!
NOPE. STILL SLEEPING.
TSK! TSK!
THAT GIRL'S GOING TO SLEEP PAST LUNCH!

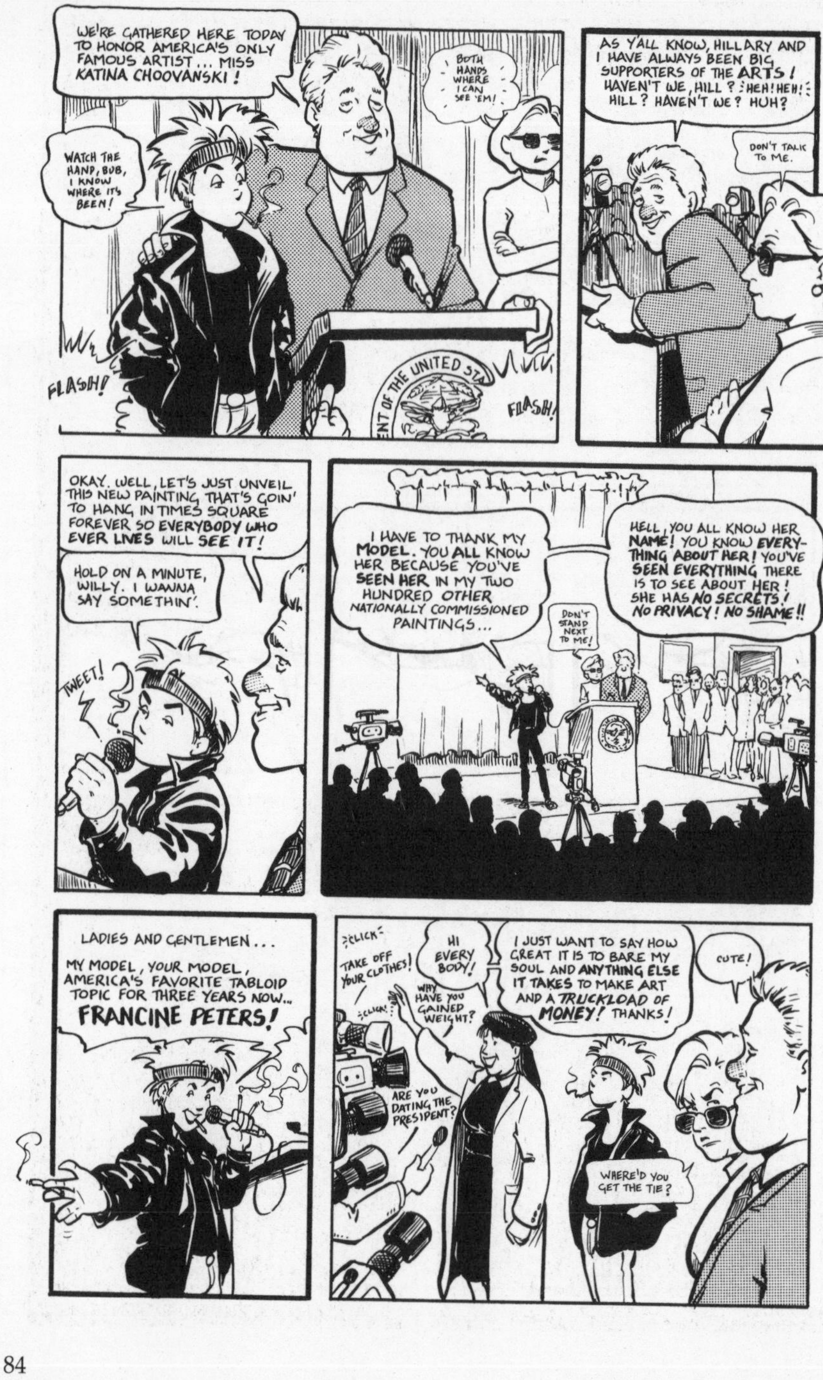
WE'RE GATHERED HERE TODAY TO HONOR AMERICA'S ONLY FAMOUS ARTIST ... MISS KATINA CHOOVANSKI!
BOTH HANDS WHERE I CAN SEE 'EM!
WATCH THE HAND, BUB, I KNOW WHERE IT'S BEEN!
FLASH!
FLASH!
AS Y'ALL KNOW, HILLARY AND I HAVE ALWAYS BEEN BIG SUPPORTERS OF THE ARTS! HAVEN'T WE, HILL? HEH! HEH! HILL? HAVEN'T WE? HUH?
DON'T TALK TO ME.
OKAY. WELL, LET'S JUST UNVEIL THIS NEW PAINTING THAT'S GOIN' TO HANG IN TIMES SQUARE FOREVER SO EVERYBODY WHO EVER LIVES WILL SEE IT!
HOLD ON A MINUTE, WILLY. I WANNA SAY SOMETHIN'.
TWEET!
I HAVE TO THANK MY MODEL. YOU ALL KNOW HER BECAUSE YOU'VE SEEN HER IN MY TWO HUNDRED OTHER NATIONALLY COMMISSIONED PAINTINGS...
HELL, YOU ALL KNOW HER NAME! YOU KNOW EVERYTHING ABOUT HER! YOU'VE SEEN EVERYTHING THERE IS TO SEE ABOUT HER! SHE HAS NO SECRETS! NO PRIVACY! NO SHAME!!
DON'T STAND NEXT TO ME!
LADIES AND GENTLEMEN...
MY MODEL, YOUR MODEL, AMERICA'S FAVORITE TABLOID TOPIC FOR THREE YEARS NOW... FRANCINE PETERS!
CLICK
TAKE OFF YOUR CLOTHES!
CLICK
HI EVERY BODY!
WHY HAVE YOU GAINED WEIGHT?
I JUST WANT TO SAY HOW GREAT IT IS TO BARE MY SOUL AND ANYTHING ELSE IT TAKES TO MAKE ART AND A TRUCKLOAD OF MONEY! THANKS!
CUTE!
ARE YOU DATING THE PRESIDENT?
WHERE'D YOU GET THE TIE?

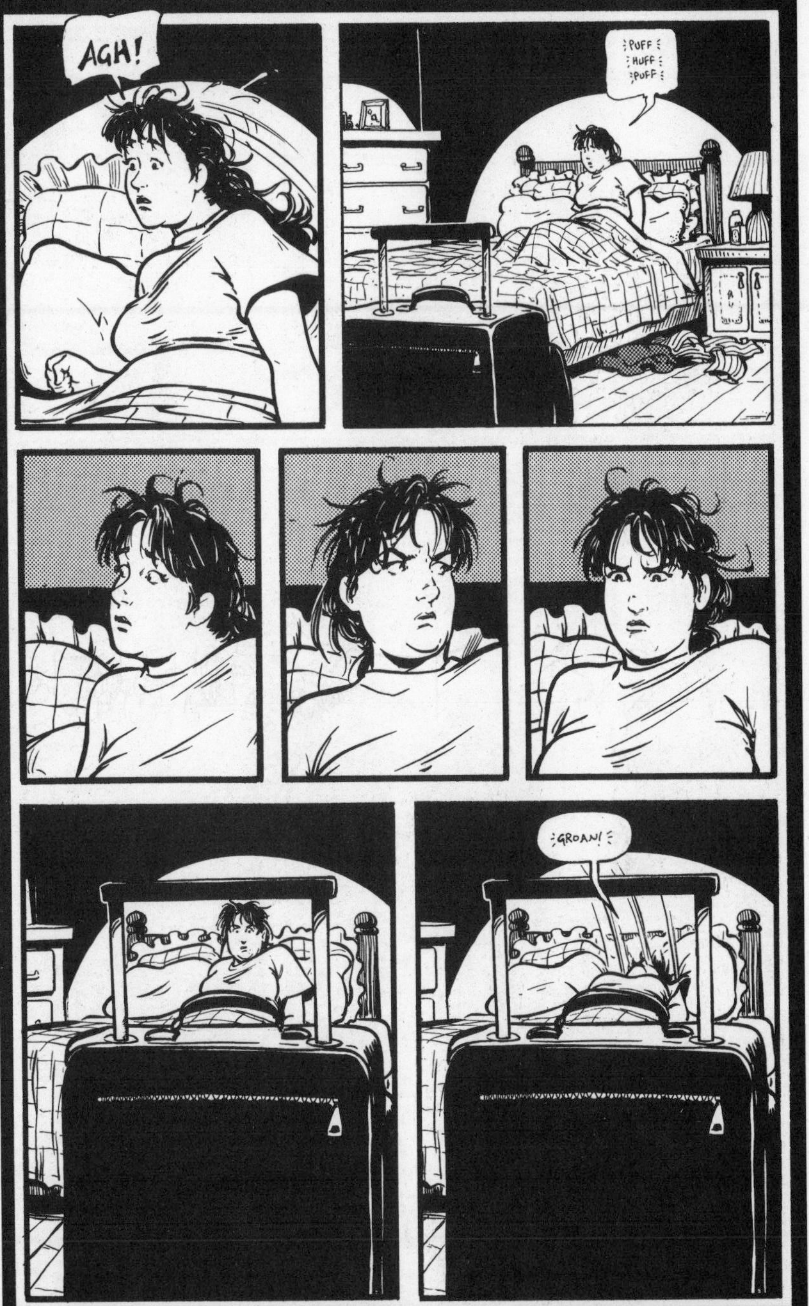
AGH!
PUFF HUFF PUFF
GROAN!

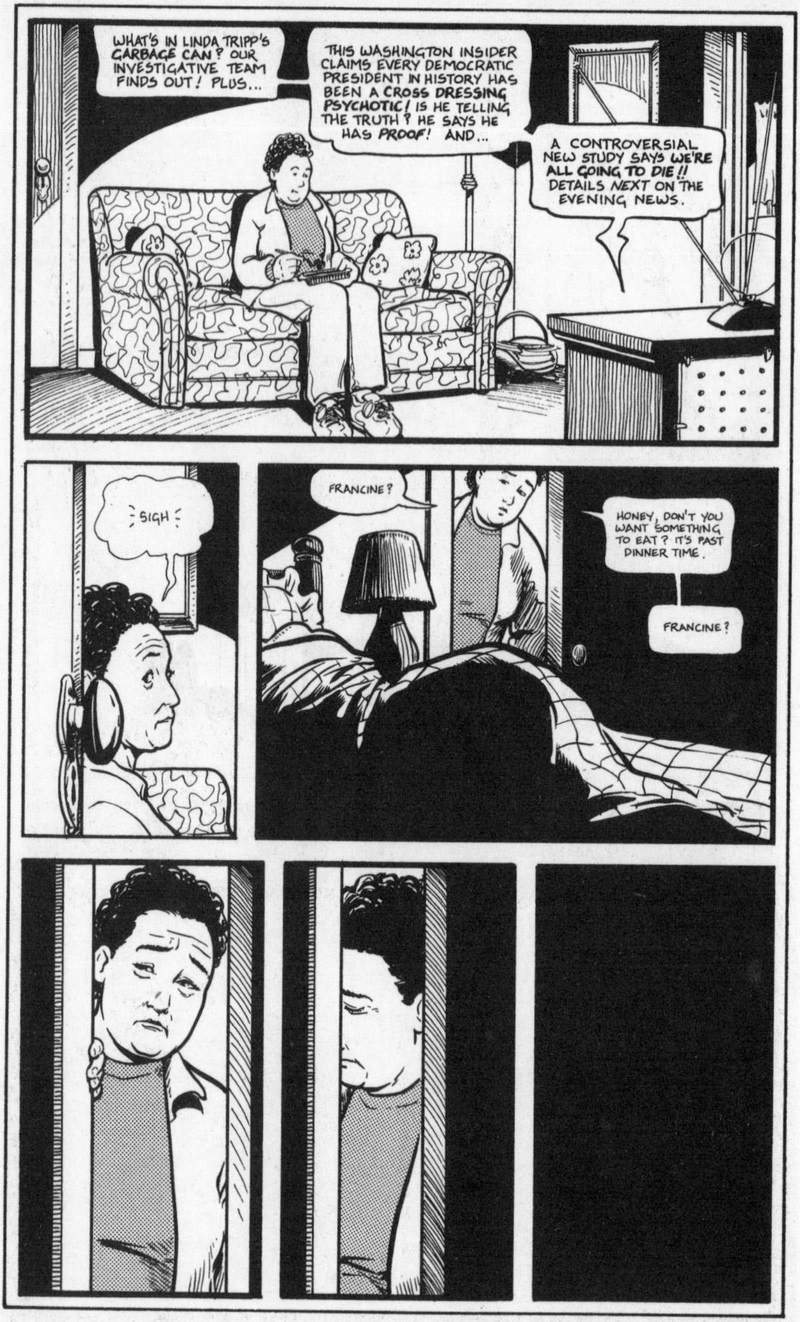
WHAT'S IN LINDA TRIPP'S GARBAGE CAN? OUR INVESTIGATIVE TEAM FINDS OUT! PLUS...
THIS WASHINGTON INSIDER CLAIMS EVERY DEMOCRATIC PRESIDENT IN HISTORY HAS BEEN A CROSS DRESSING PSYCHOTIC! IS HE TELLING THE TRUTH? HE SAYS HE HAS PROOF! AND...
A CONTROVERSIAL NEW STUDY SAYS WE'RE ALL GOING TO DIE!! DETAILS NEXT ON THE EVENING NEWS.
SIGH
FRANCINE?
HONEY, DON'T YOU WANT SOMETHING TO EAT? IT'S PAST DINNER TIME.
FRANCINE?

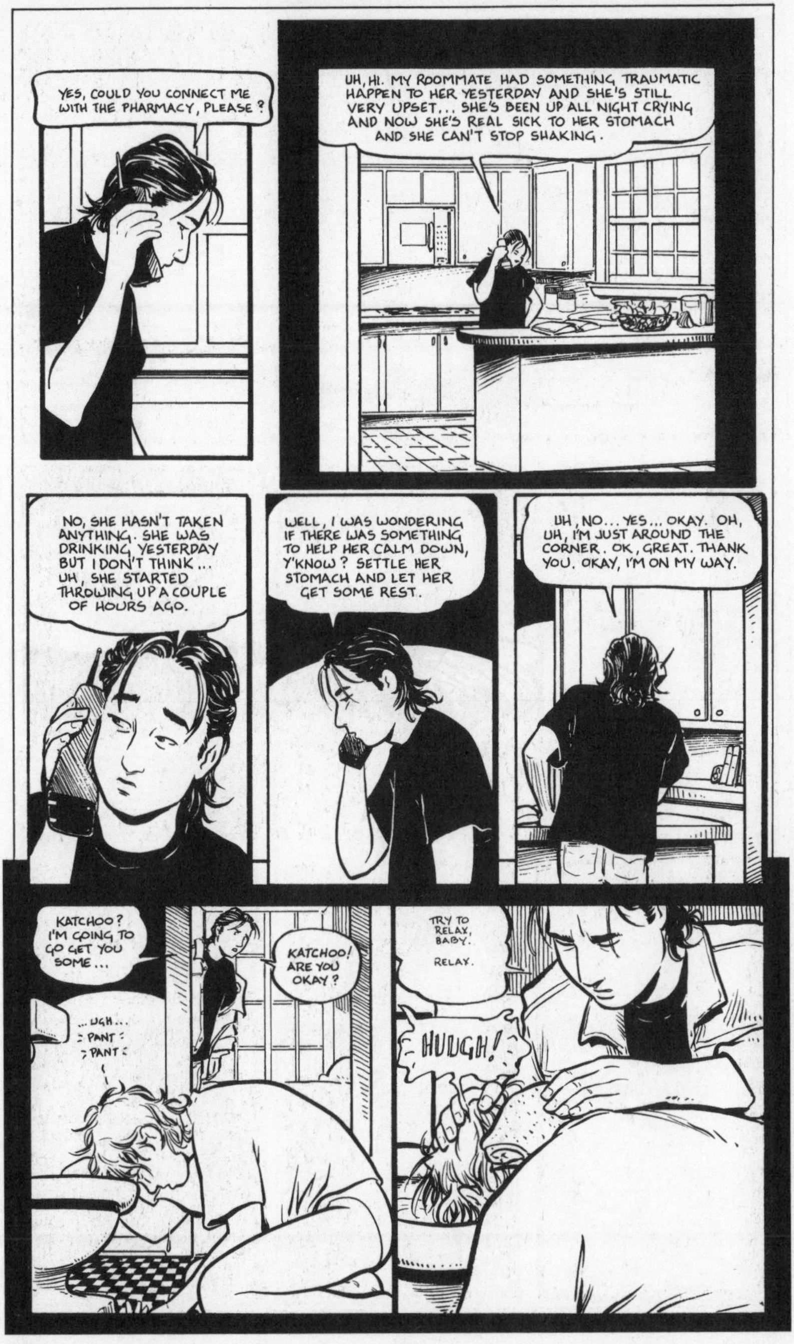
YES, COULD YOU CONNECT ME WITH THE PHARMACY, PLEASE?
UH, HI. MY ROOMMATE HAD SOMETHING TRAUMATIC HAPPEN TO HER YESTERDAY AND SHE'S STILL VERY UPSET... SHE'S BEEN UP ALL NIGHT CRYING AND NOW SHE'S REAL SICK TO HER STOMACH AND SHE CAN'T STOP SHAKING.
NO, SHE HASN'T TAKEN ANYTHING. SHE WAS DRINKING YESTERDAY BUT I DON'T THINK... UH, SHE STARTED THROWING UP A COUPLE OF HOURS AGO.
WELL, I WAS WONDERING IF THERE WAS SOMETHING TO HELP HER CALM DOWN, Y'KNOW? SETTLE HER STOMACH AND LET HER GET SOME REST.
UH, NO... YES... OKAY. OH, UH, I'M JUST AROUND THE CORNER. OK, GREAT. THANK YOU. OKAY, I'M ON MY WAY.
KATCHOO? I'M GOING TO GO GET YOU SOME...
...UGH... PANT PANT
KATCHOO! ARE YOU OKAY?
TRY TO RELAX, BABY.
RELAX.
HUUGH!

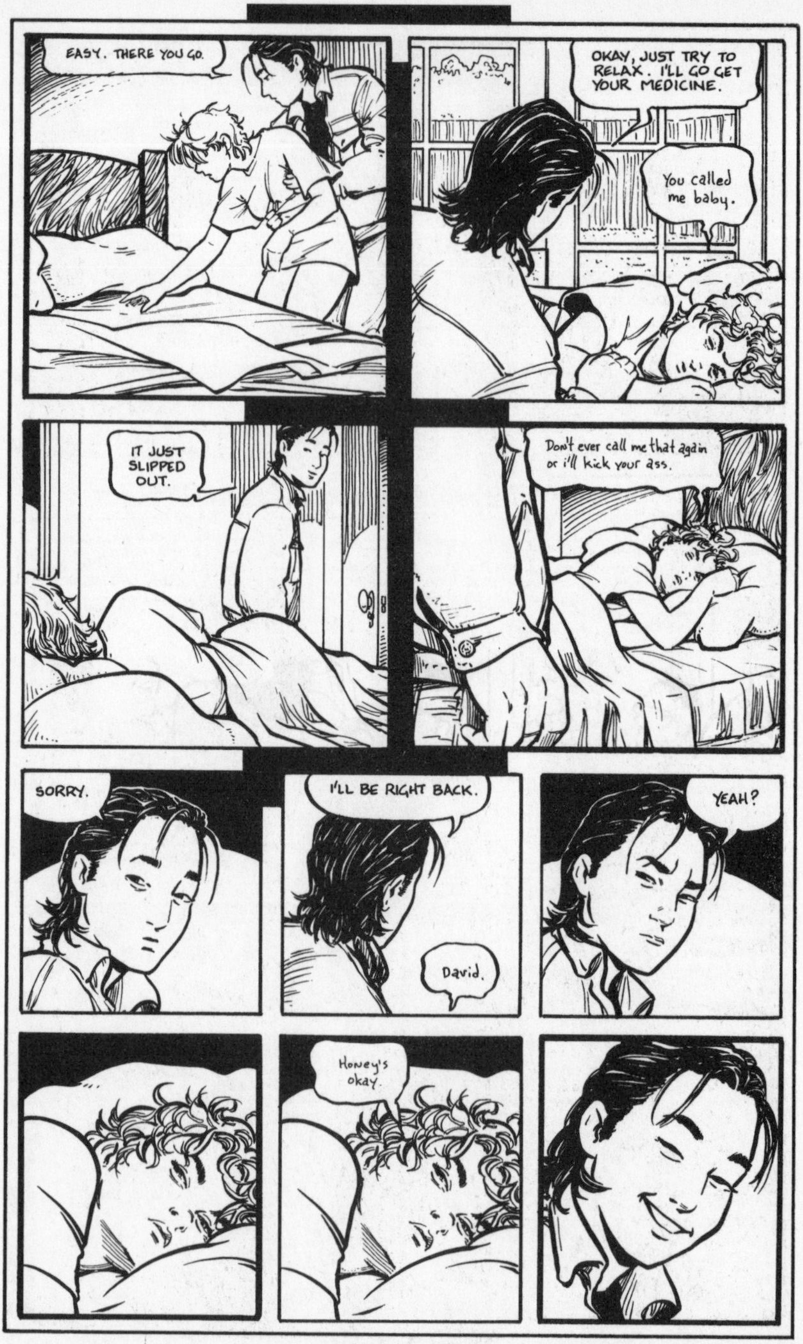
EASY. THERE YOU GO.
OKAY, JUST TRY TO RELAX. I'LL GO GET YOUR MEDICINE.
You called me baby.
IT JUST SLIPPED OUT.
Don't ever call me that again or i'll kick your ass.
SORRY.
I'LL BE RIGHT BACK.
David.
YEAH?
Honey's okay.

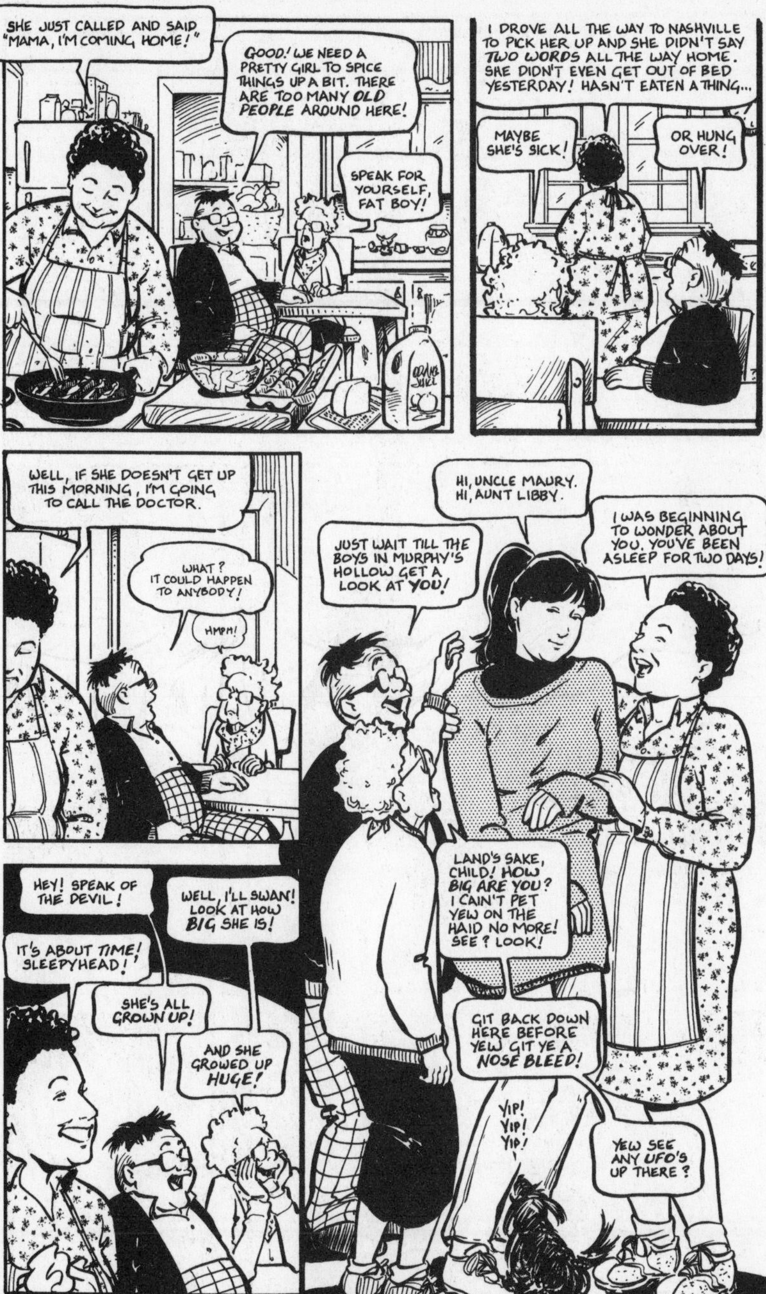

SHE JUST CALLED AND SAID "MAMA, I'M COMING HOME!"
GOOD! WE NEED A PRETTY GIRL TO SPICE THINGS UP A BIT. THERE ARE TOO MANY OLD PEOPLE AROUND HERE!
SPEAK FOR YOURSELF, FAT BOY!
I DROVE ALL THE WAY TO NASHVILLE TO PICK HER UP AND SHE DIDN'T SAY TWO WORDS ALL THE WAY HOME. SHE DIDN'T EVEN GET OUT OF BED YESTERDAY! HASN'T EATEN A THING...
MAYBE SHE'S SICK!
OR HUNG OVER!
WELL, IF SHE DOESN'T GET UP THIS MORNING, I'M GOING TO CALL THE DOCTOR.
WHAT? IT COULD HAPPEN TO ANYBODY!
HMPH!
HEY! SPEAK OF THE DEVIL!
WELL, I'LL SWAN! LOOK AT HOW BIG SHE IS!
IT'S ABOUT TIME! SLEEPYHEAD!
SHE'S ALL GROWN UP!
AND SHE GROWED UP HUGE!
HI, UNCLE MAURY. HI, AUNT LIBBY.
JUST WAIT TILL THE BOYS IN MURPHY'S HOLLOW GET A LOOK AT YOU!
I WAS BEGINNING TO WONDER ABOUT YOU. YOU'VE BEEN ASLEEP FOR TWO DAYS!
LAND'S SAKE, CHILD! HOW BIG ARE YOU? I CAIN'T PET YEW ON THE HAID NO MORE! SEE? LOOK!
GIT BACK DOWN HERE BEFORE YEW GIT YE A NOSE BLEED!
YIP! YIP! YIP!
YEW SEE ANY UFO'S UP THERE?

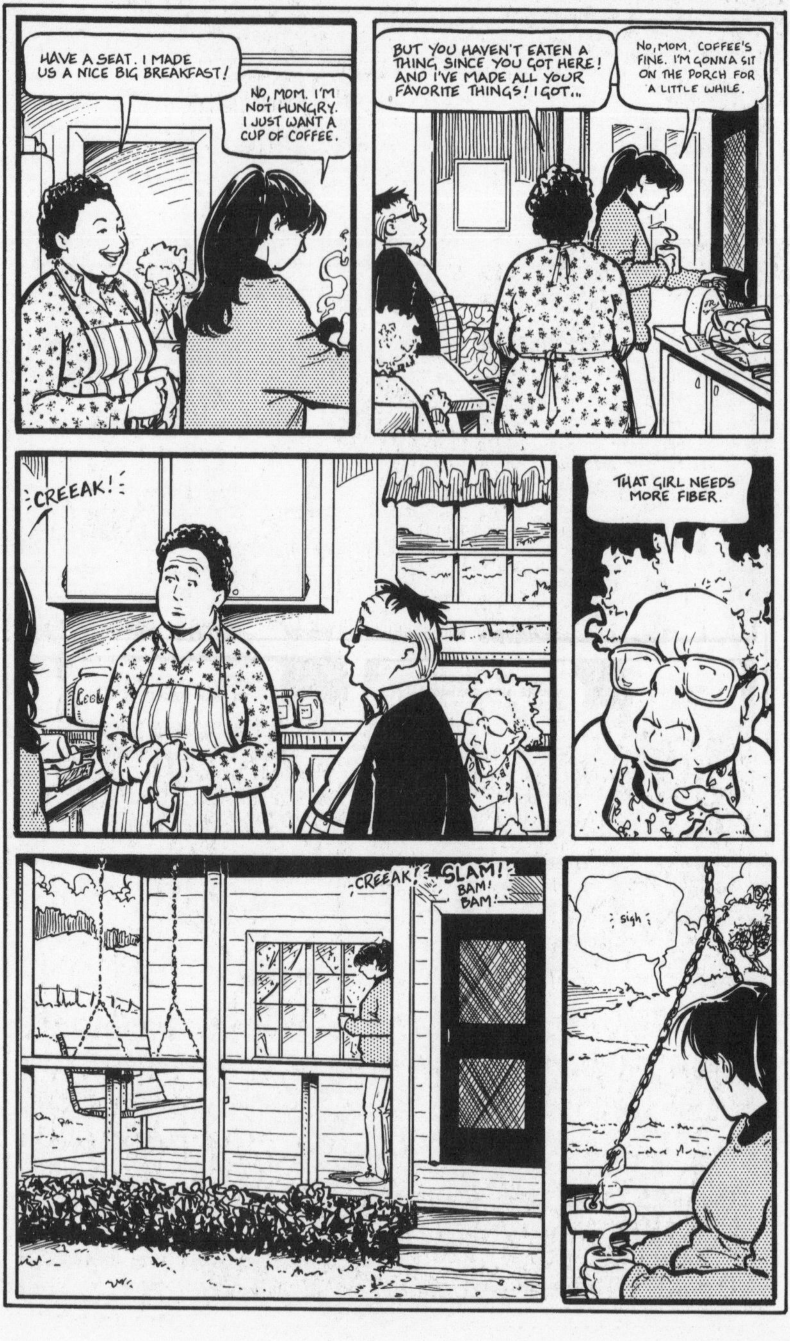
HAVE A SEAT. I MADE US A NICE BIG BREAKFAST!
NO, MOM. I'M NOT HUNGRY. I JUST WANT A CUP OF COFFEE.
BUT YOU HAVEN'T EATEN A THING SINCE YOU GOT HERE! AND I'VE MADE ALL YOUR FAVORITE THINGS! I GOT...
NO, MOM. COFFEE'S FINE. I'M GONNA SIT ON THE PORCH FOR A LITTLE WHILE.
CREEAK!
THAT GIRL NEEDS MORE FIBER.
CREEAK!
SLAM!
BAM! BAM!
sigh

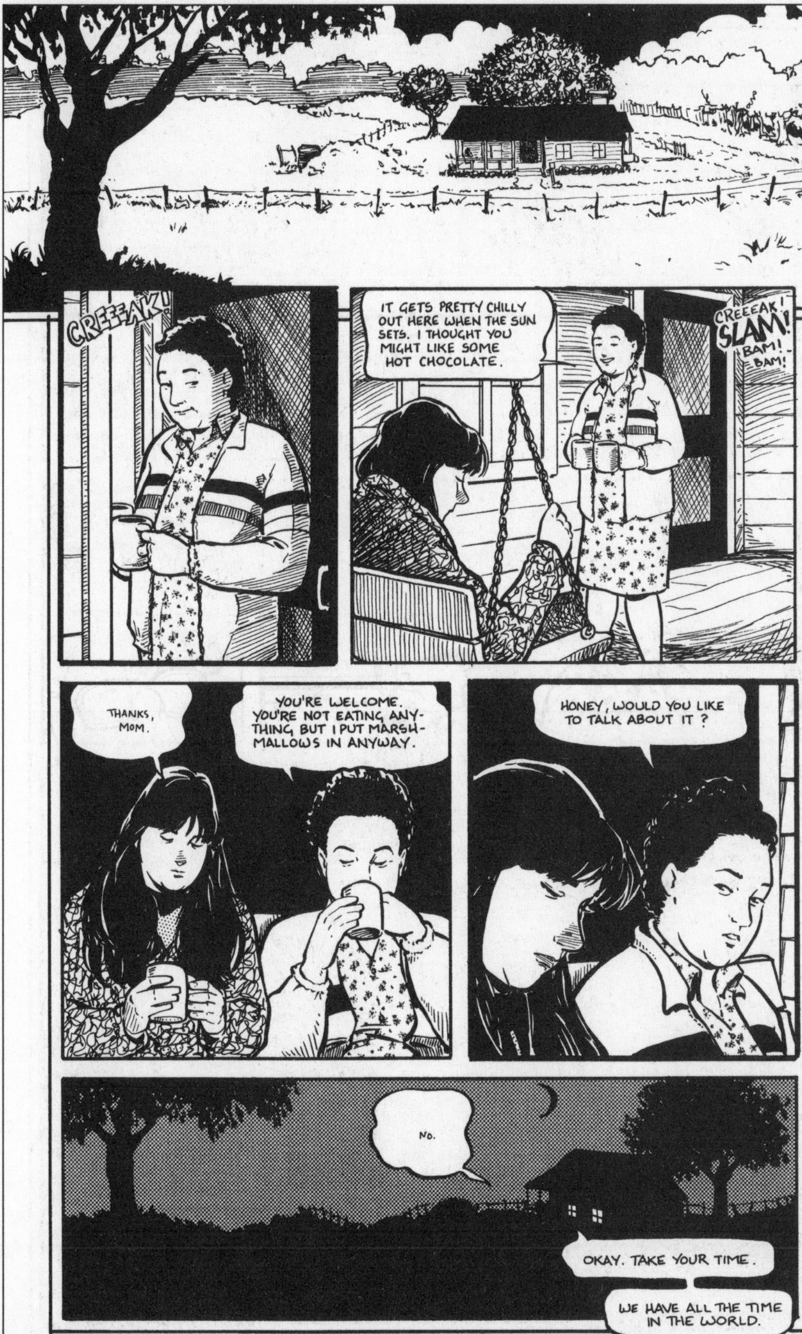
CREEEAK!
IT GETS PRETTY CHILLY OUT HERE WHEN THE SUN SETS. I THOUGHT YOU MIGHT LIKE SOME HOT CHOCOLATE.
CREEEAK! SLAM! BAM! BAM!
THANKS, MOM.
YOU'RE WELCOME. YOU'RE NOT EATING ANY-THING, BUT I PUT MARSH-MALLOWS IN ANYWAY.
HONEY, WOULD YOU LIKE TO TALK ABOUT IT?
NO.
OKAY. TAKE YOUR TIME.
WE HAVE ALL THE TIME IN THE WORLD.

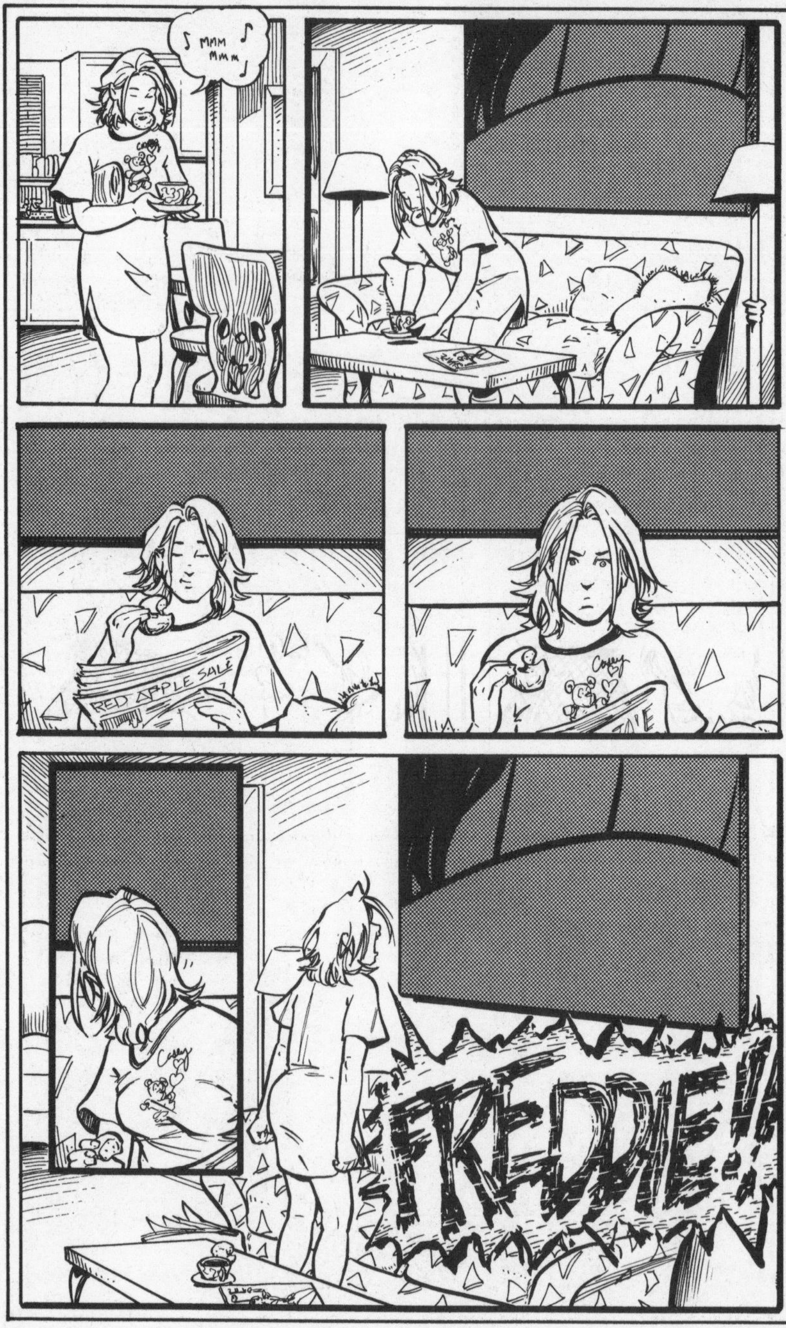
MMM MMM
RED APPLE SALE
FREDDIE!!

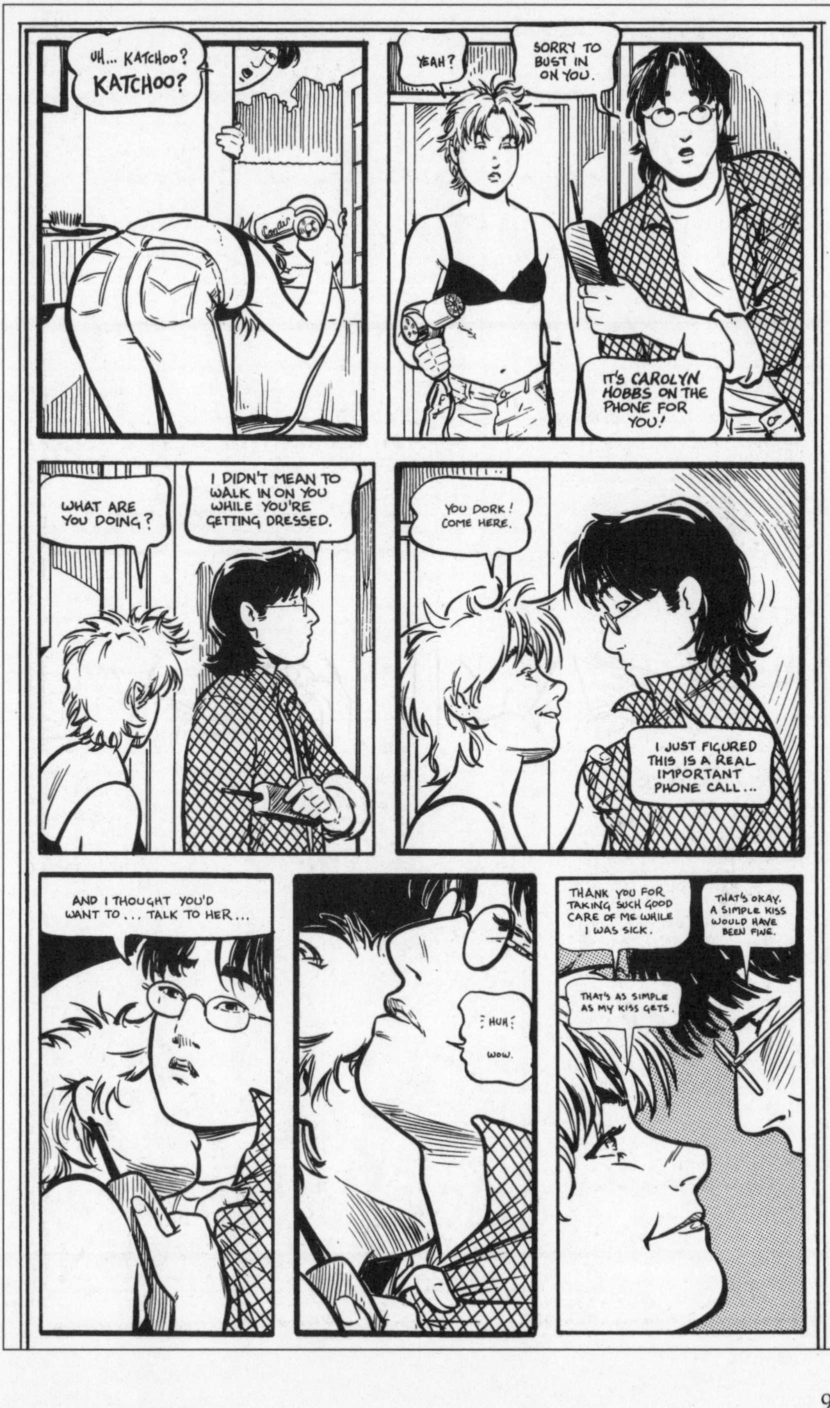
UH... KATCHOO?
KATCHOO?
YEAH?
SORRY TO BUST IN ON YOU.
IT'S CAROLYN HOBBS ON THE PHONE FOR YOU!
WHAT ARE YOU DOING?
I DIDN'T MEAN TO WALK IN ON YOU WHILE YOU'RE GETTING DRESSED.
YOU DORK! COME HERE.
I JUST FIGURED THIS IS A REAL IMPORTANT PHONE CALL...
AND I THOUGHT YOU'D WANT TO... TALK TO HER...
HUH
WOW.
THANK YOU FOR TAKING SUCH GOOD CARE OF ME WHILE I WAS SICK.
THAT'S OKAY. A SIMPLE KISS WOULD HAVE BEEN FINE.
THAT'S AS SIMPLE AS MY KISS GETS.

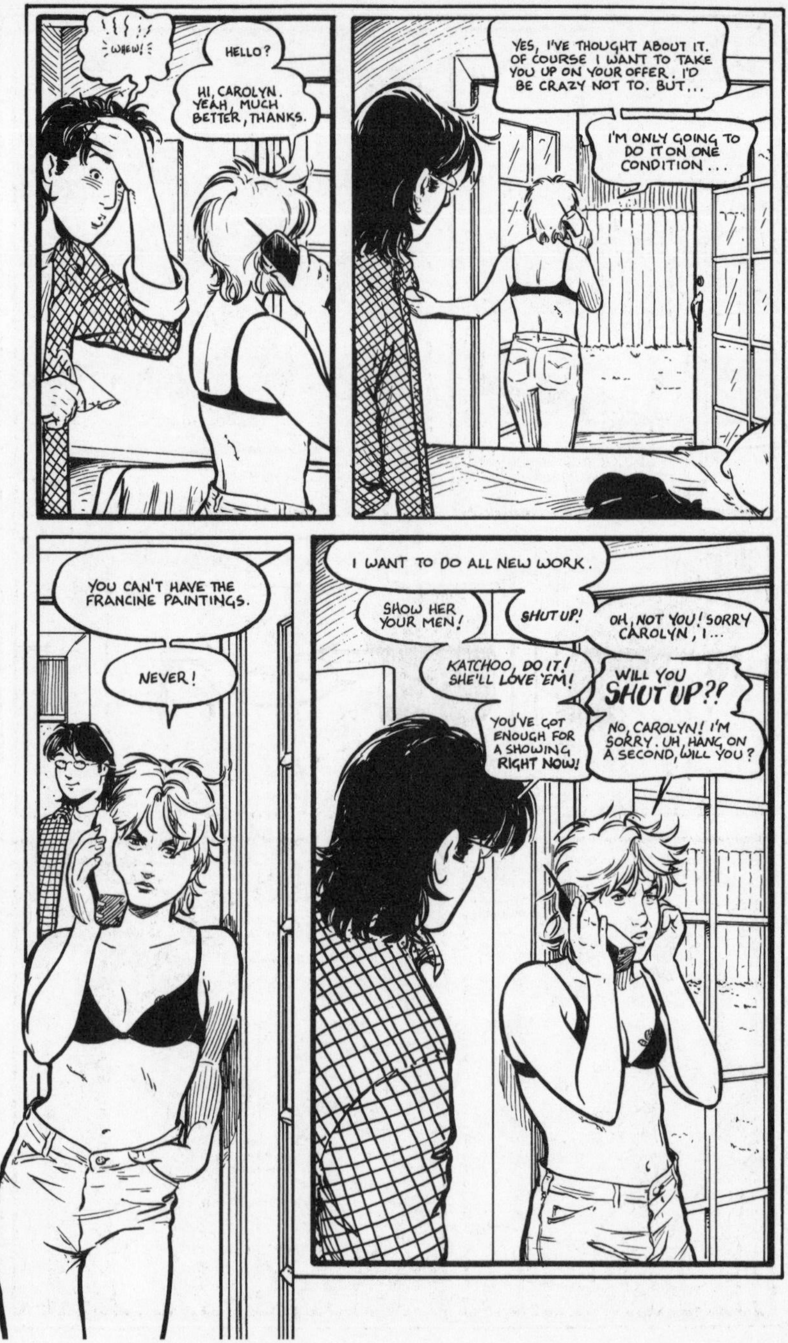
WHEW!
HELLO?
HI, CAROLYN. YEAH, MUCH BETTER, THANKS.
YES, I'VE THOUGHT ABOUT IT. OF COURSE I WANT TO TAKE YOU UP ON YOUR OFFER. I'D BE CRAZY NOT TO. BUT...
I'M ONLY GOING TO DO IT ON ONE CONDITION...
YOU CAN'T HAVE THE FRANCINE PAINTINGS.
NEVER!
I WANT TO DO ALL NEW WORK.
SHOW HER YOUR MEN!
SHUT UP!
KATCHOO, DO IT! SHE'LL LOVE 'EM!
YOU'VE GOT ENOUGH FOR A SHOWING RIGHT NOW!
OH, NOT YOU! SORRY CAROLYN, I...
WILL YOU SHUT UP?!
NO, CAROLYN! I'M SORRY. UH, HANG ON A SECOND, WILL YOU?

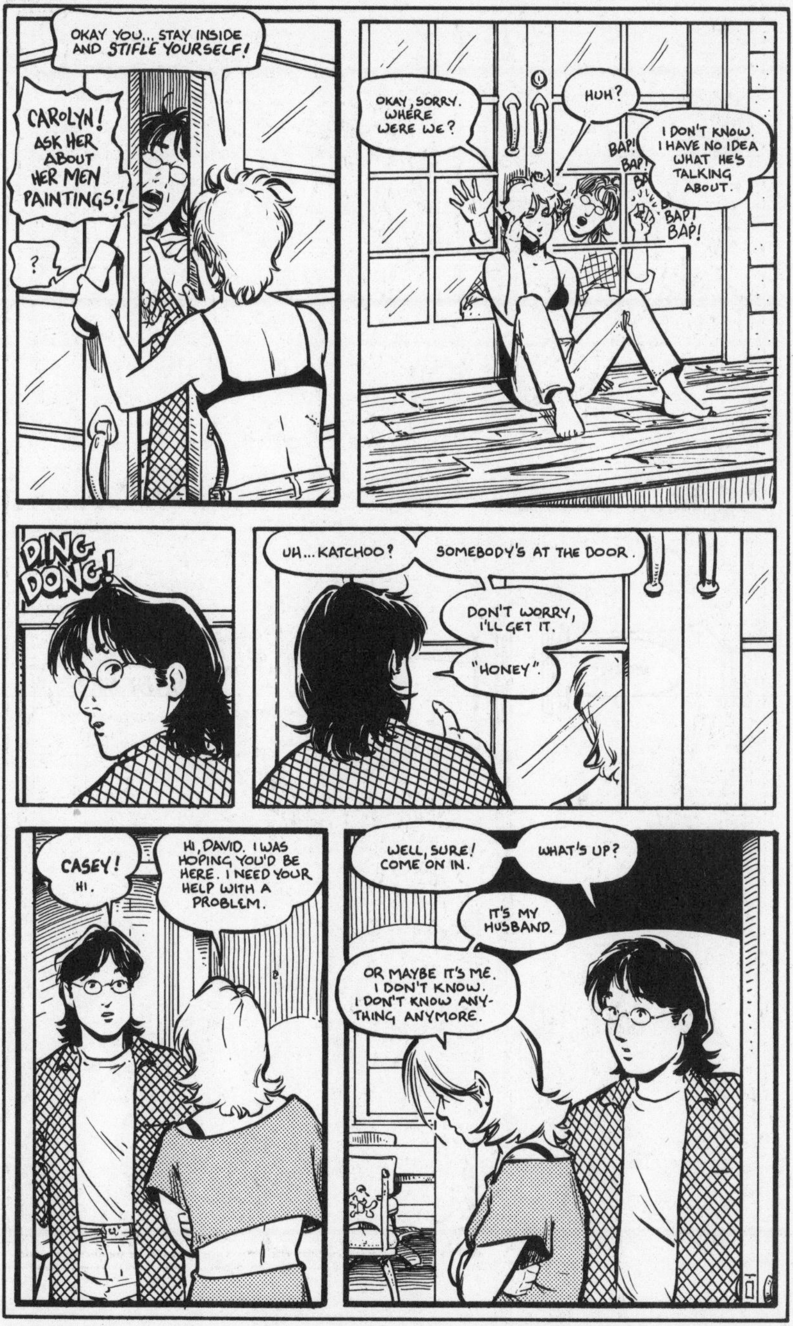
OKAY YOU... STAY INSIDE AND STIFLE YOURSELF!
CAROLYN! ASK HER ABOUT HER MEN PAINTINGS!
?
OKAY, SORRY. WHERE WERE WE?
HUH?
BAP! BAP! BAP! BAP! BAP!
I DON'T KNOW. I HAVE NO IDEA WHAT HE'S TALKING ABOUT.
DING DONG!
UH... KATCHOO?
SOMEBODY'S AT THE DOOR.
DON'T WORRY, I'LL GET IT.
"HONEY".
CASEY! HI.
HI, DAVID. I WAS HOPING YOU'D BE HERE. I NEED YOUR HELP WITH A PROBLEM.
WELL, SURE! COME ON IN.
WHAT'S UP?
IT'S MY HUSBAND.
OR MAYBE IT'S ME. I DON'T KNOW. I DON'T KNOW ANY-THING ANYMORE.

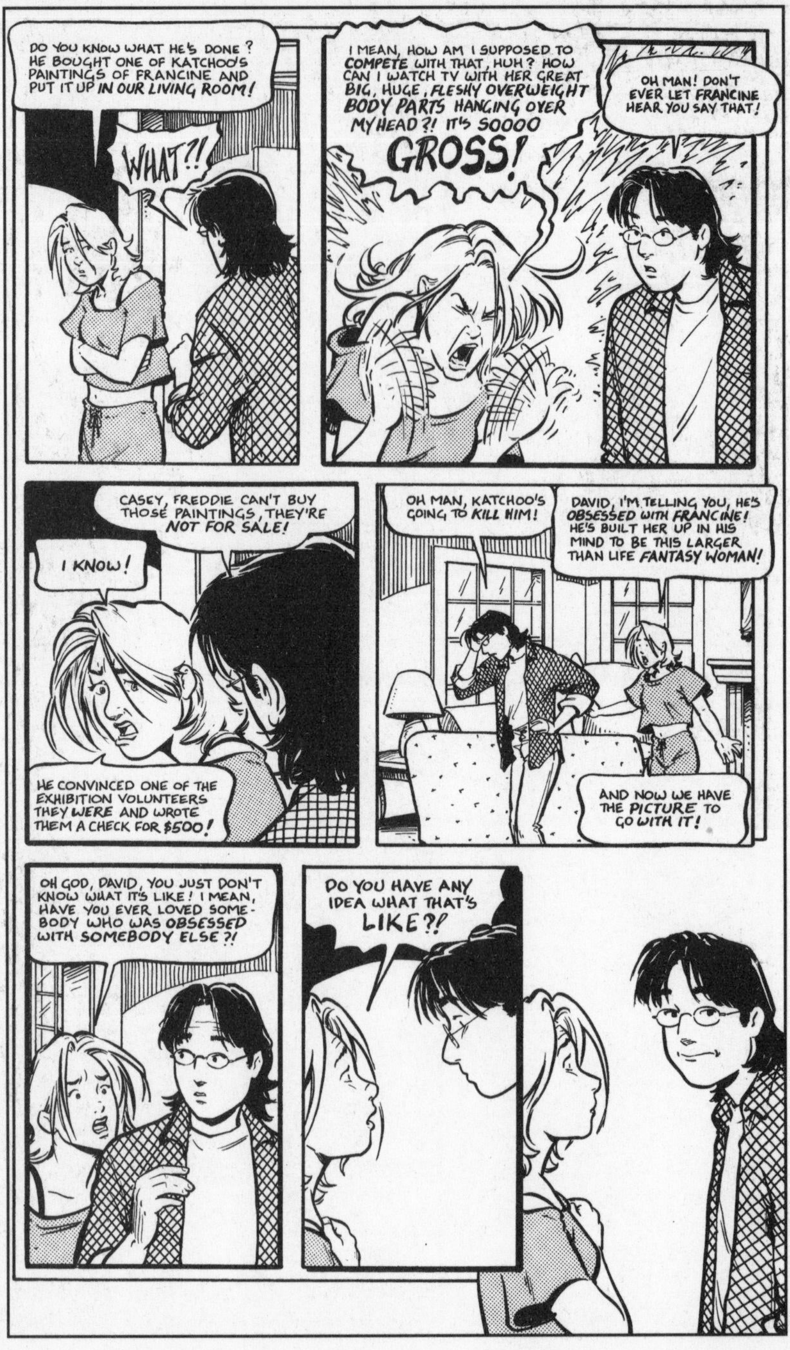

DO YOU KNOW WHAT HE'S DONE? HE BOUGHT ONE OF KATCHOO'S PAINTINGS OF FRANCINE AND PUT IT UP IN OUR LIVING ROOM!
WHAT?!
I MEAN, HOW AM I SUPPOSED TO COMPETE WITH THAT, HUH? HOW CAN I WATCH TV WITH HER GREAT BIG, HUGE, FLESHY OVERWEIGHT BODY PARTS HANGING OVER MY HEAD?! IT'S SOOOO GROSS!
OH MAN! DON'T EVER LET FRANCINE HEAR YOU SAY THAT!
CASEY, FREDDIE CAN'T BUY THOSE PAINTINGS, THEY'RE NOT FOR SALE!
I KNOW!
HE CONVINCED ONE OF THE EXHIBITION VOLUNTEERS THEY WERE AND WROTE THEM A CHECK FOR $500!
OH MAN, KATCHOO'S GOING TO KILL HIM!
DAVID, I'M TELLING YOU, HE'S OBSESSED WITH FRANCINE! HE'S BUILT HER UP IN HIS MIND TO BE THIS LARGER THAN LIFE FANTASY WOMAN!
AND NOW WE HAVE THE PICTURE TO GO WITH IT!
OH GOD, DAVID, YOU JUST DON'T KNOW WHAT IT'S LIKE! I MEAN, HAVE YOU EVER LOVED SOMEBODY WHO WAS OBSESSED WITH SOMEBODY ELSE?!
DO YOU HAVE ANY IDEA WHAT THAT'S LIKE?!

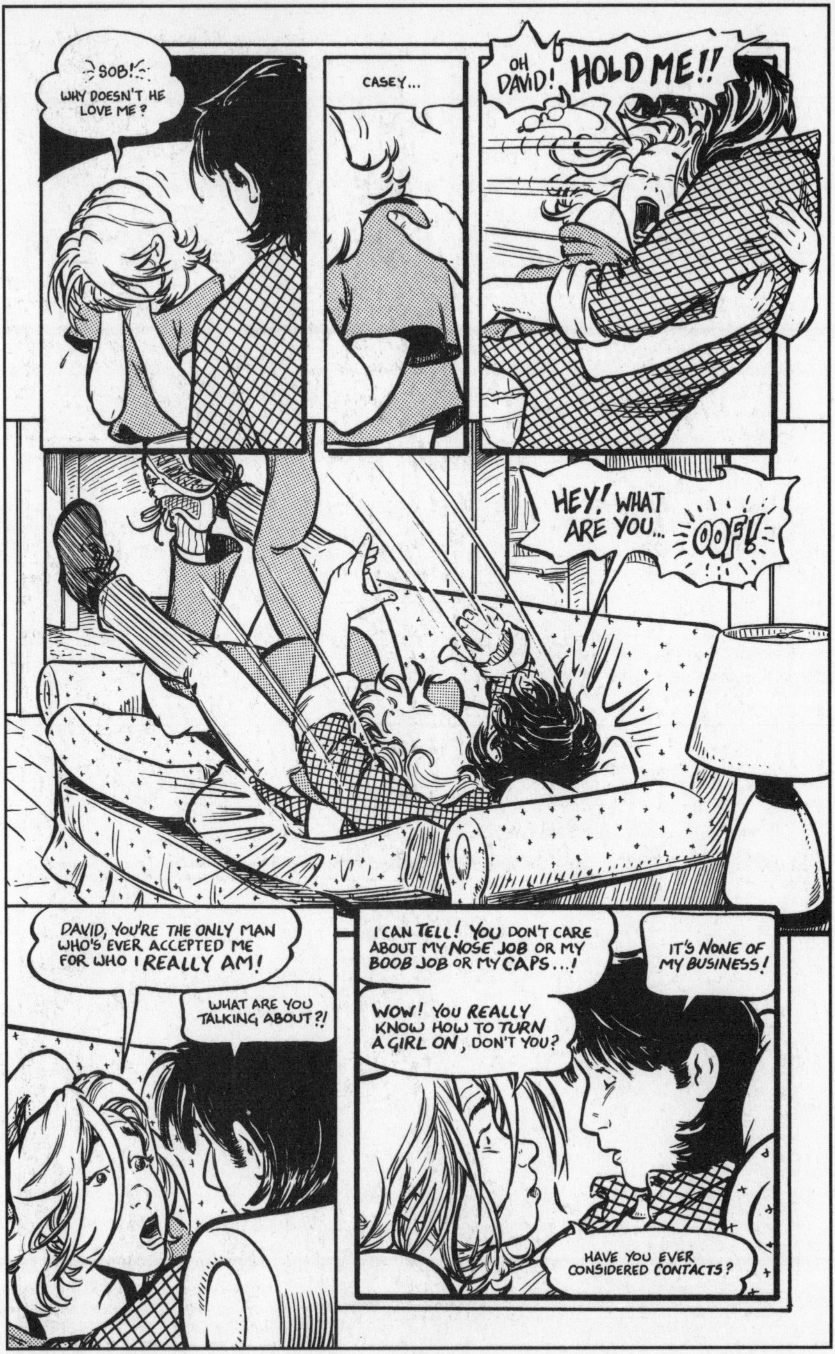
SOB!
WHY DOESN'T HE LOVE ME?
CASEY...
OH DAVID! HOLD ME!!
HEY! WHAT ARE YOU... OOF!
DAVID, YOU'RE THE ONLY MAN WHO'S EVER ACCEPTED ME FOR WHO I REALLY AM!
WHAT ARE YOU TALKING ABOUT?!
I CAN TELL! YOU DON'T CARE ABOUT MY NOSE JOB OR MY BOOB JOB OR MY CAPS...!
IT'S NONE OF MY BUSINESS!
WOW! YOU REALLY KNOW HOW TO TURN A GIRL ON, DON'T YOU?
HAVE YOU EVER CONSIDERED CONTACTS?

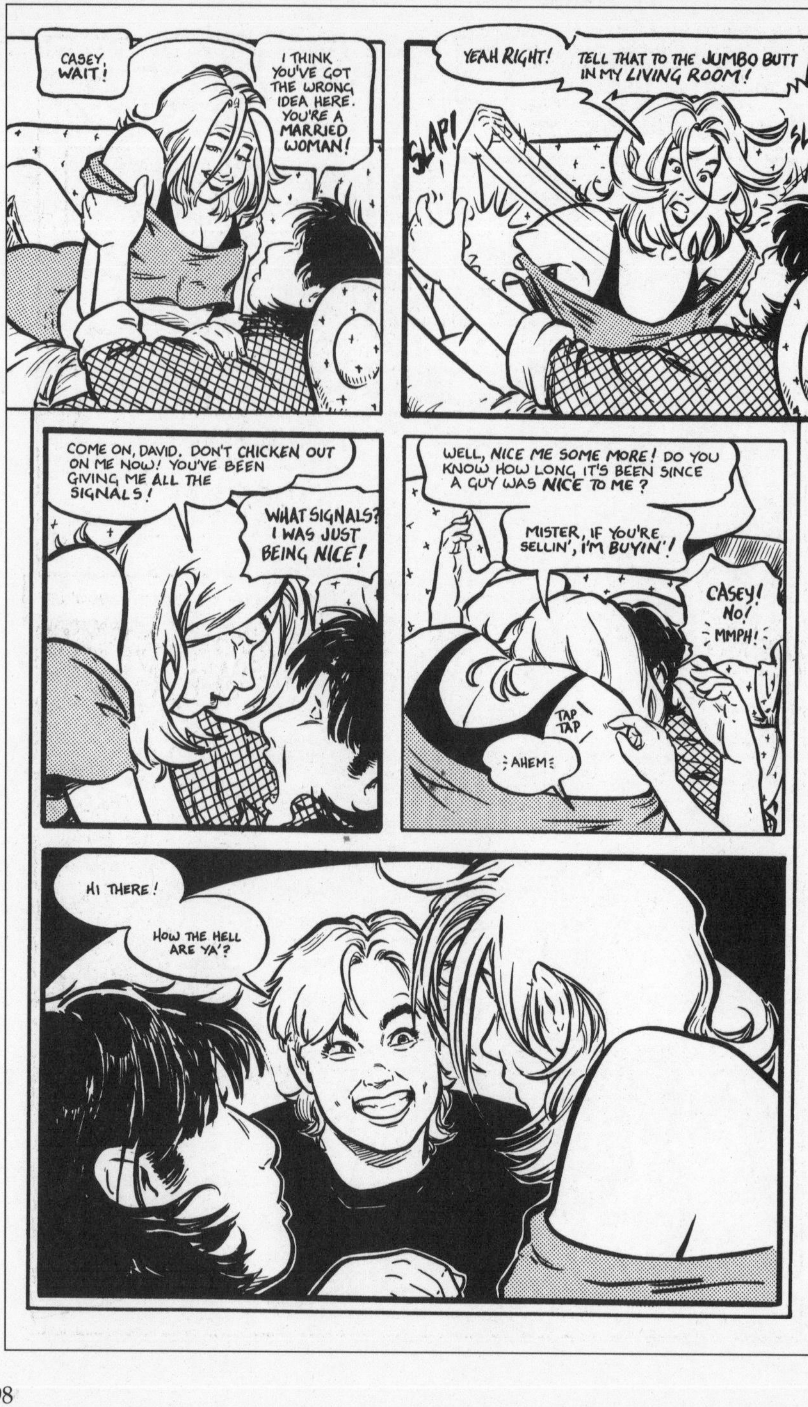
CASEY, WAIT!
I THINK YOU'VE GOT THE WRONG IDEA HERE. YOU'RE A MARRIED WOMAN!
YEAH RIGHT!
TELL THAT TO THE JUMBO BUTT IN MY LIVING ROOM!
SLAP!
COME ON, DAVID. DON'T CHICKEN OUT ON ME NOW! YOU'VE BEEN GIVING ME ALL THE SIGNALS!
WHAT SIGNALS? I WAS JUST BEING NICE!
WELL, NICE ME SOME MORE! DO YOU KNOW HOW LONG IT'S BEEN SINCE A GUY WAS NICE TO ME?
MISTER, IF YOU'RE SELLIN', I'M BUYIN'!
CASEY! NO!
MMPH!
TAP TAP
AHEM
HI THERE!
HOW THE HELL ARE YA'?

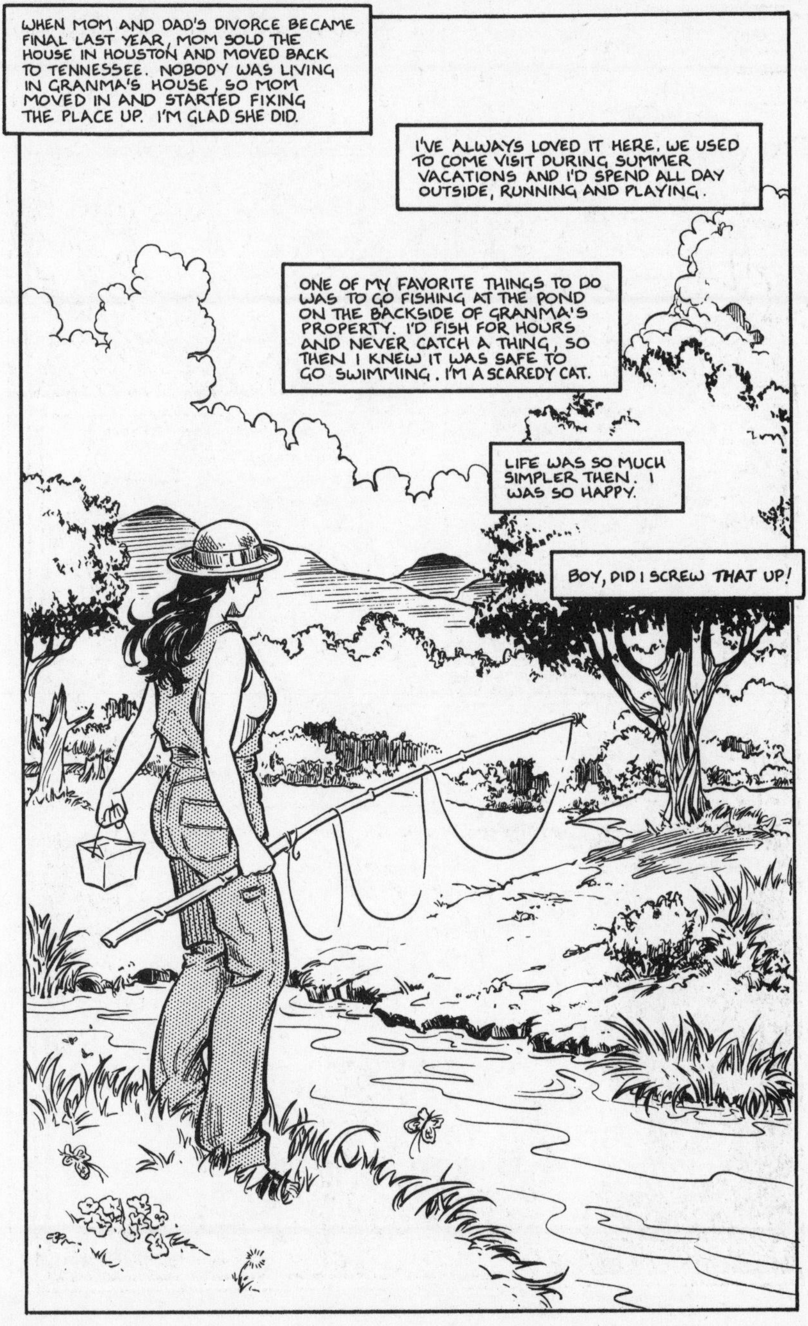
WHEN MOM AND DAD'S DIVORCE BECAME FINAL LAST YEAR, MOM SOLD THE HOUSE IN HOUSTON AND MOVED BACK TO TENNESSEE. NOBODY WAS LIVING IN GRANMA'S HOUSE, SO MOM MOVED IN AND STARTED FIXING THE PLACE UP. I'M GLAD SHE DID.
I'VE ALWAYS LOVED IT HERE. WE USED TO COME VISIT DURING SUMMER VACATIONS AND I'D SPEND ALL DAY OUTSIDE, RUNNING AND PLAYING.
ONE OF MY FAVORITE THINGS TO DO WAS TO GO FISHING AT THE POND ON THE BACKSIDE OF GRANMA'S PROPERTY. I'D FISH FOR HOURS AND NEVER CATCH A THING, SO THEN I KNEW IT WAS SAFE TO GO SWIMMING. I'M A SCAREDY CAT.
LIFE WAS SO MUCH SIMPLER THEN. I WAS SO HAPPY.
BOY, DID I SCREW THAT UP!

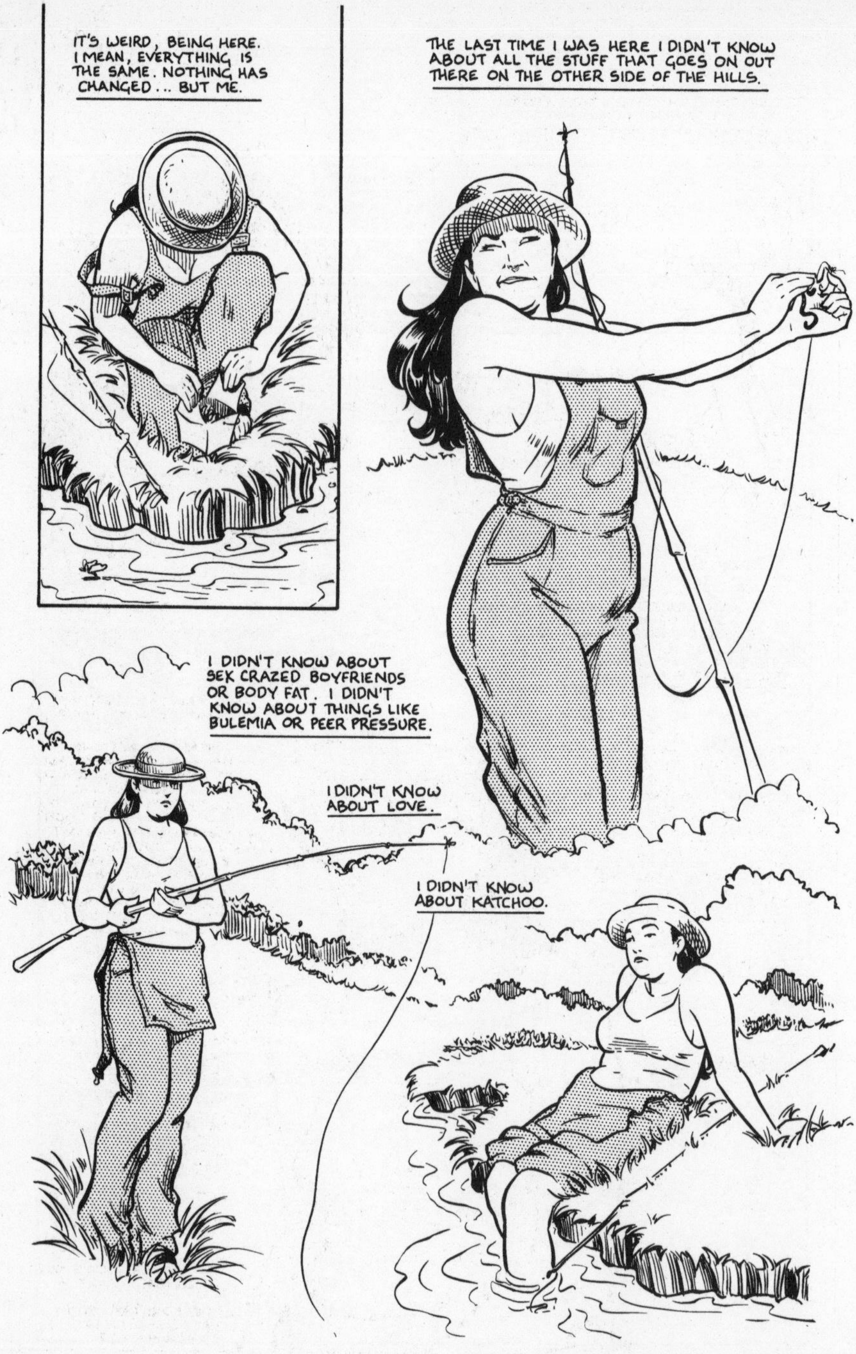
IT'S WEIRD, BEING HERE. I MEAN, EVERYTHING IS THE SAME. NOTHING HAS CHANGED... BUT ME.
THE LAST TIME I WAS HERE I DIDN'T KNOW ABOUT ALL THE STUFF THAT GOES ON OUT THERE ON THE OTHER SIDE OF THE HILLS.
I DIDN'T KNOW ABOUT SEK CRAZED BOYFRIENDS OR BODY FAT. I DIDN'T KNOW ABOUT THINGS LIKE BULEMIA OR PEER PRESSURE.
I DIDN'T KNOW ABOUT LOVE.
I DIDN'T KNOW ABOUT KATCHOO.

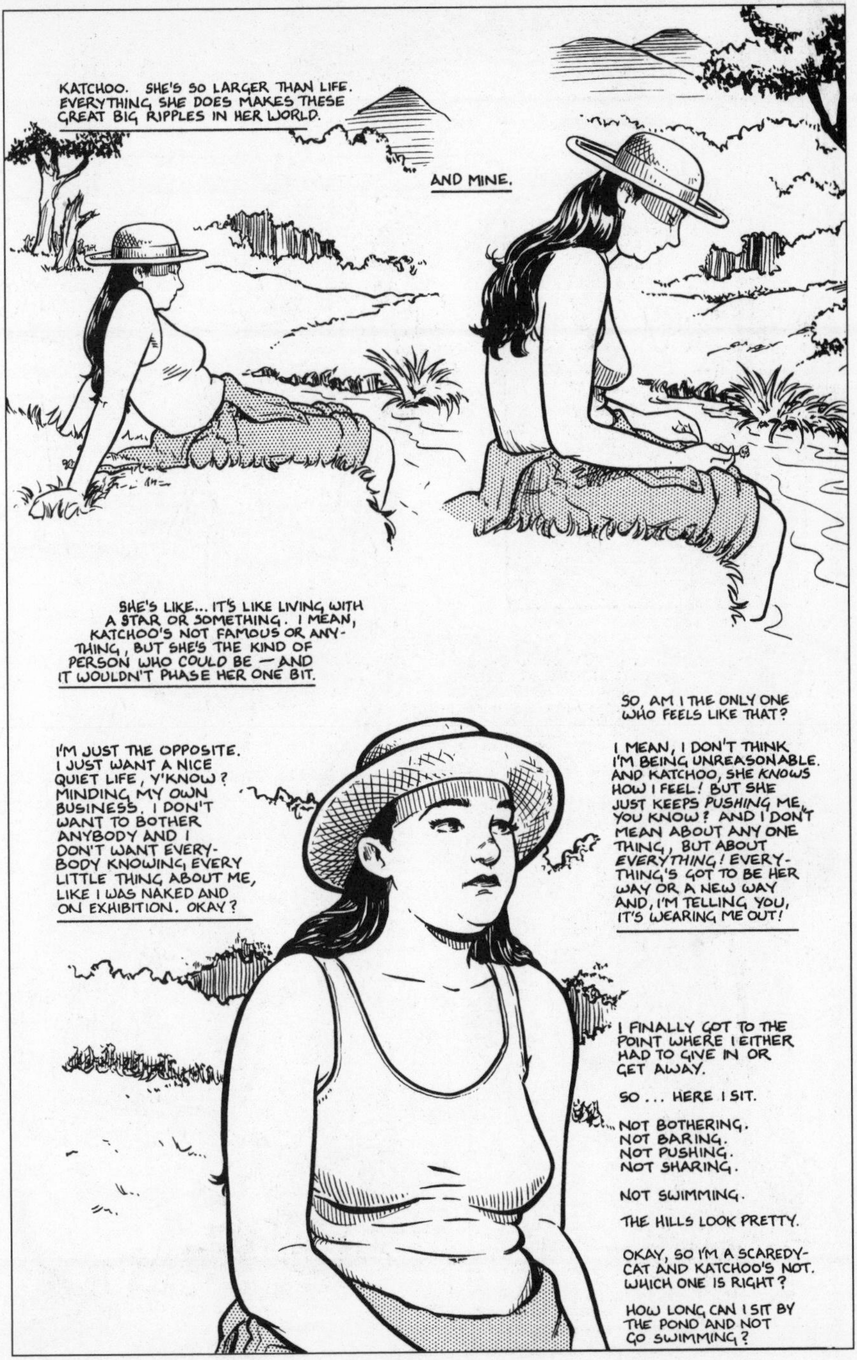
KATCHOO. SHE'S SO LARGER THAN LIFE. EVERYTHING SHE DOES MAKES THESE GREAT BIG RIPPLES IN HER WORLD.
AND MINE.
SHE'S LIKE... IT'S LIKE LIVING WITH A STAR OR SOMETHING. I MEAN, KATCHOO'S NOT FAMOUS OR ANY-THING, BUT SHE'S THE KIND OF PERSON WHO COULD BE — AND IT WOULDN'T PHASE HER ONE BIT.
I'M JUST THE OPPOSITE. I JUST WANT A NICE QUIET LIFE, Y'KNOW? MINDING MY OWN BUSINESS. I DON'T WANT TO BOTHER ANYBODY AND I DON'T WANT EVERY-BODY KNOWING EVERY LITTLE THING ABOUT ME, LIKE I WAS NAKED AND ON EXHIBITION. OKAY?
SO, AM I THE ONLY ONE WHO FEELS LIKE THAT?
I MEAN, I DON'T THINK I'M BEING UNREASONABLE. AND KATCHOO, SHE *KNOWS* HOW I FEEL! BUT SHE JUST KEEPS *PUSHING* ME, YOU KNOW? AND I DON'T MEAN ABOUT ANY ONE THING, BUT ABOUT *EVERYTHING*! EVERY-THING'S GOT TO BE HER WAY OR A NEW WAY AND, I'M TELLING YOU, IT'S WEARING ME OUT!
I FINALLY GOT TO THE POINT WHERE I EITHER HAD TO GIVE IN OR GET AWAY.
SO ... HERE I SIT.
NOT BOTHERING. NOT BARING. NOT PUSHING. NOT SHARING.
NOT SWIMMING.
THE HILLS LOOK PRETTY.
OKAY, SO I'M A SCAREDY-CAT AND KATCHOO'S NOT. WHICH ONE IS RIGHT?
HOW LONG CAN I SIT BY THE POND AND NOT GO SWIMMING?

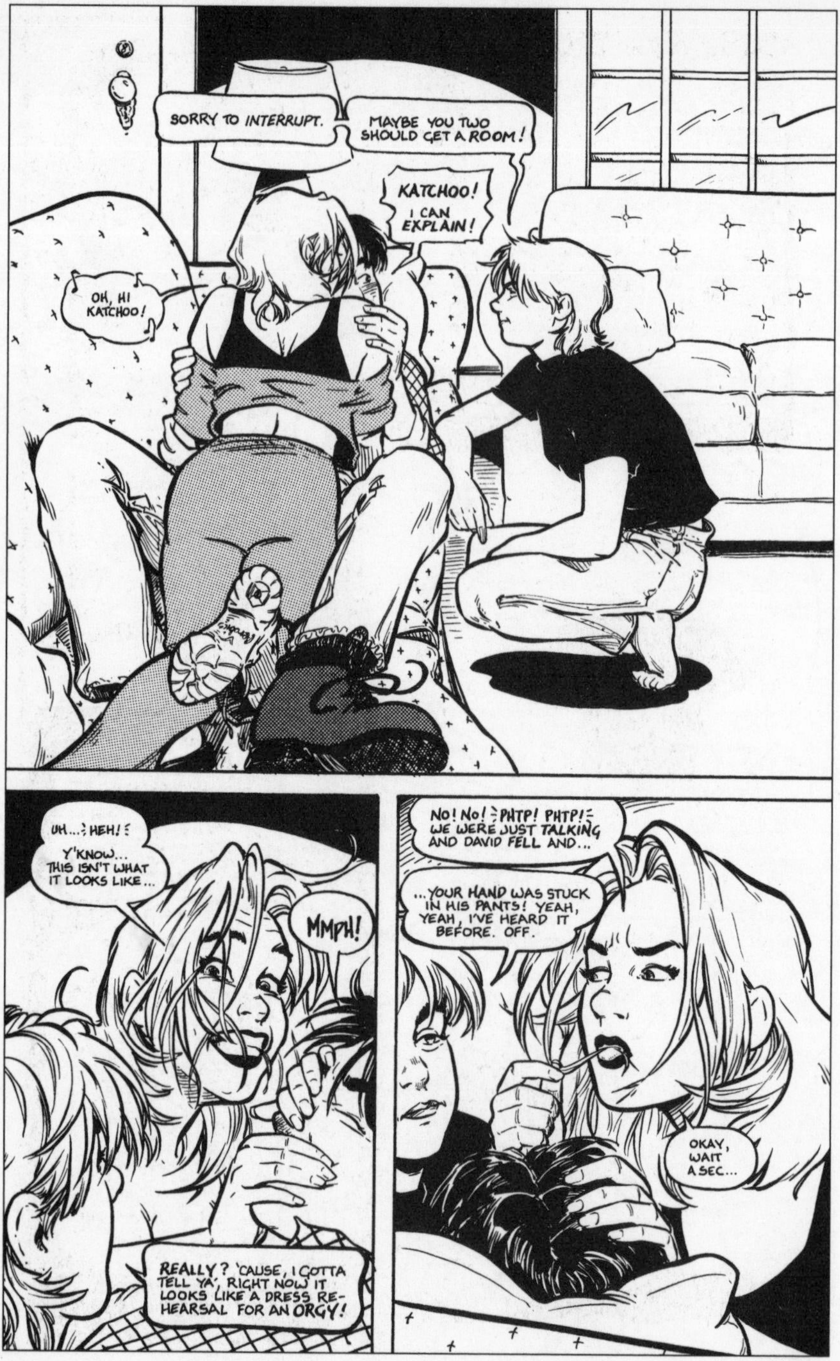
SORRY TO INTERRUPT.
MAYBE YOU TWO SHOULD GET A ROOM!
KATCHOO! I CAN EXPLAIN!
OH, HI KATCHOO!
UH... HEH!
Y'KNOW... THIS ISN'T WHAT IT LOOKS LIKE...
MMPH!
REALLY? 'CAUSE, I GOTTA TELL YA', RIGHT NOW IT LOOKS LIKE A DRESS RE-HEARSAL FOR AN ORGY!
NO! NO! PHTP! PHTP! WE WERE JUST TALKING AND DAVID FELL AND...
...YOUR HAND WAS STUCK IN HIS PANTS! YEAH, YEAH, I'VE HEARD IT BEFORE. OFF.
OKAY, WAIT A SEC...

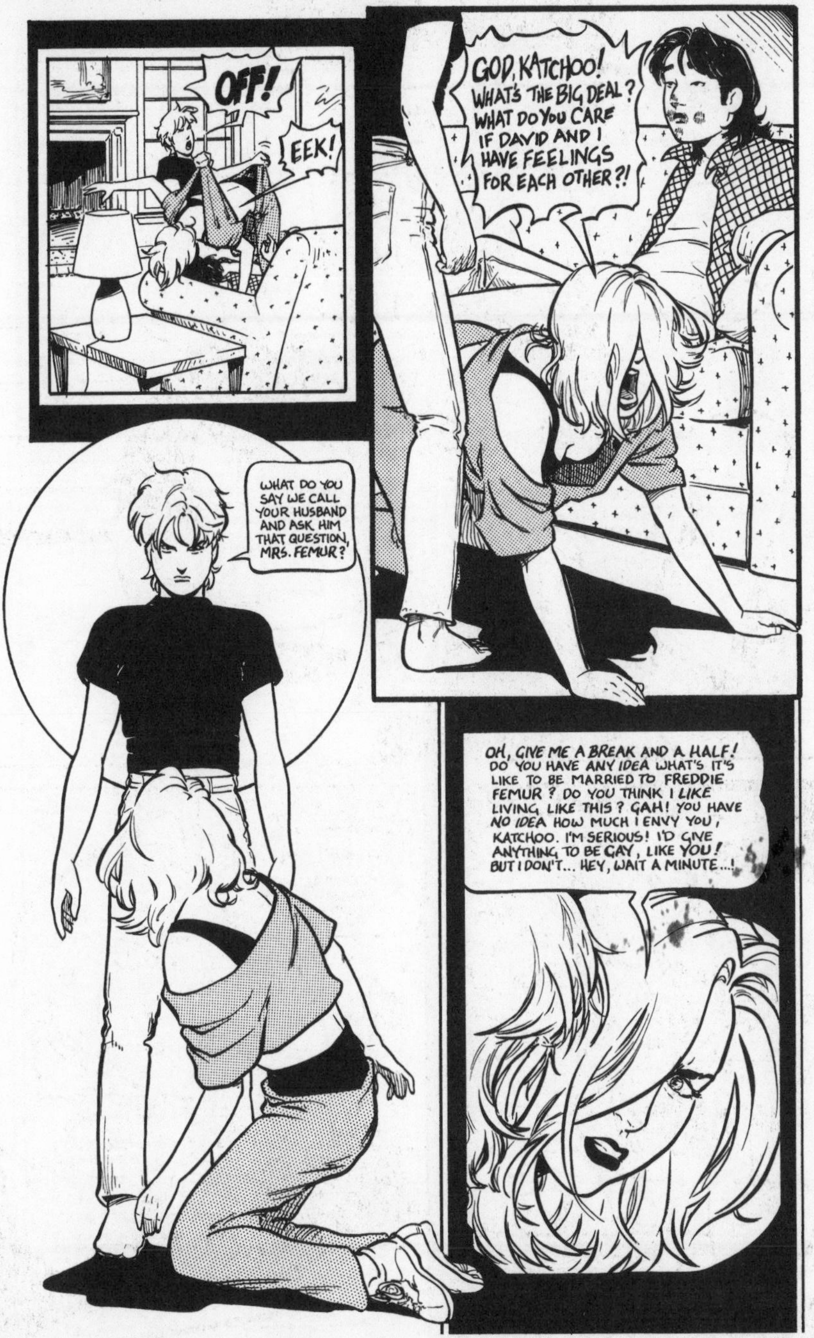
OFF!
EEK!
GOD, KATCHOO! WHAT'S THE BIG DEAL? WHAT DO YOU CARE IF DAVID AND I HAVE FEELINGS FOR EACH OTHER?!
WHAT DO YOU SAY WE CALL YOUR HUSBAND AND ASK HIM THAT QUESTION, MRS. FEMUR?
OH, GIVE ME A BREAK AND A HALF! DO YOU HAVE ANY IDEA WHAT'S IT'S LIKE TO BE MARRIED TO FREDDIE FEMUR? DO YOU THINK I LIKE LIVING LIKE THIS? GAH! YOU HAVE NO IDEA HOW MUCH I ENVY YOU, KATCHOO. I'M SERIOUS! I'D GIVE ANYTHING TO BE GAY, LIKE YOU! BUT I DON'T... HEY, WAIT A MINUTE...!

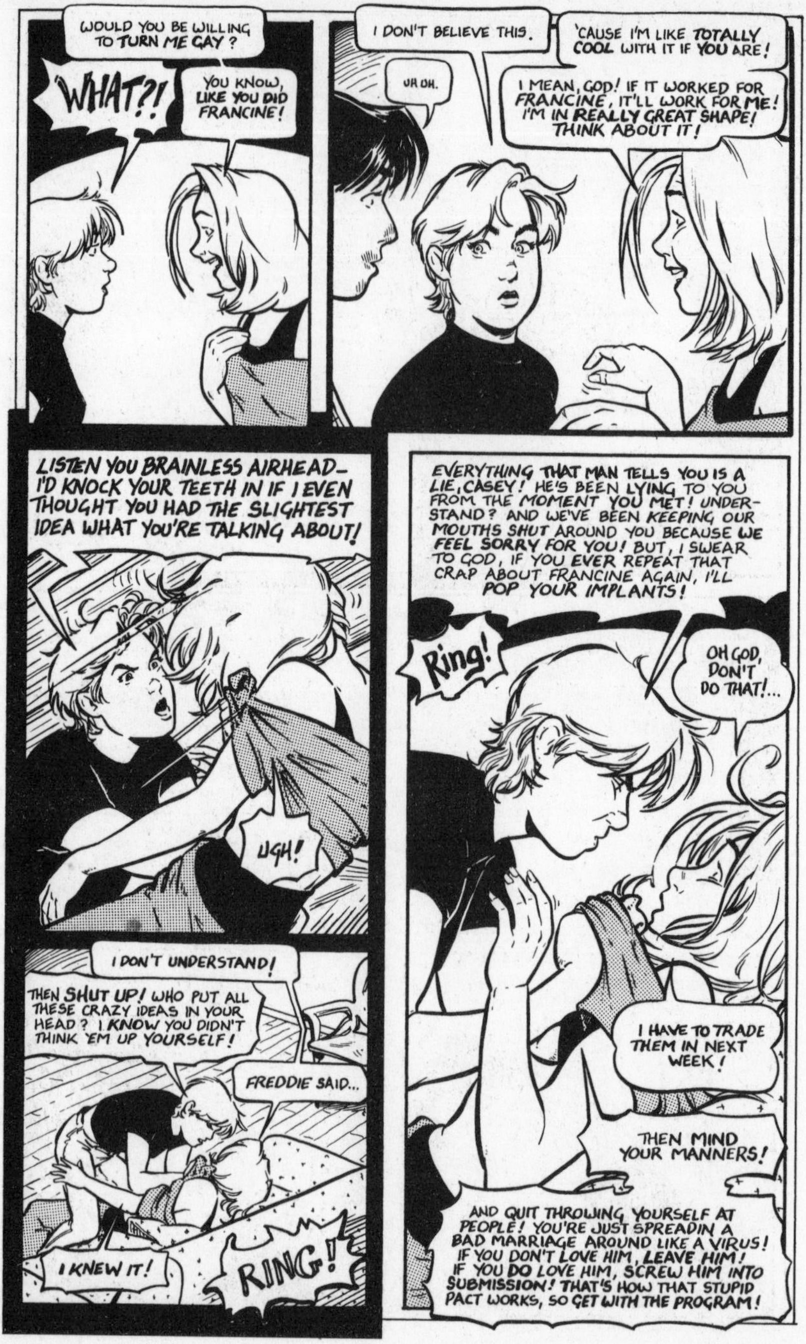
WOULD YOU BE WILLING TO TURN ME GAY?
WHAT?!
YOU KNOW, LIKE YOU DID FRANCINE!
I DON'T BELIEVE THIS.
UH OH.
'CAUSE I'M LIKE TOTALLY COOL WITH IT IF YOU ARE!
I MEAN, GOD! IF IT WORKED FOR FRANCINE, IT'LL WORK FOR ME! I'M IN REALLY GREAT SHAPE! THINK ABOUT IT!
LISTEN YOU BRAINLESS AIRHEAD- I'D KNOCK YOUR TEETH IN IF I EVEN THOUGHT YOU HAD THE SLIGHTEST IDEA WHAT YOU'RE TALKING ABOUT!
UGH!
I DON'T UNDERSTAND!
THEN SHUT UP! WHO PUT ALL THESE CRAZY IDEAS IN YOUR HEAD? I KNOW YOU DIDN'T THINK 'EM UP YOURSELF!
FREDDIE SAID...
I KNEW IT!
RING!
EVERYTHING THAT MAN TELLS YOU IS A LIE, CASEY! HE'S BEEN LYING TO YOU FROM THE MOMENT YOU MET! UNDERSTAND? AND WE'VE BEEN KEEPING OUR MOUTHS SHUT AROUND YOU BECAUSE WE FEEL SORRY FOR YOU! BUT, I SWEAR TO GOD, IF YOU EVER REPEAT THAT CRAP ABOUT FRANCINE AGAIN, I'LL POP YOUR IMPLANTS!
Ring!
OH GOD, DON'T DO THAT!...
I HAVE TO TRADE THEM IN NEXT WEEK!
THEN MIND YOUR MANNERS!
AND QUIT THROWING YOURSELF AT PEOPLE! YOU'RE JUST SPREADIN A BAD MARRIAGE AROUND LIKE A VIRUS! IF YOU DON'T LOVE HIM, LEAVE HIM! IF YOU DO LOVE HIM, SCREW HIM INTO SUBMISSION! THAT'S HOW THAT STUPID PACT WORKS, SO GET WITH THE PROGRAM!

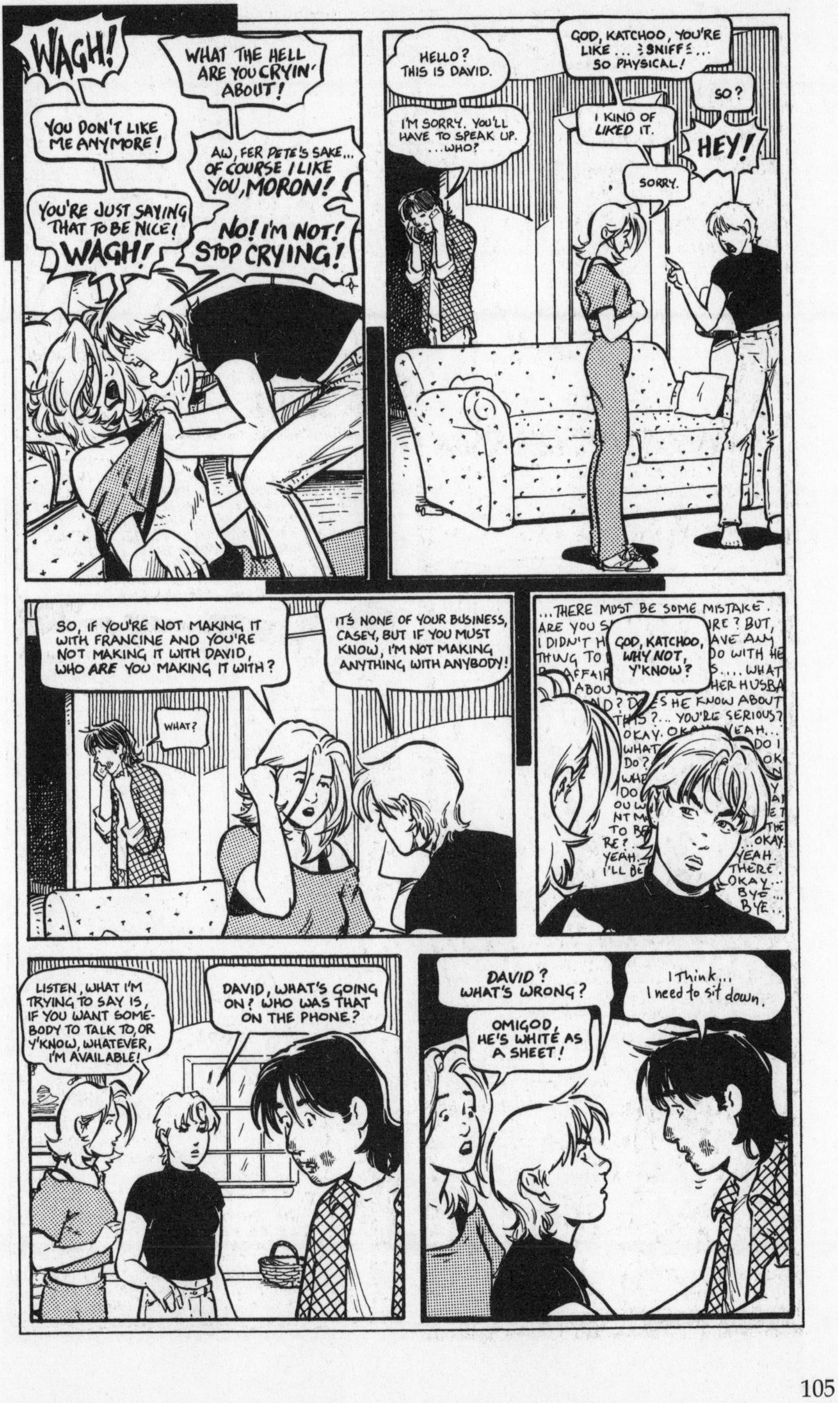
WAGH!
YOU DON'T LIKE ME ANYMORE!
WHAT THE HELL ARE YOU CRYIN' ABOUT!
AW, FER PETE'S SAKE... OF COURSE I LIKE YOU, MORON!
YOU'RE JUST SAYING THAT TO BE NICE! WAGH!
NO! I'M NOT! STOP CRYING!
HELLO? THIS IS DAVID.
I'M SORRY. YOU'LL HAVE TO SPEAK UP. ...WHO?
GOD, KATCHOO, YOU'RE LIKE... SNIFF... SO PHYSICAL!
I KIND OF LIKED IT.
SORRY.
SO?
HEY!
SO, IF YOU'RE NOT MAKING IT WITH FRANCINE AND YOU'RE NOT MAKING IT WITH DAVID, WHO ARE YOU MAKING IT WITH?
IT'S NONE OF YOUR BUSINESS, CASEY, BUT IF YOU MUST KNOW, I'M NOT MAKING ANYTHING WITH ANYBODY!
WHAT?
...THERE MUST BE SOME MISTAKE.
ARE YOU S
RE? BUT,
I DIDN'T H
AVE ANY
THING TO
DO WITH HE
AFFAIR
S.... WHAT
ABOU
HER HUSBA
ND? DOES HE KNOW ABOUT
THIS?... YOU'RE SERIOUS?
OKAY. OKAY. YEAH...
WHAT
DO I
DO?
YEAH.
I'LL BE
...OKAY.
YEAH.
THERE.
OKAY...
BYE...
BYE...
GOD, KATCHOO, WHY NOT, Y'KNOW?
LISTEN, WHAT I'M TRYING TO SAY IS, IF YOU WANT SOMEBODY TO TALK TO, OR Y'KNOW, WHATEVER, I'M AVAILABLE!
DAVID, WHAT'S GOING ON? WHO WAS THAT ON THE PHONE?
DAVID? WHAT'S WRONG?
OMIGOD, HE'S WHITE AS A SHEET!
I Think... I need to sit down.

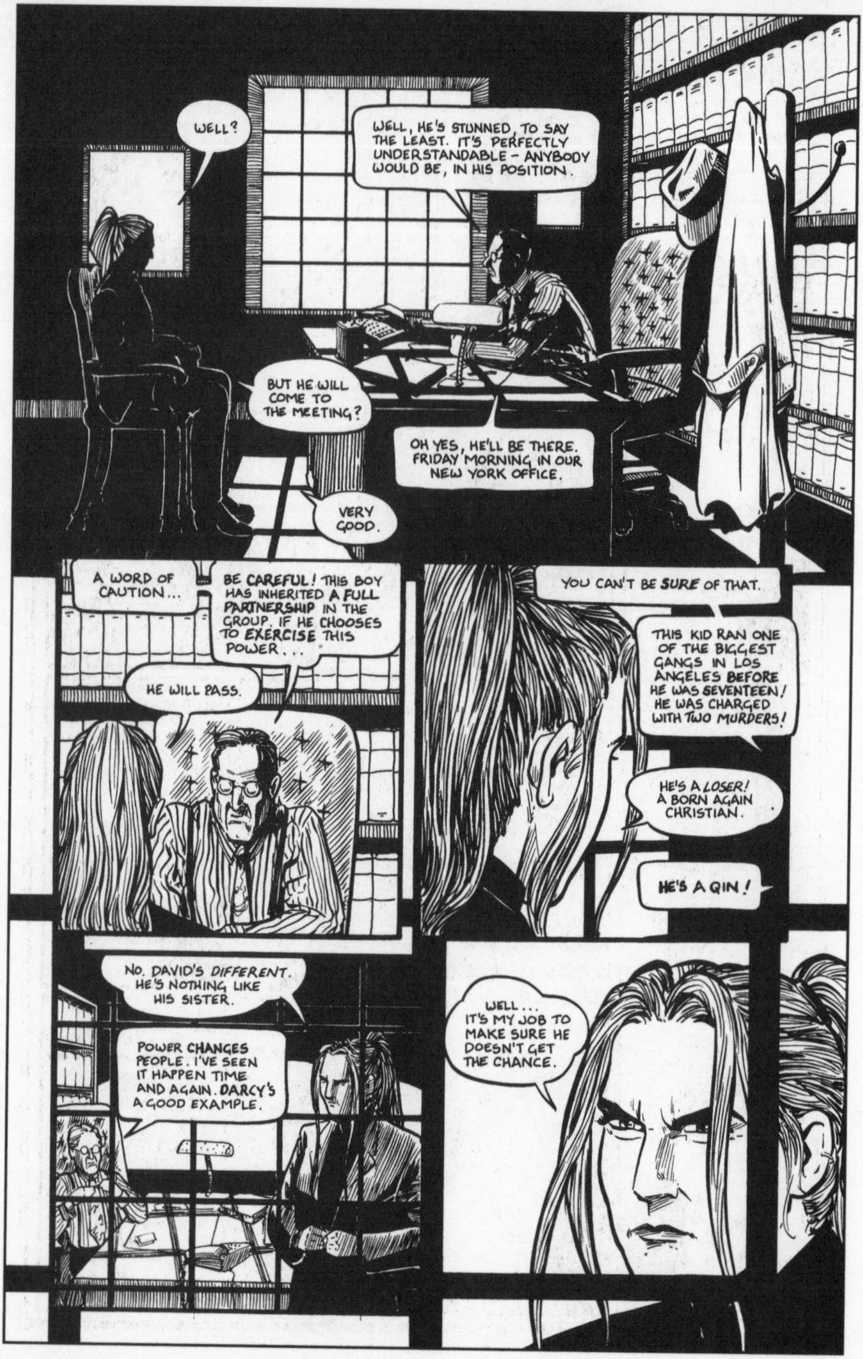
WELL?
WELL, HE'S STUNNED, TO SAY THE LEAST. IT'S PERFECTLY UNDERSTANDABLE - ANYBODY WOULD BE, IN HIS POSITION.
BUT HE WILL COME TO THE MEETING?
OH YES, HE'LL BE THERE. FRIDAY MORNING IN OUR NEW YORK OFFICE.
VERY GOOD.
A WORD OF CAUTION...
BE CAREFUL! THIS BOY HAS INHERITED A FULL PARTNERSHIP IN THE GROUP. IF HE CHOOSES TO EXERCISE THIS POWER...
HE WILL PASS.
YOU CAN'T BE SURE OF THAT.
THIS KID RAN ONE OF THE BIGGEST GANGS IN LOS ANGELES BEFORE HE WAS SEVENTEEN! HE WAS CHARGED WITH TWO MURDERS!
HE'S A LOSER! A BORN AGAIN CHRISTIAN.
HE'S A QIN!
NO. DAVID'S DIFFERENT. HE'S NOTHING LIKE HIS SISTER.
POWER CHANGES PEOPLE. I'VE SEEN IT HAPPEN TIME AND AGAIN. DARCY'S A GOOD EXAMPLE.
WELL... IT'S MY JOB TO MAKE SURE HE DOESN'T GET THE CHANCE.

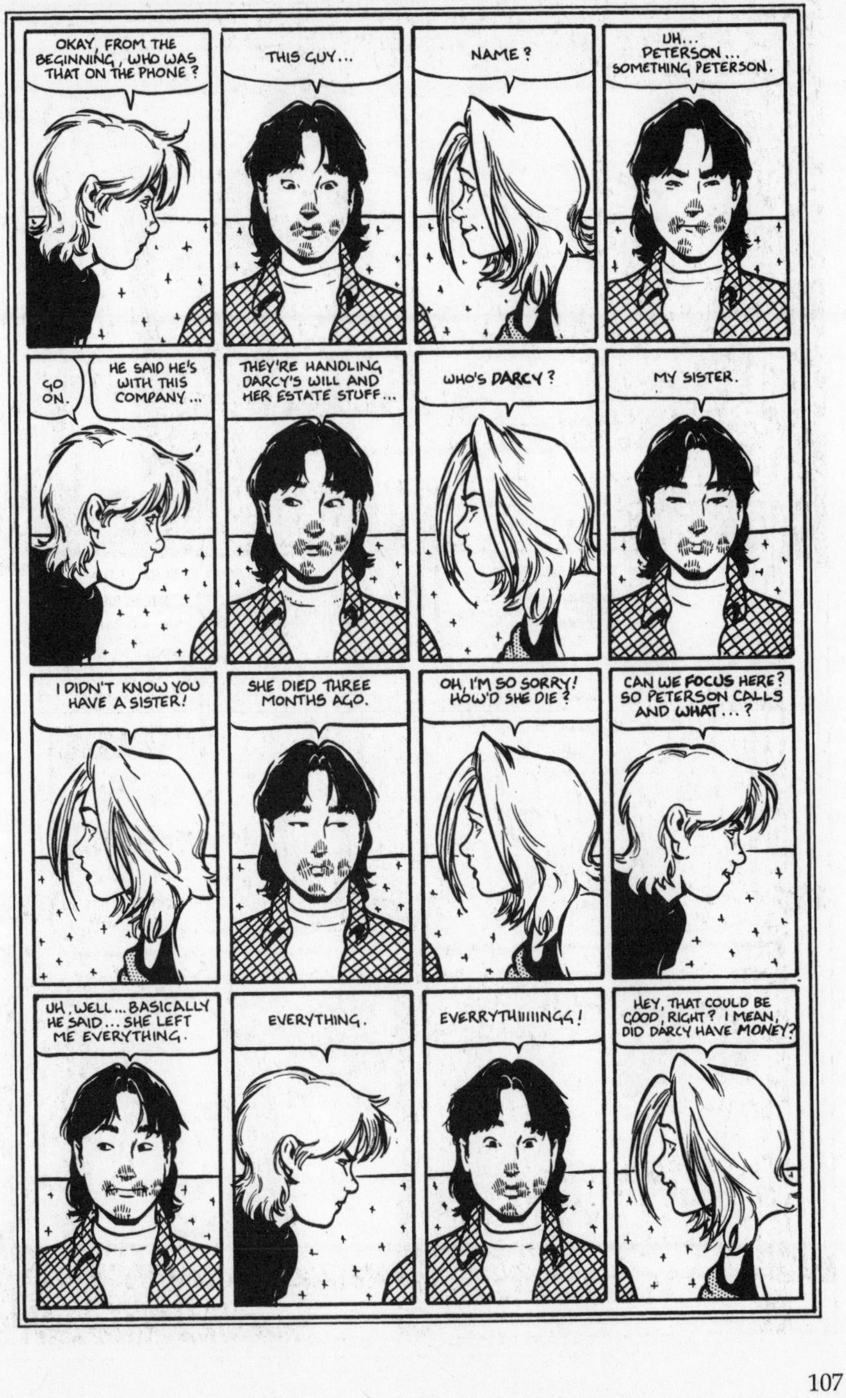
OKAY, FROM THE BEGINNING, WHO WAS THAT ON THE PHONE?
THIS GUY...
NAME?
UH... PETERSON... SOMETHING PETERSON.
GO ON.
HE SAID HE'S WITH THIS COMPANY...
THEY'RE HANDLING DARCY'S WILL AND HER ESTATE STUFF...
WHO'S DARCY?
MY SISTER.
I DIDN'T KNOW YOU HAVE A SISTER!
SHE DIED THREE MONTHS AGO.
OH, I'M SO SORRY! HOW'D SHE DIE?
CAN WE FOCUS HERE? SO PETERSON CALLS AND WHAT...?
UH, WELL... BASICALLY HE SAID... SHE LEFT ME EVERYTHING.
EVERYTHING.
EVERRYTHIIIIINGG!
HEY, THAT COULD BE GOOD, RIGHT? I MEAN, DID DARCY HAVE MONEY?

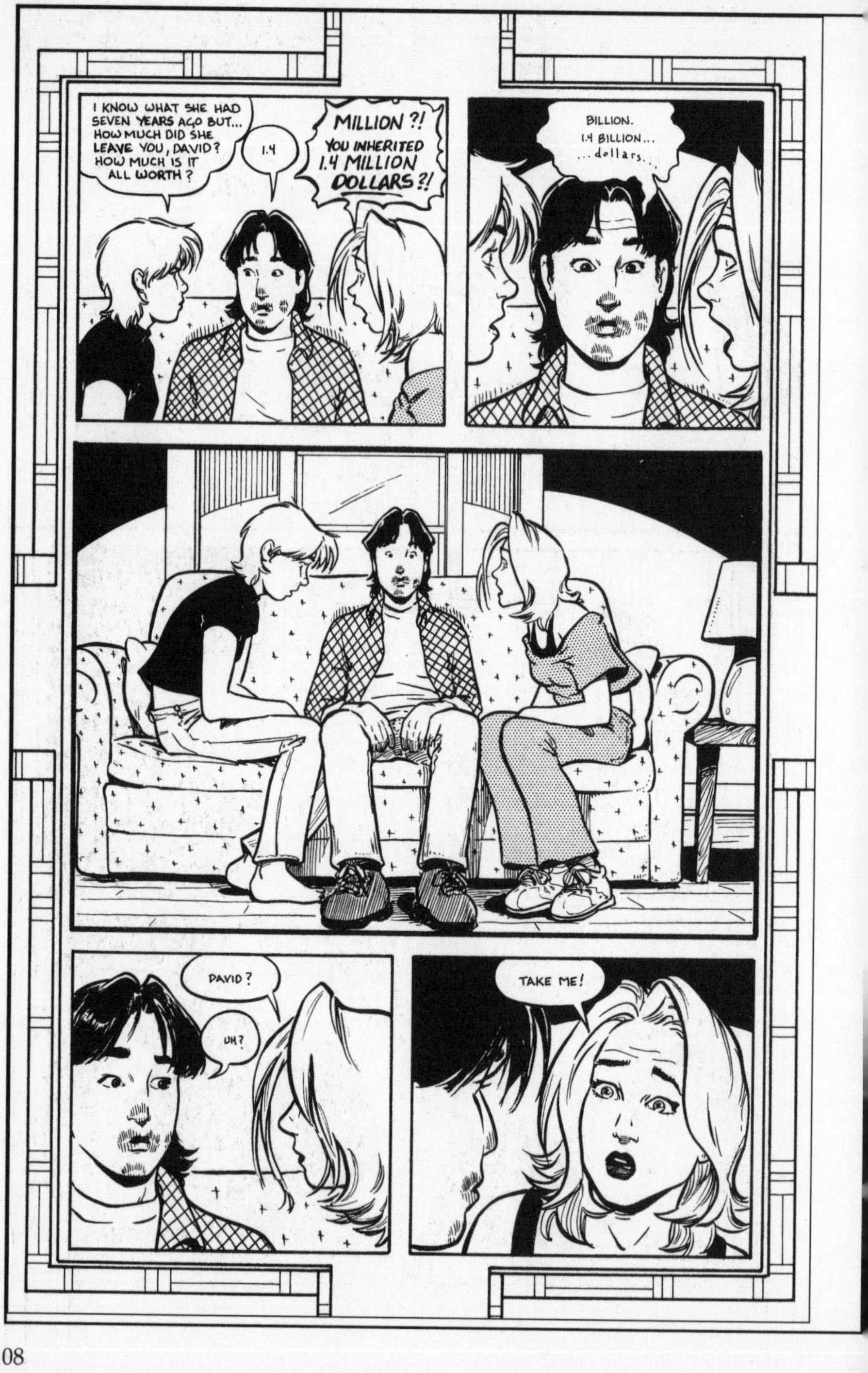
I KNOW WHAT SHE HAD SEVEN YEARS AGO BUT... HOW MUCH DID SHE LEAVE YOU, DAVID? HOW MUCH IS IT ALL WORTH?
1.4
MILLION?! YOU INHERITED 1.4 MILLION DOLLARS?!
BILLION. 1.4 BILLION... ...dollars...
DAVID?
UH?
TAKE ME!

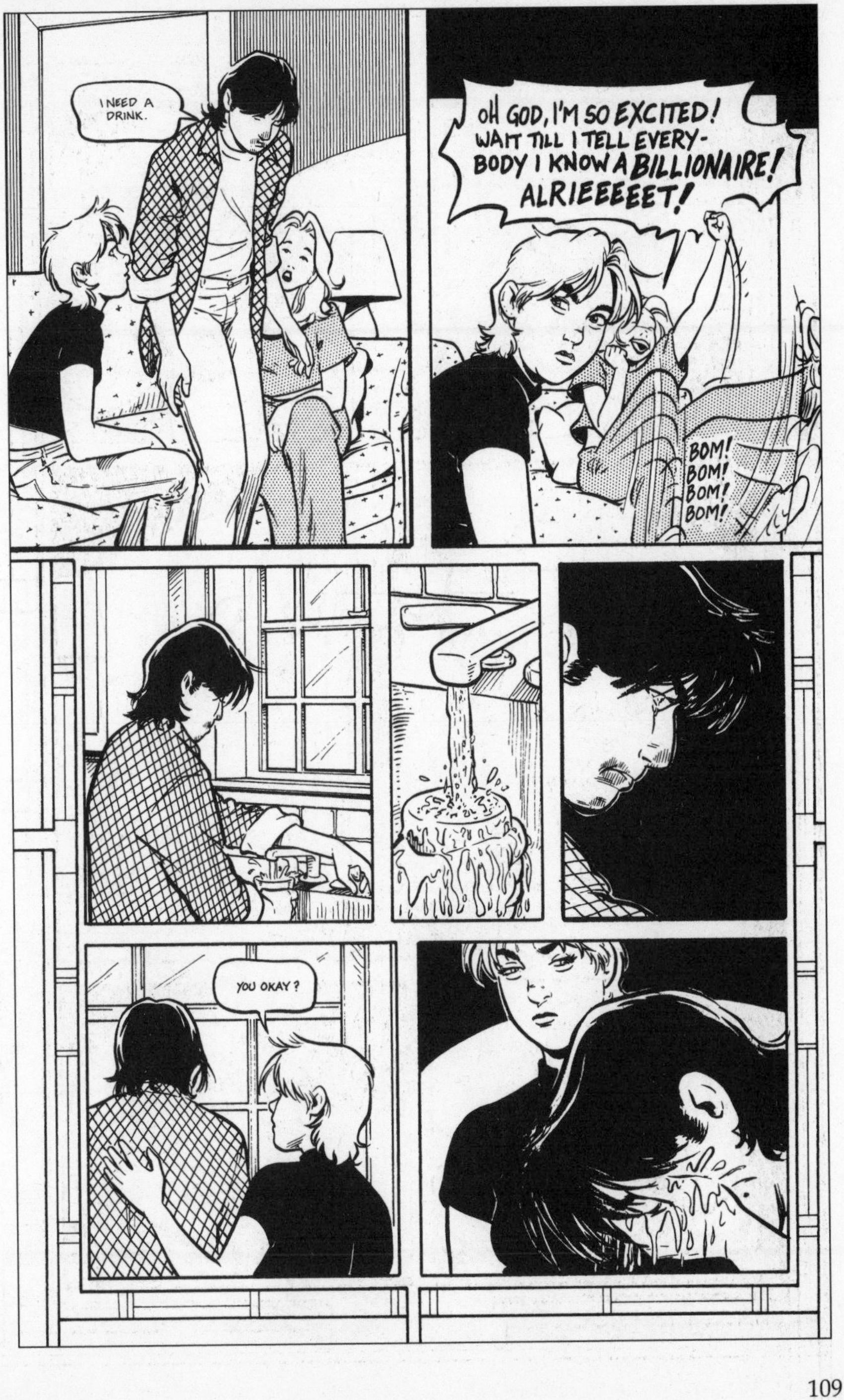
I NEED A DRINK.
OH GOD, I'M SO EXCITED! WAIT TILL I TELL EVERYBODY I KNOW A BILLIONAIRE! ALRIEEEEEET!
BOM! BOM! BOM! BOM!
YOU OKAY?

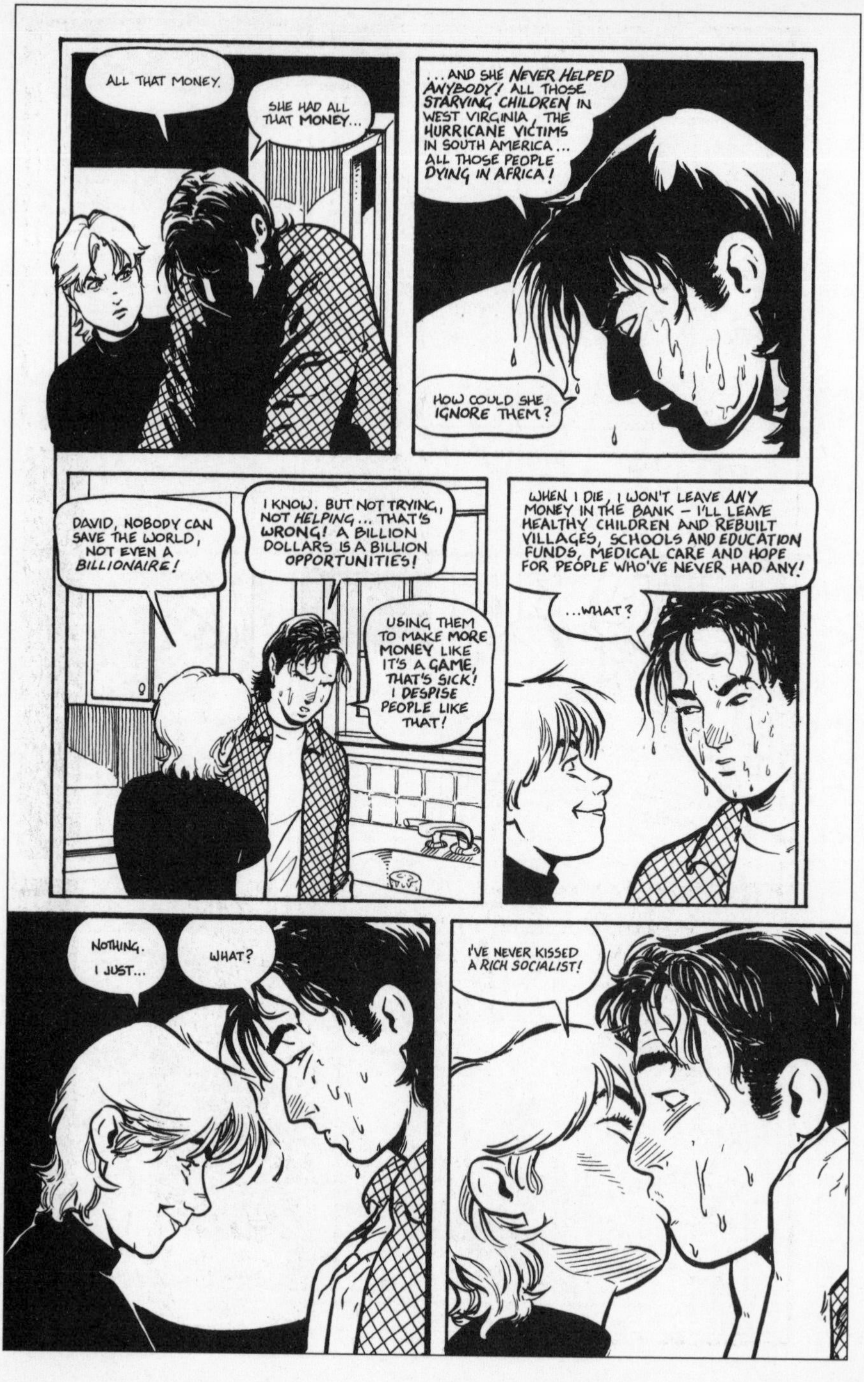
ALL THAT MONEY.
SHE HAD ALL THAT MONEY...
...AND SHE NEVER HELPED ANYBODY! ALL THOSE STARVING CHILDREN IN WEST VIRGINIA, THE HURRICANE VICTIMS IN SOUTH AMERICA... ALL THOSE PEOPLE DYING IN AFRICA!
HOW COULD SHE IGNORE THEM?
DAVID, NOBODY CAN SAVE THE WORLD, NOT EVEN A BILLIONAIRE!
I KNOW. BUT NOT TRYING, NOT HELPING... THAT'S WRONG! A BILLION DOLLARS IS A BILLION OPPORTUNITIES!
USING THEM TO MAKE MORE MONEY LIKE IT'S A GAME, THAT'S SICK! I DESPISE PEOPLE LIKE THAT!
WHEN I DIE, I WON'T LEAVE ANY MONEY IN THE BANK - I'LL LEAVE HEALTHY CHILDREN AND REBUILT VILLAGES, SCHOOLS AND EDUCATION FUNDS, MEDICAL CARE AND HOPE FOR PEOPLE WHO'VE NEVER HAD ANY!
...WHAT?
NOTHING. I JUST...
WHAT?
I'VE NEVER KISSED A RICH SOCIALIST!

DAVID?
KATCHOO?
YOO-HOO?
WHERE DID EVERYBODY GO?
GIGGLE!
Baby you're a rich man...
goo goo goo joob!
One of the beautiful people!
yeah, right!
NOW YOU CAN LIVE NEXT TO BILL GATES.
WHO?
...AND GET THAT HEARING PROBLEM FIXED!
HAH! HAH!

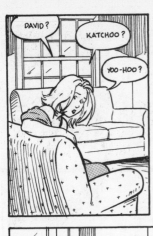

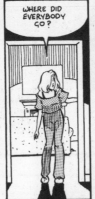

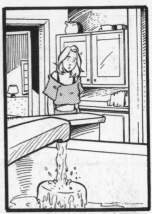

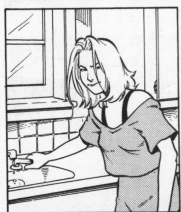

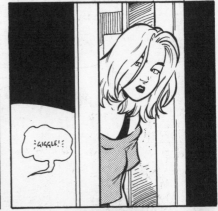

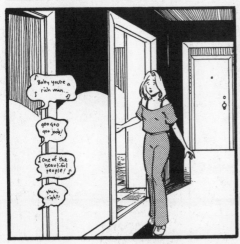

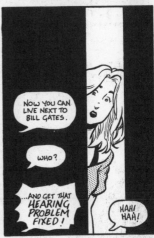

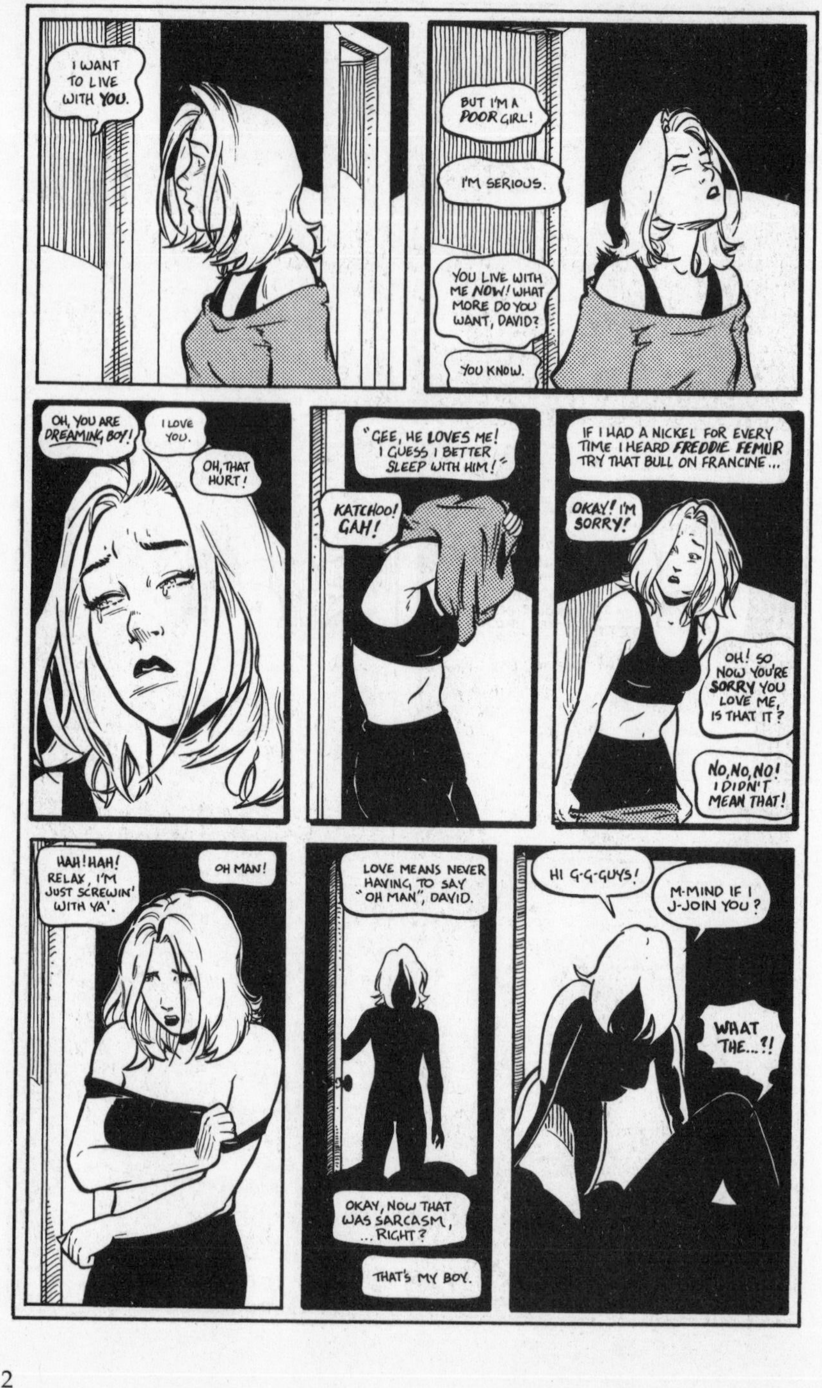
I WANT TO LIVE WITH YOU.
BUT I'M A POOR GIRL!
I'M SERIOUS.
YOU LIVE WITH ME NOW! WHAT MORE DO YOU WANT, DAVID?
YOU KNOW.
OH, YOU ARE DREAMING BOY!
I LOVE YOU.
OH, THAT HURT!
"GEE, HE LOVES ME! I GUESS I BETTER SLEEP WITH HIM!"
KATCHOO! GAH!
IF I HAD A NICKEL FOR EVERY TIME I HEARD FREDDIE FEMUR TRY THAT BULL ON FRANCINE...
OKAY! I'M SORRY!
OH! SO NOW YOU'RE SORRY YOU LOVE ME, IS THAT IT?
NO, NO, NO! I DIDN'T MEAN THAT!
HAH! HAH! RELAX, I'M JUST SCREWIN' WITH YA'.
OH MAN!
LOVE MEANS NEVER HAVING TO SAY "OH MAN", DAVID.
OKAY, NOW THAT WAS SARCASM, ... RIGHT?
THAT'S MY BOY.
HI G-G-GUYS!
M-MIND IF I J-JOIN YOU?
WHAT THE...?!

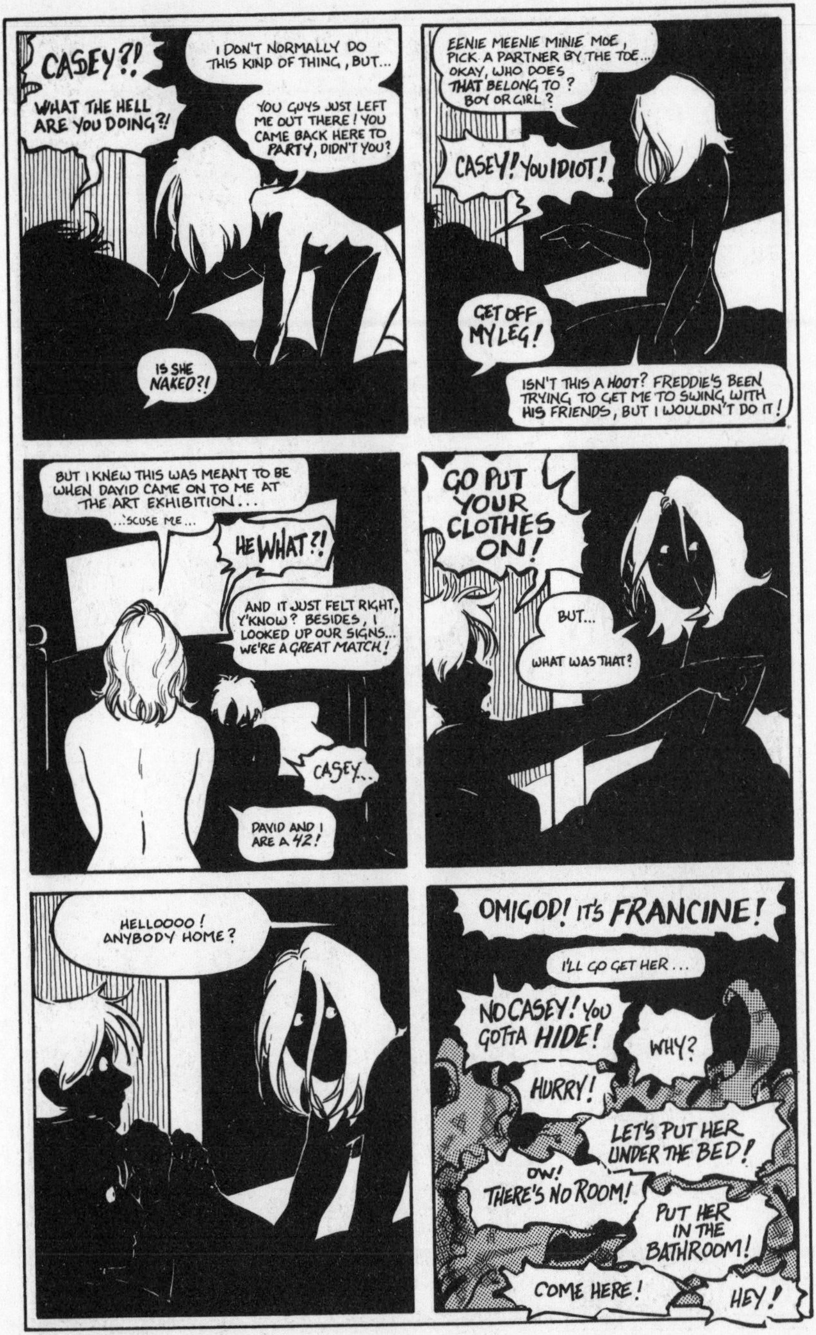
CASEY?!
WHAT THE HELL ARE YOU DOING?!
I DON'T NORMALLY DO THIS KIND OF THING, BUT...
YOU GUYS JUST LEFT ME OUT THERE! YOU CAME BACK HERE TO PARTY, DIDN'T YOU?
IS SHE NAKED?!
EENIE MEENIE MINIE MOE, PICK A PARTNER BY THE TOE... OKAY, WHO DOES THAT BELONG TO? BOY OR GIRL?
CASEY! YOU IDIOT!
GET OFF MY LEG!
ISN'T THIS A HOOT? FREDDIE'S BEEN TRYING TO GET ME TO SWING WITH HIS FRIENDS, BUT I WOULDN'T DO IT!
BUT I KNEW THIS WAS MEANT TO BE WHEN DAVID CAME ON TO ME AT THE ART EXHIBITION...
...'SCUSE ME...
HE WHAT?!
AND IT JUST FELT RIGHT, Y'KNOW? BESIDES, I LOOKED UP OUR SIGNS... WE'RE A GREAT MATCH!
CASEY...
DAVID AND I ARE A 42!
GO PUT YOUR CLOTHES ON!
BUT...
WHAT WAS THAT?
HELLOOOO! ANYBODY HOME?
OMIGOD! IT'S FRANCINE!
I'LL GO GET HER...
NO CASEY! YOU GOTTA HIDE!
WHY?
HURRY!
LET'S PUT HER UNDER THE BED!
OW! THERE'S NO ROOM!
PUT HER IN THE BATHROOM!
COME HERE!
HEY!

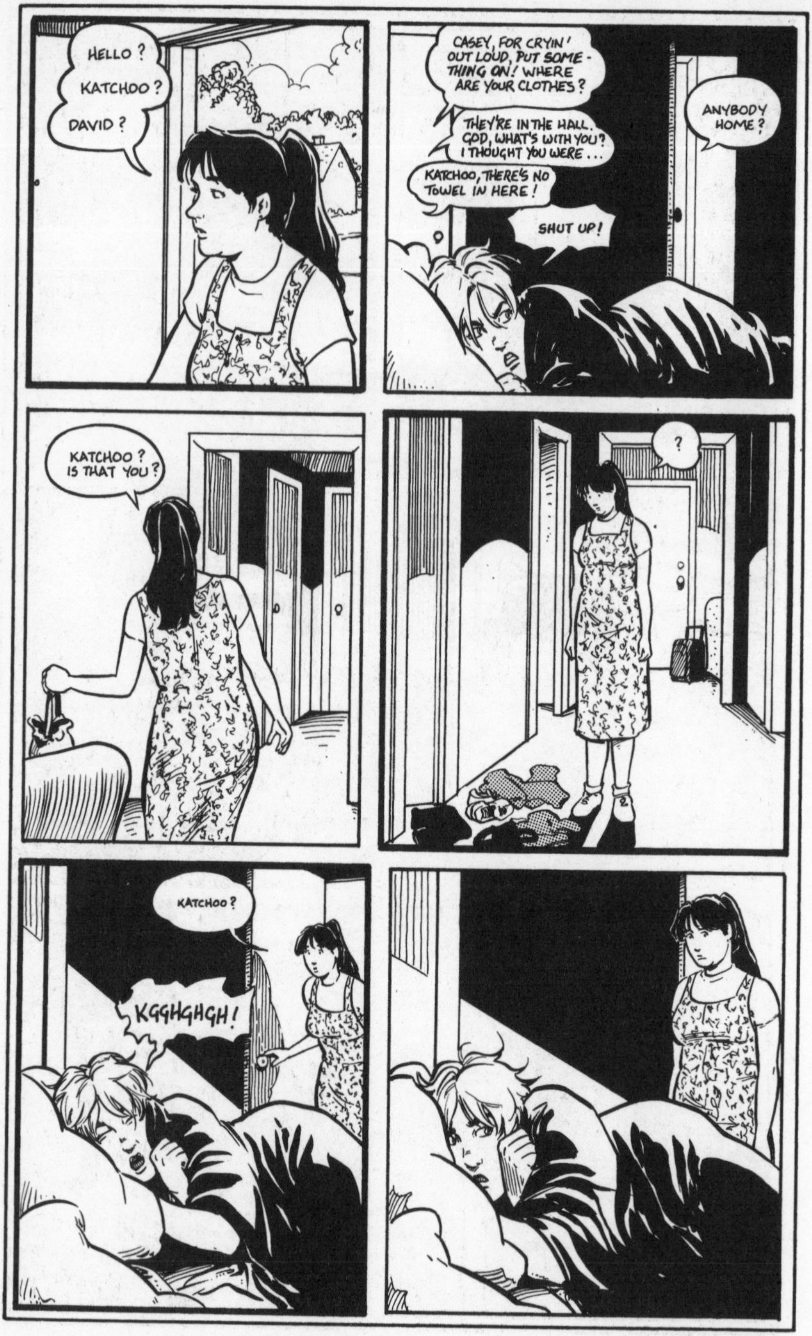
HELLO ?
KATCHOO ?
DAVID ?
CASEY, FOR CRYIN' OUT LOUD, PUT SOME-THING ON! WHERE ARE YOUR CLOTHES ?
THEY'RE IN THE HALL. GOD, WHAT'S WITH YOU? I THOUGHT YOU WERE ...
KATCHOO, THERE'S NO TOWEL IN HERE !
SHUT UP!
ANYBODY HOME ?
KATCHOO ? IS THAT YOU ?
?
KATCHOO ?
KGGHGHGH!

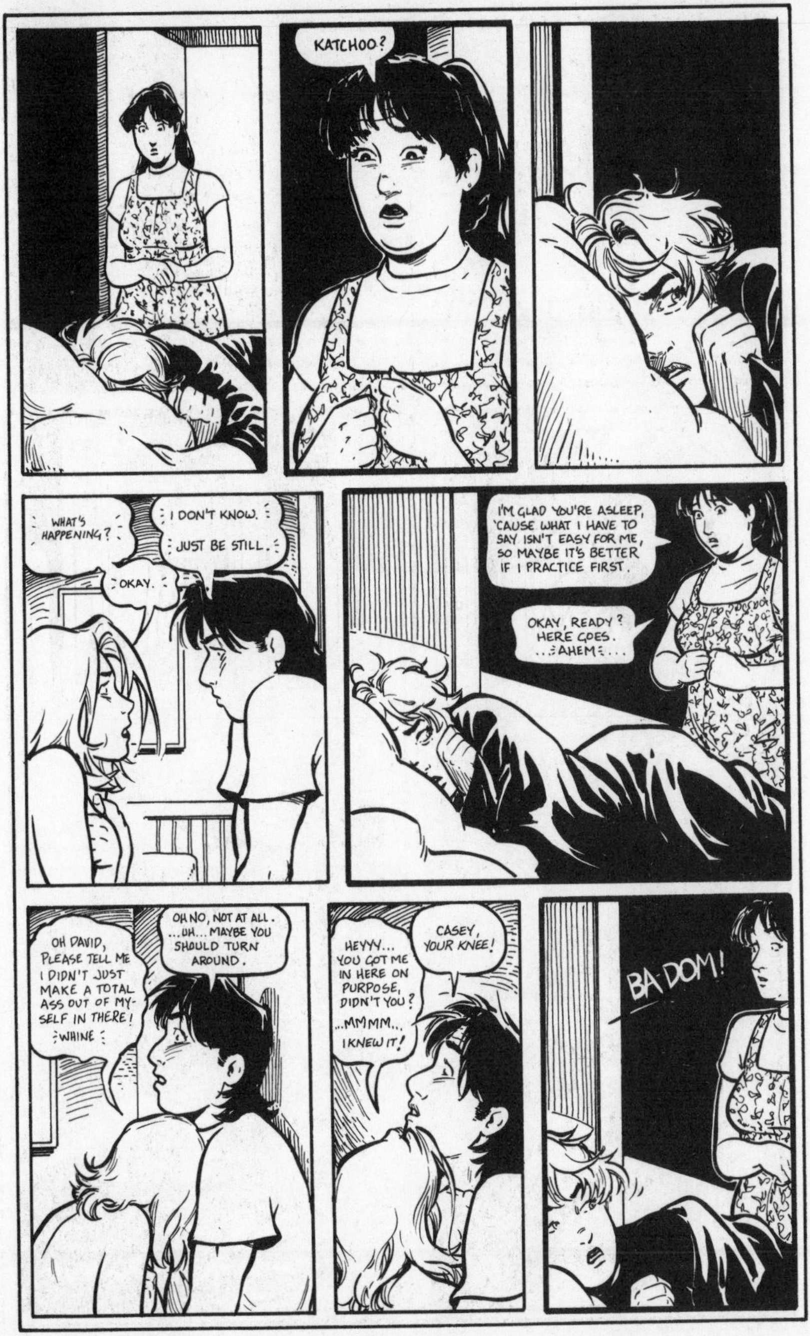

KATCHOO?
WHAT'S HAPPENING?
I DON'T KNOW.
JUST BE STILL.
OKAY.
I'M GLAD YOU'RE ASLEEP, 'CAUSE WHAT I HAVE TO SAY ISN'T EASY FOR ME, SO MAYBE IT'S BETTER IF I PRACTICE FIRST.
OKAY, READY? HERE GOES. ...AHEM...
OH DAVID, PLEASE TELL ME I DIDN'T JUST MAKE A TOTAL ASS OUT OF MYSELF IN THERE! WHINE
OH NO, NOT AT ALL. ...UH... MAYBE YOU SHOULD TURN AROUND.
HEYYY... YOU GOT ME IN HERE ON PURPOSE, DIDN'T YOU? ...MMMM... I KNEW IT!
CASEY, YOUR KNEE!
BA-DOM!

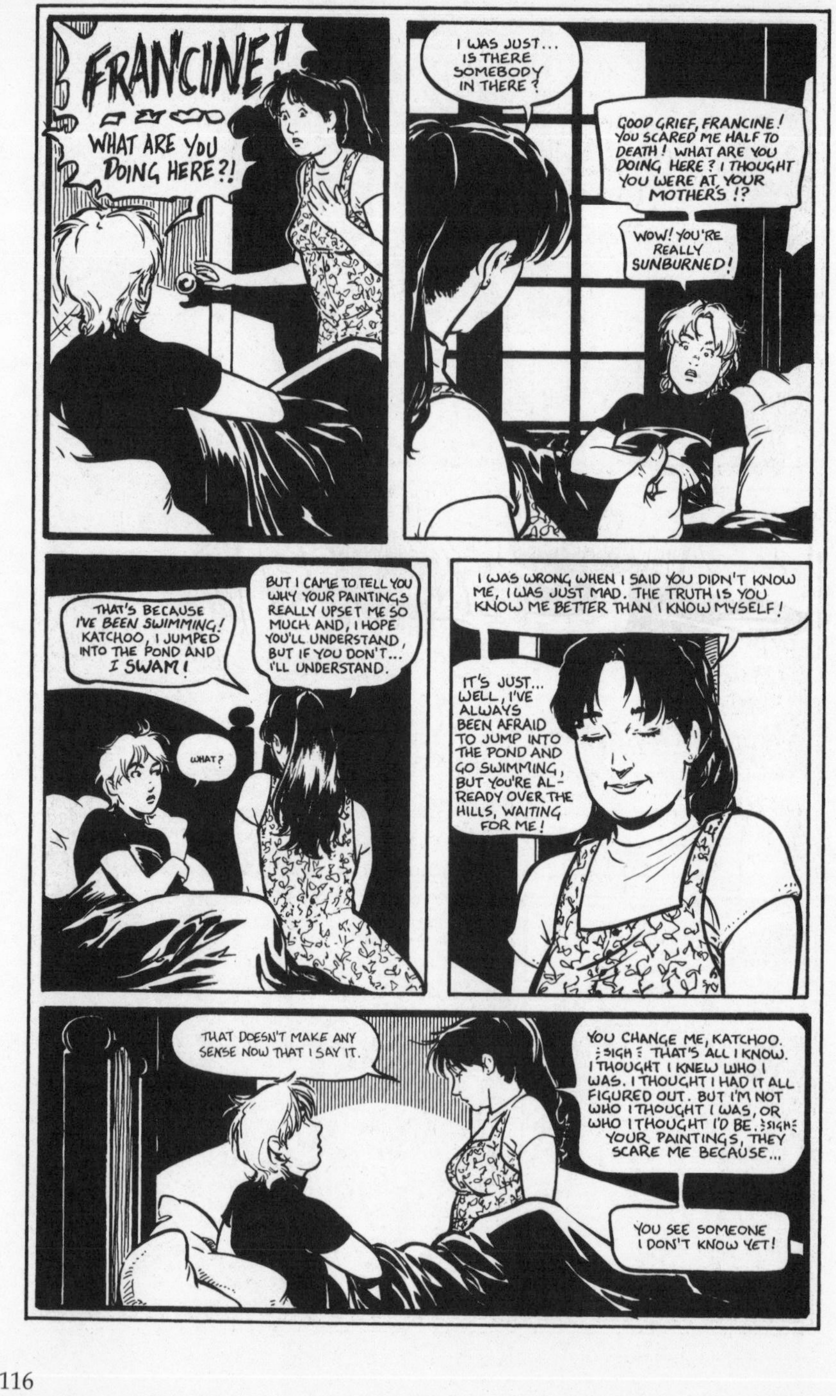
FRANCINE!
WHAT ARE YOU DOING HERE?!
I WAS JUST... IS THERE SOMEBODY IN THERE?
GOOD GRIEF, FRANCINE! YOU SCARED ME HALF TO DEATH! WHAT ARE YOU DOING HERE? I THOUGHT YOU WERE AT YOUR MOTHER'S!?
WOW! YOU'RE REALLY SUNBURNED!
THAT'S BECAUSE I'VE BEEN SWIMMING! KATCHOO, I JUMPED INTO THE POND AND I SWAM!
WHAT?
BUT I CAME TO TELL YOU WHY YOUR PAINTINGS REALLY UPSET ME SO MUCH AND, I HOPE YOU'LL UNDERSTAND, BUT IF YOU DON'T... I'LL UNDERSTAND.
I WAS WRONG WHEN I SAID YOU DIDN'T KNOW ME, I WAS JUST MAD. THE TRUTH IS YOU KNOW ME BETTER THAN I KNOW MYSELF!
IT'S JUST... WELL, I'VE ALWAYS BEEN AFRAID TO JUMP INTO THE POND AND GO SWIMMING, BUT YOU'RE ALREADY OVER THE HILLS, WAITING FOR ME!
THAT DOESN'T MAKE ANY SENSE NOW THAT I SAY IT.
YOU CHANGE ME, KATCHOO. SIGH THAT'S ALL I KNOW. I THOUGHT I KNEW WHO I WAS. I THOUGHT I HAD IT ALL FIGURED OUT. BUT I'M NOT WHO I THOUGHT I WAS, OR WHO I THOUGHT I'D BE. SIGH YOUR PAINTINGS, THEY SCARE ME BECAUSE...
YOU SEE SOMEONE I DON'T KNOW YET!

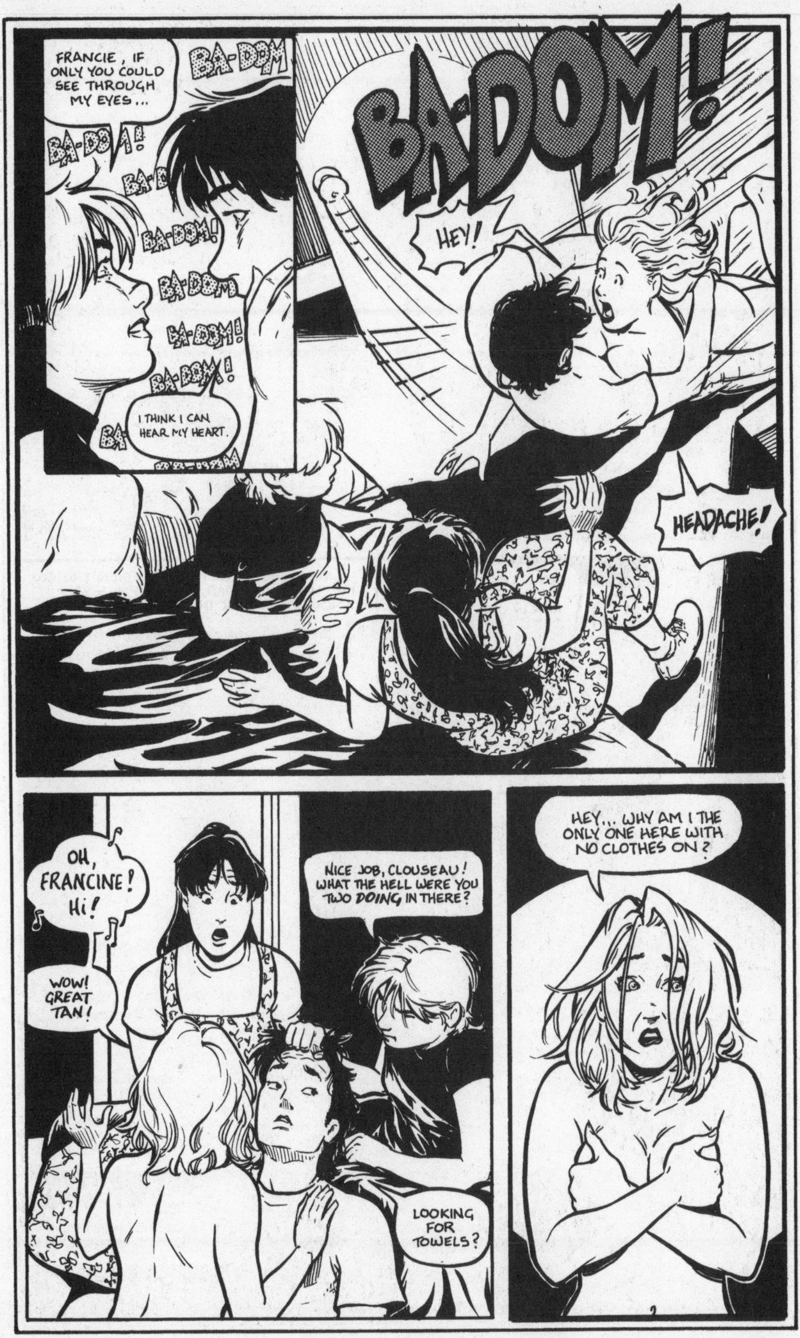
FRANCIE, IF ONLY YOU COULD SEE THROUGH MY EYES...
BA-DOM
BA-DOM!
BA-DOM!
BA-DOM
BA-DOM!
BA-DOM!
I THINK I CAN HEAR MY HEART.
BA-DOM!
HEY!
HEADACHE!
OH, FRANCINE! Hi!
WOW! GREAT TAN!
NICE JOB, CLOUSEAU! WHAT THE HELL WERE YOU TWO DOING IN THERE?
LOOKING FOR TOWELS?
HEY... WHY AM I THE ONLY ONE HERE WITH NO CLOTHES ON?

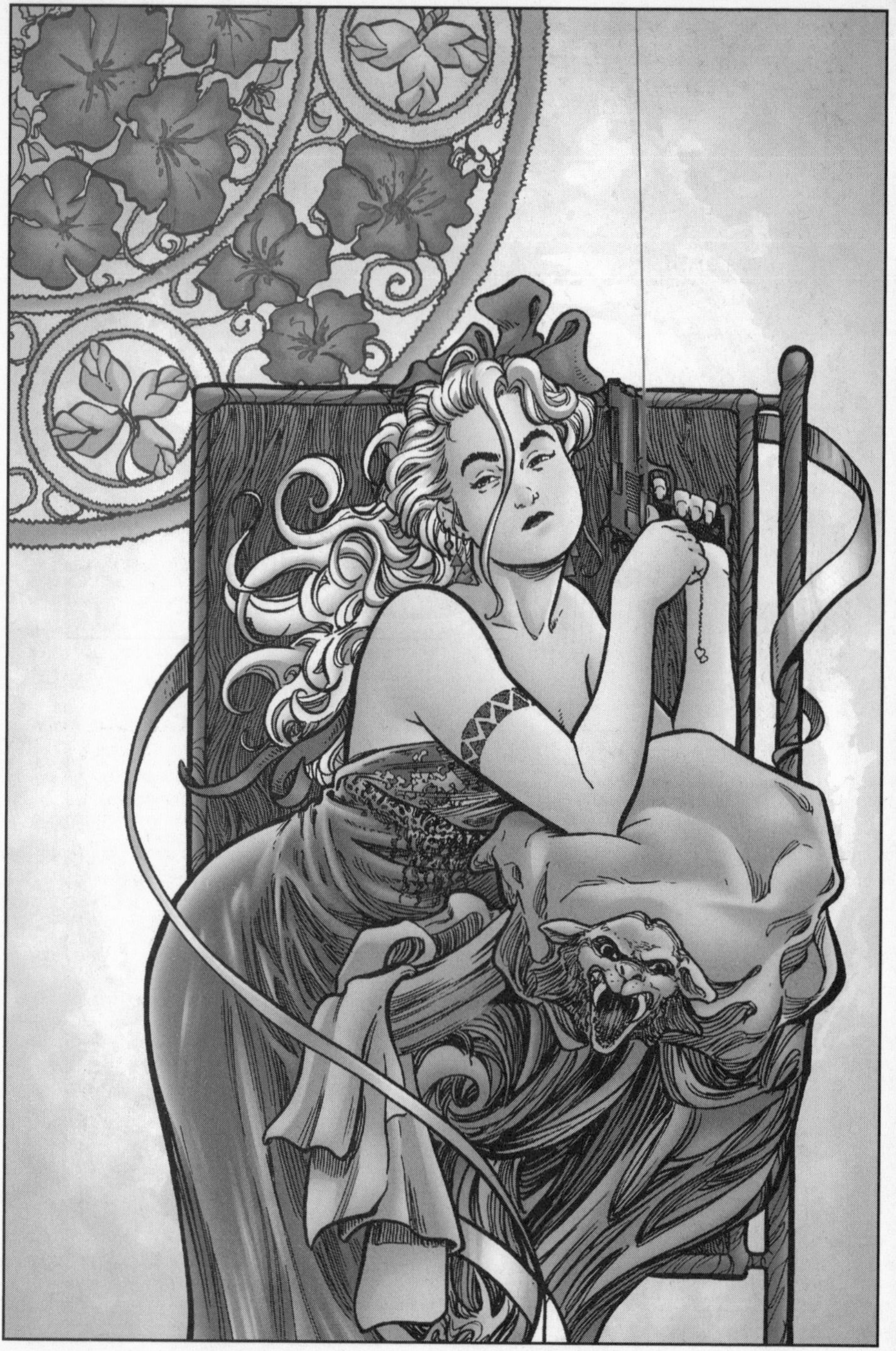

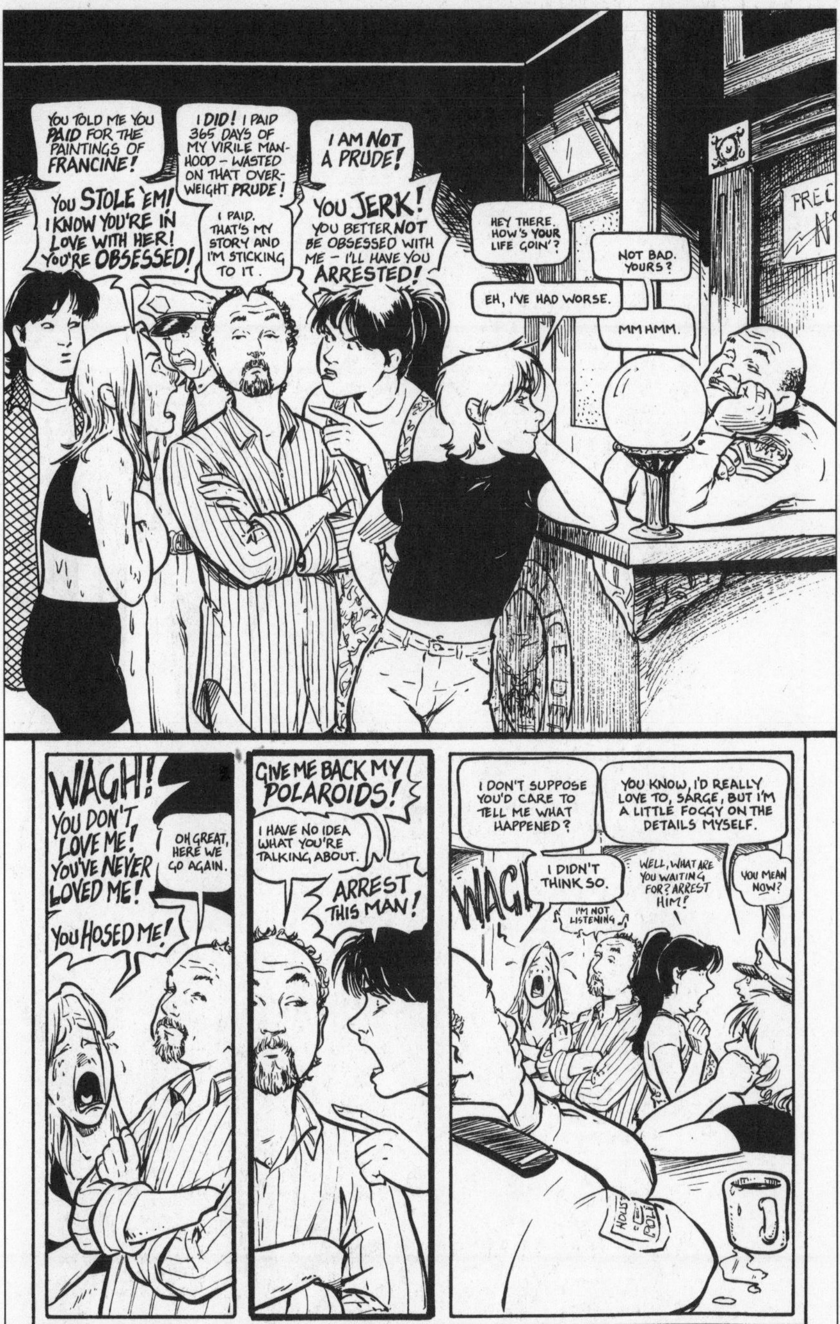
YOU TOLD ME YOU PAID FOR THE PAINTINGS OF FRANCINE!
YOU STOLE 'EM! I KNOW YOU'RE IN LOVE WITH HER! YOU'RE OBSESSED!
I DID! I PAID 365 DAYS OF MY VIRILE MAN-HOOD - WASTED ON THAT OVER-WEIGHT PRUDE!
I PAID. THAT'S MY STORY AND I'M STICKING TO IT.
I AM NOT A PRUDE!
YOU JERK! YOU BETTER NOT BE OBSESSED WITH ME - I'LL HAVE YOU ARRESTED!
HEY THERE. HOW'S YOUR LIFE GOIN'?
NOT BAD. YOURS?
EH, I'VE HAD WORSE.
MM HMM.
WAGH! YOU DON'T LOVE ME! YOU'VE NEVER LOVED ME!
OH GREAT, HERE WE GO AGAIN.
YOU HOSED ME!
GIVE ME BACK MY POLAROIDS!
I HAVE NO IDEA WHAT YOU'RE TALKING ABOUT.
ARREST THIS MAN!
I DON'T SUPPOSE YOU'D CARE TO TELL ME WHAT HAPPENED?
YOU KNOW, I'D REALLY LOVE TO, SARGE, BUT I'M A LITTLE FOGGY ON THE DETAILS MYSELF.
WAGH
I DIDN'T THINK SO.
I'M NOT LISTENING
WELL, WHAT ARE YOU WAITING FOR? ARREST HIM!
YOU MEAN NOW?

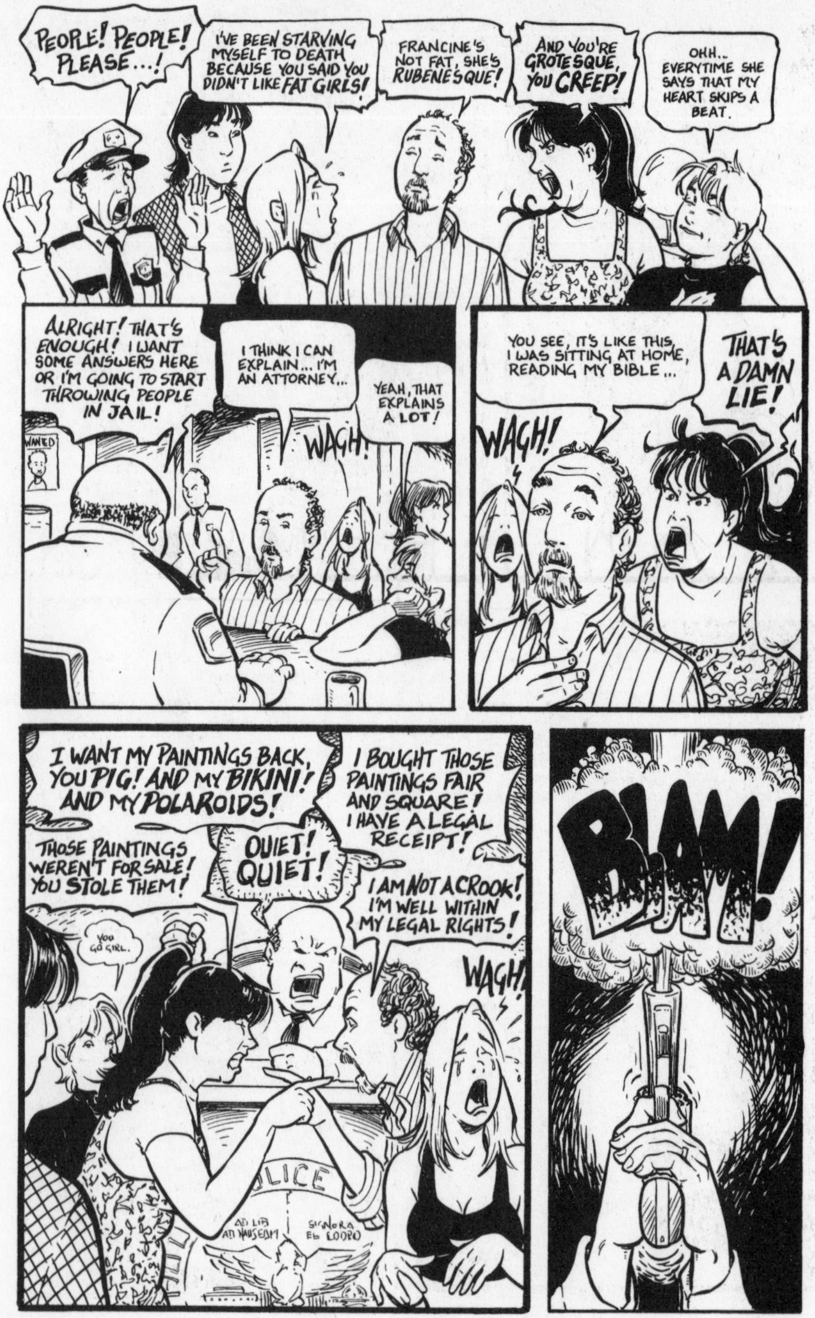
PEOPLE! PEOPLE! PLEASE...!
I'VE BEEN STARVING MYSELF TO DEATH BECAUSE YOU SAID YOU DIDN'T LIKE FAT GIRLS!
FRANCINE'S NOT FAT, SHE'S RUBENESQUE!
AND YOU'RE GROTESQUE, YOU CREEP!
OHH... EVERYTIME SHE SAYS THAT MY HEART SKIPS A BEAT.
ALRIGHT! THAT'S ENOUGH! I WANT SOME ANSWERS HERE OR I'M GOING TO START THROWING PEOPLE IN JAIL!
WANTED
I THINK I CAN EXPLAIN... I'M AN ATTORNEY...
YEAH, THAT EXPLAINS A LOT!
WAGH!
YOU SEE, IT'S LIKE THIS, I WAS SITTING AT HOME, READING MY BIBLE...
THAT'S A DAMN LIE!
WAGH!
I WANT MY PAINTINGS BACK, YOU PIG! AND MY BIKINI! AND MY POLAROIDS!
I BOUGHT THOSE PAINTINGS FAIR AND SQUARE! I HAVE A LEGAL RECEIPT!
THOSE PAINTINGS WEREN'T FOR SALE! YOU STOLE THEM!
QUIET! QUIET!
I AM NOT A CROOK! I'M WELL WITHIN MY LEGAL RIGHTS!
YOU GO GIRL.
WAGH!
OLICE
BLAM!

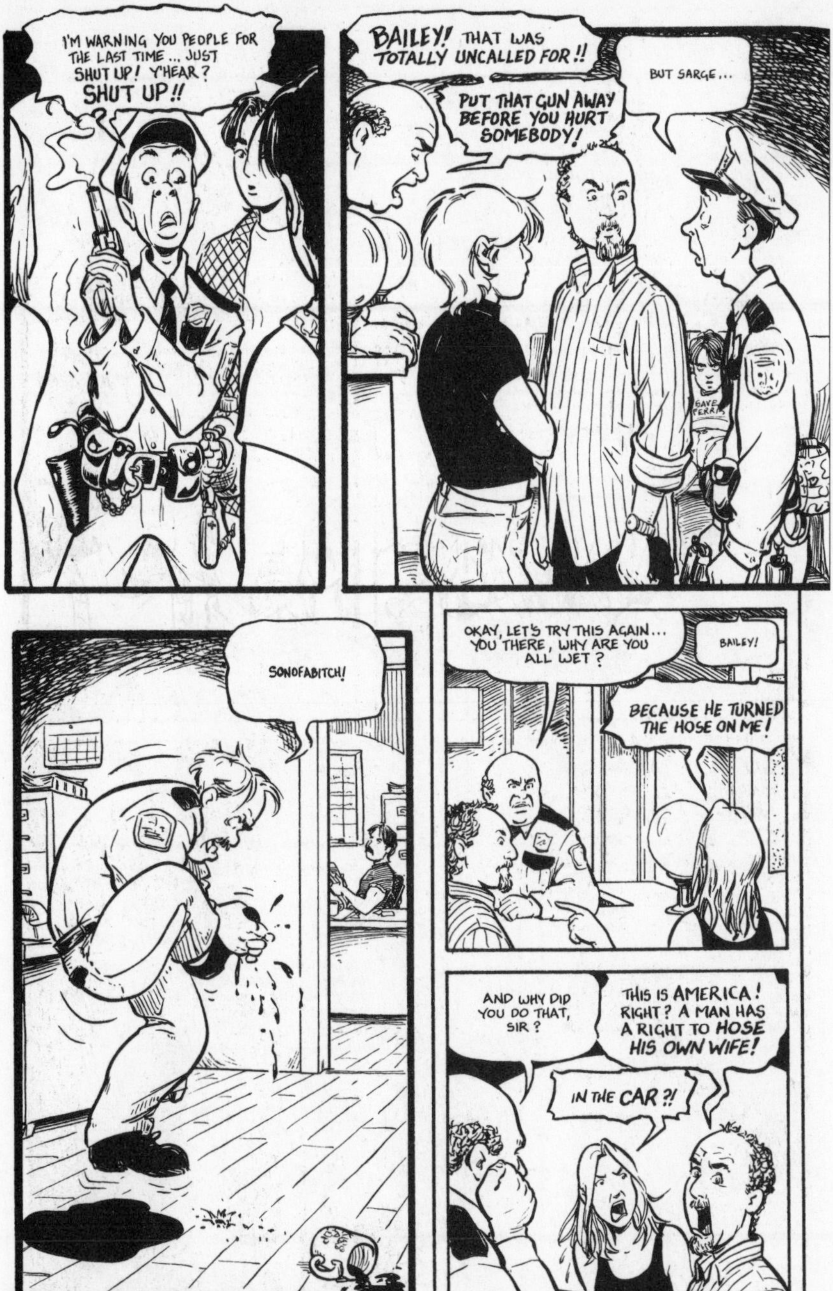
I'M WARNING YOU PEOPLE FOR THE LAST TIME ... JUST SHUT UP! Y'HEAR? SHUT UP!!
BAILEY! THAT WAS TOTALLY UNCALLED FOR!!
PUT THAT GUN AWAY BEFORE YOU HURT SOMEBODY!
BUT SARGE...
SONOFABITCH!
OKAY, LET'S TRY THIS AGAIN... YOU THERE, WHY ARE YOU ALL WET?
BAILEY!
BECAUSE HE TURNED THE HOSE ON ME!
AND WHY DID YOU DO THAT, SIR?
THIS IS AMERICA! RIGHT? A MAN HAS A RIGHT TO HOSE HIS OWN WIFE!
IN THE CAR?!

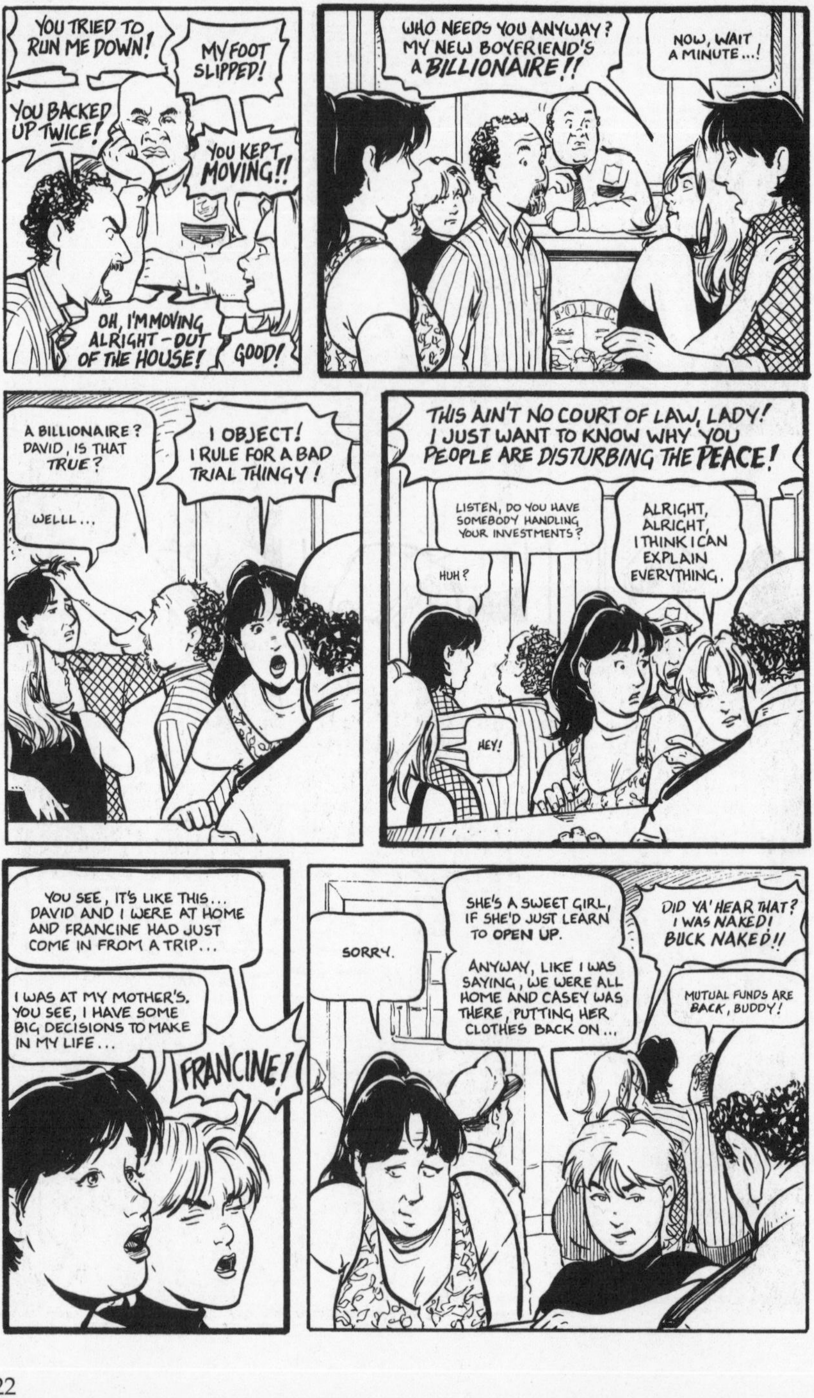
YOU TRIED TO RUN ME DOWN!
MY FOOT SLIPPED!
YOU BACKED UP TWICE!
YOU KEPT MOVING!!
OH, I'M MOVING ALRIGHT - OUT OF THE HOUSE!
GOOD!
WHO NEEDS YOU ANYWAY? MY NEW BOYFRIEND'S A BILLIONAIRE!!
NOW, WAIT A MINUTE...!
A BILLIONAIRE? DAVID, IS THAT TRUE?
I OBJECT! I RULE FOR A BAD TRIAL THINGY!
WELLL...
THIS AIN'T NO COURT OF LAW, LADY! I JUST WANT TO KNOW WHY YOU PEOPLE ARE DISTURBING THE PEACE!
LISTEN, DO YOU HAVE SOMEBODY HANDLING YOUR INVESTMENTS?
ALRIGHT, ALRIGHT, I THINK I CAN EXPLAIN EVERYTHING.
HUH?
HEY!
YOU SEE, IT'S LIKE THIS... DAVID AND I WERE AT HOME AND FRANCINE HAD JUST COME IN FROM A TRIP...
I WAS AT MY MOTHER'S. YOU SEE, I HAVE SOME BIG DECISIONS TO MAKE IN MY LIFE...
FRANCINE!
SORRY.
SHE'S A SWEET GIRL, IF SHE'D JUST LEARN TO OPEN UP.
ANYWAY, LIKE I WAS SAYING, WE WERE ALL HOME AND CASEY WAS THERE, PUTTING HER CLOTHES BACK ON...
DID YA' HEAR THAT? I WAS NAKED! BUCK NAKED!!
MUTUAL FUNDS ARE BACK, BUDDY!

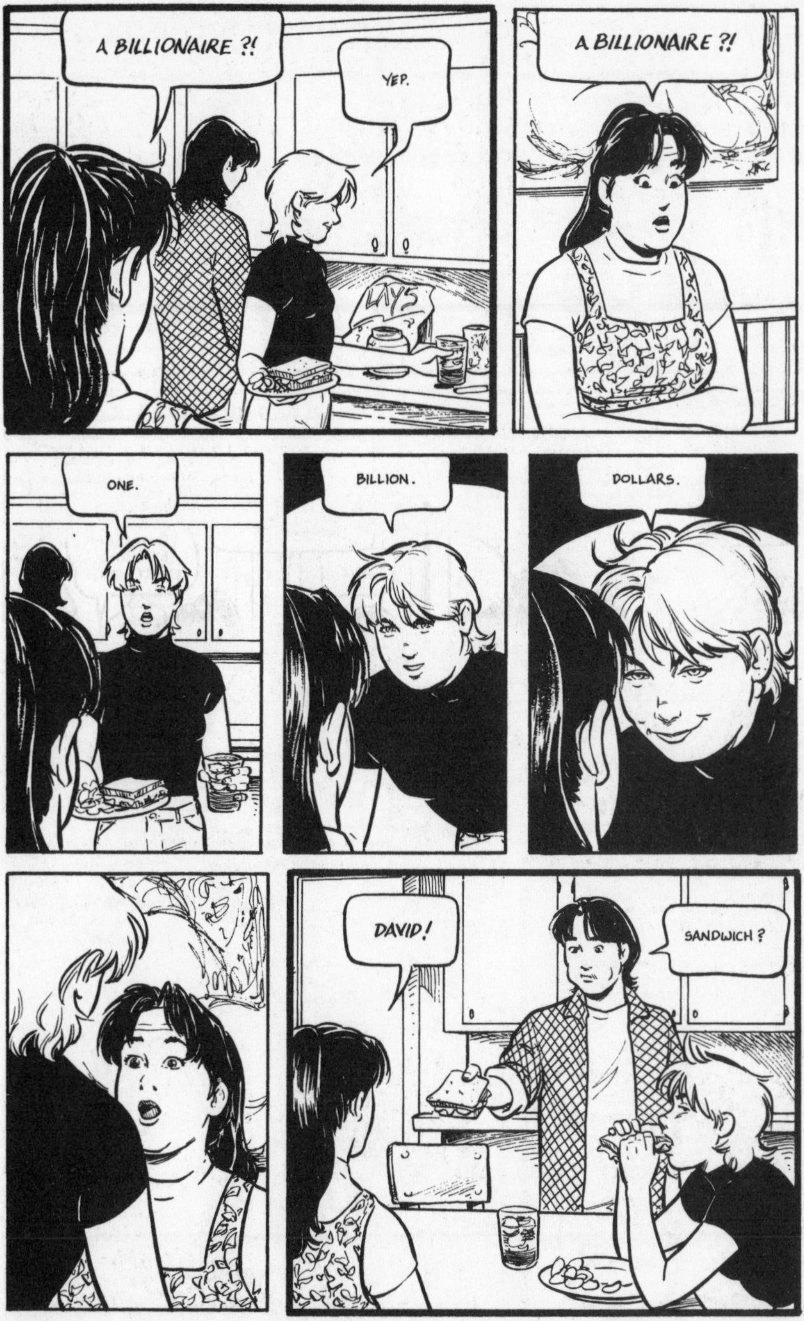
A BILLIONAIRE ?!
YEP.
A BILLIONAIRE ?!
ONE.
BILLION.
DOLLARS.
DAVID!
SANDWICH ?

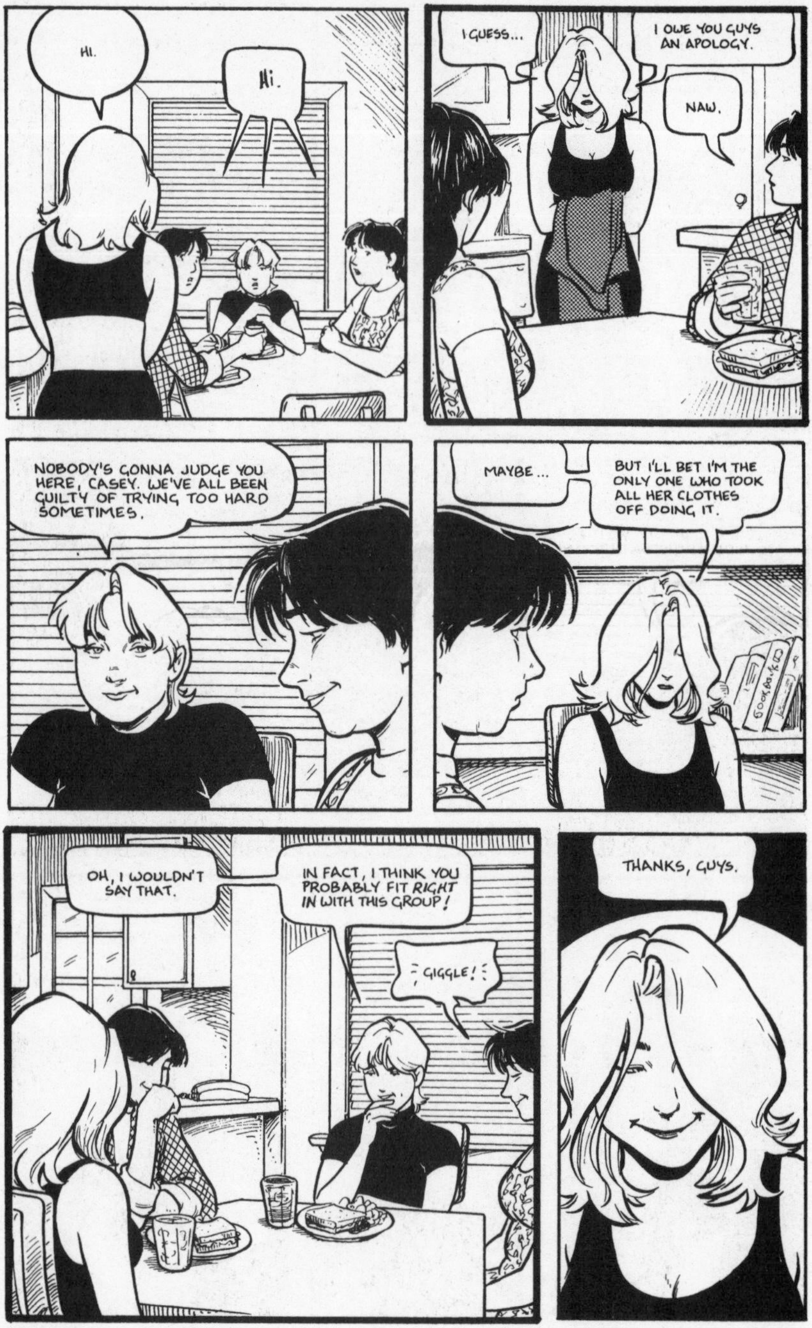
HI.
Hi.
I GUESS...
I OWE YOU GUYS AN APOLOGY.
NAW.
NOBODY'S GONNA JUDGE YOU HERE, CASEY. WE'VE ALL BEEN GUILTY OF TRYING TOO HARD SOMETIMES.
MAYBE...
BUT I'LL BET I'M THE ONLY ONE WHO TOOK ALL HER CLOTHES OFF DOING IT.
OH, I WOULDN'T SAY THAT.
IN FACT, I THINK YOU PROBABLY FIT RIGHT IN WITH THIS GROUP!
GIGGLE!
THANKS, GUYS.

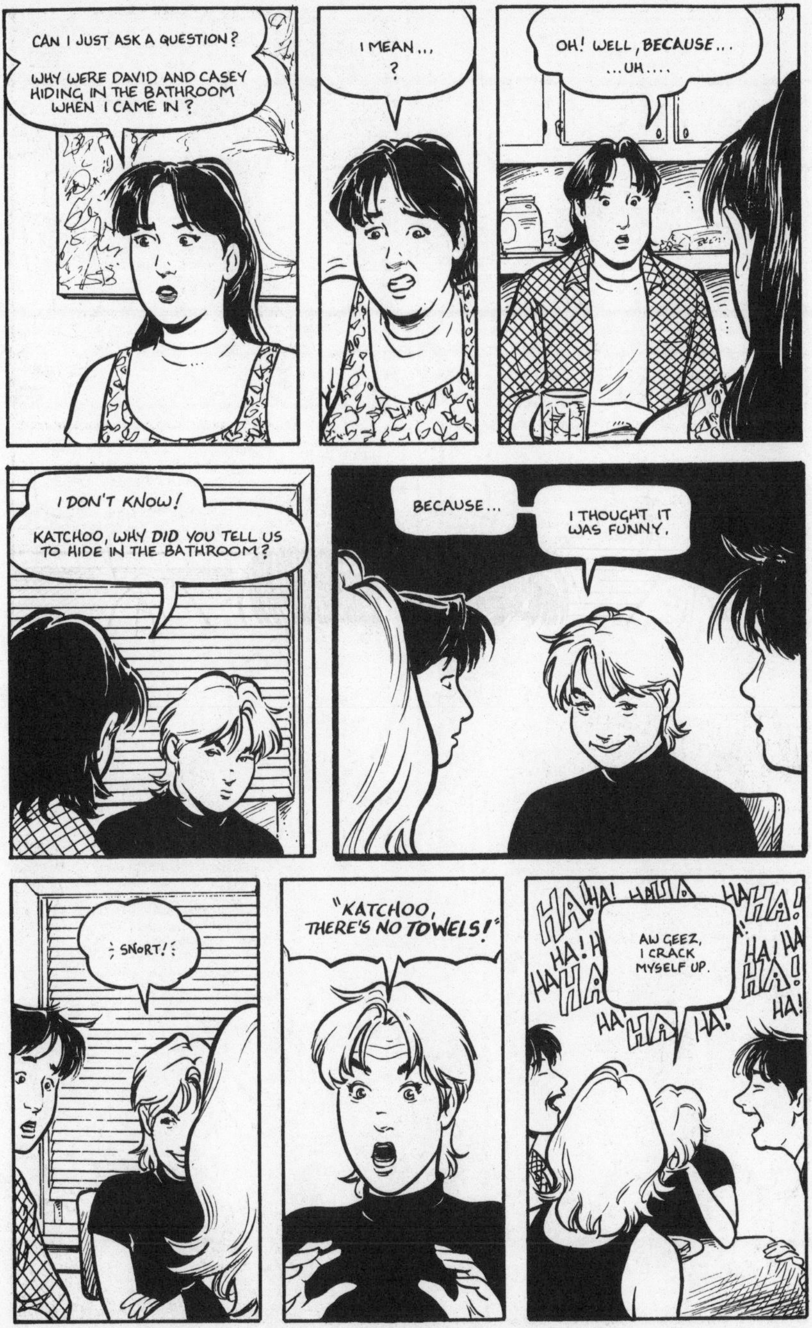
CAN I JUST ASK A QUESTION?
WHY WERE DAVID AND CASEY HIDING IN THE BATHROOM WHEN I CAME IN?
I MEAN... ?
OH! WELL, BECAUSE... ...UH....
I DON'T KNOW!
KATCHOO, WHY DID YOU TELL US TO HIDE IN THE BATHROOM?
BECAUSE...
I THOUGHT IT WAS FUNNY.
SNORT!
"KATCHOO, THERE'S NO TOWELS!"
HA! HA! HA! HA! HA! HA! HA! HA! HA! HA! HA! HA! HA! HA!
AW GEEZ, I CRACK MYSELF UP.

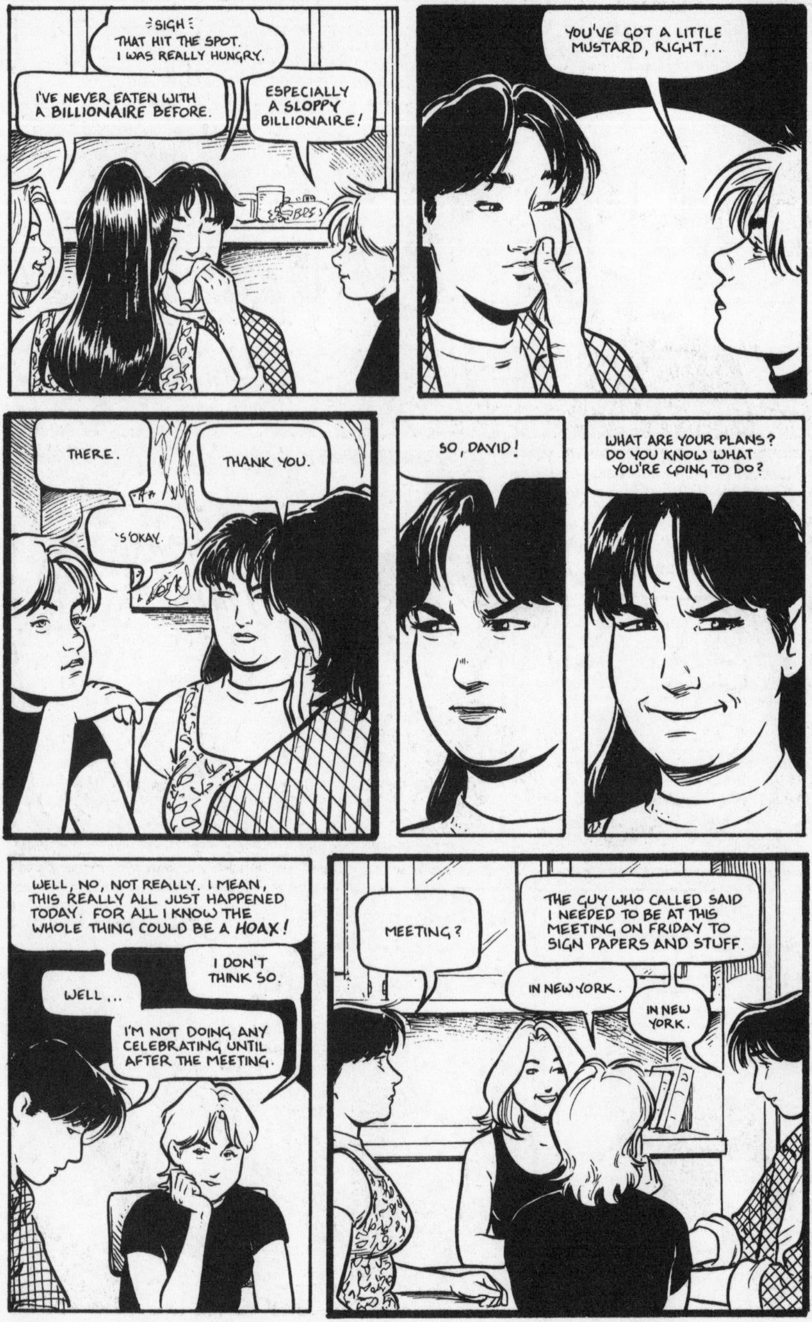

SIGH
THAT HIT THE SPOT. I WAS REALLY HUNGRY.
I'VE NEVER EATEN WITH A BILLIONAIRE BEFORE.
ESPECIALLY A SLOPPY BILLIONAIRE!
YOU'VE GOT A LITTLE MUSTARD, RIGHT...
THERE.
THANK YOU.
'S OKAY.
SO, DAVID!
WHAT ARE YOUR PLANS? DO YOU KNOW WHAT YOU'RE GOING TO DO?
WELL, NO, NOT REALLY. I MEAN, THIS REALLY ALL JUST HAPPENED TODAY. FOR ALL I KNOW THE WHOLE THING COULD BE A HOAX!
I DON'T THINK SO.
WELL...
I'M NOT DOING ANY CELEBRATING UNTIL AFTER THE MEETING.
MEETING?
THE GUY WHO CALLED SAID I NEEDED TO BE AT THIS MEETING ON FRIDAY TO SIGN PAPERS AND STUFF.
IN NEW YORK.
IN NEW YORK.

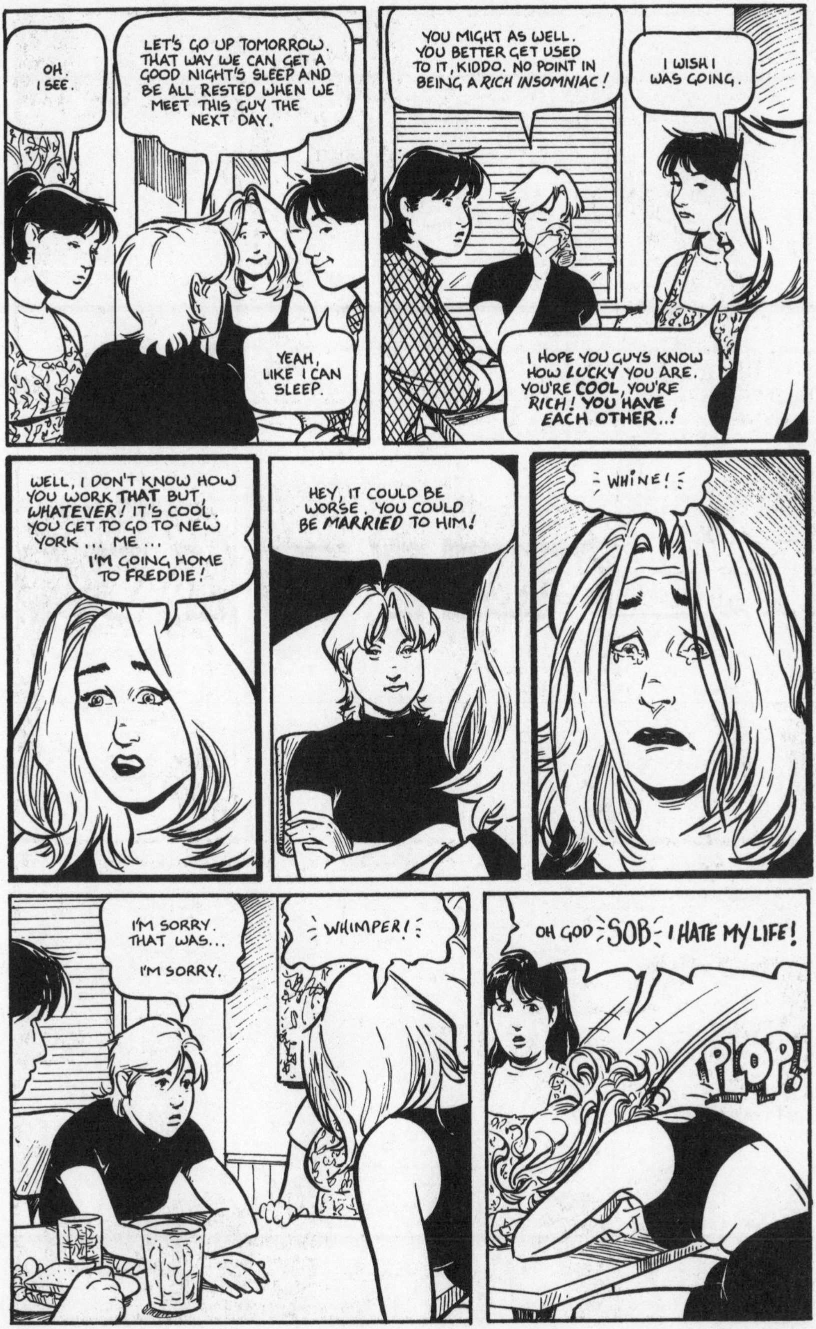
OH. I SEE.
LET'S GO UP TOMORROW. THAT WAY WE CAN GET A GOOD NIGHT'S SLEEP AND BE ALL RESTED WHEN WE MEET THIS GUY THE NEXT DAY.
YEAH, LIKE I CAN SLEEP.
YOU MIGHT AS WELL. YOU BETTER GET USED TO IT, KIDDO. NO POINT IN BEING A RICH INSOMNIAC!
I WISH I WAS GOING.
I HOPE YOU GUYS KNOW HOW LUCKY YOU ARE. YOU'RE COOL, YOU'RE RICH! YOU HAVE EACH OTHER...!
WELL, I DON'T KNOW HOW YOU WORK THAT BUT, WHATEVER! IT'S COOL. YOU GET TO GO TO NEW YORK ... ME ... I'M GOING HOME TO FREDDIE!
HEY, IT COULD BE WORSE. YOU COULD BE MARRIED TO HIM!
WHINE!
I'M SORRY. THAT WAS... I'M SORRY.
WHIMPER!
OH GOD SOB I HATE MY LIFE!
PLOP!

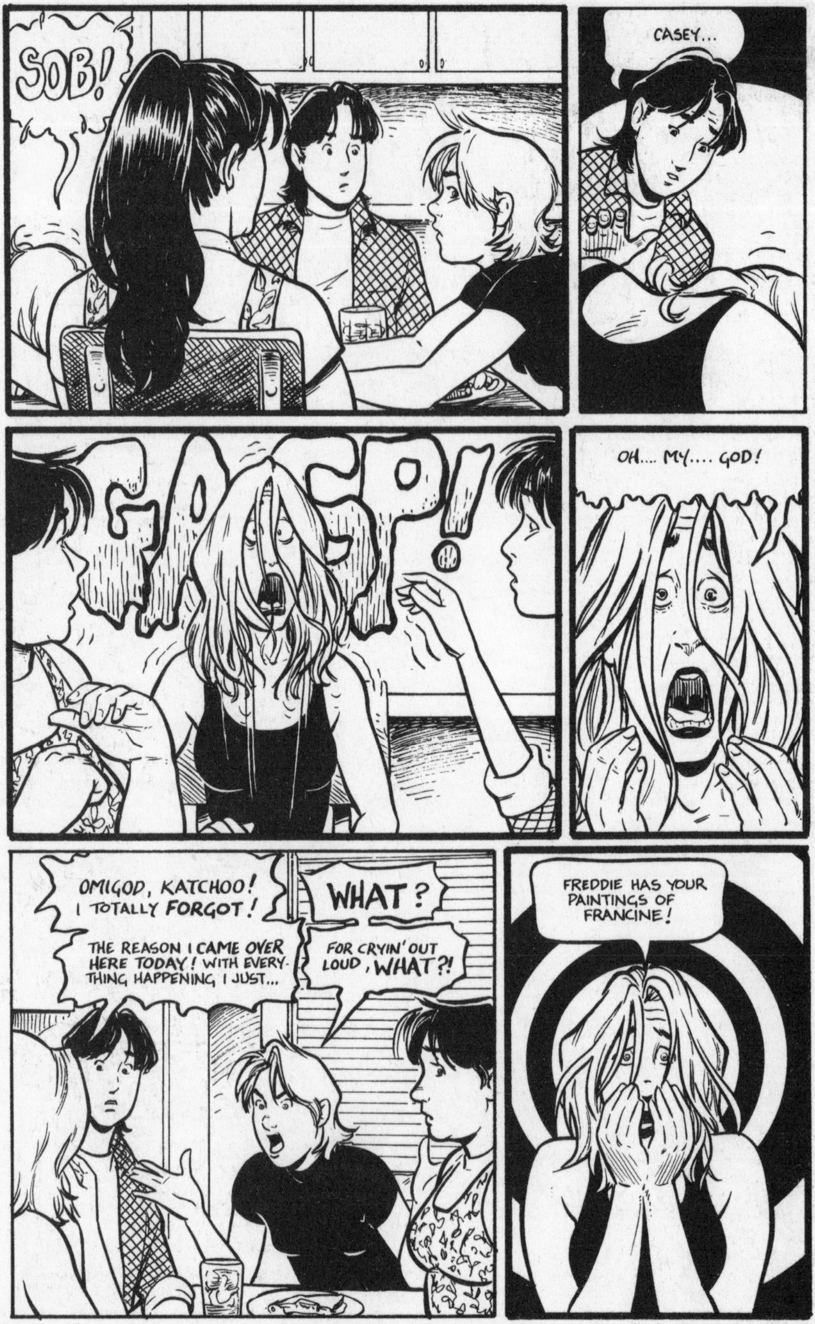
SOB!
CASEY...
GASP!
OH.... MY.... GOD!
OMIGOD, KATCHOO! I TOTALLY FORGOT!
THE REASON I CAME OVER HERE TODAY! WITH EVERYTHING HAPPENING I JUST...
WHAT?
FOR CRYIN' OUT LOUD, WHAT?!
FREDDIE HAS YOUR PAINTINGS OF FRANCINE!

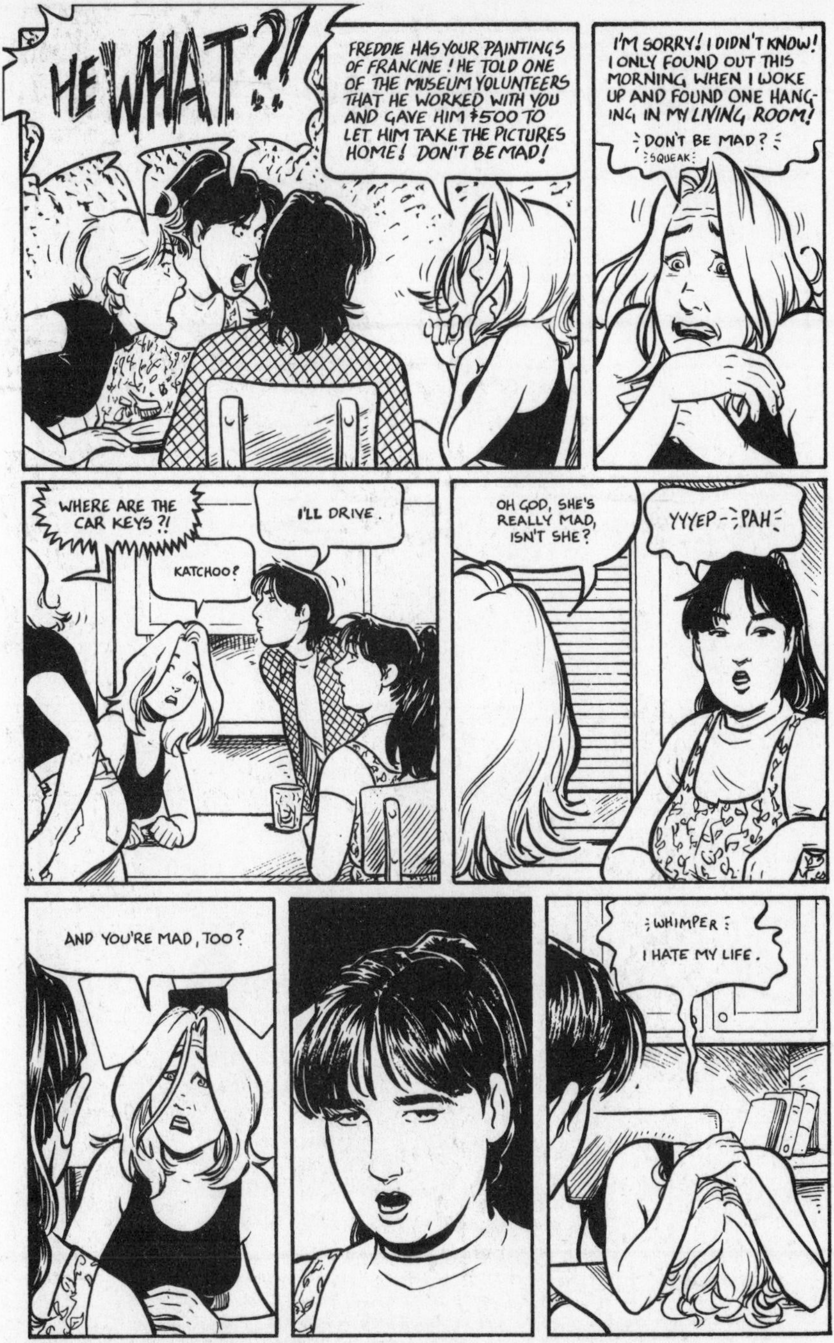
HE WHAT?!
FREDDIE HAS YOUR PAINTINGS OF FRANCINE! HE TOLD ONE OF THE MUSEUM VOLUNTEERS THAT HE WORKED WITH YOU AND GAVE HIM $500 TO LET HIM TAKE THE PICTURES HOME! DON'T BE MAD!
I'M SORRY! I DIDN'T KNOW! I ONLY FOUND OUT THIS MORNING WHEN I WOKE UP AND FOUND ONE HANGING IN MY LIVING ROOM!
DON'T BE MAD?
SQUEAK
WHERE ARE THE CAR KEYS?!
I'LL DRIVE.
KATCHOO?
OH GOD, SHE'S REALLY MAD, ISN'T SHE?
YYYEP-- PAH
AND YOU'RE MAD, TOO?
WHIMPER
I HATE MY LIFE.

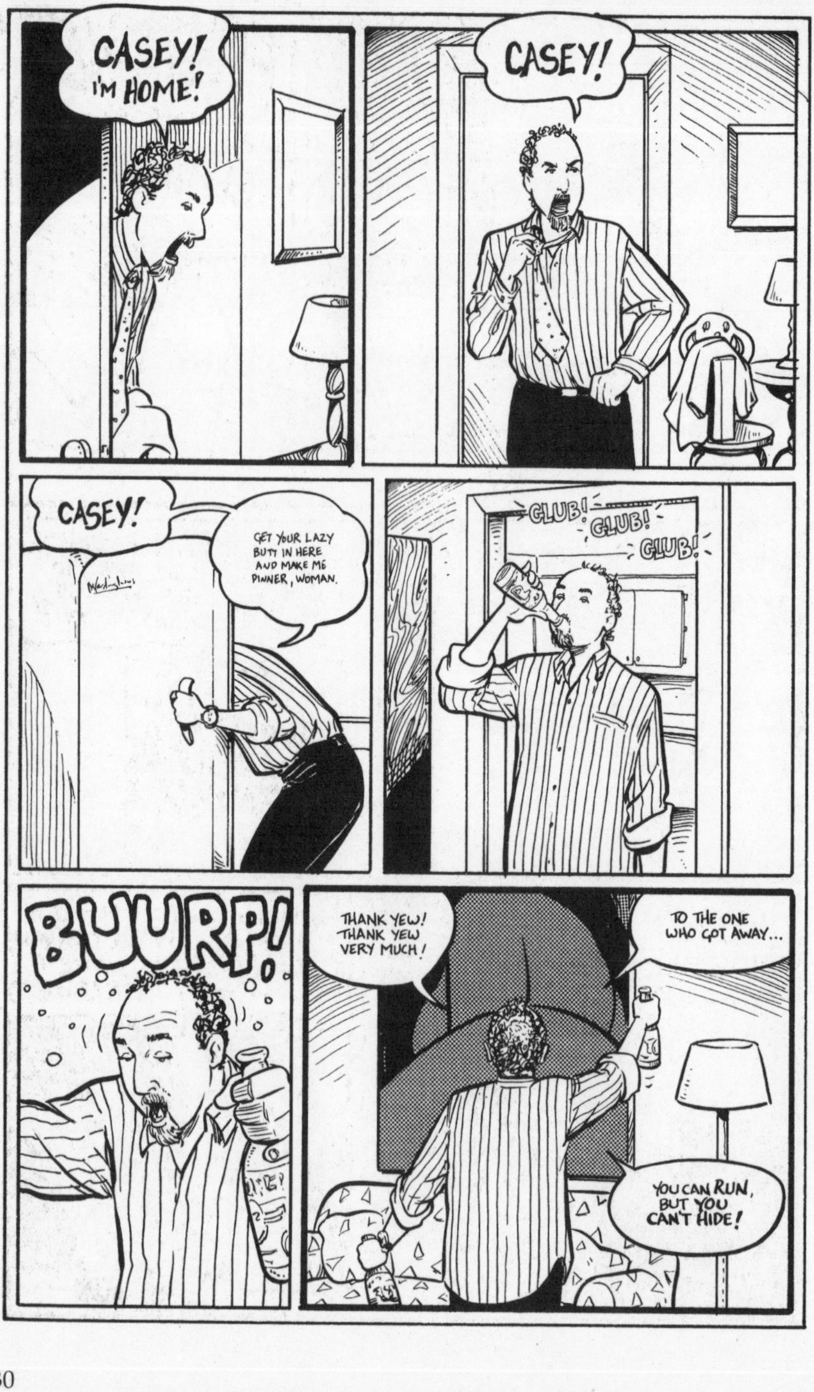
CASEY! I'M HOME!
CASEY!
CASEY!
GET YOUR LAZY BUTT IN HERE AND MAKE ME DINNER, WOMAN.
GLUB! GLUB! GLUB!
BUURP!
THANK YEW! THANK YEW VERY MUCH!
TO THE ONE WHO GOT AWAY...
YOU CAN RUN, BUT YOU CAN'T HIDE!

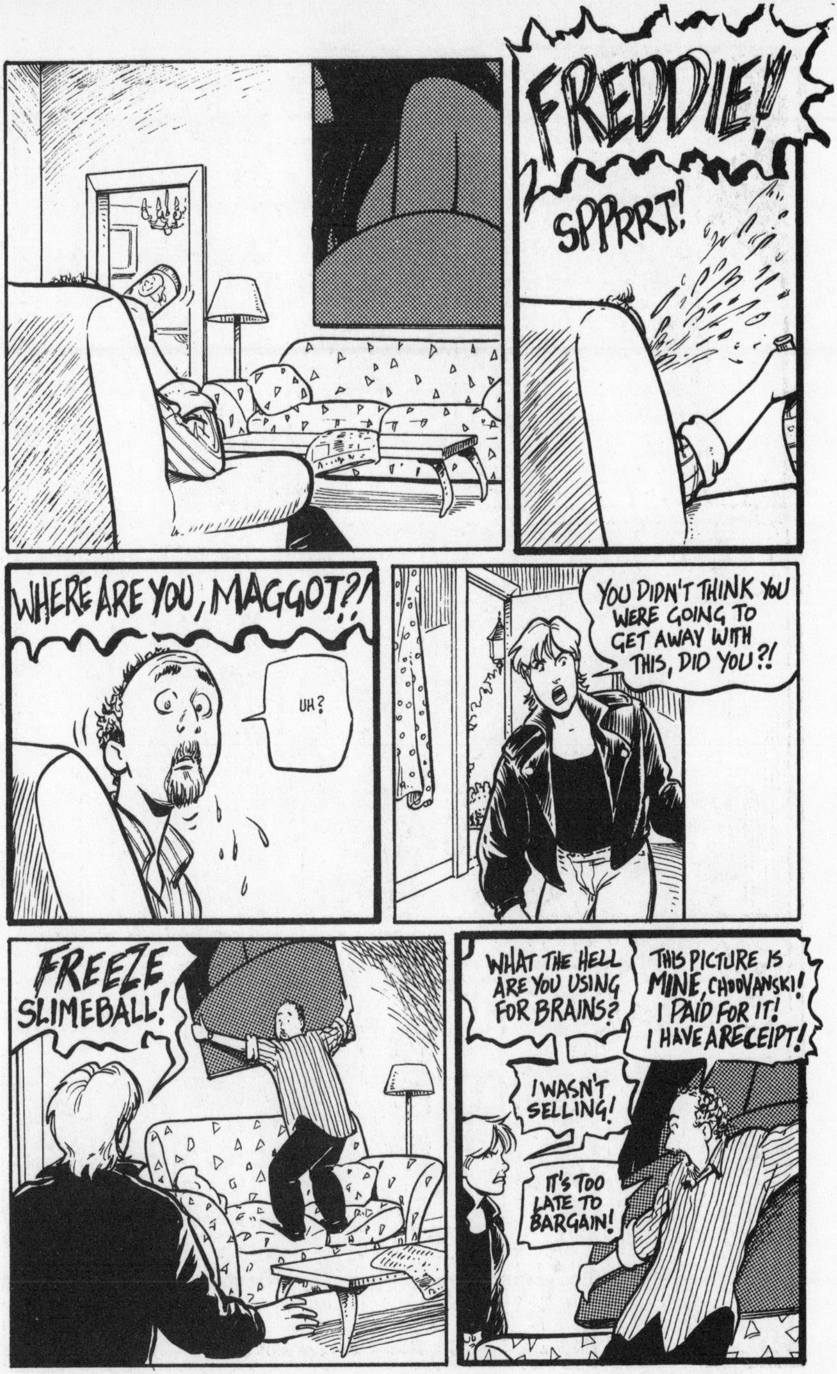
FREDDIE!
SPPRRT!
WHERE ARE YOU, MAGGOT?!
UH?
YOU DIDN'T THINK YOU WERE GOING TO GET AWAY WITH THIS, DID YOU?!
FREEZE SLIMEBALL!
WHAT THE HELL ARE YOU USING FOR BRAINS?
THIS PICTURE IS MINE, CHOOVANSKI! I PAID FOR IT! I HAVE A RECEIPT!
I WASN'T SELLING!
IT'S TOO LATE TO BARGAIN!

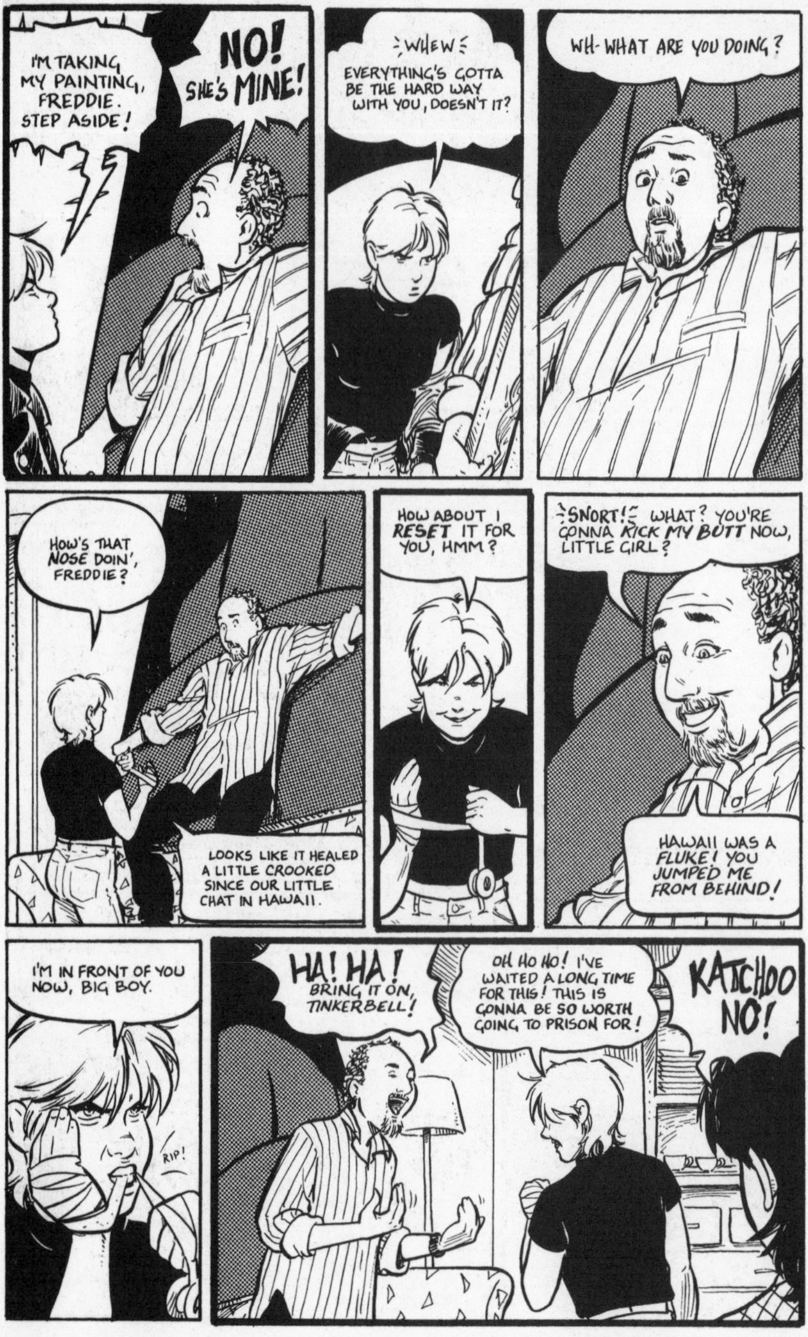
I'M TAKING MY PAINTING, FREDDIE. STEP ASIDE!
NO! SHE'S MINE!
WHEW
EVERYTHING'S GOTTA BE THE HARD WAY WITH YOU, DOESN'T IT?
WH- WHAT ARE YOU DOING?
HOW'S THAT NOSE DOIN', FREDDIE?
LOOKS LIKE IT HEALED A LITTLE CROOKED SINCE OUR LITTLE CHAT IN HAWAII.
HOW ABOUT I RESET IT FOR YOU, HMM?
SNORT! WHAT? YOU'RE GONNA KICK MY BUTT NOW, LITTLE GIRL?
HAWAII WAS A FLUKE! YOU JUMPED ME FROM BEHIND!
I'M IN FRONT OF YOU NOW, BIG BOY.
RIP!
HA! HA! BRING IT ON, TINKERBELL!
OH HO HO! I'VE WAITED A LONG TIME FOR THIS! THIS IS GONNA BE SO WORTH GOING TO PRISON FOR!
KATCHOO NO!

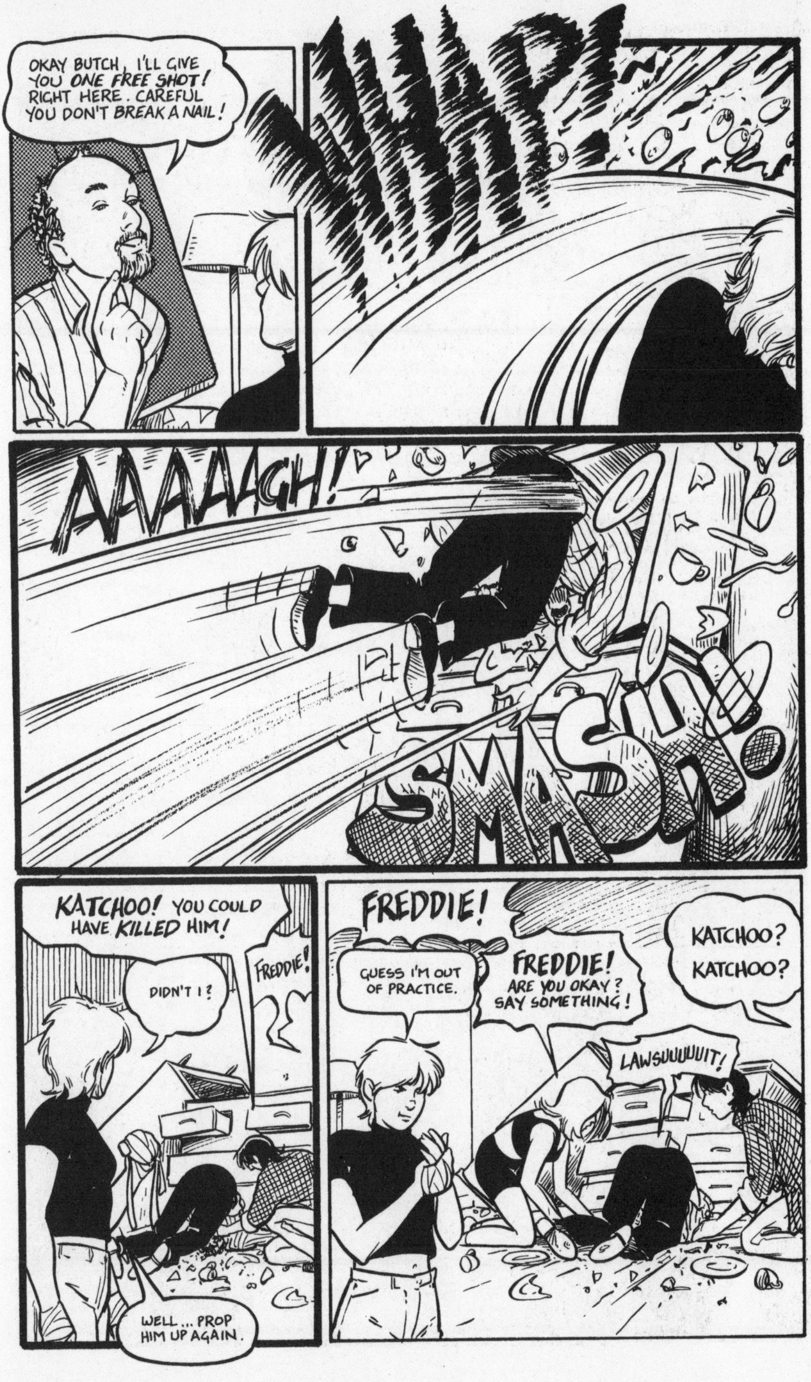
OKAY BUTCH, I'LL GIVE YOU ONE FREE SHOT! RIGHT HERE. CAREFUL YOU DON'T BREAK A NAIL!
WHAP!
AAAAAGH!
SMASH!
KATCHOO! YOU COULD HAVE KILLED HIM!
DIDN'T I?
FREDDIE!
WELL... PROP HIM UP AGAIN.
FREDDIE!
GUESS I'M OUT OF PRACTICE.
FREDDIE! ARE YOU OKAY? SAY SOMETHING!
KATCHOO? KATCHOO?
LAWSUUUUUIT!

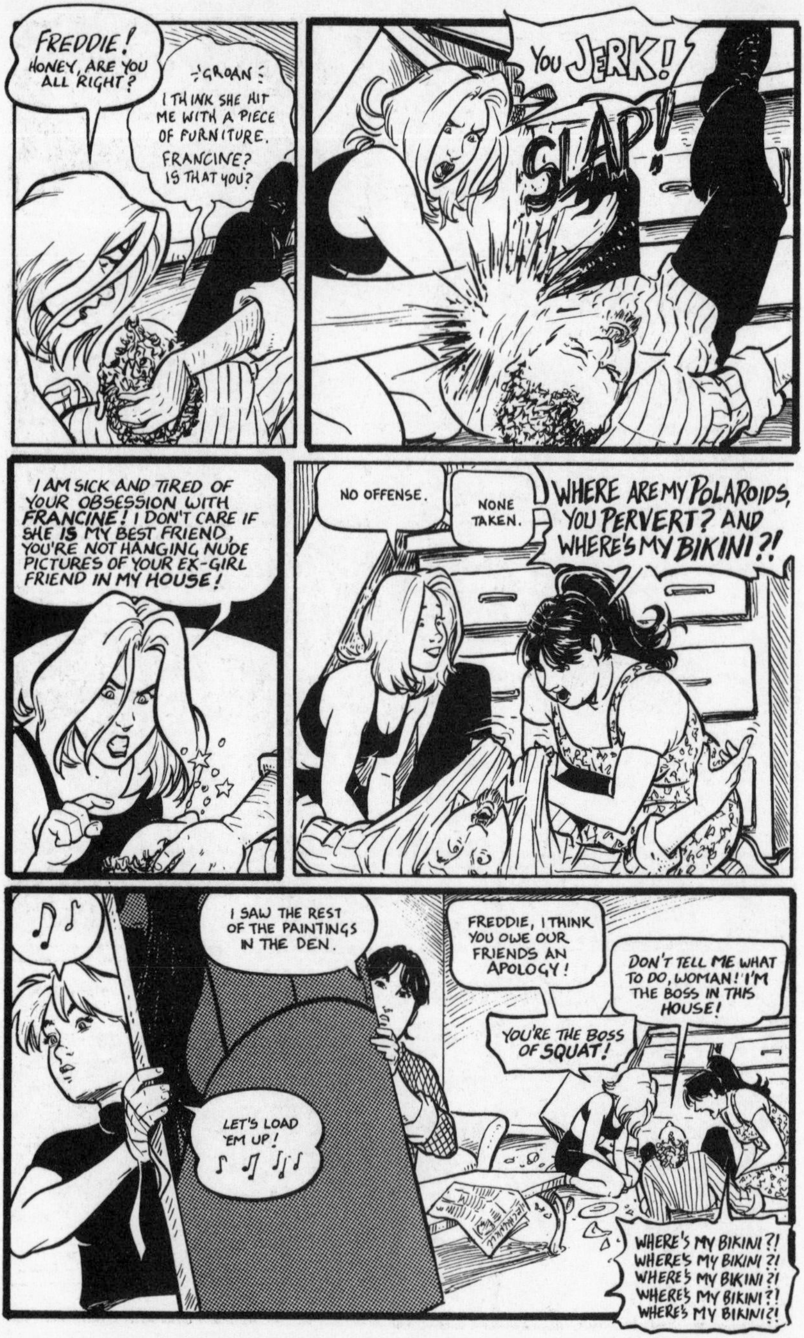
FREDDIE! HONEY, ARE YOU ALL RIGHT?
GROAN
I THINK SHE HIT ME WITH A PIECE OF FURNITURE. FRANCINE? IS THAT YOU?
YOU JERK!
SLAP!
I AM SICK AND TIRED OF YOUR OBSESSION WITH FRANCINE! I DON'T CARE IF SHE IS MY BEST FRIEND, YOU'RE NOT HANGING NUDE PICTURES OF YOUR EX-GIRL FRIEND IN MY HOUSE!
NO OFFENSE.
NONE TAKEN.
WHERE ARE MY POLAROIDS, YOU PERVERT? AND WHERE'S MY BIKINI?!
I SAW THE REST OF THE PAINTINGS IN THE DEN.
LET'S LOAD 'EM UP!
FREDDIE, I THINK YOU OWE OUR FRIENDS AN APOLOGY!
YOU'RE THE BOSS OF SQUAT!
DON'T TELL ME WHAT TO DO, WOMAN! I'M THE BOSS IN THIS HOUSE!
WHERE'S MY BIKINI?!
WHERE'S MY BIKINI?!
WHERE'S MY BIKINI?!
WHERE'S MY BIKINI?!
WHERE'S MY BIKINI?!

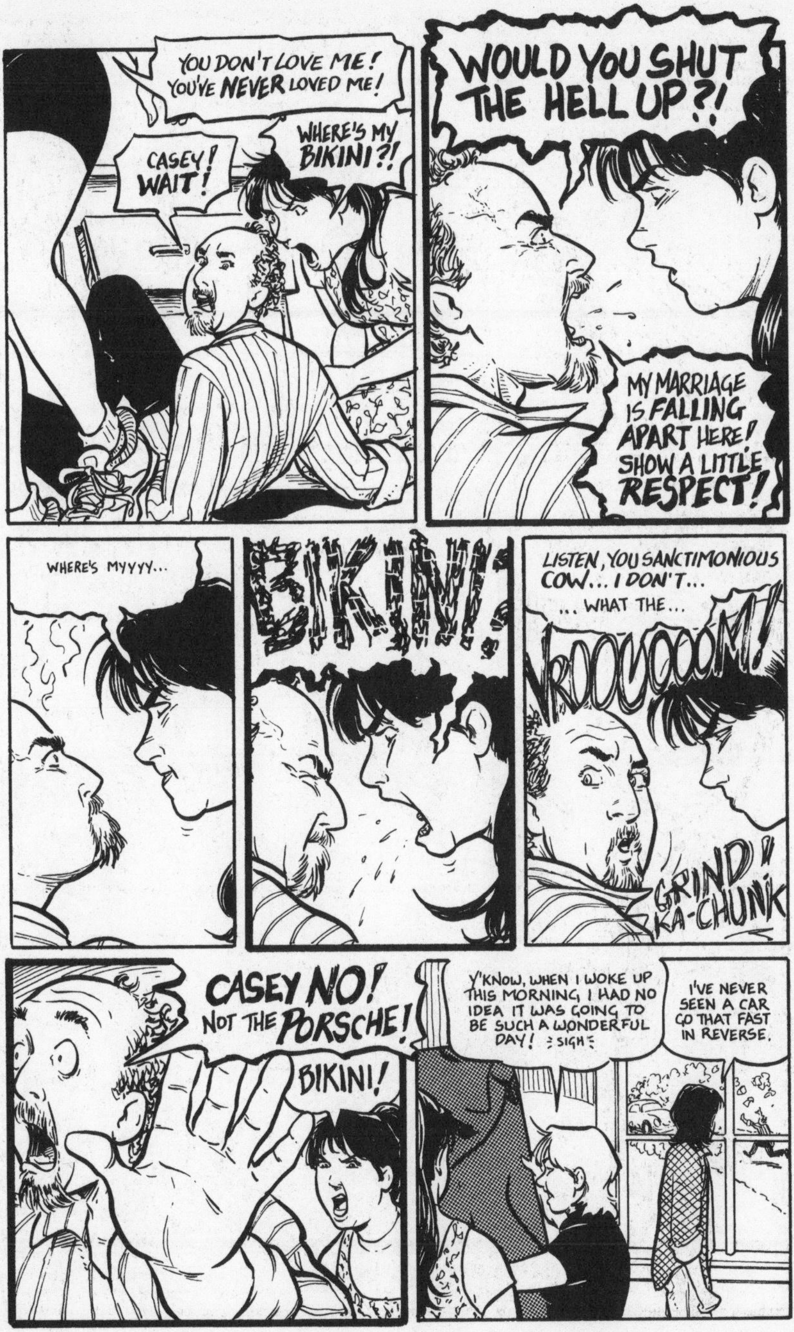
YOU DON'T LOVE ME! YOU'VE NEVER LOVED ME!
CASEY! WAIT!
WHERE'S MY BIKINI?!
WOULD YOU SHUT THE HELL UP?!
MY MARRIAGE IS FALLING APART HERE! SHOW A LITTLE RESPECT!
WHERE'S MYYYY...
BIKINI!
LISTEN, YOU SANCTIMONIOUS COW... I DON'T...
... WHAT THE...
VROOOOOOM!
GRIND! KA-CHUNK
CASEY NO! NOT THE PORSCHE!
BIKINI!
Y'KNOW, WHEN I WOKE UP THIS MORNING, I HAD NO IDEA IT WAS GOING TO BE SUCH A WONDERFUL DAY! SIGH
I'VE NEVER SEEN A CAR GO THAT FAST IN REVERSE.

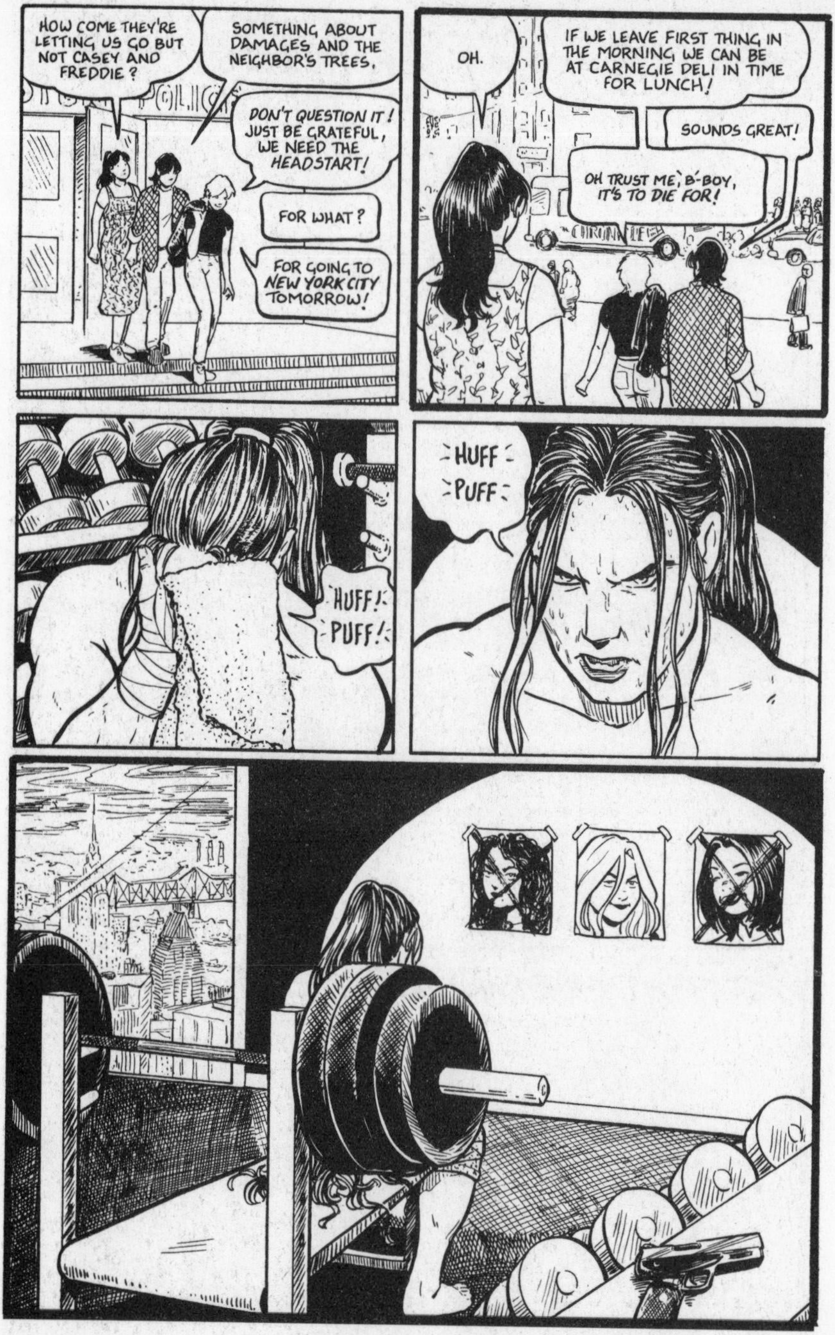
HOW COME THEY'RE LETTING US GO BUT NOT CASEY AND FREDDIE ?
SOMETHING ABOUT DAMAGES AND THE NEIGHBOR'S TREES.
DON'T QUESTION IT! JUST BE GRATEFUL, WE NEED THE HEADSTART!
FOR WHAT ?
FOR GOING TO NEW YORK CITY TOMORROW!
OH.
IF WE LEAVE FIRST THING IN THE MORNING WE CAN BE AT CARNEGIE DELI IN TIME FOR LUNCH!
SOUNDS GREAT!
OH TRUST ME, B-BOY, IT'S TO DIE FOR!
HUFF! PUFF!
HUFF PUFF

I am waiting for you to see
What you do to me and to stop it
    Running late

I am waiting for you to love me
Please come and touch me
  I'll thank you
    Running late

Desperate running to
Catch you briefly to
Let you see me
When I can be wrong

Count the pennies you give to me
Days I dare to say what I'm thinking
    Running late

I hold wonders in dreams and slumbers
I work to want to release them
    Running late

Blazed and blasting they swear it's lasting to
Hear the footsteps behind me
    Running late

Desperate running to
Catch my dream globe I
See my heart in
The middle on fire

    Running late

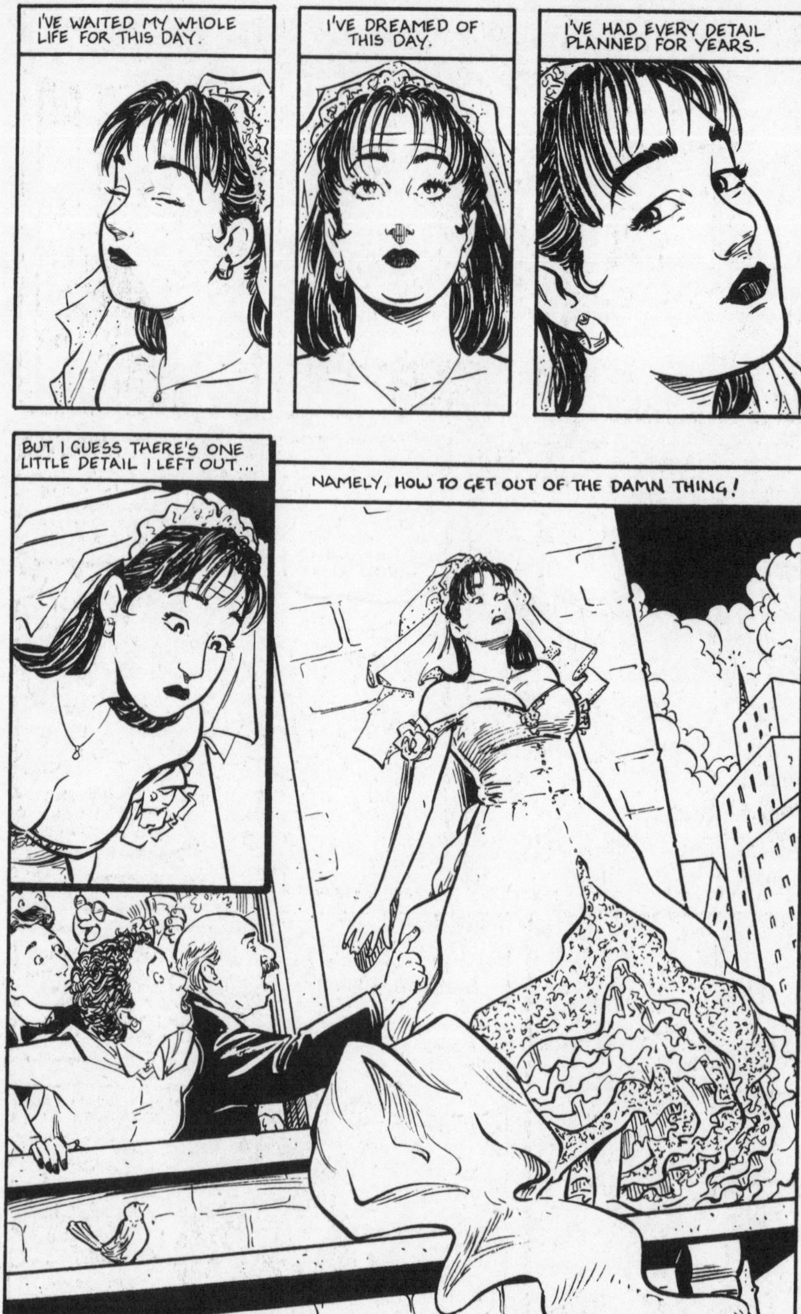
I'VE WAITED MY WHOLE LIFE FOR THIS DAY.
I'VE DREAMED OF THIS DAY.
I'VE HAD EVERY DETAIL PLANNED FOR YEARS.
BUT I GUESS THERE'S ONE LITTLE DETAIL I LEFT OUT...
NAMELY, HOW TO GET OUT OF THE DAMN THING!

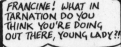

FRANCINE! WHAT IN TARNATION DO YOU THINK YOU'RE DOING OUT THERE, YOUNG LADY?!

I'M THINKING!

THINKING?! WELL, YOU'RE DOIN' A PRETTY LOUSY JOB OF IT! DO YOU REALIZE I HAVE FIFTY POUNDS OF SHRIMP TURNING INTO A POISON COCKTAIL IN HERE?!

OH HUSH! LET ME TALK TO HER.

FRANCINE, SWEETHEART... TELL MOTHER, DEAR... IS SOMETHING WRONG?

OH, MOM... AGH!

AHA! GOTCHA!

GET BACK IN HERE! YOU'RE GOING DOWN THE AISLE IF I HAVE TO THROW YOU!

LET GO OF ME!

FRANCINE! LOOK AT THAT AWFUL UNDERWEAR! WHAT IF YOU GET HIT BY A BUS?

NOT GONNA GET HIT BY A BUS!

I'M TOO YOUNG TO DIE! I'M TOO YOUNG TO GET MARRIED!

HELLO, BOO'FUL. PLAYIN WITH THE DUCKS AGAIN?

HUH?

THIS IS NOT CONDUCT BECOMING A BRIDE!

GET BACK IN HERE!

THIS WEDDING IS COSTING ME A BLOODY FORTUNE AND YOU'RE GOING TO GO THROUGH WITH IT!

BUT WHAT IF HE DOESN'T REALLY LOVE ME? WHAT IF HE ENDS UP LIVING TWO LIVES SOMEDAY, AND I'M THE BORING DOMESTIC HALF!?!

THEN YOU'LL DO WHAT WE ALL DO TO PASS THE TIME, DEAR...

DIET, DRINK AND DECORATE!

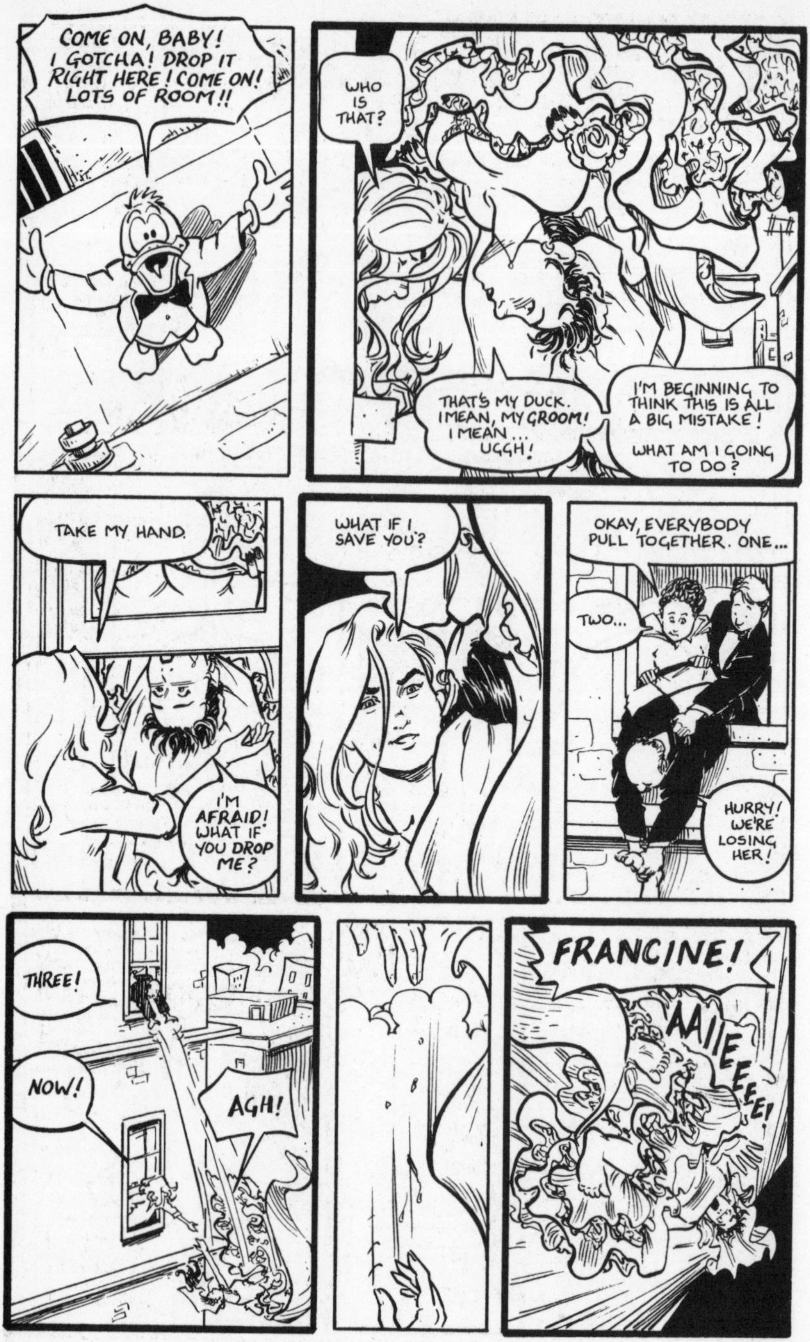
COME ON, BABY! I GOTCHA! DROP IT RIGHT HERE! COME ON! LOTS OF ROOM!!
WHO IS THAT?
THAT'S MY DUCK. I MEAN, MY GROOM! I MEAN... UGGH!
I'M BEGINNING TO THINK THIS IS ALL A BIG MISTAKE!
WHAT AM I GOING TO DO?
TAKE MY HAND.
I'M AFRAID! WHAT IF YOU DROP ME?
WHAT IF I SAVE YOU?
OKAY, EVERYBODY PULL TOGETHER. ONE...
TWO...
HURRY! WE'RE LOSING HER!
THREE!
NOW!
AGH!
FRANCINE!
AAIIEEEEE!

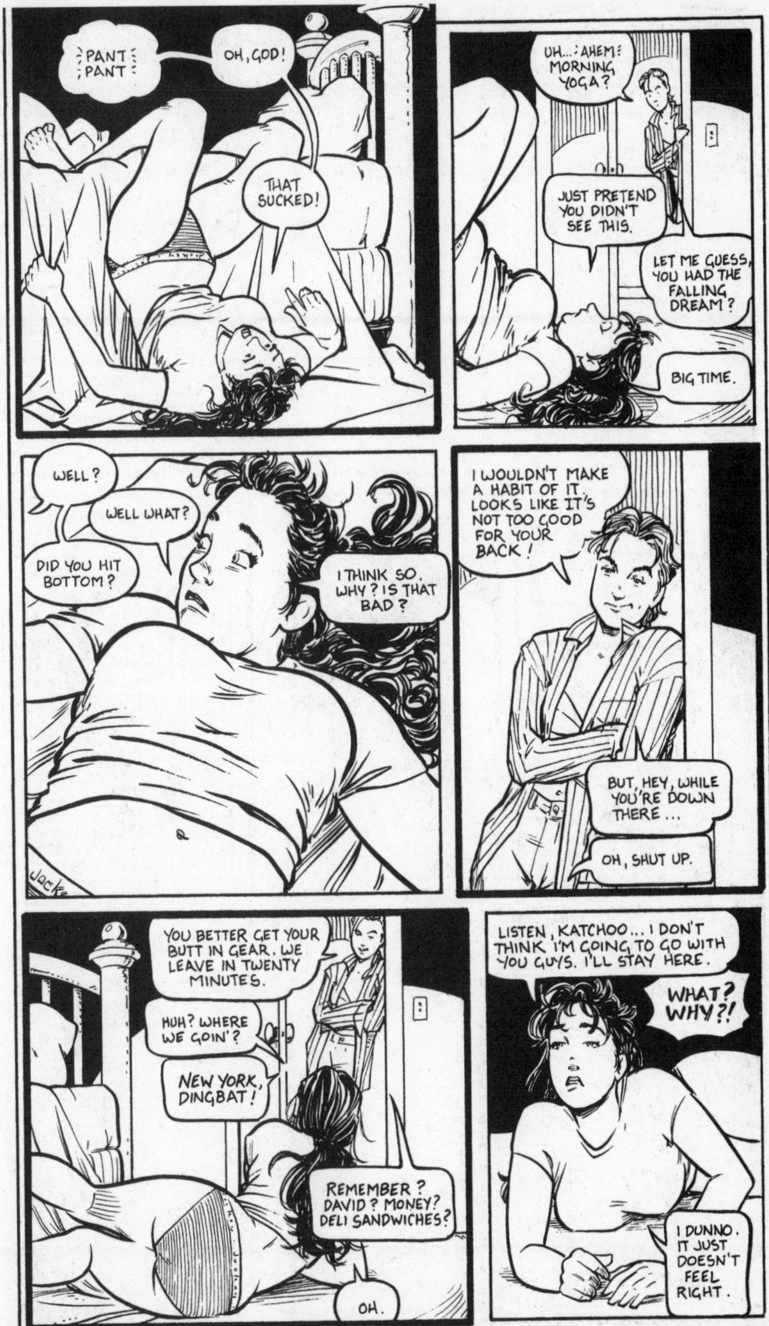
PANT PANT
OH, GOD!
THAT SUCKED!
UH... AHEM MORNING YOGA?
JUST PRETEND YOU DIDN'T SEE THIS.
LET ME GUESS, YOU HAD THE FALLING DREAM?
BIG TIME.
WELL?
WELL WHAT?
DID YOU HIT BOTTOM?
I THINK SO. WHY? IS THAT BAD?
I WOULDN'T MAKE A HABIT OF IT. LOOKS LIKE IT'S NOT TOO GOOD FOR YOUR BACK!
BUT, HEY, WHILE YOU'RE DOWN THERE...
OH, SHUT UP.
YOU BETTER GET YOUR BUTT IN GEAR. WE LEAVE IN TWENTY MINUTES.
HUH? WHERE WE GOIN'?
NEW YORK, DINGBAT!
REMEMBER? DAVID? MONEY? DELI SANDWICHES?
OH.
LISTEN, KATCHOO... I DON'T THINK I'M GOING TO GO WITH YOU GUYS. I'LL STAY HERE.
WHAT? WHY?!
I DUNNO. IT JUST DOESN'T FEEL RIGHT.

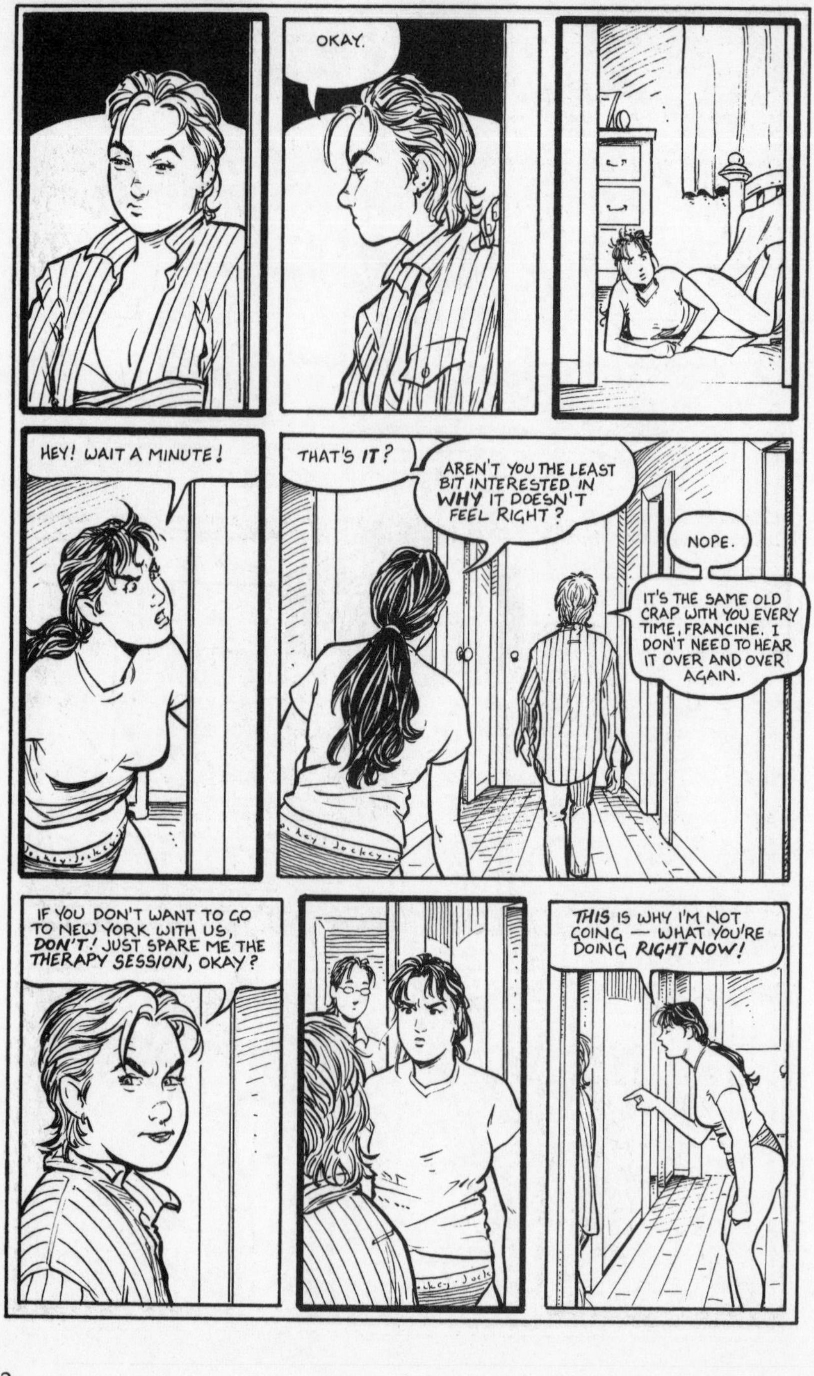
OKAY.
HEY! WAIT A MINUTE!
THAT'S IT?
AREN'T YOU THE LEAST BIT INTERESTED IN WHY IT DOESN'T FEEL RIGHT?
NOPE.
IT'S THE SAME OLD CRAP WITH YOU EVERY TIME, FRANCINE. I DON'T NEED TO HEAR IT OVER AND OVER AGAIN.
IF YOU DON'T WANT TO GO TO NEW YORK WITH US, DON'T! JUST SPARE ME THE THERAPY SESSION, OKAY?
THIS IS WHY I'M NOT GOING — WHAT YOU'RE DOING RIGHT NOW!

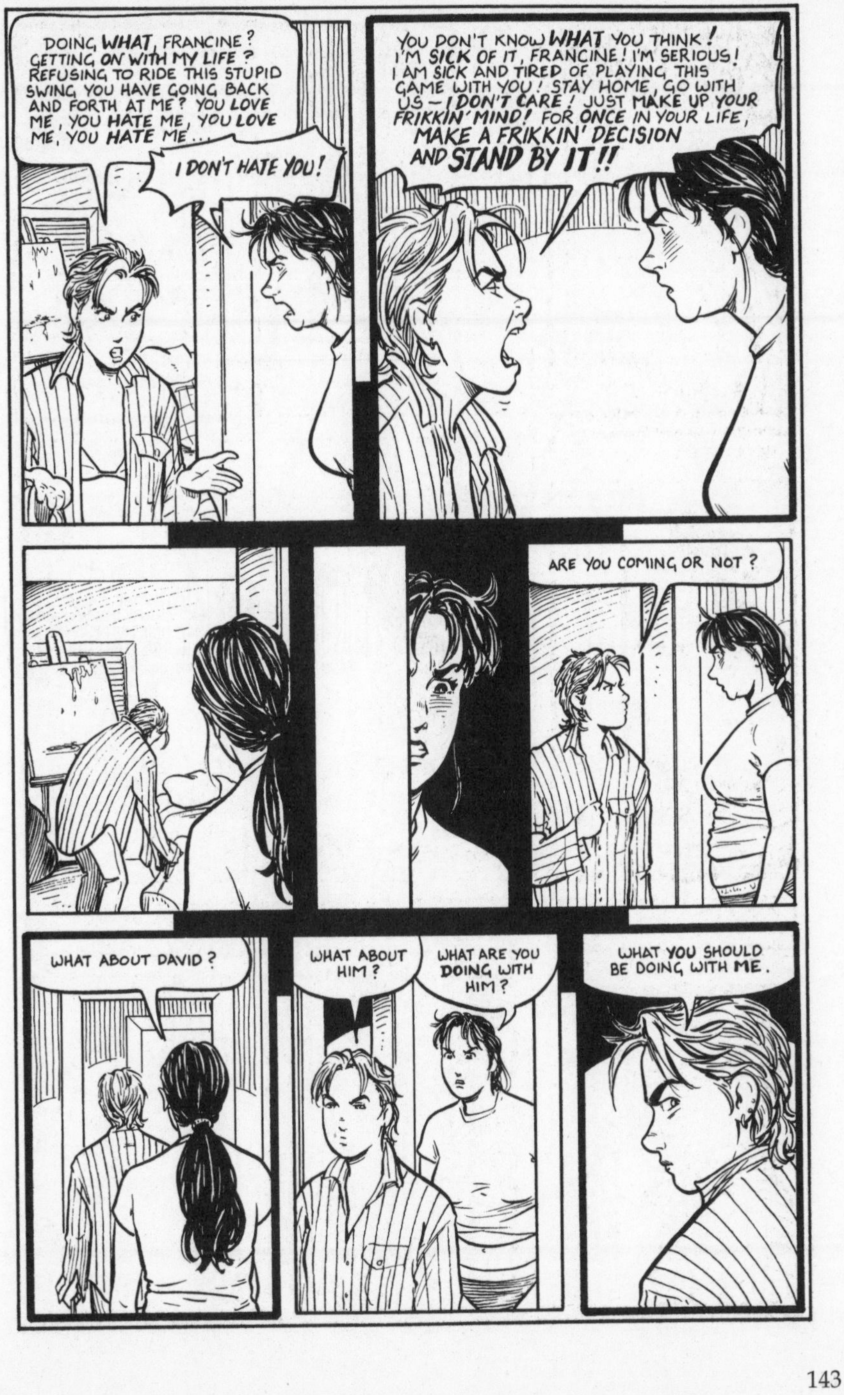
DOING WHAT, FRANCINE? GETTING ON WITH MY LIFE? REFUSING TO RIDE THIS STUPID SWING YOU HAVE GOING BACK AND FORTH AT ME? YOU LOVE ME, YOU HATE ME, YOU LOVE ME, YOU HATE ME...
I DON'T HATE YOU!
YOU DON'T KNOW WHAT YOU THINK! I'M SICK OF IT, FRANCINE! I'M SERIOUS! I AM SICK AND TIRED OF PLAYING THIS GAME WITH YOU! STAY HOME, GO WITH US — I DON'T CARE! JUST MAKE UP YOUR FRIKKIN' MIND! FOR ONCE IN YOUR LIFE, MAKE A FRIKKIN' DECISION AND STAND BY IT!!
ARE YOU COMING OR NOT?
WHAT ABOUT DAVID?
WHAT ABOUT HIM?
WHAT ARE YOU DOING WITH HIM?
WHAT YOU SHOULD BE DOING WITH ME.

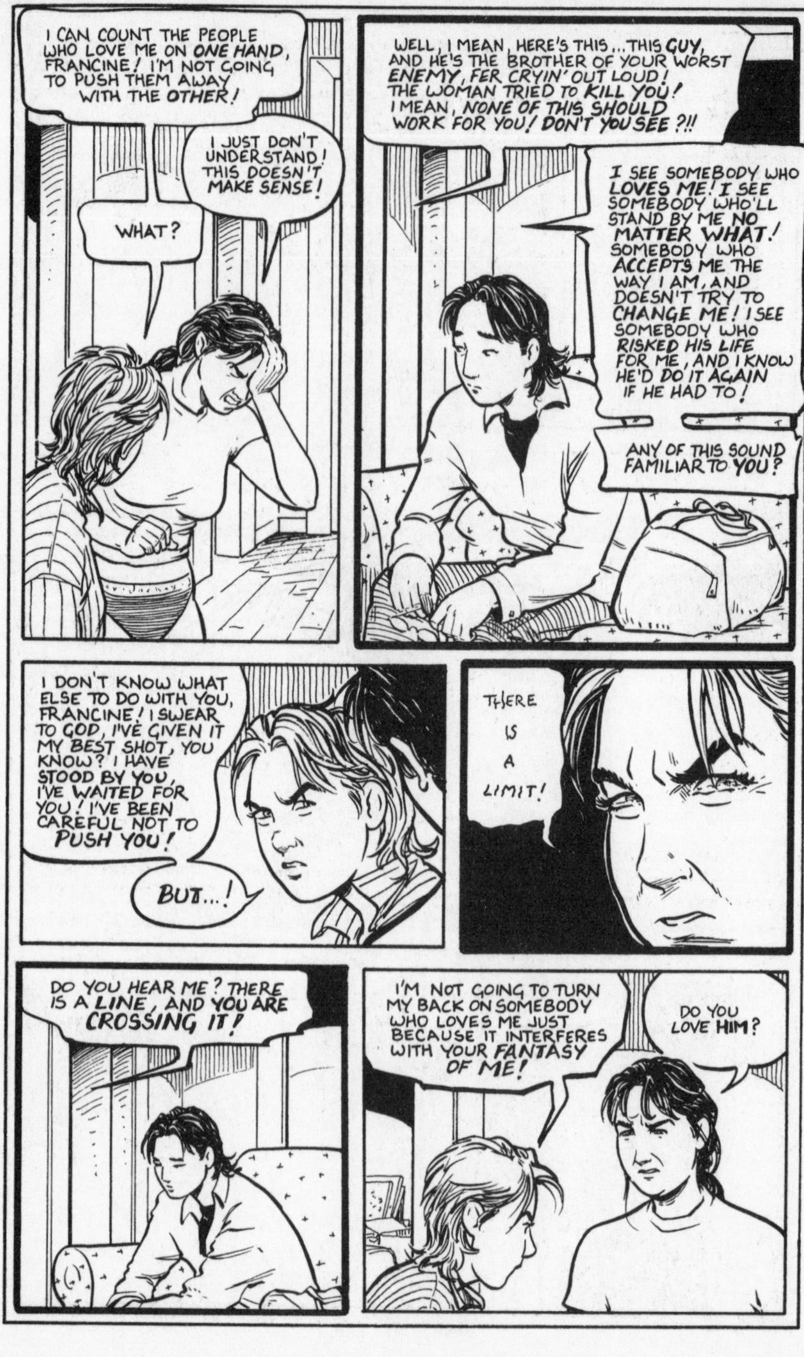
I CAN COUNT THE PEOPLE WHO LOVE ME ON ONE HAND, FRANCINE! I'M NOT GOING TO PUSH THEM AWAY WITH THE OTHER!
WHAT?
I JUST DON'T UNDERSTAND! THIS DOESN'T MAKE SENSE!
WELL, I MEAN, HERE'S THIS... THIS GUY, AND HE'S THE BROTHER OF YOUR WORST ENEMY, FER CRYIN' OUT LOUD! THE WOMAN TRIED TO KILL YOU! I MEAN, NONE OF THIS SHOULD WORK FOR YOU! DON'T YOU SEE?!!
I SEE SOMEBODY WHO LOVES ME! I SEE SOMEBODY WHO'LL STAND BY ME NO MATTER WHAT! SOMEBODY WHO ACCEPTS ME THE WAY I AM, AND DOESN'T TRY TO CHANGE ME! I SEE SOMEBODY WHO RISKED HIS LIFE FOR ME, AND I KNOW HE'D DO IT AGAIN IF HE HAD TO!
ANY OF THIS SOUND FAMILIAR TO YOU?
I DON'T KNOW WHAT ELSE TO DO WITH YOU, FRANCINE! I SWEAR TO GOD, I'VE GIVEN IT MY BEST SHOT, YOU KNOW? I HAVE STOOD BY YOU, I'VE WAITED FOR YOU! I'VE BEEN CAREFUL NOT TO PUSH YOU!
BUT...!
THERE IS A LIMIT!
DO YOU HEAR ME? THERE IS A LINE, AND YOU ARE CROSSING IT!
I'M NOT GOING TO TURN MY BACK ON SOMEBODY WHO LOVES ME JUST BECAUSE IT INTERFERES WITH YOUR FANTASY OF ME!
DO YOU LOVE HIM?

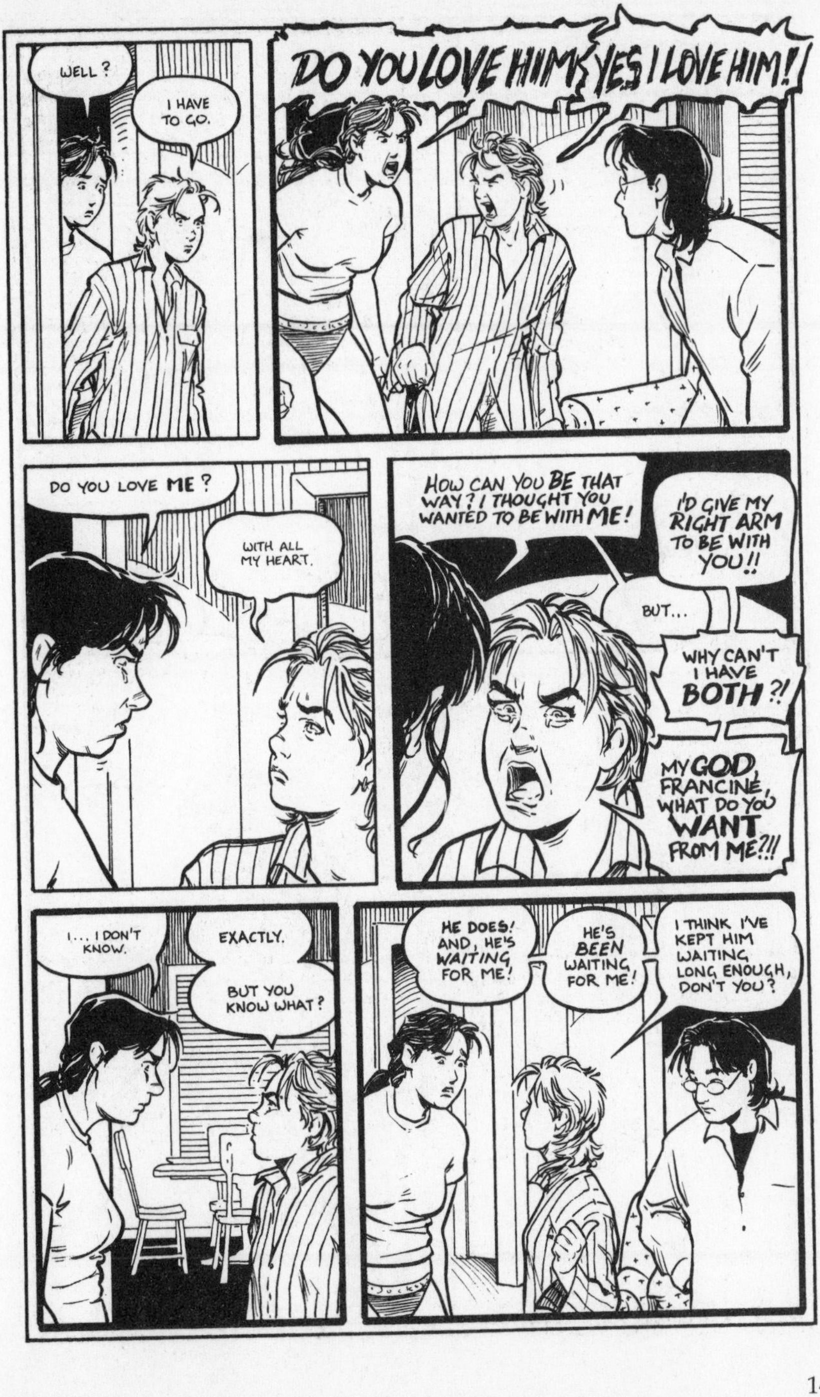
WELL ?
I HAVE TO GO.
DO YOU LOVE HIM? YES I LOVE HIM!!
DO YOU LOVE ME ?
WITH ALL MY HEART.
HOW CAN YOU BE THAT WAY? I THOUGHT YOU WANTED TO BE WITH ME!
I'D GIVE MY RIGHT ARM TO BE WITH YOU!!
BUT...
WHY CAN'T I HAVE BOTH ?!
MY GOD, FRANCINE, WHAT DO YOU WANT FROM ME?!!
I... I DON'T KNOW.
EXACTLY.
BUT YOU KNOW WHAT ?
HE DOES! AND, HE'S WAITING FOR ME!
HE'S BEEN WAITING FOR ME!
I THINK I'VE KEPT HIM WAITING LONG ENOUGH, DON'T YOU ?

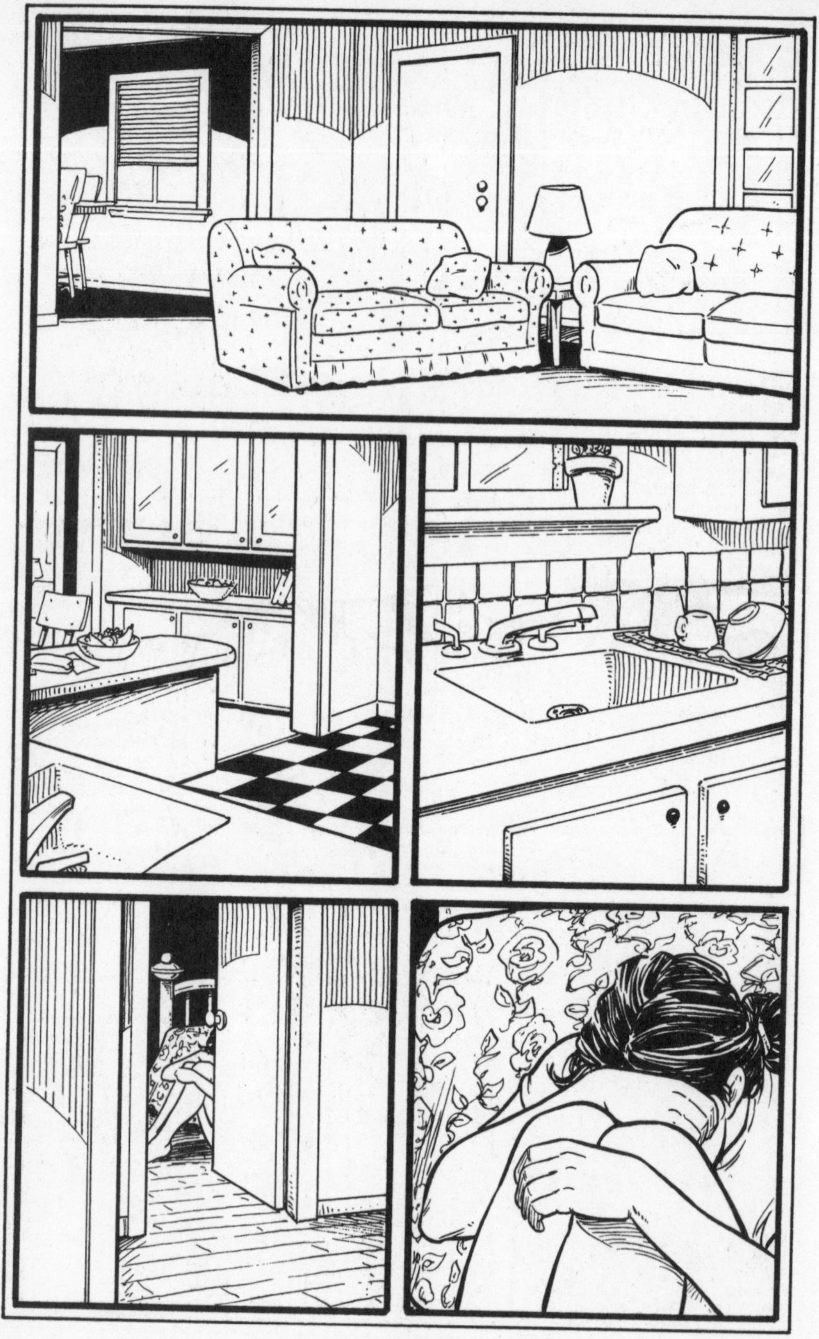

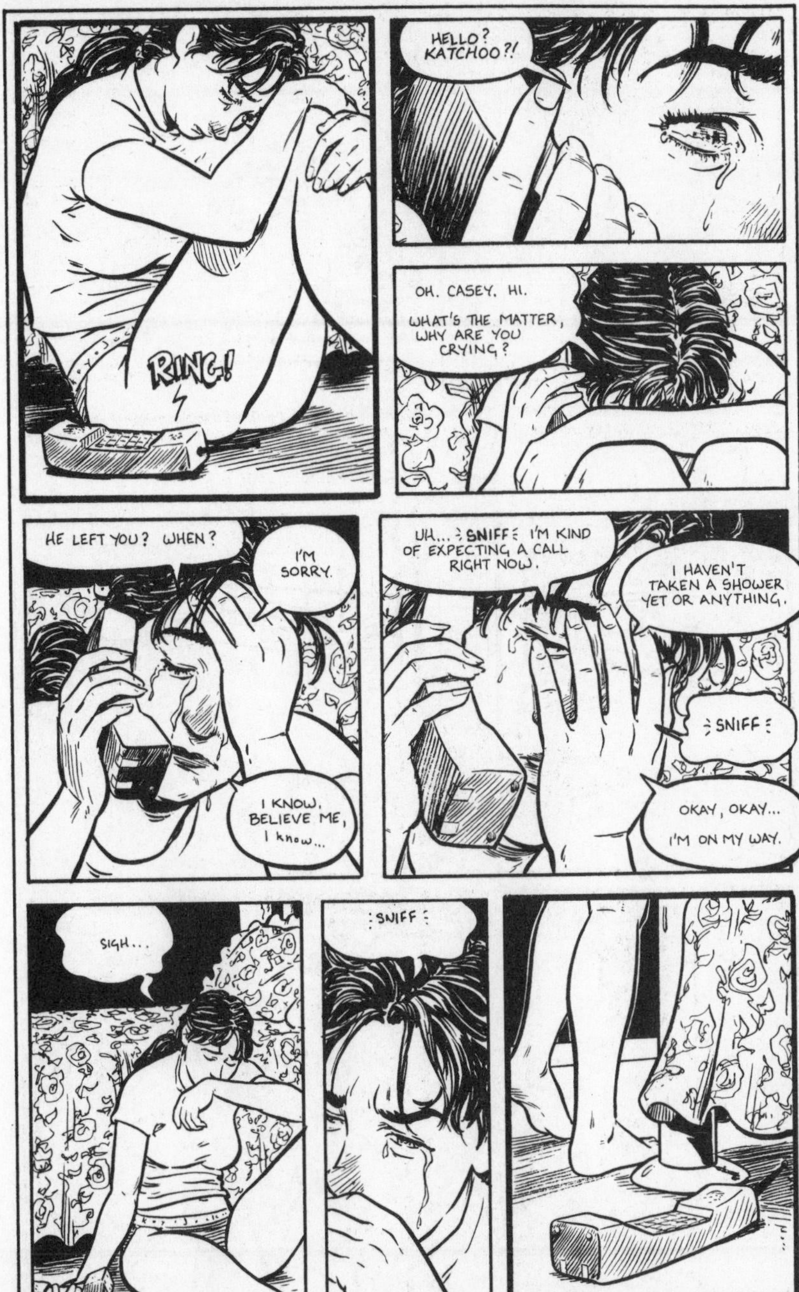
RING!
HELLO? KATCHOO?!
OH. CASEY. HI.
WHAT'S THE MATTER, WHY ARE YOU CRYING?
HE LEFT YOU? WHEN?
I'M SORRY.
I KNOW. BELIEVE ME, I know...
UH... SNIFF I'M KIND OF EXPECTING A CALL RIGHT NOW.
I HAVEN'T TAKEN A SHOWER YET OR ANYTHING.
SNIFF
OKAY, OKAY...
I'M ON MY WAY.
SIGH...
SNIFF

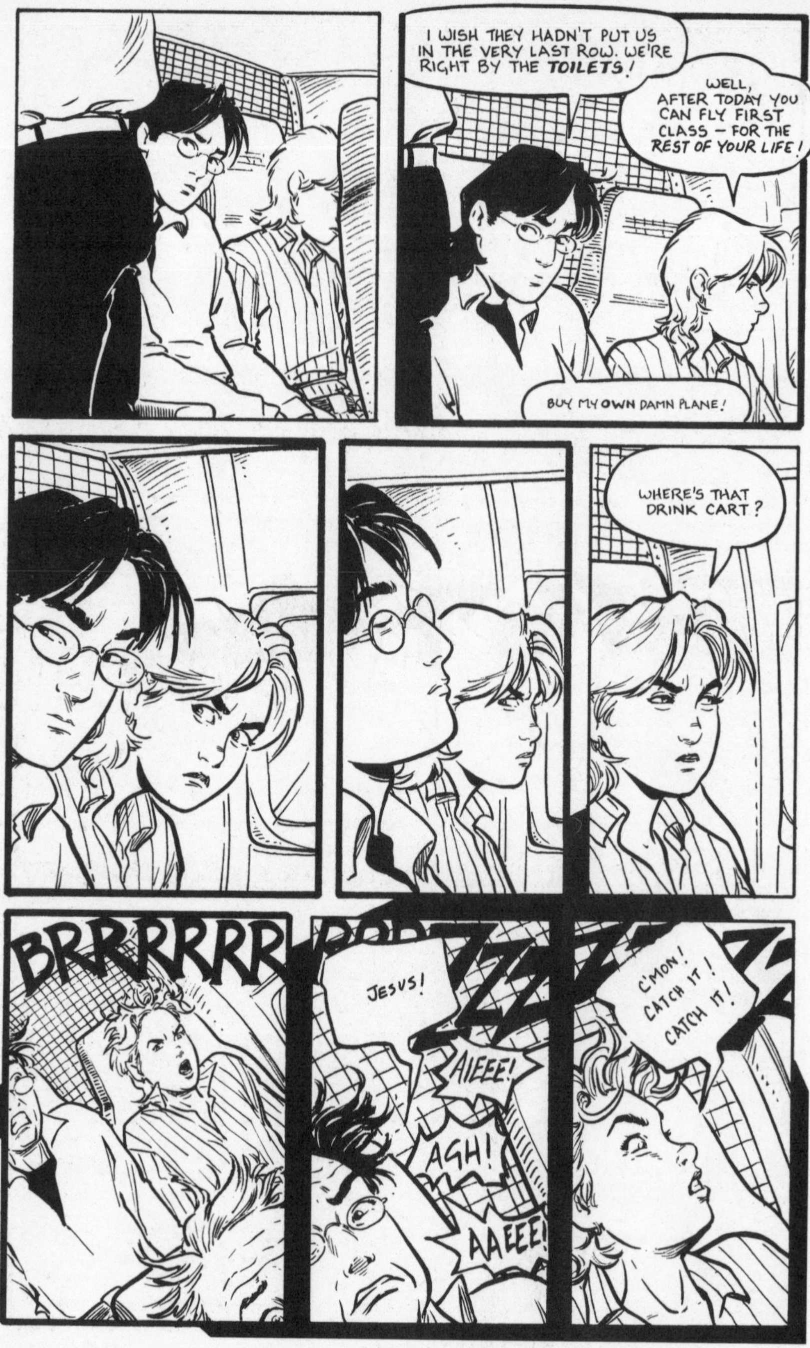
I WISH THEY HADN'T PUT US IN THE VERY LAST ROW. WE'RE RIGHT BY THE TOILETS!
WELL, AFTER TODAY YOU CAN FLY FIRST CLASS – FOR THE REST OF YOUR LIFE!
BUY MY OWN DAMN PLANE!
WHERE'S THAT DRINK CART?
BRRRRRRR
JESUS!
AIEEE!
AGH!
AAEEE!
C'MON! CATCH IT! CATCH IT!

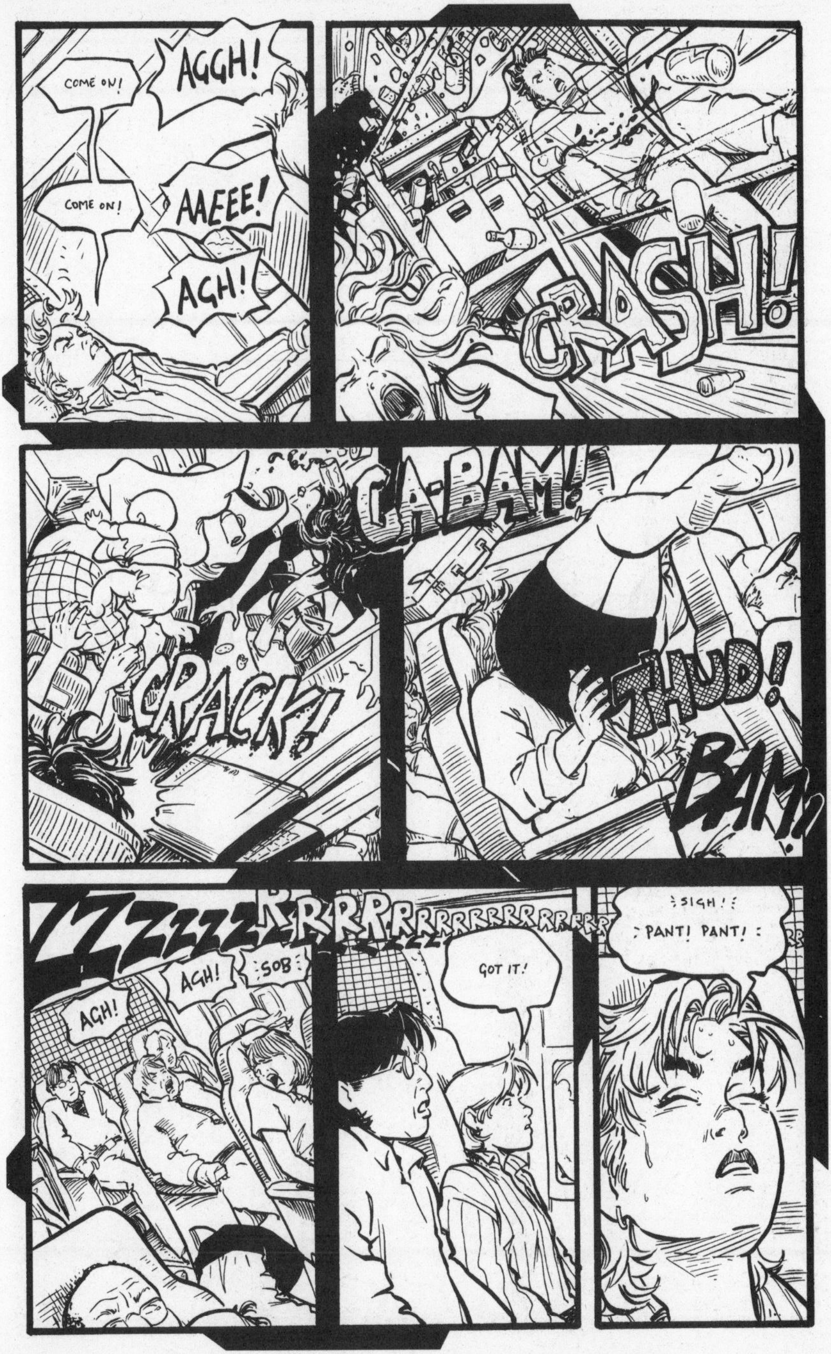

COME ON!
AGGH!
COME ON!
AAEEE!
AGH!
CRASH!
CA-BAM!
CRACK!
THUD!
BAM!
ZZZZZZZRRRRRRRRRRRRRRRR
AGH!
AGH!
SOB
GOT IT!
SIGH!
PANT! PANT!

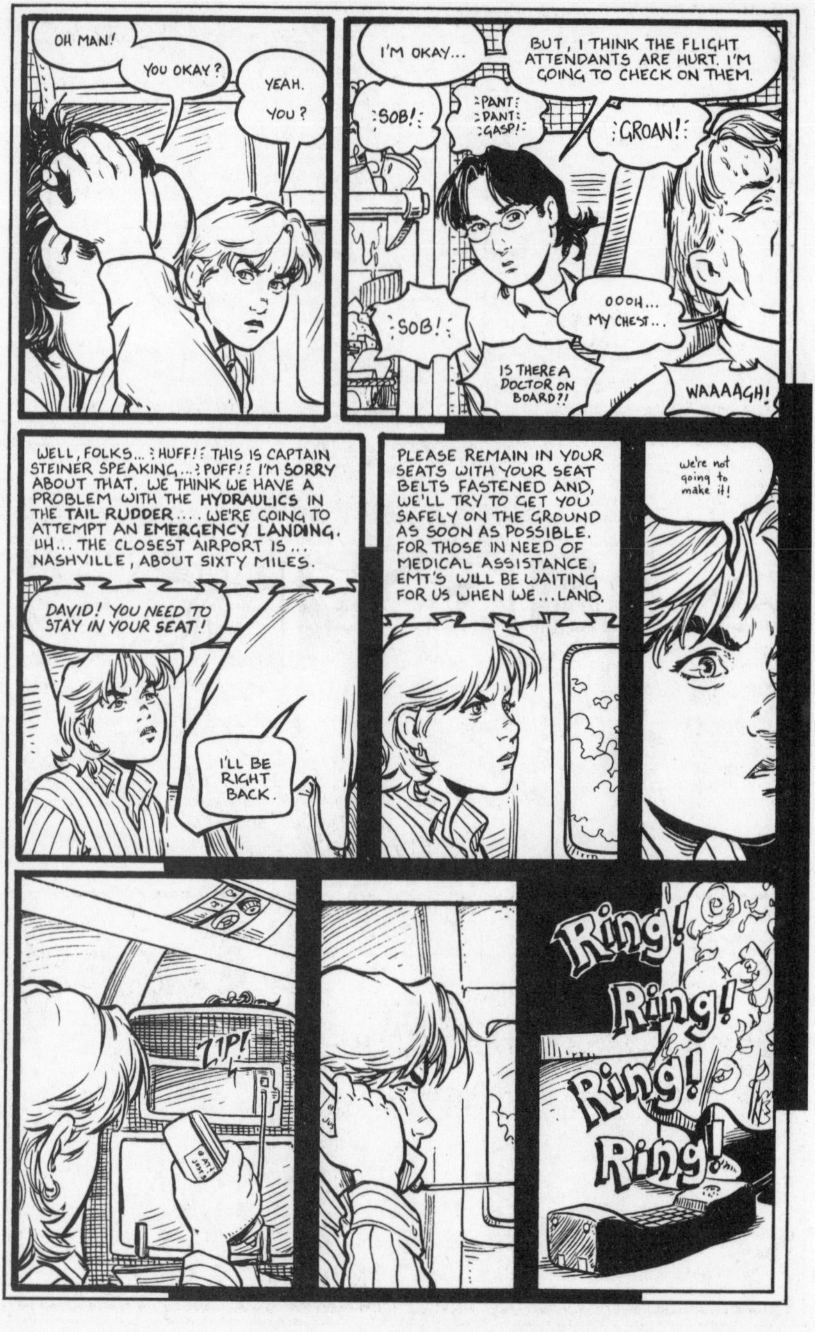
OH MAN!
YOU OKAY?
YEAH.
YOU?
I'M OKAY...
BUT, I THINK THE FLIGHT ATTENDANTS ARE HURT. I'M GOING TO CHECK ON THEM.
SOB!
PANT PANT GASP!
GROAN!
SOB!
OOOH... MY CHEST...
IS THERE A DOCTOR ON BOARD?!
WAAAAGH!
WELL, FOLKS... HUFF! THIS IS CAPTAIN STEINER SPEAKING... PUFF! I'M SORRY ABOUT THAT. WE THINK WE HAVE A PROBLEM WITH THE HYDRAULICS IN THE TAIL RUDDER.... WE'RE GOING TO ATTEMPT AN EMERGENCY LANDING. UH... THE CLOSEST AIRPORT IS... NASHVILLE, ABOUT SIXTY MILES.
DAVID! YOU NEED TO STAY IN YOUR SEAT!
I'LL BE RIGHT BACK.
PLEASE REMAIN IN YOUR SEATS WITH YOUR SEAT BELTS FASTENED AND, WE'LL TRY TO GET YOU SAFELY ON THE GROUND AS SOON AS POSSIBLE. FOR THOSE IN NEED OF MEDICAL ASSISTANCE, EMT'S WILL BE WAITING FOR US WHEN WE... LAND.
we're not going to make it!
ZIP!
Ring!
Ring!
Ring!
Ring!

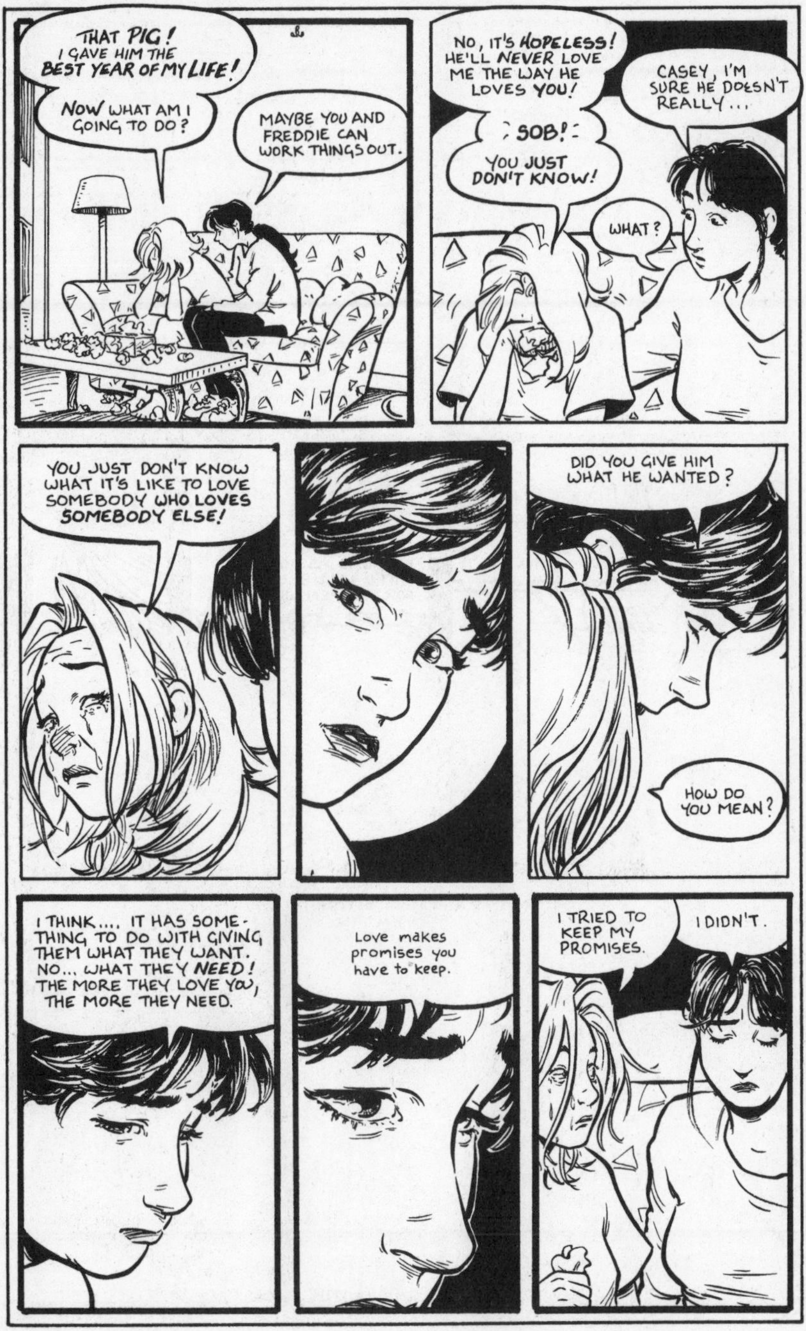
THAT PIG! I GAVE HIM THE BEST YEAR OF MY LIFE!
NOW WHAT AM I GOING TO DO?
MAYBE YOU AND FREDDIE CAN WORK THINGS OUT.
NO, IT'S HOPELESS! HE'LL NEVER LOVE ME THE WAY HE LOVES YOU!
SOB!
YOU JUST DON'T KNOW!
CASEY, I'M SURE HE DOESN'T REALLY...
WHAT?
YOU JUST DON'T KNOW WHAT IT'S LIKE TO LOVE SOMEBODY WHO LOVES SOMEBODY ELSE!
DID YOU GIVE HIM WHAT HE WANTED?
HOW DO YOU MEAN?
I THINK...., IT HAS SOMETHING TO DO WITH GIVING THEM WHAT THEY WANT. NO... WHAT THEY NEED! THE MORE THEY LOVE YOU, THE MORE THEY NEED.
Love makes promises you have to keep.
I TRIED TO KEEP MY PROMISES.
I DIDN'T.

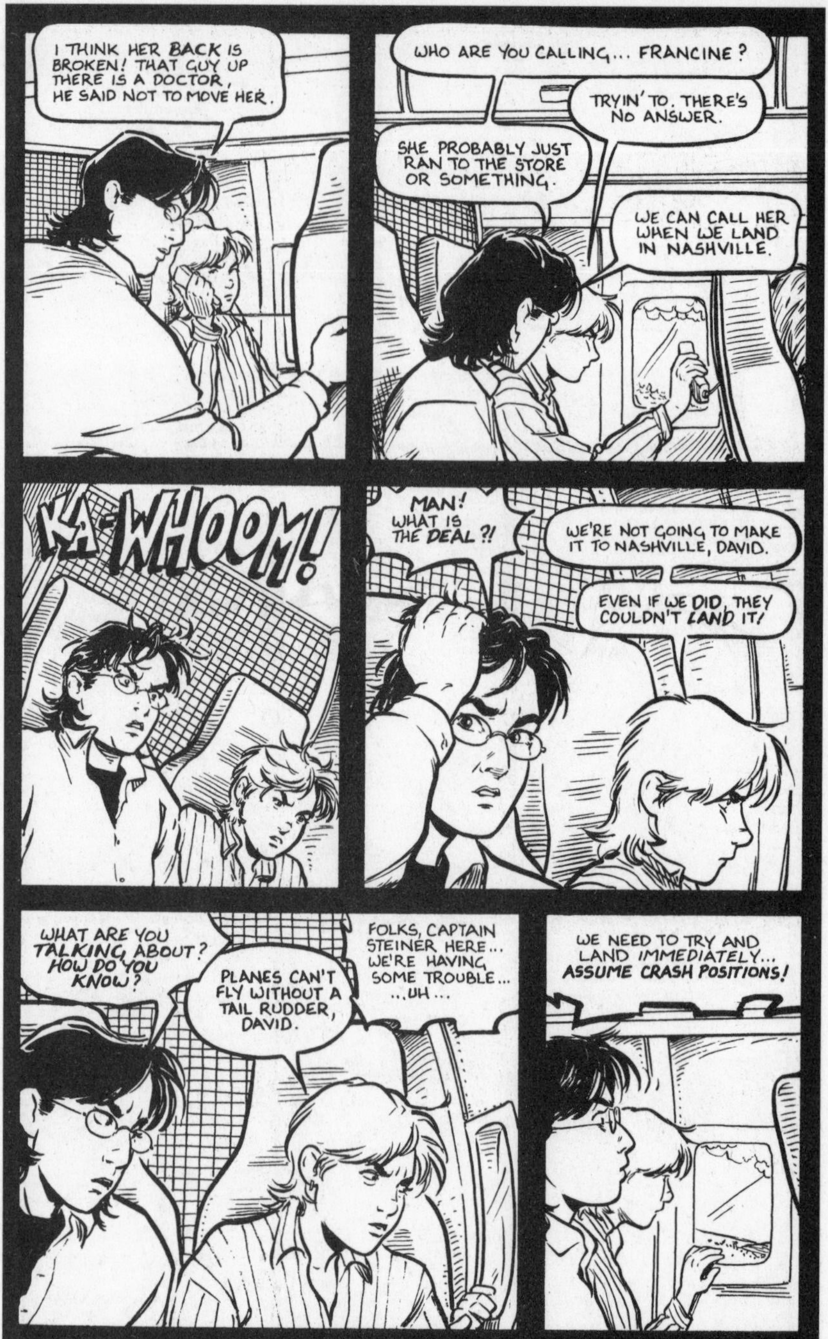

I THINK HER BACK IS BROKEN! THAT GUY UP THERE IS A DOCTOR, HE SAID NOT TO MOVE HER.
WHO ARE YOU CALLING... FRANCINE?
TRYIN' TO. THERE'S NO ANSWER.
SHE PROBABLY JUST RAN TO THE STORE OR SOMETHING.
WE CAN CALL HER WHEN WE LAND IN NASHVILLE.
KA-WHOOM!
MAN! WHAT IS THE DEAL?!
WE'RE NOT GOING TO MAKE IT TO NASHVILLE, DAVID.
EVEN IF WE DID, THEY COULDN'T LAND IT!
WHAT ARE YOU TALKING ABOUT? HOW DO YOU KNOW?
PLANES CAN'T FLY WITHOUT A TAIL RUDDER, DAVID.
FOLKS, CAPTAIN STEINER HERE... WE'RE HAVING SOME TROUBLE... ...UH ...
WE NEED TO TRY AND LAND IMMEDIATELY... ASSUME CRASH POSITIONS!

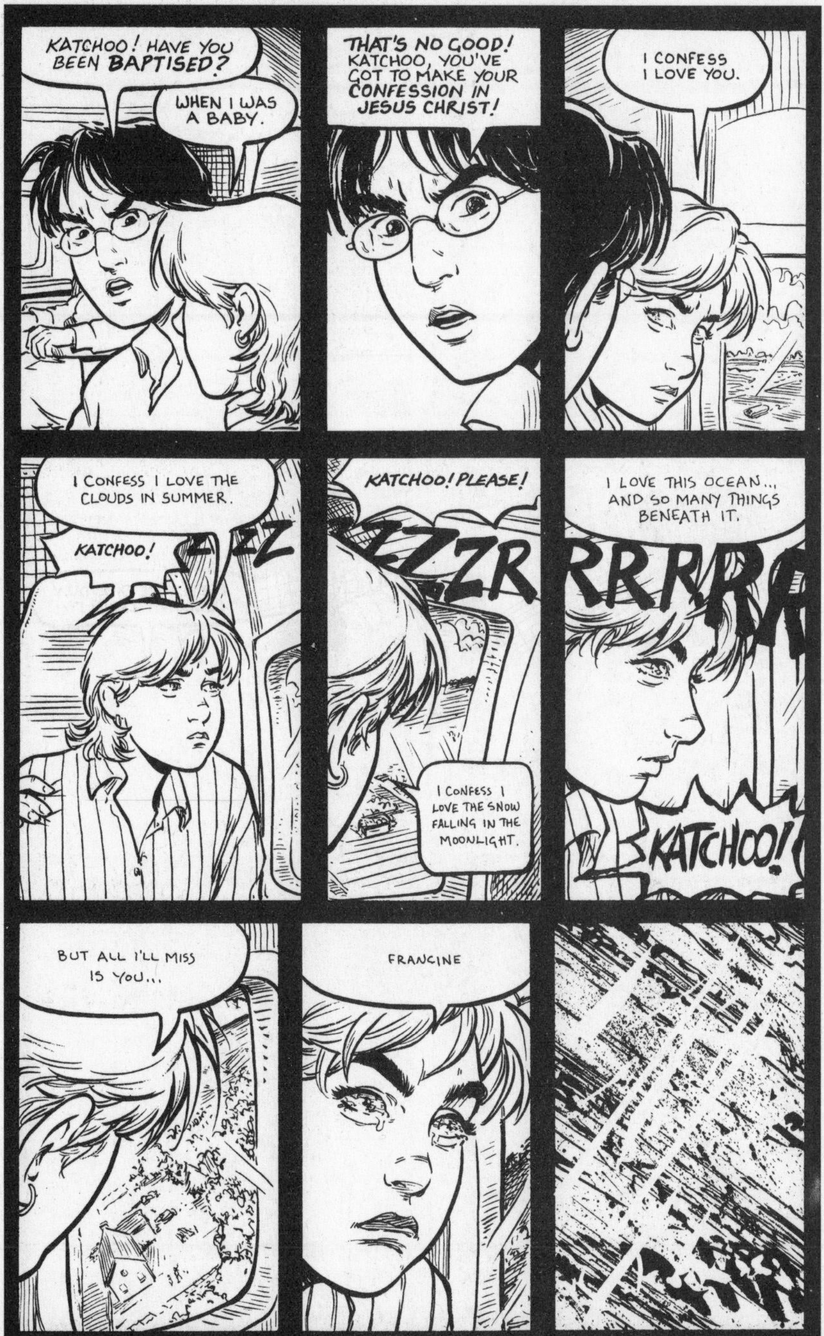
KATCHOO! HAVE YOU BEEN BAPTISED?
WHEN I WAS A BABY.
THAT'S NO GOOD! KATCHOO, YOU'VE GOT TO MAKE YOUR CONFESSION IN JESUS CHRIST!
I CONFESS I LOVE YOU.
I CONFESS I LOVE THE CLOUDS IN SUMMER.
KATCHOO!
KATCHOO! PLEASE!
I CONFESS I LOVE THE SNOW FALLING IN THE MOONLIGHT.
I LOVE THIS OCEAN... AND SO MANY THINGS BENEATH IT.
ZZZZZZRRRRRR
KATCHOO!
BUT ALL I'LL MISS IS YOU...
FRANCINE

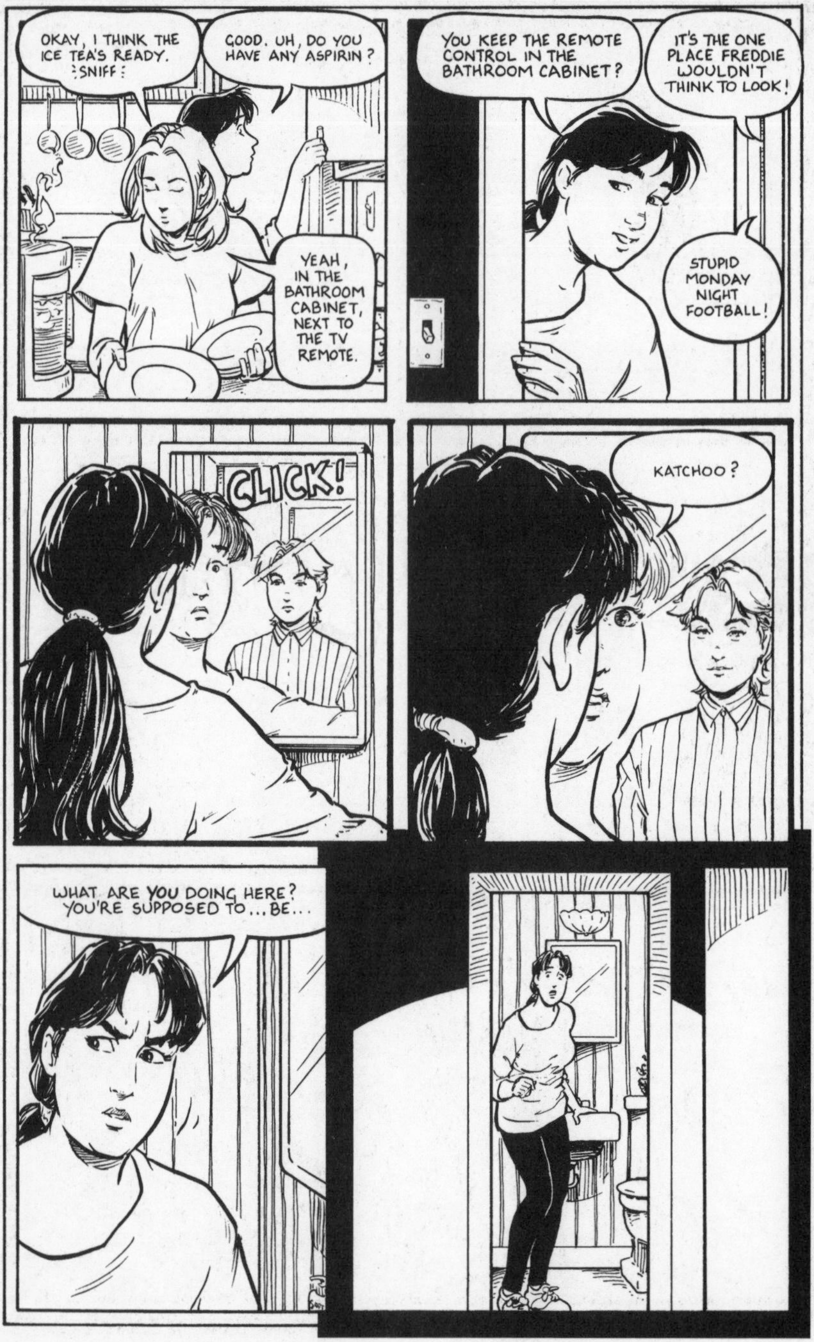
OKAY, I THINK THE ICE TEA'S READY. :SNIFF:
GOOD. UH, DO YOU HAVE ANY ASPIRIN?
YEAH, IN THE BATHROOM CABINET, NEXT TO THE TV REMOTE.
YOU KEEP THE REMOTE CONTROL IN THE BATHROOM CABINET?
IT'S THE ONE PLACE FREDDIE WOULDN'T THINK TO LOOK!
STUPID MONDAY NIGHT FOOTBALL!
CLICK!
KATCHOO?
WHAT ARE YOU DOING HERE? YOU'RE SUPPOSED TO... BE...

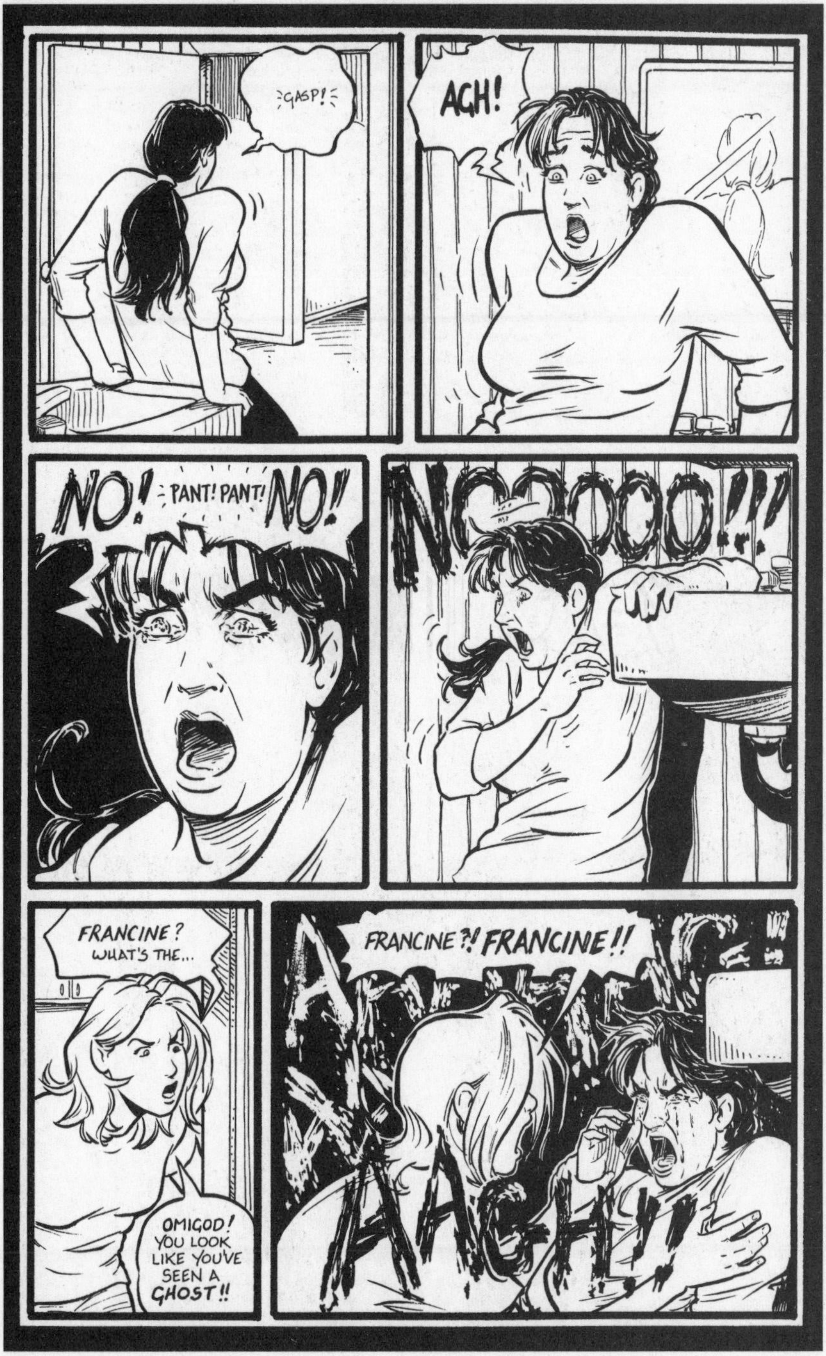
GASP!
AGH!
NO! PANT! PANT! NO!
NOOOOOO!!!
FRANCINE? WHAT'S THE...
OMIGOD! YOU LOOK LIKE YOU'VE SEEN A GHOST!!
FRANCINE?! FRANCINE!!
AAGH!!

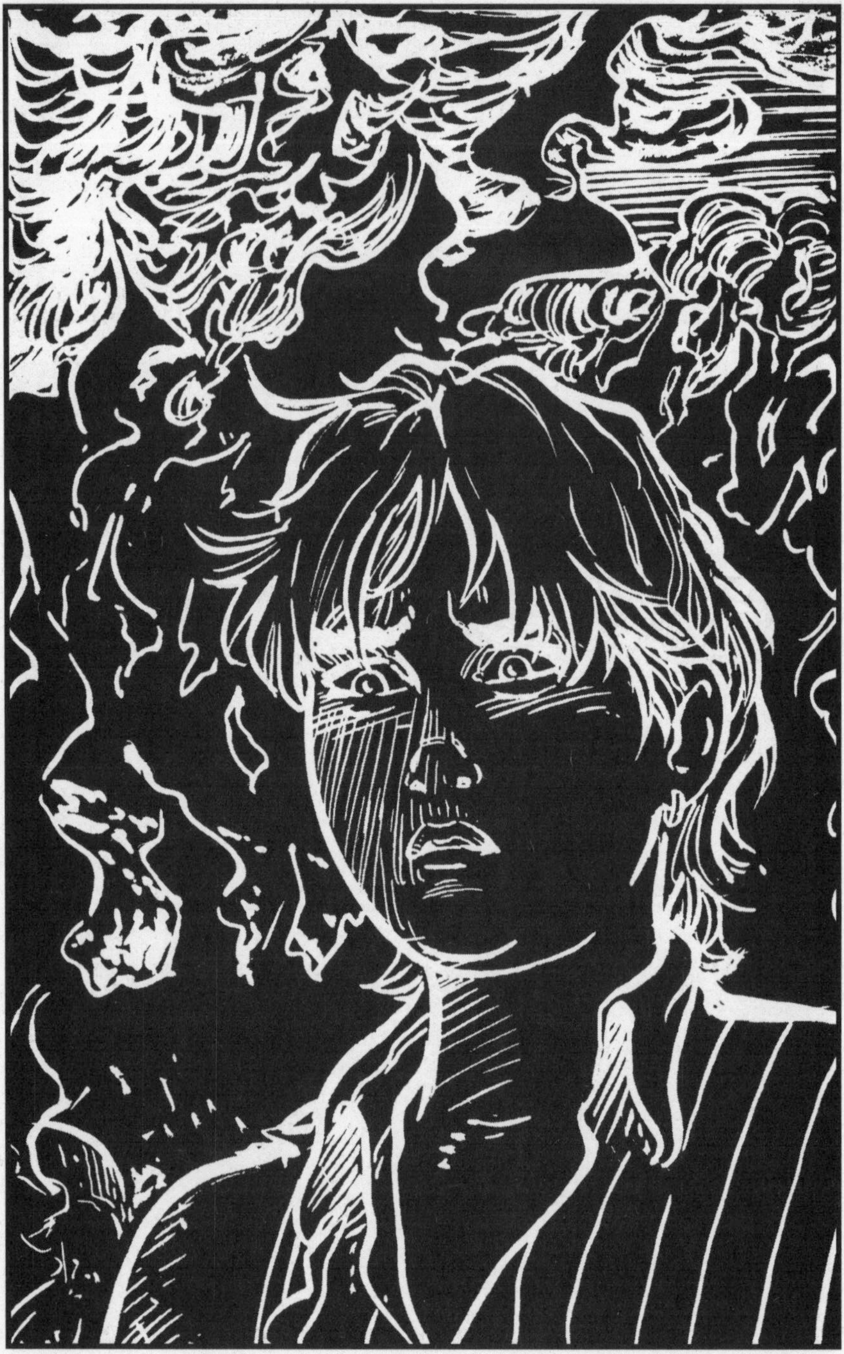

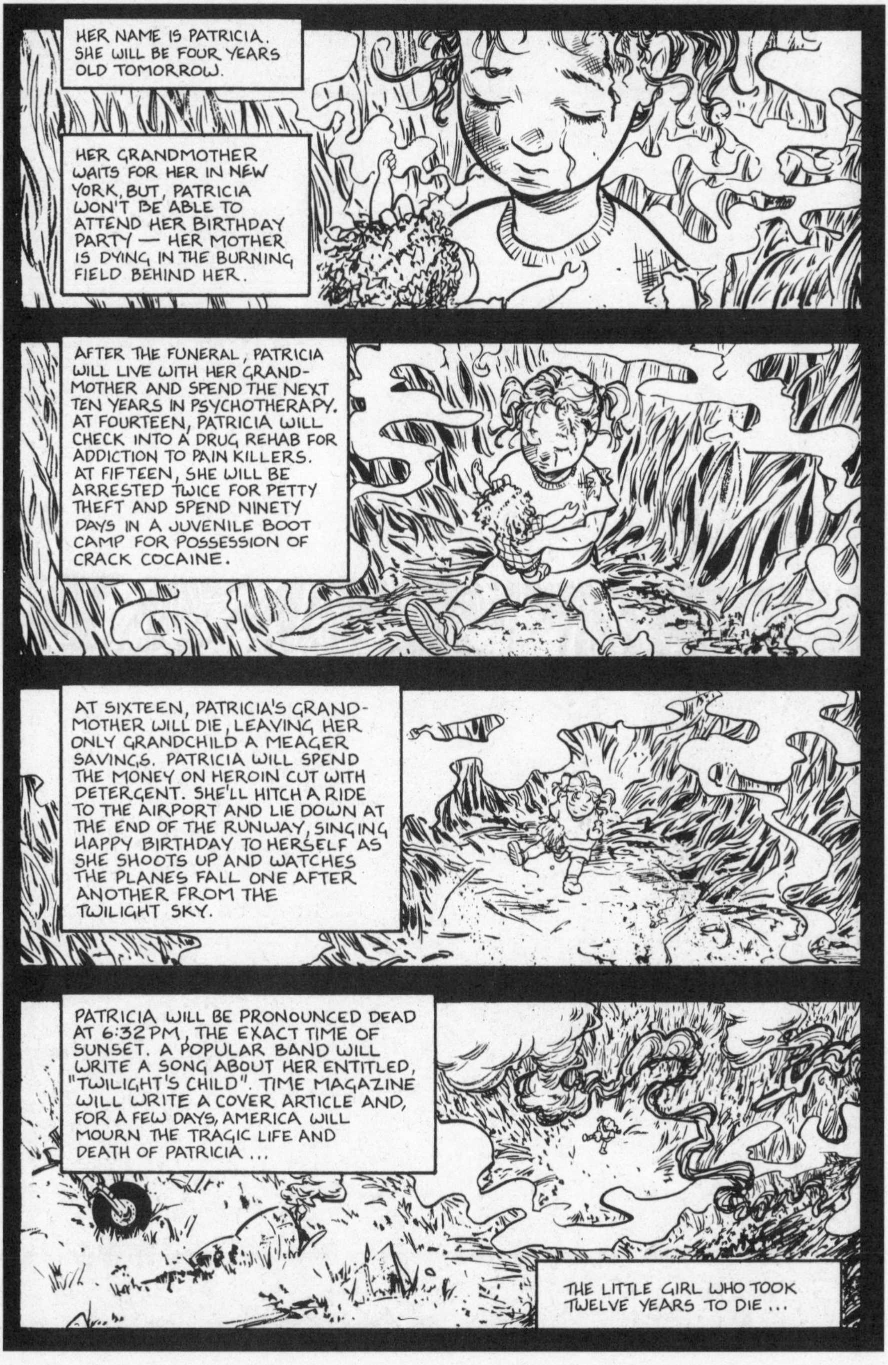
HER NAME IS PATRICIA. SHE WILL BE FOUR YEARS OLD TOMORROW.
HER GRANDMOTHER WAITS FOR HER IN NEW YORK, BUT, PATRICIA WON'T BE ABLE TO ATTEND HER BIRTHDAY PARTY — HER MOTHER IS DYING IN THE BURNING FIELD BEHIND HER.
AFTER THE FUNERAL, PATRICIA WILL LIVE WITH HER GRAND-MOTHER AND SPEND THE NEXT TEN YEARS IN PSYCHOTHERAPY. AT FOURTEEN, PATRICIA WILL CHECK INTO A DRUG REHAB FOR ADDICTION TO PAIN KILLERS. AT FIFTEEN, SHE WILL BE ARRESTED TWICE FOR PETTY THEFT AND SPEND NINETY DAYS IN A JUVENILE BOOT CAMP FOR POSSESSION OF CRACK COCAINE.
AT SIXTEEN, PATRICIA'S GRAND-MOTHER WILL DIE, LEAVING HER ONLY GRANDCHILD A MEAGER SAVINGS. PATRICIA WILL SPEND THE MONEY ON HEROIN CUT WITH DETERGENT. SHE'LL HITCH A RIDE TO THE AIRPORT AND LIE DOWN AT THE END OF THE RUNWAY, SINGING HAPPY BIRTHDAY TO HERSELF AS SHE SHOOTS UP AND WATCHES THE PLANES FALL ONE AFTER ANOTHER FROM THE TWILIGHT SKY.
PATRICIA WILL BE PRONOUNCED DEAD AT 6:32 PM, THE EXACT TIME OF SUNSET. A POPULAR BAND WILL WRITE A SONG ABOUT HER ENTITLED, "TWILIGHT'S CHILD". TIME MAGAZINE WILL WRITE A COVER ARTICLE AND, FOR A FEW DAYS, AMERICA WILL MOURN THE TRAGIC LIFE AND DEATH OF PATRICIA ...
THE LITTLE GIRL WHO TOOK TWELVE YEARS TO DIE ...

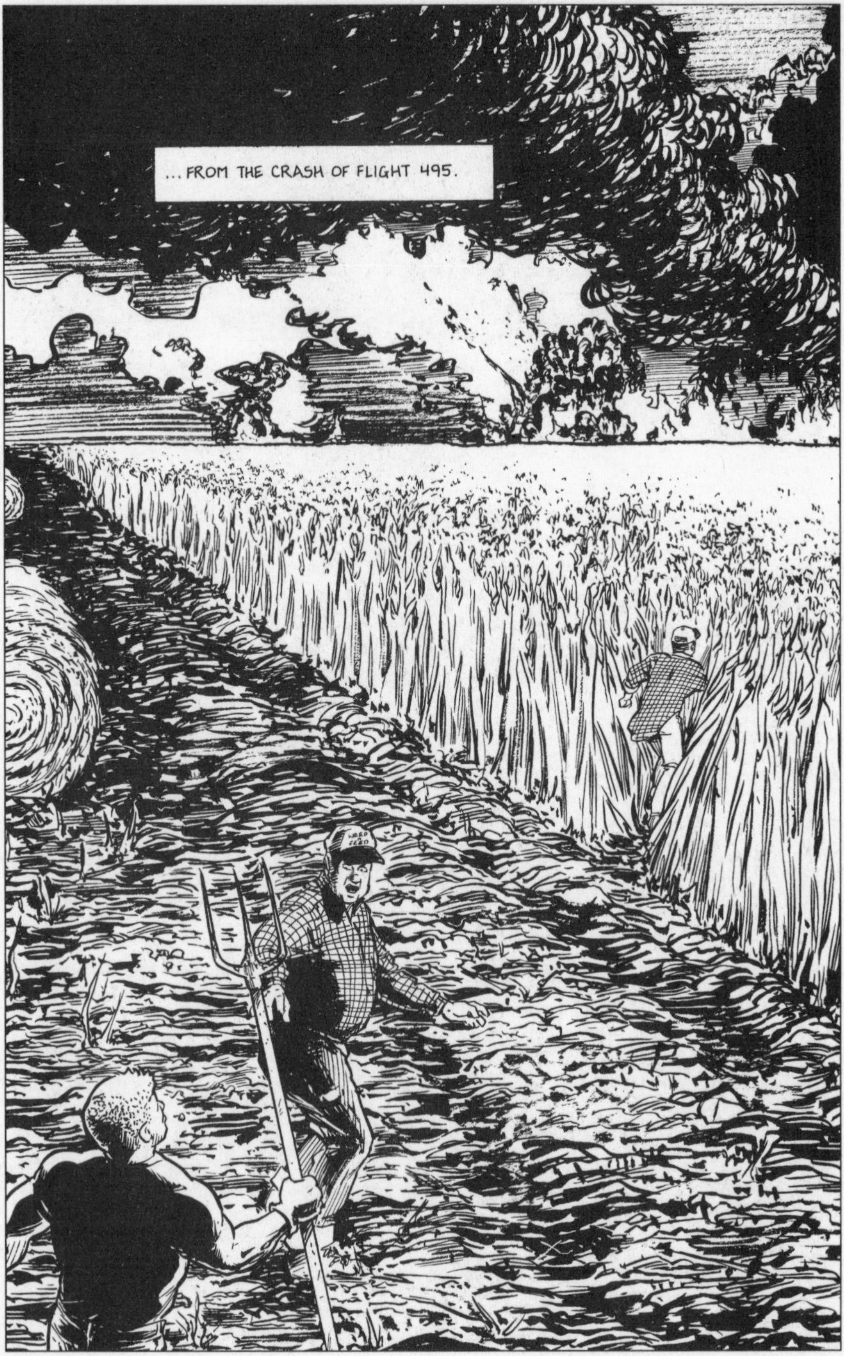
... FROM THE CRASH OF FLIGHT 495.

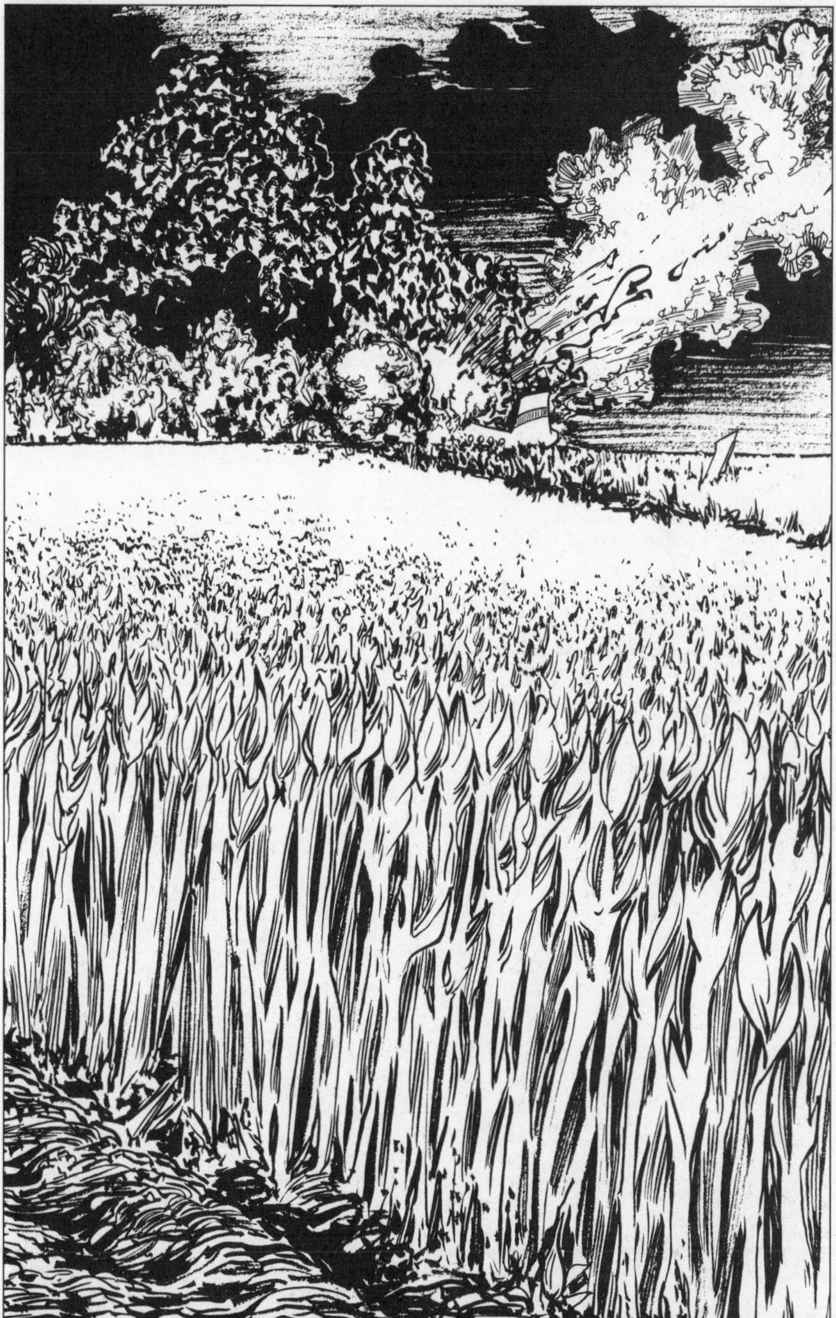

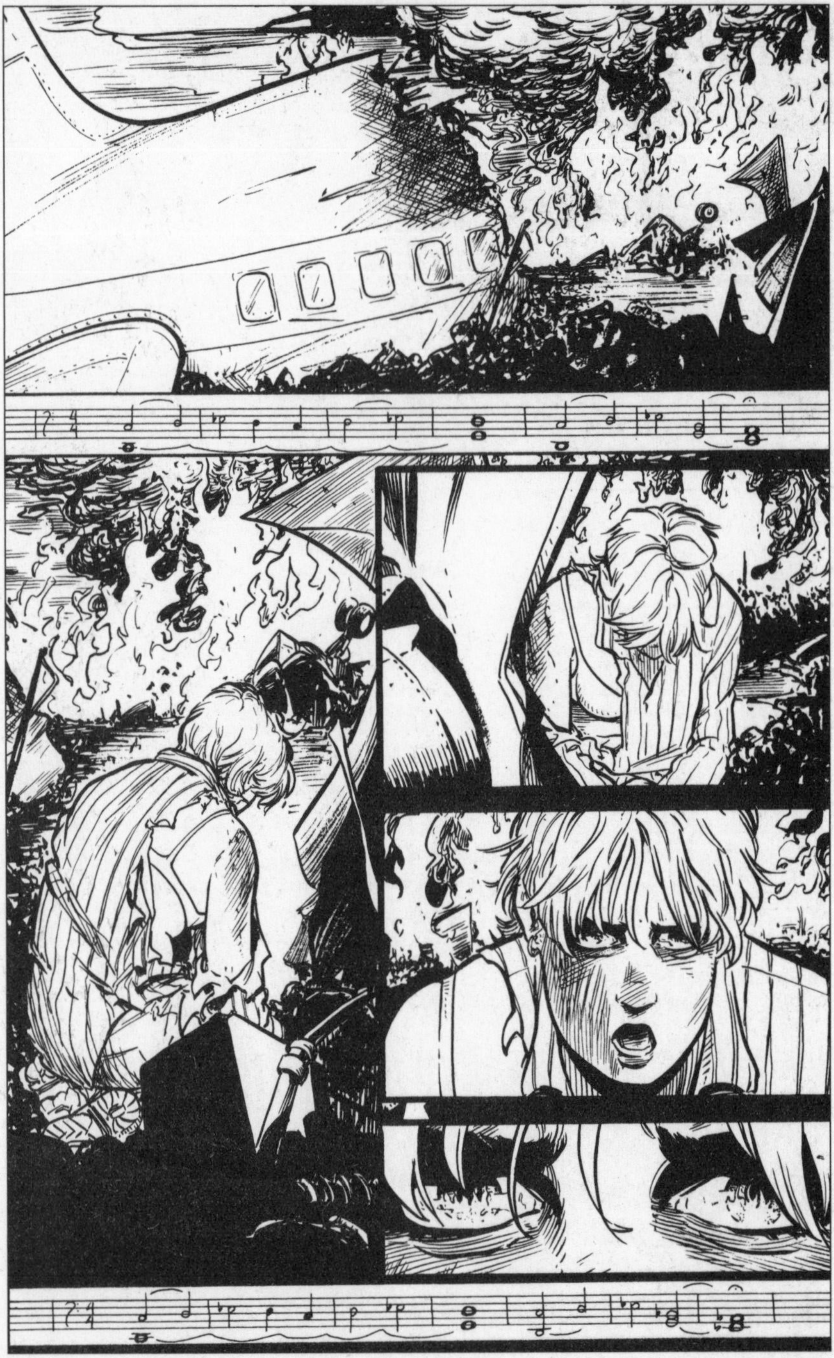

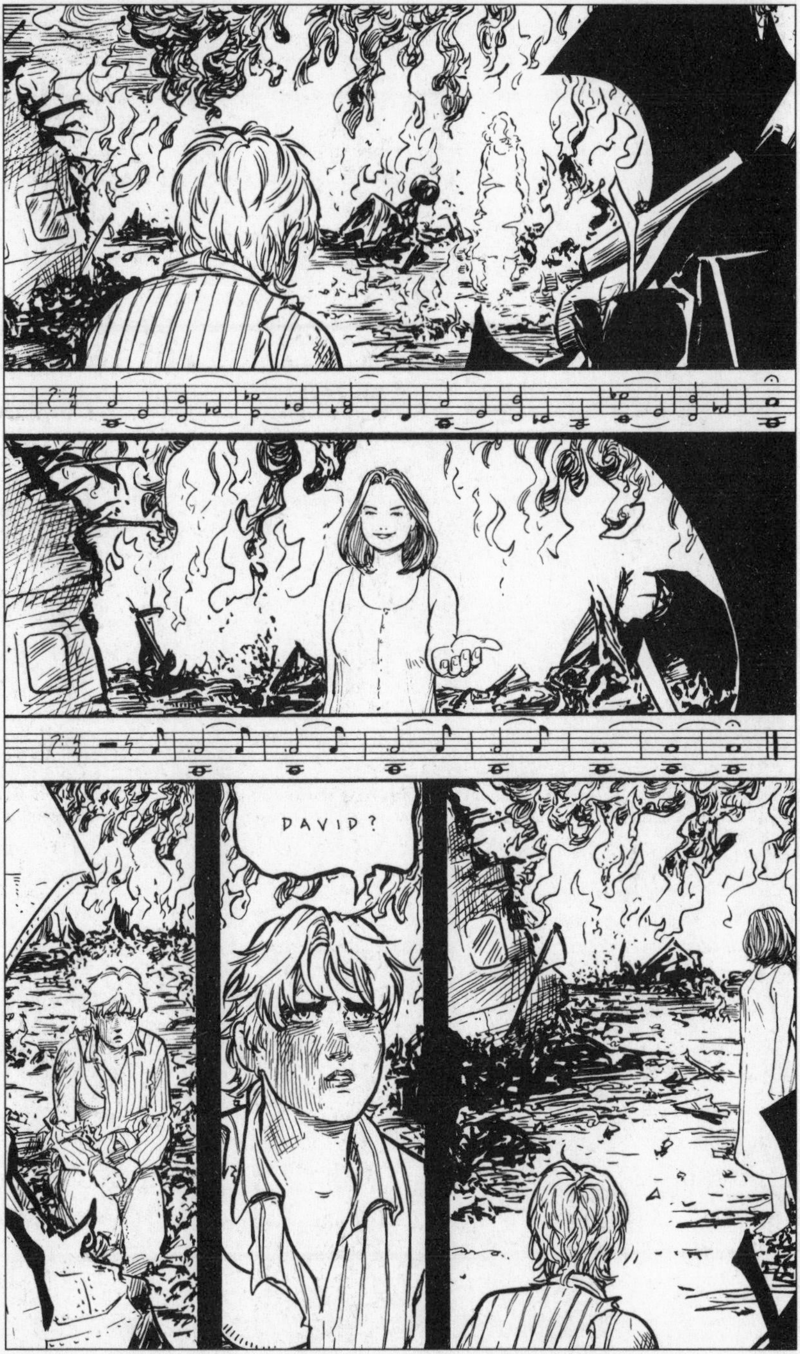
DAVID?

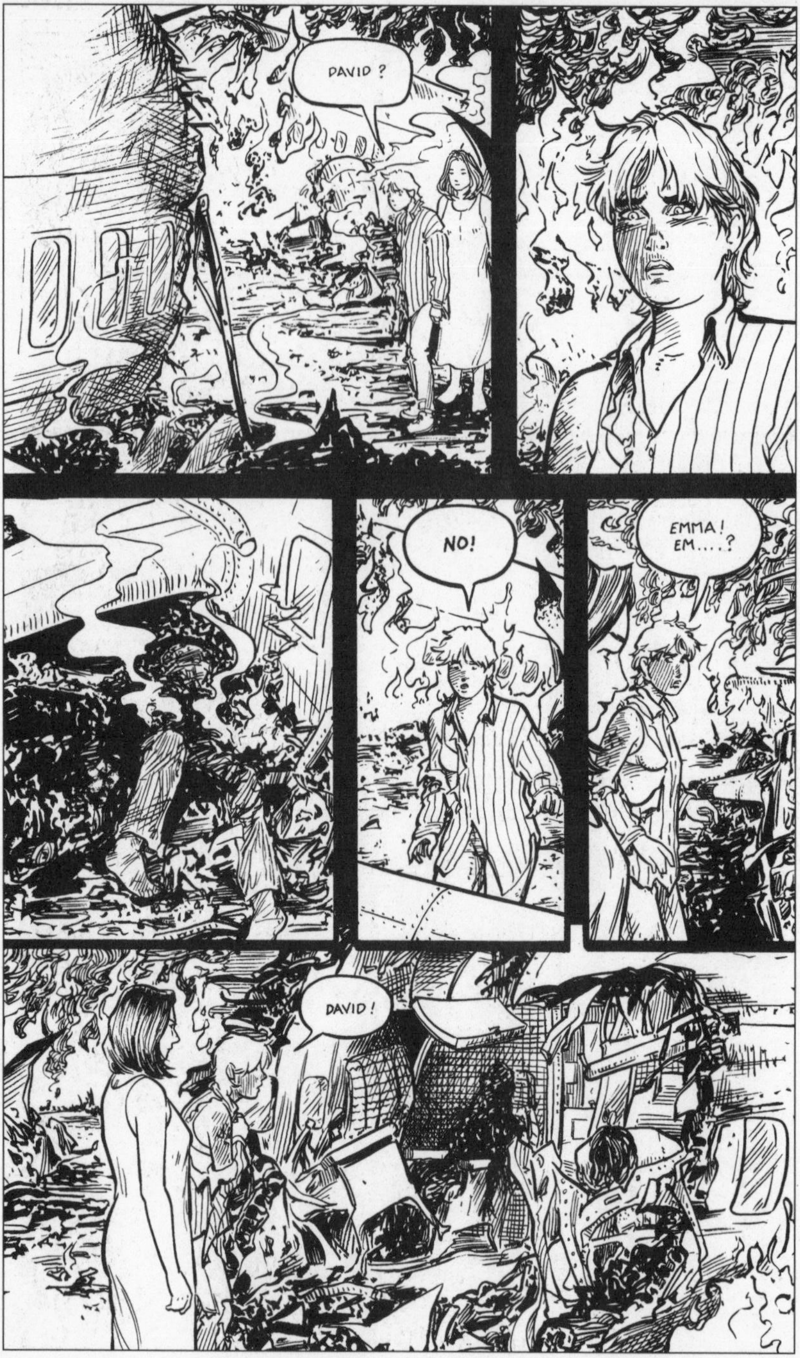
DAVID ?
NO!
EMMA! EM....?
DAVID!

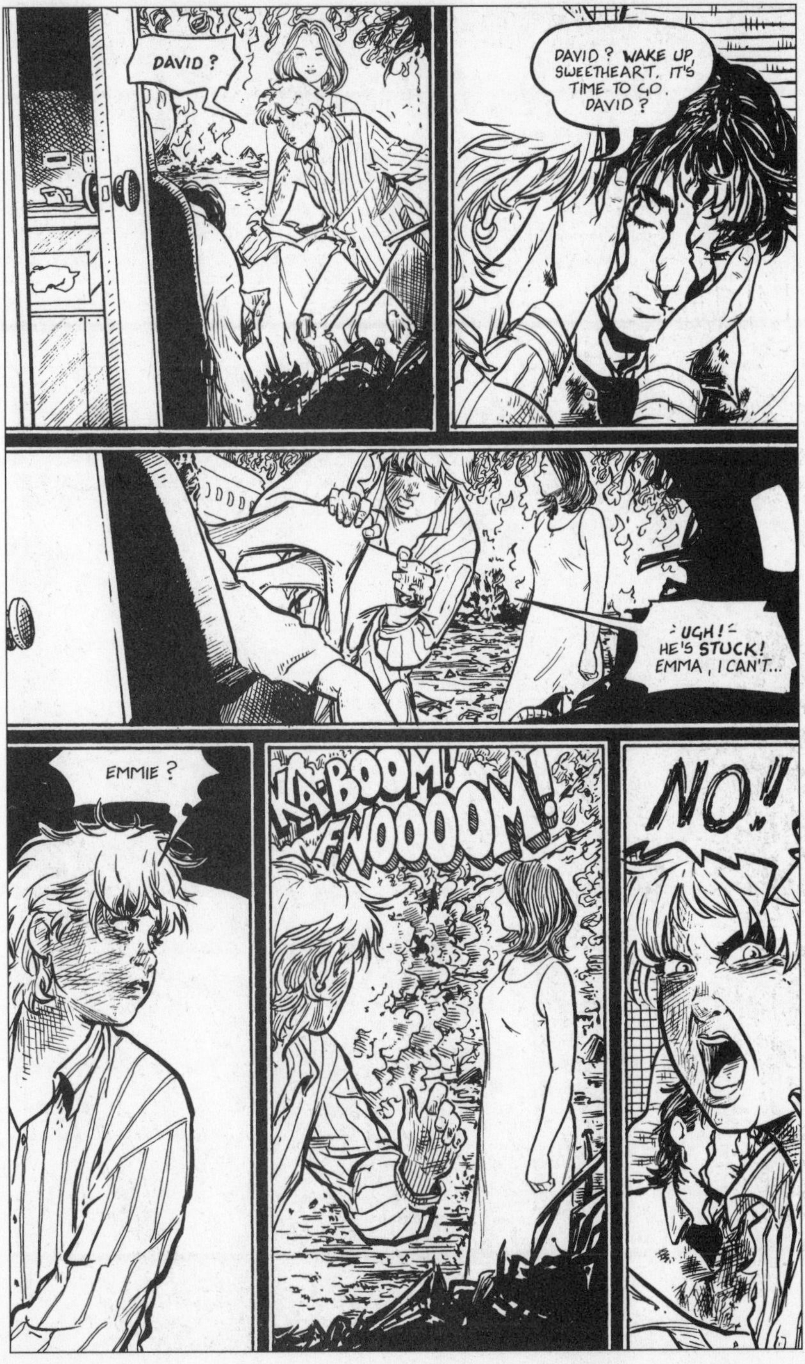

DAVID ?
DAVID ? WAKE UP, SWEETHEART. IT'S TIME TO GO. DAVID ?
UGH! HE'S STUCK! EMMA, I CAN'T...
EMMIE ?
KA-BOOM! FWOOOOM!
NO!!

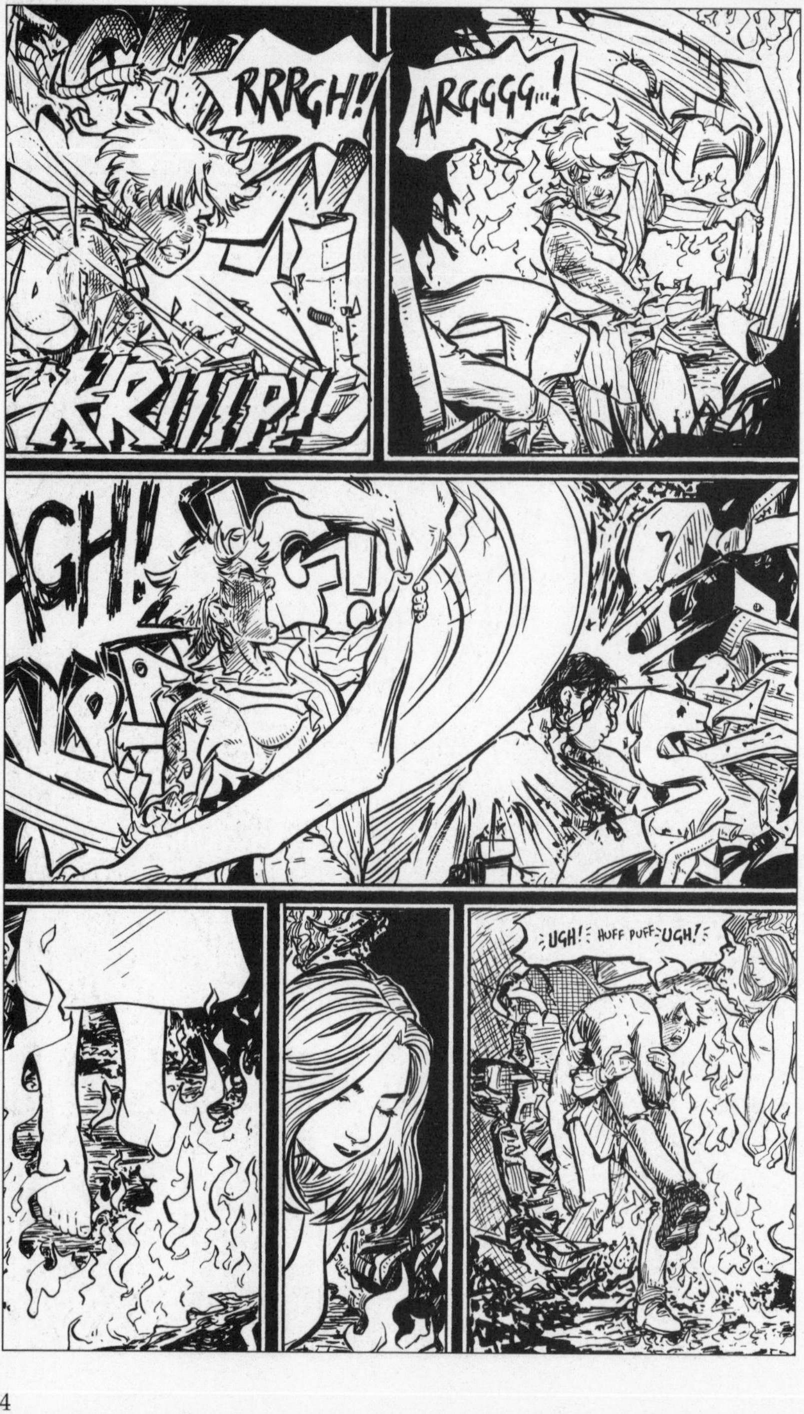
RRRGH!!
KRIIIIP!!
ARGGGG...!
UGH! HUFF PUFF UGH!

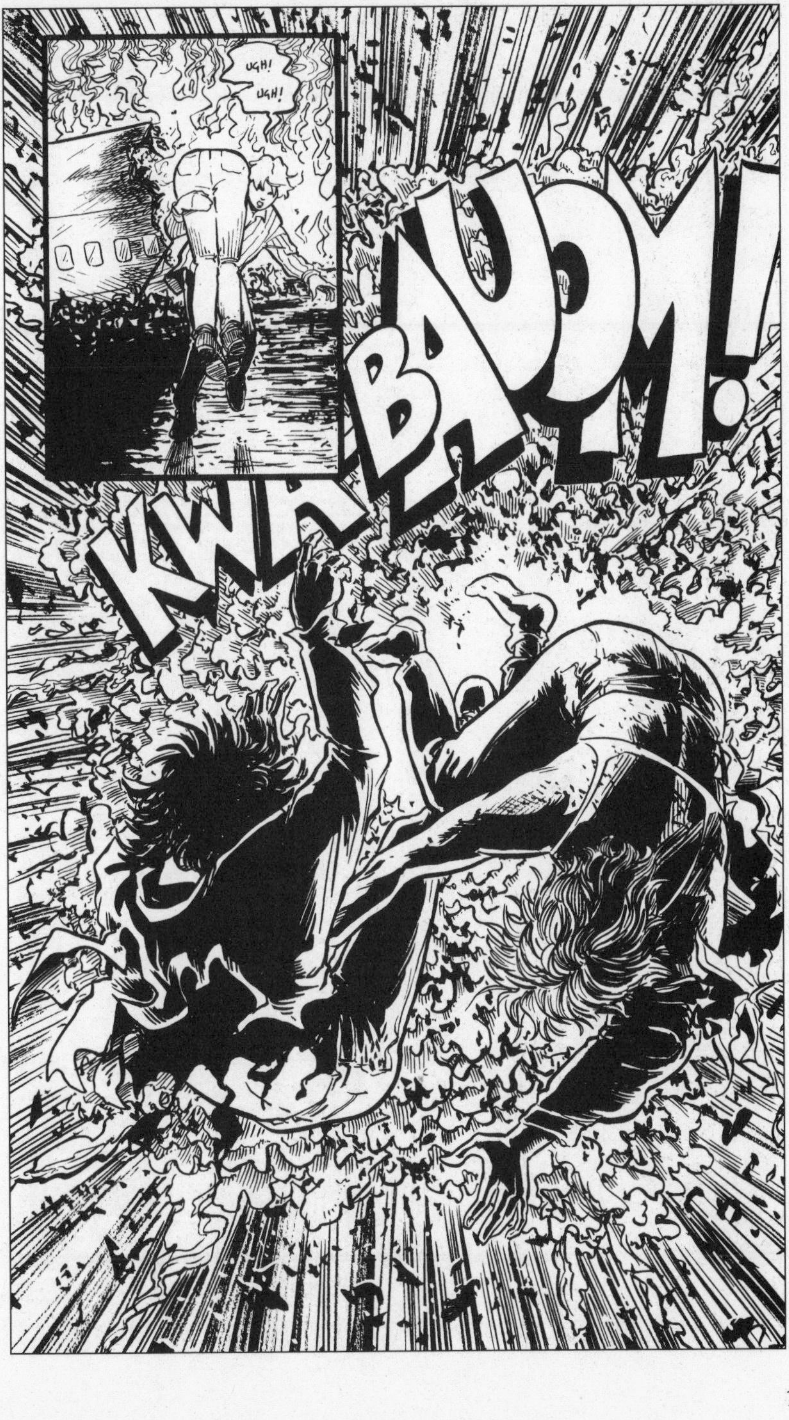
UGH!
UGH!
KWA-BAOOM!

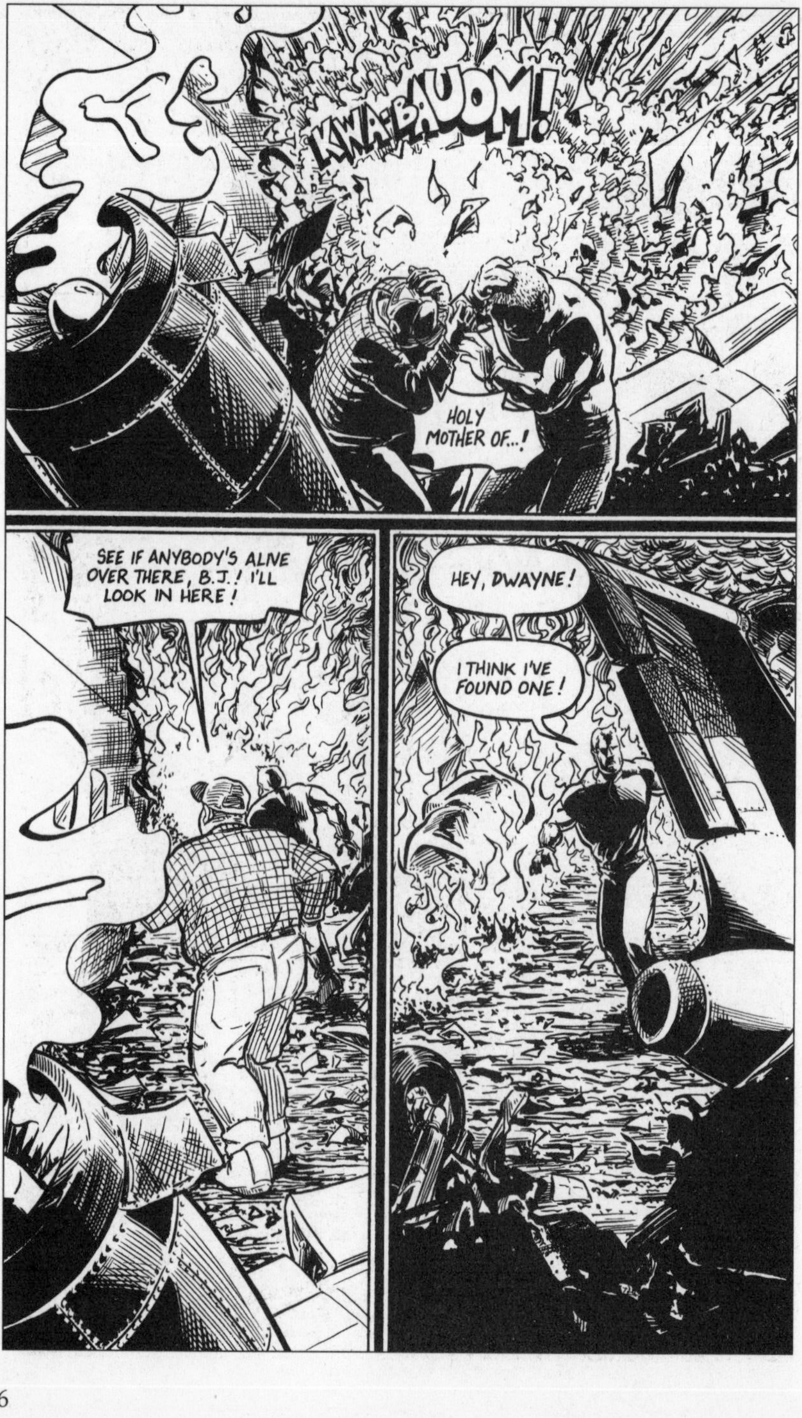
KWA-BAUOM!
HOLY MOTHER OF...!
SEE IF ANYBODY'S ALIVE OVER THERE, B.J.! I'LL LOOK IN HERE!
HEY, DWAYNE!
I THINK I'VE FOUND ONE!

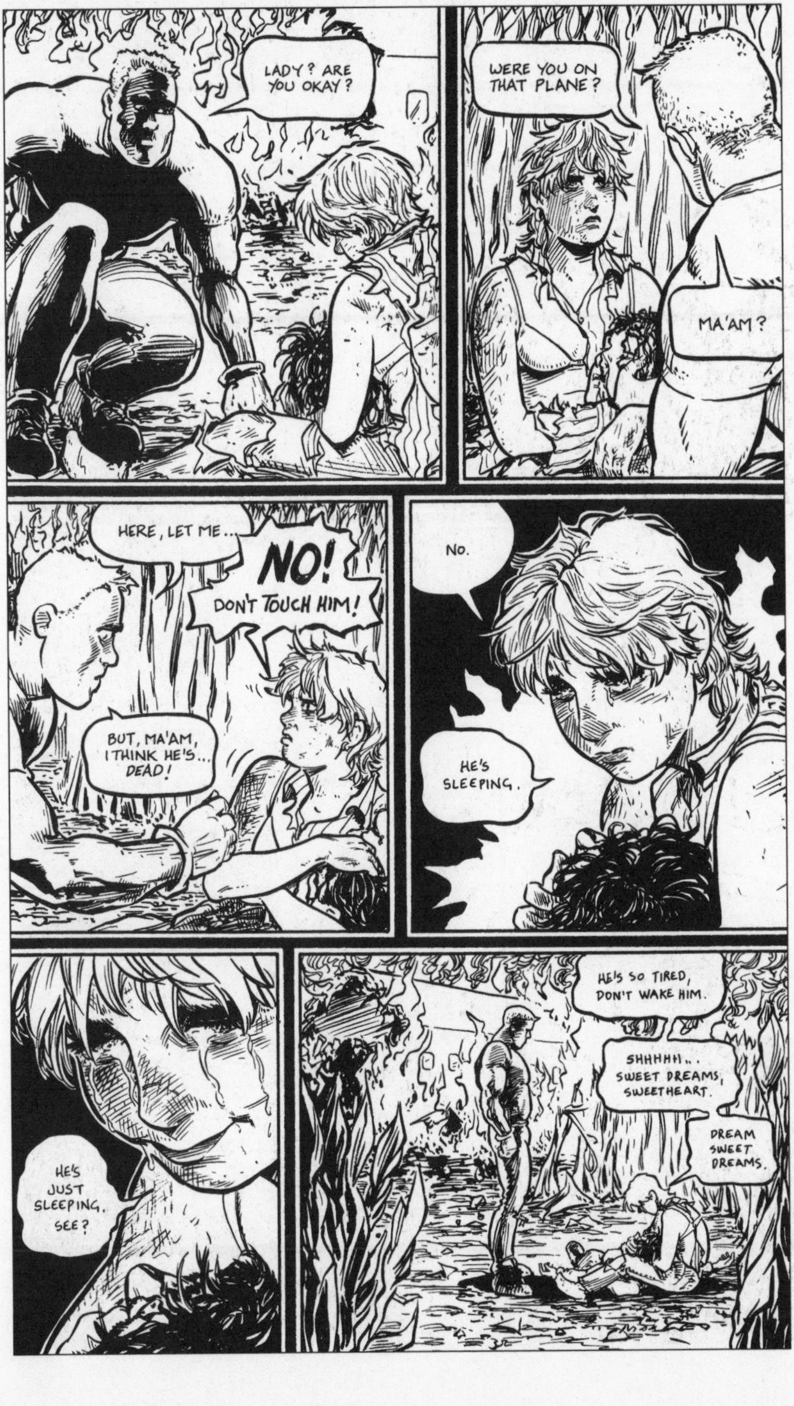
LADY? ARE YOU OKAY?
WERE YOU ON THAT PLANE?
MA'AM?
HERE, LET ME...
NO! DON'T TOUCH HIM!
BUT, MA'AM, I THINK HE'S... DEAD!
NO.
HE'S SLEEPING.
HE'S JUST SLEEPING. SEE?
HE'S SO TIRED, DON'T WAKE HIM.
SHHHHH.. SWEET DREAMS, SWEETHEART.
DREAM SWEET DREAMS.

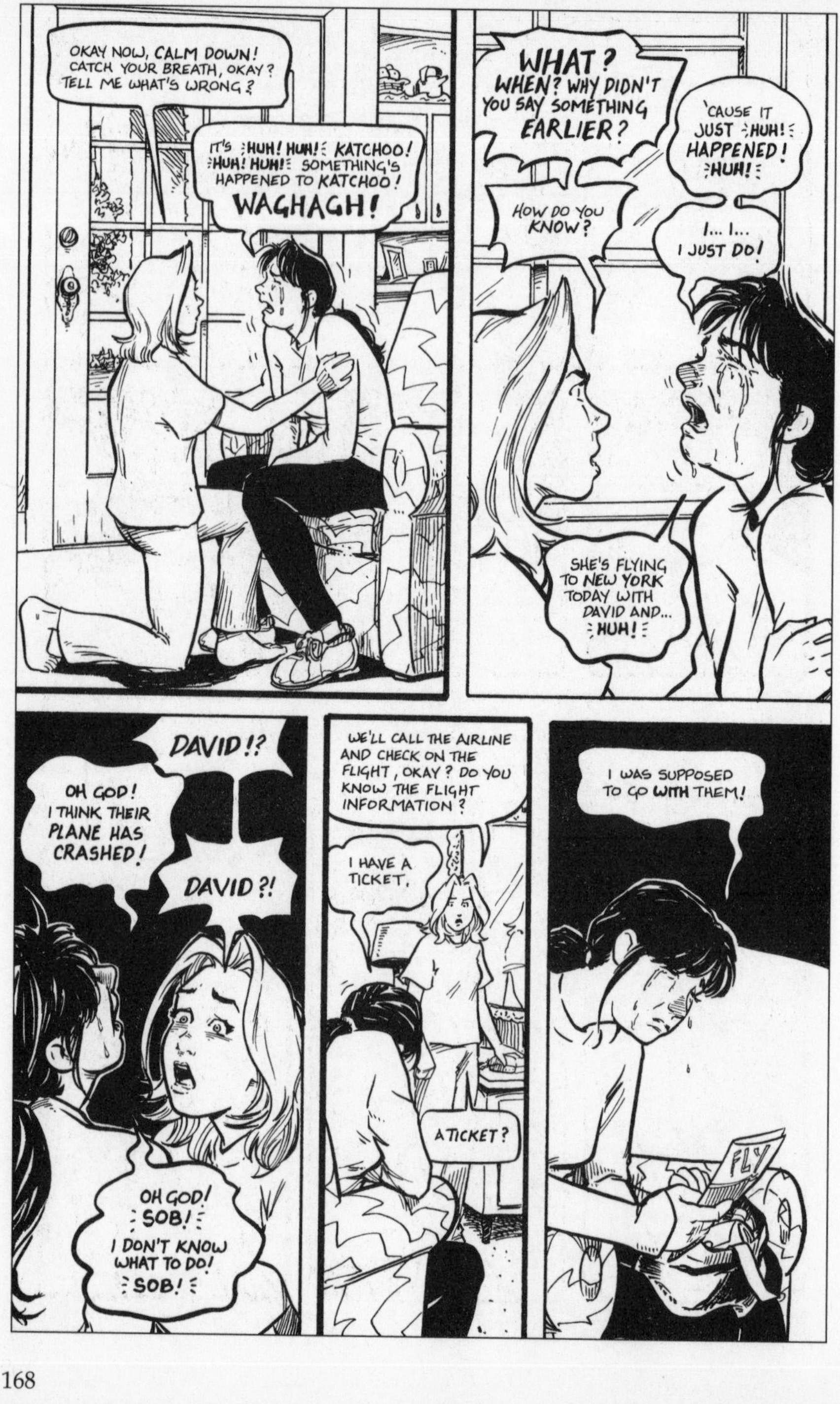
OKAY NOW, CALM DOWN! CATCH YOUR BREATH, OKAY? TELL ME WHAT'S WRONG?
IT'S HUH! HUH! KATCHOO! HUH! HUH! SOMETHING'S HAPPENED TO KATCHOO! WAGHAGH!
WHAT? WHEN? WHY DIDN'T YOU SAY SOMETHING EARLIER?
'CAUSE IT JUST HUH! HAPPENED! HUH!
HOW DO YOU KNOW?
I... I... I JUST DO!
SHE'S FLYING TO NEW YORK TODAY WITH DAVID AND... HUH!
DAVID!?
OH GOD! I THINK THEIR PLANE HAS CRASHED!
DAVID?!
OH GOD! SOB! I DON'T KNOW WHAT TO DO! SOB!
WE'LL CALL THE AIRLINE AND CHECK ON THE FLIGHT, OKAY? DO YOU KNOW THE FLIGHT INFORMATION?
I HAVE A TICKET.
A TICKET?
I WAS SUPPOSED TO GO WITH THEM!
FLY

WHY DIDN'T YOU?

BECAUSE :HUH!: I DON'T KEEP MY PROMISES!

OH, YES. HI. I WANT TO CHECK ON A FLIGHT FROM HOUSTON INTERCONTINENTAL TO NEW YORK.... OH NO, I MEAN ONE THAT'S FLYING TODAY, RIGHT NOW.

FLIGHT NUMBER 495.

FLIGHT 495.

OH GOD!

OKAY... OKAY... DO YOU HAVE ANY MORE INFORMATION THAN THAT? OKAY.... WHERE?

NO!

PUBLIC RELATIONS OFFICE, TERMINAL G, 2ND FLOOR, BETWEEN GATES 20 AND 21. OKAY, THANK YOU.

WHAT ARE THEY SAYING?

THE PLANE EXPERIENCED TROUBLE AND WAS FORCED TO ATTEMPT AN EMERGENCY LANDING NEAR NASHVILLE. THEY'RE ASKING FAMILY MEMBERS TO COME TO THE AIRPORT FOR MORE INFORMATION!

OH GOD! WHY DID I LET HER GO?!

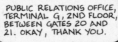

169

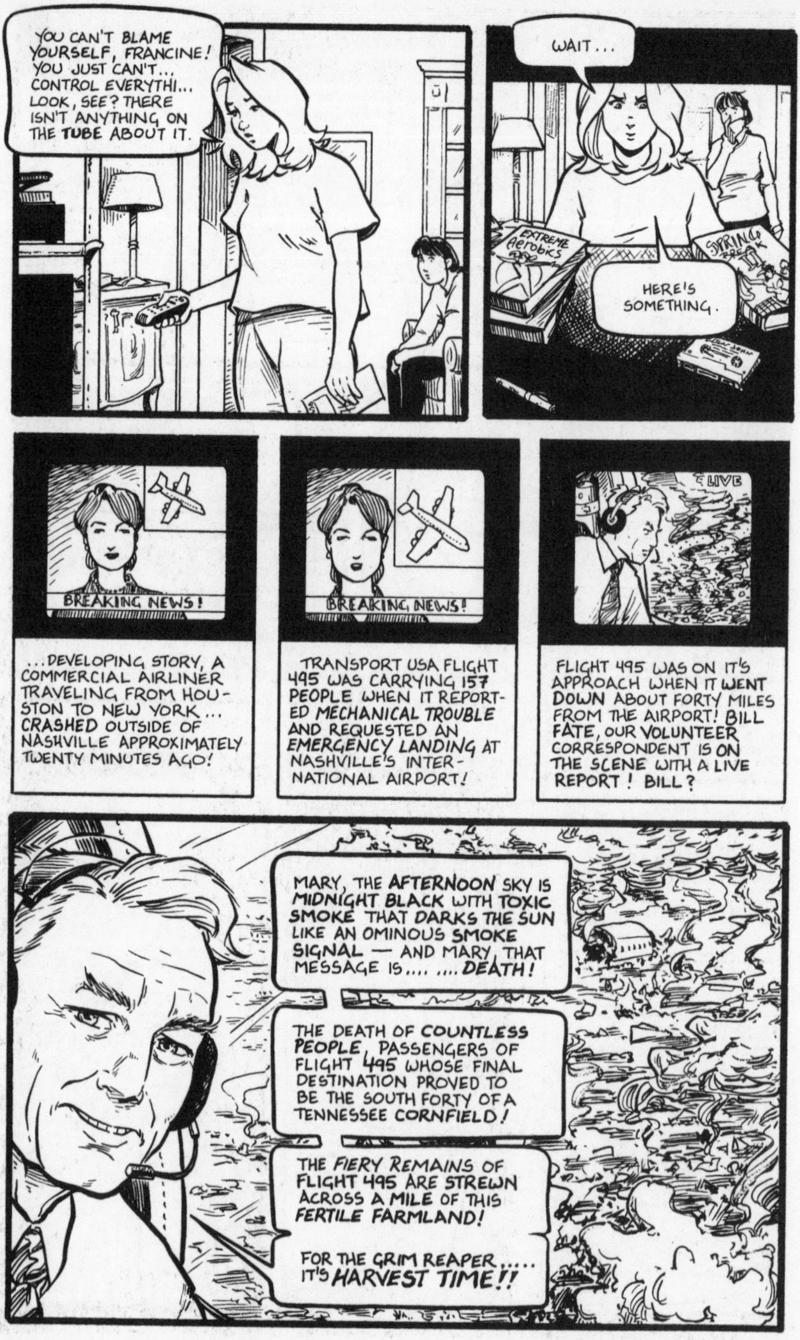

YOU CAN'T BLAME YOURSELF, FRANCINE! YOU JUST CAN'T... CONTROL EVERYTHI... LOOK, SEE? THERE ISN'T ANYTHING ON THE TUBE ABOUT IT.
WAIT...
EXTREME Aerobics
SPRING BREAK II
HERE'S SOMETHING.
BREAKING NEWS!
...DEVELOPING STORY, A COMMERCIAL AIRLINER TRAVELING FROM HOUSTON TO NEW YORK... CRASHED OUTSIDE OF NASHVILLE APPROXIMATELY TWENTY MINUTES AGO!
BREAKING NEWS!
TRANSPORT USA FLIGHT 495 WAS CARRYING 157 PEOPLE WHEN IT REPORTED MECHANICAL TROUBLE AND REQUESTED AN EMERGENCY LANDING AT NASHVILLE'S INTERNATIONAL AIRPORT!
LIVE
FLIGHT 495 WAS ON IT'S APPROACH WHEN IT WENT DOWN ABOUT FORTY MILES FROM THE AIRPORT! BILL FATE, OUR VOLUNTEER CORRESPONDENT IS ON THE SCENE WITH A LIVE REPORT! BILL?
MARY, THE AFTERNOON SKY IS MIDNIGHT BLACK WITH TOXIC SMOKE THAT DARKS THE SUN LIKE AN OMINOUS SMOKE SIGNAL — AND MARY, THAT MESSAGE IS.... ....DEATH!
THE DEATH OF COUNTLESS PEOPLE, PASSENGERS OF FLIGHT 495 WHOSE FINAL DESTINATION PROVED TO BE THE SOUTH FORTY OF A TENNESSEE CORNFIELD!
THE FIERY REMAINS OF FLIGHT 495 ARE STREWN ACROSS A MILE OF THIS FERTILE FARMLAND!
FOR THE GRIM REAPER..... IT'S HARVEST TIME!!

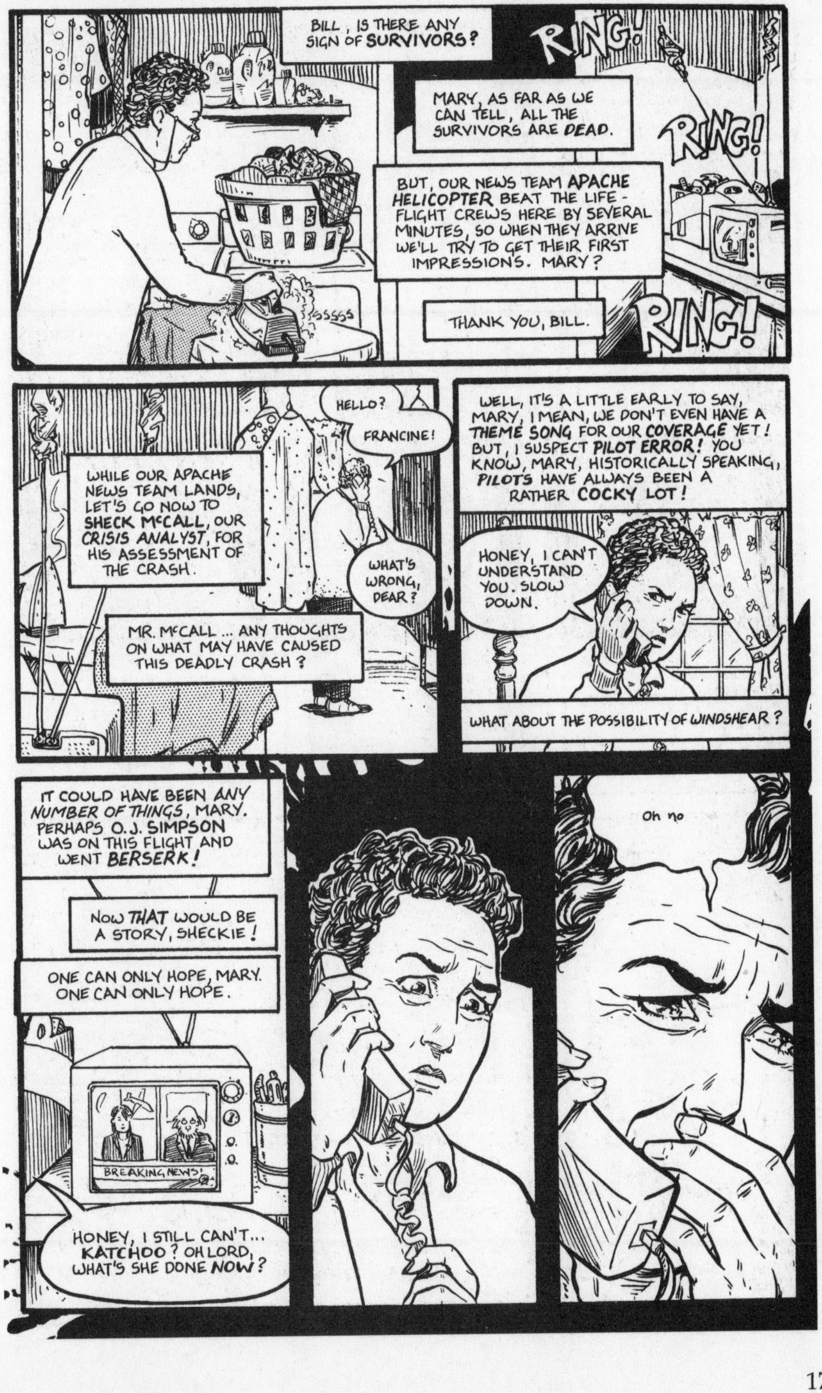
BILL, IS THERE ANY SIGN OF SURVIVORS?
RING!
MARY, AS FAR AS WE CAN TELL, ALL THE SURVIVORS ARE DEAD.
RING!
BUT, OUR NEWS TEAM APACHE HELICOPTER BEAT THE LIFE-FLIGHT CREWS HERE BY SEVERAL MINUTES, SO WHEN THEY ARRIVE WE'LL TRY TO GET THEIR FIRST IMPRESSIONS. MARY?
SSSSS
THANK YOU, BILL.
RING!
HELLO?
FRANCINE!
WHILE OUR APACHE NEWS TEAM LANDS, LET'S GO NOW TO SHECK McCALL, OUR CRISIS ANALYST, FOR HIS ASSESSMENT OF THE CRASH.
WHAT'S WRONG, DEAR?
MR. McCALL ... ANY THOUGHTS ON WHAT MAY HAVE CAUSED THIS DEADLY CRASH?
WELL, IT'S A LITTLE EARLY TO SAY, MARY, I MEAN, WE DON'T EVEN HAVE A THEME SONG FOR OUR COVERAGE YET! BUT, I SUSPECT PILOT ERROR! YOU KNOW, MARY, HISTORICALLY SPEAKING, PILOTS HAVE ALWAYS BEEN A RATHER COCKY LOT!
HONEY, I CAN'T UNDERSTAND YOU. SLOW DOWN.
WHAT ABOUT THE POSSIBILITY OF WINDSHEAR?
IT COULD HAVE BEEN ANY NUMBER OF THINGS, MARY. PERHAPS O.J. SIMPSON WAS ON THIS FLIGHT AND WENT BERSERK!
NOW THAT WOULD BE A STORY, SHECKIE!
ONE CAN ONLY HOPE, MARY. ONE CAN ONLY HOPE.
BREAKING NEWS!
HONEY, I STILL CAN'T... KATCHOO? OH LORD, WHAT'S SHE DONE NOW?
Oh no

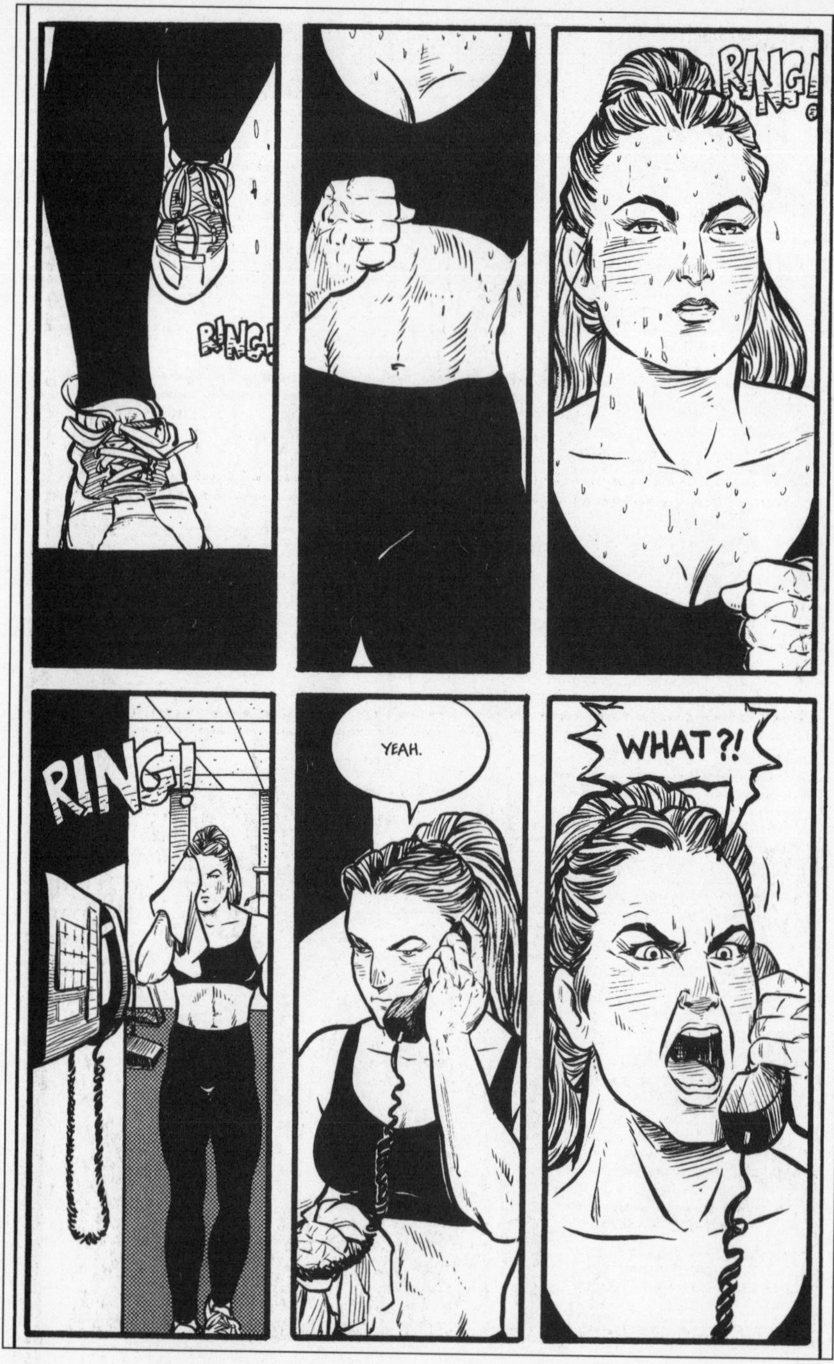
RING!
RING!
RING!
YEAH.
WHAT?!

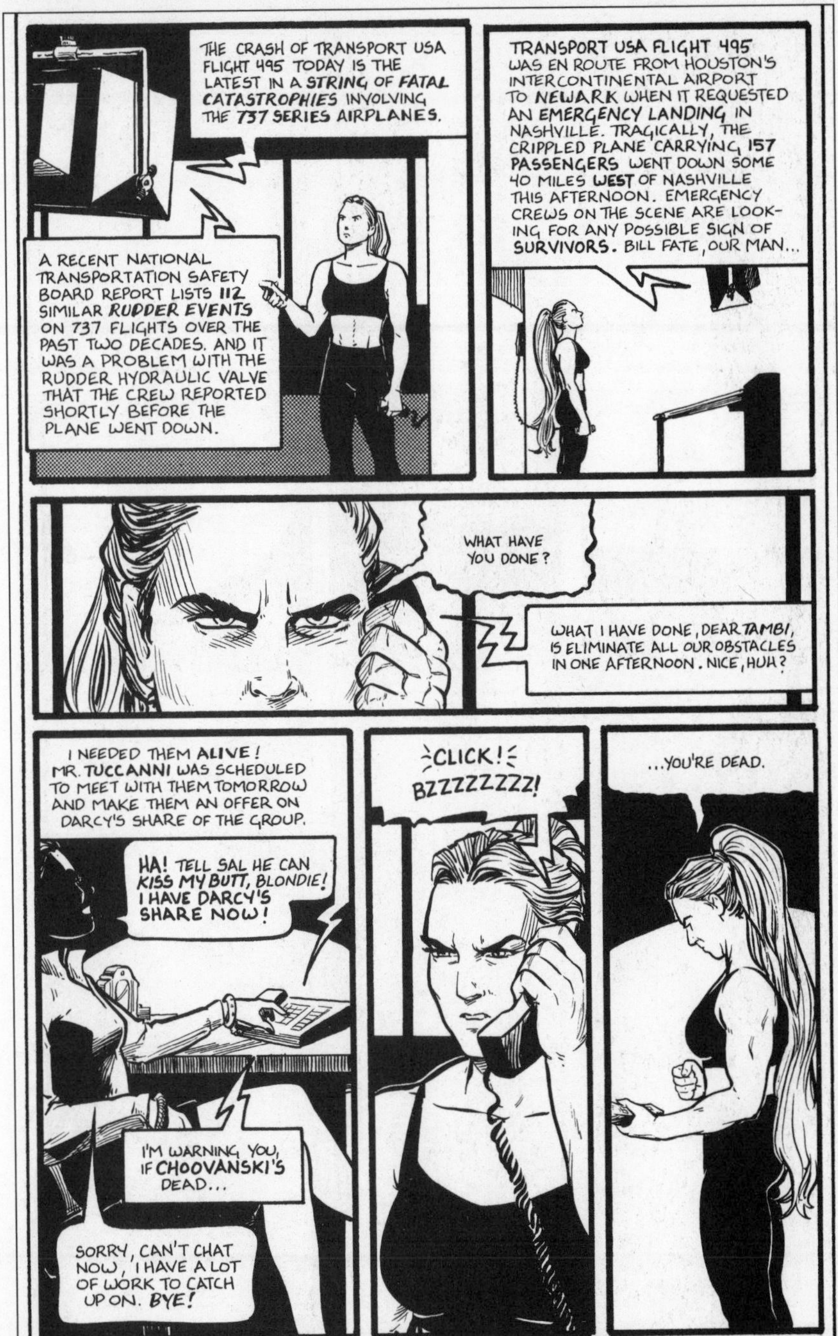
THE CRASH OF TRANSPORT USA FLIGHT 495 TODAY IS THE LATEST IN A STRING OF FATAL CATASTROPHIES INVOLVING THE 737 SERIES AIRPLANES.
A RECENT NATIONAL TRANSPORTATION SAFETY BOARD REPORT LISTS 112 SIMILAR RUDDER EVENTS ON 737 FLIGHTS OVER THE PAST TWO DECADES. AND IT WAS A PROBLEM WITH THE RUDDER HYDRAULIC VALVE THAT THE CREW REPORTED SHORTLY BEFORE THE PLANE WENT DOWN.
TRANSPORT USA FLIGHT 495 WAS EN ROUTE FROM HOUSTON'S INTERCONTINENTAL AIRPORT TO NEWARK WHEN IT REQUESTED AN EMERGENCY LANDING IN NASHVILLE. TRAGICALLY, THE CRIPPLED PLANE CARRYING 157 PASSENGERS WENT DOWN SOME 40 MILES WEST OF NASHVILLE THIS AFTERNOON. EMERGENCY CREWS ON THE SCENE ARE LOOKING FOR ANY POSSIBLE SIGN OF SURVIVORS. BILL FATE, OUR MAN...
WHAT HAVE YOU DONE?
WHAT I HAVE DONE, DEAR TAMBI, IS ELIMINATE ALL OUR OBSTACLES IN ONE AFTERNOON. NICE, HUH?
I NEEDED THEM ALIVE! MR. TUCCANNI WAS SCHEDULED TO MEET WITH THEM TOMORROW AND MAKE THEM AN OFFER ON DARCY'S SHARE OF THE GROUP.
HA! TELL SAL HE CAN KISS MY BUTT, BLONDIE! I HAVE DARCY'S SHARE NOW!
I'M WARNING YOU, IF CHOOVANSKI'S DEAD...
SORRY, CAN'T CHAT NOW, I HAVE A LOT OF WORK TO CATCH UP ON. BYE!
CLICK!
BZZZZZZZZ!
...YOU'RE DEAD.

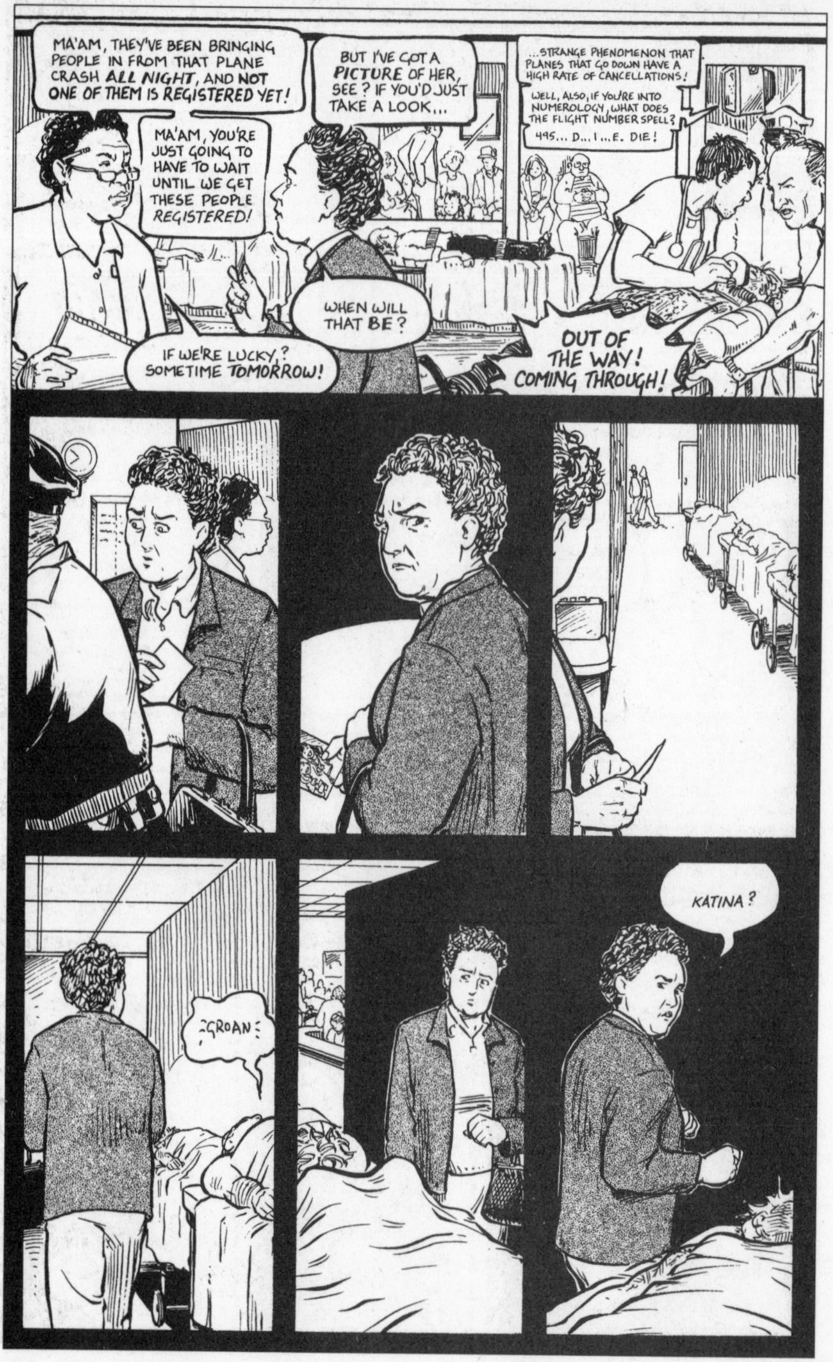

MA'AM, THEY'VE BEEN BRINGING PEOPLE IN FROM THAT PLANE CRASH ALL NIGHT, AND NOT ONE OF THEM IS REGISTERED YET!
MA'AM, YOU'RE JUST GOING TO HAVE TO WAIT UNTIL WE GET THESE PEOPLE REGISTERED!
BUT I'VE GOT A PICTURE OF HER, SEE? IF YOU'D JUST TAKE A LOOK...
WHEN WILL THAT BE?
IF WE'RE LUCKY? SOMETIME TOMORROW!
...STRANGE PHENOMENON THAT PLANES THAT GO DOWN HAVE A HIGH RATE OF CANCELLATIONS!
WELL, ALSO, IF YOU'RE INTO NUMEROLOGY, WHAT DOES THE FLIGHT NUMBER SPELL?
495... D... I... E. DIE!
OUT OF THE WAY! COMING THROUGH!
GROAN
KATINA?

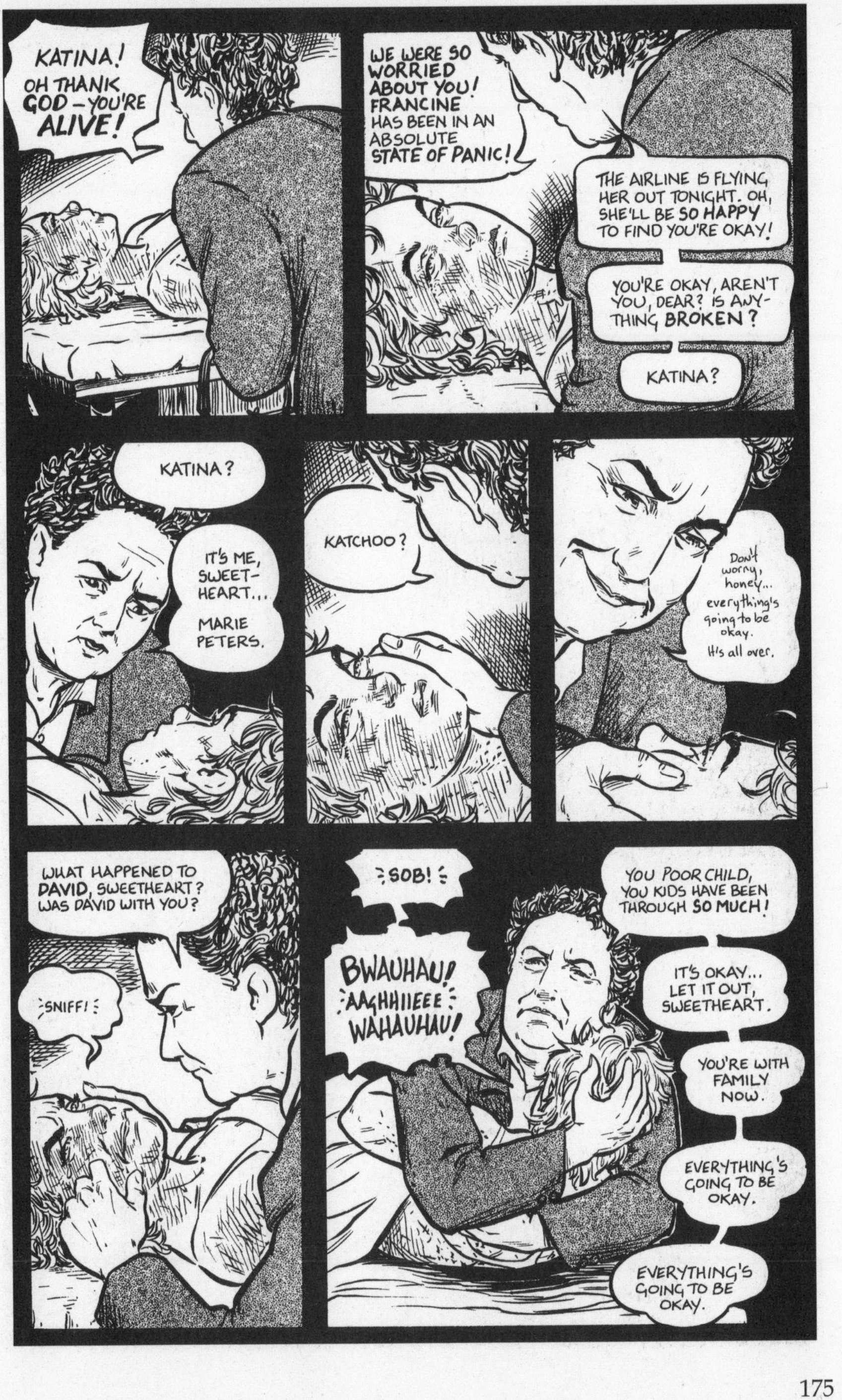
KATINA! OH THANK GOD—YOU'RE ALIVE!
WE WERE SO WORRIED ABOUT YOU! FRANCINE HAS BEEN IN AN ABSOLUTE STATE OF PANIC!
THE AIRLINE IS FLYING HER OUT TONIGHT. OH, SHE'LL BE SO HAPPY TO FIND YOU'RE OKAY!
YOU'RE OKAY, AREN'T YOU, DEAR? IS ANYTHING BROKEN?
KATINA?
KATINA?
IT'S ME, SWEETHEART... MARIE PETERS.
KATCHOO?
Don't worry, honey... everything's going to be okay. It's all over.
WHAT HAPPENED TO DAVID, SWEETHEART? WAS DAVID WITH YOU?
SNIFF!
SOB!
BWAUHAU! AAGHHIIEEE WAHAUHAU!
YOU POOR CHILD, YOU KIDS HAVE BEEN THROUGH SO MUCH!
IT'S OKAY... LET IT OUT, SWEETHEART.
YOU'RE WITH FAMILY NOW.
EVERYTHING'S GOING TO BE OKAY.
EVERYTHING'S GOING TO BE OKAY.

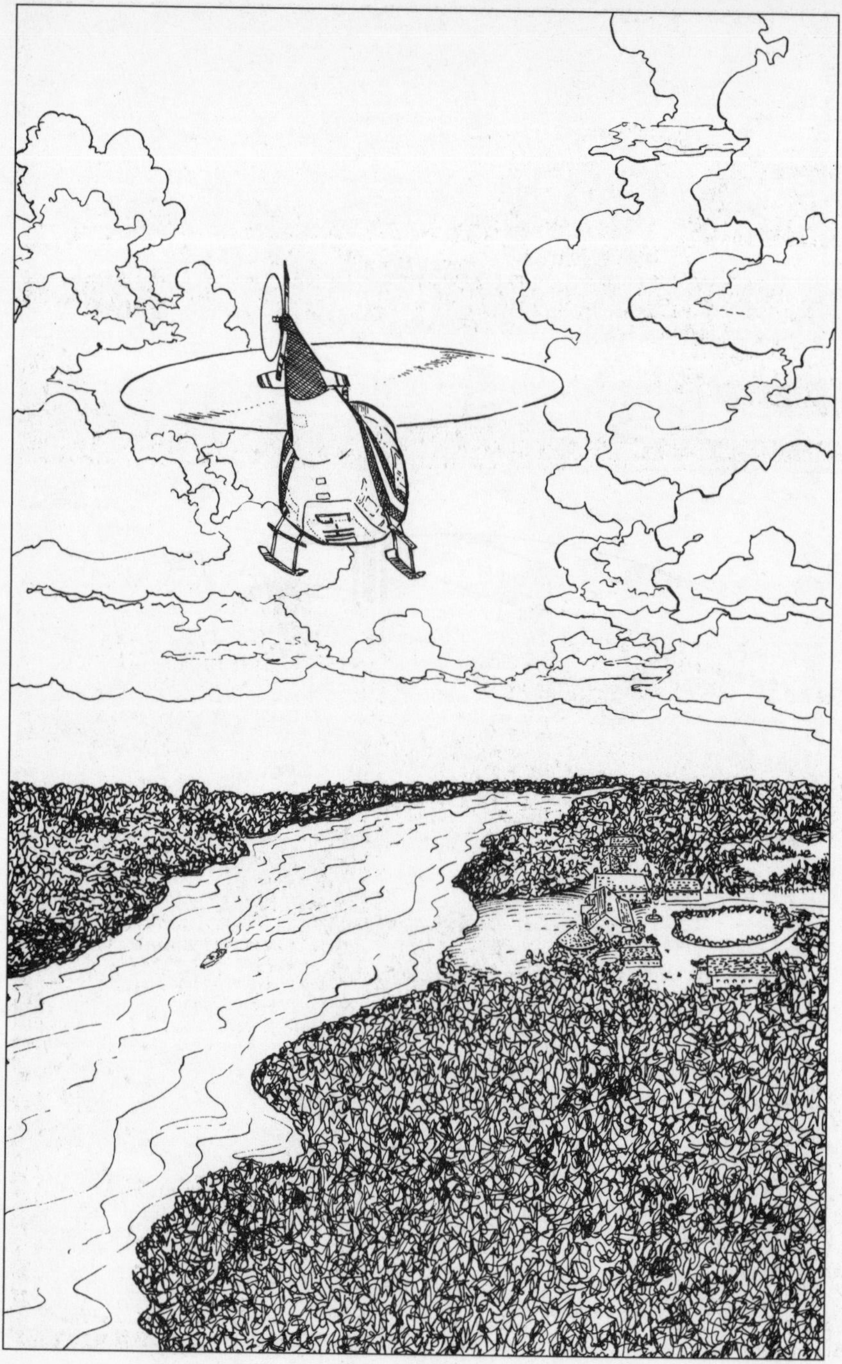

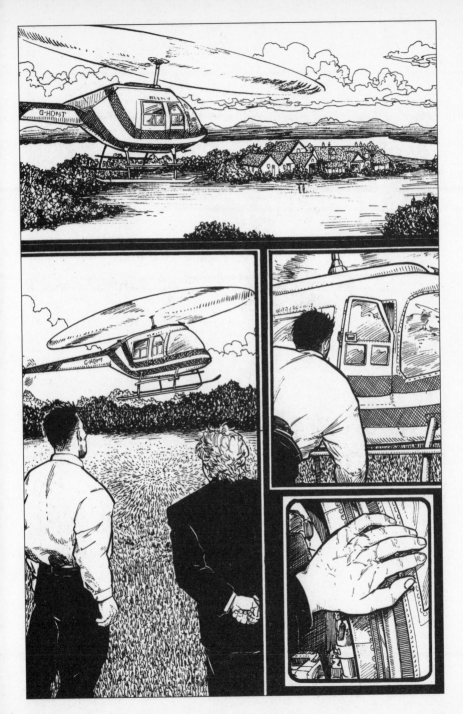

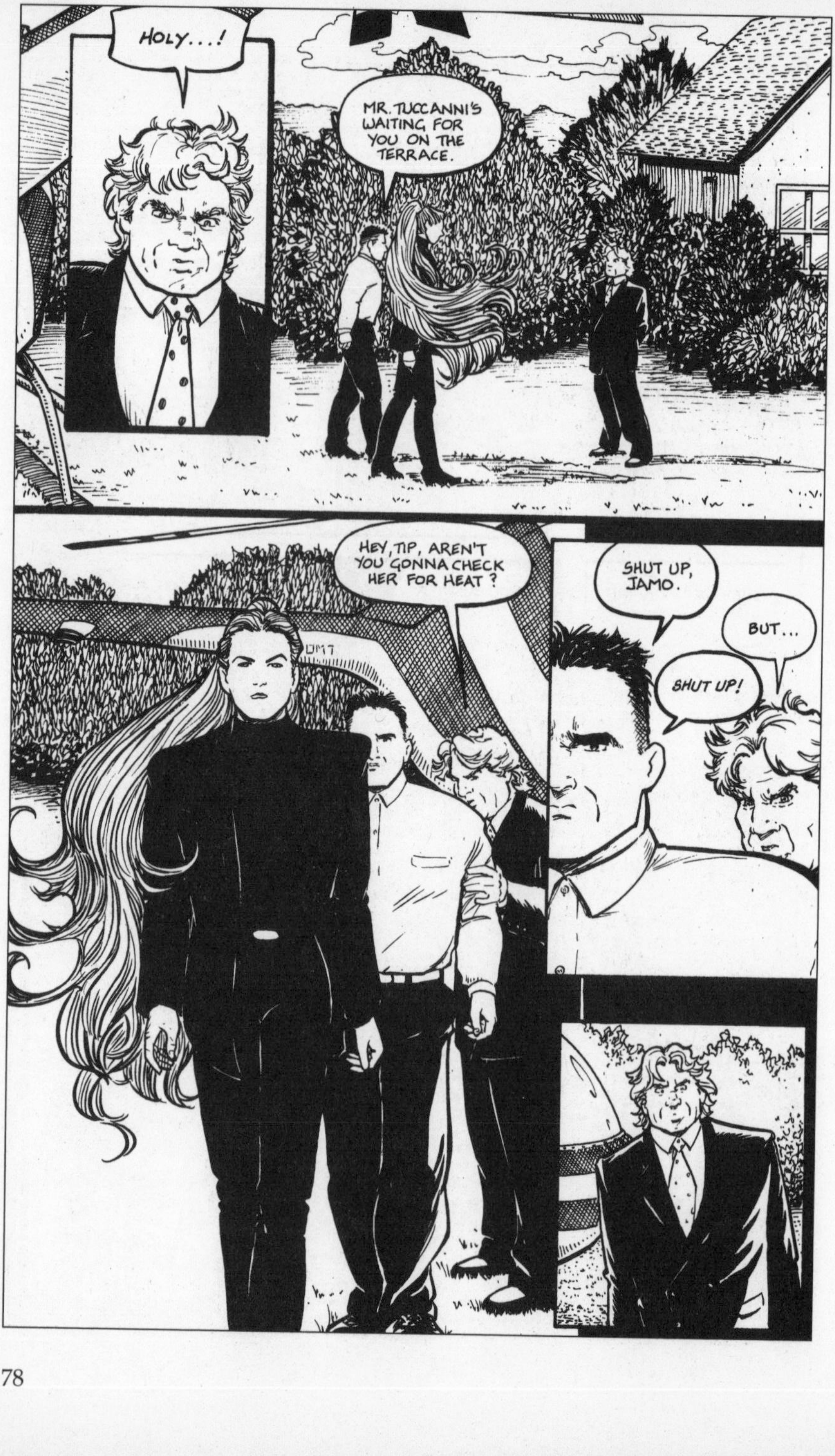
HOLY...!
MR. TUCCANNI'S WAITING FOR YOU ON THE TERRACE.
HEY, TIP, AREN'T YOU GONNA CHECK HER FOR HEAT?
SHUT UP, JAMO.
BUT...
SHUT UP!

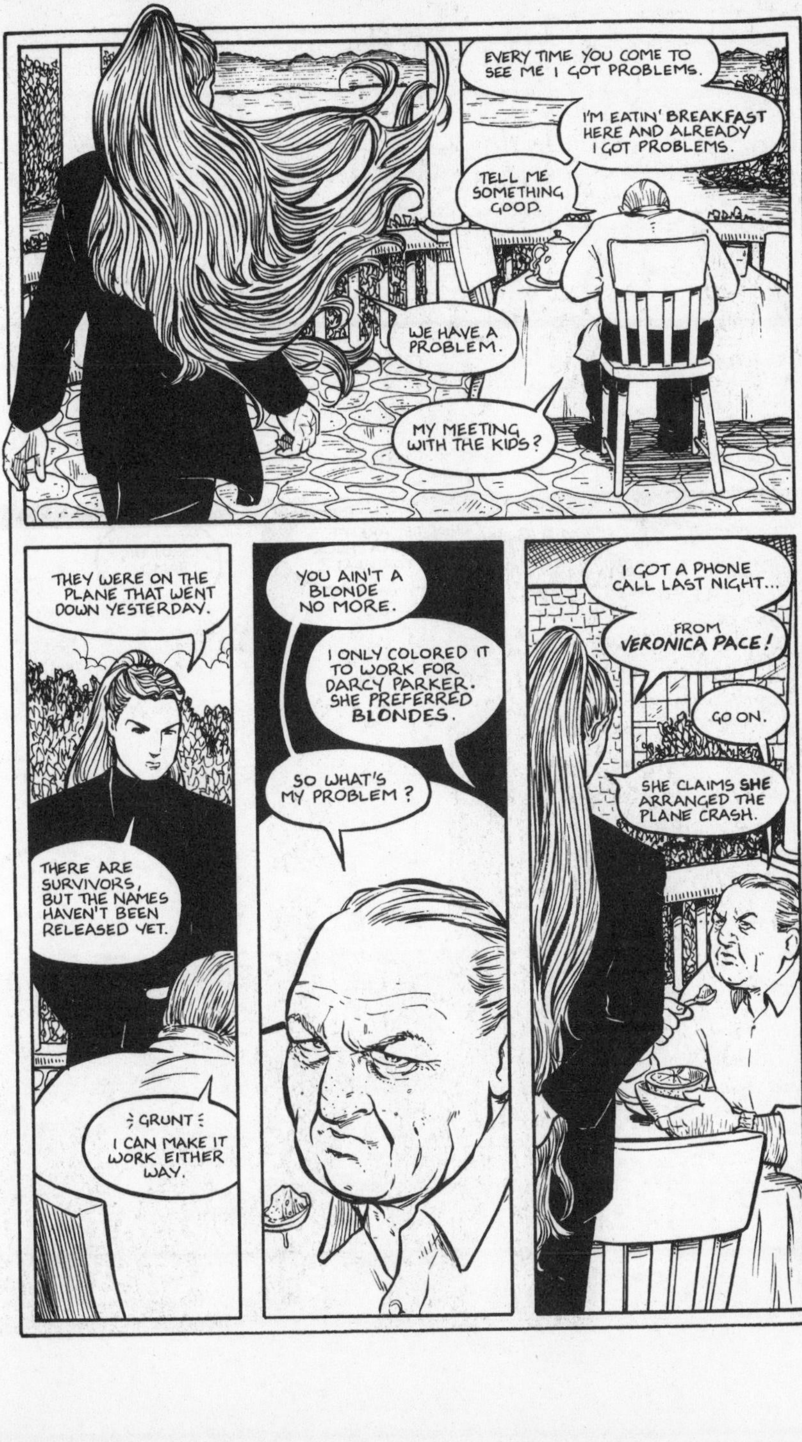
EVERY TIME YOU COME TO SEE ME I GOT PROBLEMS.
I'M EATIN' BREAKFAST HERE AND ALREADY I GOT PROBLEMS.
TELL ME SOMETHING GOOD.
WE HAVE A PROBLEM.
MY MEETING WITH THE KIDS?
THEY WERE ON THE PLANE THAT WENT DOWN YESTERDAY.
THERE ARE SURVIVORS, BUT THE NAMES HAVEN'T BEEN RELEASED YET.
GRUNT
I CAN MAKE IT WORK EITHER WAY.
YOU AIN'T A BLONDE NO MORE.
I ONLY COLORED IT TO WORK FOR DARCY PARKER. SHE PREFERRED BLONDES.
SO WHAT'S MY PROBLEM?
I GOT A PHONE CALL LAST NIGHT...
FROM VERONICA PACE!
GO ON.
SHE CLAIMS SHE ARRANGED THE PLANE CRASH.

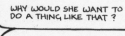

WHY WOULD SHE WANT TO DO A THING LIKE THAT?

SHE CONSIDERED DAVID QIN AND KATINA CHOOVANSKI TO BE HER KEY OBSTACLES... SHE WANTS TO REORGANIZE THE *PARKER GIRLS!*

-KLING!

CRASH!

I *TOLD* LOU NOT TO HELP THAT WOMAN WITH *HER LEGAL PROBLEMS!*

I DON'T GOT *ENOUGH* PROBLEMS RUNNIN' THE COMPANY, NOW I GOT SOME *JUNIOR PSYCHO* WANTS TO START THAT *PARKER CRAP* AGAIN?!

THE PARKER GIRLS DON'T EXIST NO MORE! PERIOD! I BURIED THAT FREAKIN' PSYCHO AND I'LL BURY HER FREAKIN' PROTEGEE, TOO!

I'LL BURY EVERY *FREAKIN'* ONE OF 'EM IF I HAVE TO!!

THAT PARKER WITCH ALMOST TOOK THE *ENTIRE COMPANY* DOWN WITH HER – NOW HER FLUNKY'S SCREWIN' WITH ME AND CAUSIN' A FEDERAL INVESTIGATION?!

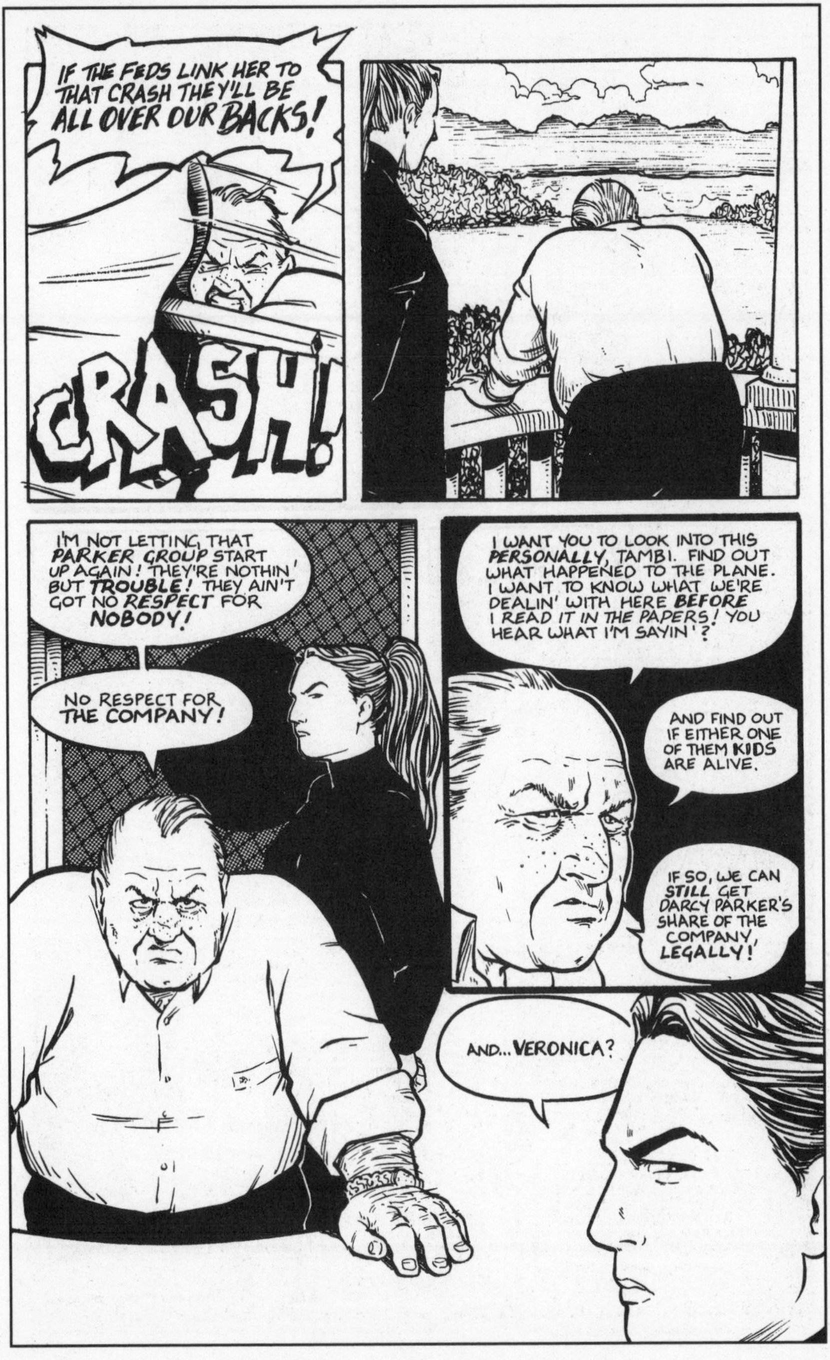
IF THE FEDS LINK HER TO THAT CRASH THEY'LL BE ALL OVER OUR BACKS!
CRASH!
I'M NOT LETTING THAT PARKER GROUP START UP AGAIN! THEY'RE NOTHIN' BUT TROUBLE! THEY AIN'T GOT NO RESPECT FOR NOBODY!
NO RESPECT FOR THE COMPANY!
I WANT YOU TO LOOK INTO THIS PERSONALLY, TAMBI. FIND OUT WHAT HAPPENED TO THE PLANE. I WANT TO KNOW WHAT WE'RE DEALIN' WITH HERE BEFORE I READ IT IN THE PAPERS! YOU HEAR WHAT I'M SAYIN'?
AND FIND OUT IF EITHER ONE OF THEM KIDS ARE ALIVE.
IF SO, WE CAN STILL GET DARCY PARKER'S SHARE OF THE COMPANY, LEGALLY!
AND... VERONICA?

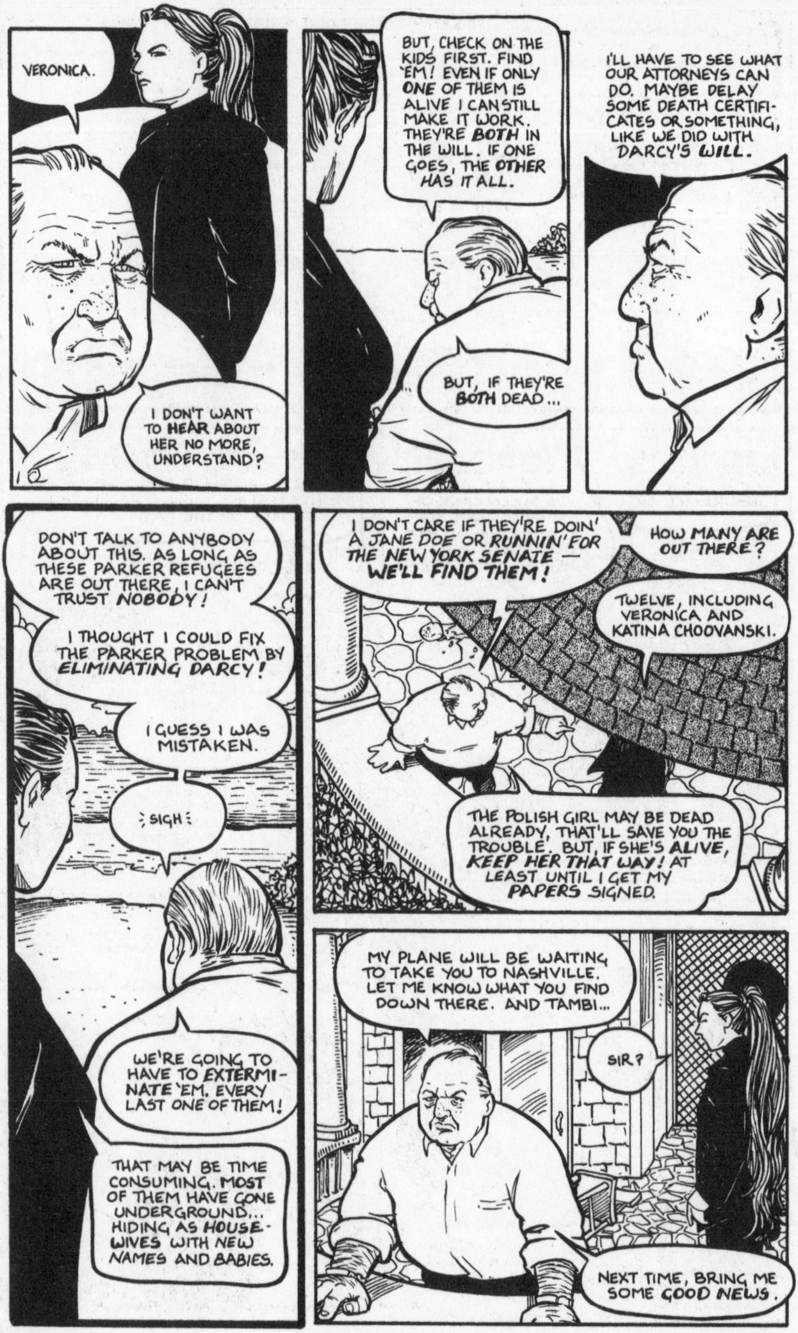
VERONICA.
I DON'T WANT TO HEAR ABOUT HER NO MORE, UNDERSTAND?
BUT, CHECK ON THE KIDS FIRST. FIND 'EM! EVEN IF ONLY ONE OF THEM IS ALIVE I CAN STILL MAKE IT WORK. THEY'RE BOTH IN THE WILL. IF ONE GOES, THE OTHER HAS IT ALL.
BUT, IF THEY'RE BOTH DEAD...
I'LL HAVE TO SEE WHAT OUR ATTORNEYS CAN DO. MAYBE DELAY SOME DEATH CERTIFICATES OR SOMETHING, LIKE WE DID WITH DARCY'S WILL.
DON'T TALK TO ANYBODY ABOUT THIS. AS LONG AS THESE PARKER REFUGEES ARE OUT THERE, I CAN'T TRUST NOBODY!
I THOUGHT I COULD FIX THE PARKER PROBLEM BY ELIMINATING DARCY!
I GUESS I WAS MISTAKEN.
SIGH
WE'RE GOING TO HAVE TO EXTERMINATE 'EM. EVERY LAST ONE OF THEM!
THAT MAY BE TIME CONSUMING. MOST OF THEM HAVE GONE UNDERGROUND... HIDING AS HOUSEWIVES WITH NEW NAMES AND BABIES.
I DON'T CARE IF THEY'RE DOIN' A JANE DOE OR RUNNIN' FOR THE NEW YORK SENATE— WE'LL FIND THEM!
HOW MANY ARE OUT THERE?
TWELVE, INCLUDING VERONICA AND KATINA CHOOVANSKI.
THE POLISH GIRL MAY BE DEAD ALREADY, THAT'LL SAVE YOU THE TROUBLE. BUT, IF SHE'S ALIVE, KEEP HER THAT WAY! AT LEAST UNTIL I GET MY PAPERS SIGNED.
MY PLANE WILL BE WAITING TO TAKE YOU TO NASHVILLE. LET ME KNOW WHAT YOU FIND DOWN THERE. AND TAMBI...
SIR?
NEXT TIME, BRING ME SOME GOOD NEWS.

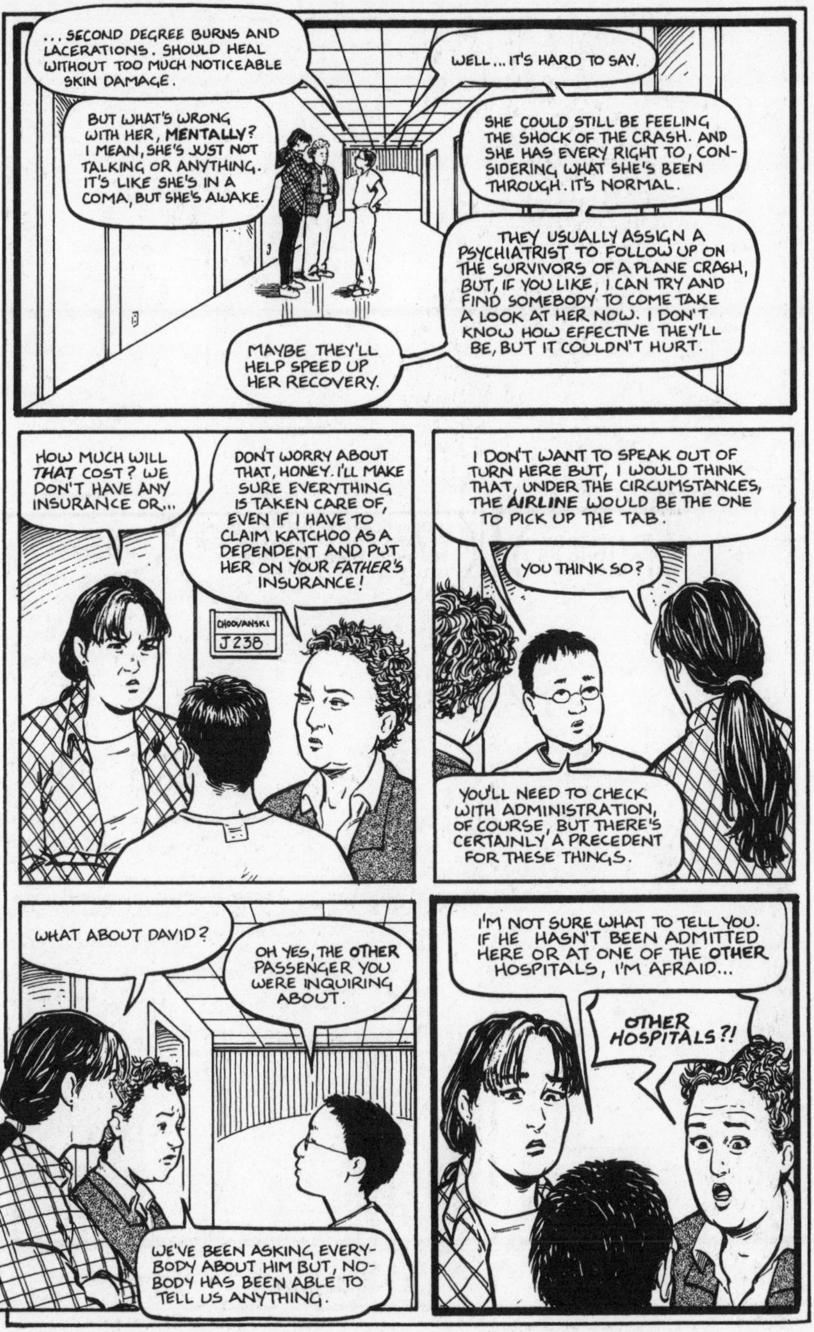
...SECOND DEGREE BURNS AND LACERATIONS. SHOULD HEAL WITHOUT TOO MUCH NOTICEABLE SKIN DAMAGE.
BUT WHAT'S WRONG WITH HER, MENTALLY? I MEAN, SHE'S JUST NOT TALKING OR ANYTHING. IT'S LIKE SHE'S IN A COMA, BUT SHE'S AWAKE.
WELL... IT'S HARD TO SAY.
SHE COULD STILL BE FEELING THE SHOCK OF THE CRASH. AND SHE HAS EVERY RIGHT TO, CONSIDERING WHAT SHE'S BEEN THROUGH. IT'S NORMAL.
THEY USUALLY ASSIGN A PSYCHIATRIST TO FOLLOW UP ON THE SURVIVORS OF A PLANE CRASH, BUT, IF YOU LIKE, I CAN TRY AND FIND SOMEBODY TO COME TAKE A LOOK AT HER NOW. I DON'T KNOW HOW EFFECTIVE THEY'LL BE, BUT IT COULDN'T HURT.
MAYBE THEY'LL HELP SPEED UP HER RECOVERY.
HOW MUCH WILL THAT COST? WE DON'T HAVE ANY INSURANCE OR...
DON'T WORRY ABOUT THAT, HONEY. I'LL MAKE SURE EVERYTHING IS TAKEN CARE OF, EVEN IF I HAVE TO CLAIM KATCHOO AS A DEPENDENT AND PUT HER ON YOUR FATHER'S INSURANCE!
CHOOVANSKI
J238
I DON'T WANT TO SPEAK OUT OF TURN HERE BUT, I WOULD THINK THAT, UNDER THE CIRCUMSTANCES, THE AIRLINE WOULD BE THE ONE TO PICK UP THE TAB.
YOU THINK SO?
YOU'LL NEED TO CHECK WITH ADMINISTRATION, OF COURSE, BUT THERE'S CERTAINLY A PRECEDENT FOR THESE THINGS.
WHAT ABOUT DAVID?
OH YES, THE OTHER PASSENGER YOU WERE INQUIRING ABOUT.
WE'VE BEEN ASKING EVERYBODY ABOUT HIM BUT, NOBODY HAS BEEN ABLE TO TELL US ANYTHING.
I'M NOT SURE WHAT TO TELL YOU. IF HE HASN'T BEEN ADMITTED HERE OR AT ONE OF THE OTHER HOSPITALS, I'M AFRAID...
OTHER HOSPITALS?!

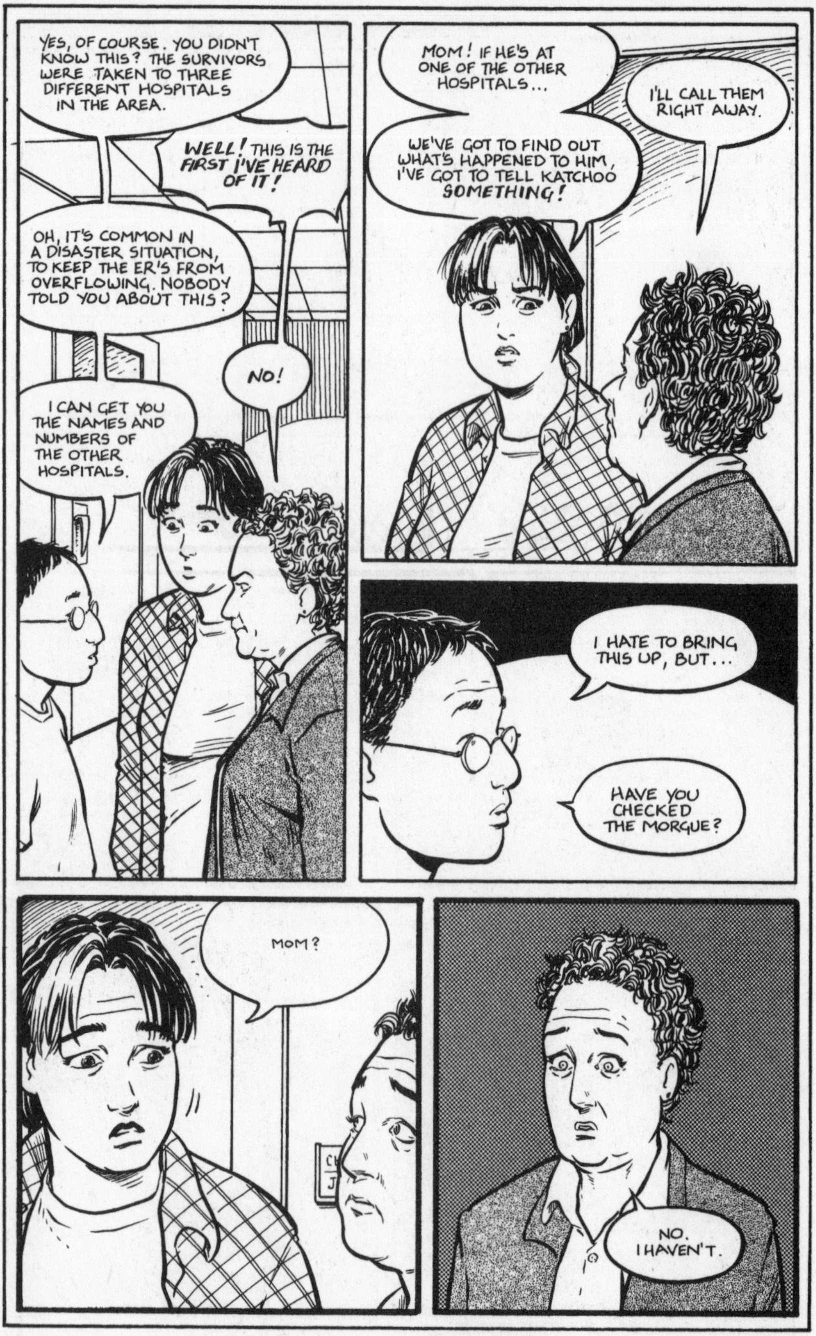
YES, OF COURSE. YOU DIDN'T KNOW THIS? THE SURVIVORS WERE TAKEN TO THREE DIFFERENT HOSPITALS IN THE AREA.
WELL! THIS IS THE FIRST I'VE HEARD OF IT!
OH, IT'S COMMON IN A DISASTER SITUATION, TO KEEP THE ER'S FROM OVERFLOWING. NOBODY TOLD YOU ABOUT THIS?
NO!
I CAN GET YOU THE NAMES AND NUMBERS OF THE OTHER HOSPITALS.
MOM! IF HE'S AT ONE OF THE OTHER HOSPITALS...
WE'VE GOT TO FIND OUT WHAT'S HAPPENED TO HIM, I'VE GOT TO TELL KATCHOO SOMETHING!
I'LL CALL THEM RIGHT AWAY.
I HATE TO BRING THIS UP, BUT...
HAVE YOU CHECKED THE MORGUE?
MOM?
NO. I HAVEN'T.

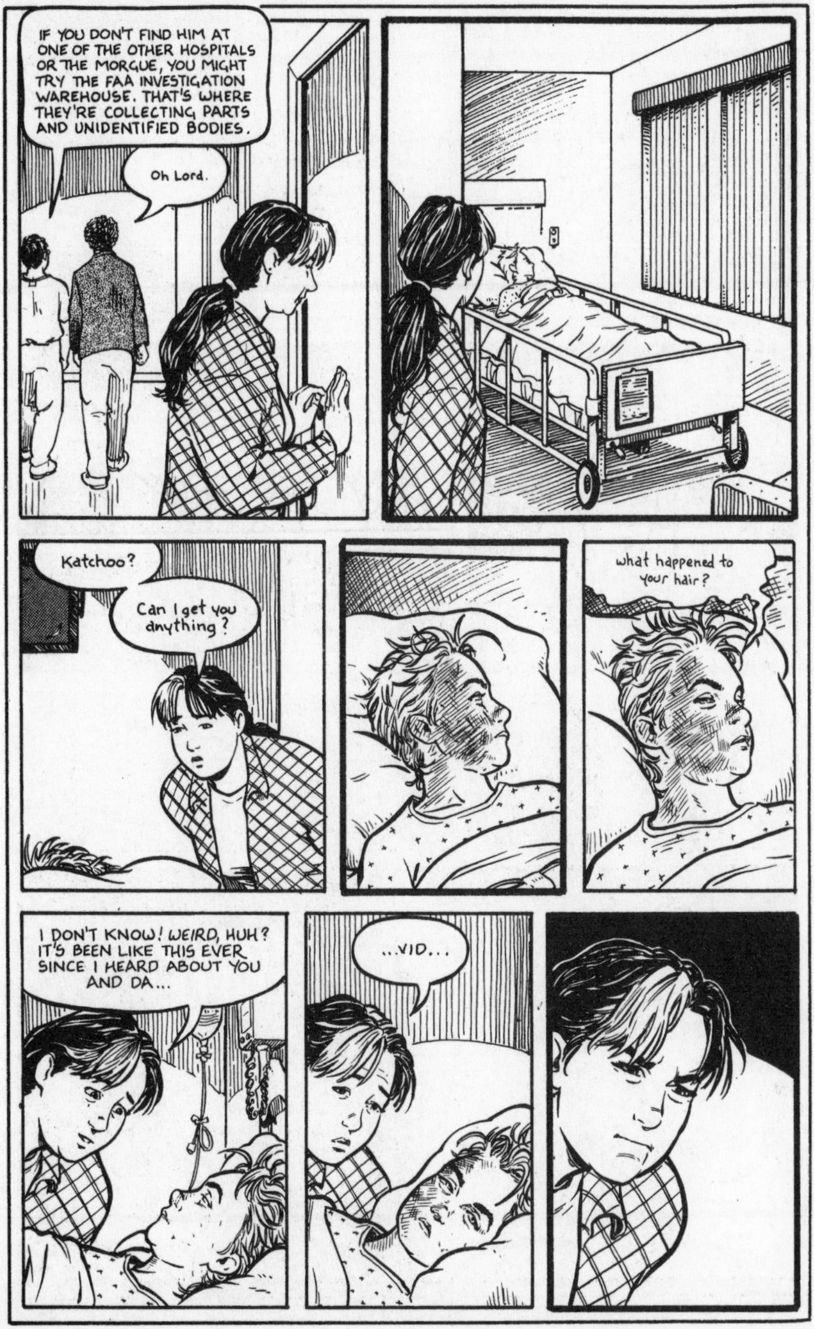
IF YOU DON'T FIND HIM AT ONE OF THE OTHER HOSPITALS OR THE MORGUE, YOU MIGHT TRY THE FAA INVESTIGATION WAREHOUSE. THAT'S WHERE THEY'RE COLLECTING PARTS AND UNIDENTIFIED BODIES.
Oh Lord.
Katchoo?
Can I get you anything?
what happened to your hair?
I DON'T KNOW! *WEIRD*, HUH? IT'S BEEN LIKE THIS EVER SINCE I HEARD ABOUT YOU AND DA...
...VID...

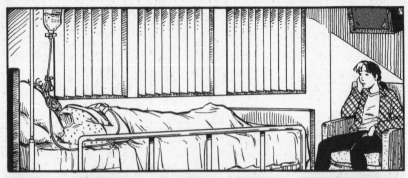

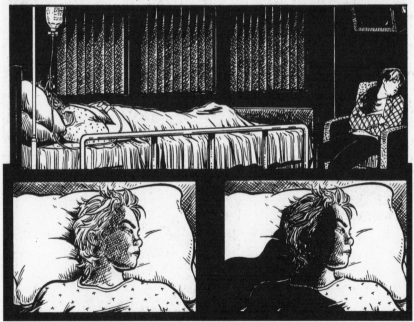

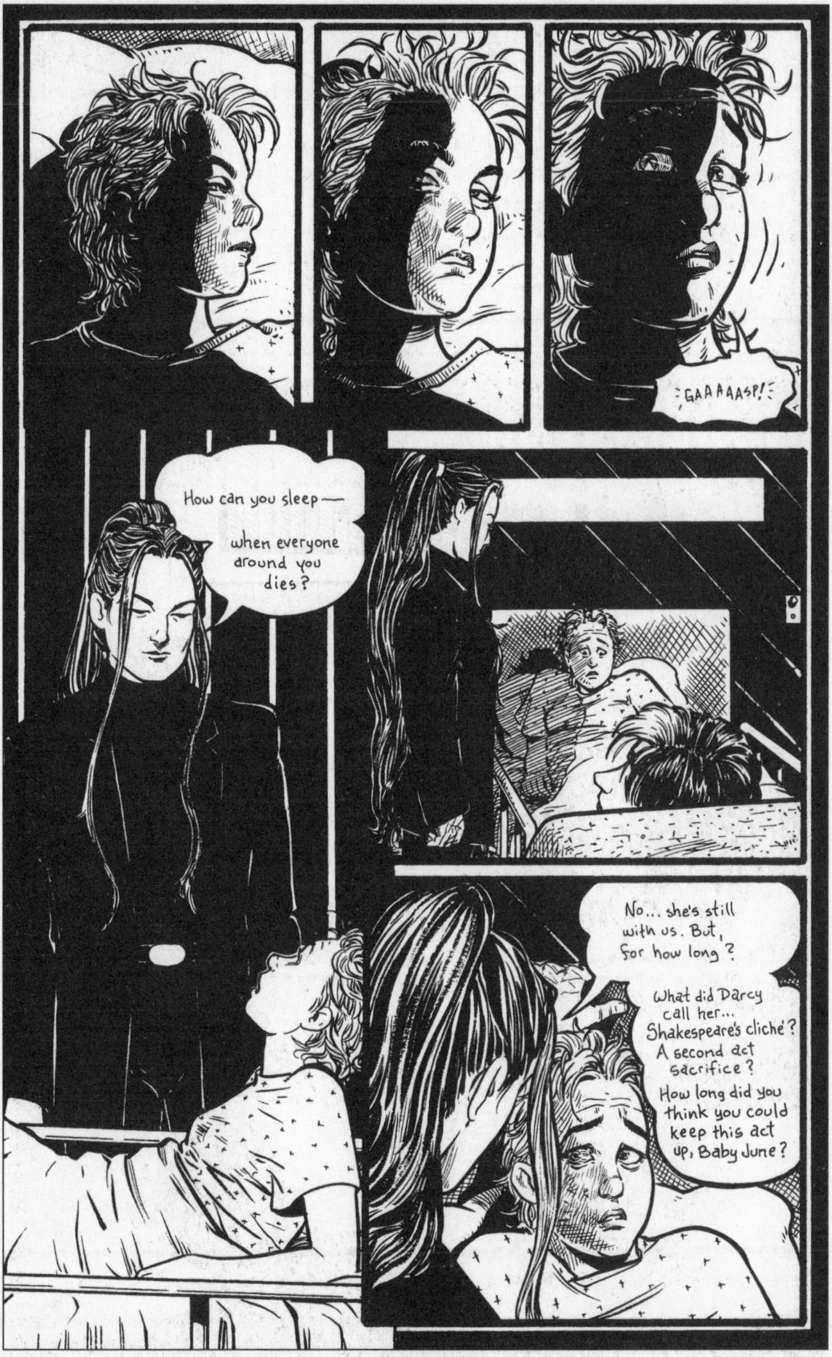
GAAAAASP!
How can you sleep—
when everyone around you dies?
No... she's still with us. But, for how long?
What did Darcy call her... Shakespeare's cliché? A second act sacrifice?
How long did you think you could keep this act up, Baby June?

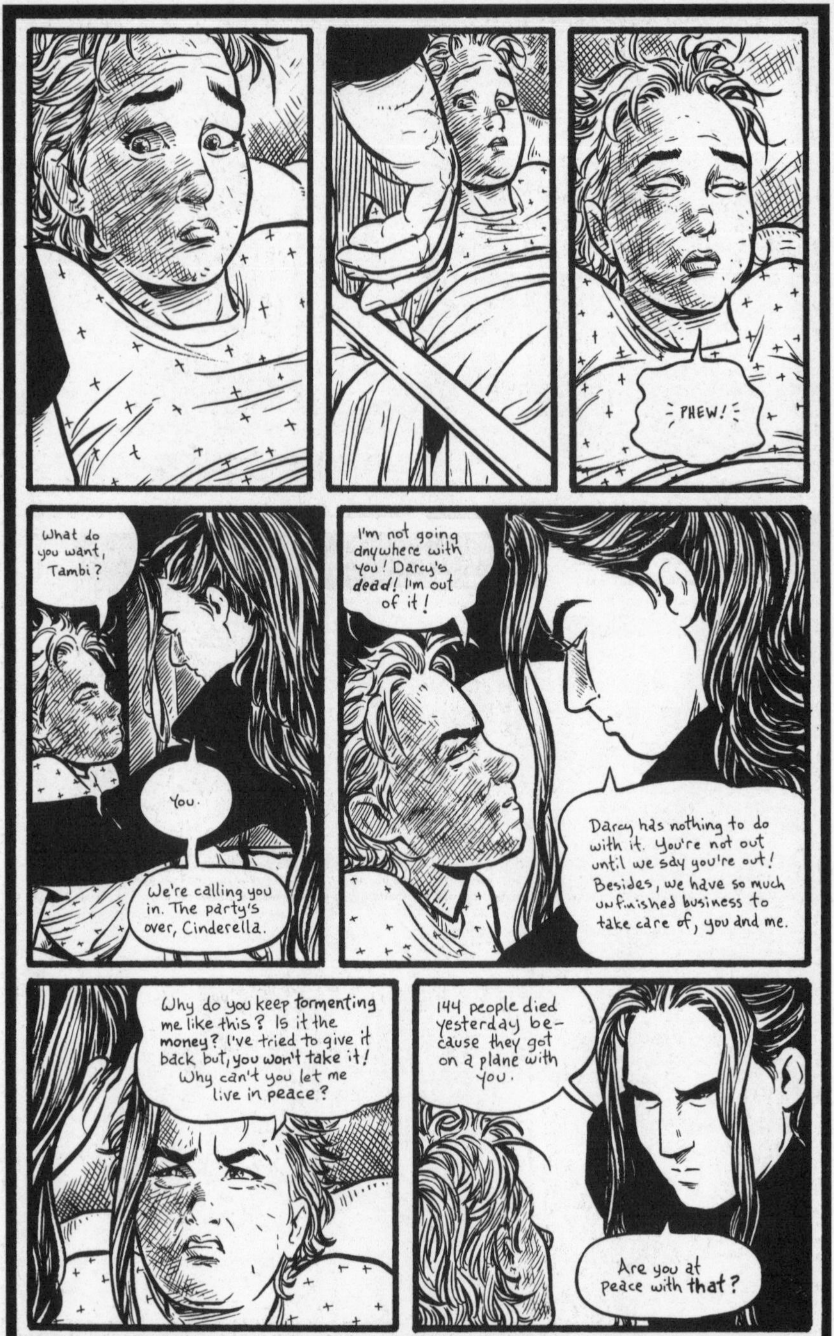
PHEW!
What do you want, Tambi?
You.
We're calling you in. The party's over, Cinderella.
I'm not going anywhere with you! Darcy's dead! I'm out of it!
Darcy has nothing to do with it. You're not out until we say you're out! Besides, we have so much unfinished business to take care of, you and me.
Why do you keep tormenting me like this? Is it the money? I've tried to give it back but, you won't take it! Why can't you let me live in peace?
144 people died yesterday because they got on a plane with you.
Are you at peace with that?

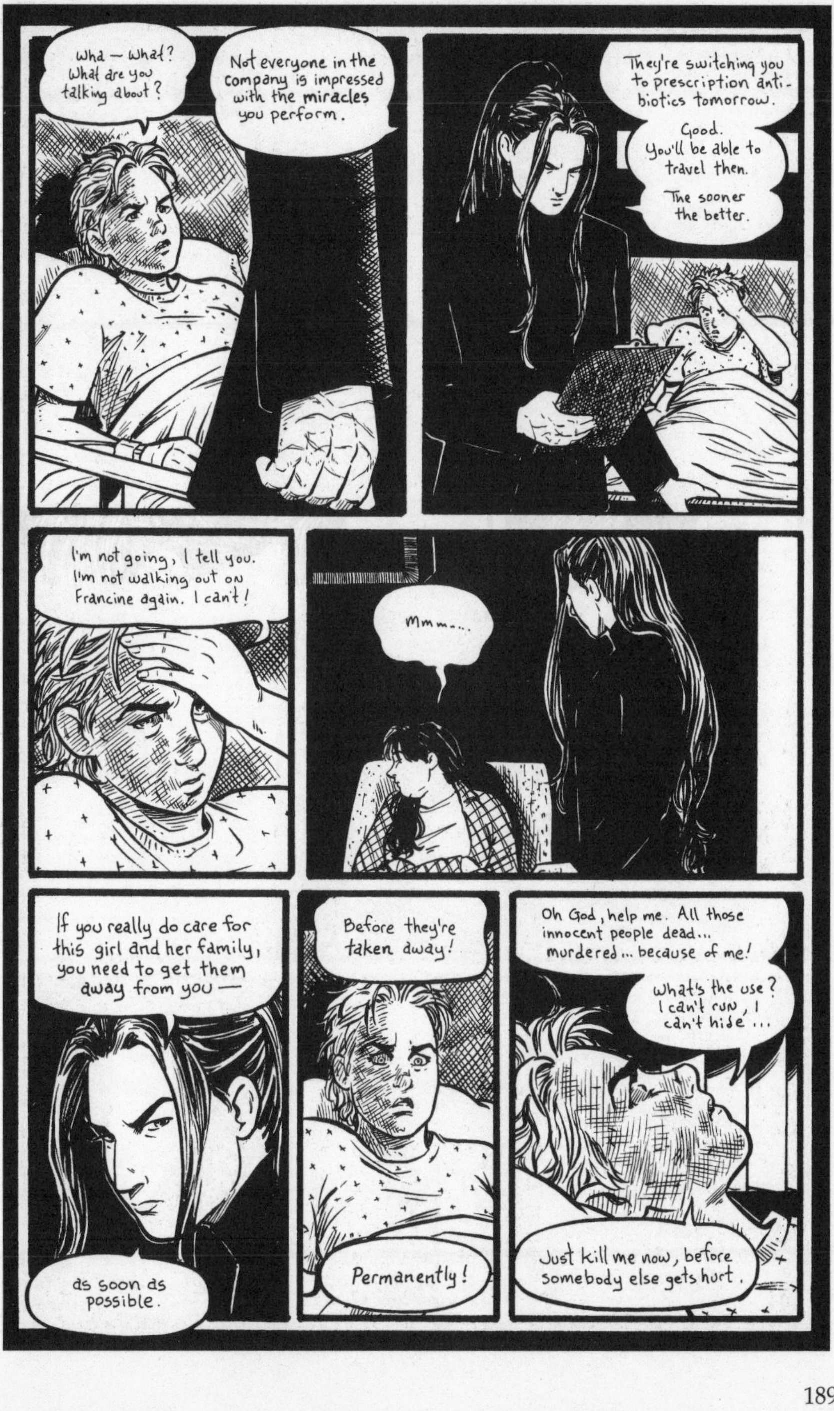
Wha — What? What are you talking about?
Not everyone in the company is impressed with the miracles you perform.
They're switching you to prescription antibiotics tomorrow.
Good. You'll be able to travel then.
The sooner the better.
I'm not going, I tell you. I'm not walking out on Francine again. I can't!
Mmm....
If you really do care for this girl and her family, you need to get them away from you —
as soon as possible.
Before they're taken away!
Permanently!
Oh God, help me. All those innocent people dead... murdered... because of me!
What's the use? I can't run, I can't hide...
Just kill me now, before somebody else gets hurt.

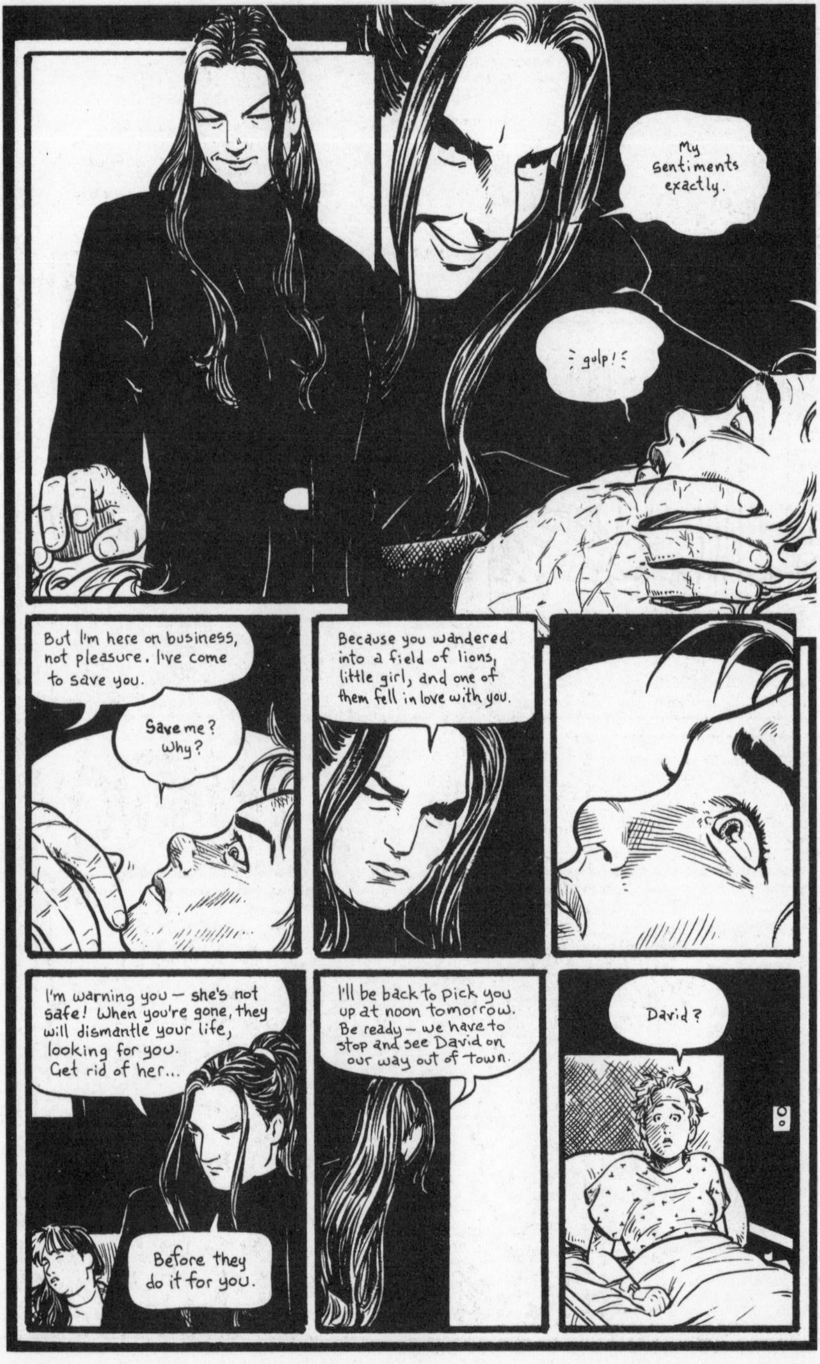
My sentiments exactly.
gulp!
But I'm here on business, not pleasure. I've come to save you.
Save me? Why?
Because you wandered into a field of lions, little girl, and one of them fell in love with you.
I'm warning you — she's not safe! When you're gone, they will dismantle your life, looking for you. Get rid of her...
Before they do it for you.
I'll be back to pick you up at noon tomorrow. Be ready — we have to stop and see David on our way out of town.
David?

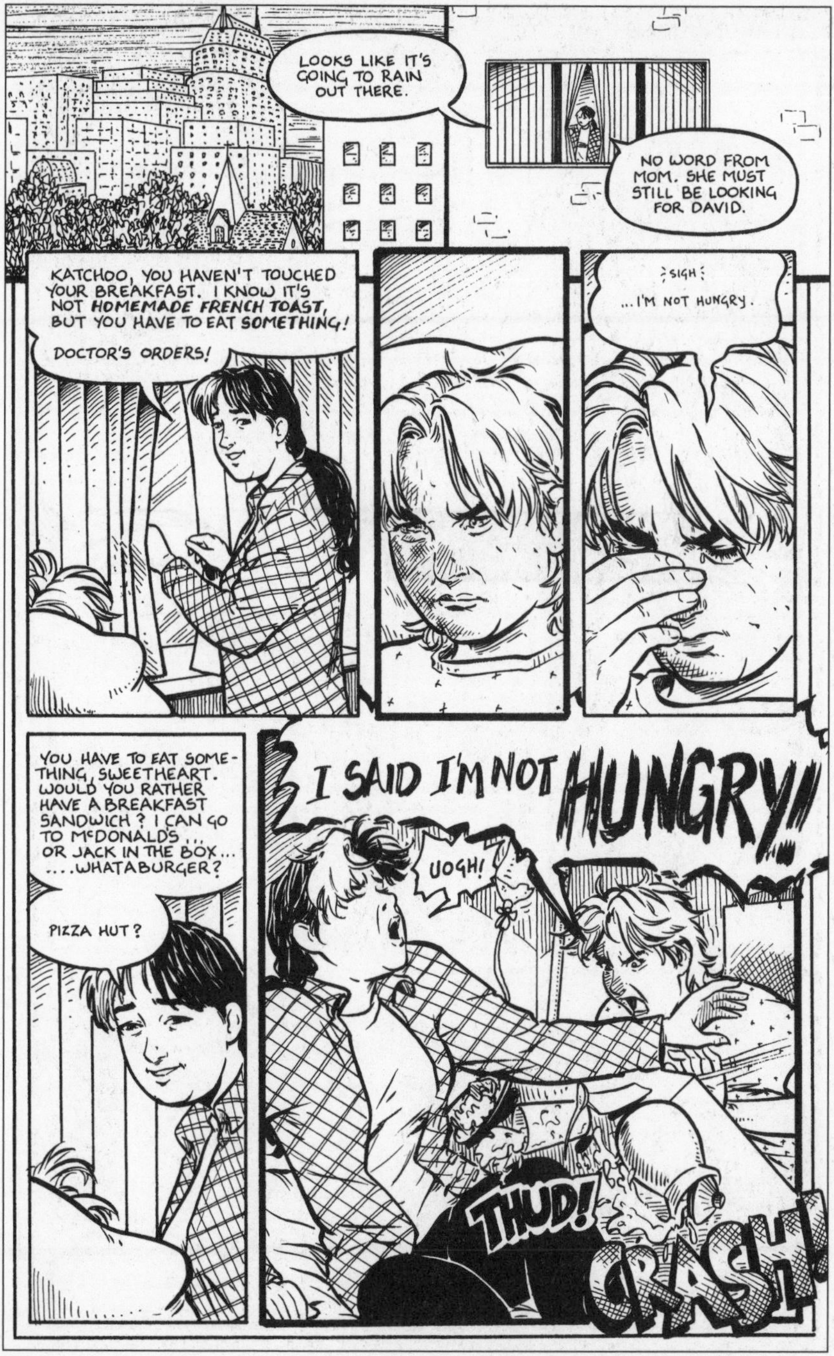
LOOKS LIKE IT'S GOING TO RAIN OUT THERE.
NO WORD FROM MOM. SHE MUST STILL BE LOOKING FOR DAVID.
KATCHOO, YOU HAVEN'T TOUCHED YOUR BREAKFAST. I KNOW IT'S NOT HOMEMADE FRENCH TOAST, BUT YOU HAVE TO EAT SOMETHING!
DOCTOR'S ORDERS!
SIGH
...I'M NOT HUNGRY.
YOU HAVE TO EAT SOMETHING, SWEETHEART. WOULD YOU RATHER HAVE A BREAKFAST SANDWICH? I CAN GO TO McDONALD'S... OR JACK IN THE BOX... ....WHATABURGER?
PIZZA HUT?
I SAID I'M NOT HUNGRY!!
UOGH!
THUD!
CRASH!

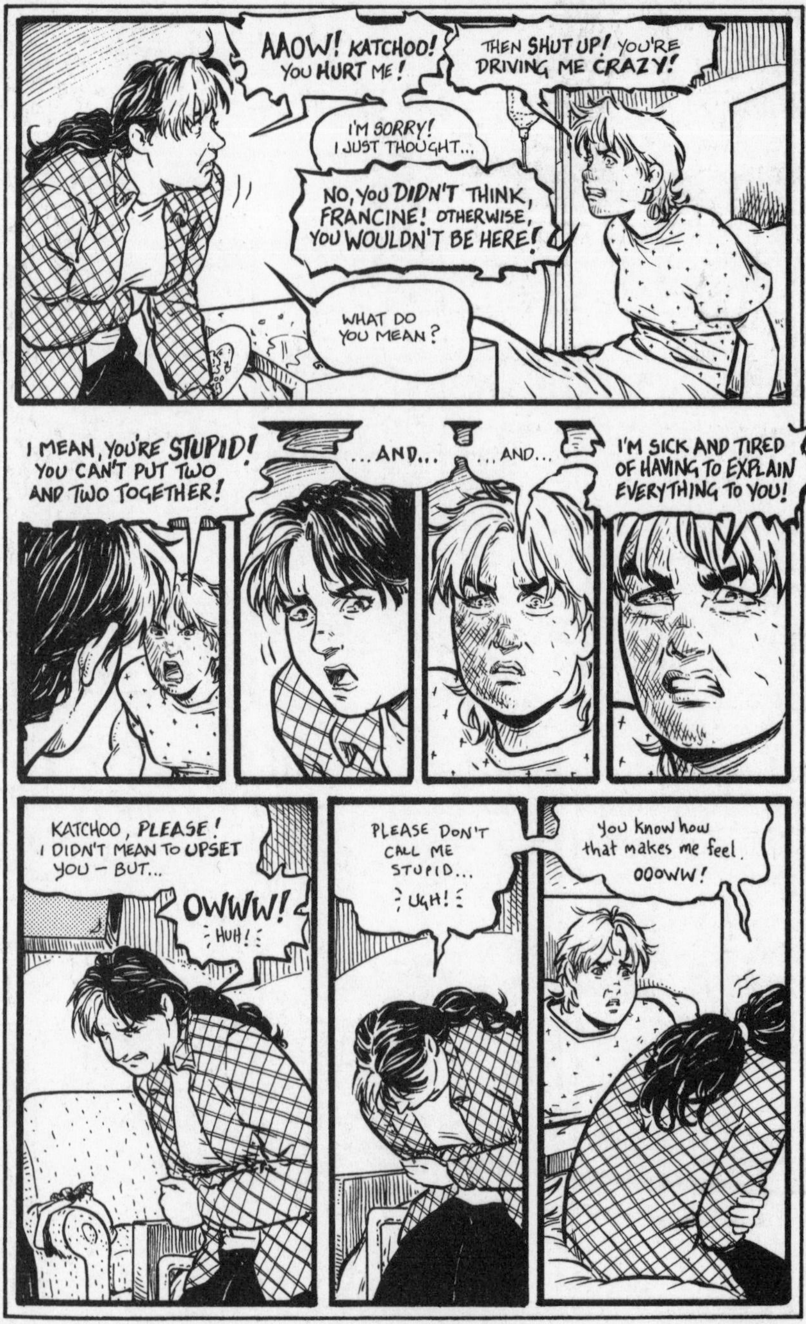
AAOW! KATCHOO! YOU HURT ME!
THEN SHUT UP! YOU'RE DRIVING ME CRAZY!
I'M SORRY! I JUST THOUGHT...
NO, YOU DIDN'T THINK, FRANCINE! OTHERWISE, YOU WOULDN'T BE HERE!
WHAT DO YOU MEAN?
I MEAN, YOU'RE STUPID! YOU CAN'T PUT TWO AND TWO TOGETHER!
...AND...
...AND...
I'M SICK AND TIRED OF HAVING TO EXPLAIN EVERYTHING TO YOU!
KATCHOO, PLEASE! I DIDN'T MEAN TO UPSET YOU — BUT...
OWWW!
HUH!
PLEASE DON'T CALL ME STUPID...
UGH!
You know how that makes me feel.
OOOWW!

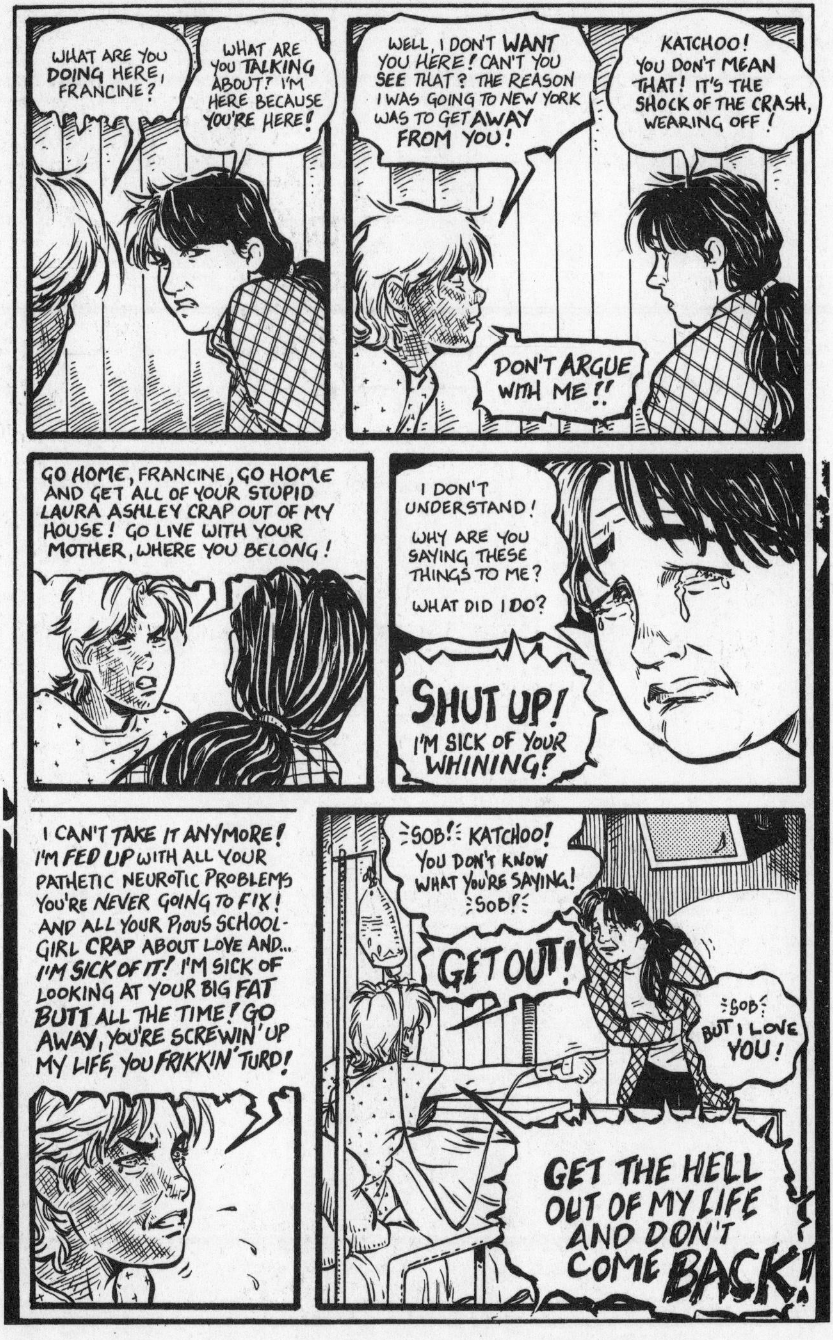
WHAT ARE YOU DOING HERE, FRANCINE?
WHAT ARE YOU TALKING ABOUT? I'M HERE BECAUSE YOU'RE HERE!
WELL, I DON'T WANT YOU HERE! CAN'T YOU SEE THAT? THE REASON I WAS GOING TO NEW YORK WAS TO GET AWAY FROM YOU!
KATCHOO! YOU DON'T MEAN THAT! IT'S THE SHOCK OF THE CRASH, WEARING OFF!
DON'T ARGUE WITH ME!!
GO HOME, FRANCINE, GO HOME AND GET ALL OF YOUR STUPID LAURA ASHLEY CRAP OUT OF MY HOUSE! GO LIVE WITH YOUR MOTHER, WHERE YOU BELONG!
I DON'T UNDERSTAND!
WHY ARE YOU SAYING THESE THINGS TO ME?
WHAT DID I DO?
SHUT UP! I'M SICK OF YOUR WHINING!
I CAN'T TAKE IT ANYMORE! I'M FED UP WITH ALL YOUR PATHETIC NEUROTIC PROBLEMS YOU'RE NEVER GOING TO FIX! AND ALL YOUR PIOUS SCHOOL-GIRL CRAP ABOUT LOVE AND... I'M SICK OF IT! I'M SICK OF LOOKING AT YOUR BIG FAT BUTT ALL THE TIME! GO AWAY, YOU'RE SCREWIN' UP MY LIFE, YOU FRIKKIN' TURD!
SOB! KATCHOO! YOU DON'T KNOW WHAT YOU'RE SAYING! SOB!
GET OUT!
SOB BUT I LOVE YOU!
GET THE HELL OUT OF MY LIFE AND DON'T COME BACK!

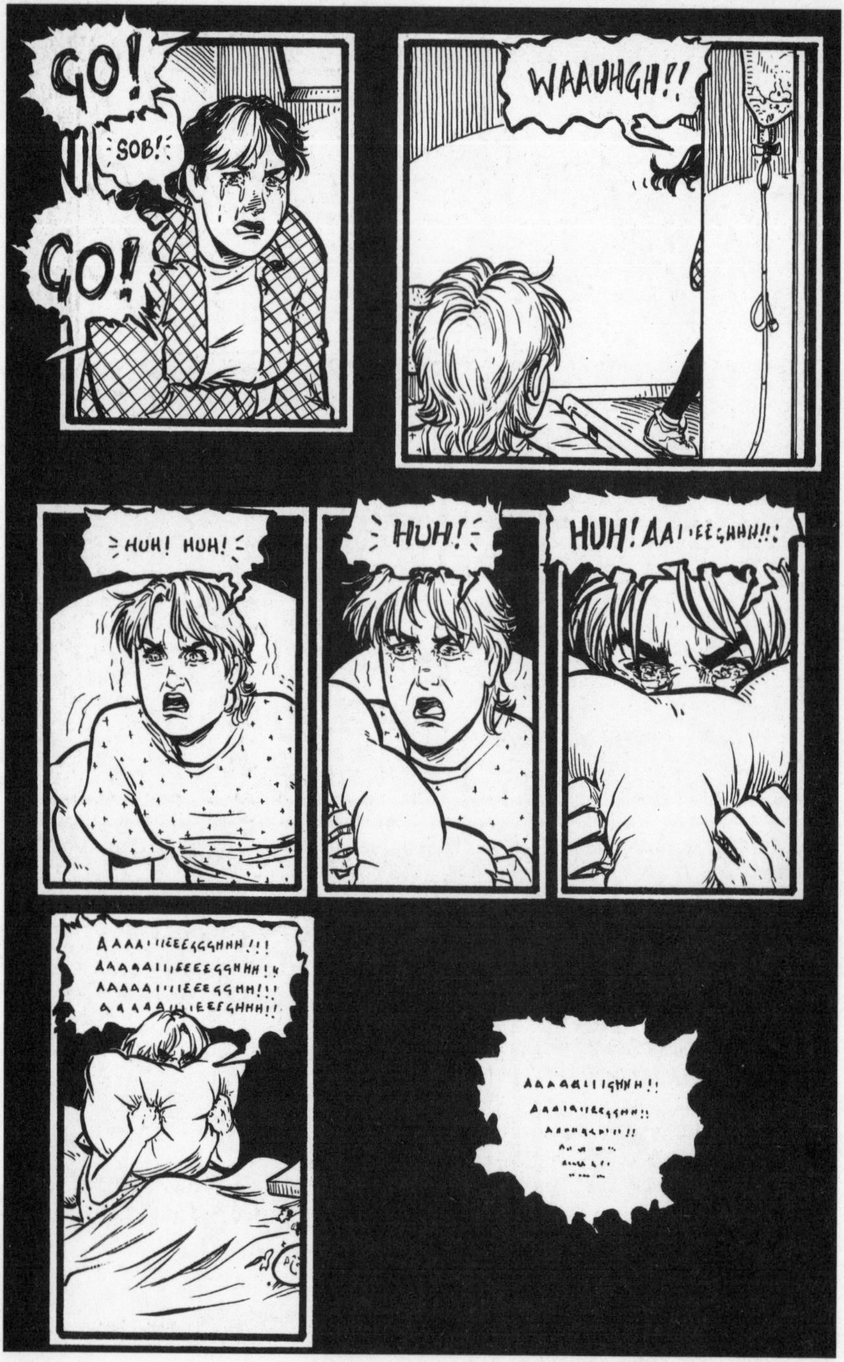
GO!
SOB!
GO!
WAAUHGH!!
HUH! HUH!
HUH!
HUH! AAIEEGHHH!!!
AAAAIIIEEEGGGHHH!!!
AAAAAIIIEEEEGGHHH!!
AAAAAIIIIEEEGGHH!!!
AAAAAIIIIEEEGHHH!!
AAAAAIIIGHHH!!

When I wake up at night
Remembering my other life,
I scream.
If I could find a way don't you believe
That I'd be there today?
But for my clever mind, to punish me,
I'm trapped inside this black design
My eyes are gallows and my heart's a nervous wreck
Trapped in confusion all around me I forget
My real name,
But they call me profane.

When I had angry eyes
To see beyond the veil of lies was nothing,
But now they're baby blue and don't see any answers,
I'm as blind as you.
If what they say is true then anything can happen
There are no border lines.
Tho' deep inside I hold the child I think I am,
My hands were midwife to the hell I'm living in.
Oh believe me,
I'm running out of time.

When I wake up at night
Remembering my other life,
I scream.
But every dawning day the faith in me
beyond my reach more distant fades.
My eyes are gallows and my heart's a nervous wreck;
My cries are fondled by the hangman's deadly kiss.
Oh believe me,
I'm running out of

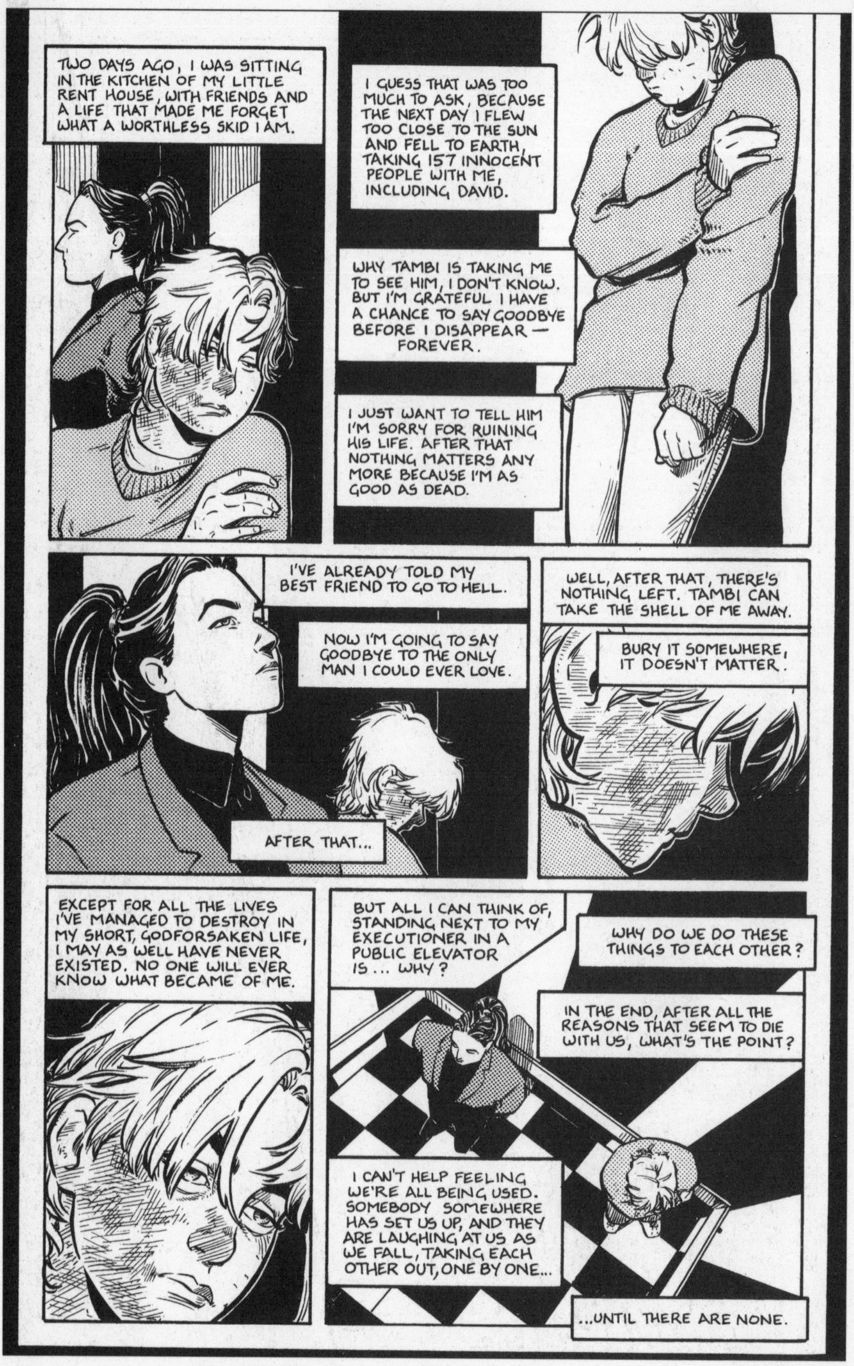
TWO DAYS AGO, I WAS SITTING IN THE KITCHEN OF MY LITTLE RENT HOUSE, WITH FRIENDS AND A LIFE THAT MADE ME FORGET WHAT A WORTHLESS SKID I AM.
I GUESS THAT WAS TOO MUCH TO ASK, BECAUSE THE NEXT DAY I FLEW TOO CLOSE TO THE SUN AND FELL TO EARTH, TAKING 157 INNOCENT PEOPLE WITH ME, INCLUDING DAVID.
WHY TAMBI IS TAKING ME TO SEE HIM, I DON'T KNOW. BUT I'M GRATEFUL I HAVE A CHANCE TO SAY GOODBYE BEFORE I DISAPPEAR — FOREVER.
I JUST WANT TO TELL HIM I'M SORRY FOR RUINING HIS LIFE. AFTER THAT NOTHING MATTERS ANY MORE BECAUSE I'M AS GOOD AS DEAD.
I'VE ALREADY TOLD MY BEST FRIEND TO GO TO HELL.
NOW I'M GOING TO SAY GOODBYE TO THE ONLY MAN I COULD EVER LOVE.
AFTER THAT...
WELL, AFTER THAT, THERE'S NOTHING LEFT. TAMBI CAN TAKE THE SHELL OF ME AWAY.
BURY IT SOMEWHERE, IT DOESN'T MATTER.
EXCEPT FOR ALL THE LIVES I'VE MANAGED TO DESTROY IN MY SHORT, GODFORSAKEN LIFE, I MAY AS WELL HAVE NEVER EXISTED. NO ONE WILL EVER KNOW WHAT BECAME OF ME.
BUT ALL I CAN THINK OF, STANDING NEXT TO MY EXECUTIONER IN A PUBLIC ELEVATOR IS ... WHY?
WHY DO WE DO THESE THINGS TO EACH OTHER?
IN THE END, AFTER ALL THE REASONS THAT SEEM TO DIE WITH US, WHAT'S THE POINT?
I CAN'T HELP FEELING WE'RE ALL BEING USED. SOMEBODY SOMEWHERE HAS SET US UP, AND THEY ARE LAUGHING AT US AS WE FALL, TAKING EACH OTHER OUT, ONE BY ONE...
...UNTIL THERE ARE NONE.

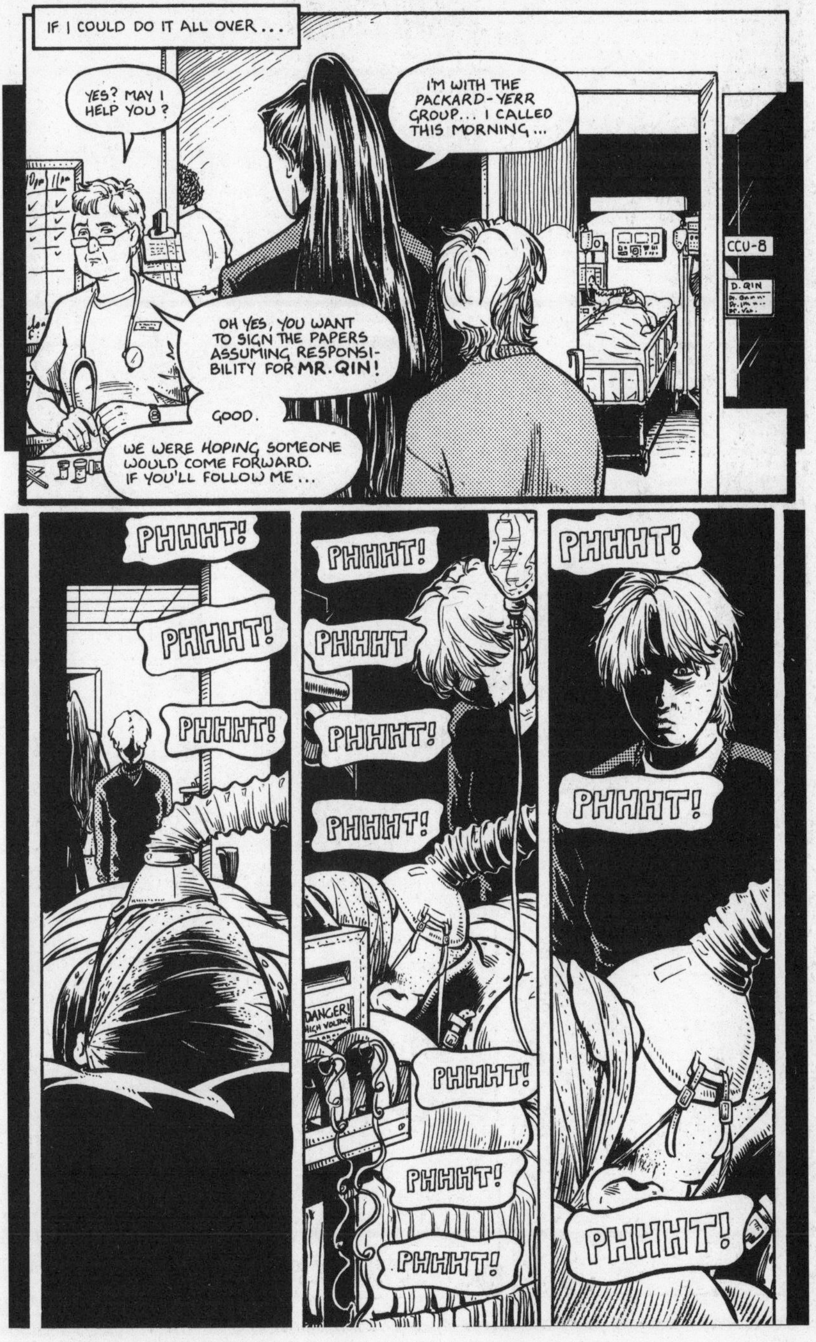
IF I COULD DO IT ALL OVER...
YES? MAY I HELP YOU?
I'M WITH THE PACKARD-YERR GROUP... I CALLED THIS MORNING...
CCU-8
D. QIN
OH YES, YOU WANT TO SIGN THE PAPERS ASSUMING RESPONSIBILITY FOR MR. QIN!
GOOD.
WE WERE HOPING SOMEONE WOULD COME FORWARD. IF YOU'LL FOLLOW ME...
PHHHT!
PHHHT!
PHHHT!
PHHHT!
PHHHT
PHHHT!
PHHHT!
DANGER! HIGH VOLTAGE
PHHHT!
PHHHT!
PHHHT!
PHHHT!
PHHHT!
PHHHT!

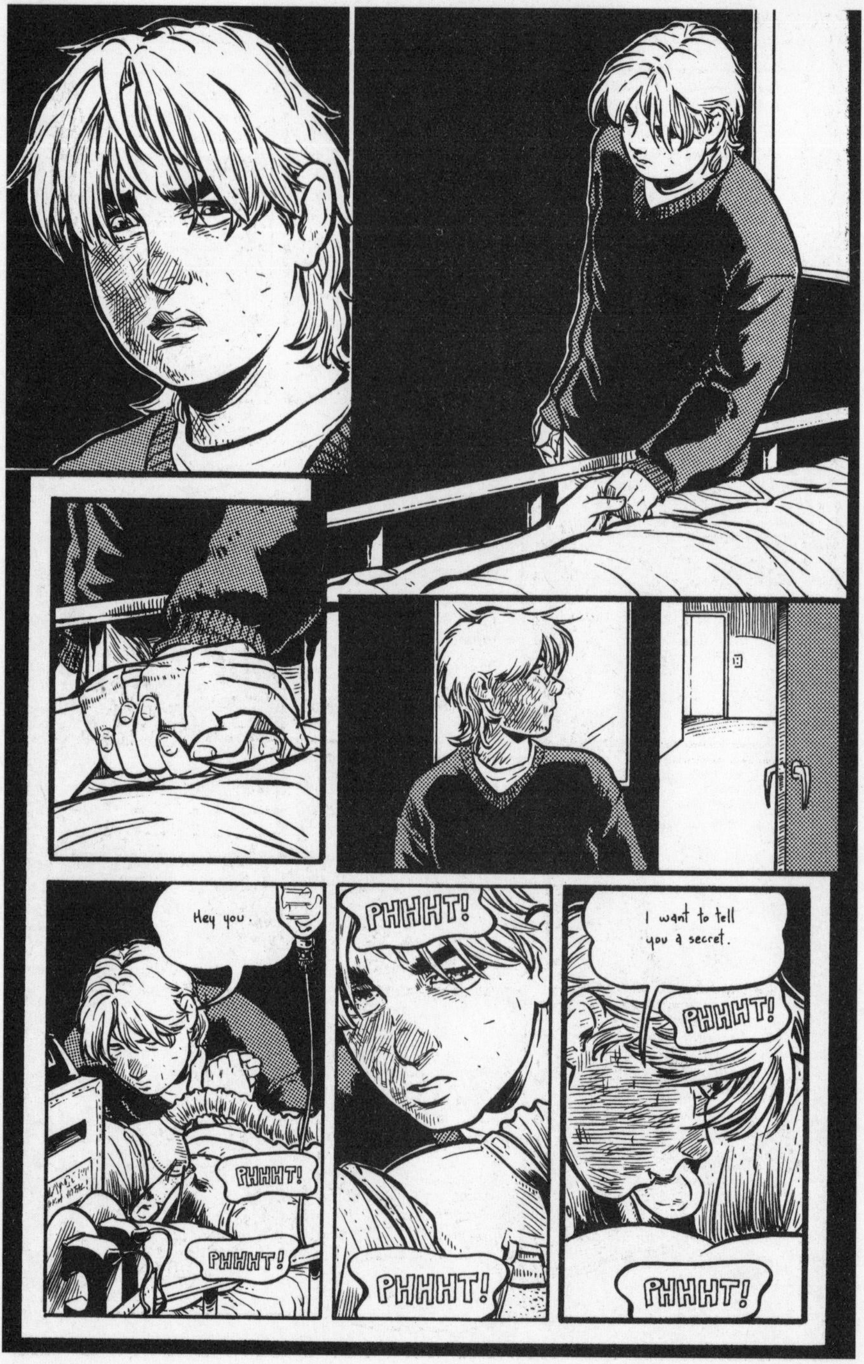
Hey you.
PHHHT!
PHHHT!
PHHHT!
PHHHT!
I want to tell you a secret.
PHHHT!
PHHHT!

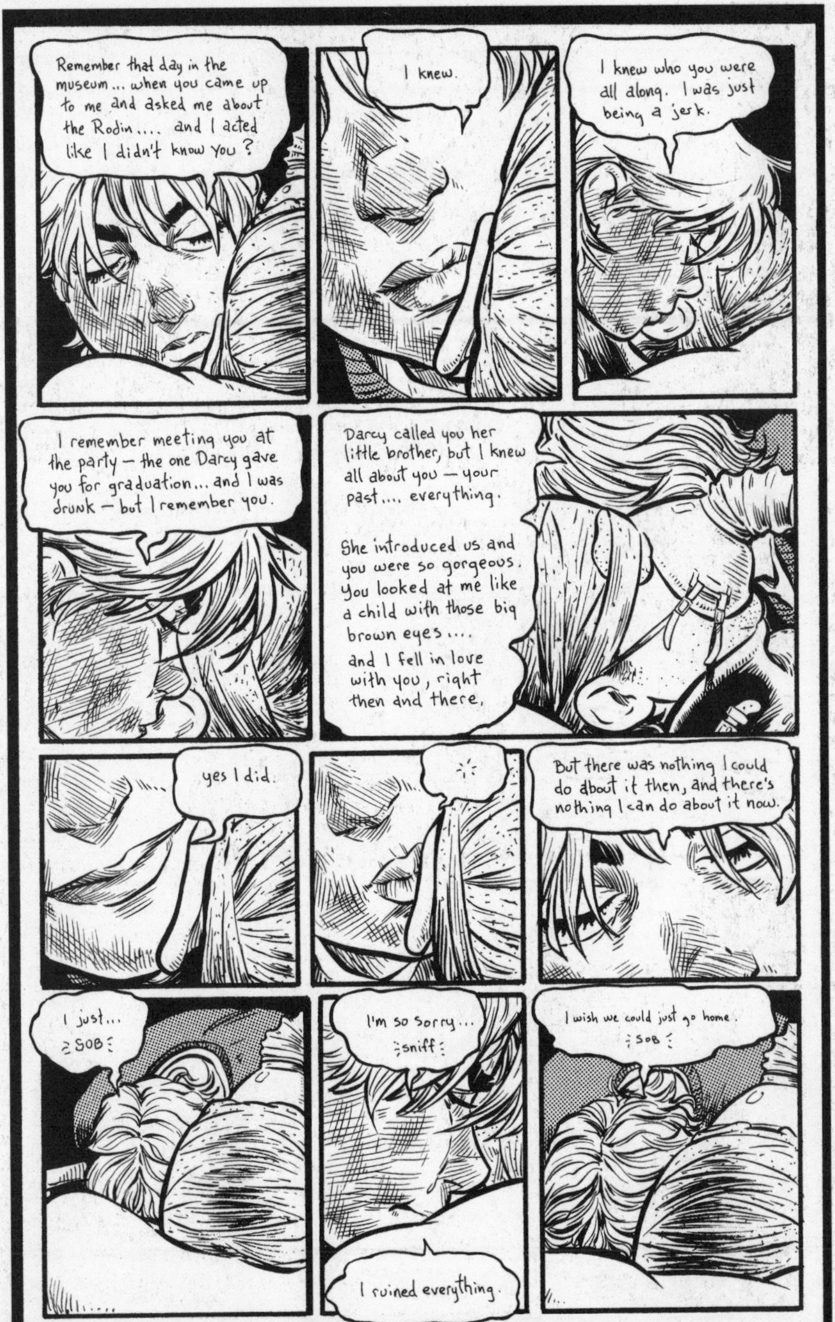

Remember that day in the museum... when you came up to me and asked me about the Rodin.... and I acted like I didn't know you?
I knew.
I knew who you were all along. I was just being a jerk.
I remember meeting you at the party — the one Darcy gave you for graduation... and I was drunk — but I remember you.
Darcy called you her little brother, but I knew all about you — your past.... everything.
She introduced us and you were so gorgeous. You looked at me like a child with those big brown eyes....
and I fell in love with you, right then and there,
yes I did.
But there was nothing I could do about it then, and there's nothing I can do about it now.
I just...
SOB
I'm so sorry...
sniff
I ruined everything.
I wish we could just go home.
SOB

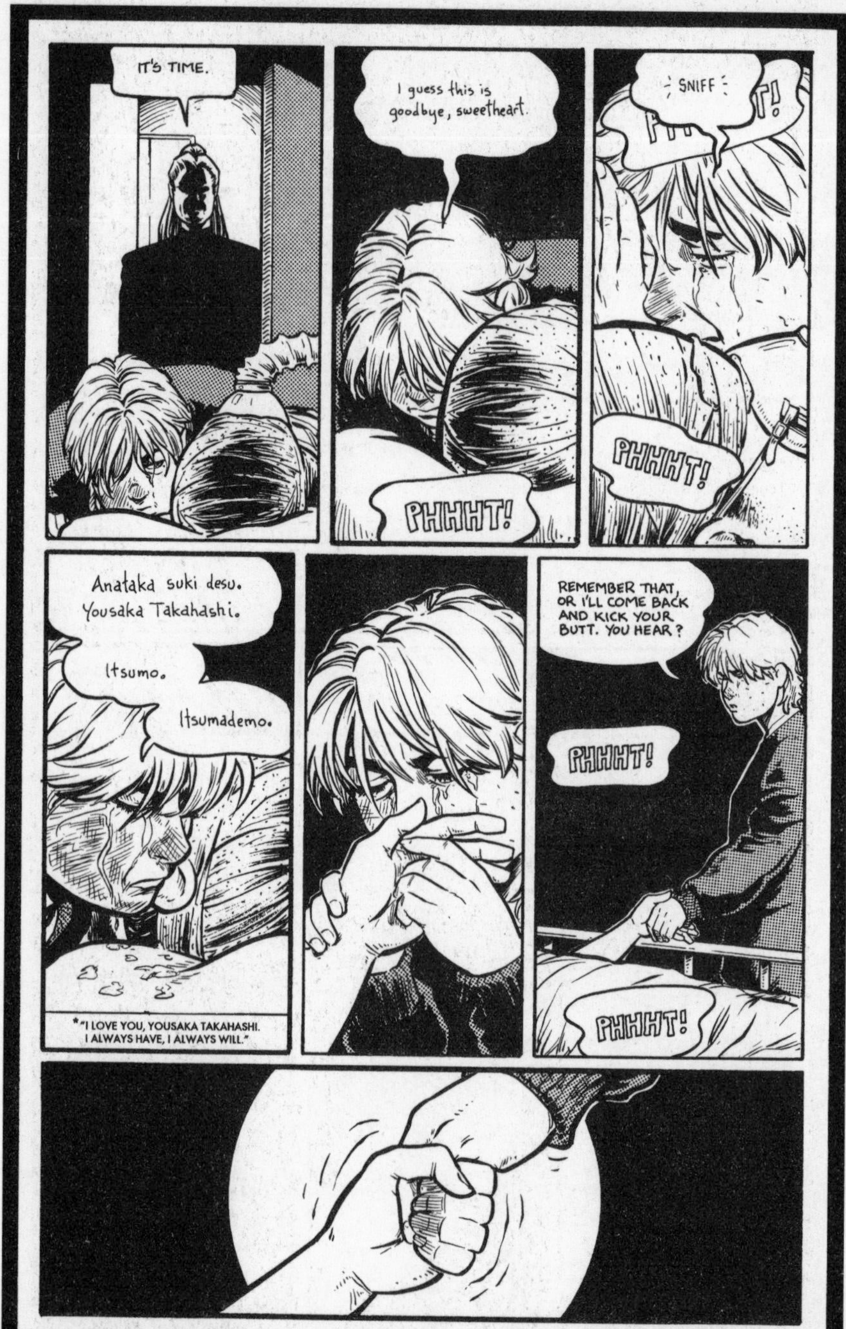

IT'S TIME.
I guess this is goodbye, sweetheart.
PHHHT!
SNIFF
PHHHT!
Anataka suki desu. Yousaka Takahashi.
Itsumo.
Itsumademo.
*"I LOVE YOU, YOUSAKA TAKAHASHI. I ALWAYS HAVE, I ALWAYS WILL."
REMEMBER THAT, OR I'LL COME BACK AND KICK YOUR BUTT. YOU HEAR?
PHHHT!
PHHHT!

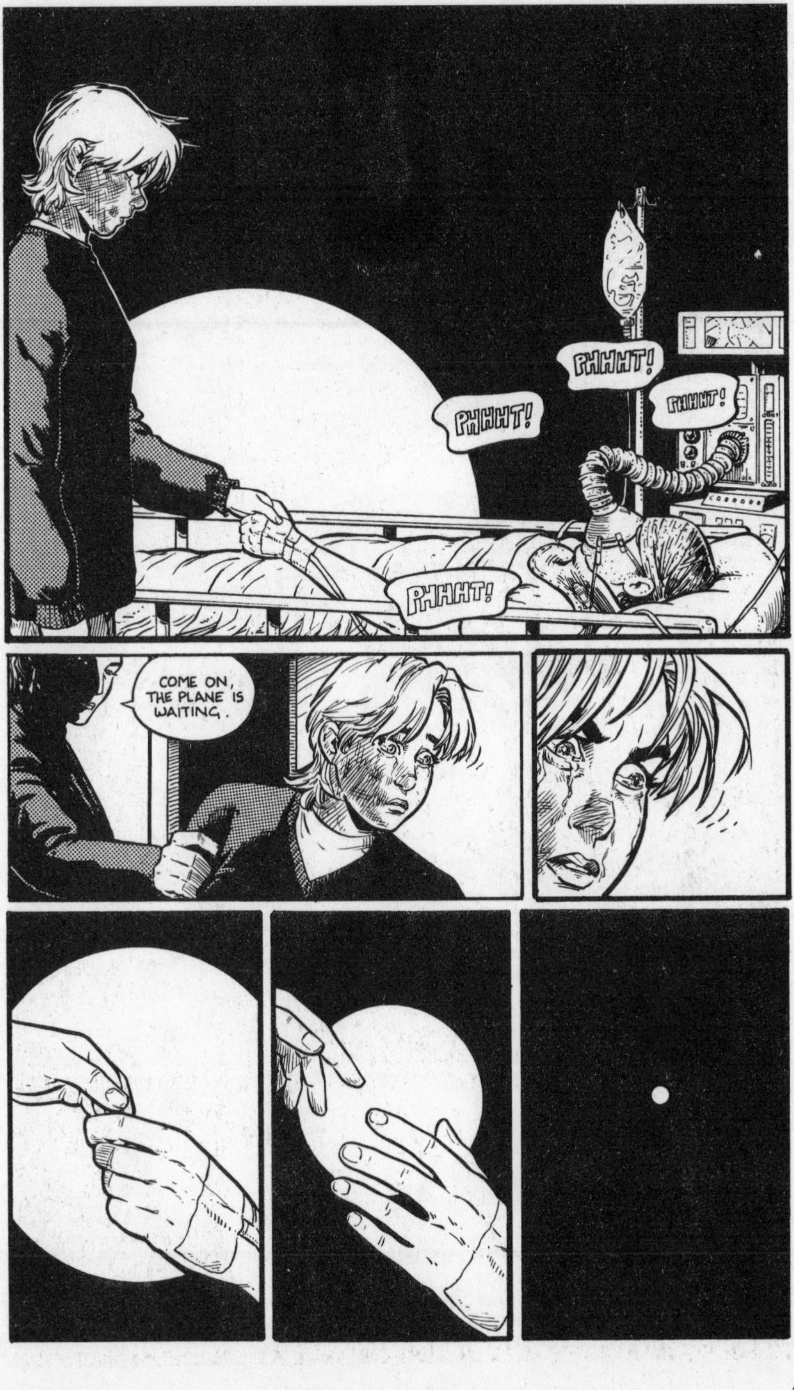
PHHHT!
PHHHT!
PHHHT!
PHHHT!
COME ON, THE PLANE IS WAITING.

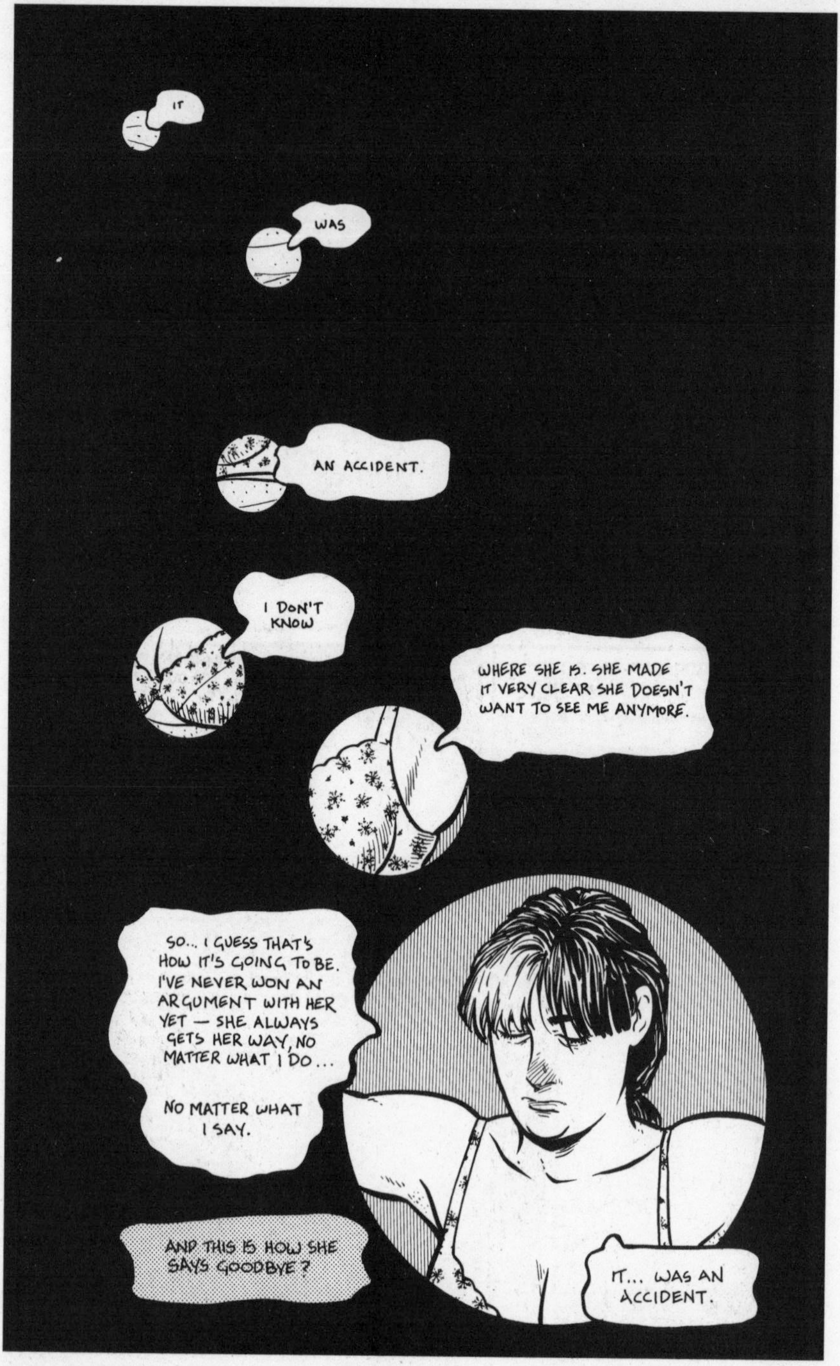
IT
WAS
AN ACCIDENT.
I DON'T KNOW
WHERE SHE IS. SHE MADE IT VERY CLEAR SHE DOESN'T WANT TO SEE ME ANYMORE.
SO... I GUESS THAT'S HOW IT'S GOING TO BE. I'VE NEVER WON AN ARGUMENT WITH HER YET — SHE ALWAYS GETS HER WAY, NO MATTER WHAT I DO...
NO MATTER WHAT I SAY.
AND THIS IS HOW SHE SAYS GOODBYE?
IT... WAS AN ACCIDENT.

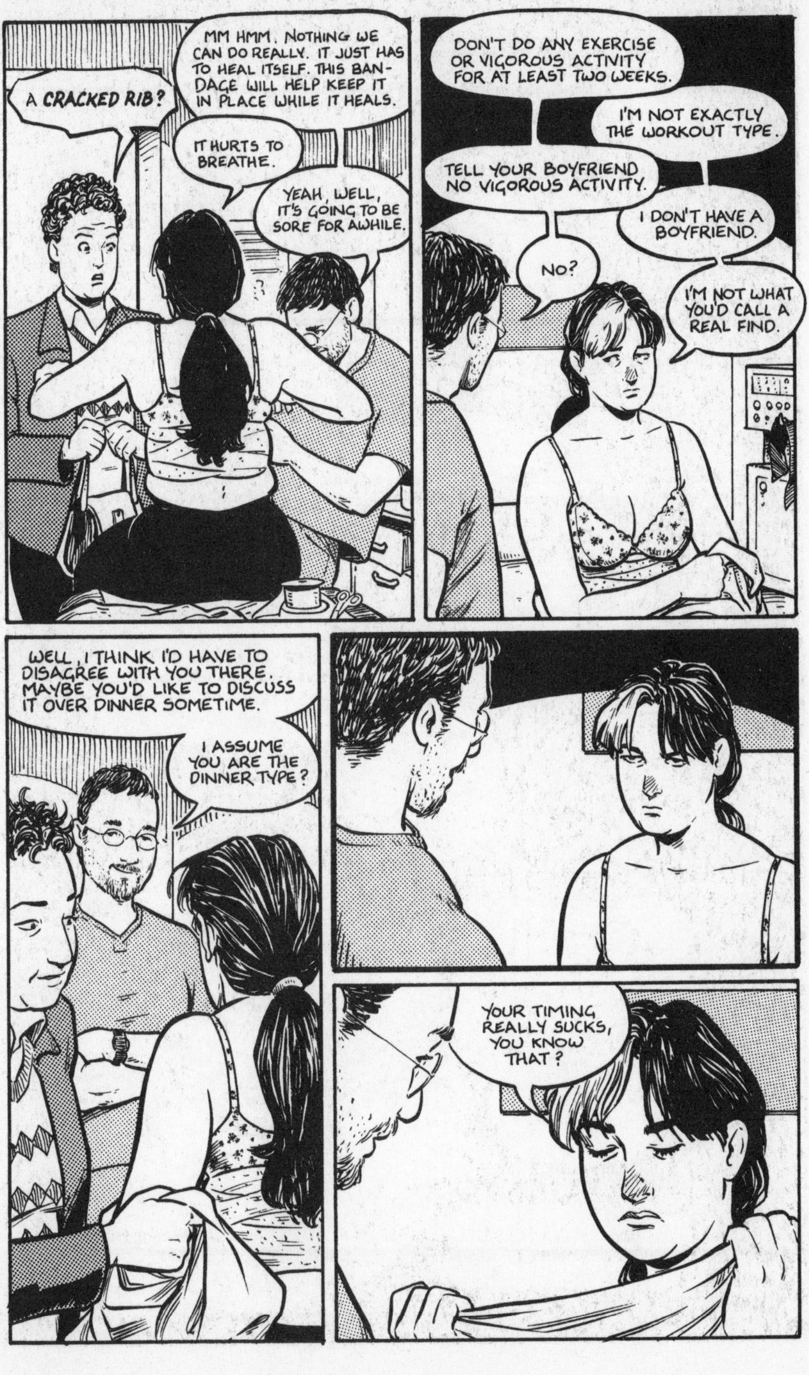
A CRACKED RIB?
MM HMM. NOTHING WE CAN DO REALLY. IT JUST HAS TO HEAL ITSELF. THIS BANDAGE WILL HELP KEEP IT IN PLACE WHILE IT HEALS.
IT HURTS TO BREATHE.
YEAH, WELL, IT'S GOING TO BE SORE FOR AWHILE.
DON'T DO ANY EXERCISE OR VIGOROUS ACTIVITY FOR AT LEAST TWO WEEKS.
I'M NOT EXACTLY THE WORKOUT TYPE.
TELL YOUR BOYFRIEND NO VIGOROUS ACTIVITY.
I DON'T HAVE A BOYFRIEND.
NO?
I'M NOT WHAT YOU'D CALL A REAL FIND.
WELL, I THINK I'D HAVE TO DISAGREE WITH YOU THERE. MAYBE YOU'D LIKE TO DISCUSS IT OVER DINNER SOMETIME.
I ASSUME YOU ARE THE DINNER TYPE?
YOUR TIMING REALLY SUCKS, YOU KNOW THAT?

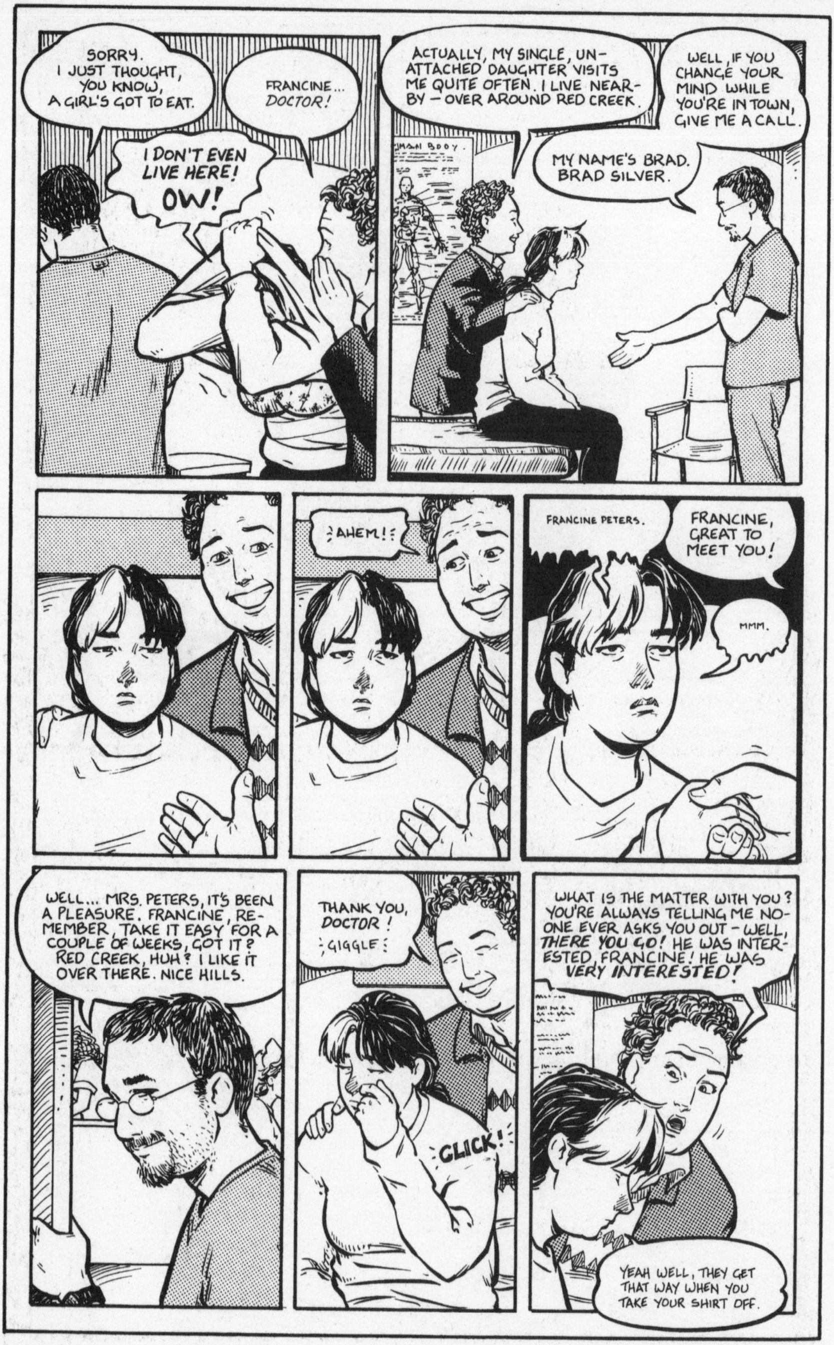
SORRY. I JUST THOUGHT, YOU KNOW, A GIRL'S GOT TO EAT.
FRANCINE... DOCTOR!
I DON'T EVEN LIVE HERE! OW!
ACTUALLY, MY SINGLE, UN-ATTACHED DAUGHTER VISITS ME QUITE OFTEN. I LIVE NEAR-BY — OVER AROUND RED CREEK.
WELL, IF YOU CHANGE YOUR MIND WHILE YOU'RE IN TOWN, GIVE ME A CALL.
MY NAME'S BRAD. BRAD SILVER.
AHEM!
FRANCINE PETERS.
FRANCINE, GREAT TO MEET YOU!
MMM.
WELL... MRS. PETERS, IT'S BEEN A PLEASURE. FRANCINE, RE-MEMBER, TAKE IT EASY FOR A COUPLE OF WEEKS, GOT IT? RED CREEK, HUH? I LIKE IT OVER THERE. NICE HILLS.
THANK YOU, DOCTOR! GIGGLE
CLICK!
WHAT IS THE MATTER WITH YOU? YOU'RE ALWAYS TELLING ME NO-ONE EVER ASKS YOU OUT — WELL, THERE YOU GO! HE WAS INTER-ESTED, FRANCINE! HE WAS VERY INTERESTED!
YEAH WELL, THEY GET THAT WAY WHEN YOU TAKE YOUR SHIRT OFF.

HE'S A DOCTOR. YOU CAN'T SHOW HIM ANYTHING HE HASN'T SEEN A THOUSAND TIMES BEFORE.

KATCHOO'S RIGHT — THEY DO ALL LOOK ALIKE WITH THOSE STUPID GOATEES.

NONSENSE. I THOUGHT HE LOOKED VERY HIP. VERY STYLISH!

HE LOOKS LIKE FREDDIE FEMUR. THEY ALL LOOK LIKE FREDDIE FEMUR WITH THAT STUPID COPY-CAT FASHION FLUNKY GAY WARLOCK WANNABE MINI-BEARD AND THAT MATCHING PRISON CAMP CASTRATE ME HAIRCUT.

FRIKKIN' SHEEP!

FRANCINE! I'VE NEVER HEARD SUCH LANGUAGE!

THEN YOU HAVEN'T SPENT MUCH TIME AROUND KATCHOO.

I COME BACK HERE WITH NEWS ABOUT DAVID AND I FIND YOU IN THE EMERGENCY ROOM WITH A BROKE RIB AND FOUL MOUTH! ;SIGH; I SWEAR...

YOU FOUND DAVID? WHERE? IS HE ALRIGHT?

NO, HONEY, HE'S NOT. DAVID IS IN CRITICAL CONDITION AT A NEARBY HOSPITAL... HE HAS A FRACTURED SKULL... THE DOCTORS... THEY'RE DOING ALL THEY CAN, BUT....

I SHOULD SAY NOT! WHAT IS THE MEANING OF ALL THIS?

I DON'T KNOW, MOM. I DON'T KNOW. SORRY.

THEY DON'T THINK HE WILL LIVE THROUGH THE WEEKEND, DEAR.

I'M SO SORRY, SWEETHEART. I KNOW YOU KIDS HAVE HAD MORE THAN YOUR SHARE OF T... BLE AND GR... YOUR FA... TH IS ALL YO... DEPEND... ON ME FO... ANY... NG. (W... YOU... TO THI... ABO... MOV... THIS... AND... COME... LIVE... WITH M... FOR A... WHILE... JUST L... YOU HAV... TIME TO... THINK... OVE... AND...

what is happening?

ABO... YOU... LM... LI... TH... O... SI... UP... AN... C... LL PER... KATCHOO... UPBRING... JUST WAS... NOBODY SH... SO SAD. BUT... TEN YEARS FR... NOW, THIS WILL... NOTHING FROM...

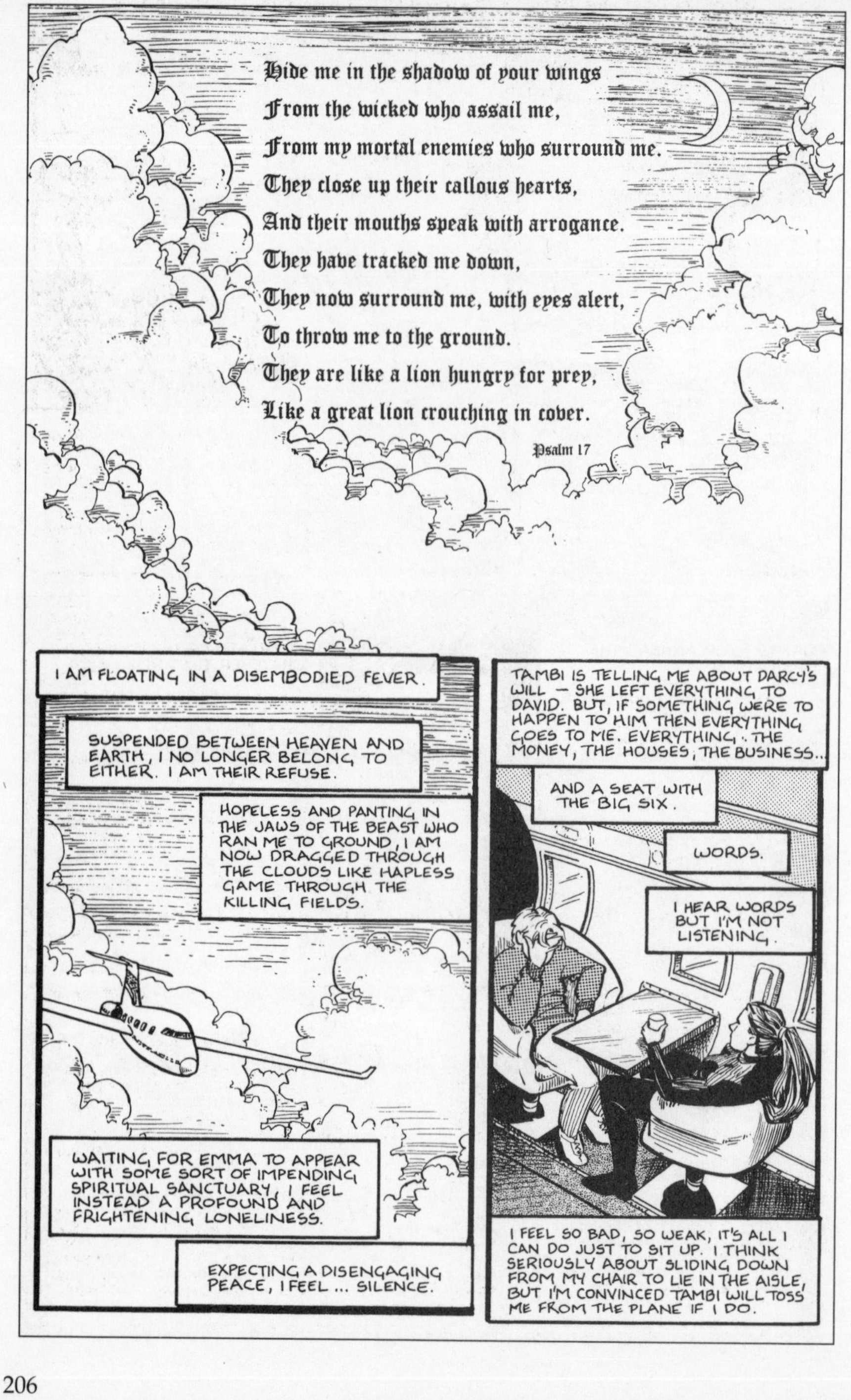
Hide me in the shadow of your wings
From the wicked who assail me,
From my mortal enemies who surround me.
They close up their callous hearts,
And their mouths speak with arrogance.
They have tracked me down,
They now surround me, with eyes alert,
To throw me to the ground.
They are like a lion hungry for prey,
Like a great lion crouching in cover.
Psalm 17
I AM FLOATING IN A DISEMBODIED FEVER.
SUSPENDED BETWEEN HEAVEN AND EARTH, I NO LONGER BELONG TO EITHER. I AM THEIR REFUSE.
HOPELESS AND PANTING IN THE JAWS OF THE BEAST WHO RAN ME TO GROUND, I AM NOW DRAGGED THROUGH THE CLOUDS LIKE HAPLESS GAME THROUGH THE KILLING FIELDS.
WAITING FOR EMMA TO APPEAR WITH SOME SORT OF IMPENDING SPIRITUAL SANCTUARY, I FEEL INSTEAD A PROFOUND AND FRIGHTENING LONELINESS.
EXPECTING A DISENGAGING PEACE, I FEEL ... SILENCE.
TAMBI IS TELLING ME ABOUT DARCY'S WILL — SHE LEFT EVERYTHING TO DAVID. BUT, IF SOMETHING WERE TO HAPPEN TO HIM THEN EVERYTHING GOES TO ME. EVERYTHING . THE MONEY, THE HOUSES, THE BUSINESS...
AND A SEAT WITH THE BIG SIX.
WORDS.
I HEAR WORDS BUT I'M NOT LISTENING.
I FEEL SO BAD, SO WEAK, IT'S ALL I CAN DO JUST TO SIT UP. I THINK SERIOUSLY ABOUT SLIDING DOWN FROM MY CHAIR TO LIE IN THE AISLE, BUT I'M CONVINCED TAMBI WILL TOSS ME FROM THE PLANE IF I DO.

I FIGURE AS LONG AS I PRETEND I'M LISTENING, SHE'LL KEEP TALKING BUT, HOW LONG I CAN KEEP IT UP, I DON'T KNOW.

THEN SHE SAYS SOMETHING THAT CATCHES MY ATTENTION — SOMETHING THAT DOESN'T ADD UP.

Wait...

Wha...

Veronica?

VERONICA PACE — YOUR SUCCESSOR.

You mean Veronica BOUEDAUES?

THAT'S AN ALIAS.

BUT THE FBI...

KNOWS WHAT WE WANT THEM TO KNOW.

No. what's the point of all this?

VERONICA PACE, ALIAS VERONICA BOUEDAUES OF HUMBLE NEW ORLEANS UPBRINGING, ALIAS BEVERLY PACE OF THE UPPER WASHINGTON SOCIAL SET, ALIAS RACHEL HAMPTON OF PACKARD-YERR NEW YORK. THE LIST GOES ON, SHALL I CONTINUE?

VERONICA WANTS TO RESURRECT THE PARKER GIRLS — AND SHE WANTS TO SPEARHEAD THE OPERATION.

PRETTY AMBITIOUS FOR A CHAUFFEUR.

NEVER TRUST THE QUIET, CONTRITE ONES.

HOW LONG HAS THIS BEEN GOING ON?

THIS GOES BACK TO BEFORE YOU CAME IN. VERONICA AND SAM WERE PLANNING A COUP D'ETAT TO SEIZE THE OPERATION FROM DARCY. THEY KNEW THAT SAL TUCCIANI AND THE OTHERS IN THE BIG SIX WERE NOT HAPPY WITH DARCY'S LACK OF RESPECT AND... DISCRETION, SO THEY OFFERED HIM A DEAL... HELP THEM REMOVE DARCY AND SANCTION THEIR NEW MANAGEMENT AND, IN RETURN, THEY ASSURED HIM A SIGNIFICANT INCREASE IN BRANCH COOPERATION, PLUS A HIGHER PERCENTAGE OF THE TAKE.

:SIGH: IDIOTS.

THAT'S WHEN SAL SENT ME IN.

TO HELP THEM?

TO WATCH THEM. SAL'S NOT STUPID, HE WASN'T ABOUT TO WASTE TIME WITH A COUPLE OF ZEALOUS FOOT SOLDIERS, BUT HE KNEW THEY WERE A

PRECURSOR OF THINGS TO COME. MY JOB WAS TO PROTECT THE INTERESTS OF THE COMPANY — WHATEVER THAT REQUIRED.

AND DARCY NEVER KNEW.

I DON'T THINK SO.

WHY ARE YOU TELLING ME ALL THIS?

BECAUSE THAT'S WHEN YOU CAME IN. YOU CHANGED EVERYTHING.

ME?

ALL OF THIS WAS IN PLACE WHEN EMMA INTRODUCED YOU TO DARCY. SHE KNEW DARCY HAD A FETISH FOR TEENAGE GIRLS...

WAIT A MINUTE...

AND EMMA NEEDED THE MONEY FOR CRANK...

THAT'S A *DAMN LIE!*

IS IT? WHY DO YOU THINK EMMA GOT YOU INTO PROSTITUTION? WHAT HAPPENED TO ALL THE MONEY YOU MADE?

I... EMMA HANDLED ALL THAT.

WHY DO YOU THINK SHE PULLED YOU OFF THE STREETS — BECAUSE SHE FELT SORRY FOR YOU? YOU WERE A CASH COW TO HER. DON'T TELL ME YOU'VE BEEN HARBORING SOME SORT OF ROMANTIC ILLUSION ABOUT HER. NOT YOU!

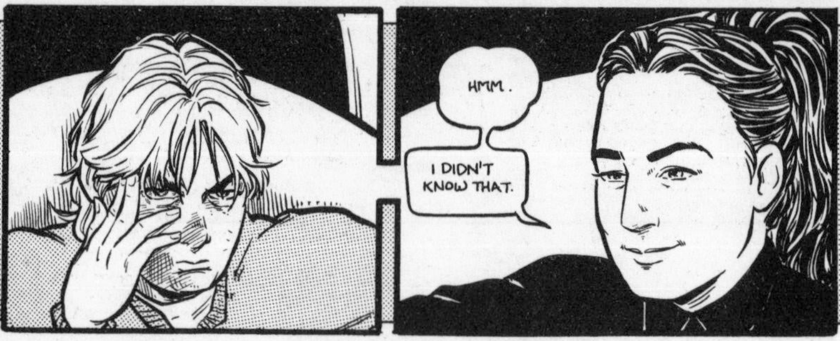
HMM.
I DIDN'T KNOW THAT.

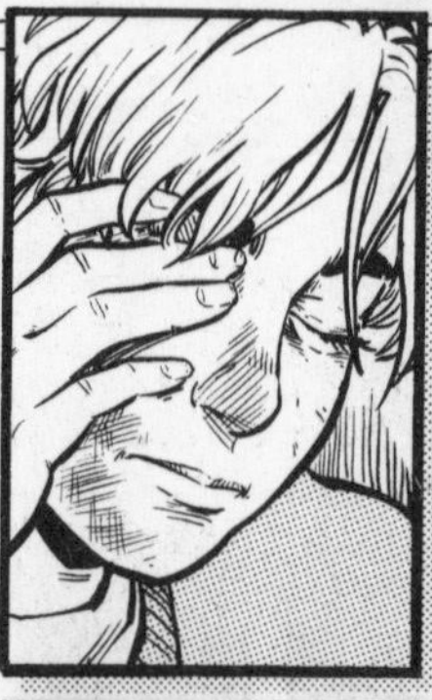

LOOK, I'M NOT IN A HURRY TO DIE BUT, WHY ARE WE HAVING THIS CONVERSATION?

MY GOAL HERE IS TO TELL YOU THE TRUTH... ABOUT EVERYTHING.

WHY? WHAT DIFFERENCE DOES IT MAKE NOW?

DARCY FELL IN LOVE WITH YOU, SHE TRUSTED YOU, SHE EVEN CONFIDED IN YOU. YOU BEGAN TO OFFER YOUR OPINION AND YOUR OBSERVATIONS WERE ASTUTE. YOU DIRECTED HER THROUGH SEVERAL COMPLICATED SITUATIONS AND YOUR INFLUENCE EVENTUALLY MADE THE PARKER OPERATION MORE POWERFUL AND COMPLEX THAN ANYONE THOUGHT POSSIBLE. IN SHORT, TO EVERYONE'S SURPRISE, IT TURNS OUT YOU HAVE A GIFT FOR THIS LINE OF WORK. THAT'S WHY SAMANTHA AND VERONICA SET YOU UP.

THAT'S WHAT I'VE BEEN SAYING, AND YOU KNEW THIS ALL ALONG?

I TOLD YOU, MY JOB WAS TO PROTECT THE COMPANY, NOT FIX YOUR PROBLEMS. DARCY HAD A PARTY FOR DAVID AND INVITED SENATOR CHALMERS, WHO WAS BRINGING HER A PAYMENT FOR A BLACKMAIL DEAL SHE WAS WORKING ON HIM. SHE SENT YOU AND EMMA UPSTAIRS UNDER THE PRETEXT OF REWARDING HIS COOPERATION, BUT THE HIDDEN CAMERAS WOULD SERVE TO PERPETUATE HIS SERVITUDE. THE SENATOR HAD THE MONEY ON HIM. WHEN SAMANTHA WENT TO SWEEP THE ROOM OF LIABILITIES AFTER YOU AND EMMA FINISHED, SHE INTENDED TO TAKE THE MONEY AND HIDE IT. YOU AND EMMA WOULD BE ACCUSED OF THE CRIME AND, IF ALL WENT ACCORDING TO PLAN, THE TWO OF YOU WOULD NEVER SEE THE LIGHT OF DAY AGAIN. SIMPLE ENOUGH, RIGHT? WHAT COULD POSSIBLY GO WRONG?

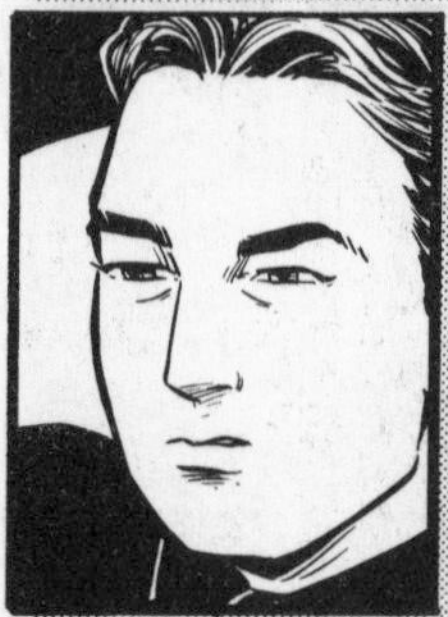

BUT YOU BEAT THEM TO THE PUNCH – YOU DISAPPEARED WITH THE MONEY BEFORE THEY HAD A CHANCE TO NAIL YOU. I MUST SAY, I WAS IMPRESSED. YOUR TIMING HAS ALWAYS BEEN IMPECCABLE, MISS CHOOVANSKI.

I DIDN'T TAKE THE MONEY.

I KNOW. EMMA TOOK IT, DIDN'T SHE? YOU DIDN'T EVEN KNOW SHE HAD IT UNTIL SHE SHOWED YOU IN HAWAII, DID YOU? YOU JUST WANTED TO RUN AWAY – BUT SHE COMPLICATED MATTERS. HOW AM I DOING SO FAR?

IT'S PISSING ME OFF YOU KNEW ALL THIS AND DIDN'T SAY SOMETHING.

YOU FLEW TO ZURICH AND OPENED AN ACCOUNT IN SAMANTHA'S NAME – A BRILLIANT MOVE BY THE WAY, VERY FARSIGHTED – AND WHEN YOU REJOINED EMMA IN HAWAII, WE WERE WAITING FOR YOU. THE MONEY WAS NOWHERE TO BE FOUND. YOU ACTED LIKE YOU DIDN'T KNOW WHAT WE WERE TALKING ABOUT, EMMA OVERDOSES ON HER NEW CRANK AND NEARLY DROWNS, SAM AND VERONICA WANT TO CRUCIFY YOU AND DARCY WANTS THE PRODIGAL DAUGHTER TO COME HOME. WOULD YOU CARE FOR A DRINK?

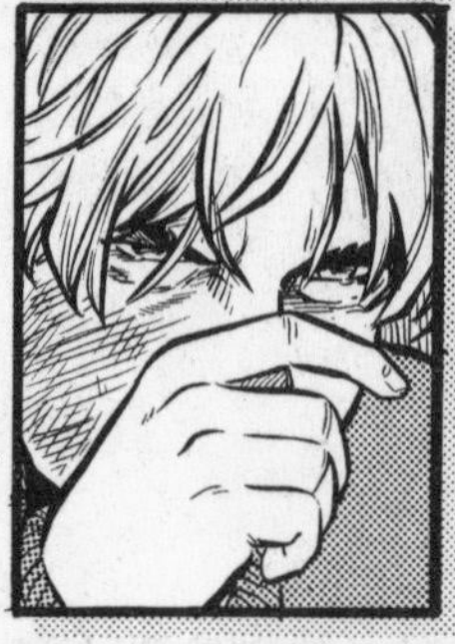

NO.

DARCY WOULDN'T LET THEM KILL YOU, SO THEY LET YOU GO. YOU AND EMMA SPLIT UP TO FORK THE TRAIL – SHE GOES HOME TO TORONTO AND YOU TO HOUSTON. SAM'S PLAN WAS TO FOLLOW YOU, CONVINCED YOU'D LEAD THEM TO THE MONEY. THEN SHE COULD USE THE WHOLE MESS TO DISCREDIT DARCY AND GET WHAT SHE WANTED. BUT YOU DO NOTHING, YOU LAY LOW, AND SAM GROWS IMPATIENT. THE MONEY SHE'S SIPHONING OFF THE COMPANY ISN'T ENOUGH. SHE VILIFIES YOU TO PARKER – SO THEY SEND DAVID.

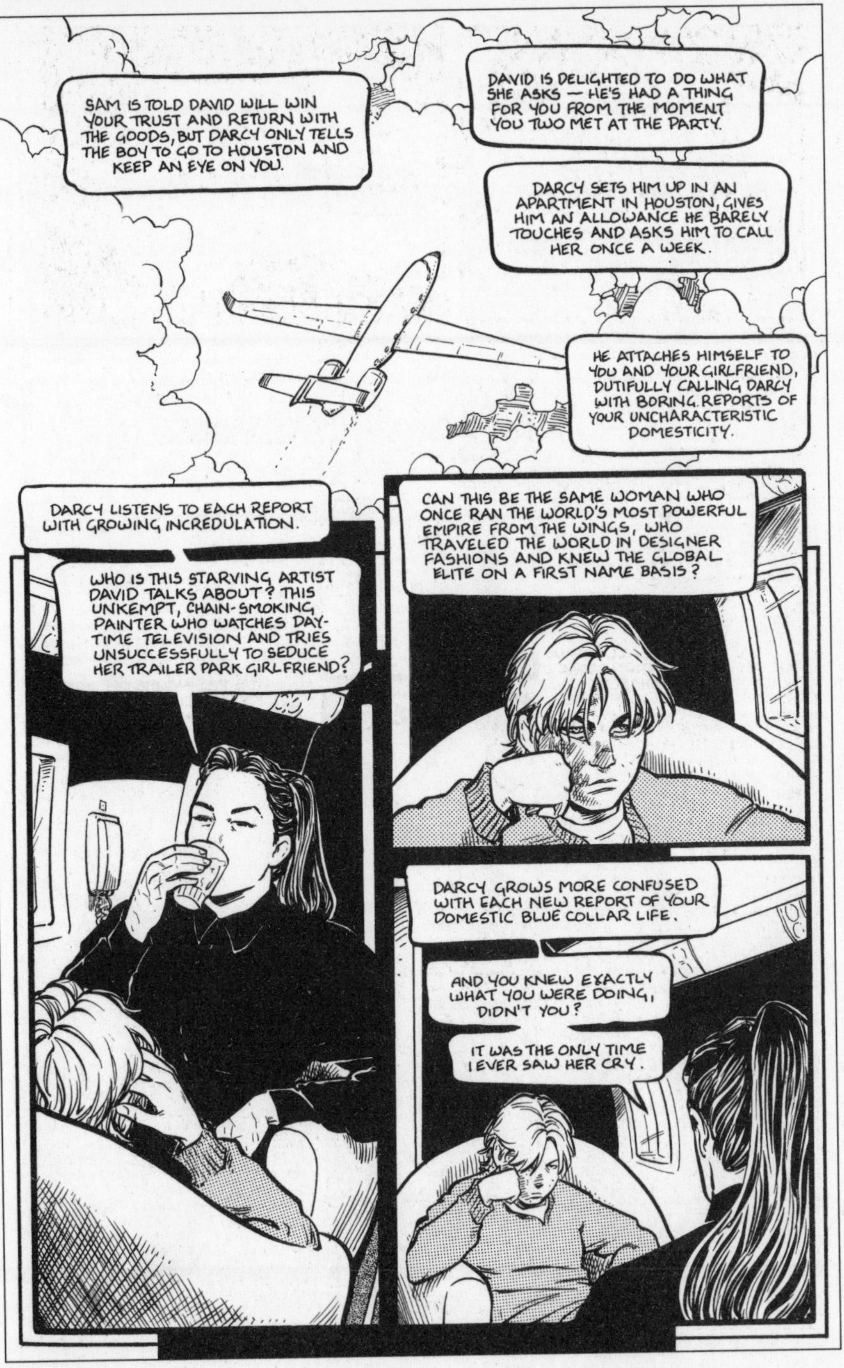
SAM IS TOLD DAVID WILL WIN YOUR TRUST AND RETURN WITH THE GOODS, BUT DARCY ONLY TELLS THE BOY TO GO TO HOUSTON AND KEEP AN EYE ON YOU.
DAVID IS DELIGHTED TO DO WHAT SHE ASKS — HE'S HAD A THING FOR YOU FROM THE MOMENT YOU TWO MET AT THE PARTY.
DARCY SETS HIM UP IN AN APARTMENT IN HOUSTON, GIVES HIM AN ALLOWANCE HE BARELY TOUCHES AND ASKS HIM TO CALL HER ONCE A WEEK.
HE ATTACHES HIMSELF TO YOU AND YOUR GIRLFRIEND, DUTIFULLY CALLING DARCY WITH BORING REPORTS OF YOUR UNCHARACTERISTIC DOMESTICITY.
DARCY LISTENS TO EACH REPORT WITH GROWING INCREDULATION.
WHO IS THIS STARVING ARTIST DAVID TALKS ABOUT? THIS UNKEMPT, CHAIN-SMOKING PAINTER WHO WATCHES DAY-TIME TELEVISION AND TRIES UNSUCCESSFULLY TO SEDUCE HER TRAILER PARK GIRLFRIEND?
CAN THIS BE THE SAME WOMAN WHO ONCE RAN THE WORLD'S MOST POWERFUL EMPIRE FROM THE WINGS, WHO TRAVELED THE WORLD IN DESIGNER FASHIONS AND KNEW THE GLOBAL ELITE ON A FIRST NAME BASIS?
DARCY GROWS MORE CONFUSED WITH EACH NEW REPORT OF YOUR DOMESTIC BLUE COLLAR LIFE.
AND YOU KNEW EXACTLY WHAT YOU WERE DOING, DIDN'T YOU?
IT WAS THE ONLY TIME I EVER SAW HER CRY.

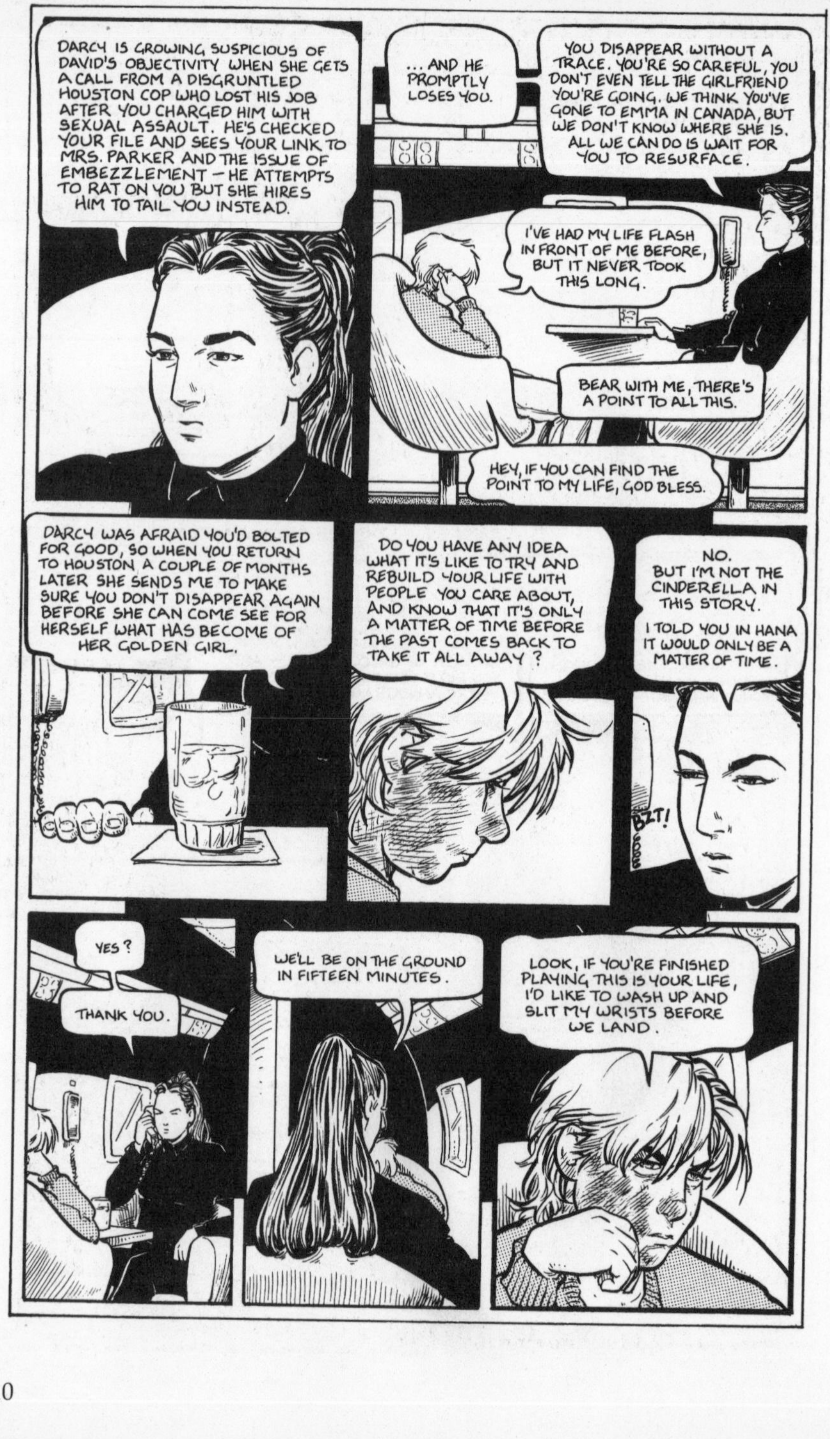
DARCY IS GROWING SUSPICIOUS OF DAVID'S OBJECTIVITY WHEN SHE GETS A CALL FROM A DISGRUNTLED HOUSTON COP WHO LOST HIS JOB AFTER YOU CHARGED HIM WITH SEXUAL ASSAULT. HE'S CHECKED YOUR FILE AND SEES YOUR LINK TO MRS. PARKER AND THE ISSUE OF EMBEZZLEMENT — HE ATTEMPTS TO RAT ON YOU BUT SHE HIRES HIM TO TAIL YOU INSTEAD.
... AND HE PROMPTLY LOSES YOU.
YOU DISAPPEAR WITHOUT A TRACE. YOU'RE SO CAREFUL, YOU DON'T EVEN TELL THE GIRLFRIEND YOU'RE GOING. WE THINK YOU'VE GONE TO EMMA IN CANADA, BUT WE DON'T KNOW WHERE SHE IS. ALL WE CAN DO IS WAIT FOR YOU TO RESURFACE.
I'VE HAD MY LIFE FLASH IN FRONT OF ME BEFORE, BUT IT NEVER TOOK THIS LONG.
BEAR WITH ME, THERE'S A POINT TO ALL THIS.
HEY, IF YOU CAN FIND THE POINT TO MY LIFE, GOD BLESS.
DARCY WAS AFRAID YOU'D BOLTED FOR GOOD, SO WHEN YOU RETURN TO HOUSTON A COUPLE OF MONTHS LATER SHE SENDS ME TO MAKE SURE YOU DON'T DISAPPEAR AGAIN BEFORE SHE CAN COME SEE FOR HERSELF WHAT HAS BECOME OF HER GOLDEN GIRL.
DO YOU HAVE ANY IDEA WHAT IT'S LIKE TO TRY AND REBUILD YOUR LIFE WITH PEOPLE YOU CARE ABOUT, AND KNOW THAT IT'S ONLY A MATTER OF TIME BEFORE THE PAST COMES BACK TO TAKE IT ALL AWAY?
NO. BUT I'M NOT THE CINDERELLA IN THIS STORY.
I TOLD YOU IN HANA IT WOULD ONLY BE A MATTER OF TIME.
BZT!
YES?
THANK YOU.
WE'LL BE ON THE GROUND IN FIFTEEN MINUTES.
LOOK, IF YOU'RE FINISHED PLAYING THIS IS YOUR LIFE, I'D LIKE TO WASH UP AND SLIT MY WRISTS BEFORE WE LAND.

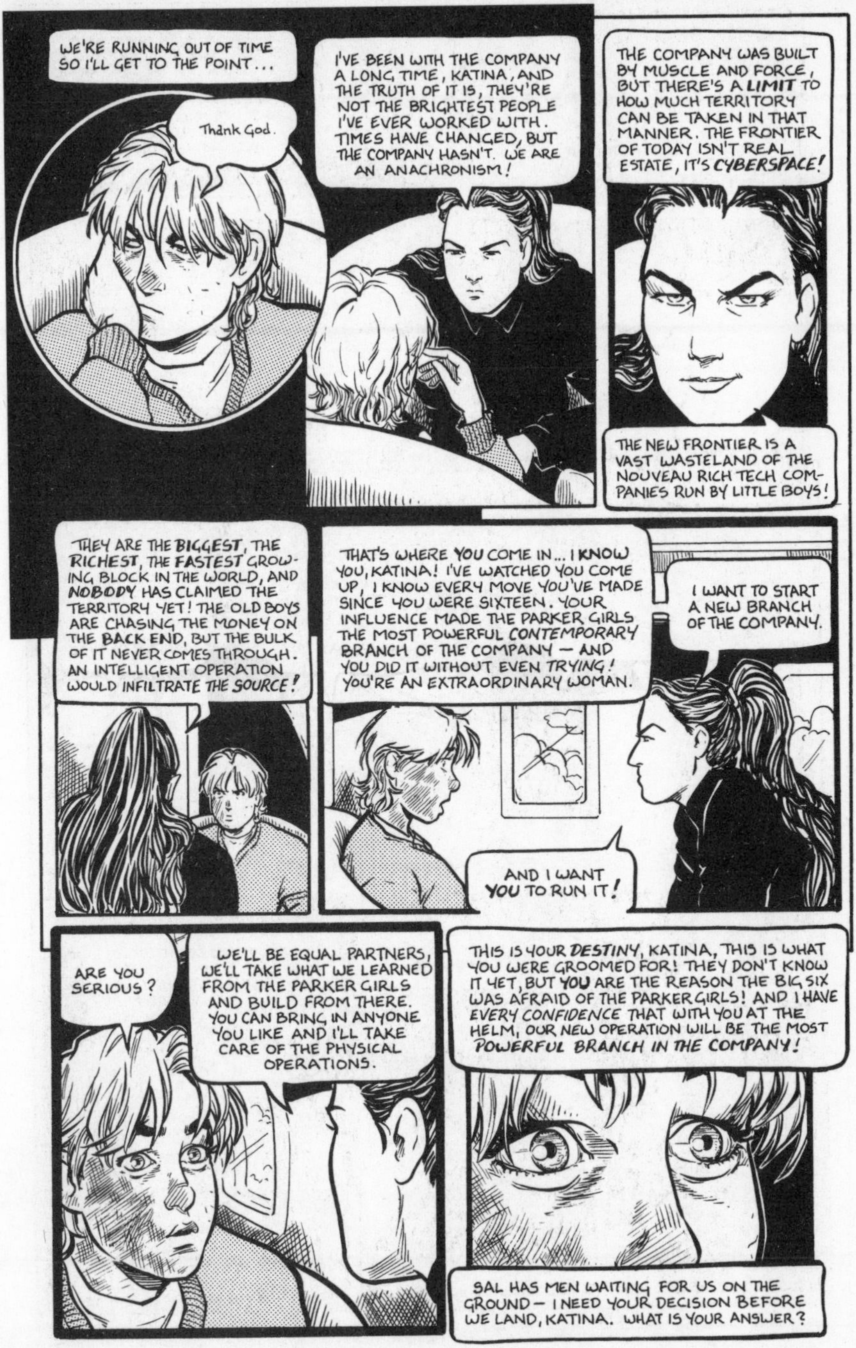
WE'RE RUNNING OUT OF TIME SO I'LL GET TO THE POINT...
Thank God.
I'VE BEEN WITH THE COMPANY A LONG TIME, KATINA, AND THE TRUTH OF IT IS, THEY'RE NOT THE BRIGHTEST PEOPLE I'VE EVER WORKED WITH. TIMES HAVE CHANGED, BUT THE COMPANY HASN'T. WE ARE AN ANACHRONISM!
THE COMPANY WAS BUILT BY MUSCLE AND FORCE, BUT THERE'S A LIMIT TO HOW MUCH TERRITORY CAN BE TAKEN IN THAT MANNER. THE FRONTIER OF TODAY ISN'T REAL ESTATE, IT'S CYBERSPACE!
THE NEW FRONTIER IS A VAST WASTELAND OF THE NOUVEAU RICH TECH COMPANIES RUN BY LITTLE BOYS!
THEY ARE THE BIGGEST, THE RICHEST, THE FASTEST GROWING BLOCK IN THE WORLD, AND NOBODY HAS CLAIMED THE TERRITORY YET! THE OLD BOYS ARE CHASING THE MONEY ON THE BACK END, BUT THE BULK OF IT NEVER COMES THROUGH. AN INTELLIGENT OPERATION WOULD INFILTRATE THE SOURCE!
THAT'S WHERE YOU COME IN... I KNOW YOU, KATINA! I'VE WATCHED YOU COME UP, I KNOW EVERY MOVE YOU'VE MADE SINCE YOU WERE SIXTEEN. YOUR INFLUENCE MADE THE PARKER GIRLS THE MOST POWERFUL CONTEMPORARY BRANCH OF THE COMPANY — AND YOU DID IT WITHOUT EVEN TRYING! YOU'RE AN EXTRAORDINARY WOMAN.
I WANT TO START A NEW BRANCH OF THE COMPANY.
AND I WANT YOU TO RUN IT!
ARE YOU SERIOUS?
WE'LL BE EQUAL PARTNERS, WE'LL TAKE WHAT WE LEARNED FROM THE PARKER GIRLS AND BUILD FROM THERE. YOU CAN BRING IN ANYONE YOU LIKE AND I'LL TAKE CARE OF THE PHYSICAL OPERATIONS.
THIS IS YOUR DESTINY, KATINA, THIS IS WHAT YOU WERE GROOMED FOR! THEY DON'T KNOW IT YET, BUT YOU ARE THE REASON THE BIG SIX WAS AFRAID OF THE PARKER GIRLS! AND I HAVE EVERY CONFIDENCE THAT WITH YOU AT THE HELM, OUR NEW OPERATION WILL BE THE MOST POWERFUL BRANCH IN THE COMPANY!
SAL HAS MEN WAITING FOR US ON THE GROUND — I NEED YOUR DECISION BEFORE WE LAND, KATINA. WHAT IS YOUR ANSWER?

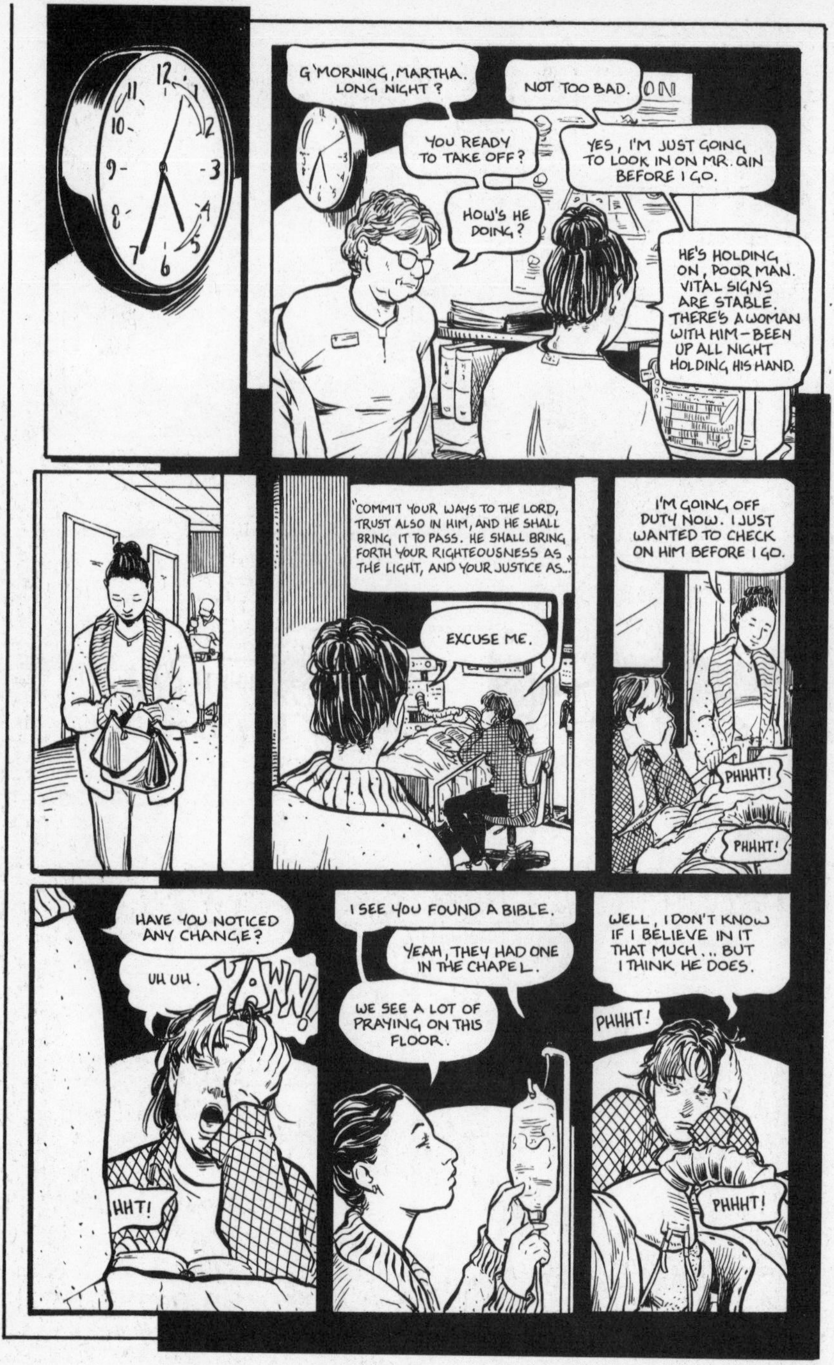
G'MORNING, MARTHA. LONG NIGHT?
NOT TOO BAD.
YOU READY TO TAKE OFF?
YES, I'M JUST GOING TO LOOK IN ON MR. QIN BEFORE I GO.
HOW'S HE DOING?
HE'S HOLDING ON, POOR MAN. VITAL SIGNS ARE STABLE. THERE'S A WOMAN WITH HIM—BEEN UP ALL NIGHT HOLDING HIS HAND.
"COMMIT YOUR WAYS TO THE LORD, TRUST ALSO IN HIM, AND HE SHALL BRING IT TO PASS. HE SHALL BRING FORTH YOUR RIGHTEOUSNESS AS THE LIGHT, AND YOUR JUSTICE AS..."
EXCUSE ME.
I'M GOING OFF DUTY NOW. I JUST WANTED TO CHECK ON HIM BEFORE I GO.
PHHHT!
PHHHT!
HAVE YOU NOTICED ANY CHANGE?
UH UH.
YAWN!
HHT!
I SEE YOU FOUND A BIBLE.
YEAH, THEY HAD ONE IN THE CHAPEL.
WE SEE A LOT OF PRAYING ON THIS FLOOR.
WELL, I DON'T KNOW IF I BELIEVE IN IT THAT MUCH... BUT I THINK HE DOES.
PHHHT!
PHHHT!

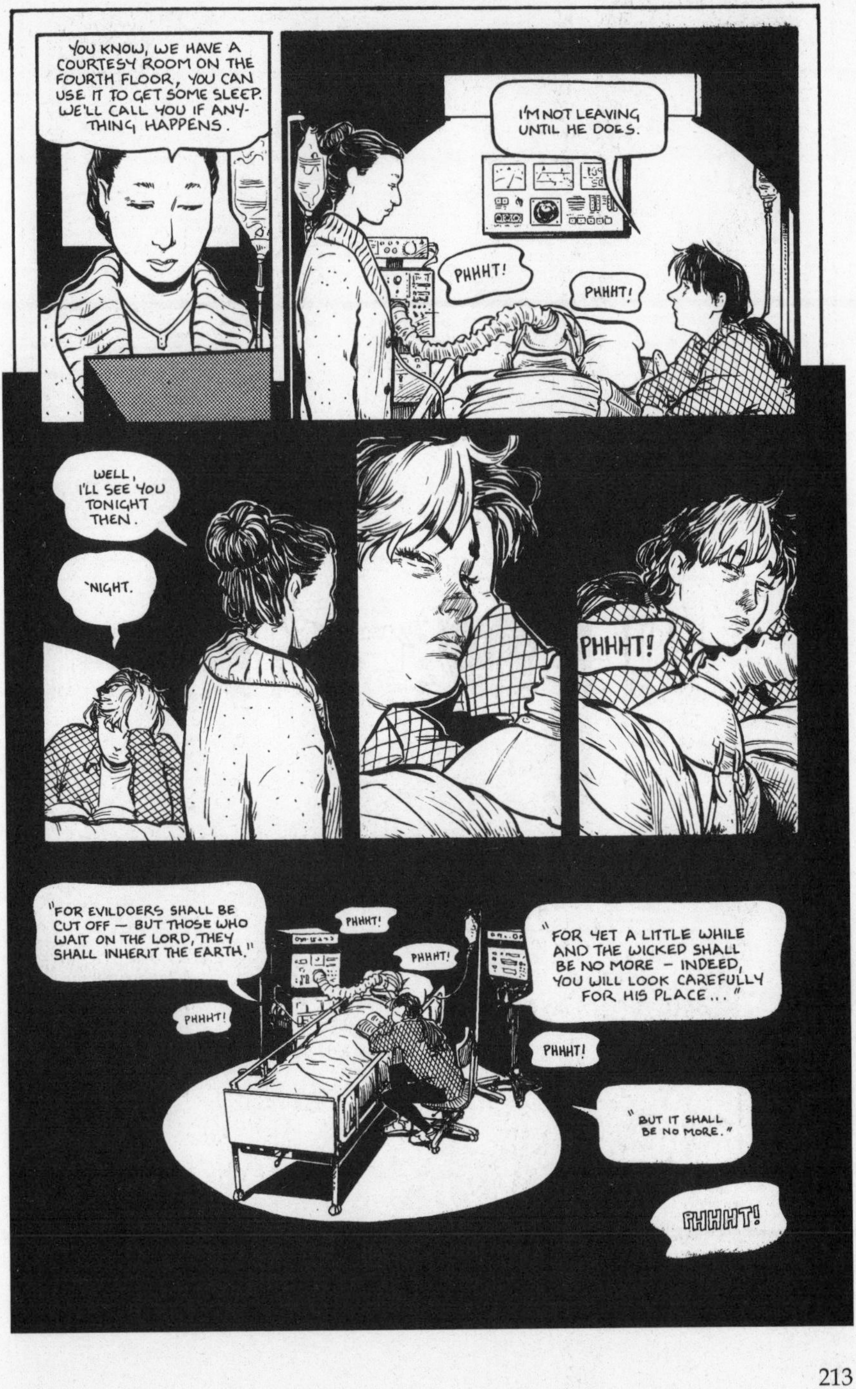
YOU KNOW, WE HAVE A COURTESY ROOM ON THE FOURTH FLOOR, YOU CAN USE IT TO GET SOME SLEEP. WE'LL CALL YOU IF ANYTHING HAPPENS.
I'M NOT LEAVING UNTIL HE DOES.
PHHHT!
PHHHT!
WELL, I'LL SEE YOU TONIGHT THEN.
'NIGHT.
PHHHT!
"FOR EVILDOERS SHALL BE CUT OFF — BUT THOSE WHO WAIT ON THE LORD, THEY SHALL INHERIT THE EARTH."
PHHHT!
PHHHT!
PHHHT!
"FOR YET A LITTLE WHILE AND THE WICKED SHALL BE NO MORE - INDEED, YOU WILL LOOK CAREFULLY FOR HIS PLACE..."
PHHHT!
"BUT IT SHALL BE NO MORE."
PHHHT!

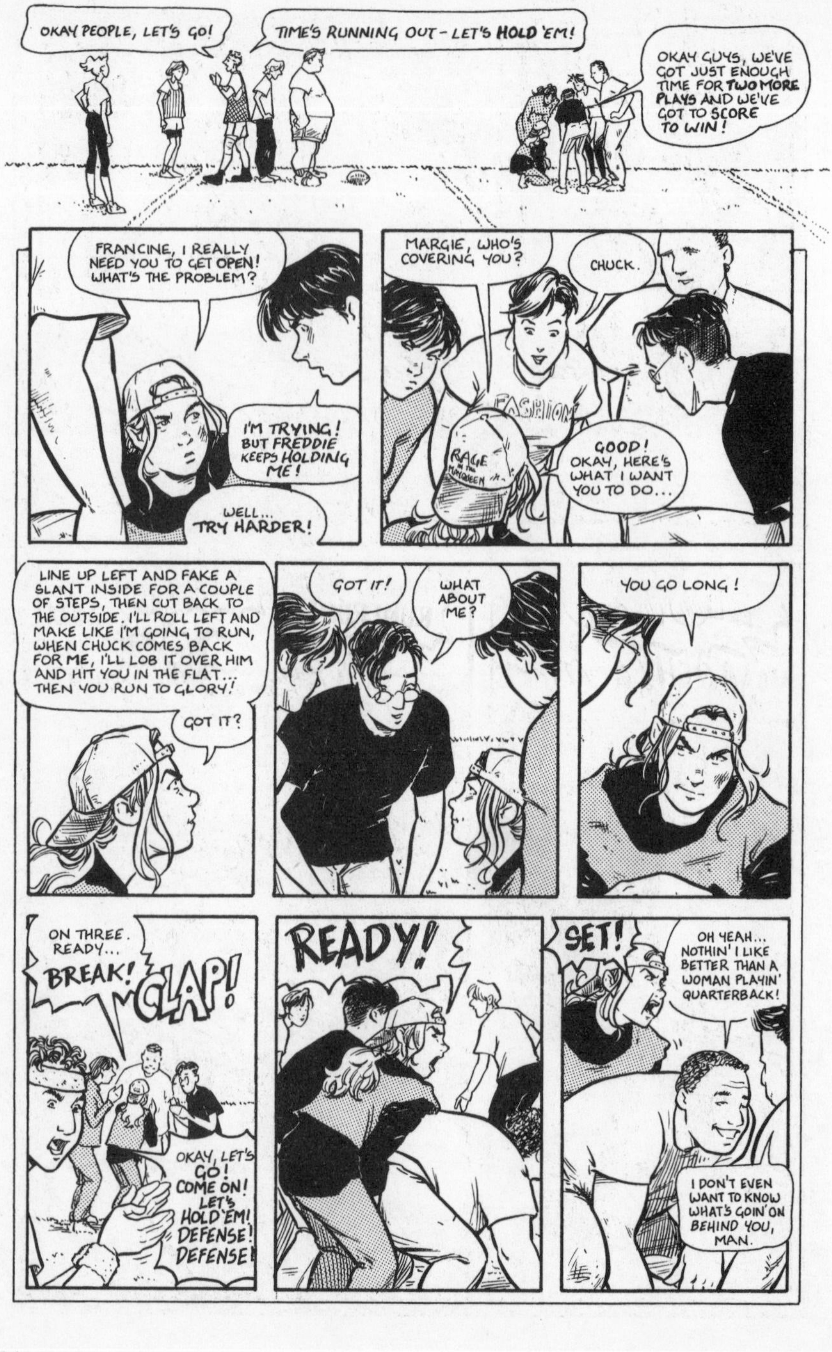
OKAY PEOPLE, LET'S GO!
TIME'S RUNNING OUT - LET'S HOLD 'EM!
OKAY GUYS, WE'VE GOT JUST ENOUGH TIME FOR TWO MORE PLAYS AND WE'VE GOT TO SCORE TO WIN!
FRANCINE, I REALLY NEED YOU TO GET OPEN! WHAT'S THE PROBLEM?
I'M TRYING! BUT FREDDIE KEEPS HOLDING ME!
WELL... TRY HARDER!
MARGIE, WHO'S COVERING YOU?
CHUCK.
GOOD! OKAY, HERE'S WHAT I WANT YOU TO DO...
FASHION
RAGE
LINE UP LEFT AND FAKE A SLANT INSIDE FOR A COUPLE OF STEPS, THEN CUT BACK TO THE OUTSIDE. I'LL ROLL LEFT AND MAKE LIKE I'M GOING TO RUN, WHEN CHUCK COMES BACK FOR ME, I'LL LOB IT OVER HIM AND HIT YOU IN THE FLAT... THEN YOU RUN TO GLORY!
GOT IT?
GOT IT!
WHAT ABOUT ME?
YOU GO LONG!
ON THREE. READY...
BREAK!
CLAP!
OKAY, LET'S GO! COME ON! LET'S HOLD 'EM! DEFENSE! DEFENSE!
READY!
SET!
OH YEAH... NOTHIN' I LIKE BETTER THAN A WOMAN PLAYIN' QUARTERBACK!
I DON'T EVEN WANT TO KNOW WHAT'S GOIN' ON BEHIND YOU, MAN.

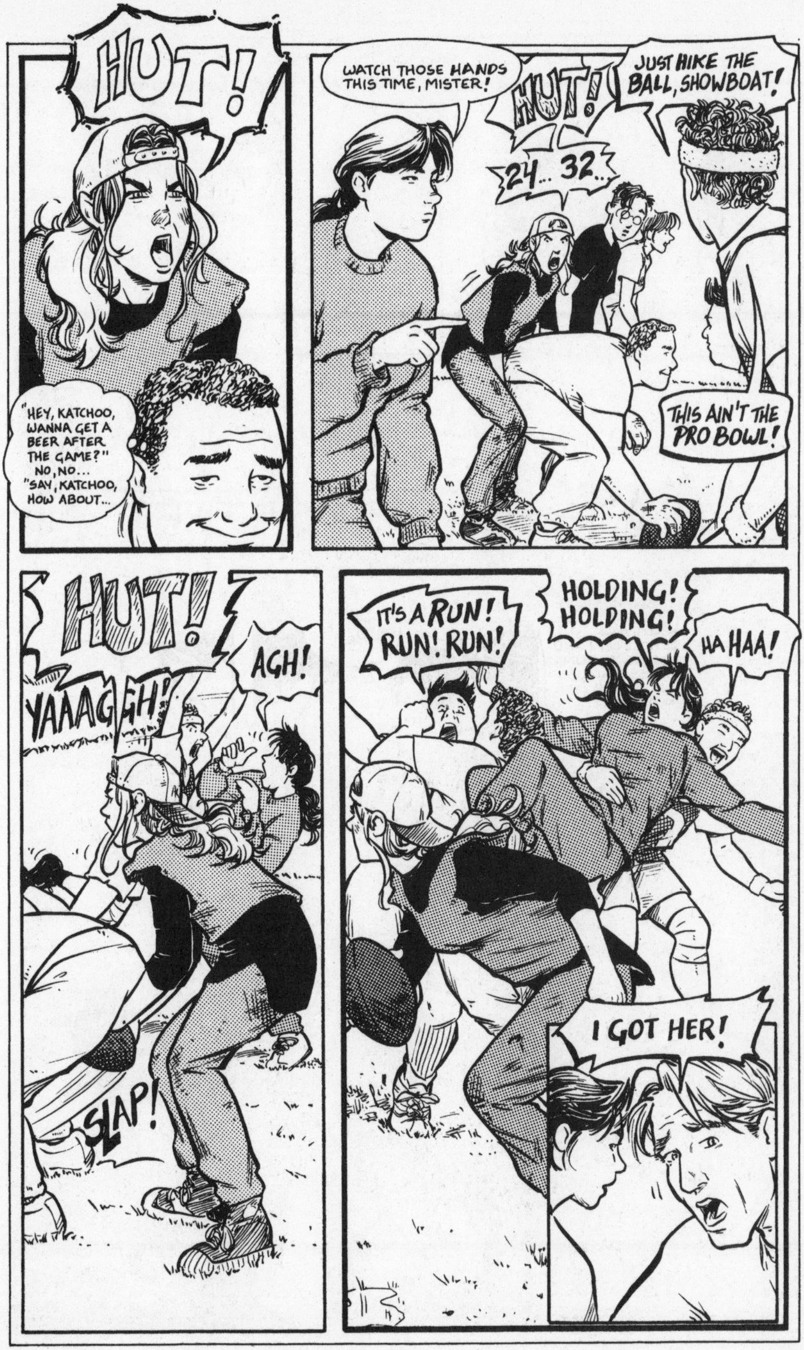
HUT!
"HEY, KATCHOO, WANNA GET A BEER AFTER THE GAME?" NO, NO... "SAY, KATCHOO, HOW ABOUT...
WATCH THOSE HANDS THIS TIME, MISTER!
HUT!
24... 32...
JUST HIKE THE BALL, SHOWBOAT!
THIS AIN'T THE PRO BOWL!
HUT!
YAAAGGH!
AGH!
SLAP!
IT'S A RUN! RUN! RUN!
HOLDING! HOLDING!
HA HAA!
I GOT HER!

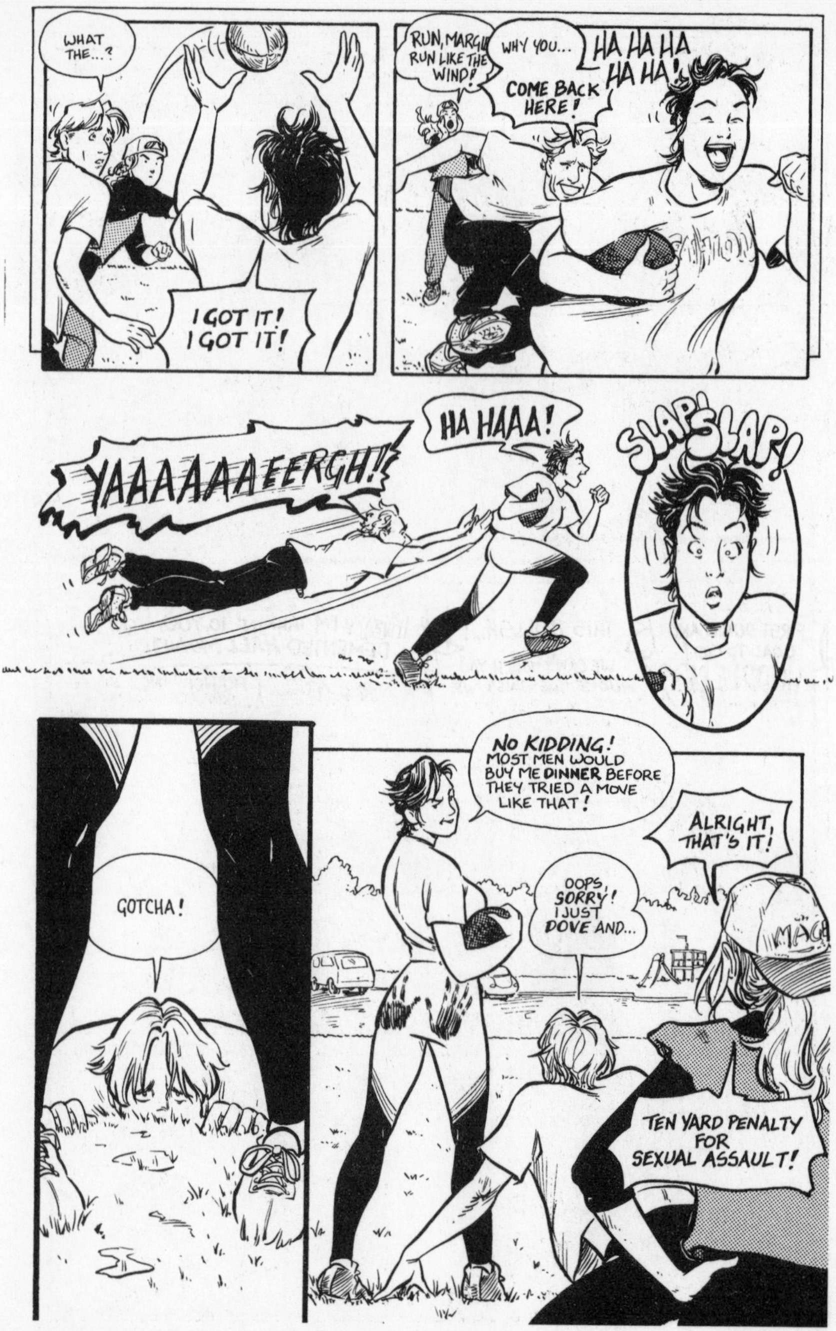
WHAT THE...?
I GOT IT! I GOT IT!
RUN, MARGIE RUN LIKE THE WIND!
WHY YOU...
COME BACK HERE!
HA HA HA HA HA!
YAAAAAAEERGH!!
HA HAAA!
SLAP! SLAP!
GOTCHA!
NO KIDDING! MOST MEN WOULD BUY ME DINNER BEFORE THEY TRIED A MOVE LIKE THAT!
OOPS, SORRY! I JUST DOVE AND...
ALRIGHT, THAT'S IT!
TEN YARD PENALTY FOR SEXUAL ASSAULT!

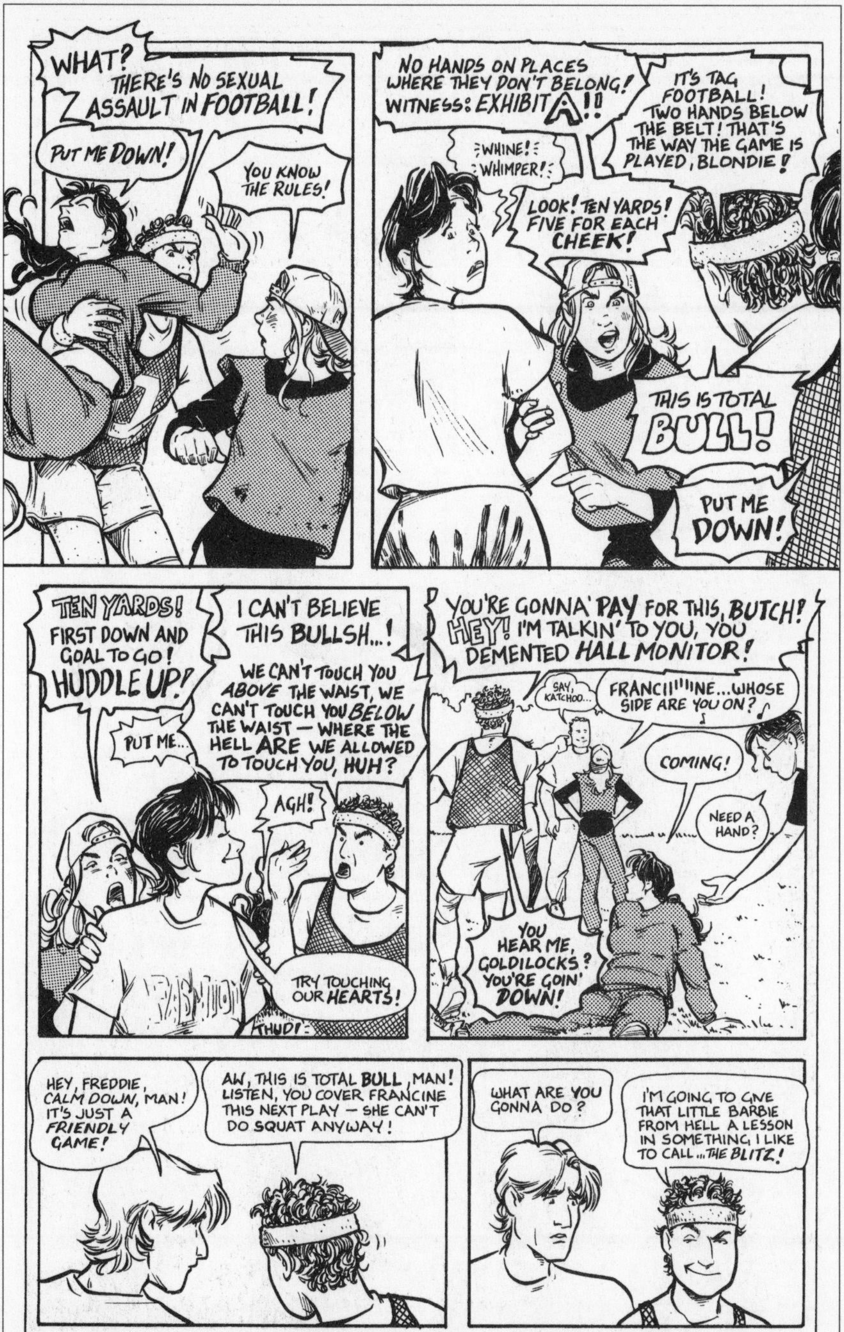
WHAT? THERE'S NO SEXUAL ASSAULT IN FOOTBALL!
PUT ME DOWN!
YOU KNOW THE RULES!
NO HANDS ON PLACES WHERE THEY DON'T BELONG! WITNESS: EXHIBIT A!!
IT'S TAG FOOTBALL! TWO HANDS BELOW THE BELT! THAT'S THE WAY THE GAME IS PLAYED, BLONDIE!
WHINE! WHIMPER!
LOOK! TEN YARDS! FIVE FOR EACH CHEEK!
THIS IS TOTAL BULL!
PUT ME DOWN!
TEN YARDS! FIRST DOWN AND GOAL TO GO! HUDDLE UP!
I CAN'T BELIEVE THIS BULLSH...!
WE CAN'T TOUCH YOU ABOVE THE WAIST, WE CAN'T TOUCH YOU BELOW THE WAIST — WHERE THE HELL ARE WE ALLOWED TO TOUCH YOU, HUH?
PUT ME...
AGH!
TRY TOUCHING OUR HEARTS!
THUD!
YOU'RE GONNA' PAY FOR THIS, BUTCH! HEY! I'M TALKIN' TO YOU, YOU DEMENTED HALL MONITOR!
SAY, KATCHOO...
FRANCIIIINE... WHOSE SIDE ARE YOU ON?
COMING!
NEED A HAND?
YOU HEAR ME, GOLDILOCKS? YOU'RE GOIN' DOWN!
HEY, FREDDIE, CALM DOWN, MAN! IT'S JUST A FRIENDLY GAME!
AW, THIS IS TOTAL BULL, MAN! LISTEN, YOU COVER FRANCINE THIS NEXT PLAY — SHE CAN'T DO SQUAT ANYWAY!
WHAT ARE YOU GONNA DO?
I'M GOING TO GIVE THAT LITTLE BARBIE FROM HELL A LESSON IN SOMETHING I LIKE TO CALL... THE BLITZ!

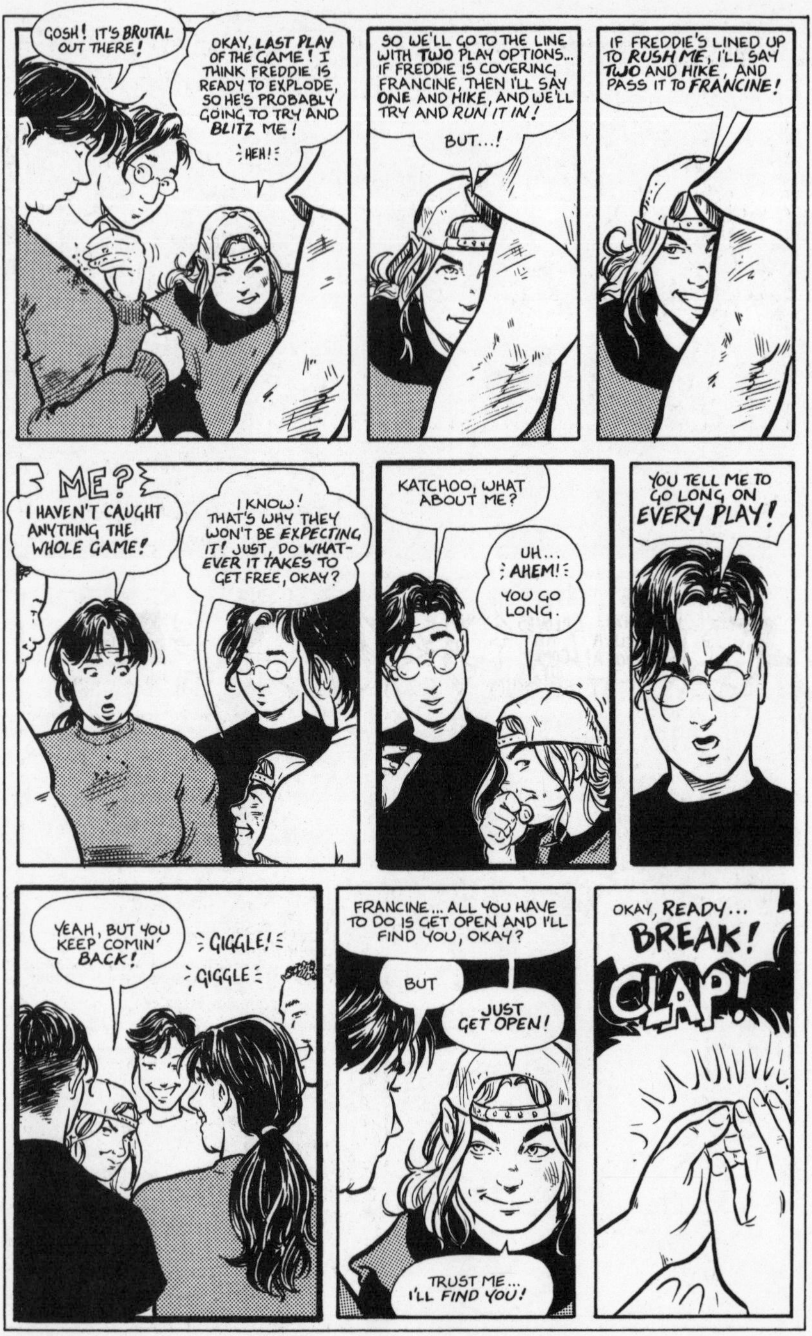
GOSH! IT'S BRUTAL OUT THERE!
OKAY, LAST PLAY OF THE GAME! I THINK FREDDIE IS READY TO EXPLODE, SO HE'S PROBABLY GOING TO TRY AND BLITZ ME!
HEH!
SO WE'LL GO TO THE LINE WITH TWO PLAY OPTIONS... IF FREDDIE IS COVERING FRANCINE, THEN I'LL SAY ONE AND HIKE, AND WE'LL TRY AND RUN IT IN!
BUT...!
IF FREDDIE'S LINED UP TO RUSH ME, I'LL SAY TWO AND HIKE, AND PASS IT TO FRANCINE!
ME?
I HAVEN'T CAUGHT ANYTHING THE WHOLE GAME!
I KNOW! THAT'S WHY THEY WON'T BE EXPECTING IT! JUST, DO WHATEVER IT TAKES TO GET FREE, OKAY?
KATCHOO, WHAT ABOUT ME?
UH... AHEM! YOU GO LONG.
YOU TELL ME TO GO LONG ON EVERY PLAY!
YEAH, BUT YOU KEEP COMIN' BACK!
GIGGLE!
GIGGLE
FRANCINE... ALL YOU HAVE TO DO IS GET OPEN AND I'LL FIND YOU, OKAY?
BUT
JUST GET OPEN!
TRUST ME... I'LL FIND YOU!
OKAY, READY... BREAK!
CLAP!

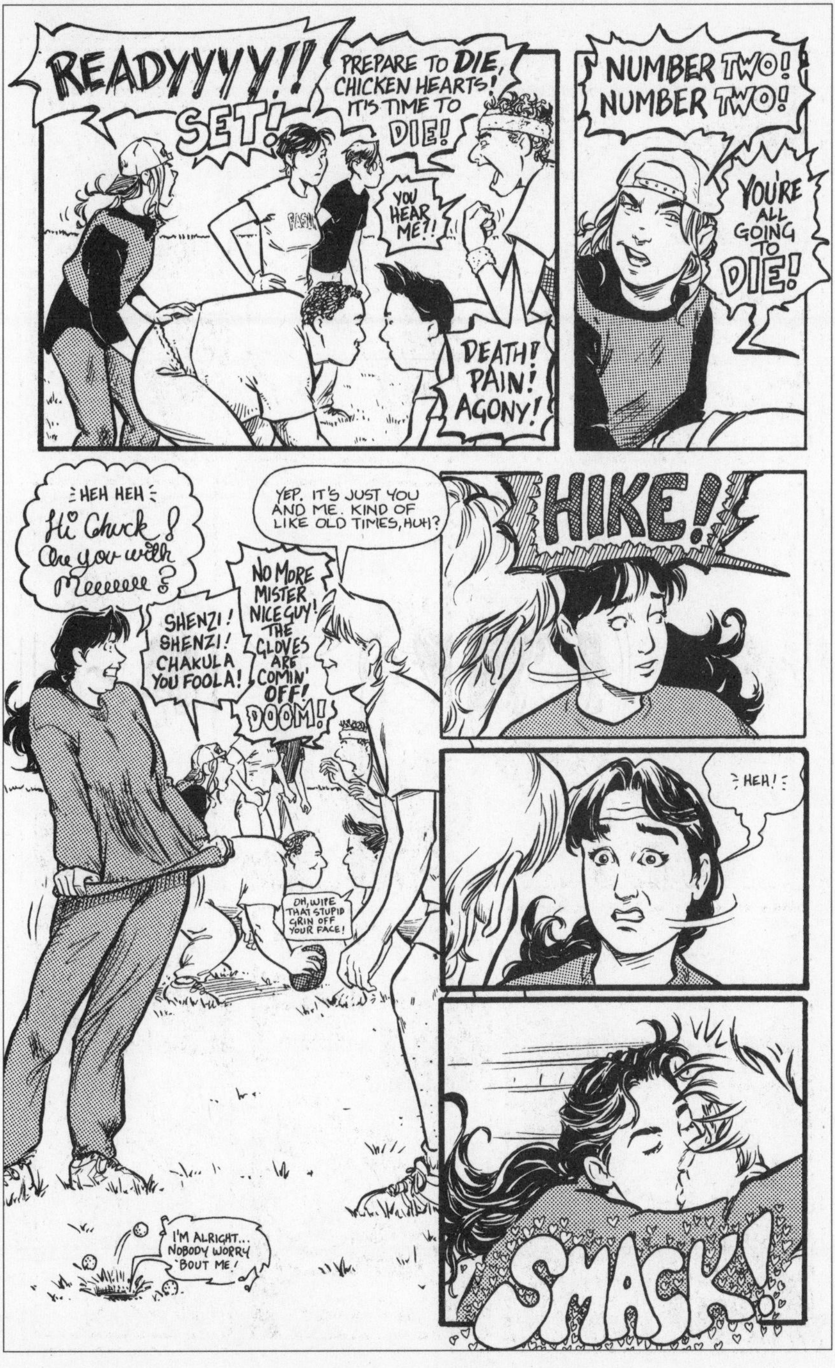
READYYYY!!
SET!
PREPARE TO DIE, CHICKEN HEARTS! IT'S TIME TO DIE!
YOU HEAR ME?!
DEATH! PAIN! AGONY!
NUMBER TWO! NUMBER TWO!
YOU'RE ALL GOING TO DIE!
HEH HEH
Hi Chuck! Are you with Meeeeee?
SHENZI! SHENZI! CHAKULA YOU FOOLA!
YEP. IT'S JUST YOU AND ME. KIND OF LIKE OLD TIMES, HUH?
NO MORE MISTER NICE GUY! THE GLOVES ARE COMIN' OFF! DOOM!
OH, WIPE THAT STUPID GRIN OFF YOUR FACE!
I'M ALRIGHT... NOBODY WORRY 'BOUT ME!
HIKE!!
HEH!
SMACK!

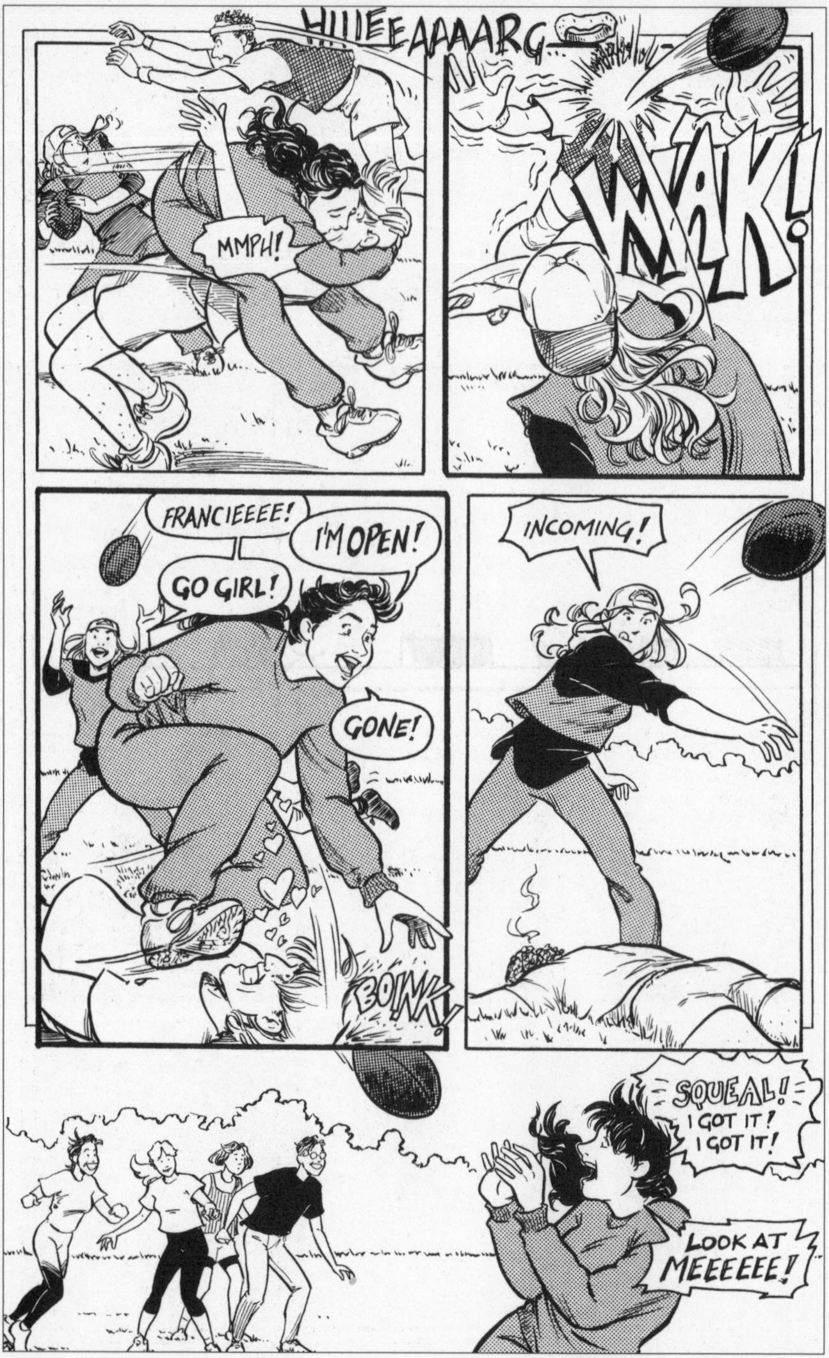
HIIIEEAAAARG
MMPH!
WAK!
FRANCIEEEE!
I'M OPEN!
GO GIRL!
GONE!
BOINK!
INCOMING!
SQUEAL! I GOT IT! I GOT IT!
LOOK AT MEEEEEE!

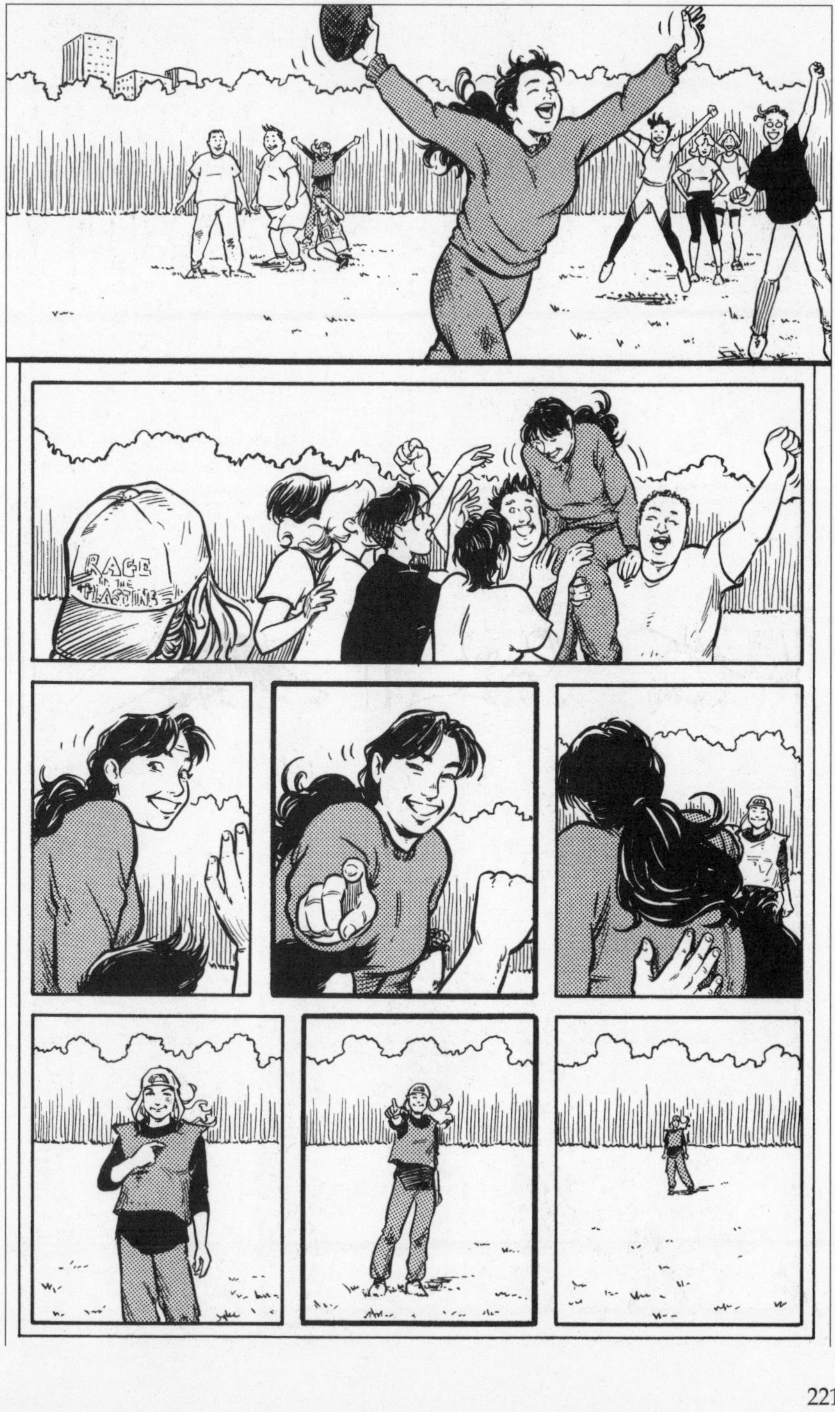

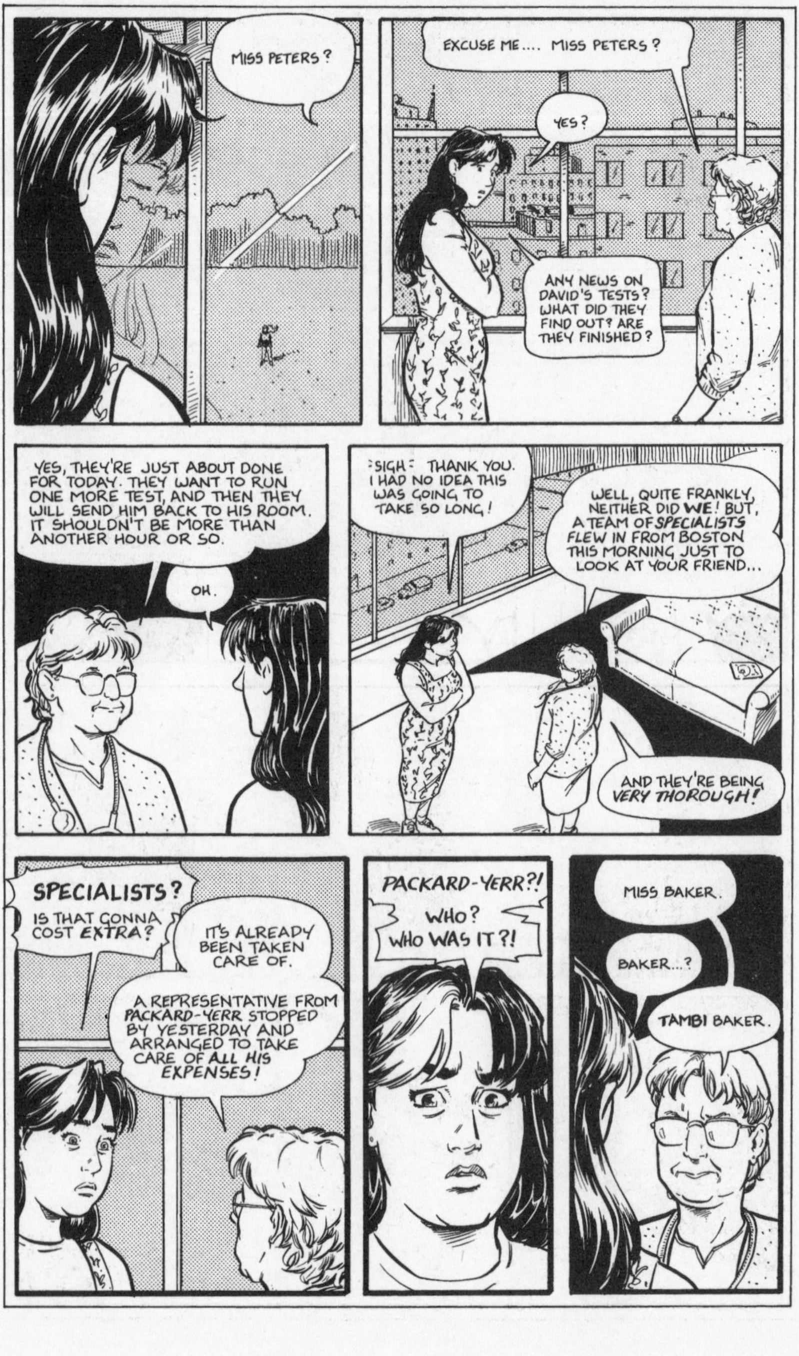
MISS PETERS ?
EXCUSE ME.... MISS PETERS ?
YES ?
ANY NEWS ON DAVID'S TESTS? WHAT DID THEY FIND OUT? ARE THEY FINISHED?
YES, THEY'RE JUST ABOUT DONE FOR TODAY. THEY WANT TO RUN ONE MORE TEST, AND THEN THEY WILL SEND HIM BACK TO HIS ROOM. IT SHOULDN'T BE MORE THAN ANOTHER HOUR OR SO.
OH.
:SIGH: THANK YOU. I HAD NO IDEA THIS WAS GOING TO TAKE SO LONG!
WELL, QUITE FRANKLY, NEITHER DID WE! BUT, A TEAM OF SPECIALISTS FLEW IN FROM BOSTON THIS MORNING JUST TO LOOK AT YOUR FRIEND...
AND THEY'RE BEING VERY THOROUGH!
SPECIALISTS? IS THAT GONNA COST EXTRA?
IT'S ALREADY BEEN TAKEN CARE OF.
A REPRESENTATIVE FROM PACKARD-YERR STOPPED BY YESTERDAY AND ARRANGED TO TAKE CARE OF ALL HIS EXPENSES!
PACKARD-YERR?! WHO? WHO WAS IT?!
MISS BAKER.
BAKER...?
TAMBI BAKER.

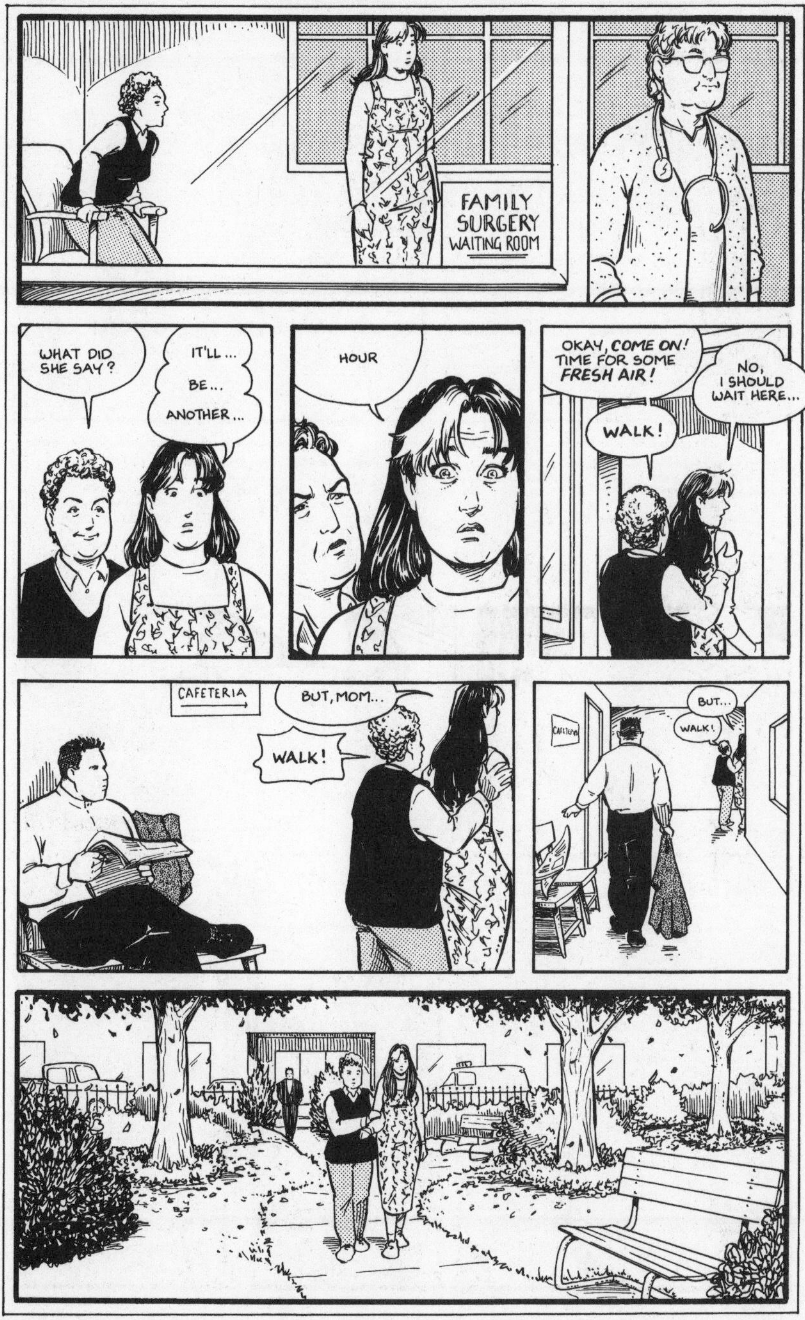
FAMILY
SURGERY
WAITING ROOM
WHAT DID SHE SAY?
IT'LL... BE... ANOTHER...
HOUR
OKAY, COME ON! TIME FOR SOME FRESH AIR!
NO, I SHOULD WAIT HERE...
WALK!
CAFETERIA
BUT, MOM...
WALK!
BUT...
WALK!

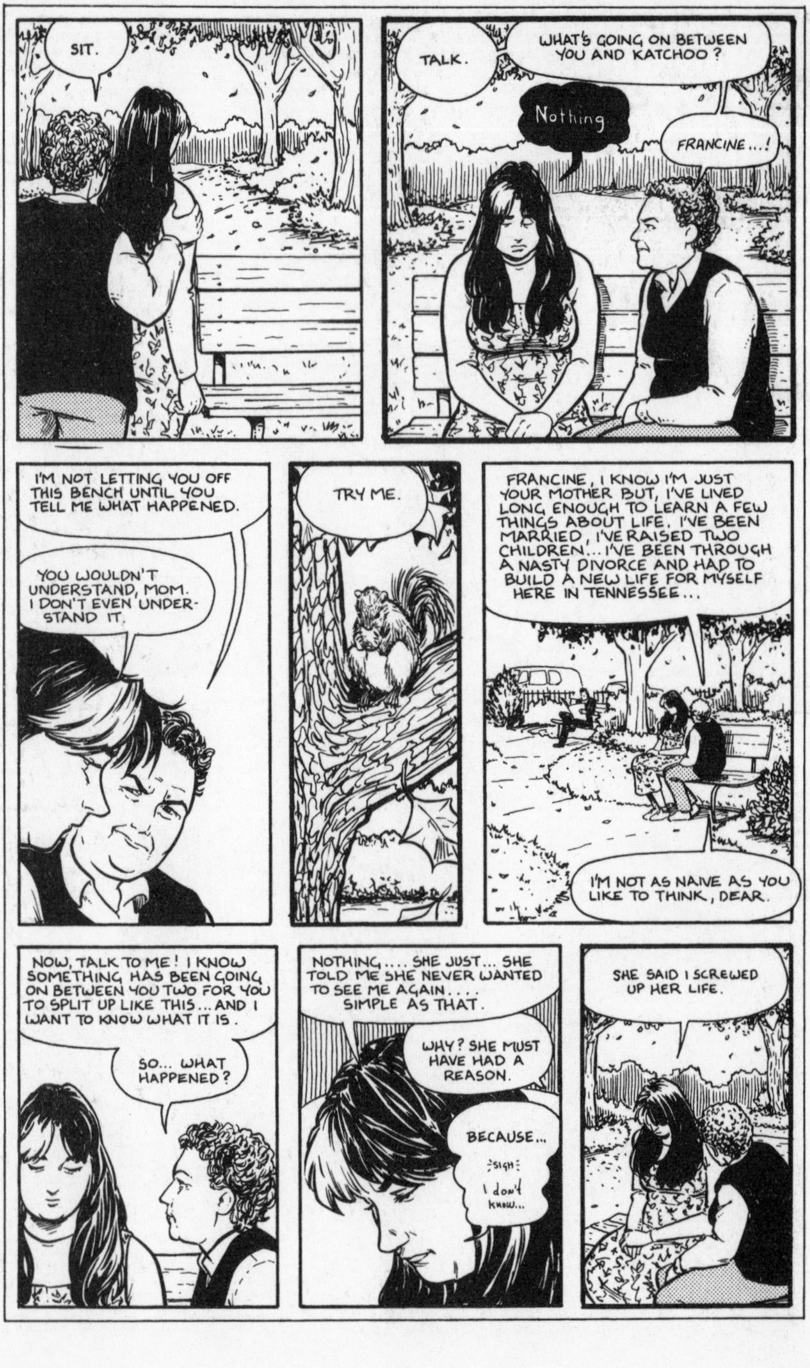
SIT.
TALK.
WHAT'S GOING ON BETWEEN YOU AND KATCHOO?
Nothing.
FRANCINE...!
I'M NOT LETTING YOU OFF THIS BENCH UNTIL YOU TELL ME WHAT HAPPENED.
YOU WOULDN'T UNDERSTAND, MOM. I DON'T EVEN UNDERSTAND IT.
TRY ME.
FRANCINE, I KNOW I'M JUST YOUR MOTHER BUT, I'VE LIVED LONG ENOUGH TO LEARN A FEW THINGS ABOUT LIFE. I'VE BEEN MARRIED, I'VE RAISED TWO CHILDREN... I'VE BEEN THROUGH A NASTY DIVORCE AND HAD TO BUILD A NEW LIFE FOR MYSELF HERE IN TENNESSEE...
I'M NOT AS NAIVE AS YOU LIKE TO THINK, DEAR.
NOW, TALK TO ME! I KNOW SOMETHING HAS BEEN GOING ON BETWEEN YOU TWO FOR YOU TO SPLIT UP LIKE THIS... AND I WANT TO KNOW WHAT IT IS.
SO... WHAT HAPPENED?
NOTHING.... SHE JUST... SHE TOLD ME SHE NEVER WANTED TO SEE ME AGAIN.... SIMPLE AS THAT.
WHY? SHE MUST HAVE HAD A REASON.
BECAUSE...
SIGH
I don't know...
SHE SAID I SCREWED UP HER LIFE.

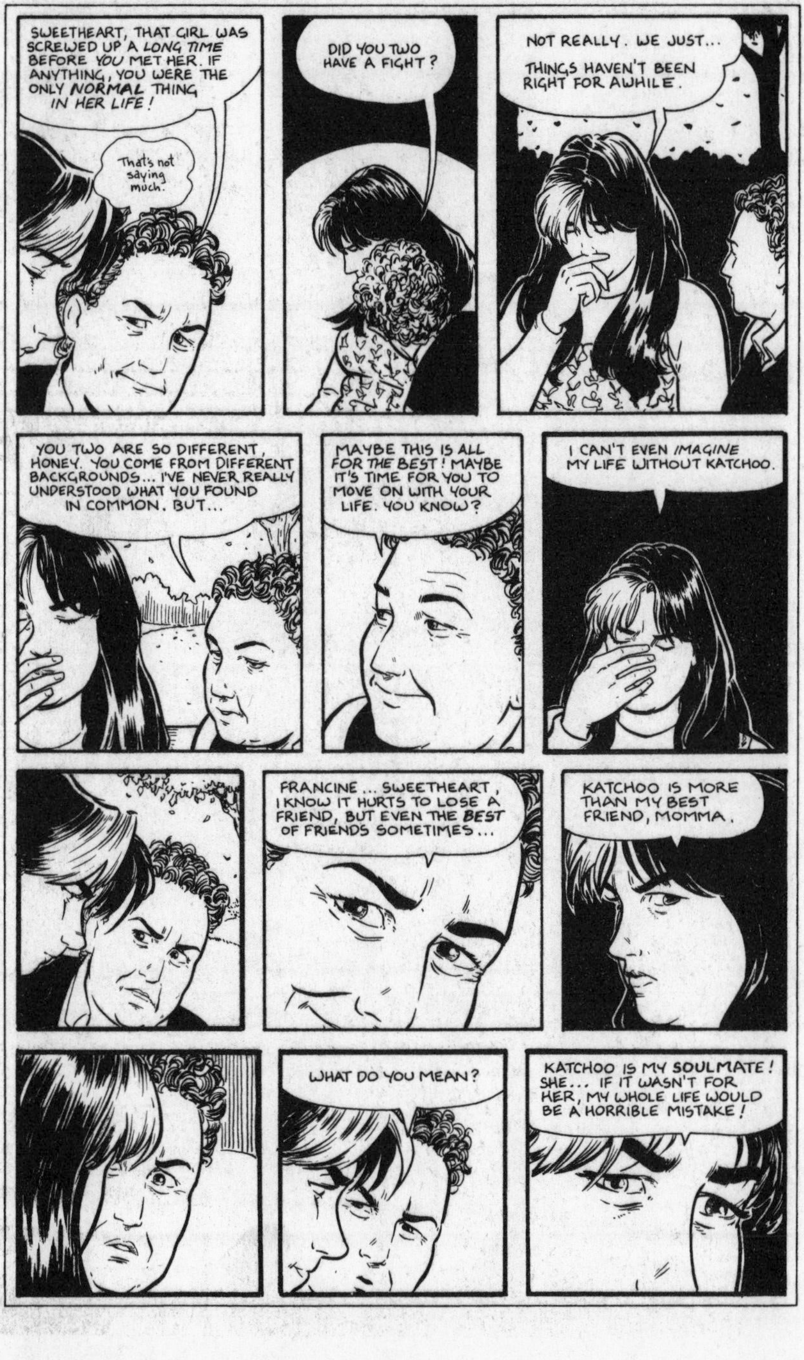
SWEETHEART, THAT GIRL WAS SCREWED UP A LONG TIME BEFORE YOU MET HER. IF ANYTHING, YOU WERE THE ONLY NORMAL THING IN HER LIFE!
That's not saying much.
DID YOU TWO HAVE A FIGHT?
NOT REALLY. WE JUST... THINGS HAVEN'T BEEN RIGHT FOR AWHILE.
YOU TWO ARE SO DIFFERENT, HONEY. YOU COME FROM DIFFERENT BACKGROUNDS... I'VE NEVER REALLY UNDERSTOOD WHAT YOU FOUND IN COMMON. BUT...
MAYBE THIS IS ALL FOR THE BEST! MAYBE IT'S TIME FOR YOU TO MOVE ON WITH YOUR LIFE. YOU KNOW?
I CAN'T EVEN IMAGINE MY LIFE WITHOUT KATCHOO.
FRANCINE... SWEETHEART, I KNOW IT HURTS TO LOSE A FRIEND, BUT EVEN THE BEST OF FRIENDS SOMETIMES...
KATCHOO IS MORE THAN MY BEST FRIEND, MOMMA.
WHAT DO YOU MEAN?
KATCHOO IS MY SOULMATE! SHE... IF IT WASN'T FOR HER, MY WHOLE LIFE WOULD BE A HORRIBLE MISTAKE!

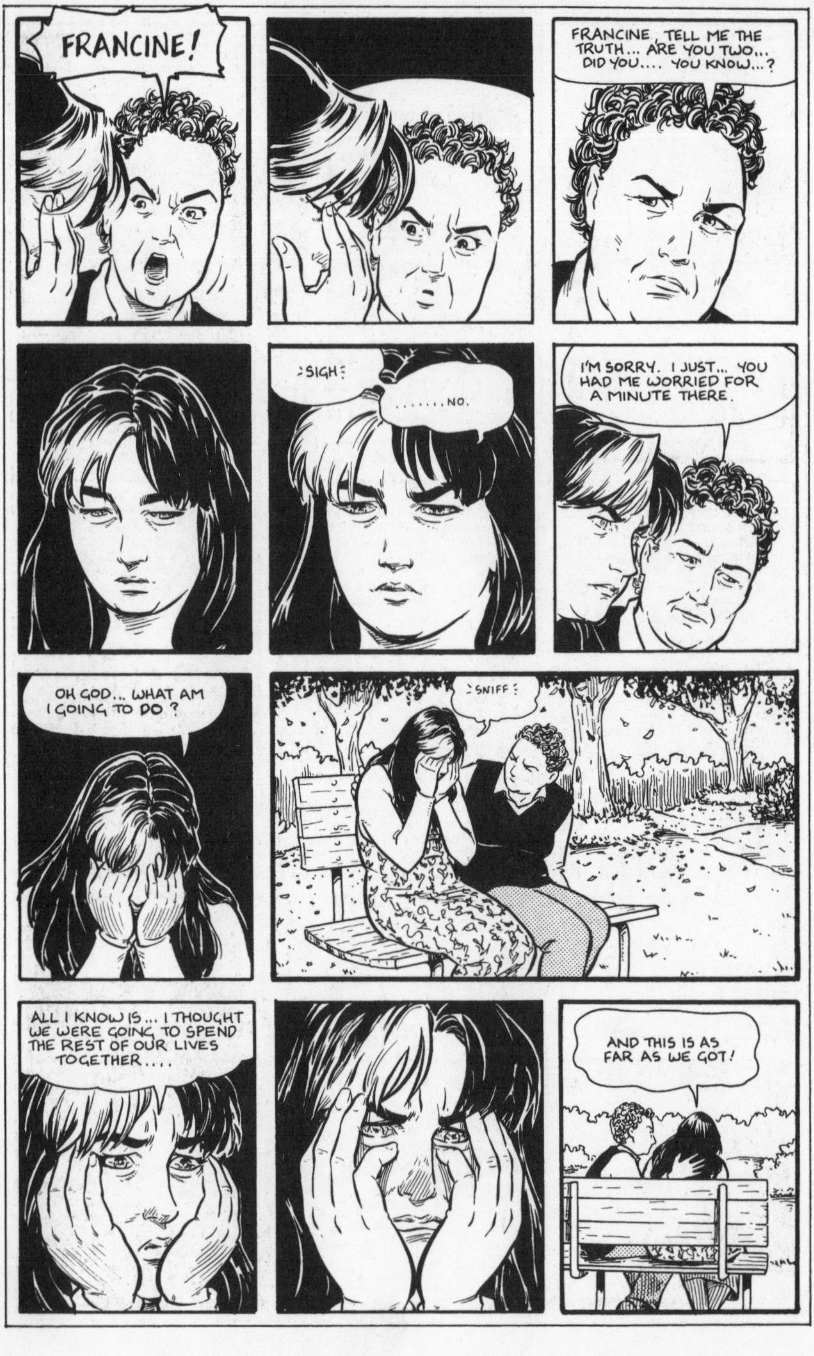
FRANCINE!
FRANCINE, TELL ME THE TRUTH... ARE YOU TWO... DID YOU.... YOU KNOW...?
SIGH
.......NO.
I'M SORRY. I JUST... YOU HAD ME WORRIED FOR A MINUTE THERE.
OH GOD... WHAT AM I GOING TO DO?
SNIFF
ALL I KNOW IS... I THOUGHT WE WERE GOING TO SPEND THE REST OF OUR LIVES TOGETHER....
AND THIS IS AS FAR AS WE GOT!

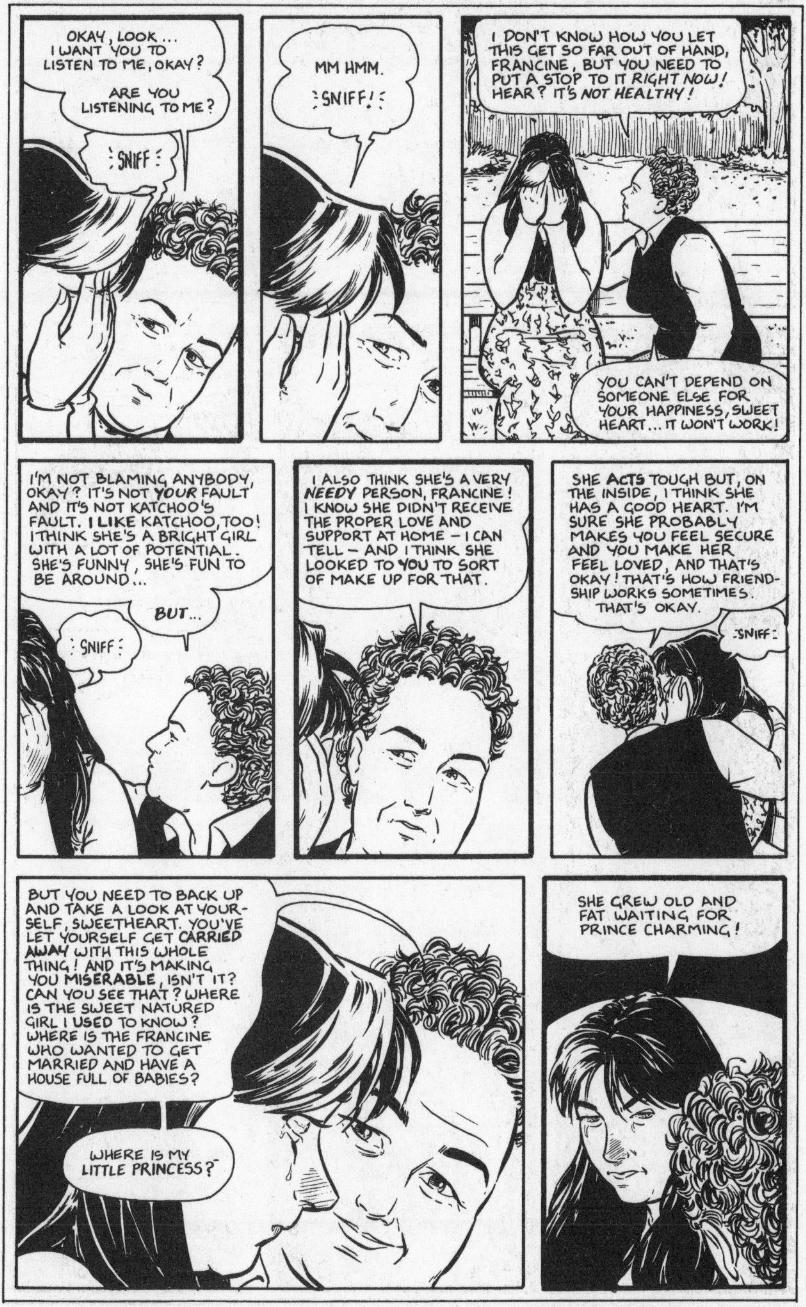
OKAY, LOOK... I WANT YOU TO LISTEN TO ME, OKAY?
ARE YOU LISTENING TO ME?
SNIFF
MM HMM.
SNIFF!
I DON'T KNOW HOW YOU LET THIS GET SO FAR OUT OF HAND, FRANCINE, BUT YOU NEED TO PUT A STOP TO IT RIGHT NOW! HEAR? IT'S NOT HEALTHY!
YOU CAN'T DEPEND ON SOMEONE ELSE FOR YOUR HAPPINESS, SWEET HEART... IT WON'T WORK!
I'M NOT BLAMING ANYBODY, OKAY? IT'S NOT YOUR FAULT AND IT'S NOT KATCHOO'S FAULT. I LIKE KATCHOO, TOO! I THINK SHE'S A BRIGHT GIRL WITH A LOT OF POTENTIAL. SHE'S FUNNY, SHE'S FUN TO BE AROUND...
BUT...
SNIFF
I ALSO THINK SHE'S A VERY NEEDY PERSON, FRANCINE! I KNOW SHE DIDN'T RECEIVE THE PROPER LOVE AND SUPPORT AT HOME - I CAN TELL - AND I THINK SHE LOOKED TO YOU TO SORT OF MAKE UP FOR THAT.
SHE ACTS TOUGH BUT, ON THE INSIDE, I THINK SHE HAS A GOOD HEART. I'M SURE SHE PROBABLY MAKES YOU FEEL SECURE AND YOU MAKE HER FEEL LOVED, AND THAT'S OKAY! THAT'S HOW FRIEND-SHIP WORKS SOMETIMES. THAT'S OKAY.
SNIFF
BUT YOU NEED TO BACK UP AND TAKE A LOOK AT YOUR-SELF, SWEETHEART. YOU'VE LET YOURSELF GET CARRIED AWAY WITH THIS WHOLE THING! AND IT'S MAKING YOU MISERABLE, ISN'T IT? CAN YOU SEE THAT? WHERE IS THE SWEET NATURED GIRL I USED TO KNOW? WHERE IS THE FRANCINE WHO WANTED TO GET MARRIED AND HAVE A HOUSE FULL OF BABIES?
WHERE IS MY LITTLE PRINCESS?
SHE GREW OLD AND FAT WAITING FOR PRINCE CHARMING!

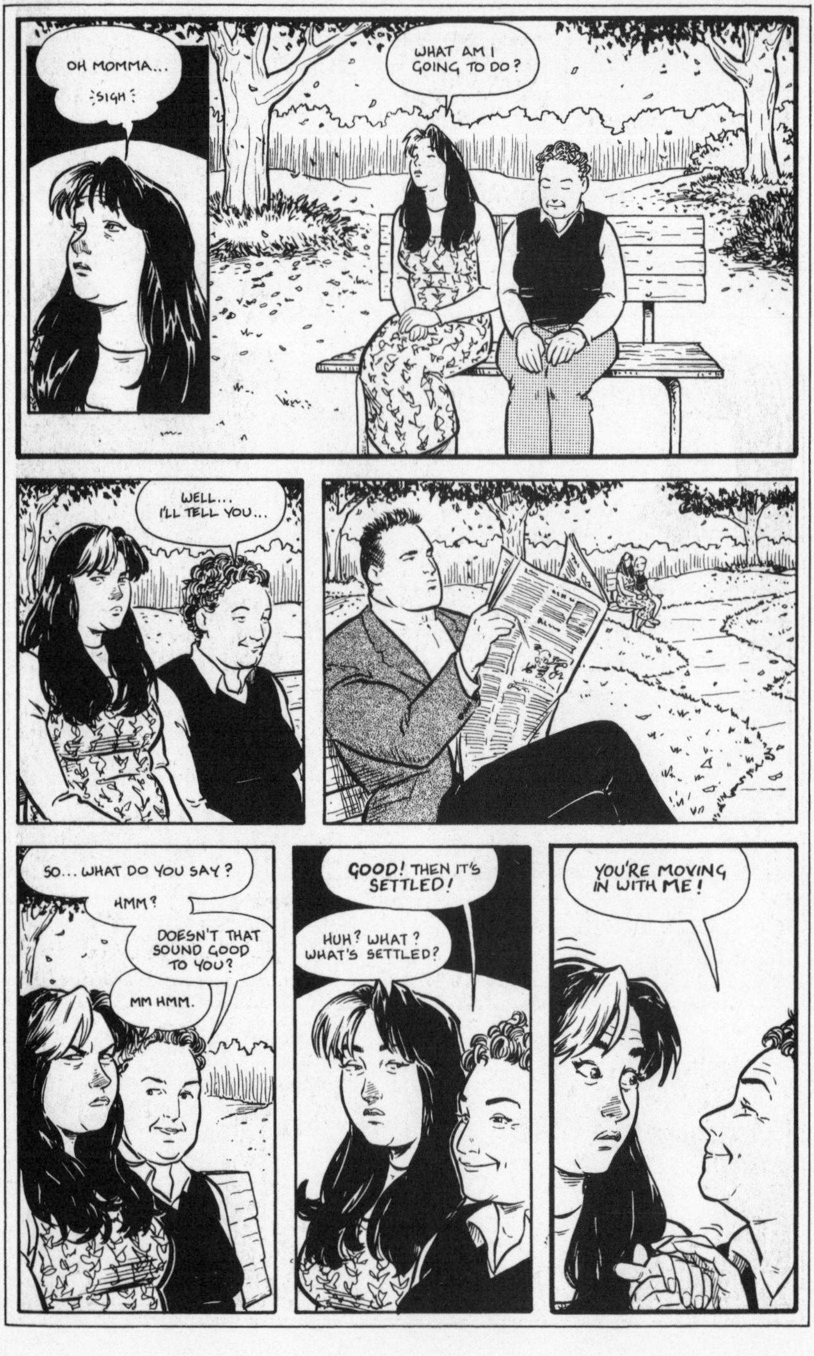
OH MOMMA...
SIGH
WHAT AM I GOING TO DO?
WELL... I'LL TELL YOU...
SO... WHAT DO YOU SAY?
HMM?
DOESN'T THAT SOUND GOOD TO YOU?
MM HMM.
GOOD! THEN IT'S SETTLED!
HUH? WHAT? WHAT'S SETTLED?
YOU'RE MOVING IN WITH ME!

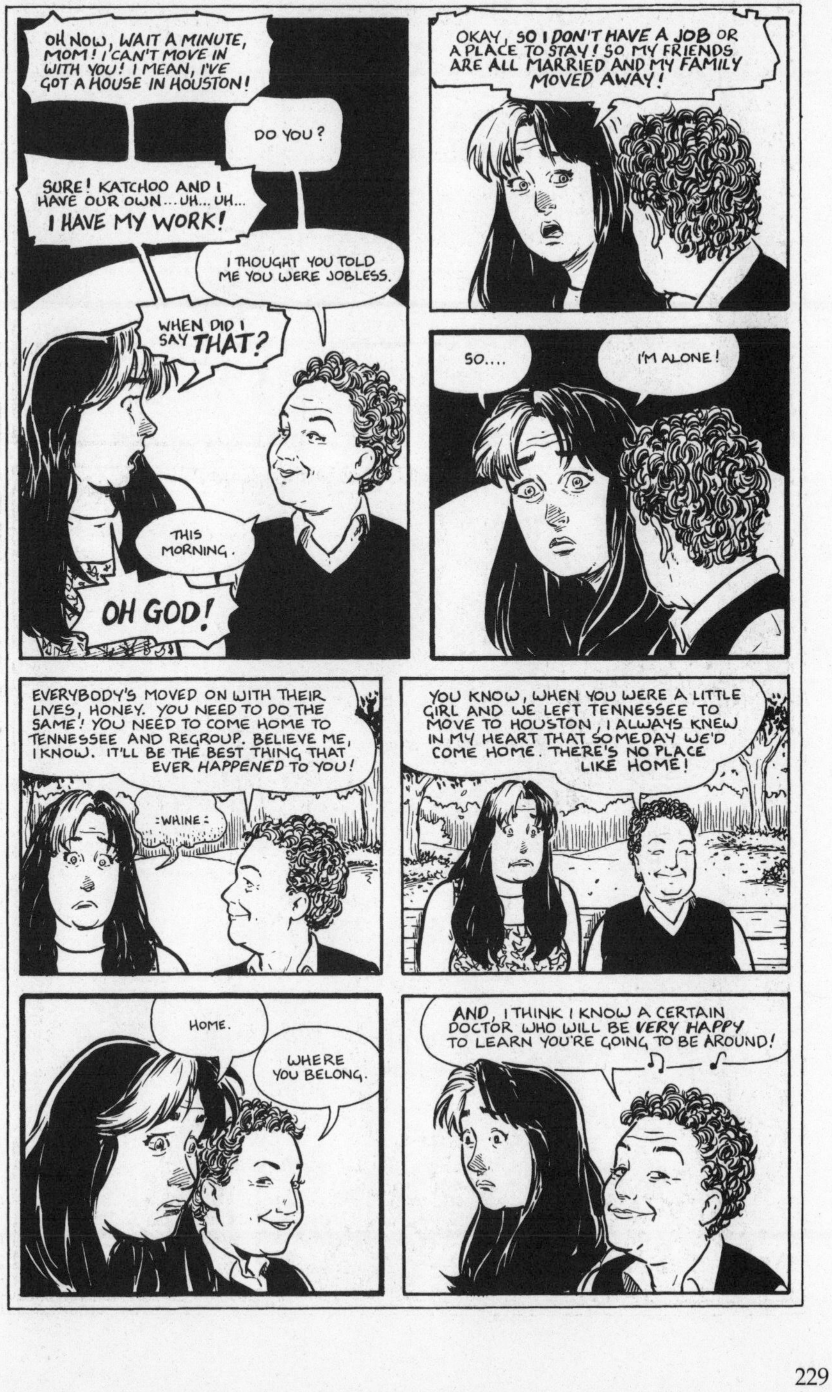
OH NOW, WAIT A MINUTE, MOM! I CAN'T MOVE IN WITH YOU! I MEAN, I'VE GOT A HOUSE IN HOUSTON!
DO YOU?
SURE! KATCHOO AND I HAVE OUR OWN... UH... UH... I HAVE MY WORK!
I THOUGHT YOU TOLD ME YOU WERE JOBLESS.
WHEN DID I SAY THAT?
THIS MORNING.
OH GOD!
OKAY, SO I DON'T HAVE A JOB OR A PLACE TO STAY! SO MY FRIENDS ARE ALL MARRIED AND MY FAMILY MOVED AWAY!
SO....
I'M ALONE!
EVERYBODY'S MOVED ON WITH THEIR LIVES, HONEY. YOU NEED TO DO THE SAME! YOU NEED TO COME HOME TO TENNESSEE AND REGROUP. BELIEVE ME, I KNOW. IT'LL BE THE BEST THING THAT EVER HAPPENED TO YOU!
:WHINE:
YOU KNOW, WHEN YOU WERE A LITTLE GIRL AND WE LEFT TENNESSEE TO MOVE TO HOUSTON, I ALWAYS KNEW IN MY HEART THAT SOMEDAY WE'D COME HOME. THERE'S NO PLACE LIKE HOME!
HOME.
WHERE YOU BELONG.
AND, I THINK I KNOW A CERTAIN DOCTOR WHO WILL BE VERY HAPPY TO LEARN YOU'RE GOING TO BE AROUND!

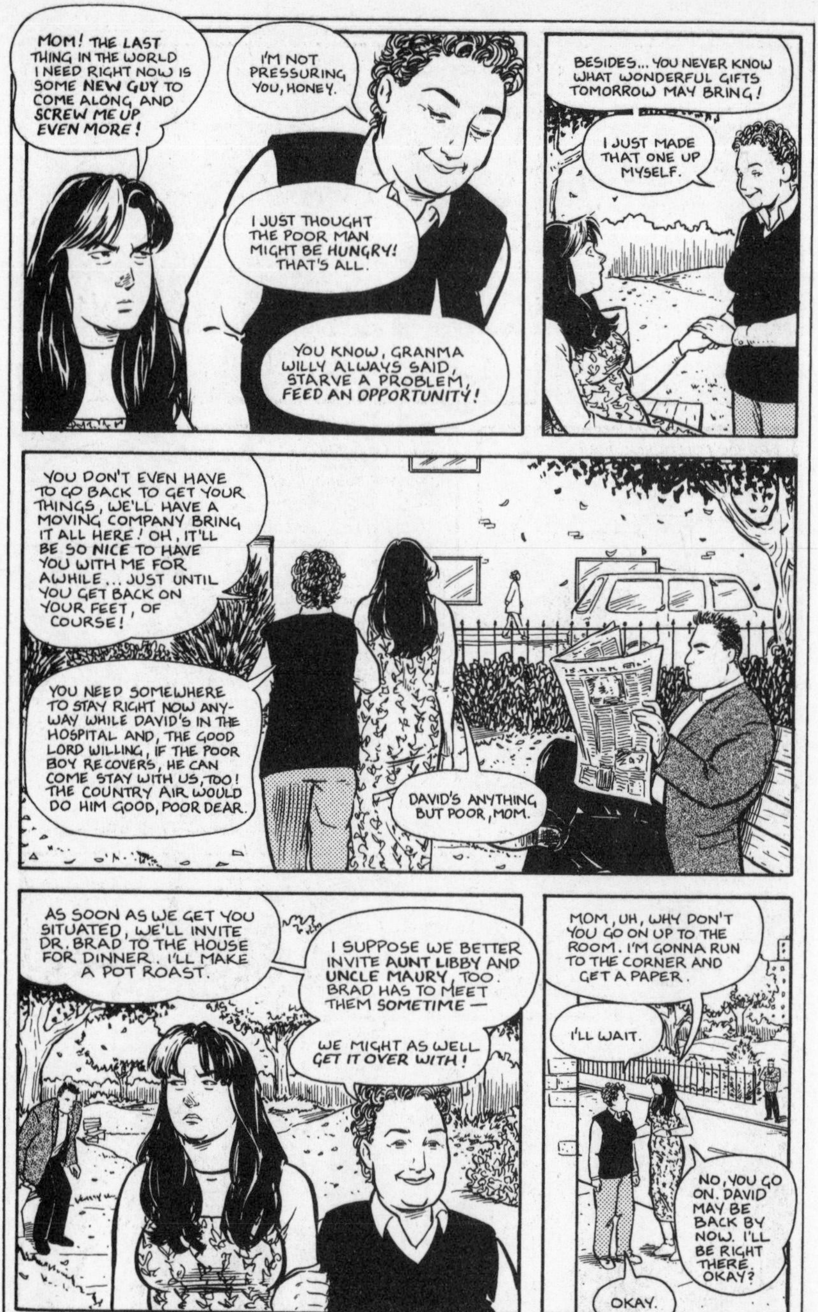
MOM! THE LAST THING IN THE WORLD I NEED RIGHT NOW IS SOME NEW GUY TO COME ALONG AND SCREW ME UP EVEN MORE!
I'M NOT PRESSURING YOU, HONEY.
I JUST THOUGHT THE POOR MAN MIGHT BE HUNGRY! THAT'S ALL.
YOU KNOW, GRANMA WILLY ALWAYS SAID, STARVE A PROBLEM, FEED AN OPPORTUNITY!
BESIDES... YOU NEVER KNOW WHAT WONDERFUL GIFTS TOMORROW MAY BRING!
I JUST MADE THAT ONE UP MYSELF.
YOU DON'T EVEN HAVE TO GO BACK TO GET YOUR THINGS, WE'LL HAVE A MOVING COMPANY BRING IT ALL HERE! OH, IT'LL BE SO NICE TO HAVE YOU WITH ME FOR AWHILE... JUST UNTIL YOU GET BACK ON YOUR FEET, OF COURSE!
YOU NEED SOMEWHERE TO STAY RIGHT NOW ANY-WAY WHILE DAVID'S IN THE HOSPITAL AND, THE GOOD LORD WILLING, IF THE POOR BOY RECOVERS, HE CAN COME STAY WITH US, TOO! THE COUNTRY AIR WOULD DO HIM GOOD, POOR DEAR.
DAVID'S ANYTHING BUT POOR, MOM.
AS SOON AS WE GET YOU SITUATED, WE'LL INVITE DR. BRAD TO THE HOUSE FOR DINNER. I'LL MAKE A POT ROAST.
I SUPPOSE WE BETTER INVITE AUNT LIBBY AND UNCLE MAURY, TOO. BRAD HAS TO MEET THEM SOMETIME —
WE MIGHT AS WELL GET IT OVER WITH!
MOM, UH, WHY DON'T YOU GO ON UP TO THE ROOM. I'M GONNA RUN TO THE CORNER AND GET A PAPER.
I'LL WAIT.
NO, YOU GO ON. DAVID MAY BE BACK BY NOW. I'LL BE RIGHT THERE. OKAY?
OKAY.

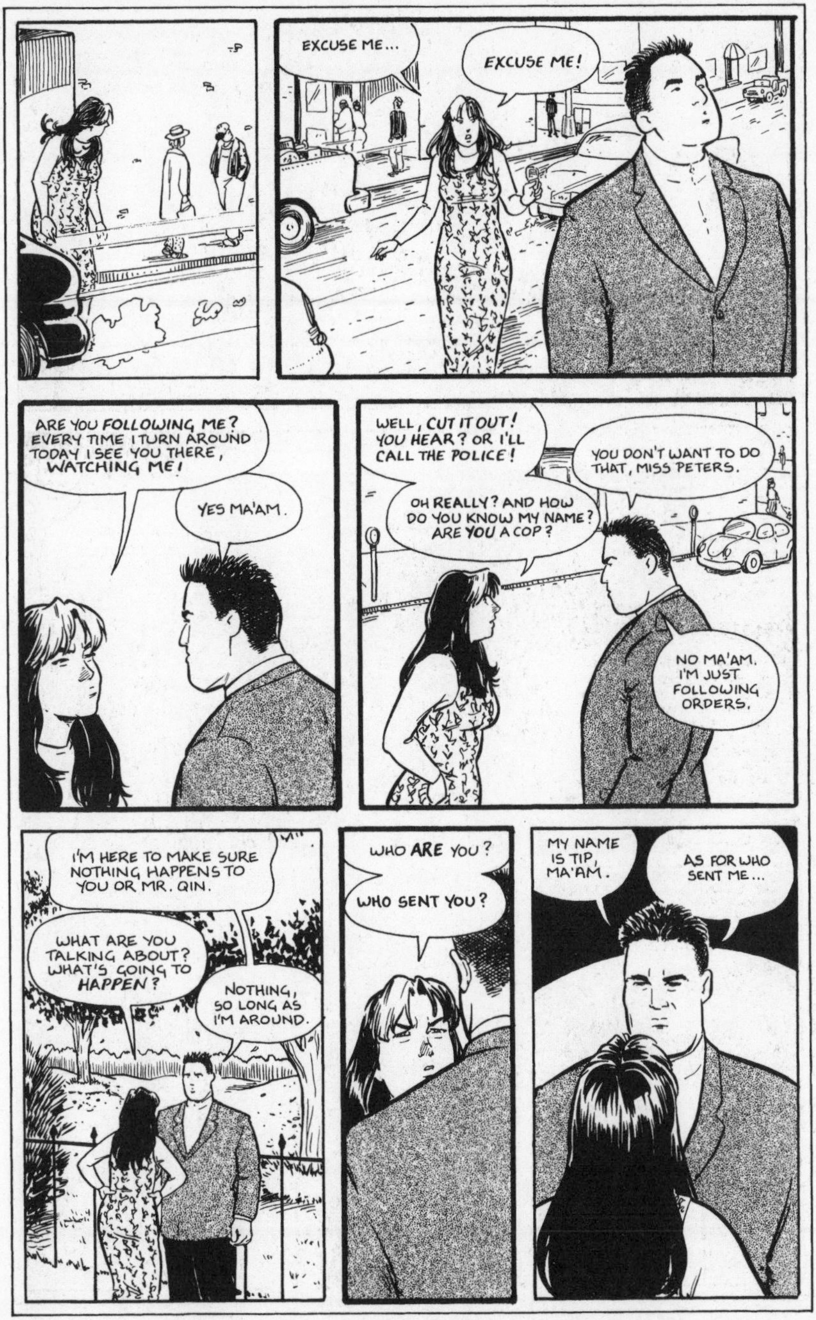
EXCUSE ME...
EXCUSE ME!
ARE YOU FOLLOWING ME? EVERY TIME I TURN AROUND TODAY I SEE YOU THERE, WATCHING ME!
YES MA'AM.
WELL, CUT IT OUT! YOU HEAR? OR I'LL CALL THE POLICE!
YOU DON'T WANT TO DO THAT, MISS PETERS.
OH REALLY? AND HOW DO YOU KNOW MY NAME? ARE YOU A COP?
NO MA'AM. I'M JUST FOLLOWING ORDERS.
I'M HERE TO MAKE SURE NOTHING HAPPENS TO YOU OR MR. QIN.
WHAT ARE YOU TALKING ABOUT? WHAT'S GOING TO HAPPEN?
NOTHING, SO LONG AS I'M AROUND.
WHO ARE YOU?
WHO SENT YOU?
MY NAME IS TIP, MA'AM.
AS FOR WHO SENT ME...

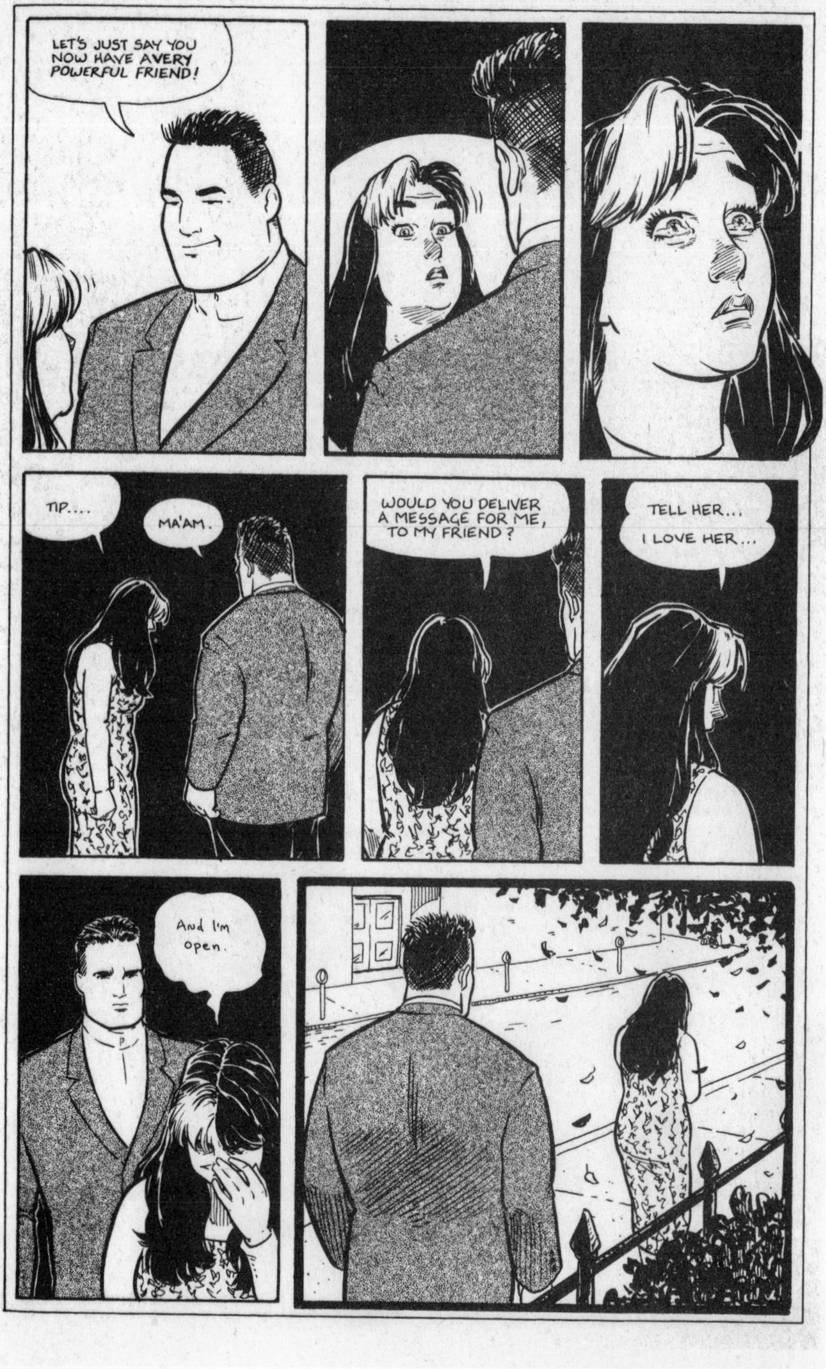
LET'S JUST SAY YOU NOW HAVE A VERY POWERFUL FRIEND!
TIP....
MA'AM.
WOULD YOU DELIVER A MESSAGE FOR ME, TO MY FRIEND?
TELL HER...
I LOVE HER...
And I'm open.

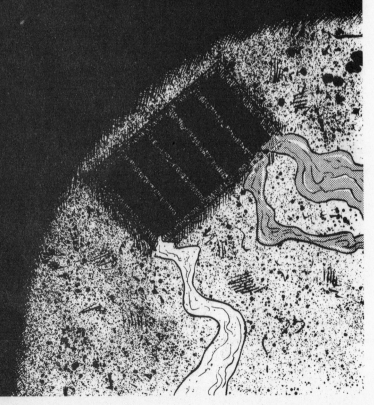

day by day we lose our civility when
night by night we play with hostility
seeding our hearts with constant desire
burning the proof in heavenly fire

hide me away in the black of your heart
hide me away and we'll make a new start
hide me away in the black of your heart
hide me away and pick me apart

hide me away in the black of your heart
hide me away in the black of your heart
hide me away in the black of your heart

in the black of your heart © 1996 griffin silver

233

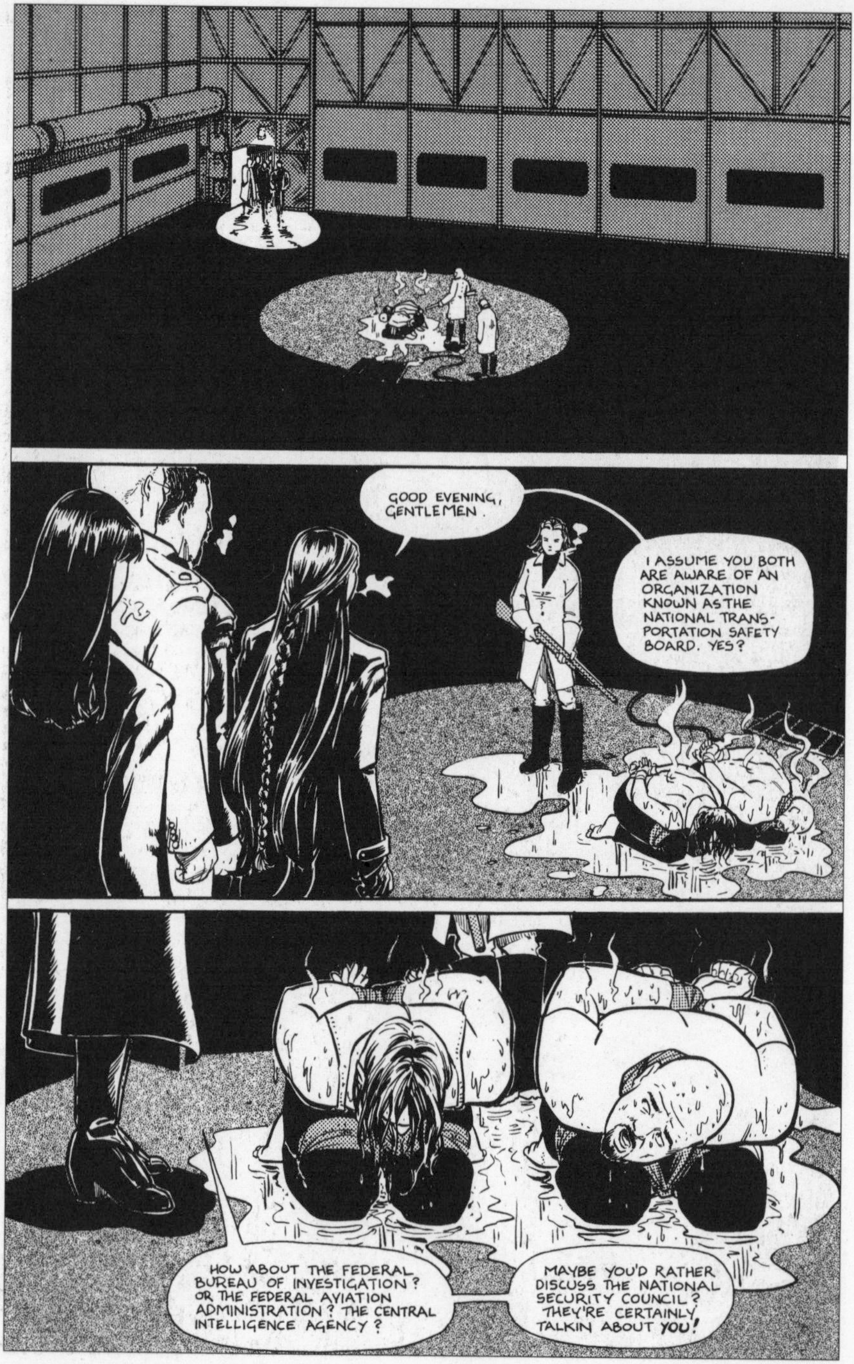
GOOD EVENING, GENTLEMEN.
I ASSUME YOU BOTH ARE AWARE OF AN ORGANIZATION KNOWN AS THE NATIONAL TRANS-PORTATION SAFETY BOARD. YES?
HOW ABOUT THE FEDERAL BUREAU OF INVESTIGATION? OR THE FEDERAL AVIATION ADMINISTRATION? THE CENTRAL INTELLIGENCE AGENCY?
MAYBE YOU'D RATHER DISCUSS THE NATIONAL SECURITY COUNCIL? THEY'RE CERTAINLY TALKIN ABOUT YOU!

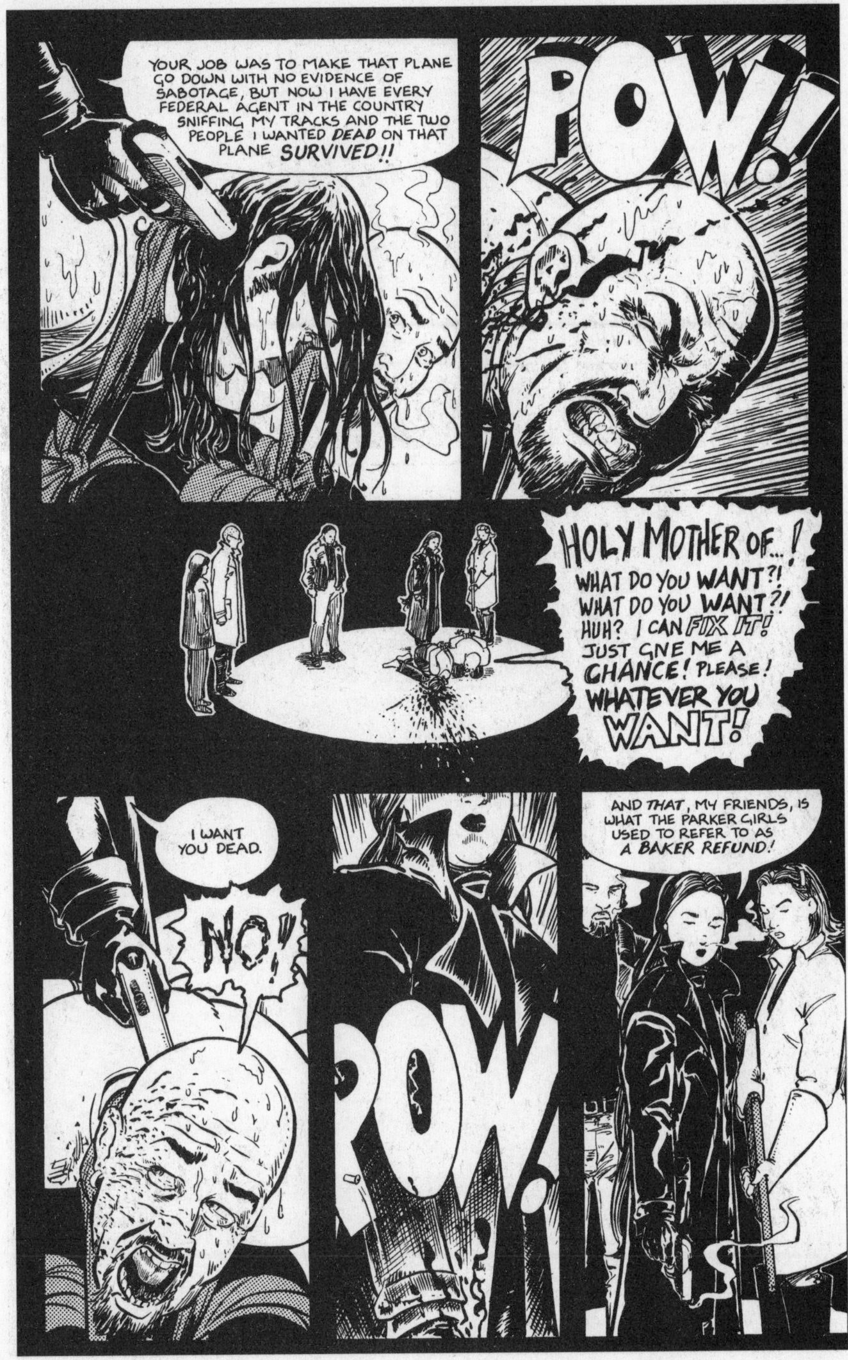
YOUR JOB WAS TO MAKE THAT PLANE GO DOWN WITH NO EVIDENCE OF SABOTAGE, BUT NOW I HAVE EVERY FEDERAL AGENT IN THE COUNTRY SNIFFING MY TRACKS AND THE TWO PEOPLE I WANTED DEAD ON THAT PLANE SURVIVED!!
POW!
HOLY MOTHER OF...! WHAT DO YOU WANT?! WHAT DO YOU WANT?! HUH? I CAN FIX IT! JUST GIVE ME A CHANCE! PLEASE! WHATEVER YOU WANT!
I WANT YOU DEAD.
NO!
POW!
AND THAT, MY FRIENDS, IS WHAT THE PARKER GIRLS USED TO REFER TO AS A BAKER REFUND!

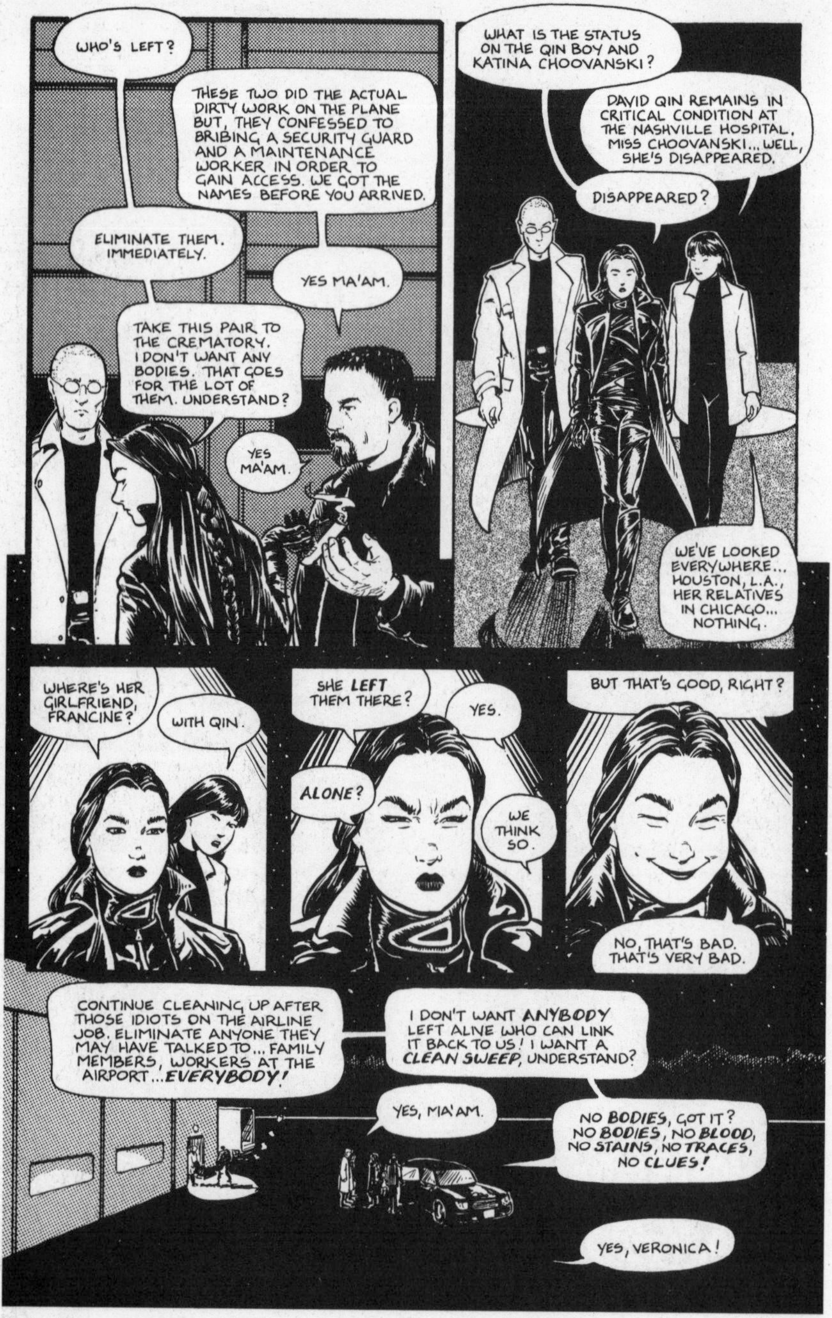
WHO'S LEFT?
THESE TWO DID THE ACTUAL DIRTY WORK ON THE PLANE BUT, THEY CONFESSED TO BRIBING A SECURITY GUARD AND A MAINTENANCE WORKER IN ORDER TO GAIN ACCESS. WE GOT THE NAMES BEFORE YOU ARRIVED.
ELIMINATE THEM. IMMEDIATELY.
YES MA'AM.
TAKE THIS PAIR TO THE CREMATORY. I DON'T WANT ANY BODIES. THAT GOES FOR THE LOT OF THEM. UNDERSTAND?
YES MA'AM.
WHAT IS THE STATUS ON THE QIN BOY AND KATINA CHOOVANSKI?
DAVID QIN REMAINS IN CRITICAL CONDITION AT THE NASHVILLE HOSPITAL. MISS CHOOVANSKI... WELL, SHE'S DISAPPEARED.
DISAPPEARED?
WE'VE LOOKED EVERYWHERE... HOUSTON, L.A., HER RELATIVES IN CHICAGO... NOTHING.
WHERE'S HER GIRLFRIEND, FRANCINE?
WITH QIN.
SHE LEFT THEM THERE?
YES.
ALONE?
WE THINK SO.
BUT THAT'S GOOD, RIGHT?
NO, THAT'S BAD. THAT'S VERY BAD.
CONTINUE CLEANING UP AFTER THOSE IDIOTS ON THE AIRLINE JOB. ELIMINATE ANYONE THEY MAY HAVE TALKED TO... FAMILY MEMBERS, WORKERS AT THE AIRPORT... EVERYBODY!
I DON'T WANT ANYBODY LEFT ALIVE WHO CAN LINK IT BACK TO US! I WANT A CLEAN SWEEP, UNDERSTAND?
YES, MA'AM.
NO BODIES, GOT IT? NO BODIES, NO BLOOD, NO STAINS, NO TRACES, NO CLUES!
YES, VERONICA!

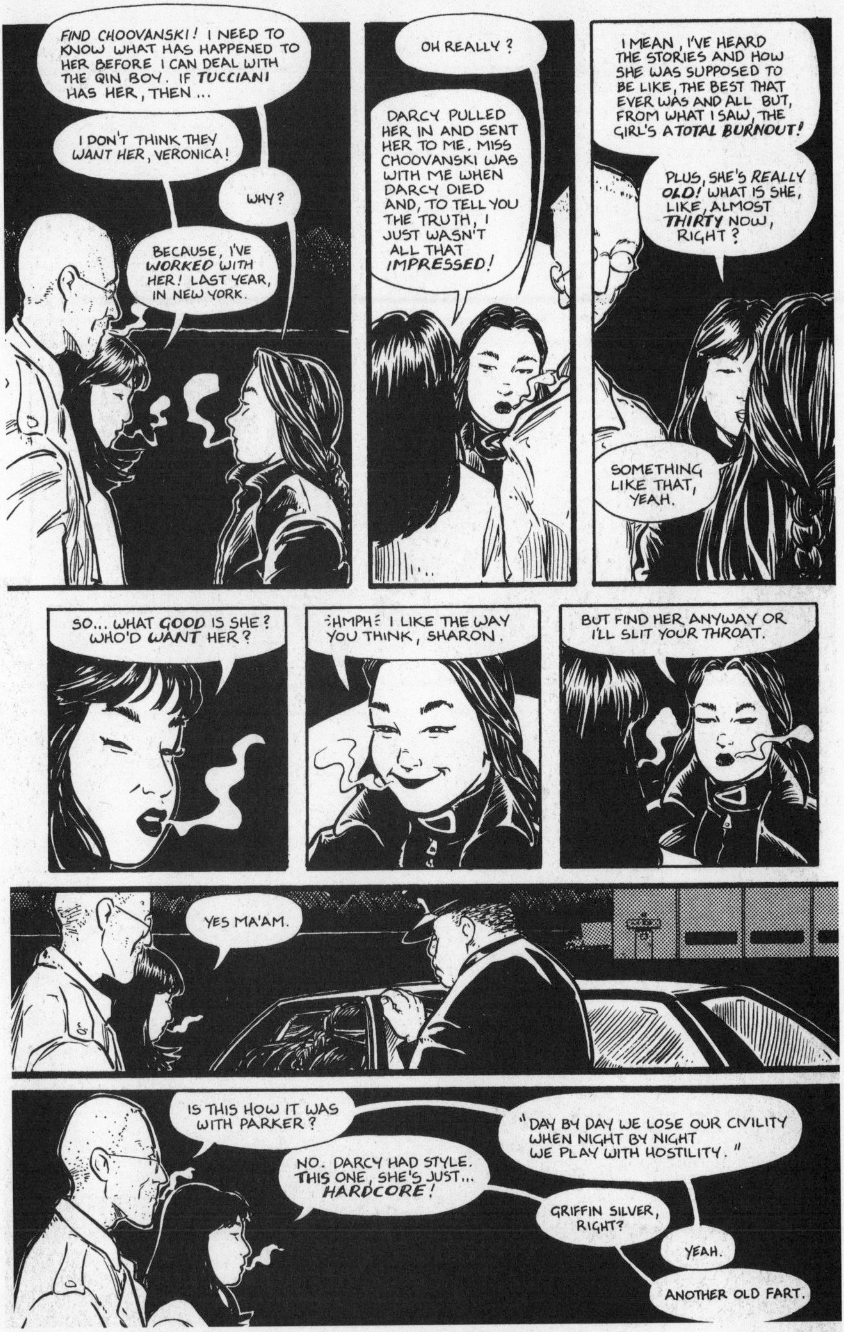

FIND CHOOVANSKI! I NEED TO KNOW WHAT HAS HAPPENED TO HER BEFORE I CAN DEAL WITH THE QIN BOY. IF TUCCIANI HAS HER, THEN ...
I DON'T THINK THEY WANT HER, VERONICA!
WHY?
BECAUSE, I'VE WORKED WITH HER! LAST YEAR, IN NEW YORK.
OH REALLY?
DARCY PULLED HER IN AND SENT HER TO ME. MISS CHOOVANSKI WAS WITH ME WHEN DARCY DIED AND, TO TELL YOU THE TRUTH, I JUST WASN'T ALL THAT IMPRESSED!
I MEAN, I'VE HEARD THE STORIES AND HOW SHE WAS SUPPOSED TO BE LIKE, THE BEST THAT EVER WAS AND ALL BUT, FROM WHAT I SAW, THE GIRL'S A TOTAL BURNOUT!
PLUS, SHE'S REALLY OLD! WHAT IS SHE, LIKE, ALMOST THIRTY NOW, RIGHT?
SOMETHING LIKE THAT, YEAH.
SO... WHAT GOOD IS SHE? WHO'D WANT HER?
HMPH I LIKE THE WAY YOU THINK, SHARON.
BUT FIND HER ANYWAY OR I'LL SLIT YOUR THROAT.
YES MA'AM.
IS THIS HOW IT WAS WITH PARKER?
NO. DARCY HAD STYLE. THIS ONE, SHE'S JUST... HARDCORE!
"DAY BY DAY WE LOSE OUR CIVILITY WHEN NIGHT BY NIGHT WE PLAY WITH HOSTILITY."
GRIFFIN SILVER, RIGHT?
YEAH.
ANOTHER OLD FART.

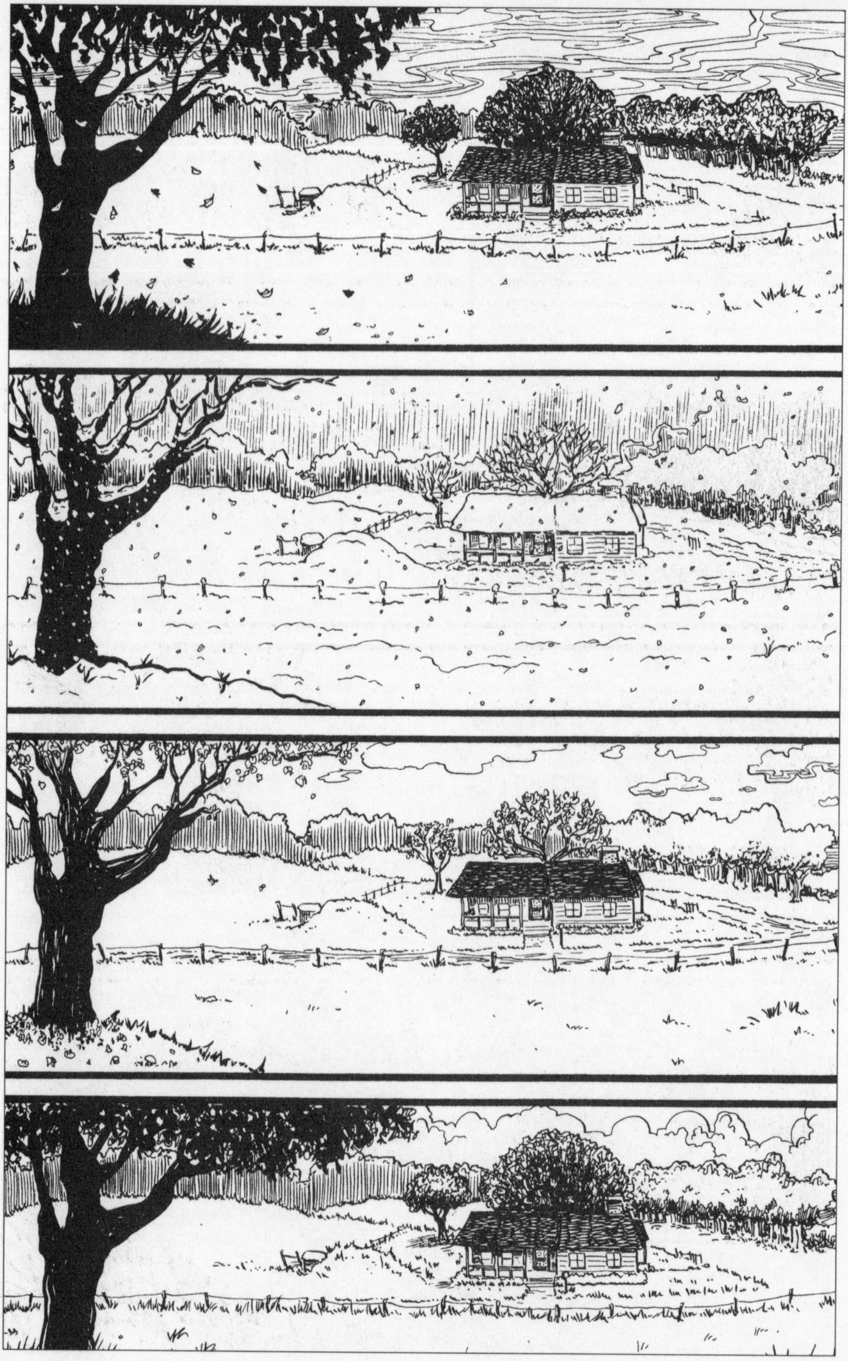

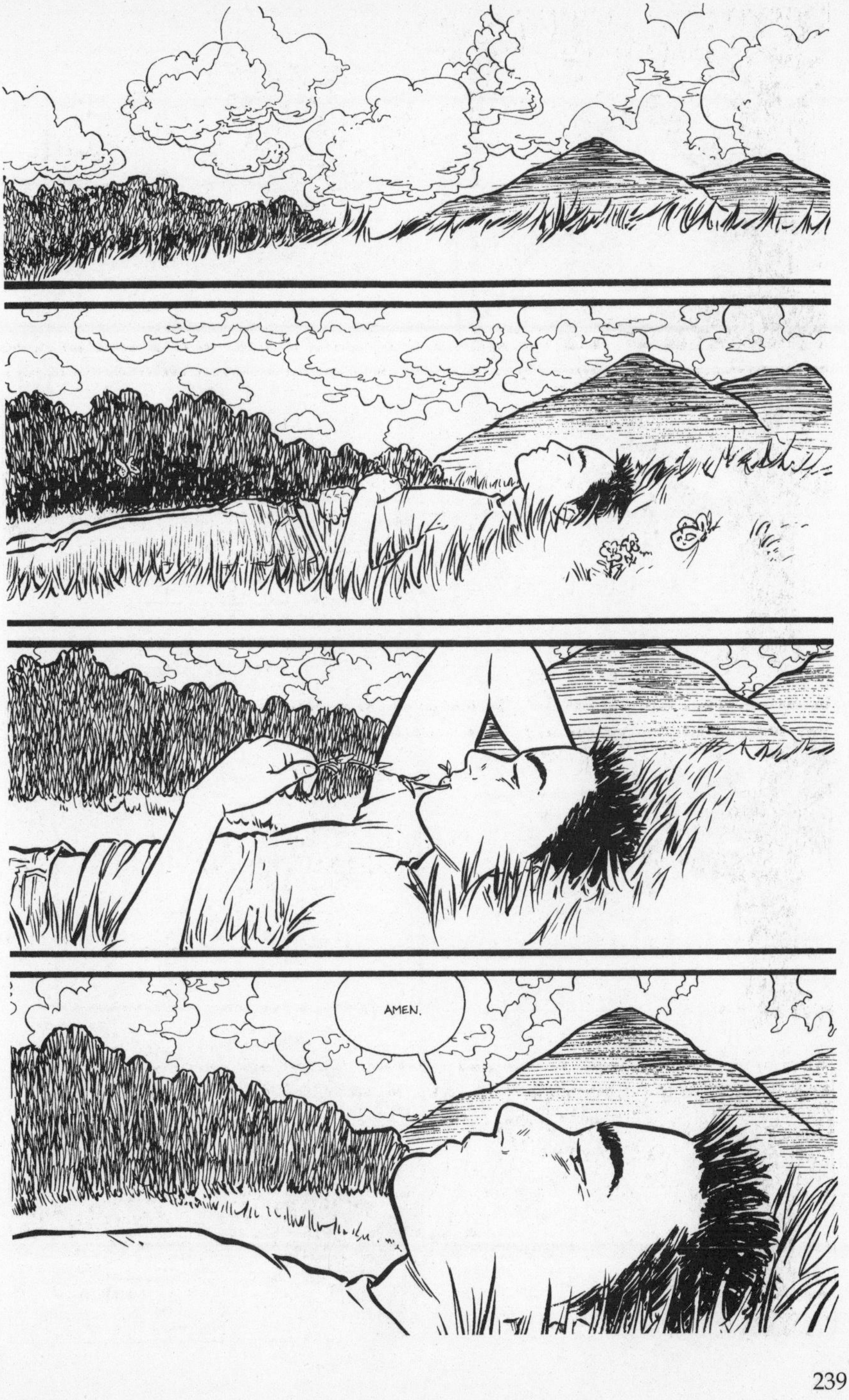
AMEN.

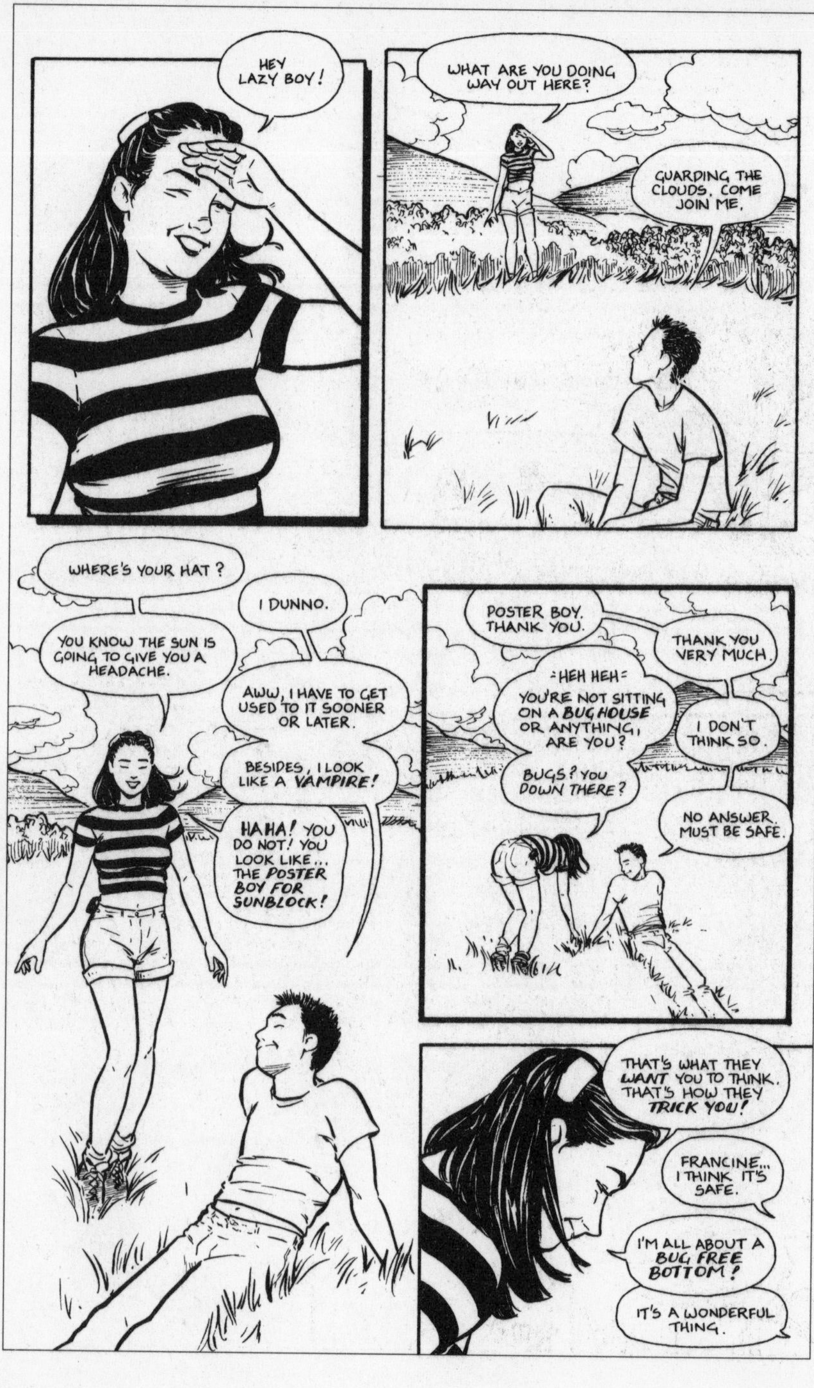
HEY LAZY BOY!
WHAT ARE YOU DOING WAY OUT HERE?
GUARDING THE CLOUDS, COME JOIN ME.
WHERE'S YOUR HAT?
YOU KNOW THE SUN IS GOING TO GIVE YOU A HEADACHE.
I DUNNO.
AWW, I HAVE TO GET USED TO IT SOONER OR LATER.
BESIDES, I LOOK LIKE A VAMPIRE!
HAHA! YOU DO NOT! YOU LOOK LIKE... THE POSTER BOY FOR SUNBLOCK!
POSTER BOY. THANK YOU.
THANK YOU VERY MUCH.
=HEH HEH=
YOU'RE NOT SITTING ON A BUG HOUSE OR ANYTHING, ARE YOU?
I DON'T THINK SO.
BUGS? YOU DOWN THERE?
NO ANSWER. MUST BE SAFE.
THAT'S WHAT THEY WANT YOU TO THINK. THAT'S HOW THEY TRICK YOU!
FRANCINE... I THINK IT'S SAFE.
I'M ALL ABOUT A BUG FREE BOTTOM!
IT'S A WONDERFUL THING.

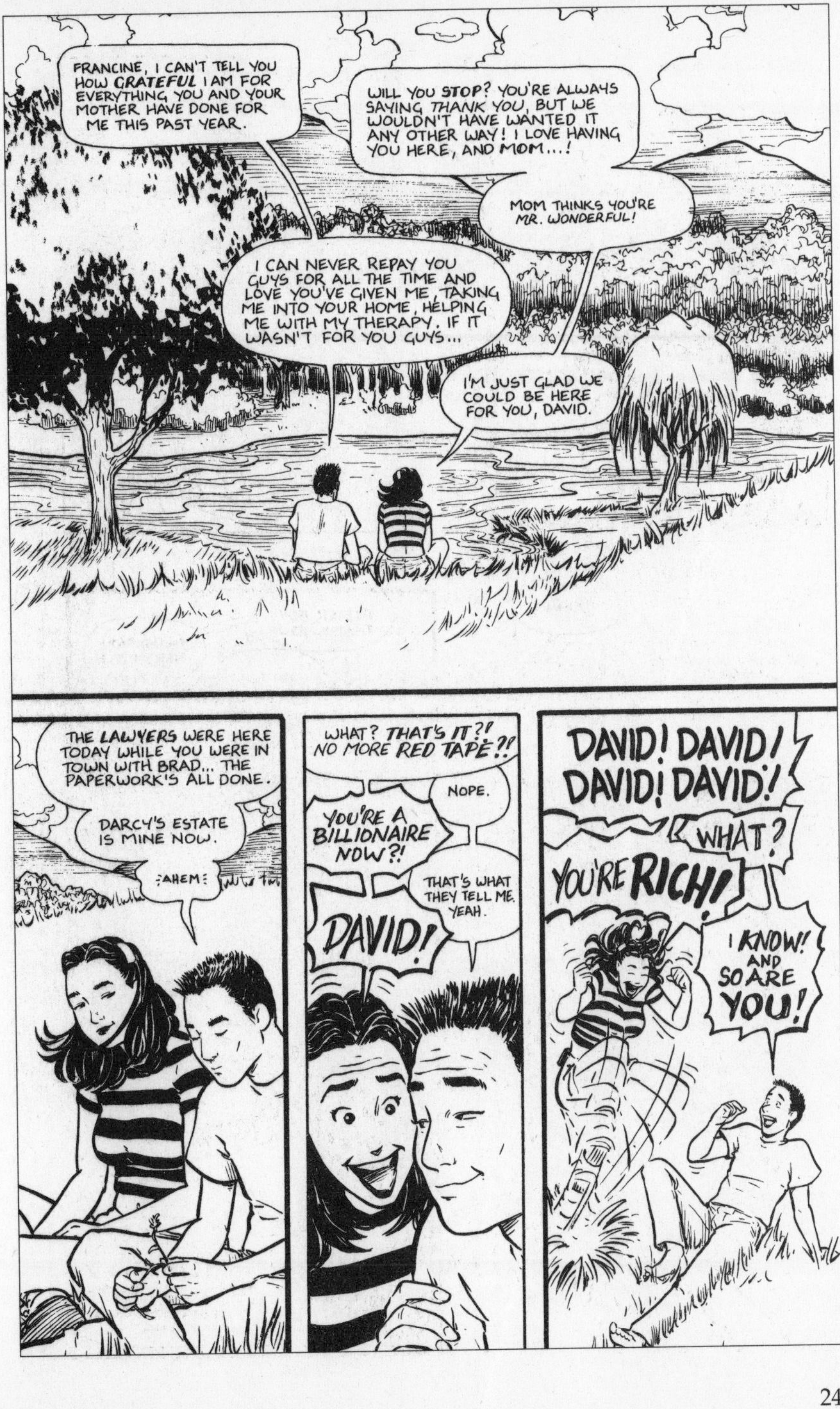
FRANCINE, I CAN'T TELL YOU HOW GRATEFUL I AM FOR EVERYTHING YOU AND YOUR MOTHER HAVE DONE FOR ME THIS PAST YEAR.
WILL YOU STOP? YOU'RE ALWAYS SAYING THANK YOU, BUT WE WOULDN'T HAVE WANTED IT ANY OTHER WAY! I LOVE HAVING YOU HERE, AND MOM...!
MOM THINKS YOU'RE MR. WONDERFUL!
I CAN NEVER REPAY YOU GUYS FOR ALL THE TIME AND LOVE YOU'VE GIVEN ME, TAKING ME INTO YOUR HOME, HELPING ME WITH MY THERAPY. IF IT WASN'T FOR YOU GUYS...
I'M JUST GLAD WE COULD BE HERE FOR YOU, DAVID.
THE LAWYERS WERE HERE TODAY WHILE YOU WERE IN TOWN WITH BRAD... THE PAPERWORK'S ALL DONE.
DARCY'S ESTATE IS MINE NOW.
AHEM
WHAT? THAT'S IT?! NO MORE RED TAPE?!
NOPE.
YOU'RE A BILLIONAIRE NOW?!
THAT'S WHAT THEY TELL ME. YEAH.
DAVID!
DAVID! DAVID! DAVID! DAVID!
WHAT?
YOU'RE RICH!
I KNOW! AND SO ARE YOU!

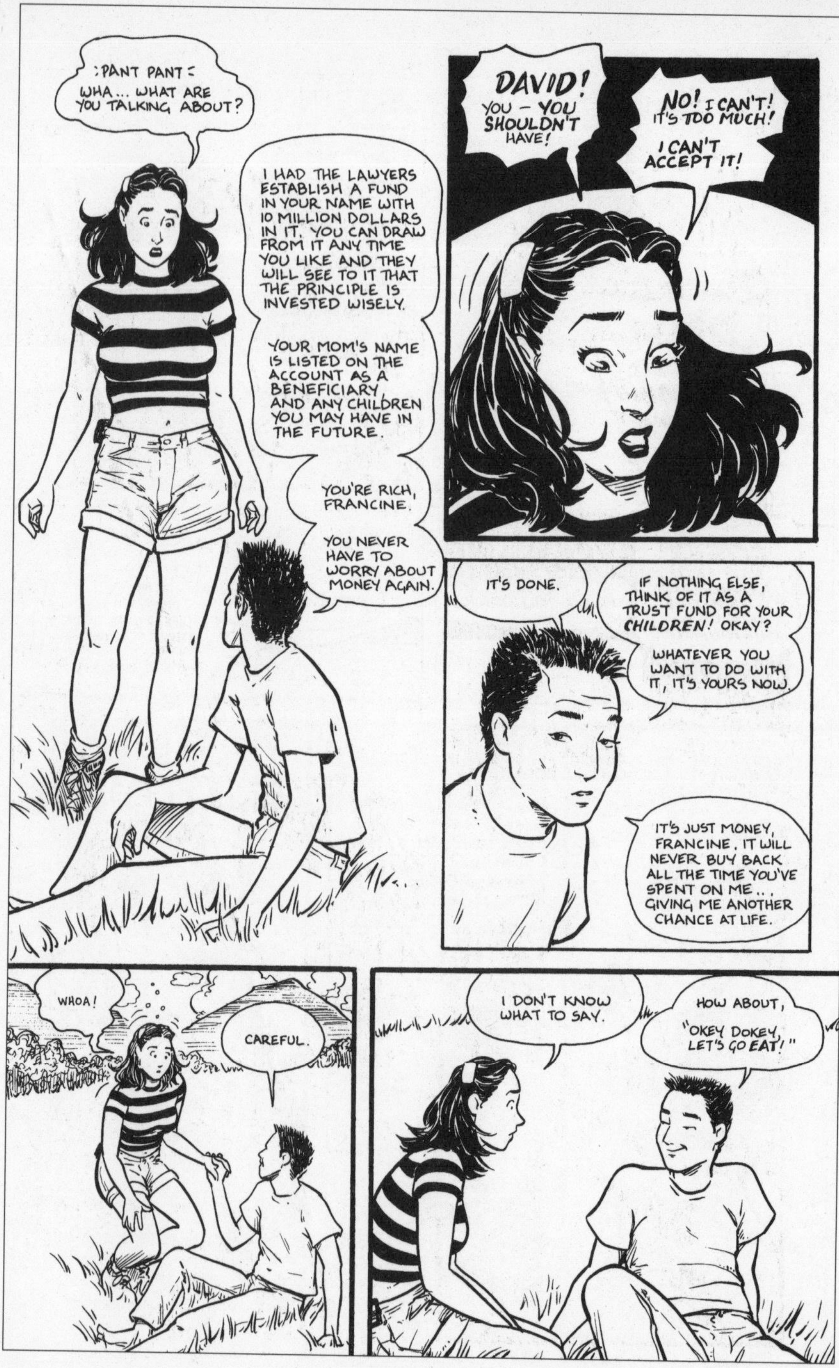
:PANT PANT: WHA... WHAT ARE YOU TALKING ABOUT?
I HAD THE LAWYERS ESTABLISH A FUND IN YOUR NAME WITH 10 MILLION DOLLARS IN IT. YOU CAN DRAW FROM IT ANY TIME YOU LIKE AND THEY WILL SEE TO IT THAT THE PRINCIPLE IS INVESTED WISELY.
YOUR MOM'S NAME IS LISTED ON THE ACCOUNT AS A BENEFICIARY AND ANY CHILDREN YOU MAY HAVE IN THE FUTURE.
YOU'RE RICH, FRANCINE.
YOU NEVER HAVE TO WORRY ABOUT MONEY AGAIN.
DAVID! YOU - YOU SHOULDN'T HAVE!
NO! I CAN'T! IT'S TOO MUCH!
I CAN'T ACCEPT IT!
IT'S DONE.
IF NOTHING ELSE, THINK OF IT AS A TRUST FUND FOR YOUR CHILDREN! OKAY?
WHATEVER YOU WANT TO DO WITH IT, IT'S YOURS NOW.
IT'S JUST MONEY, FRANCINE. IT WILL NEVER BUY BACK ALL THE TIME YOU'VE SPENT ON ME... GIVING ME ANOTHER CHANCE AT LIFE.
WHOA!
CAREFUL.
I DON'T KNOW WHAT TO SAY.
HOW ABOUT,
"OKEY DOKEY, LET'S GO EAT!"

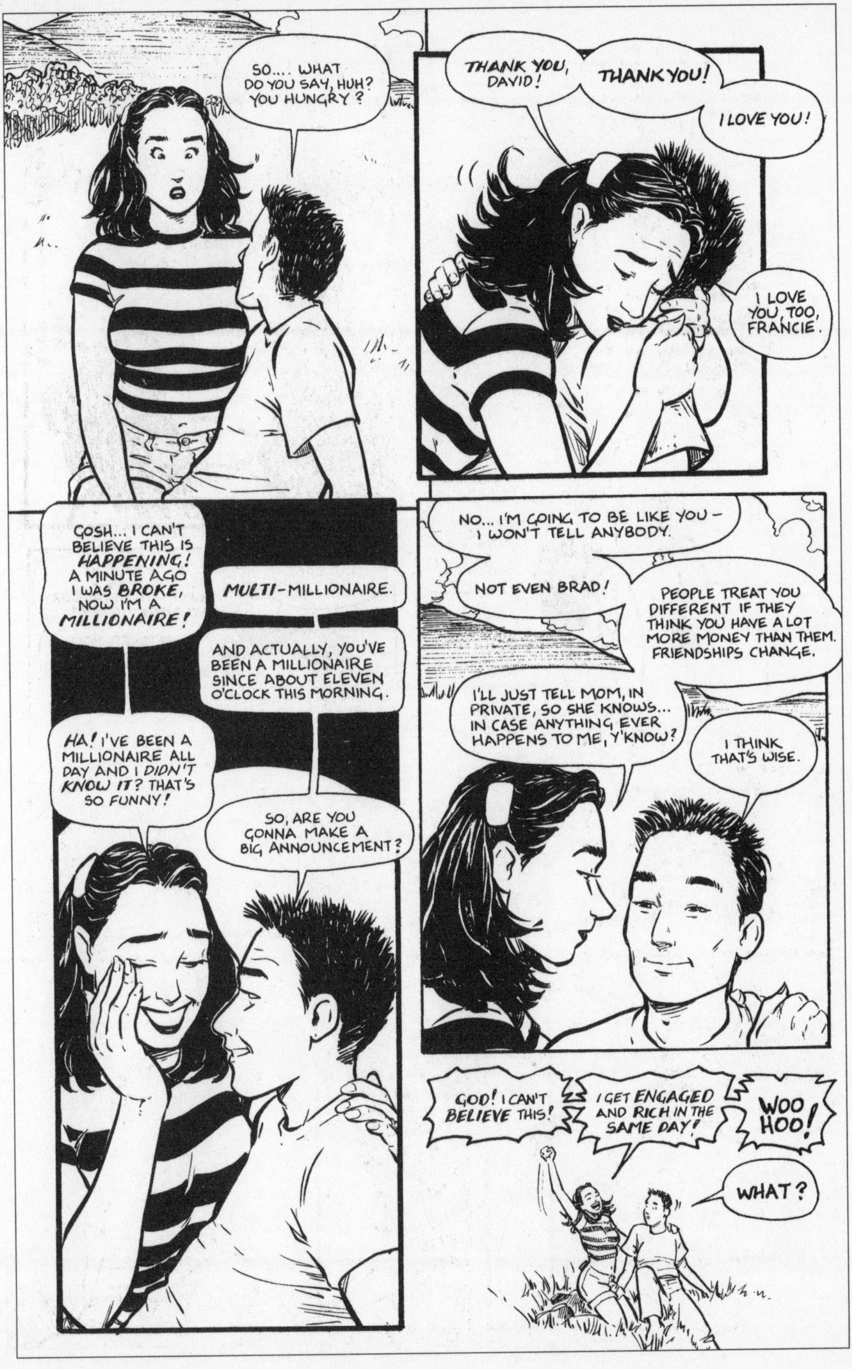
SO.... WHAT DO YOU SAY, HUH? YOU HUNGRY?
THANK YOU, DAVID!
THANK YOU!
I LOVE YOU!
I LOVE YOU, TOO, FRANCIE.
GOSH... I CAN'T BELIEVE THIS IS HAPPENING! A MINUTE AGO I WAS BROKE, NOW I'M A MILLIONAIRE!
MULTI-MILLIONAIRE.
AND ACTUALLY, YOU'VE BEEN A MILLIONAIRE SINCE ABOUT ELEVEN O'CLOCK THIS MORNING.
HA! I'VE BEEN A MILLIONAIRE ALL DAY AND I DIDN'T KNOW IT? THAT'S SO FUNNY!
SO, ARE YOU GONNA MAKE A BIG ANNOUNCEMENT?
NO... I'M GOING TO BE LIKE YOU - I WON'T TELL ANYBODY.
NOT EVEN BRAD!
PEOPLE TREAT YOU DIFFERENT IF THEY THINK YOU HAVE A LOT MORE MONEY THAN THEM. FRIENDSHIPS CHANGE.
I'LL JUST TELL MOM, IN PRIVATE, SO SHE KNOWS... IN CASE ANYTHING EVER HAPPENS TO ME, Y'KNOW?
I THINK THAT'S WISE.
GOD! I CAN'T BELIEVE THIS!
I GET ENGAGED AND RICH IN THE SAME DAY!
WOO HOO!
WHAT?

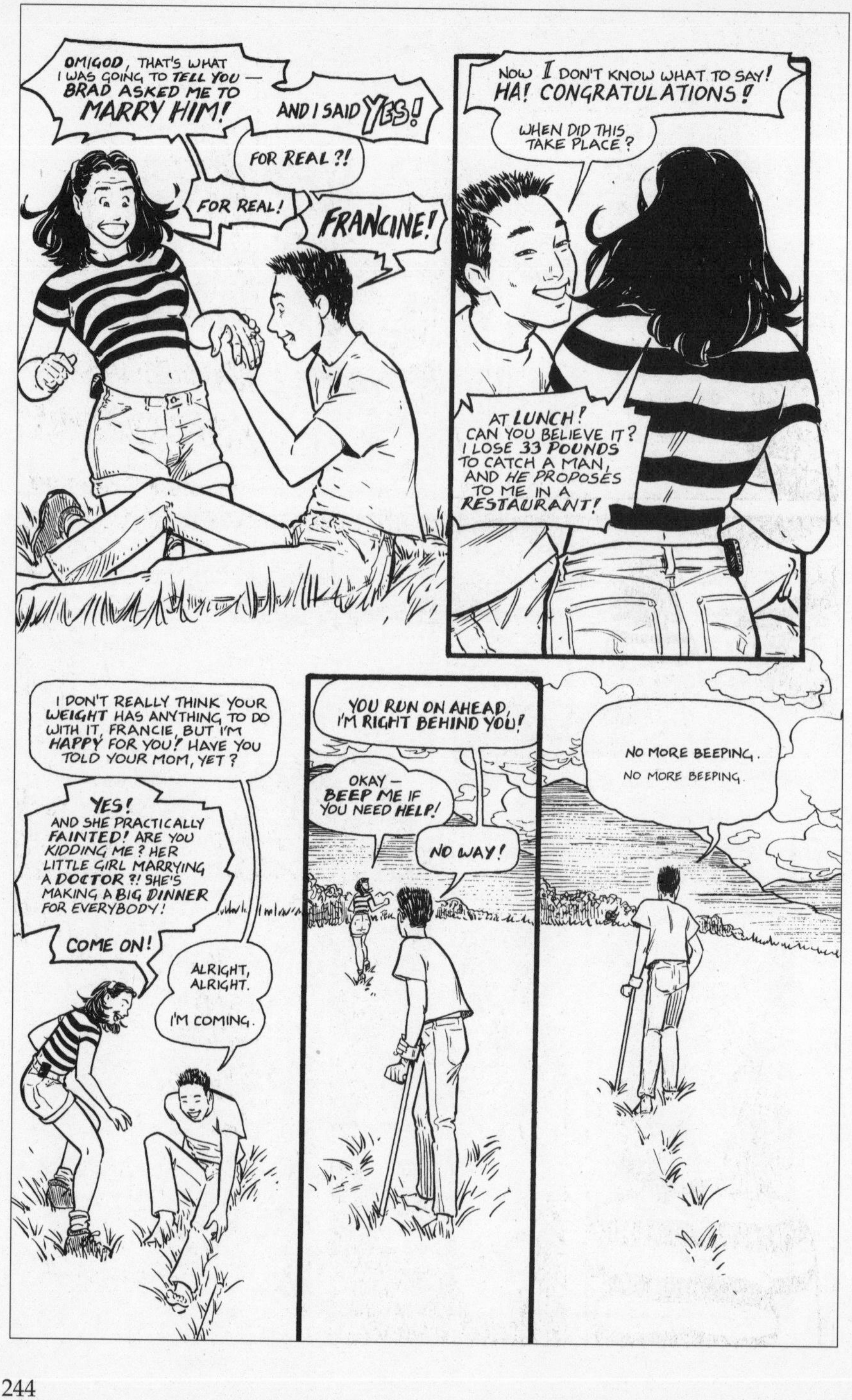
OMIGOD, THAT'S WHAT I WAS GOING TO TELL YOU — BRAD ASKED ME TO MARRY HIM!
AND I SAID YES!
FOR REAL?!
FOR REAL!
FRANCINE!
NOW I DON'T KNOW WHAT TO SAY! HA! CONGRATULATIONS!
WHEN DID THIS TAKE PLACE?
AT LUNCH! CAN YOU BELIEVE IT? I LOSE 33 POUNDS TO CATCH A MAN, AND HE PROPOSES TO ME IN A RESTAURANT!
I DON'T REALLY THINK YOUR WEIGHT HAS ANYTHING TO DO WITH IT, FRANCIE, BUT I'M HAPPY FOR YOU! HAVE YOU TOLD YOUR MOM, YET?
YES! AND SHE PRACTICALLY FAINTED! ARE YOU KIDDING ME? HER LITTLE GIRL MARRYING A DOCTOR?! SHE'S MAKING A BIG DINNER FOR EVERYBODY!
COME ON!
ALRIGHT, ALRIGHT.
I'M COMING.
YOU RUN ON AHEAD, I'M RIGHT BEHIND YOU!
OKAY — BEEP ME IF YOU NEED HELP!
NO WAY!
NO MORE BEEPING.
NO MORE BEEPING.

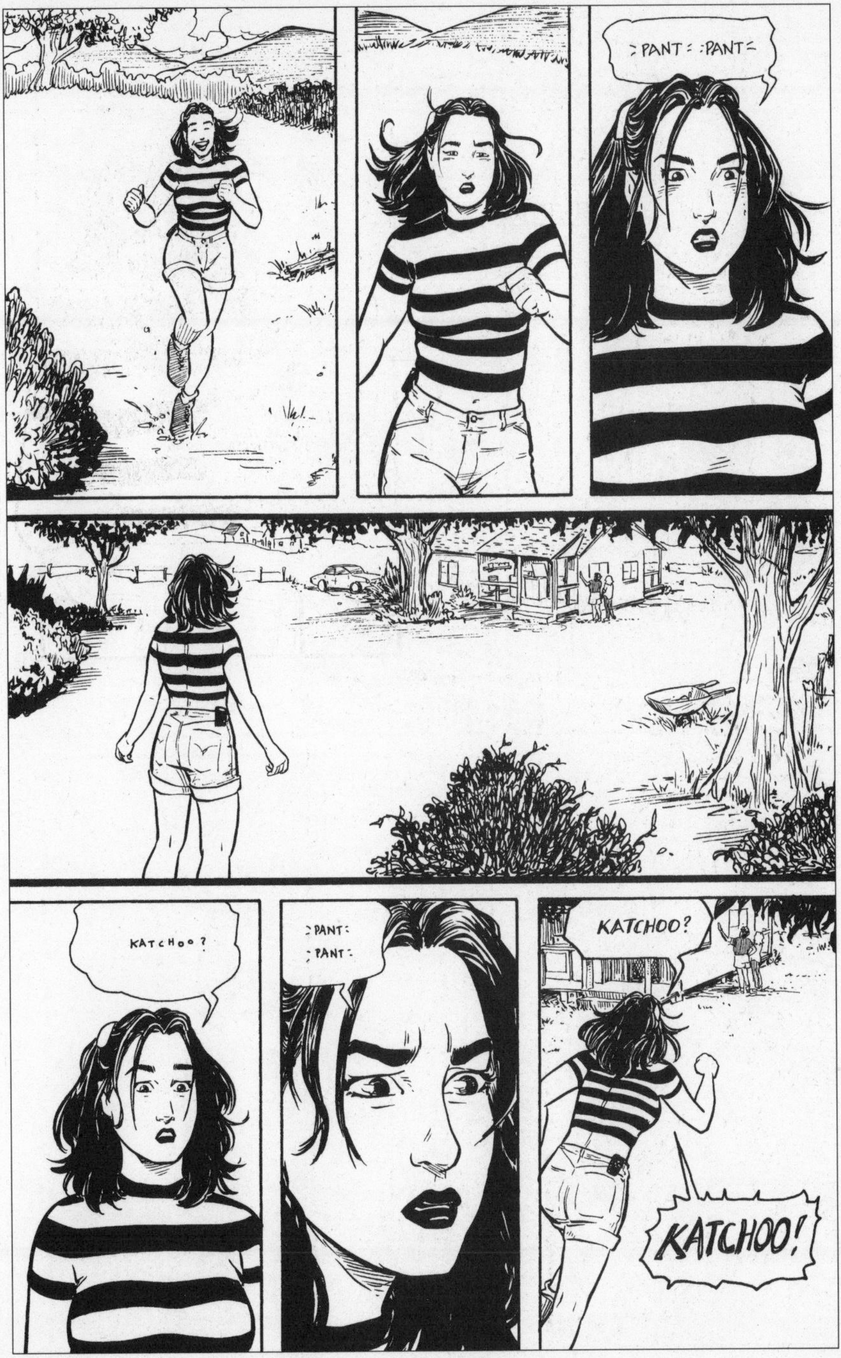
:PANT: :PANT:
KATCHOO?
:PANT:
:PANT:
KATCHOO?
KATCHOO!

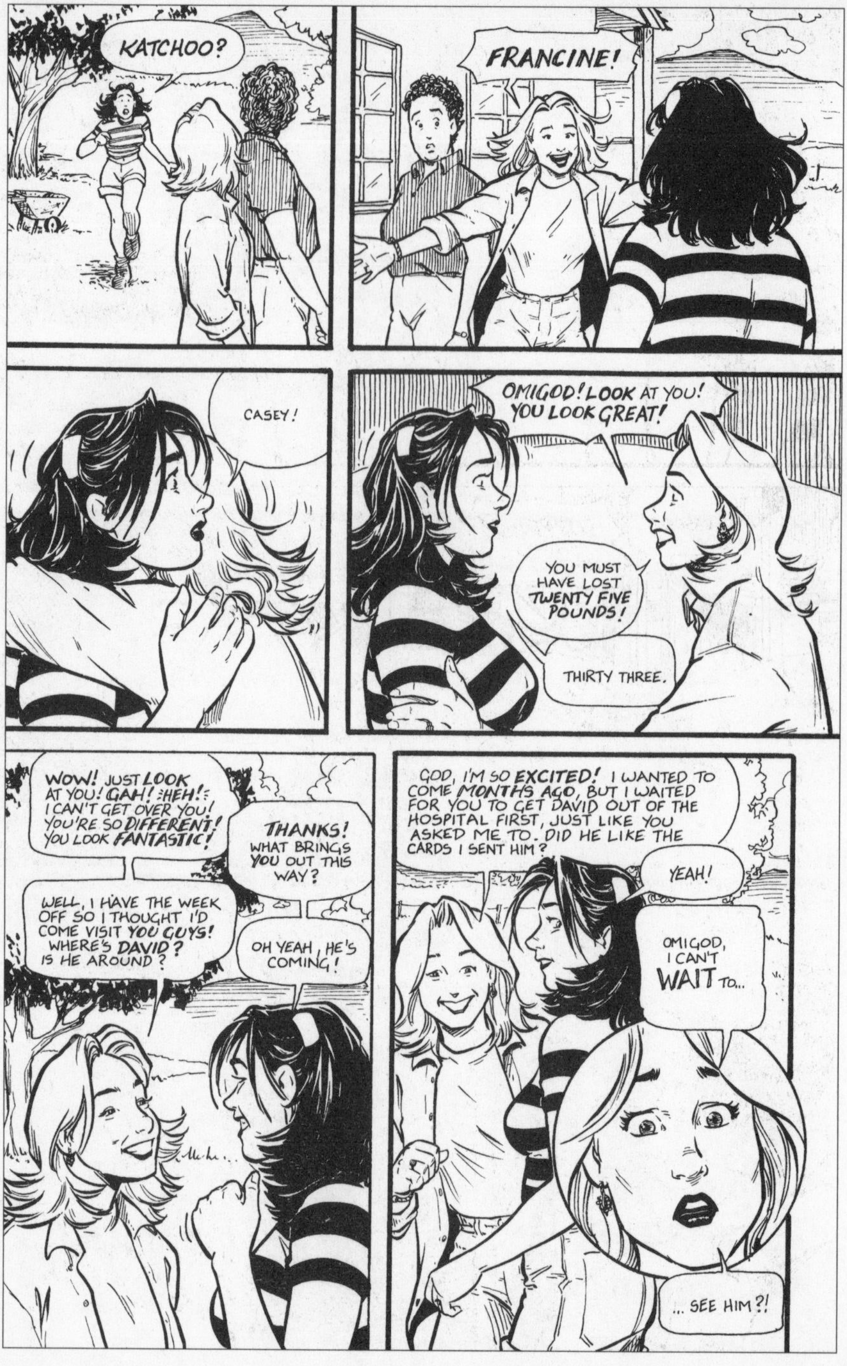
KATCHOO?
FRANCINE!
CASEY!
OMIGOD! LOOK AT YOU! YOU LOOK GREAT!
YOU MUST HAVE LOST TWENTY FIVE POUNDS!
THIRTY THREE.
WOW! JUST LOOK AT YOU! GAH! HEH! I CAN'T GET OVER YOU! YOU'RE SO DIFFERENT! YOU LOOK FANTASTIC!
THANKS! WHAT BRINGS YOU OUT THIS WAY?
WELL, I HAVE THE WEEK OFF SO I THOUGHT I'D COME VISIT YOU GUYS! WHERE'S DAVID? IS HE AROUND?
OH YEAH, HE'S COMING!
GOD, I'M SO EXCITED! I WANTED TO COME MONTHS AGO, BUT I WAITED FOR YOU TO GET DAVID OUT OF THE HOSPITAL FIRST, JUST LIKE YOU ASKED ME TO. DID HE LIKE THE CARDS I SENT HIM?
YEAH!
OMIGOD, I CAN'T WAIT TO...
... SEE HIM?!

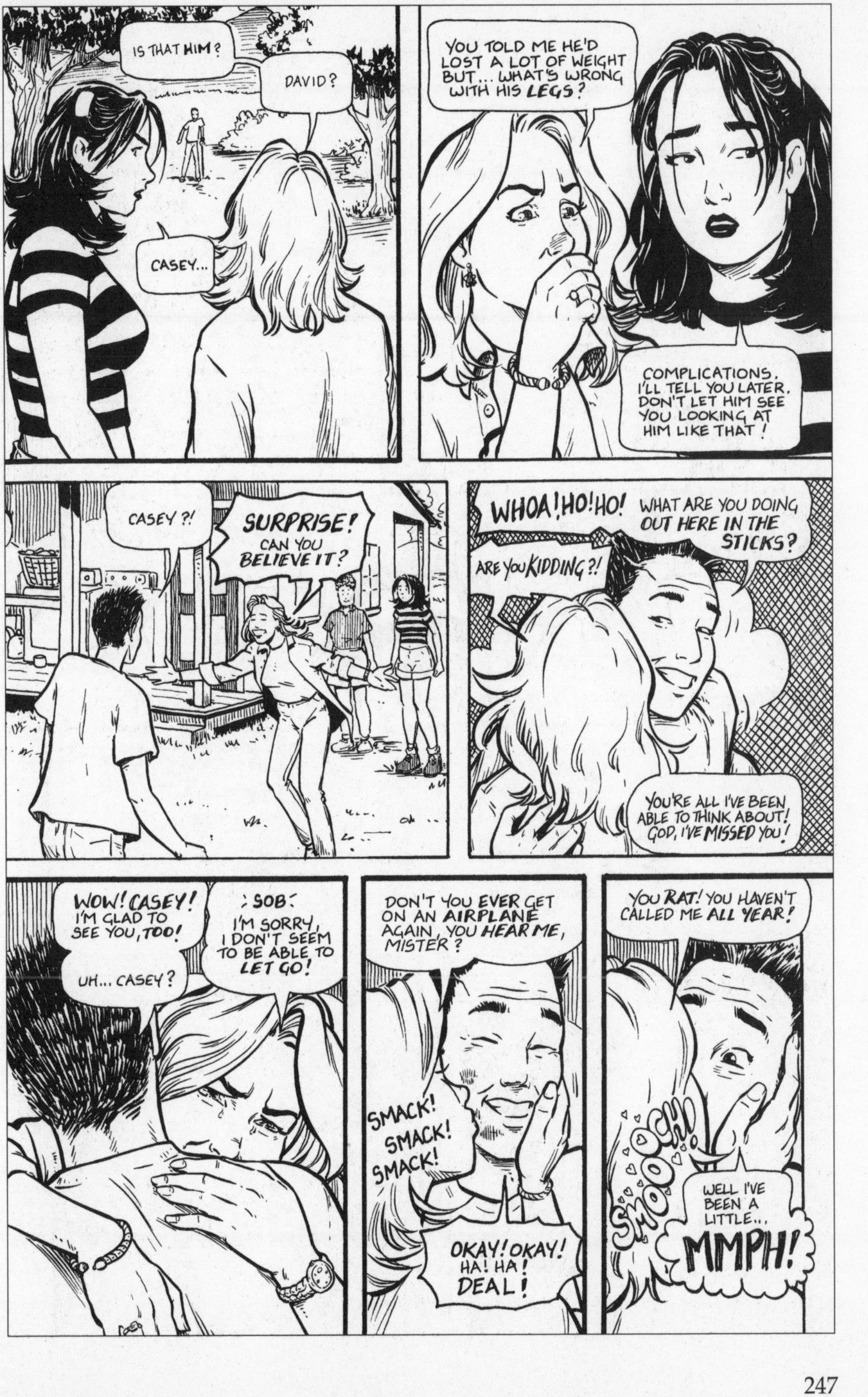
IS THAT HIM?
DAVID?
CASEY...
YOU TOLD ME HE'D LOST A LOT OF WEIGHT BUT... WHAT'S WRONG WITH HIS LEGS?
COMPLICATIONS. I'LL TELL YOU LATER. DON'T LET HIM SEE YOU LOOKING AT HIM LIKE THAT!
CASEY?!
SURPRISE! CAN YOU BELIEVE IT?
WHOA! HO! HO!
WHAT ARE YOU DOING OUT HERE IN THE STICKS?
ARE YOU KIDDING?!
YOU'RE ALL I'VE BEEN ABLE TO THINK ABOUT! GOD, I'VE MISSED YOU!
WOW! CASEY! I'M GLAD TO SEE YOU, TOO!
UH... CASEY?
:SOB:
I'M SORRY, I DON'T SEEM TO BE ABLE TO LET GO!
DON'T YOU EVER GET ON AN AIRPLANE AGAIN, YOU HEAR ME, MISTER?
SMACK! SMACK! SMACK!
OKAY! OKAY! HA! HA! DEAL!
YOU RAT! YOU HAVEN'T CALLED ME ALL YEAR!
SMOOOCH!
WELL I'VE BEEN A LITTLE...
MMPH!

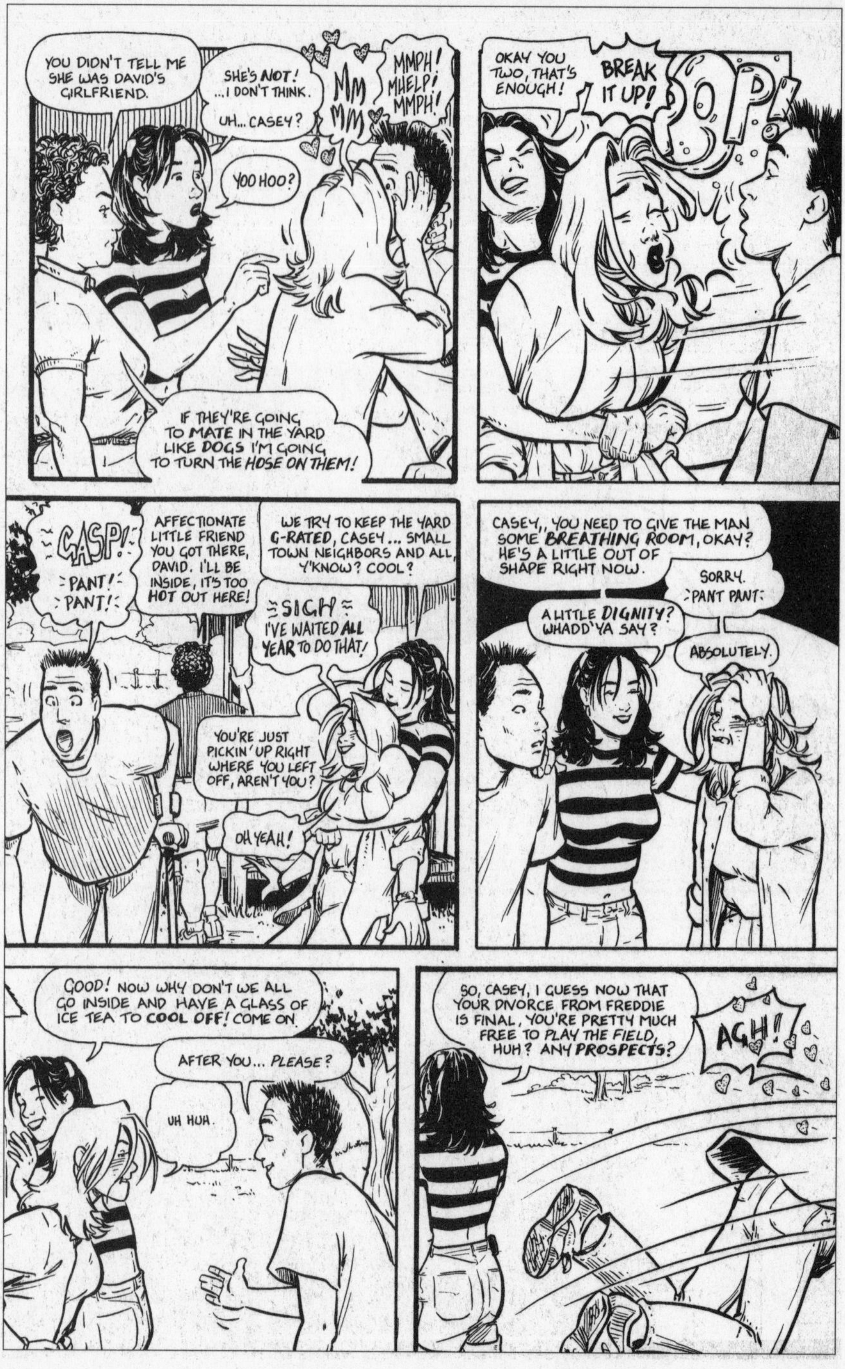

YOU DIDN'T TELL ME SHE WAS DAVID'S GIRLFRIEND.
SHE'S NOT! ...I DON'T THINK.
UH... CASEY?
MM MM
MMPH! MHELP! MMPH!
YOO HOO?
IF THEY'RE GOING TO MATE IN THE YARD LIKE DOGS I'M GOING TO TURN THE HOSE ON THEM!
OKAY YOU TWO, THAT'S ENOUGH!
BREAK IT UP!
POP!
GASP! PANT! PANT!
AFFECTIONATE LITTLE FRIEND YOU GOT THERE, DAVID. I'LL BE INSIDE, IT'S TOO HOT OUT HERE!
WE TRY TO KEEP THE YARD G-RATED, CASEY... SMALL TOWN NEIGHBORS AND ALL, Y'KNOW? COOL?
SIGH I'VE WAITED ALL YEAR TO DO THAT!
YOU'RE JUST PICKIN' UP RIGHT WHERE YOU LEFT OFF, AREN'T YOU?
OH YEAH!
CASEY, YOU NEED TO GIVE THE MAN SOME BREATHING ROOM, OKAY? HE'S A LITTLE OUT OF SHAPE RIGHT NOW.
SORRY. PANT PANT
A LITTLE DIGNITY? WHADD'YA SAY?
ABSOLUTELY.
GOOD! NOW WHY DON'T WE ALL GO INSIDE AND HAVE A GLASS OF ICE TEA TO COOL OFF! COME ON
AFTER YOU... PLEASE?
UH HUH.
SO, CASEY, I GUESS NOW THAT YOUR DIVORCE FROM FREDDIE IS FINAL, YOU'RE PRETTY MUCH FREE TO PLAY THE FIELD, HUH? ANY PROSPECTS?
AGH!

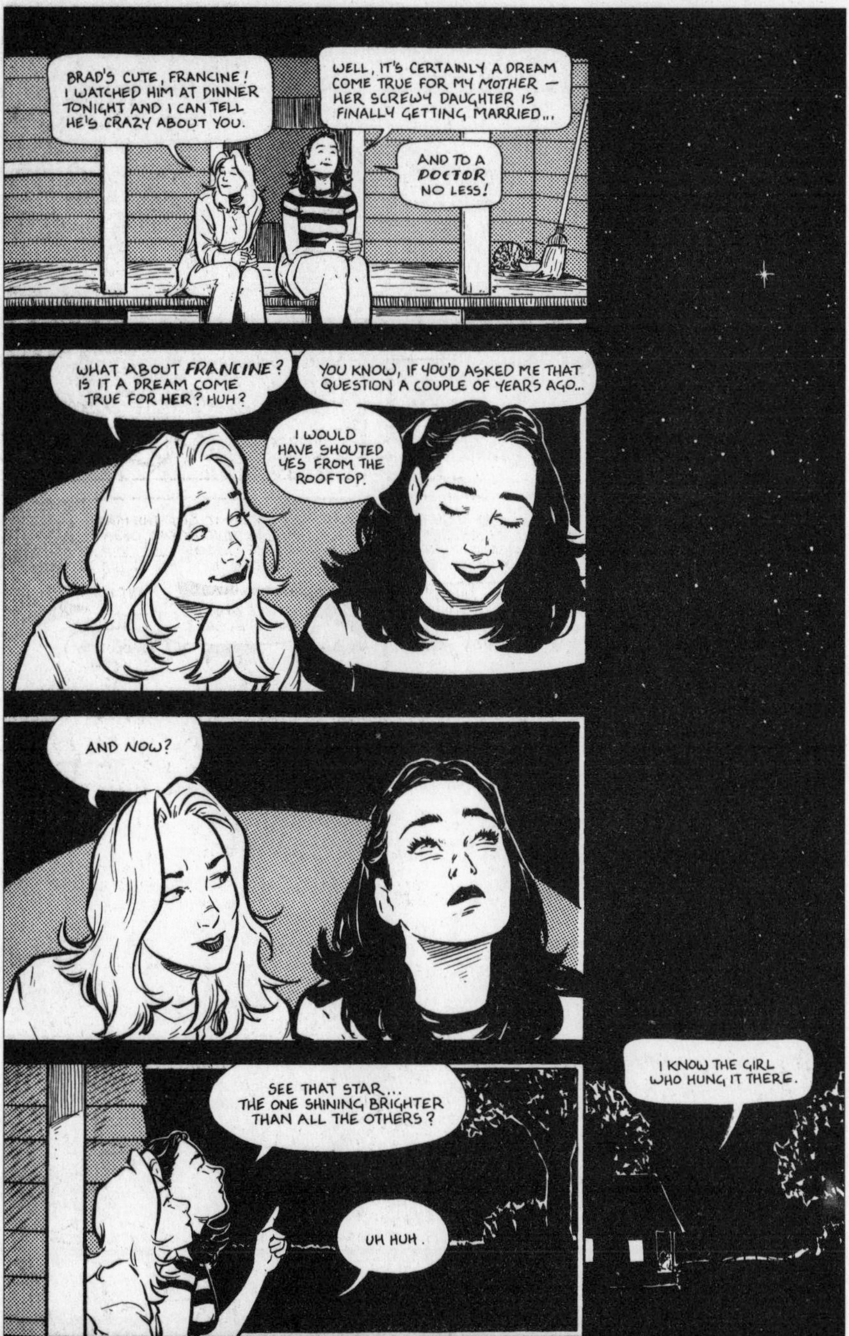
BRAD'S CUTE, FRANCINE! I WATCHED HIM AT DINNER TONIGHT AND I CAN TELL HE'S CRAZY ABOUT YOU.
WELL, IT'S CERTAINLY A DREAM COME TRUE FOR MY MOTHER — HER SCREWY DAUGHTER IS FINALLY GETTING MARRIED...
AND TO A DOCTOR NO LESS!
WHAT ABOUT FRANCINE? IS IT A DREAM COME TRUE FOR HER? HUH?
YOU KNOW, IF YOU'D ASKED ME THAT QUESTION A COUPLE OF YEARS AGO...
I WOULD HAVE SHOUTED YES FROM THE ROOFTOP.
AND NOW?
SEE THAT STAR... THE ONE SHINING BRIGHTER THAN ALL THE OTHERS?
UH HUH.
I KNOW THE GIRL WHO HUNG IT THERE.

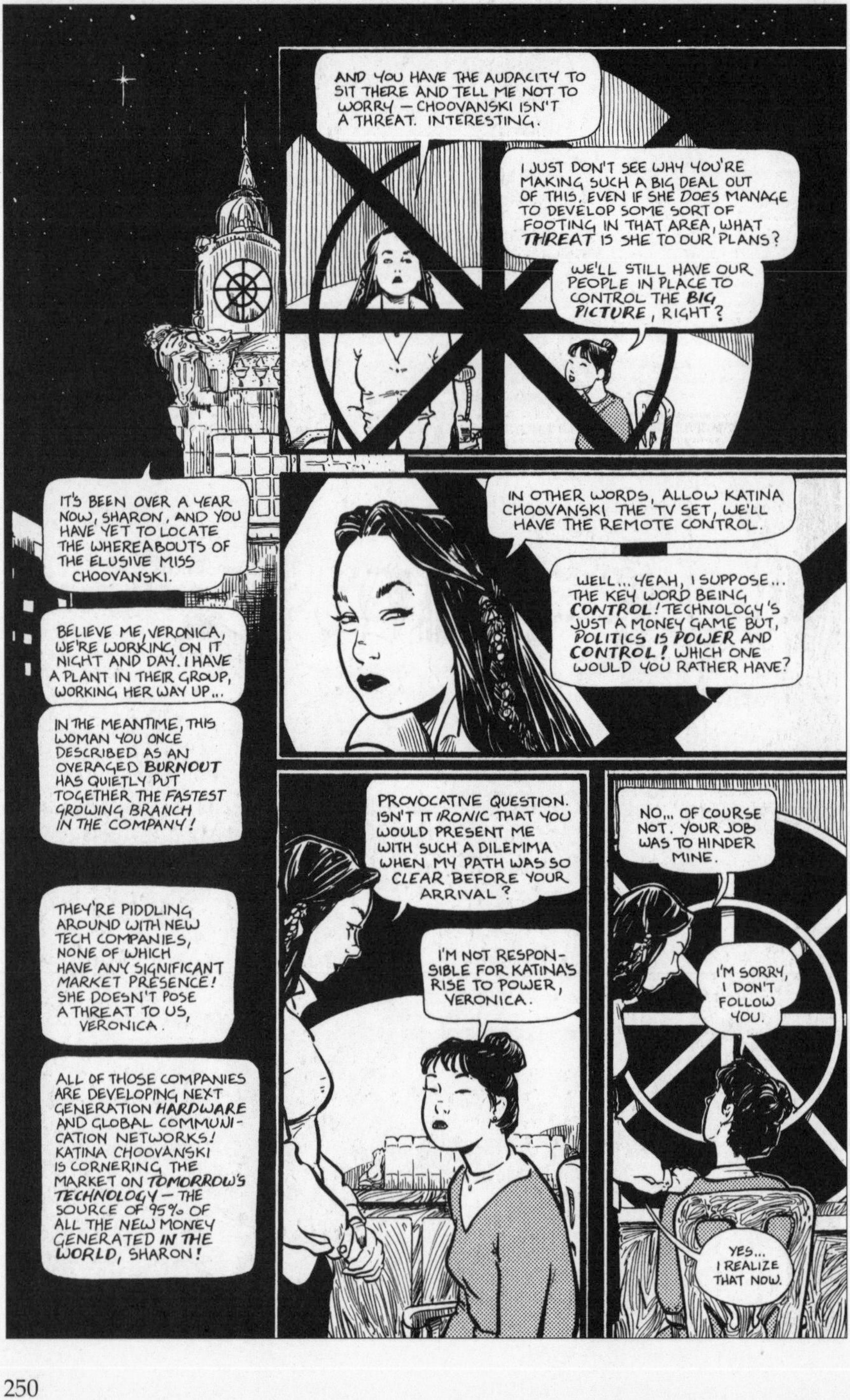

IT'S BEEN OVER A YEAR NOW, SHARON, AND YOU HAVE YET TO LOCATE THE WHEREABOUTS OF THE ELUSIVE MISS CHOOVANSKI.
BELIEVE ME, VERONICA, WE'RE WORKING ON IT NIGHT AND DAY. I HAVE A PLANT IN THEIR GROUP, WORKING HER WAY UP...
IN THE MEANTIME, THIS WOMAN YOU ONCE DESCRIBED AS AN OVERAGED **BURNOUT** HAS QUIETLY PUT TOGETHER THE *FASTEST GROWING BRANCH IN THE COMPANY!*
THEY'RE PIDDLING AROUND WITH NEW TECH COMPANIES, NONE OF WHICH HAVE ANY SIGNIFICANT MARKET PRESENCE! SHE DOESN'T POSE A THREAT TO US, VERONICA.
ALL OF THOSE COMPANIES ARE DEVELOPING NEXT GENERATION **HARDWARE** AND GLOBAL COMMUNICATION NETWORKS! KATINA CHOOVANSKI IS CORNERING THE MARKET ON *TOMORROW'S TECHNOLOGY* — THE SOURCE OF 95% OF ALL THE NEW MONEY GENERATED **IN THE WORLD**, SHARON!
AND YOU HAVE THE AUDACITY TO SIT THERE AND TELL ME NOT TO WORRY — CHOOVANSKI ISN'T A THREAT. INTERESTING.
I JUST DON'T SEE WHY YOU'RE MAKING SUCH A BIG DEAL OUT OF THIS. EVEN IF SHE *DOES* MANAGE TO DEVELOP SOME SORT OF FOOTING IN THAT AREA, WHAT **THREAT** IS SHE TO OUR PLANS?
WE'LL STILL HAVE OUR PEOPLE IN PLACE TO CONTROL THE ***BIG PICTURE***, RIGHT?
IN OTHER WORDS, ALLOW KATINA CHOOVANSKI THE TV SET, WE'LL HAVE THE REMOTE CONTROL.
WELL... YEAH, I SUPPOSE... THE KEY WORD BEING **CONTROL!** TECHNOLOGY'S JUST A MONEY GAME BUT, ***POLITICS IS POWER*** AND **CONTROL!** WHICH ONE WOULD YOU RATHER HAVE?
PROVOCATIVE QUESTION. ISN'T IT *IRONIC* THAT YOU WOULD PRESENT ME WITH SUCH A DILEMMA WHEN MY PATH WAS SO *CLEAR* BEFORE YOUR ARRIVAL?
I'M NOT RESPONSIBLE FOR KATINA'S RISE TO POWER, VERONICA.
NO... OF COURSE NOT. YOUR JOB WAS TO HINDER MINE.
I'M SORRY, I DON'T FOLLOW YOU.
YES... I REALIZE THAT NOW.

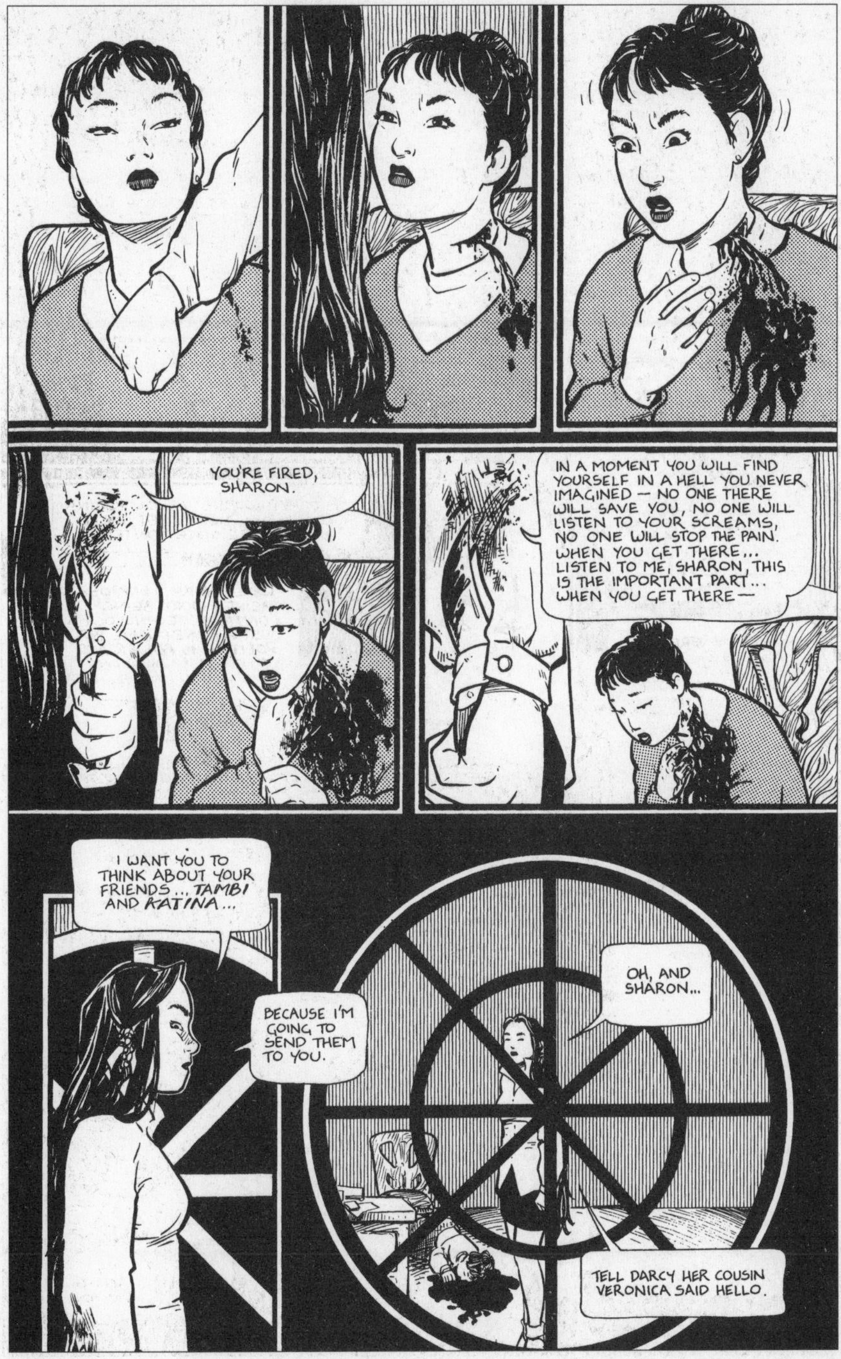
YOU'RE FIRED, SHARON.
IN A MOMENT YOU WILL FIND YOURSELF IN A HELL YOU NEVER IMAGINED — NO ONE THERE WILL SAVE YOU, NO ONE WILL LISTEN TO YOUR SCREAMS, NO ONE WILL STOP THE PAIN. WHEN YOU GET THERE... LISTEN TO ME, SHARON, THIS IS THE IMPORTANT PART... WHEN YOU GET THERE—
I WANT YOU TO THINK ABOUT YOUR FRIENDS... TAMBI AND KATINA...
BECAUSE I'M GOING TO SEND THEM TO YOU.
OH, AND SHARON...
TELL DARCY HER COUSIN VERONICA SAID HELLO.

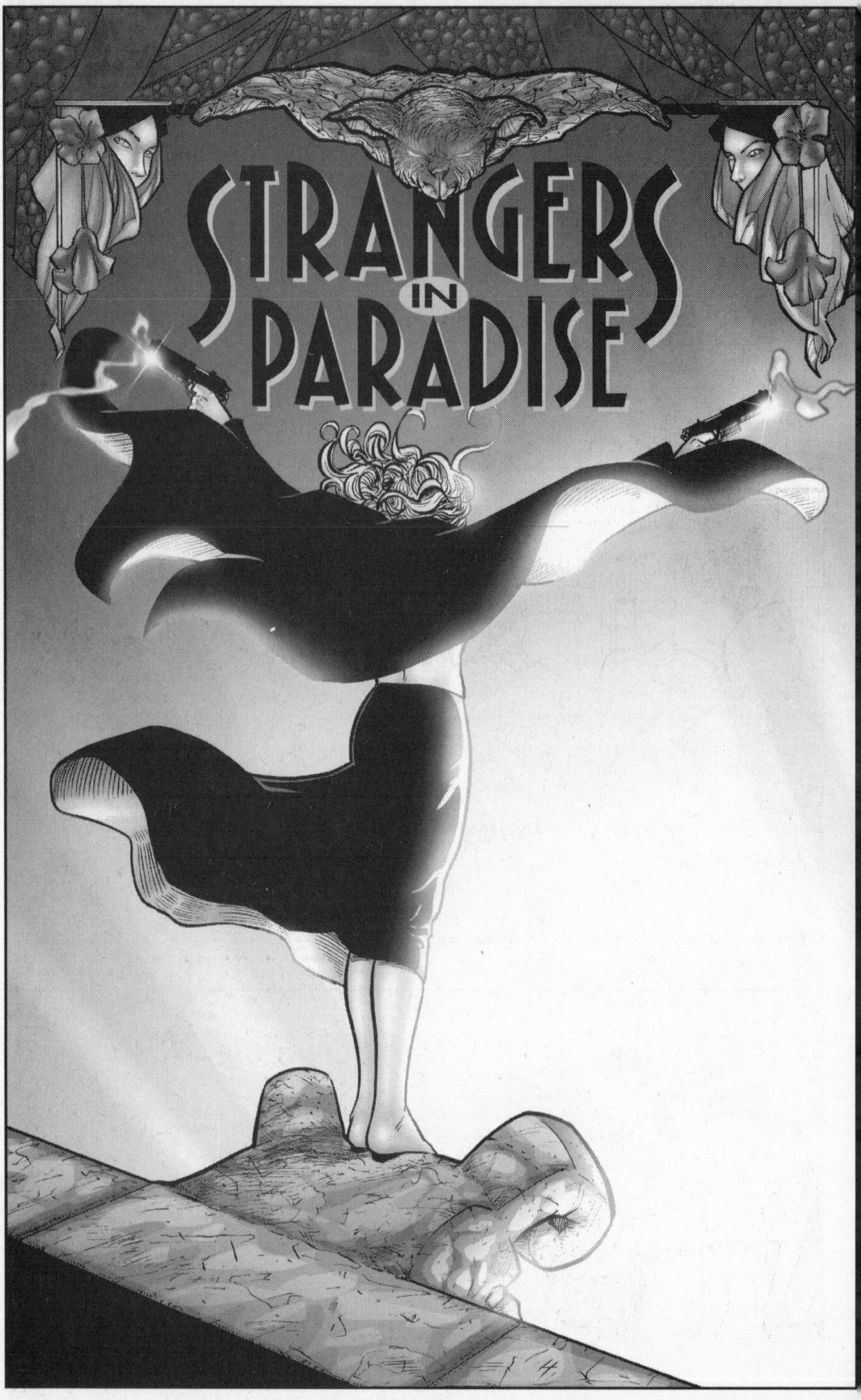
STRANGERS
IN
PARADISE

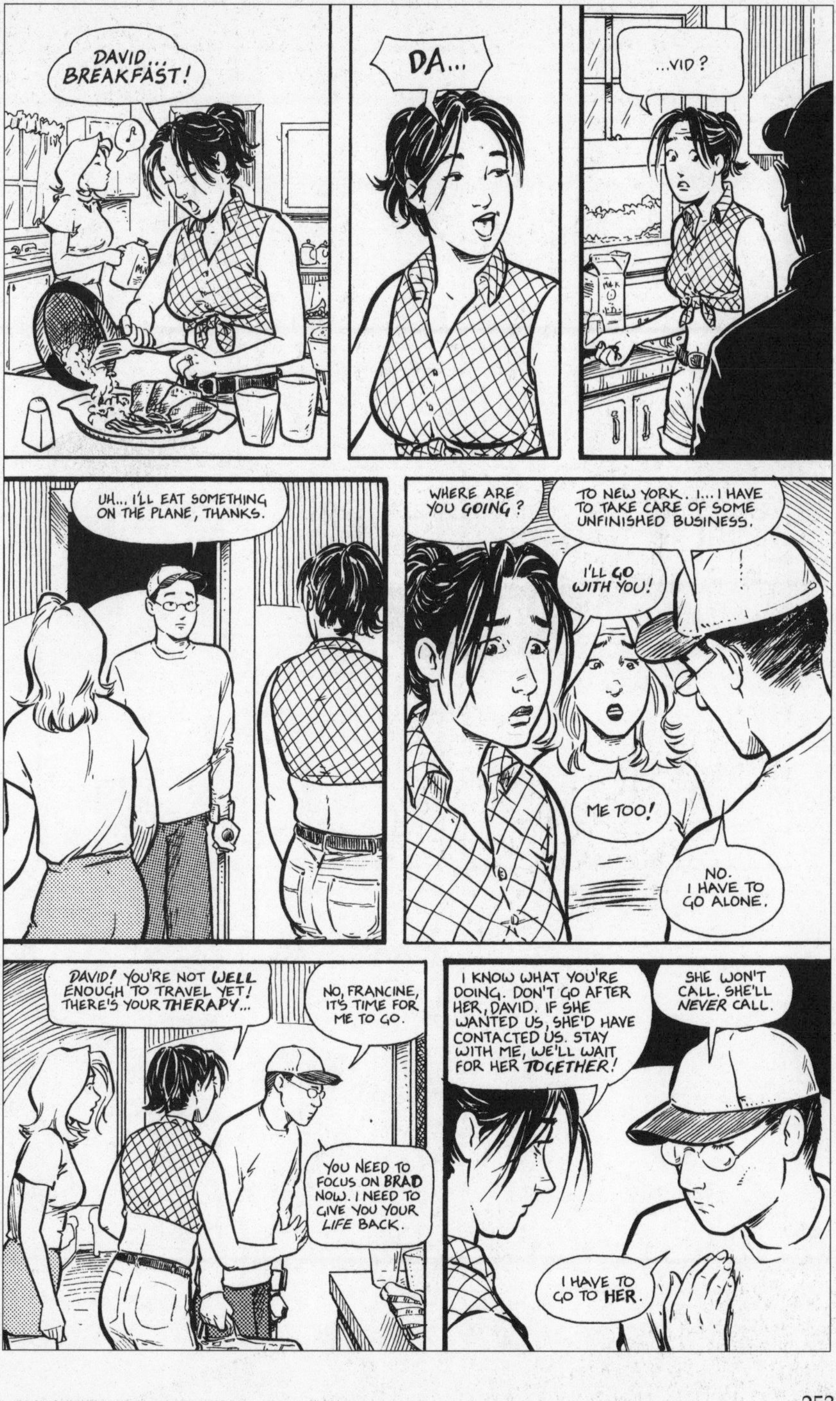
DAVID... BREAKFAST!
DA...
...VID?
UH... I'LL EAT SOMETHING ON THE PLANE, THANKS.
WHERE ARE YOU GOING?
TO NEW YORK. I... I HAVE TO TAKE CARE OF SOME UNFINISHED BUSINESS.
I'LL GO WITH YOU!
ME TOO!
NO. I HAVE TO GO ALONE.
DAVID! YOU'RE NOT WELL ENOUGH TO TRAVEL YET! THERE'S YOUR THERAPY...
NO, FRANCINE, IT'S TIME FOR ME TO GO.
YOU NEED TO FOCUS ON BRAD NOW. I NEED TO GIVE YOU YOUR LIFE BACK.
I KNOW WHAT YOU'RE DOING. DON'T GO AFTER HER, DAVID. IF SHE WANTED US, SHE'D HAVE CONTACTED US. STAY WITH ME, WE'LL WAIT FOR HER TOGETHER!
SHE WON'T CALL. SHE'LL NEVER CALL.
I HAVE TO GO TO HER.

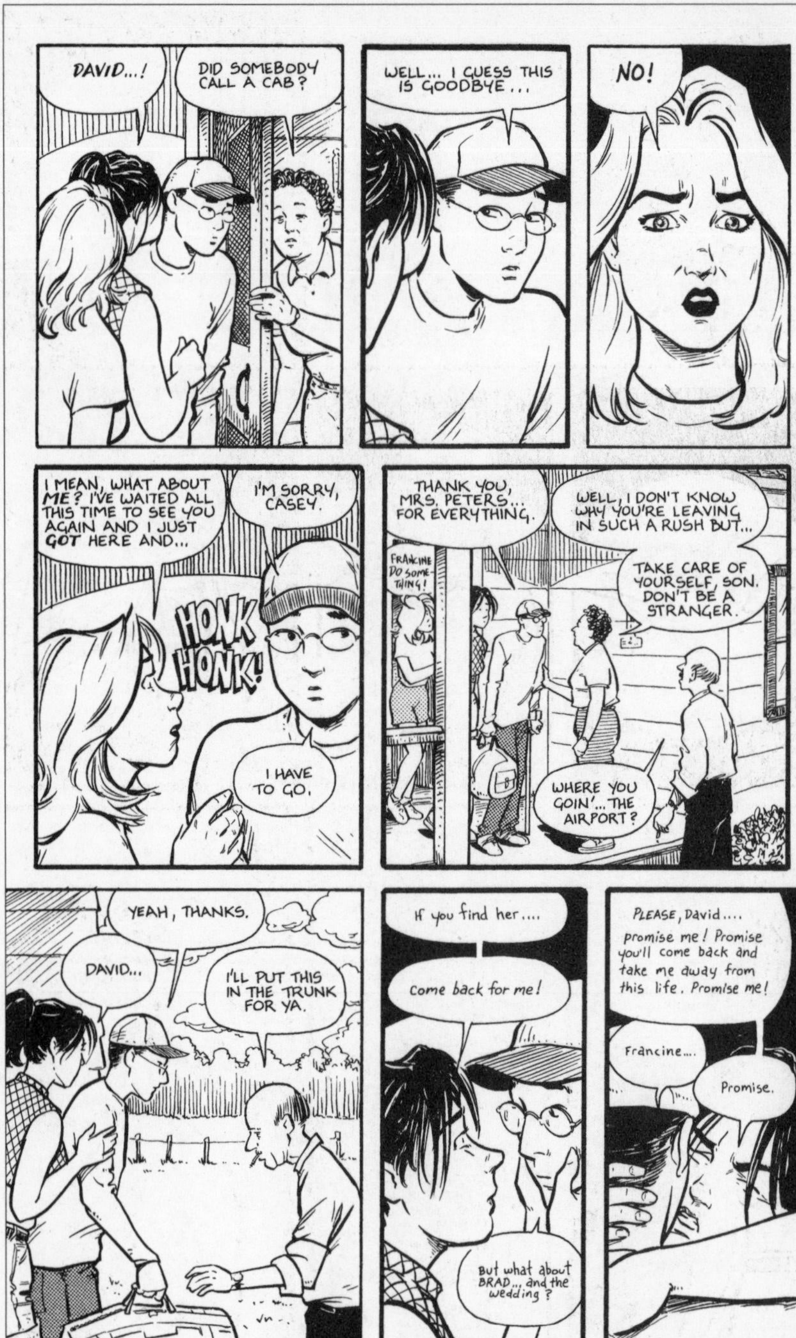
DAVID...!
DID SOMEBODY CALL A CAB?
WELL... I GUESS THIS IS GOODBYE...
NO!
I MEAN, WHAT ABOUT ME? I'VE WAITED ALL THIS TIME TO SEE YOU AGAIN AND I JUST GOT HERE AND...
I'M SORRY, CASEY.
HONK HONK!
I HAVE TO GO.
THANK YOU, MRS. PETERS... FOR EVERYTHING.
FRANCINE DO SOMETHING!
WELL, I DON'T KNOW WHY YOU'RE LEAVING IN SUCH A RUSH BUT...
TAKE CARE OF YOURSELF, SON. DON'T BE A STRANGER.
WHERE YOU GOIN'... THE AIRPORT?
YEAH, THANKS.
DAVID...
I'LL PUT THIS IN THE TRUNK FOR YA.
If you find her....
Come back for me!
But what about BRAD... and the wedding?
PLEASE, David....
promise me! Promise you'll come back and take me away from this life. Promise me!
Francine....
Promise.

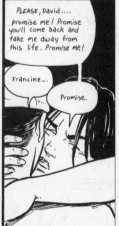

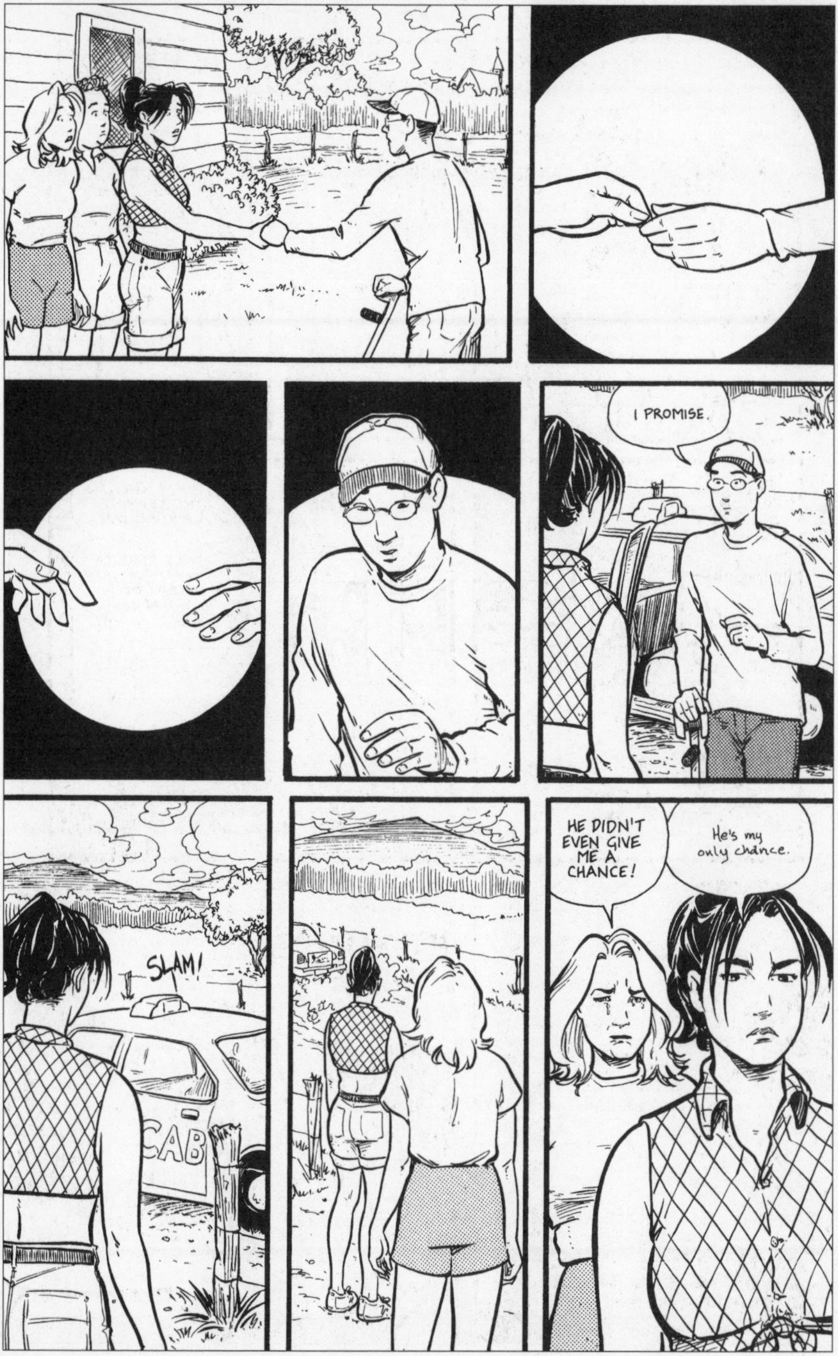
I PROMISE.
SLAM!
CAB
HE DIDN'T EVEN GIVE ME A CHANCE!
He's my only chance.

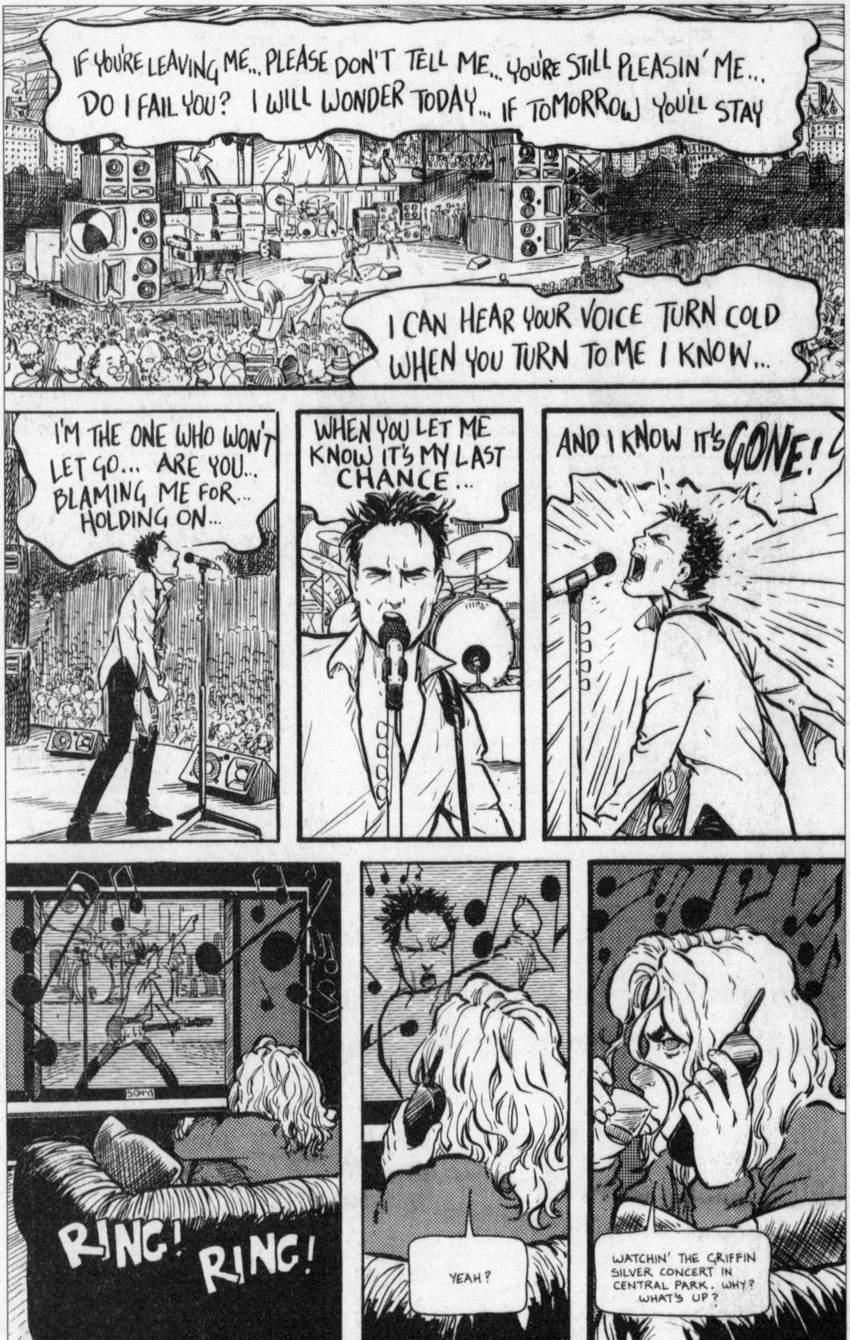
IF YOU'RE LEAVING ME... PLEASE DON'T TELL ME... YOU'RE STILL PLEASIN' ME... DO I FAIL YOU? I WILL WONDER TODAY... IF TOMORROW YOU'LL STAY
I CAN HEAR YOUR VOICE TURN COLD WHEN YOU TURN TO ME I KNOW...
I'M THE ONE WHO WON'T LET GO... ARE YOU... BLAMING ME FOR... HOLDING ON...
WHEN YOU LET ME KNOW IT'S MY LAST CHANCE...
AND I KNOW IT'S GONE!
SONY
RING! RING!
YEAH?
WATCHIN' THE GRIFFIN SILVER CONCERT IN CENTRAL PARK. WHY? WHAT'S UP?

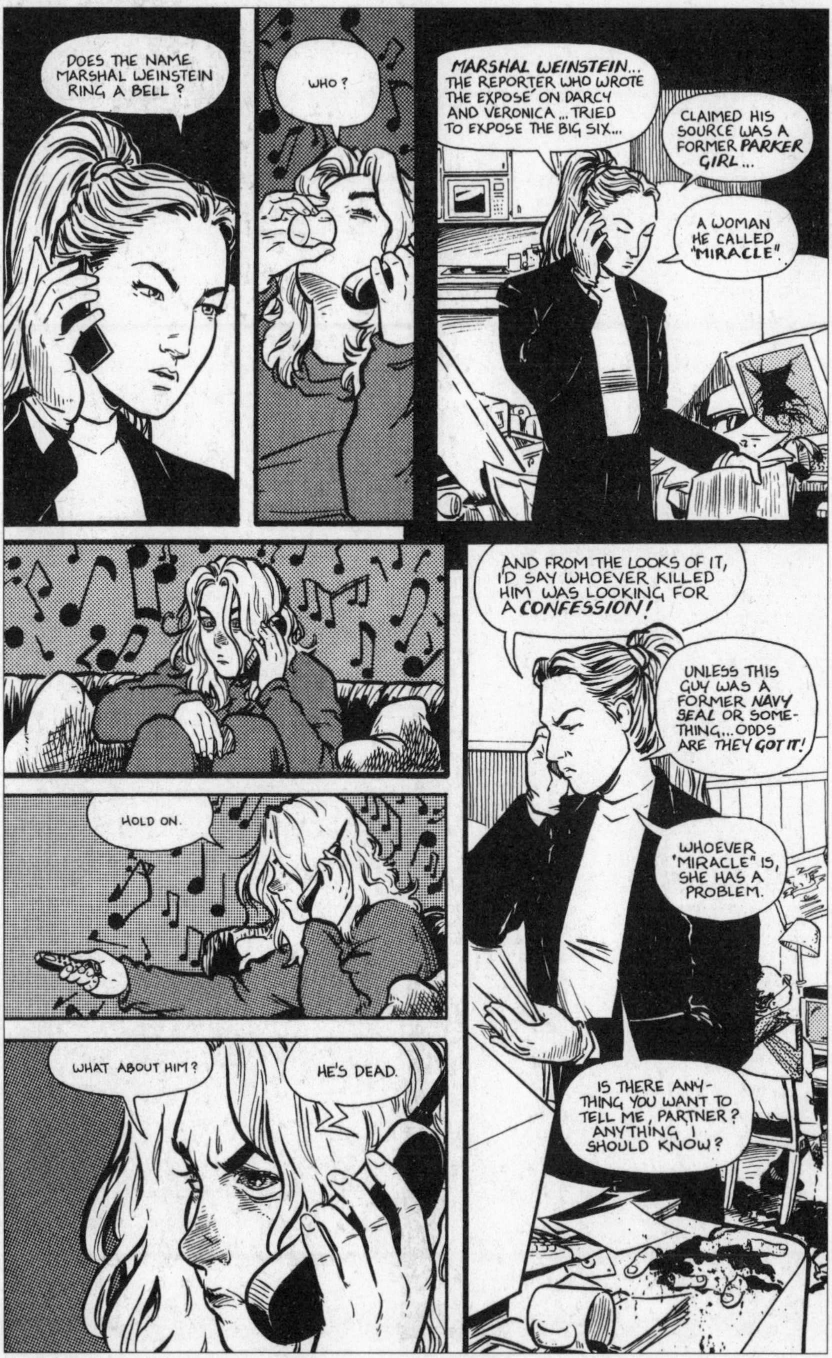
DOES THE NAME MARSHAL WEINSTEIN RING A BELL ?
WHO ?
MARSHAL WEINSTEIN... THE REPORTER WHO WROTE THE EXPOSE' ON DARCY AND VERONICA... TRIED TO EXPOSE THE BIG SIX...
CLAIMED HIS SOURCE WAS A FORMER PARKER GIRL...
A WOMAN HE CALLED "MIRACLE".
AND FROM THE LOOKS OF IT, I'D SAY WHOEVER KILLED HIM WAS LOOKING FOR A CONFESSION!
UNLESS THIS GUY WAS A FORMER NAVY SEAL OR SOMETHING... ODDS ARE THEY GOT IT!
HOLD ON.
WHOEVER "MIRACLE" IS, SHE HAS A PROBLEM.
WHAT ABOUT HIM ?
HE'S DEAD.
IS THERE ANYTHING YOU WANT TO TELL ME, PARTNER ? ANYTHING I SHOULD KNOW ?

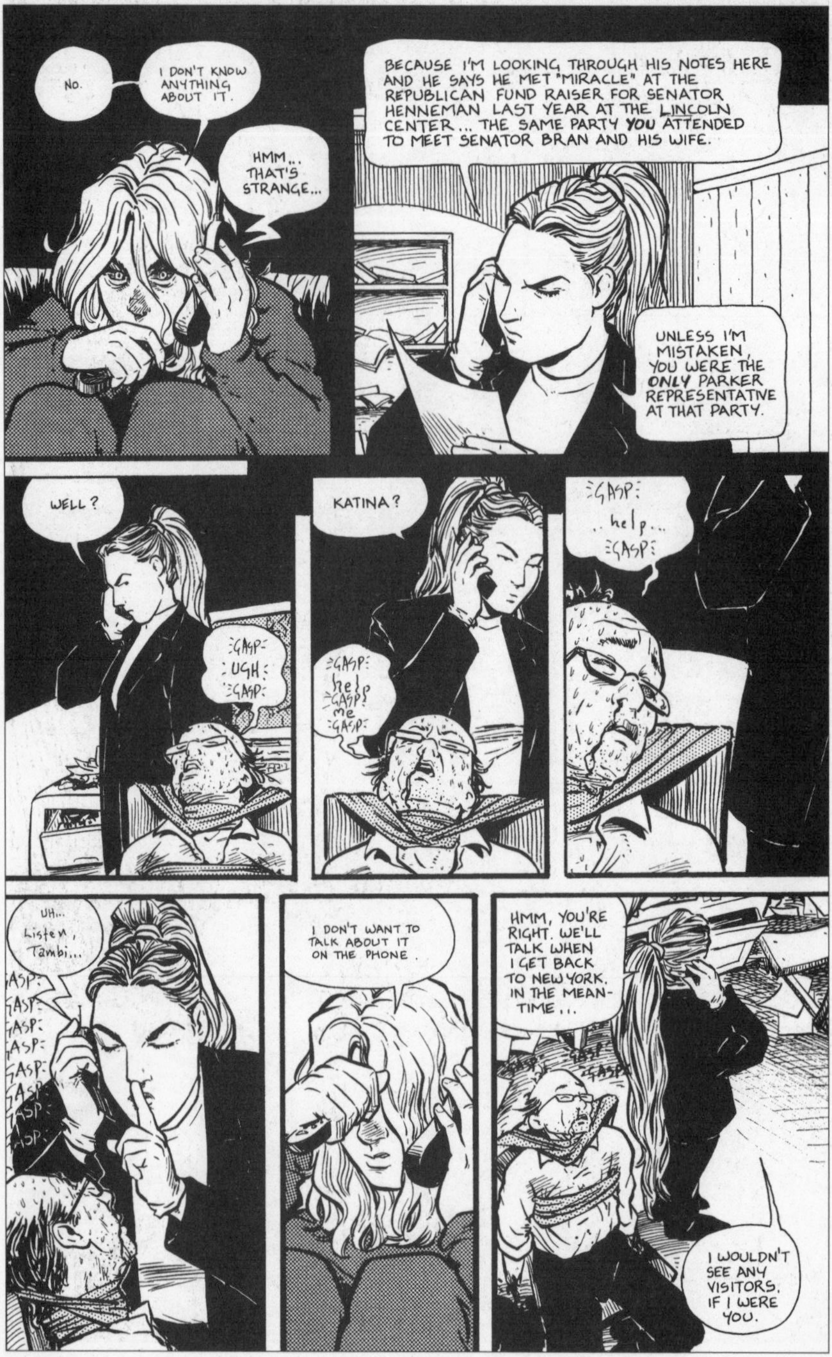
No.
I DON'T KNOW ANYTHING ABOUT IT.
HMM... THAT'S STRANGE...
BECAUSE I'M LOOKING THROUGH HIS NOTES HERE AND HE SAYS HE MET "MIRACLE" AT THE REPUBLICAN FUND RAISER FOR SENATOR HENNEMAN LAST YEAR AT THE LINCOLN CENTER... THE SAME PARTY YOU ATTENDED TO MEET SENATOR BRAN AND HIS WIFE.
UNLESS I'M MISTAKEN, YOU WERE THE ONLY PARKER REPRESENTATIVE AT THAT PARTY.
WELL?
GASP UGH GASP
KATINA?
GASP help GASP me GASP
GASP ..help... GASP
UH... Listen, Tambi...
GASP GASP GASP GASP GASP GASP GASP GASP
I DON'T WANT TO TALK ABOUT IT ON THE PHONE.
HMM, YOU'RE RIGHT. WE'LL TALK WHEN I GET BACK TO NEW YORK. IN THE MEAN-TIME...
GASP GASP GASP
I WOULDN'T SEE ANY VISITORS, IF I WERE YOU.

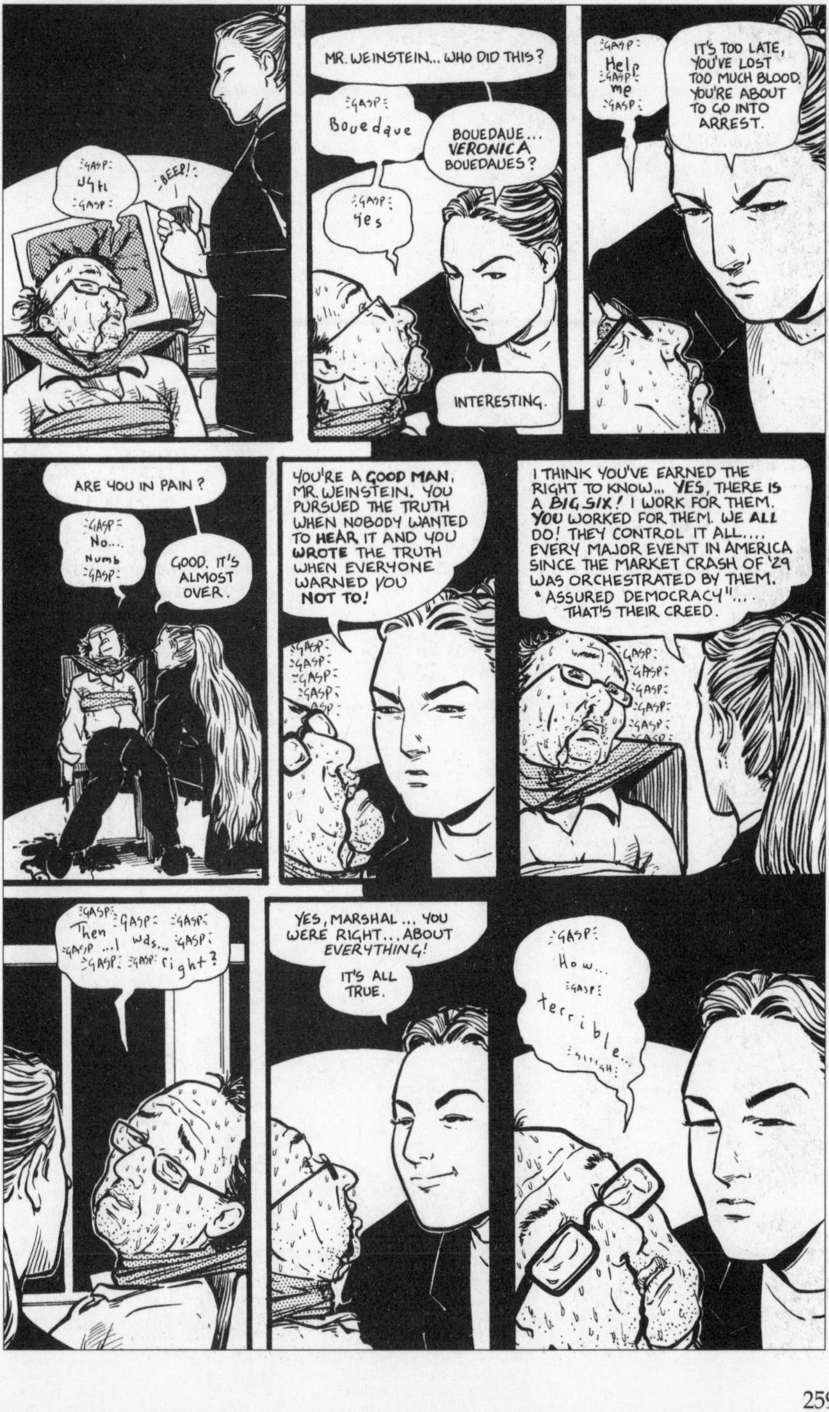
GASP
GASP
BEEP!
MR. WEINSTEIN... WHO DID THIS?
GASP Bouedaue
BOUEDAUE... VERONICA BOUEDAUES?
GASP Yes
INTERESTING.
GASP Help GASP me GASP
IT'S TOO LATE, YOU'VE LOST TOO MUCH BLOOD. YOU'RE ABOUT TO GO INTO ARREST.
ARE YOU IN PAIN?
GASP No.... Numb GASP
GOOD. IT'S ALMOST OVER.
YOU'RE A GOOD MAN, MR. WEINSTEIN. YOU PURSUED THE TRUTH WHEN NOBODY WANTED TO HEAR IT AND YOU WROTE THE TRUTH WHEN EVERYONE WARNED YOU NOT TO!
GASP GASP GASP GASP
I THINK YOU'VE EARNED THE RIGHT TO KNOW... YES, THERE IS A BIG SIX! I WORK FOR THEM. YOU WORKED FOR THEM. WE ALL DO! THEY CONTROL IT ALL.... EVERY MAJOR EVENT IN AMERICA SINCE THE MARKET CRASH OF '29 WAS ORCHESTRATED BY THEM. "ASSURED DEMOCRACY"... THAT'S THEIR CREED.
GASP GASP GASP GASP GASP
GASP Then GASP GASP GASP ...I was... GASP GASP GASP right?
YES, MARSHAL... YOU WERE RIGHT... ABOUT EVERYTHING!
IT'S ALL TRUE.
GASP How... GASP terrible...

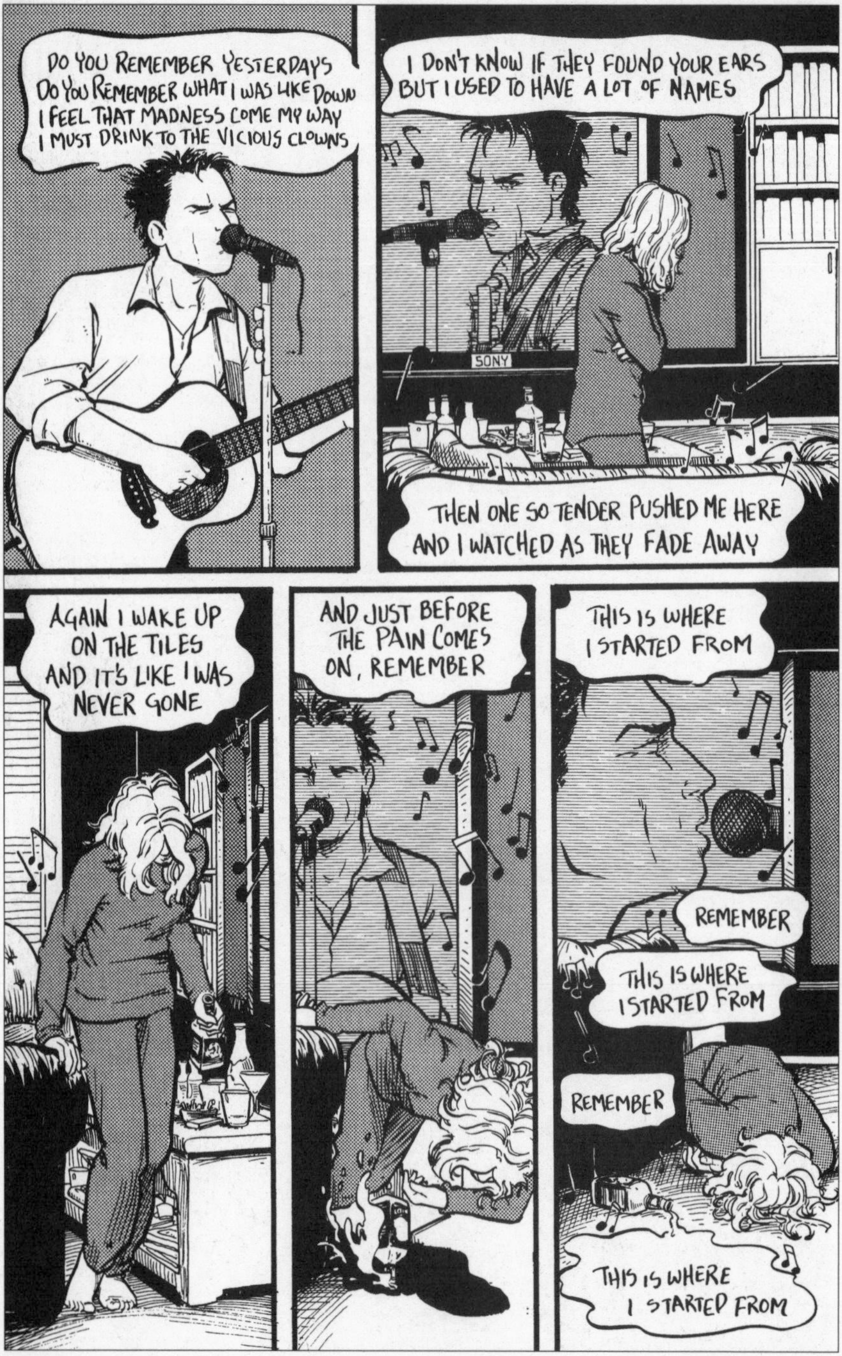
DO YOU REMEMBER YESTERDAYS
DO YOU REMEMBER WHAT I WAS LIKE DOWN
I FEEL THAT MADNESS COME MY WAY
I MUST DRINK TO THE VICIOUS CLOWNS
I DON'T KNOW IF THEY FOUND YOUR EARS
BUT I USED TO HAVE A LOT OF NAMES
SONY
THEN ONE SO TENDER PUSHED ME HERE
AND I WATCHED AS THEY FADE AWAY
AGAIN I WAKE UP ON THE TILES AND IT'S LIKE I WAS NEVER GONE
AND JUST BEFORE THE PAIN COMES ON, REMEMBER
THIS IS WHERE I STARTED FROM
REMEMBER
THIS IS WHERE I STARTED FROM
REMEMBER
THIS IS WHERE I STARTED FROM

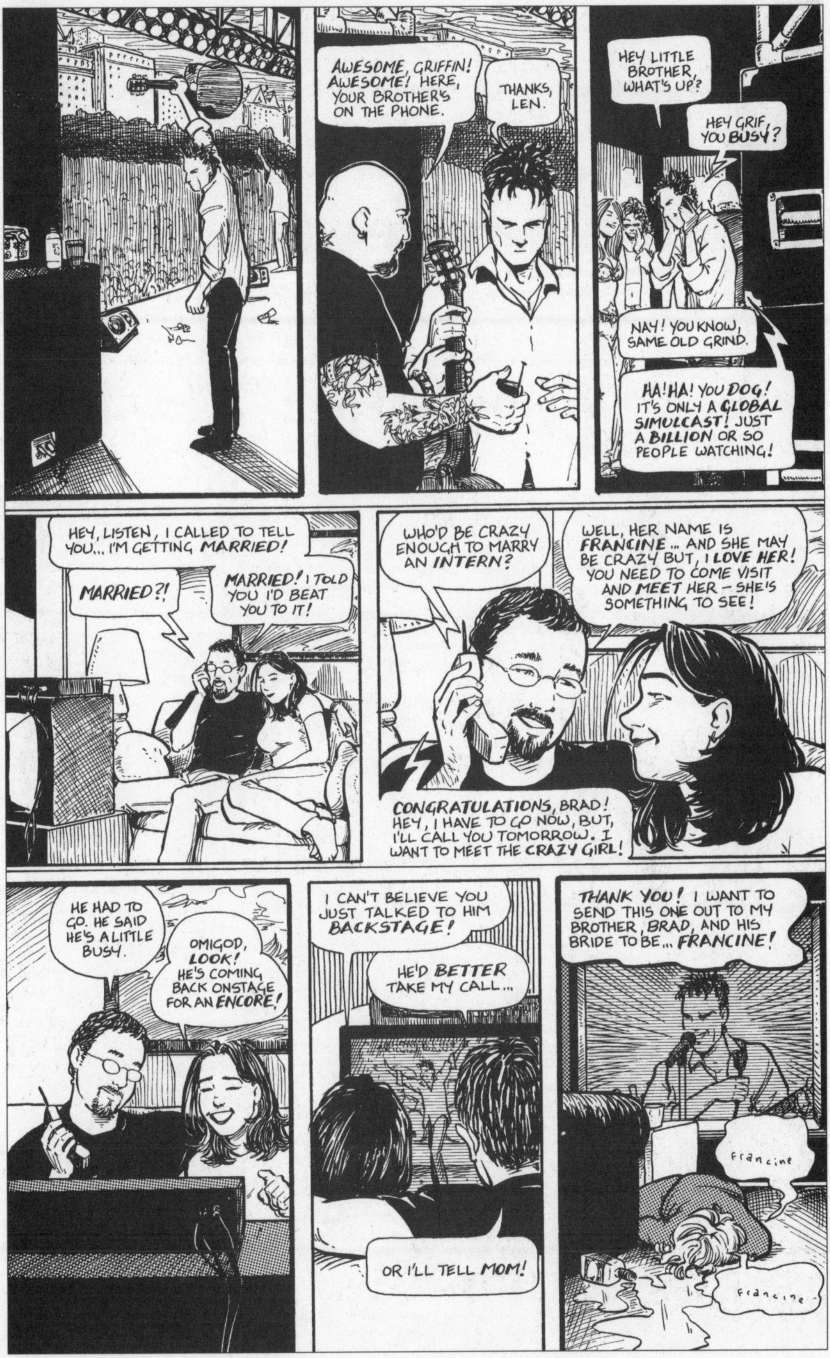
AWESOME, GRIFFIN! AWESOME! HERE, YOUR BROTHER'S ON THE PHONE.
THANKS, LEN.
HEY LITTLE BROTHER, WHAT'S UP?
HEY GRIF, YOU BUSY?
NAY! YOU KNOW, SAME OLD GRIND.
HA! HA! YOU DOG! IT'S ONLY A GLOBAL SIMULCAST! JUST A BILLION OR SO PEOPLE WATCHING!
HEY, LISTEN, I CALLED TO TELL YOU... I'M GETTING MARRIED!
MARRIED?!
MARRIED! I TOLD YOU I'D BEAT YOU TO IT!
WHO'D BE CRAZY ENOUGH TO MARRY AN INTERN?
WELL, HER NAME IS FRANCINE... AND SHE MAY BE CRAZY BUT, I LOVE HER! YOU NEED TO COME VISIT AND MEET HER – SHE'S SOMETHING TO SEE!
CONGRATULATIONS, BRAD! HEY, I HAVE TO GO NOW, BUT, I'LL CALL YOU TOMORROW. I WANT TO MEET THE CRAZY GIRL!
HE HAD TO GO. HE SAID HE'S A LITTLE BUSY.
OMIGOD, LOOK! HE'S COMING BACK ONSTAGE FOR AN ENCORE!
I CAN'T BELIEVE YOU JUST TALKED TO HIM BACKSTAGE!
HE'D BETTER TAKE MY CALL...
OR I'LL TELL MOM!
THANK YOU! I WANT TO SEND THIS ONE OUT TO MY BROTHER, BRAD, AND HIS BRIDE TO BE... FRANCINE!
francine
francine..

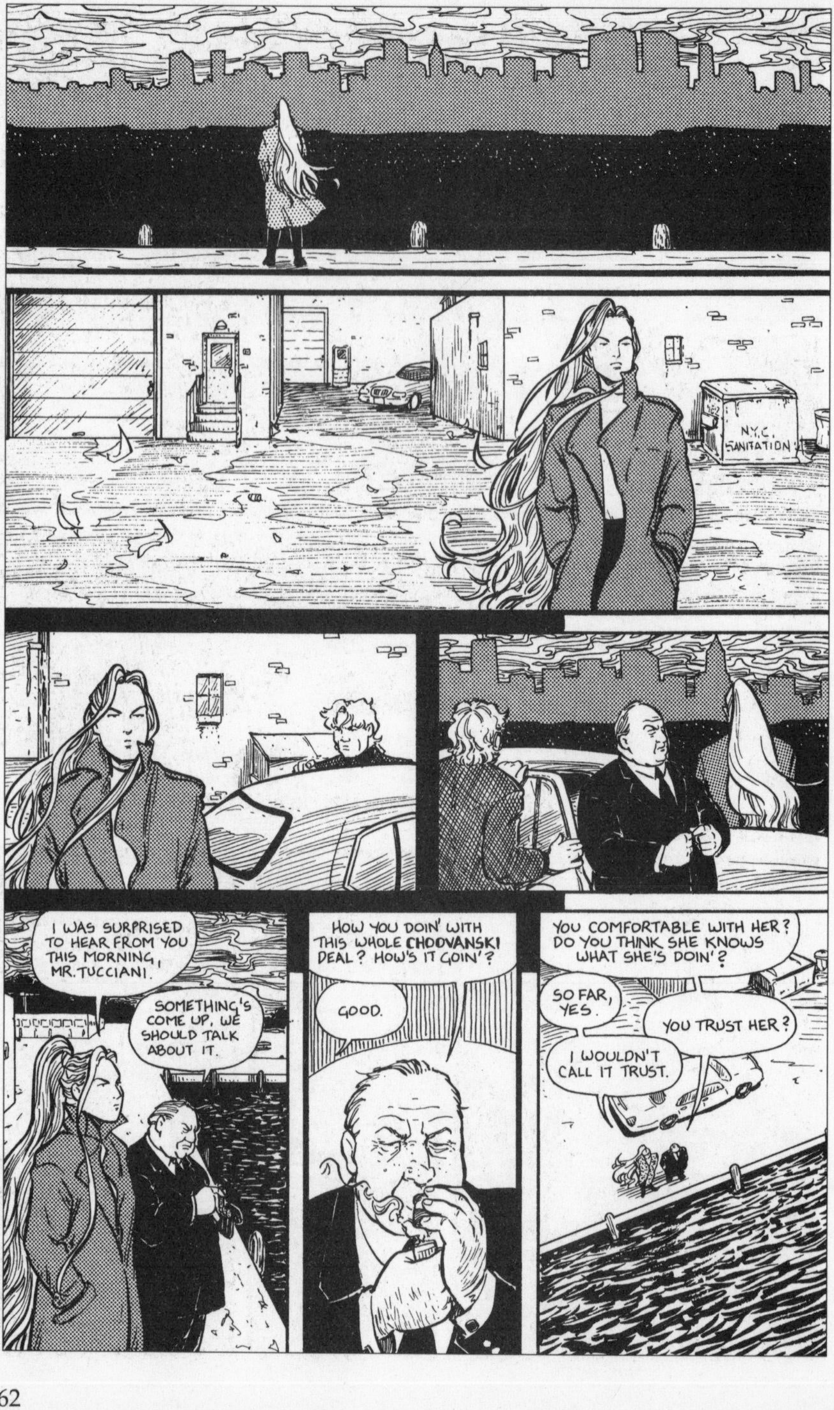
N.Y.C. SANITATION
I WAS SURPRISED TO HEAR FROM YOU THIS MORNING, MR. TUCCIANI.
SOMETHING'S COME UP, WE SHOULD TALK ABOUT IT.
HOW YOU DOIN' WITH THIS WHOLE CHOOVANSKI DEAL? HOW'S IT GOIN'?
GOOD.
YOU COMFORTABLE WITH HER? DO YOU THINK SHE KNOWS WHAT SHE'S DOIN'?
SO FAR, YES.
YOU TRUST HER?
I WOULDN'T CALL IT TRUST.

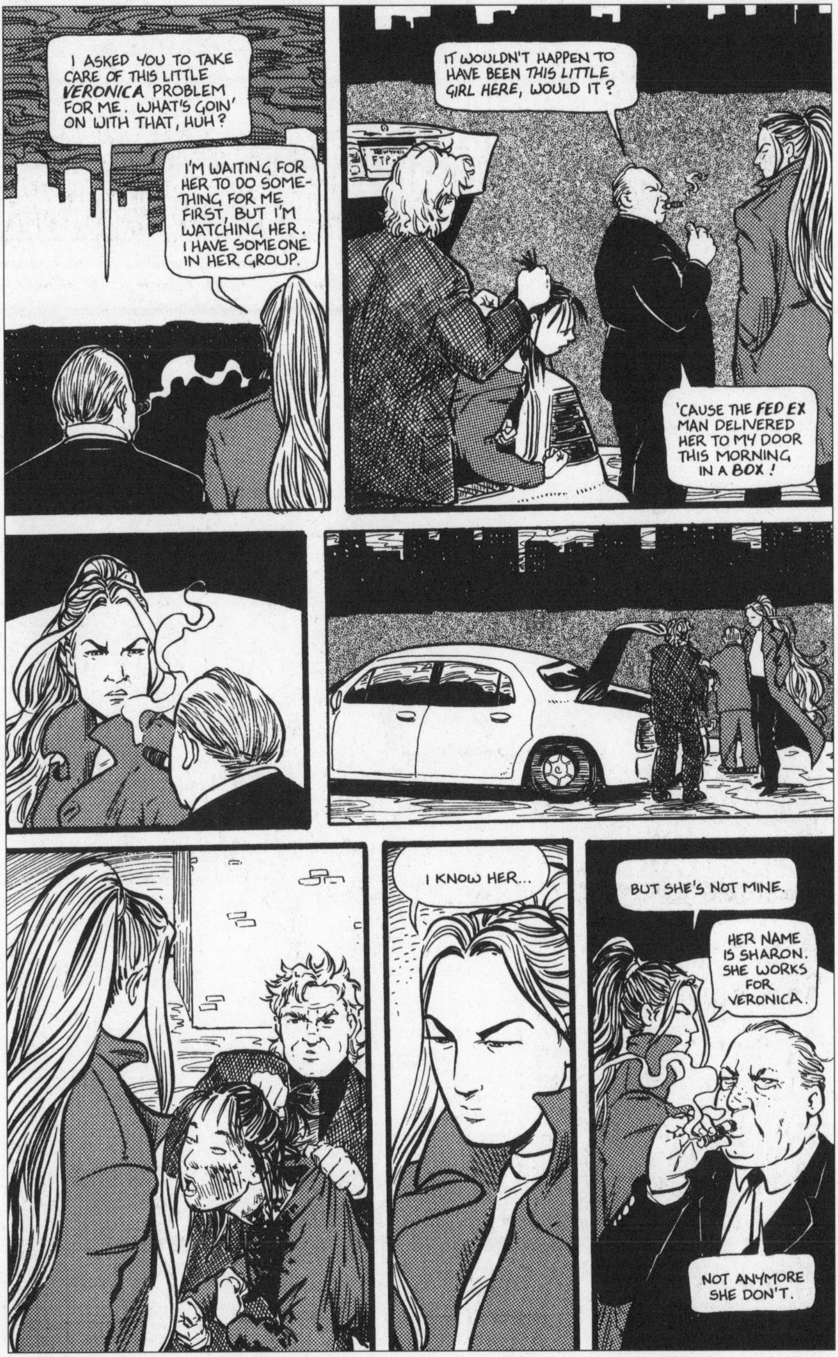
I ASKED YOU TO TAKE CARE OF THIS LITTLE VERONICA PROBLEM FOR ME. WHAT'S GOIN' ON WITH THAT, HUH?
I'M WAITING FOR HER TO DO SOME-THING FOR ME FIRST, BUT I'M WATCHING HER. I HAVE SOMEONE IN HER GROUP.
IT WOULDN'T HAPPEN TO HAVE BEEN THIS LITTLE GIRL HERE, WOULD IT?
'CAUSE THE FED EX MAN DELIVERED HER TO MY DOOR THIS MORNING IN A BOX!
I KNOW HER...
BUT SHE'S NOT MINE.
HER NAME IS SHARON. SHE WORKS FOR VERONICA.
NOT ANYMORE SHE DON'T.

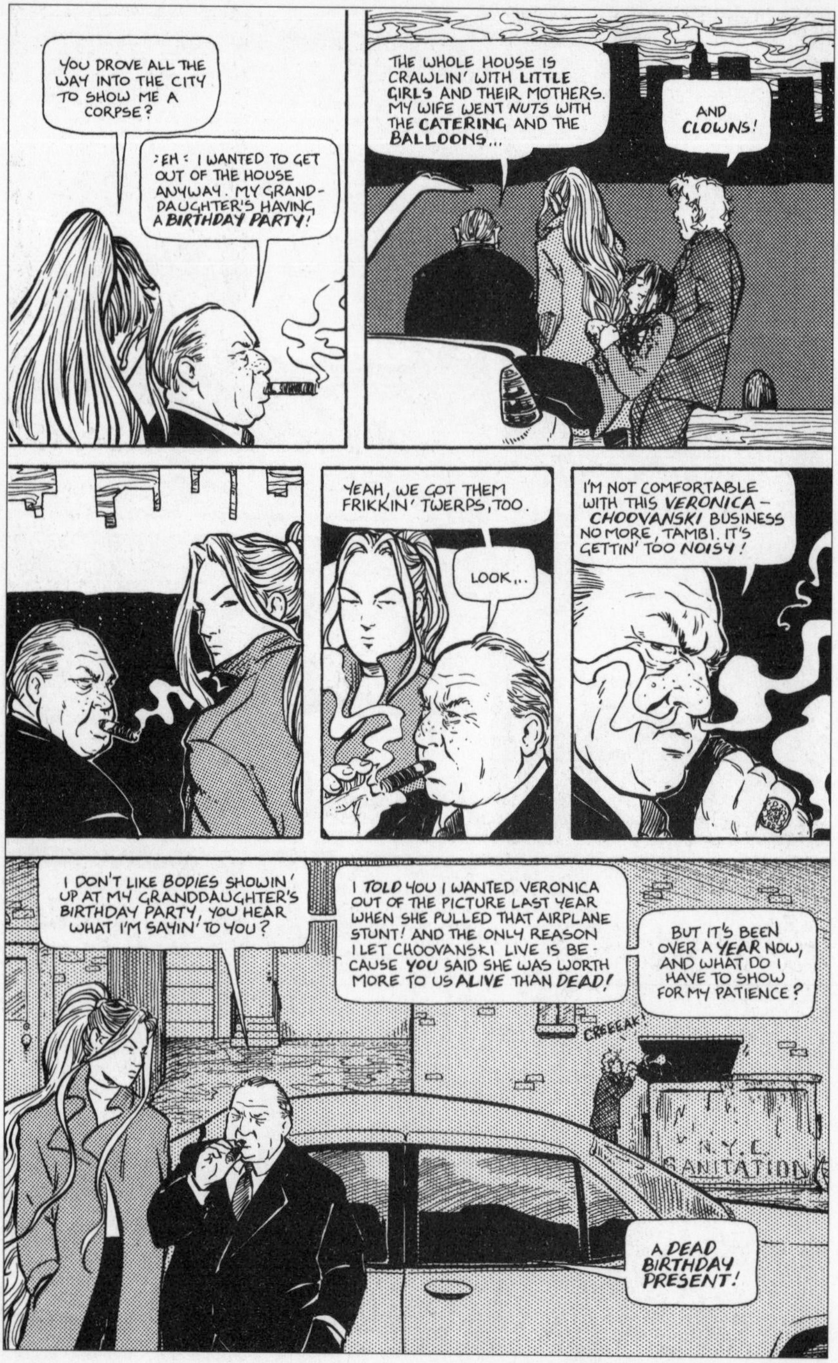
YOU DROVE ALL THE WAY INTO THE CITY TO SHOW ME A CORPSE?
:EH: I WANTED TO GET OUT OF THE HOUSE ANYWAY. MY GRAND-DAUGHTER'S HAVING A BIRTHDAY PARTY!
THE WHOLE HOUSE IS CRAWLIN' WITH LITTLE GIRLS AND THEIR MOTHERS. MY WIFE WENT NUTS WITH THE CATERING AND THE BALLOONS...
AND CLOWNS!
YEAH, WE GOT THEM FRIKKIN' TWERPS, TOO.
LOOK...
I'M NOT COMFORTABLE WITH THIS VERONICA-CHOOVANSKI BUSINESS NO MORE, TAMBI. IT'S GETTIN' TOO NOISY!
I DON'T LIKE BODIES SHOWIN' UP AT MY GRANDDAUGHTER'S BIRTHDAY PARTY, YOU HEAR WHAT I'M SAYIN' TO YOU?
I TOLD YOU I WANTED VERONICA OUT OF THE PICTURE LAST YEAR WHEN SHE PULLED THAT AIRPLANE STUNT! AND THE ONLY REASON I LET CHOOVANSKI LIVE IS BE-CAUSE YOU SAID SHE WAS WORTH MORE TO US ALIVE THAN DEAD!
BUT IT'S BEEN OVER A YEAR NOW, AND WHAT DO I HAVE TO SHOW FOR MY PATIENCE?
CREEEAK!
N.Y.C. SANITATION
A DEAD BIRTHDAY PRESENT!

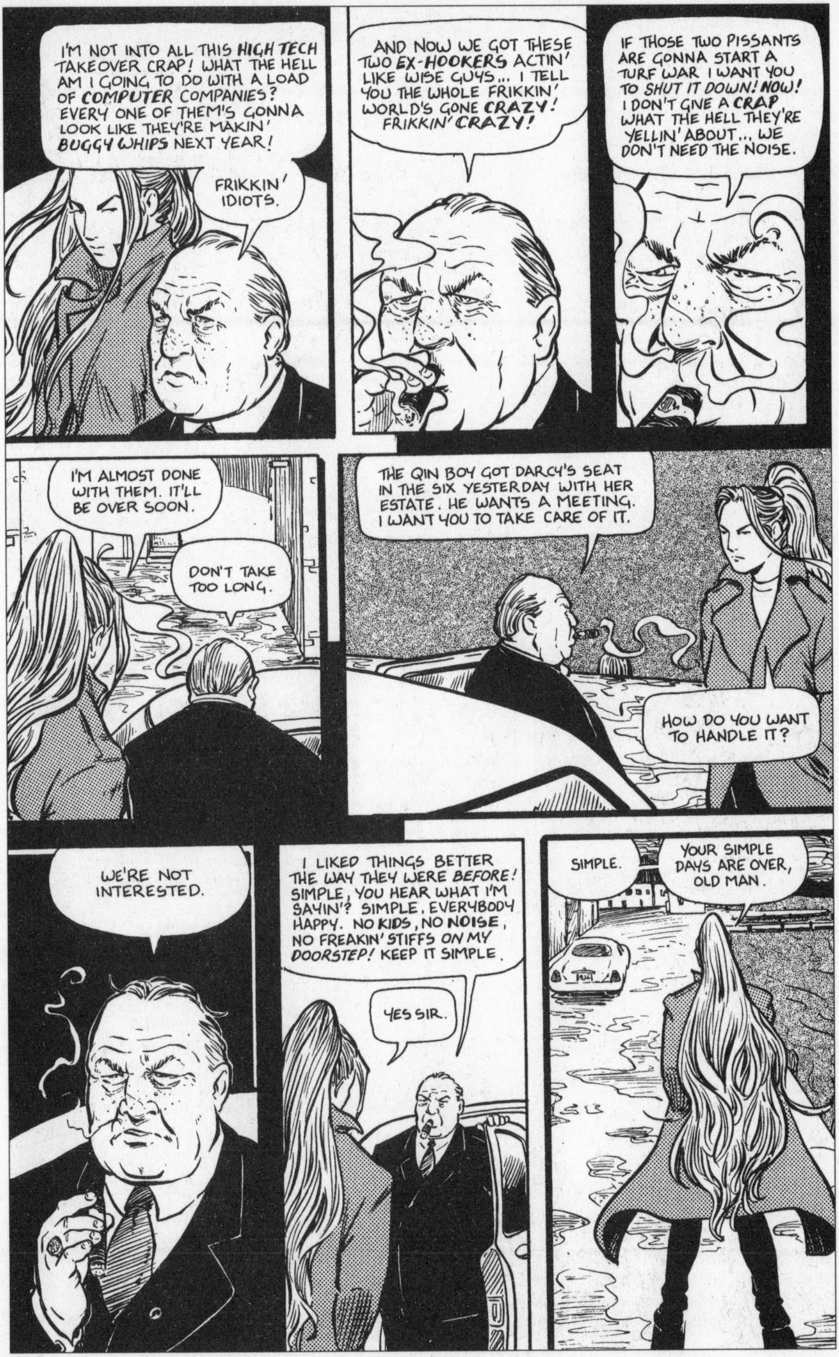
I'M NOT INTO ALL THIS HIGH TECH TAKEOVER CRAP! WHAT THE HELL AM I GOING TO DO WITH A LOAD OF COMPUTER COMPANIES? EVERY ONE OF THEM'S GONNA LOOK LIKE THEY'RE MAKIN' BUGGY WHIPS NEXT YEAR!
FRIKKIN' IDIOTS.
AND NOW WE GOT THESE TWO EX-HOOKERS ACTIN' LIKE WISE GUYS... I TELL YOU THE WHOLE FRIKKIN' WORLD'S GONE CRAZY! FRIKKIN' CRAZY!
IF THOSE TWO PISSANTS ARE GONNA START A TURF WAR I WANT YOU TO SHUT IT DOWN! NOW! I DON'T GIVE A CRAP WHAT THE HELL THEY'RE YELLIN' ABOUT... WE DON'T NEED THE NOISE.
I'M ALMOST DONE WITH THEM. IT'LL BE OVER SOON.
DON'T TAKE TOO LONG.
THE QIN BOY GOT DARCY'S SEAT IN THE SIX YESTERDAY WITH HER ESTATE. HE WANTS A MEETING. I WANT YOU TO TAKE CARE OF IT.
HOW DO YOU WANT TO HANDLE IT?
WE'RE NOT INTERESTED.
I LIKED THINGS BETTER THE WAY THEY WERE BEFORE! SIMPLE, YOU HEAR WHAT I'M SAYIN'? SIMPLE. EVERYBODY HAPPY. NO KIDS, NO NOISE, NO FREAKIN' STIFFS ON MY DOORSTEP! KEEP IT SIMPLE.
YES SIR.
SIMPLE.
YOUR SIMPLE DAYS ARE OVER, OLD MAN.

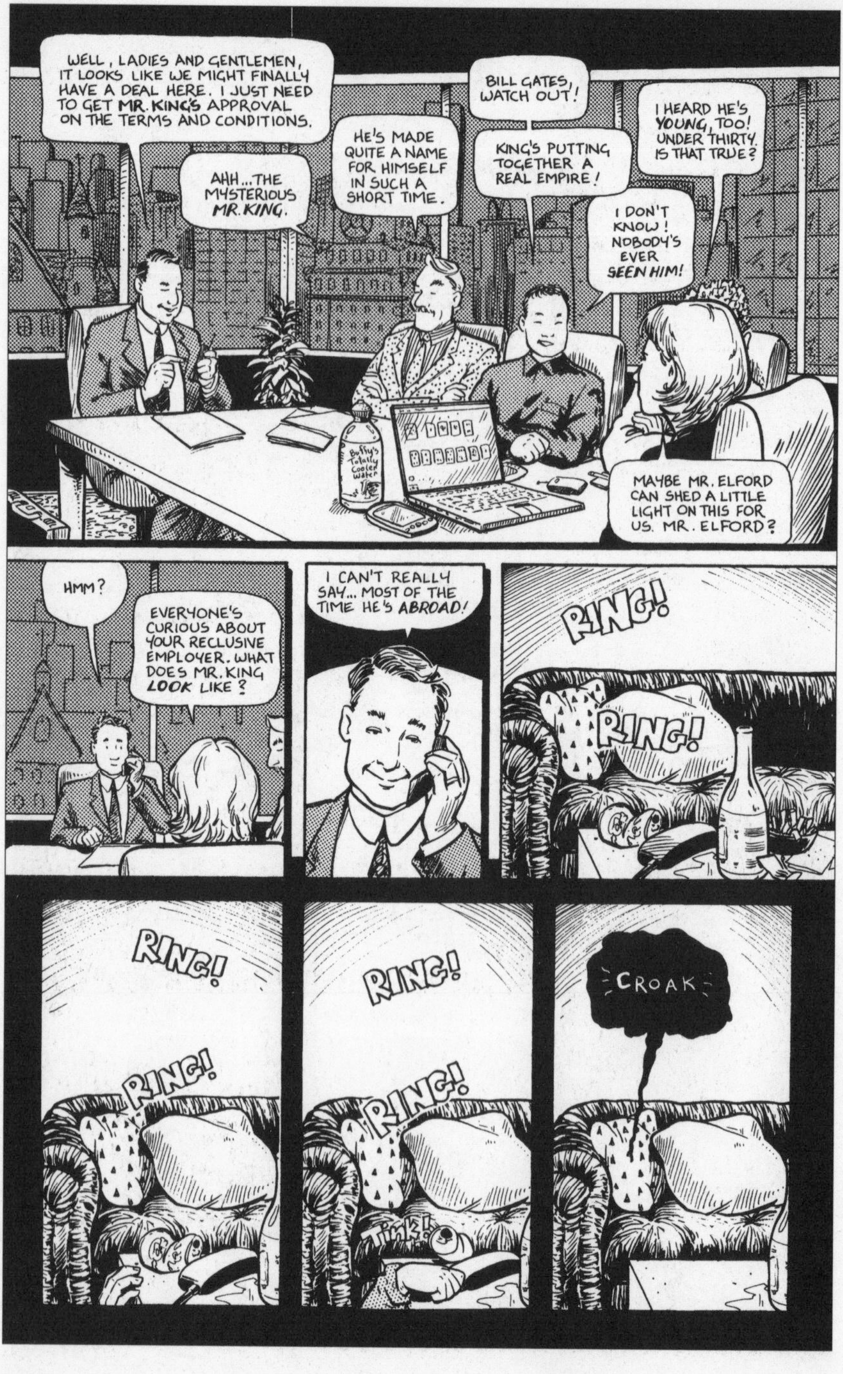

WELL, LADIES AND GENTLEMEN, IT LOOKS LIKE WE MIGHT FINALLY HAVE A DEAL HERE. I JUST NEED TO GET MR. KING'S APPROVAL ON THE TERMS AND CONDITIONS.
AHH... THE MYSTERIOUS MR. KING.
HE'S MADE QUITE A NAME FOR HIMSELF IN SUCH A SHORT TIME.
BILL GATES, WATCH OUT!
KING'S PUTTING TOGETHER A REAL EMPIRE!
I HEARD HE'S YOUNG, TOO! UNDER THIRTY. IS THAT TRUE?
I DON'T KNOW! NOBODY'S EVER SEEN HIM!
Buffy's Totally Cooler Water
MAYBE MR. ELFORD CAN SHED A LITTLE LIGHT ON THIS FOR US. MR. ELFORD?
HMM?
EVERYONE'S CURIOUS ABOUT YOUR RECLUSIVE EMPLOYER. WHAT DOES MR. KING LOOK LIKE?
I CAN'T REALLY SAY... MOST OF THE TIME HE'S ABROAD!
RING!
RING!
RING!
RING!
RING!
RING!
TINK!
CROAK

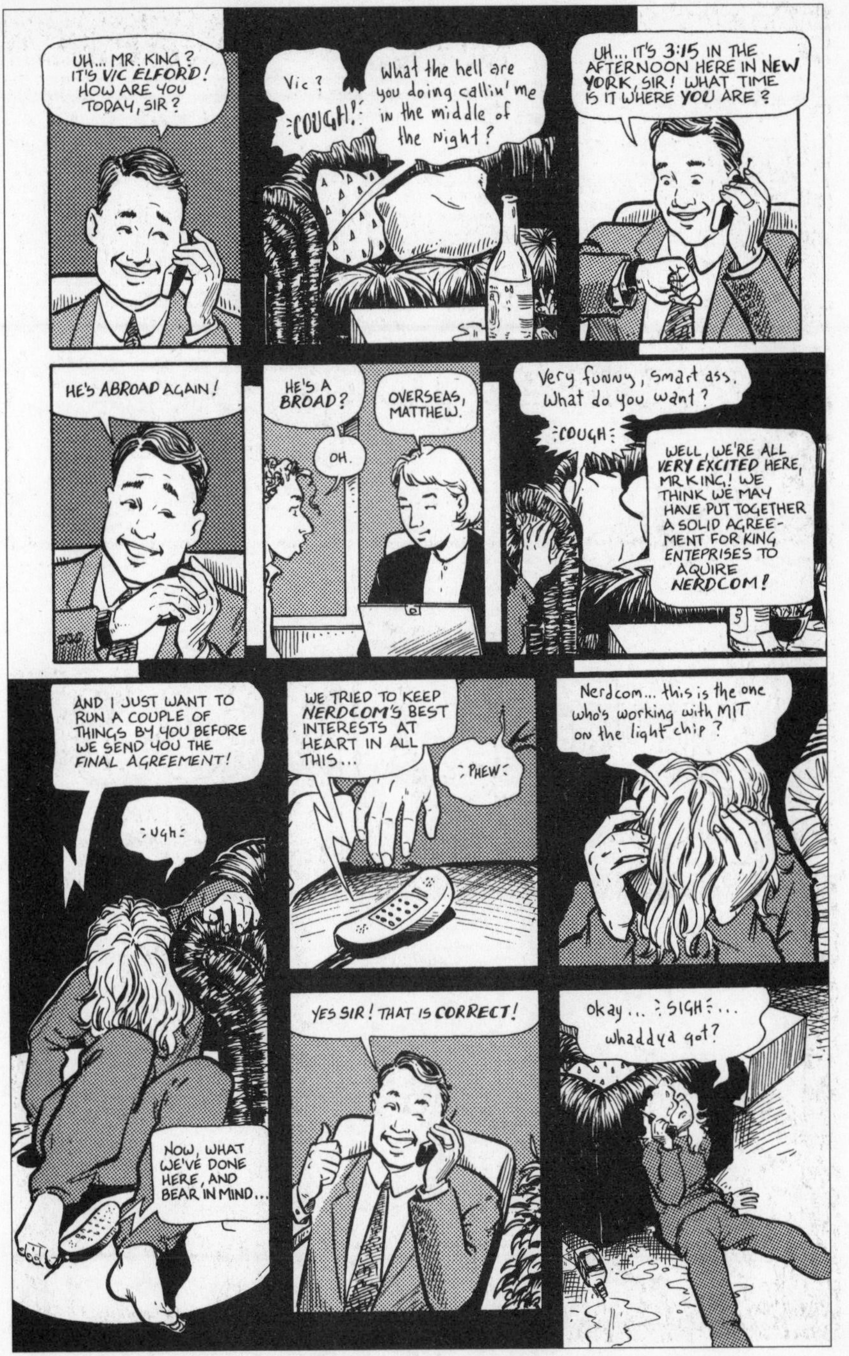
UH... MR. KING? IT'S VIC ELFORD! HOW ARE YOU TODAY, SIR?
Vic?
COUGH!
What the hell are you doing callin' me in the middle of the night?
UH... IT'S 3:15 IN THE AFTERNOON HERE IN NEW YORK, SIR! WHAT TIME IS IT WHERE YOU ARE?
HE'S ABROAD AGAIN!
HE'S A BROAD?
OVERSEAS, MATTHEW.
OH.
Very funny, smart ass. What do you want?
COUGH
WELL, WE'RE ALL VERY EXCITED HERE, MR KING! WE THINK WE MAY HAVE PUT TOGETHER A SOLID AGREEMENT FOR KING ENTEPRISES TO AQUIRE NERDCOM!
AND I JUST WANT TO RUN A COUPLE OF THINGS BY YOU BEFORE WE SEND YOU THE FINAL AGREEMENT!
ugh
WE TRIED TO KEEP NERDCOM'S BEST INTERESTS AT HEART IN ALL THIS...
PHEW
Nerdcom... this is the one who's working with MIT on the light chip?
NOW, WHAT WE'VE DONE HERE, AND BEAR IN MIND...
YES SIR! THAT IS CORRECT!
Okay... SIGH... whaddya got?

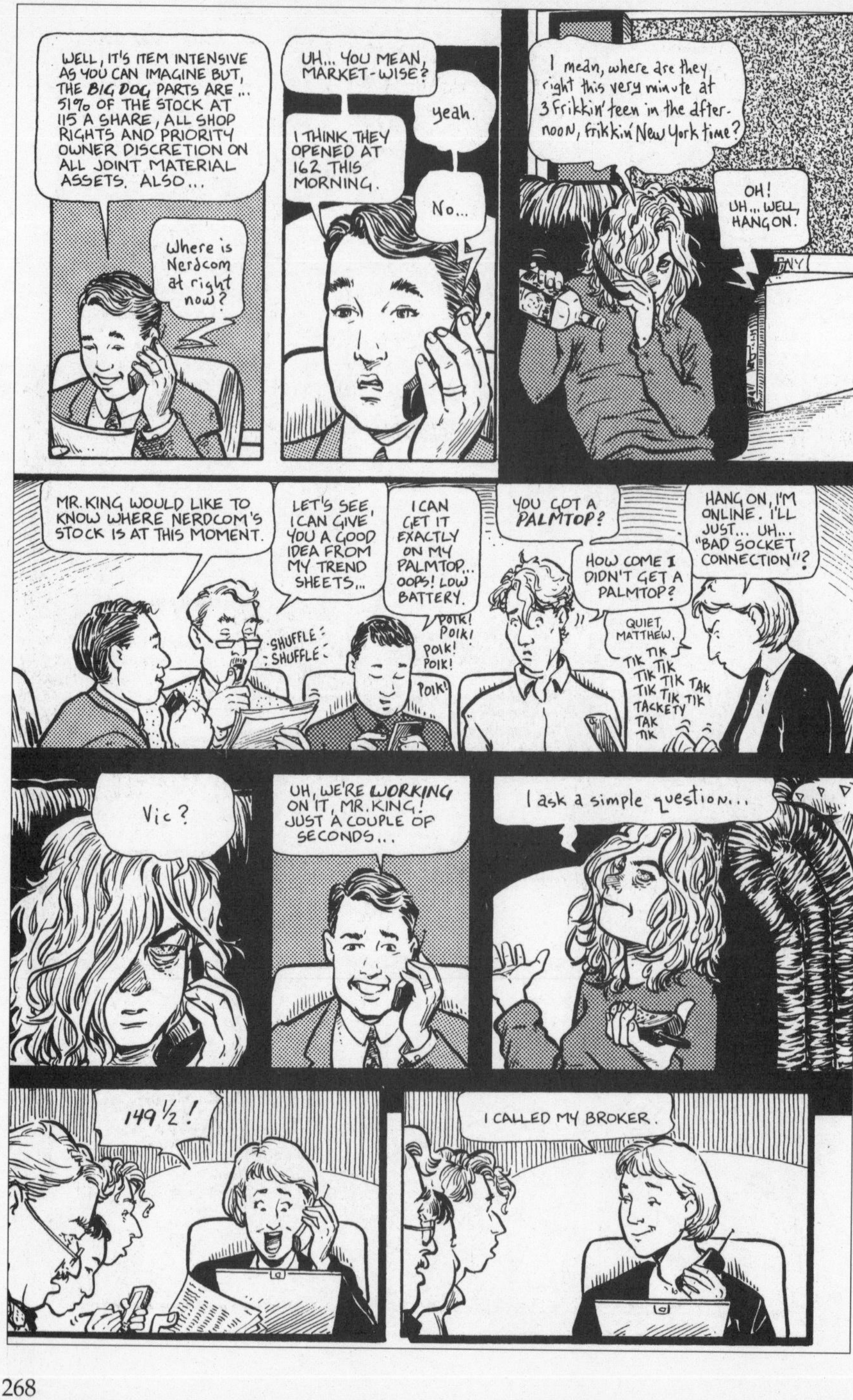
WELL, IT'S ITEM INTENSIVE AS YOU CAN IMAGINE BUT, THE BIG DOG PARTS ARE... 51% OF THE STOCK AT 115 A SHARE, ALL SHOP RIGHTS AND PRIORITY OWNER DISCRETION ON ALL JOINT MATERIAL ASSETS. ALSO...
Where is Nerdcom at right now?
UH... YOU MEAN, MARKET-WISE?
yeah.
I THINK THEY OPENED AT 162 THIS MORNING.
No...
I mean, where are they right this very minute at 3 Frikkin' teen in the after-noon, frikkin' New York time?
OH! UH... WELL, HANG ON.
MR. KING WOULD LIKE TO KNOW WHERE NERDCOM'S STOCK IS AT THIS MOMENT.
LET'S SEE, I CAN GIVE YOU A GOOD IDEA FROM MY TREND SHEETS...
SHUFFLE SHUFFLE
I CAN GET IT EXACTLY ON MY PALMTOP... OOPS! LOW BATTERY.
POIK! POIK! POIK! POIK! POIK!
YOU GOT A PALMTOP?
HOW COME I DIDN'T GET A PALMTOP?
QUIET, MATTHEW.
HANG ON, I'M ONLINE. I'LL JUST... UH... "BAD SOCKET CONNECTION"?
TIK TIK TIK TIK TIK TIK TAK TIK TIK TIK TACKETY TAK TIK
Vic?
UH, WE'RE WORKING ON IT, MR. KING! JUST A COUPLE OF SECONDS...
I ask a simple question...
149 1/2!
I CALLED MY BROKER.

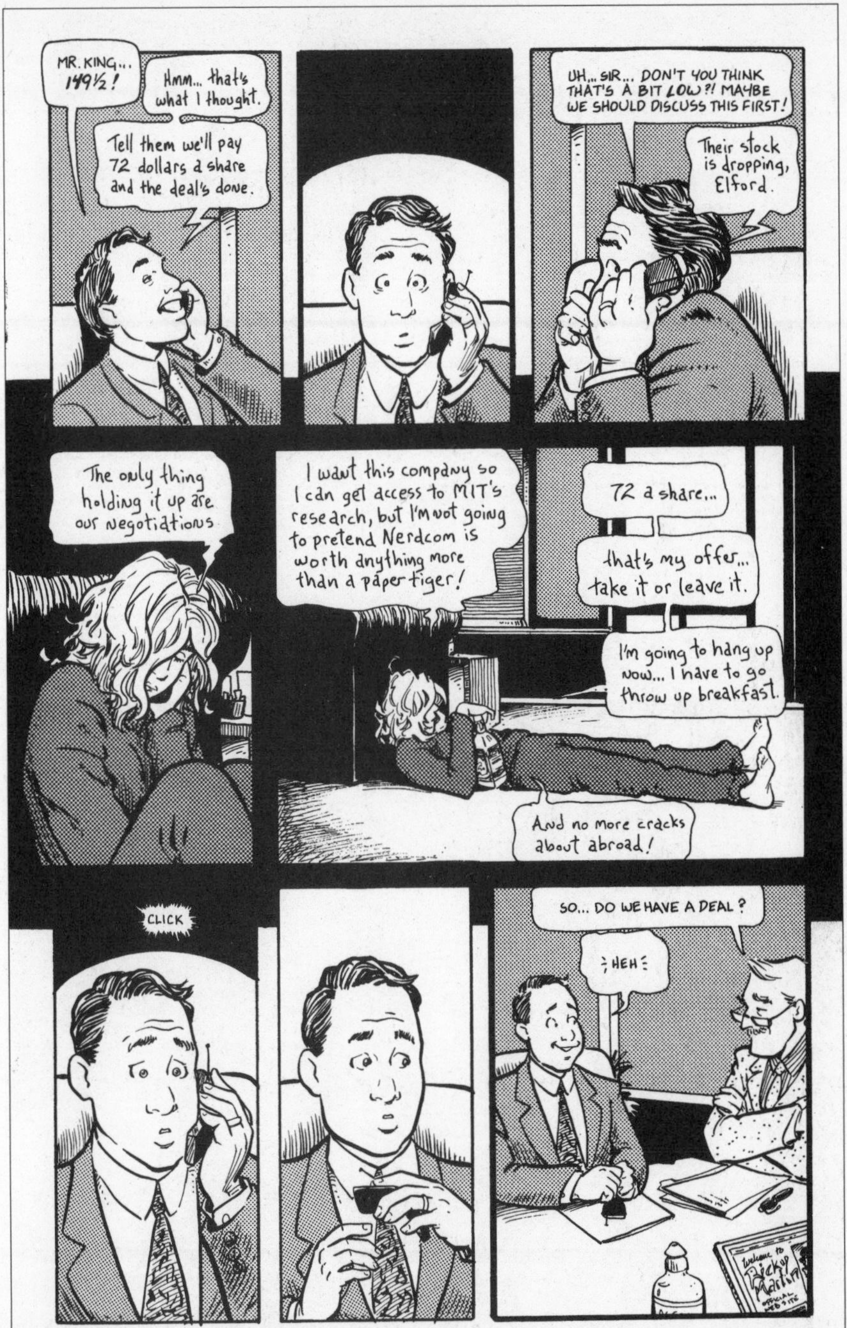
MR. KING... 149½!
Hmm... that's what I thought.
Tell them we'll pay 72 dollars a share and the deal's done.
UH... SIR... DON'T YOU THINK THAT'S A BIT LOW?! MAYBE WE SHOULD DISCUSS THIS FIRST!
Their stock is dropping, Elford.
The only thing holding it up are our negotiations
I want this company so I can get access to MIT's research, but I'm not going to pretend Nerdcom is worth anything more than a paper tiger!
72 a share...
that's my offer... take it or leave it.
I'm going to hang up now... I have to go throw up breakfast.
And no more cracks about abroad!
CLICK
SO... DO WE HAVE A DEAL?
HEH

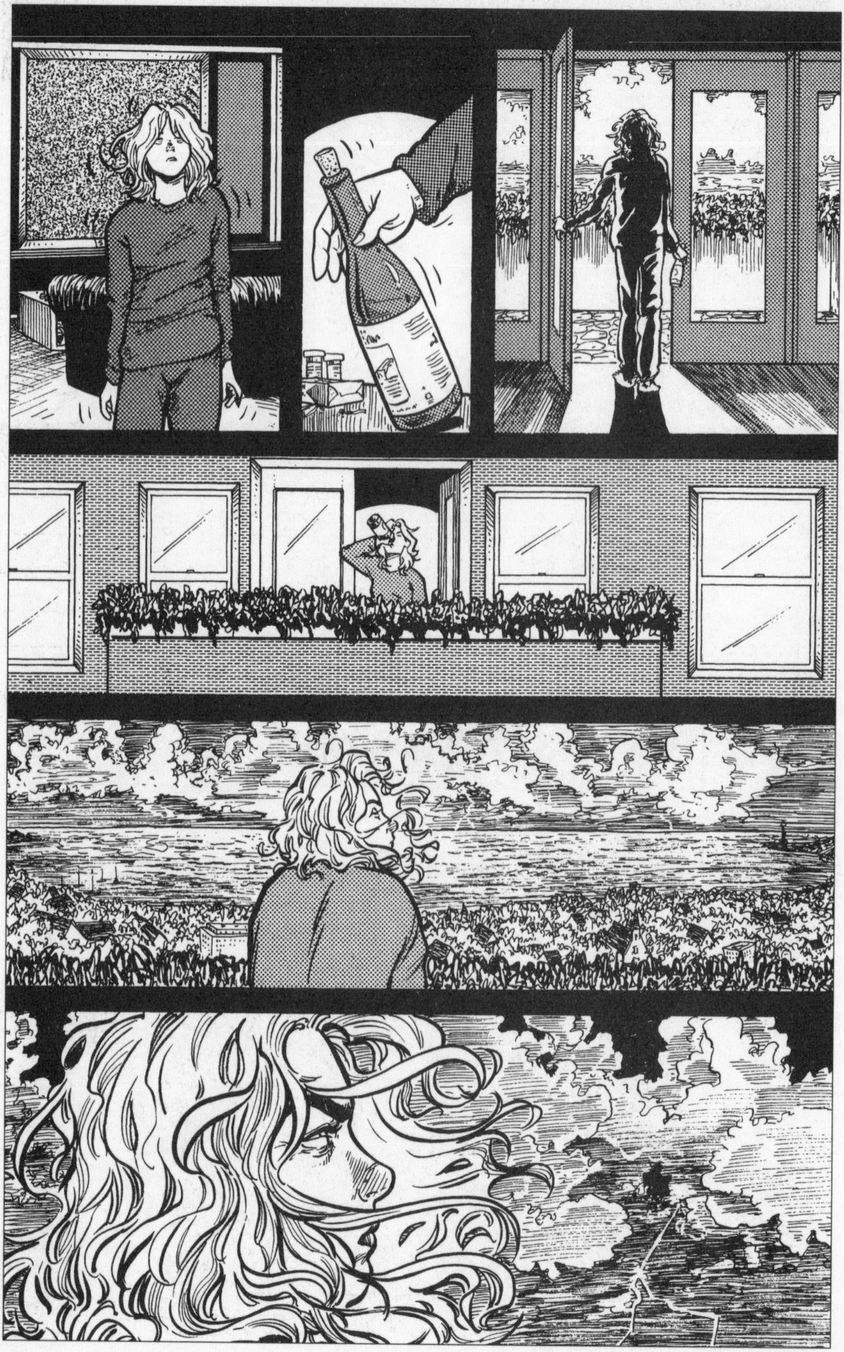

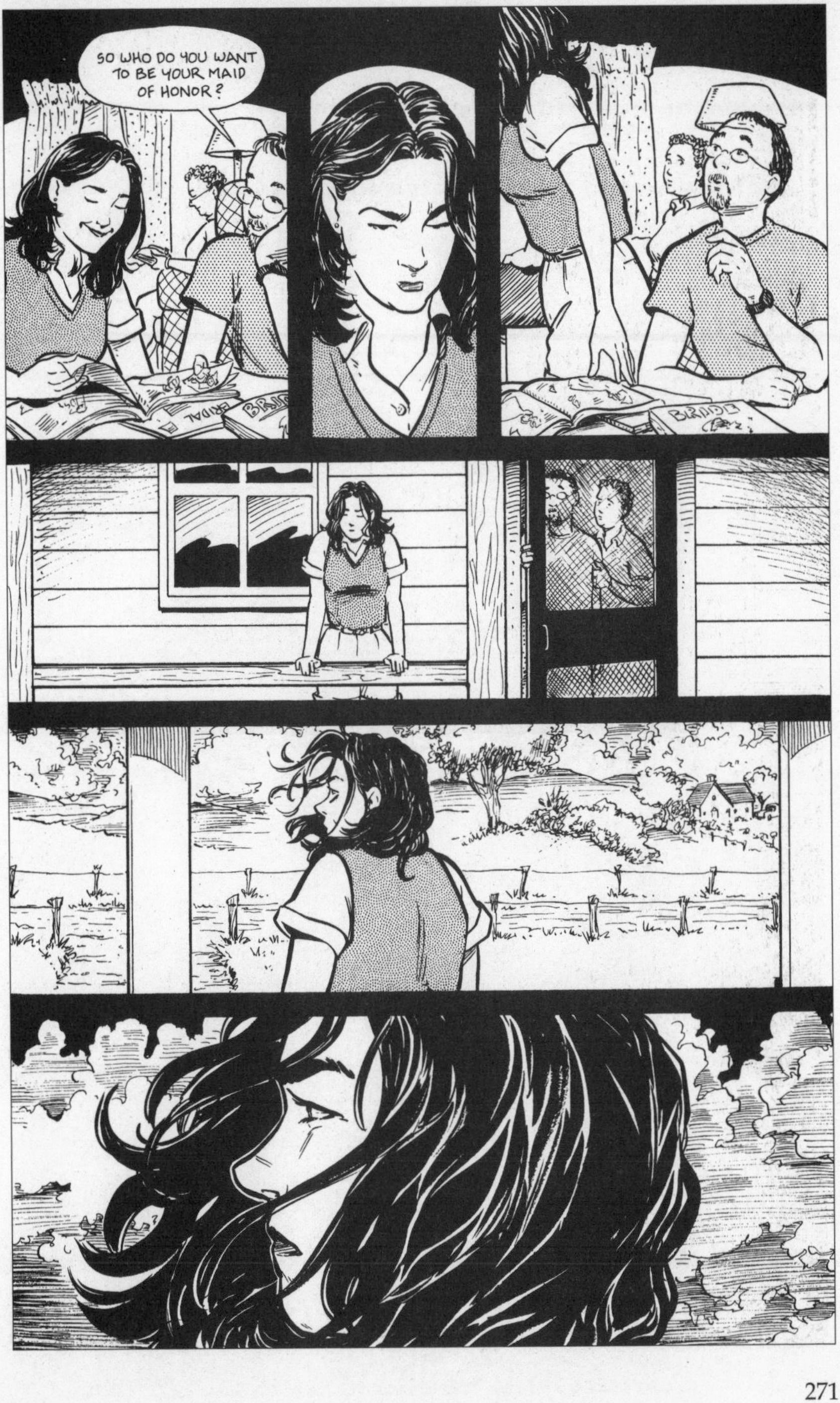
SO WHO DO YOU WANT TO BE YOUR MAID OF HONOR?
BRIDAL
BRIDE

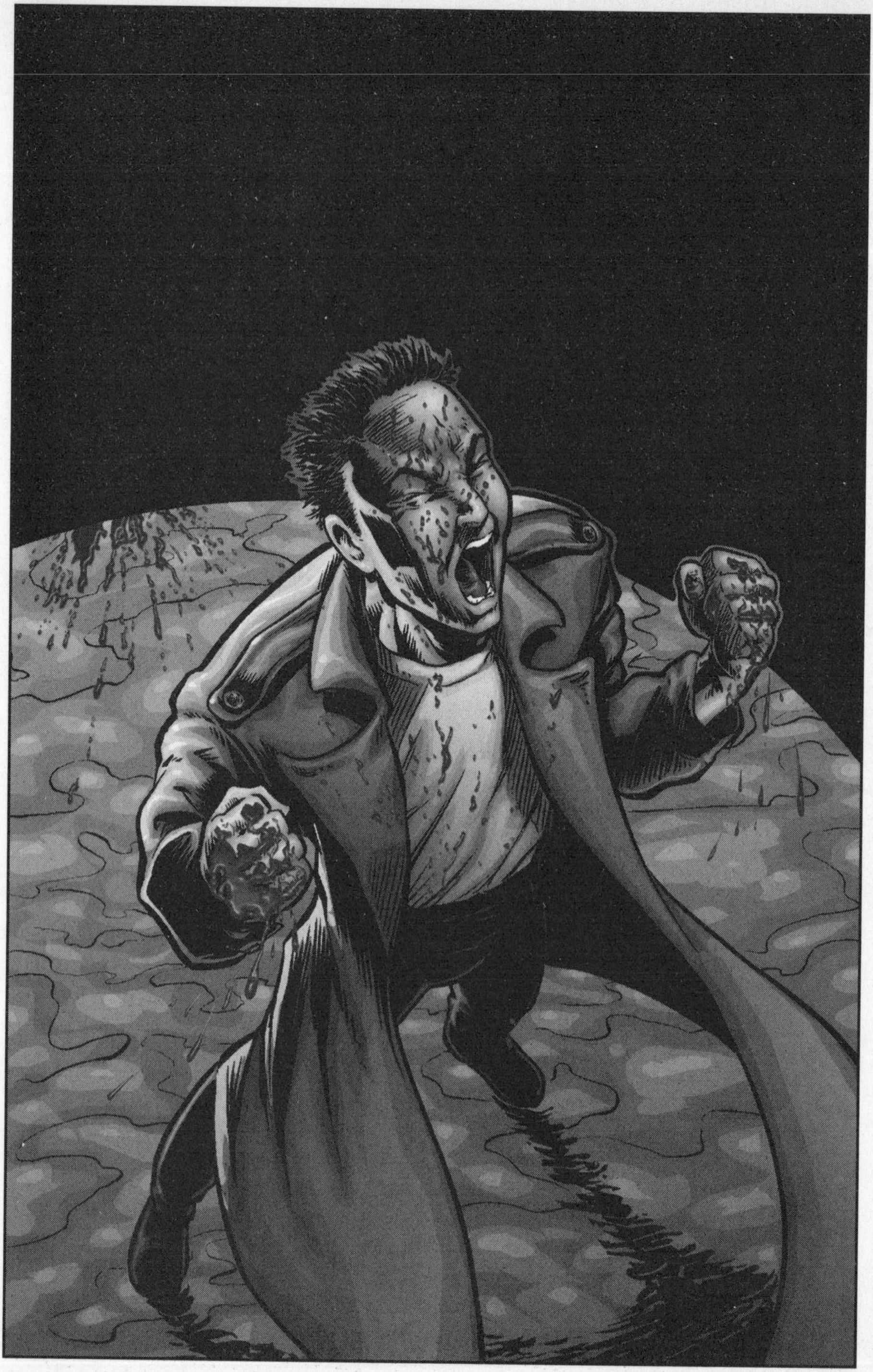

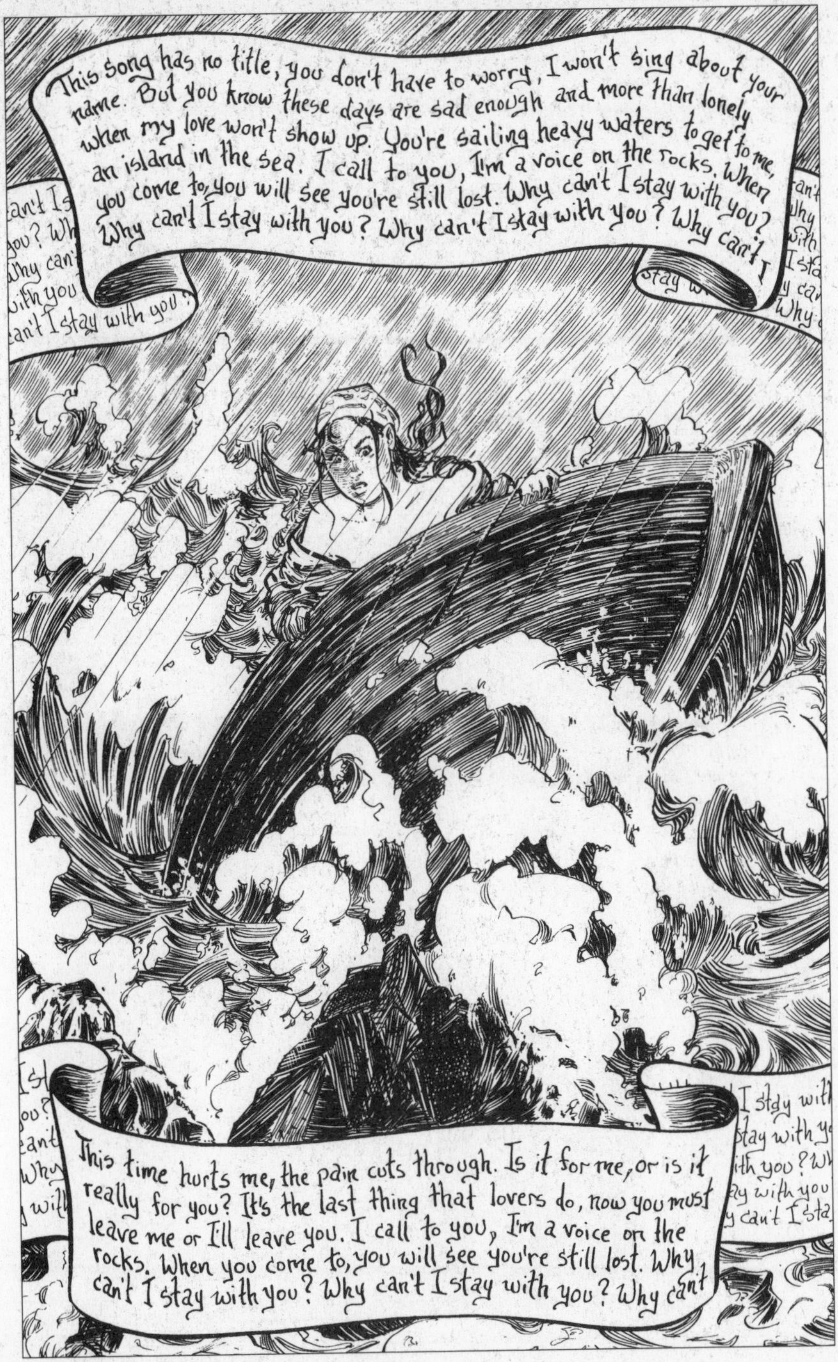
This song has no title, you don't have to worry, I won't sing about your name. But you know these days are sad enough and more than lonely when my love won't show up. You're sailing heavy waters to get to me, an island in the sea. I call to you, I'm a voice on the rocks. When you come to, you will see you're still lost. Why can't I stay with you? Why can't I stay with you? Why can't I stay with you? Why can't I
This time hurts me, the pain cuts through. Is it for me, or is it really for you? It's the last thing that lovers do, now you must leave me or I'll leave you. I call to you, I'm a voice on the rocks. When you come to, you will see you're still lost. Why can't I stay with you? Why can't I stay with you? Why can't

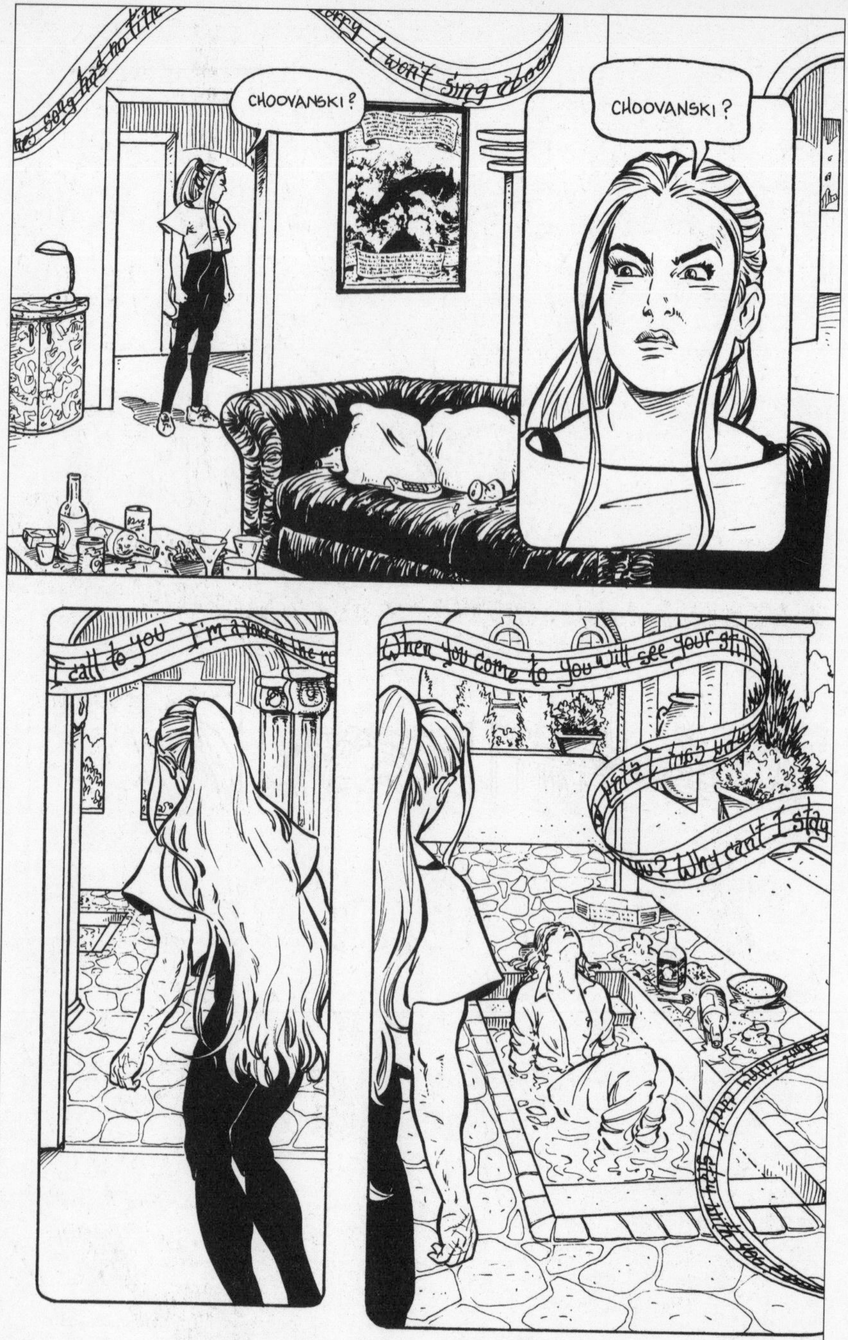
song has no title
I won't sing about
CHOOVANSKI?
CHOOVANSKI?
I call to you I'm a voice on the
When you come to you will see your
Why can't I stay

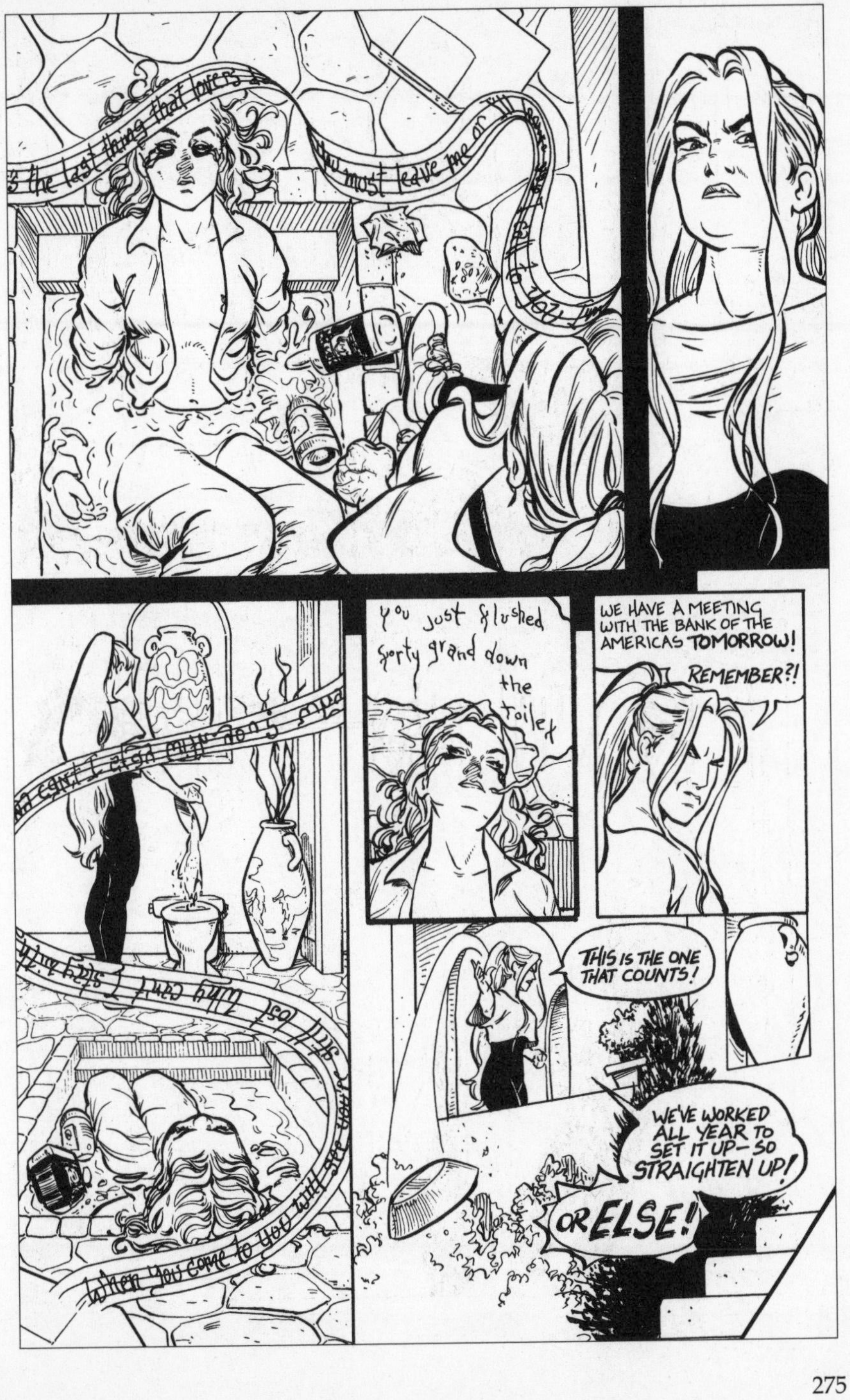
's the last thing that lovers
you most leave me or I'll leave
to you I
When you come to you
you just flushed forty grand down the toilet
WE HAVE A MEETING WITH THE BANK OF THE AMERICAS TOMORROW!
REMEMBER?!
THIS IS THE ONE THAT COUNTS!
WE'VE WORKED ALL YEAR TO SET IT UP—SO STRAIGHTEN UP!
OR ELSE!

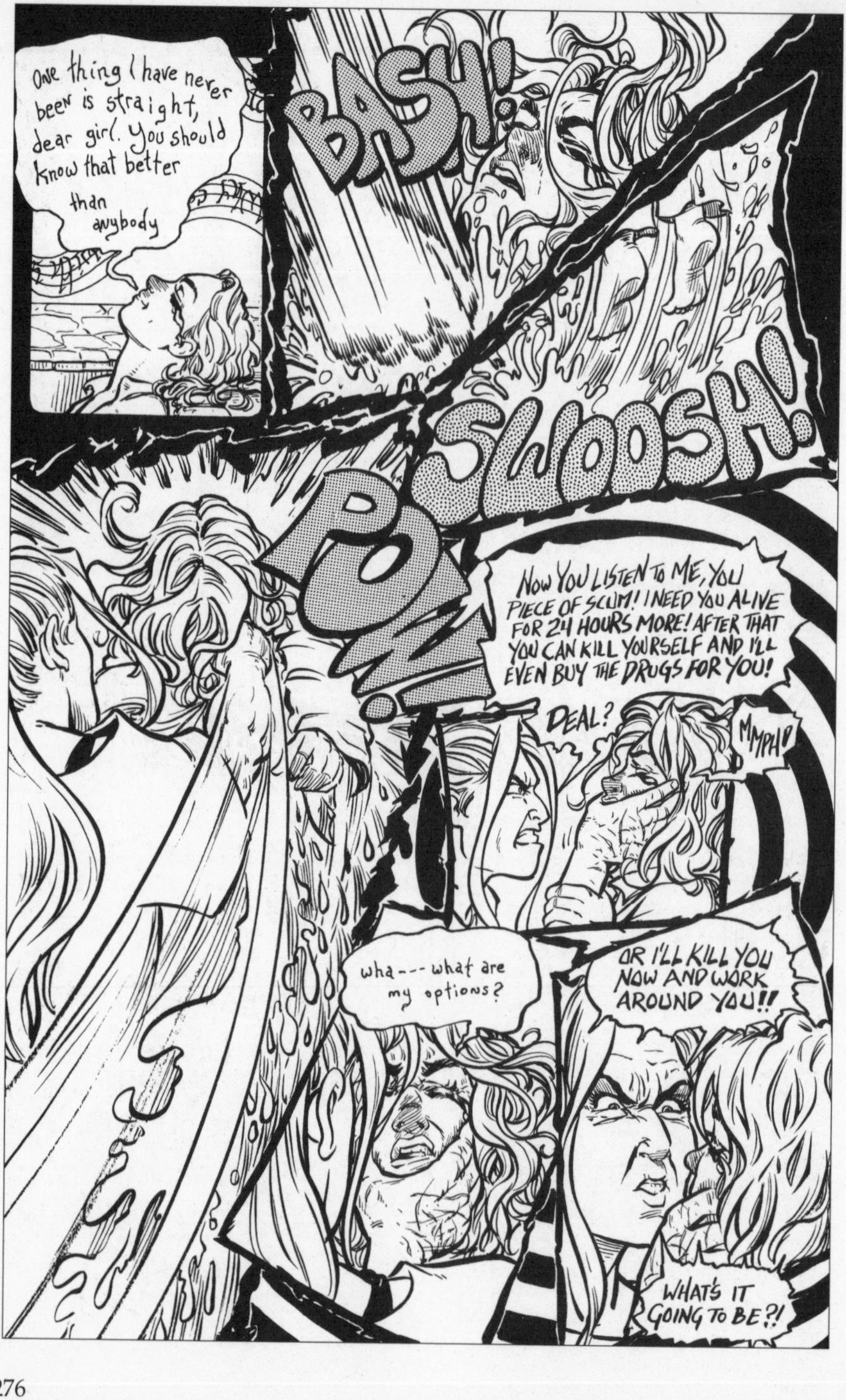
One thing I have never been is straight, dear girl. You should know that better than anybody
BASH!
SWOOSH!
POW
NOW YOU LISTEN TO ME, YOU PIECE OF SCUM! I NEED YOU ALIVE FOR 24 HOURS MORE! AFTER THAT YOU CAN KILL YOURSELF AND I'LL EVEN BUY THE DRUGS FOR YOU!
DEAL?
MMPH!
wha---what are my options?
OR I'LL KILL YOU NOW AND WORK AROUND YOU!!
WHAT'S IT GOING TO BE?!

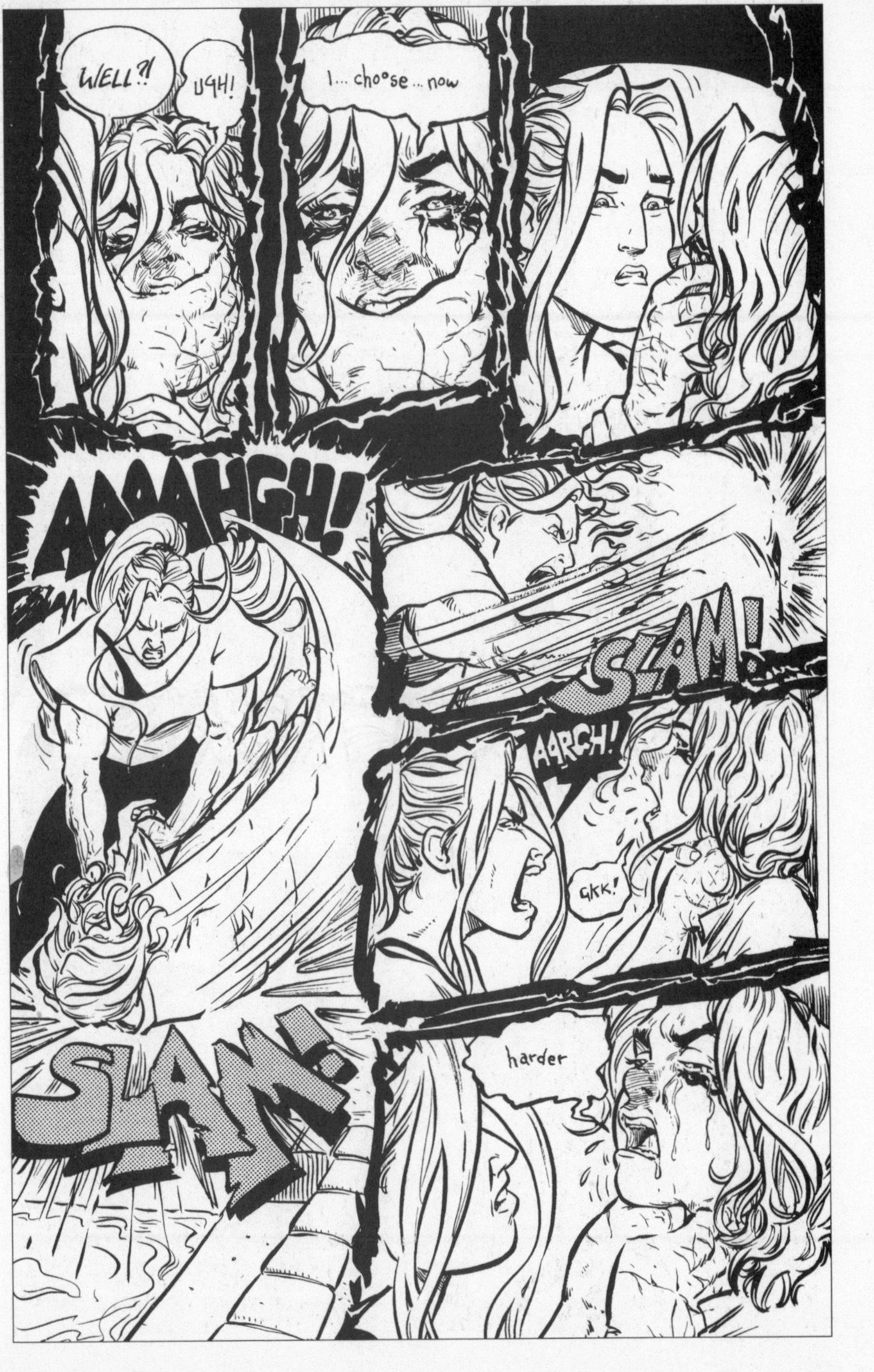
WELL?!
UGH!
I... choose... now
AAAAHGH!
SLAM!
AARGH!
GKK!
SLAM!
harder

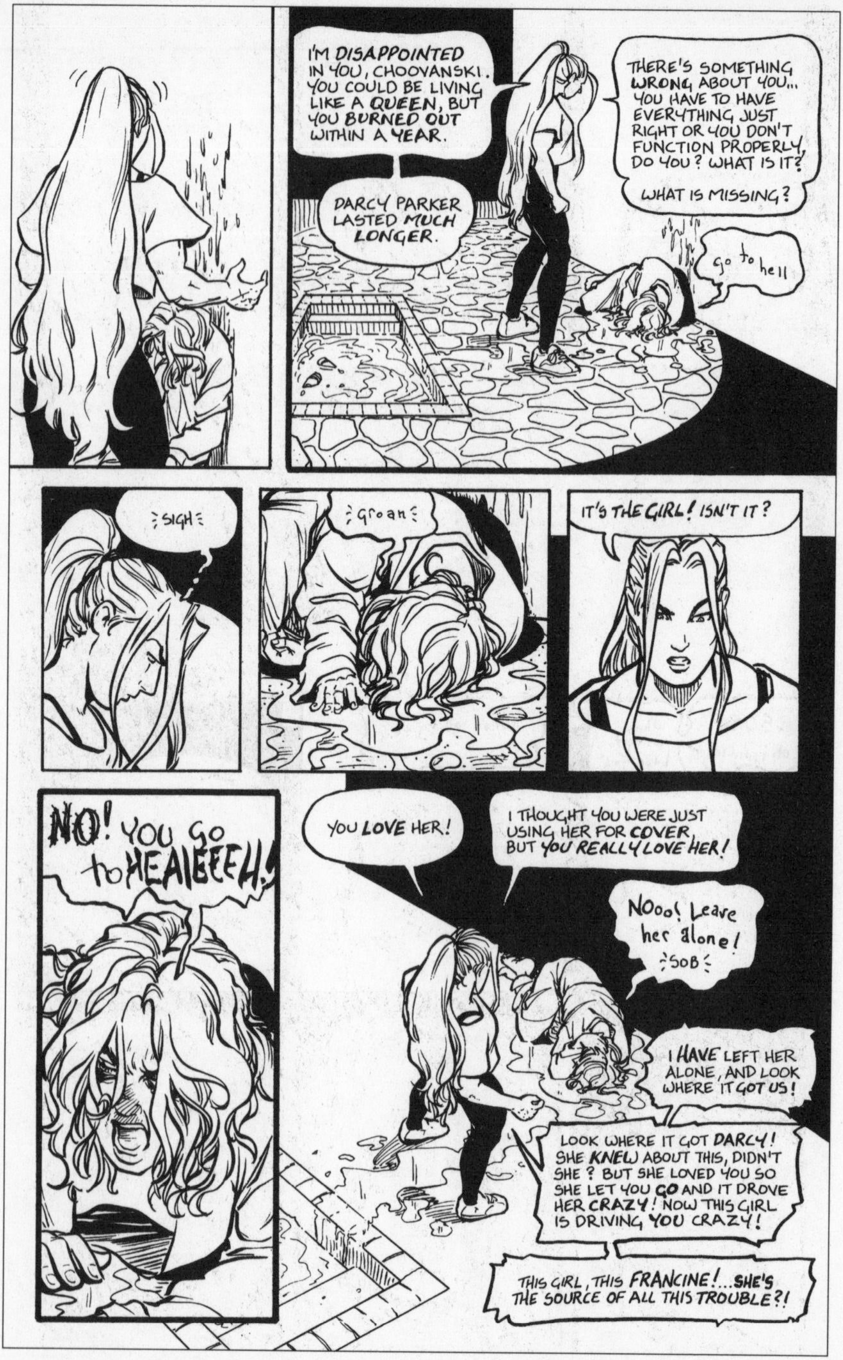
I'M DISAPPOINTED IN YOU, CHOOVANSKI. YOU COULD BE LIVING LIKE A QUEEN, BUT YOU BURNED OUT WITHIN A YEAR.
DARCY PARKER LASTED MUCH LONGER.
THERE'S SOMETHING WRONG ABOUT YOU... YOU HAVE TO HAVE EVERYTHING JUST RIGHT OR YOU DON'T FUNCTION PROPERLY, DO YOU? WHAT IS IT?
WHAT IS MISSING?
go to hell
SIGH
groan
IT'S THE GIRL! ISN'T IT?
NO! YOU GO to HEALLEEEH!
YOU LOVE HER!
I THOUGHT YOU WERE JUST USING HER FOR COVER, BUT YOU REALLY LOVE HER!
NOoo! Leave her alone!
SOB
I HAVE LEFT HER ALONE, AND LOOK WHERE IT GOT US!
LOOK WHERE IT GOT DARCY! SHE KNEW ABOUT THIS, DIDN'T SHE? BUT SHE LOVED YOU SO SHE LET YOU GO AND IT DROVE HER CRAZY! NOW THIS GIRL IS DRIVING YOU CRAZY!
THIS GIRL, THIS FRANCINE!... SHE'S THE SOURCE OF ALL THIS TROUBLE?!

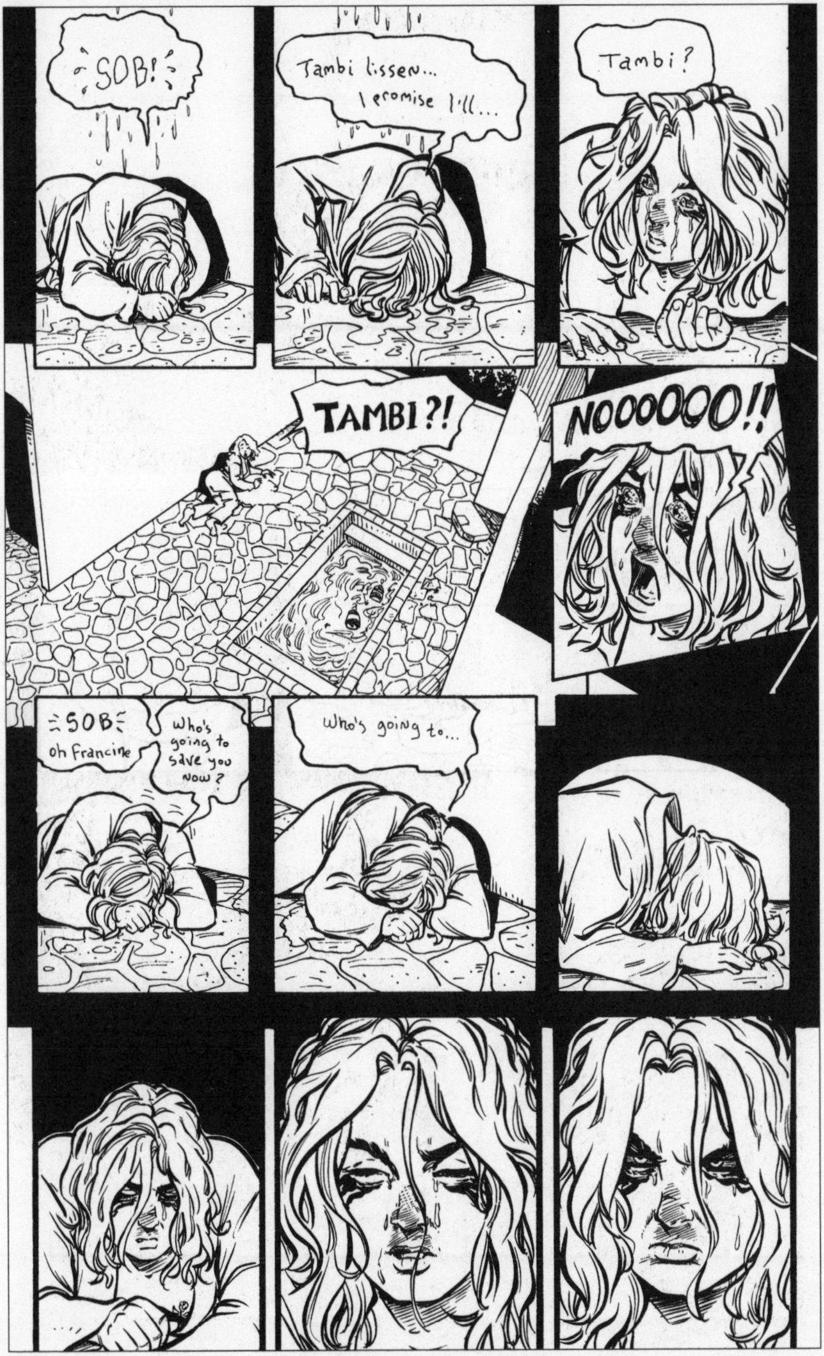
SOB!
Tambi lissen... I promise I'll...
Tambi?
TAMBI?!
NOOOOOO!!
SOB
oh Francine
Who's going to save you now?
Who's going to...
...

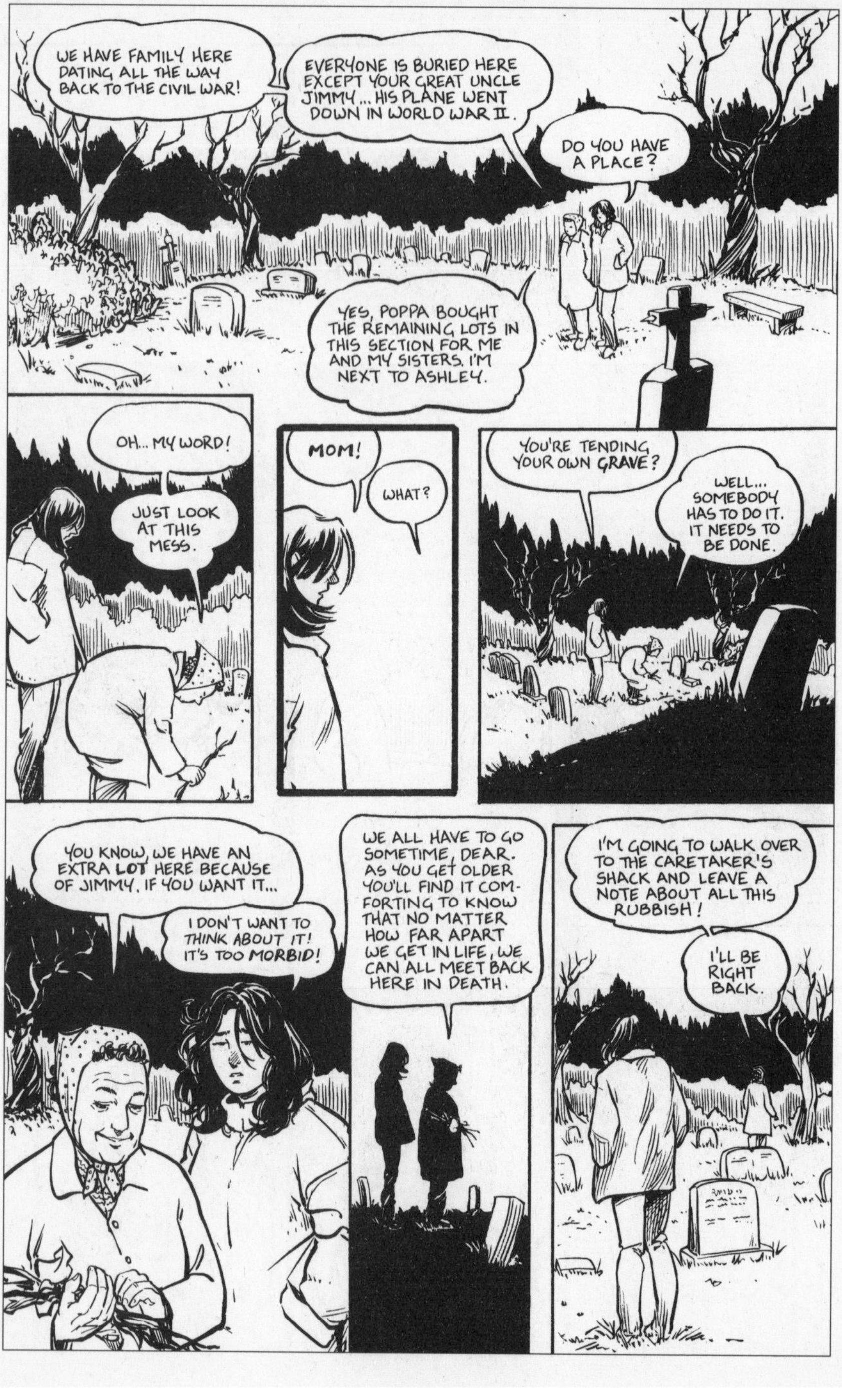
WE HAVE FAMILY HERE DATING ALL THE WAY BACK TO THE CIVIL WAR!
EVERYONE IS BURIED HERE EXCEPT YOUR GREAT UNCLE JIMMY... HIS PLANE WENT DOWN IN WORLD WAR II.
DO YOU HAVE A PLACE?
YES, POPPA BOUGHT THE REMAINING LOTS IN THIS SECTION FOR ME AND MY SISTERS. I'M NEXT TO ASHLEY.
OH... MY WORD!
JUST LOOK AT THIS MESS.
MOM!
WHAT?
YOU'RE TENDING YOUR OWN GRAVE?
WELL... SOMEBODY HAS TO DO IT. IT NEEDS TO BE DONE.
YOU KNOW, WE HAVE AN EXTRA LOT HERE BECAUSE OF JIMMY. IF YOU WANT IT...
I DON'T WANT TO THINK ABOUT IT! IT'S TOO MORBID!
WE ALL HAVE TO GO SOMETIME, DEAR. AS YOU GET OLDER YOU'LL FIND IT COMFORTING TO KNOW THAT NO MATTER HOW FAR APART WE GET IN LIFE, WE CAN ALL MEET BACK HERE IN DEATH.
I'M GOING TO WALK OVER TO THE CARETAKER'S SHACK AND LEAVE A NOTE ABOUT ALL THIS RUBBISH!
I'LL BE RIGHT BACK.

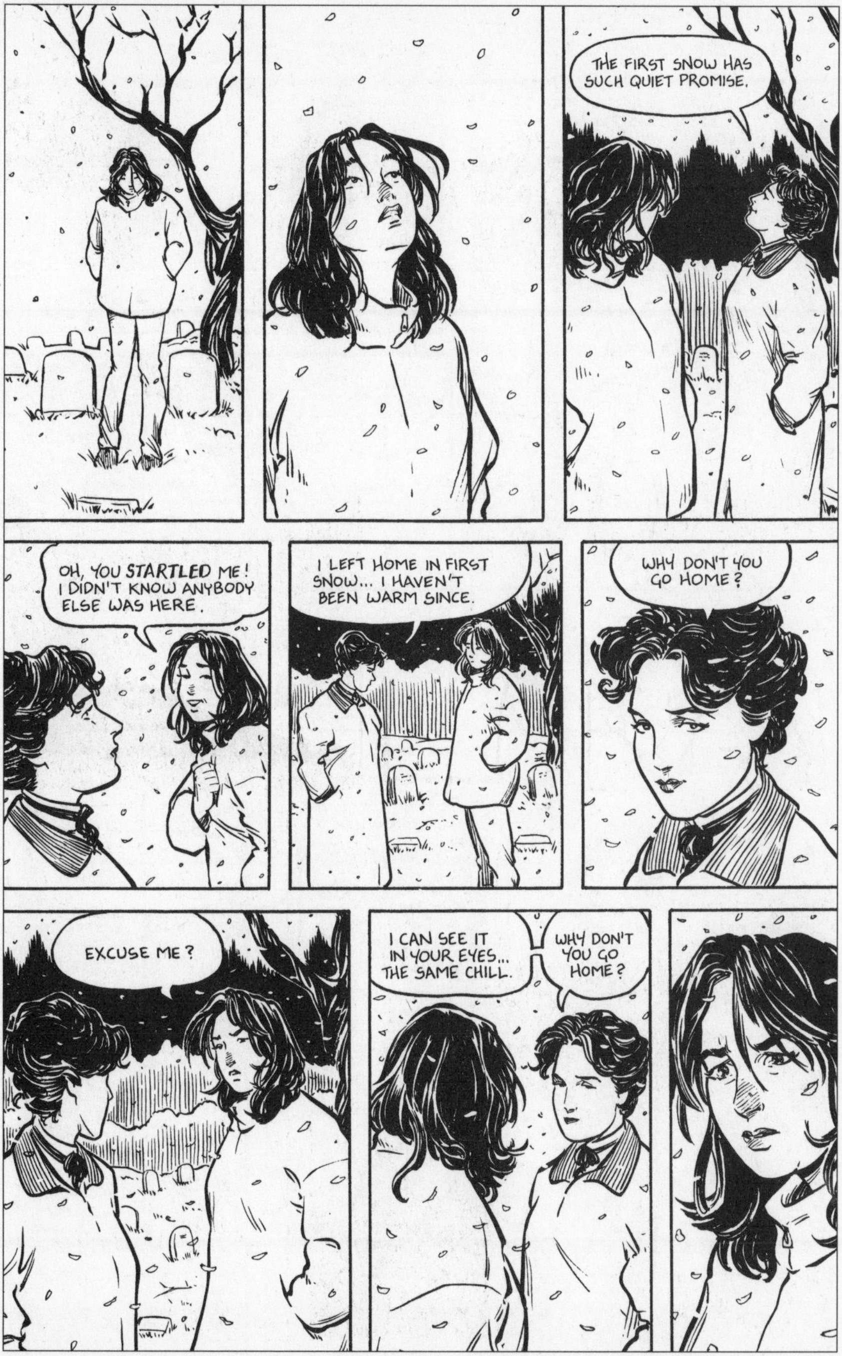
THE FIRST SNOW HAS SUCH QUIET PROMISE.
OH, YOU STARTLED ME! I DIDN'T KNOW ANYBODY ELSE WAS HERE.
I LEFT HOME IN FIRST SNOW... I HAVEN'T BEEN WARM SINCE.
WHY DON'T YOU GO HOME?
EXCUSE ME?
I CAN SEE IT IN YOUR EYES... THE SAME CHILL.
WHY DON'T YOU GO HOME?

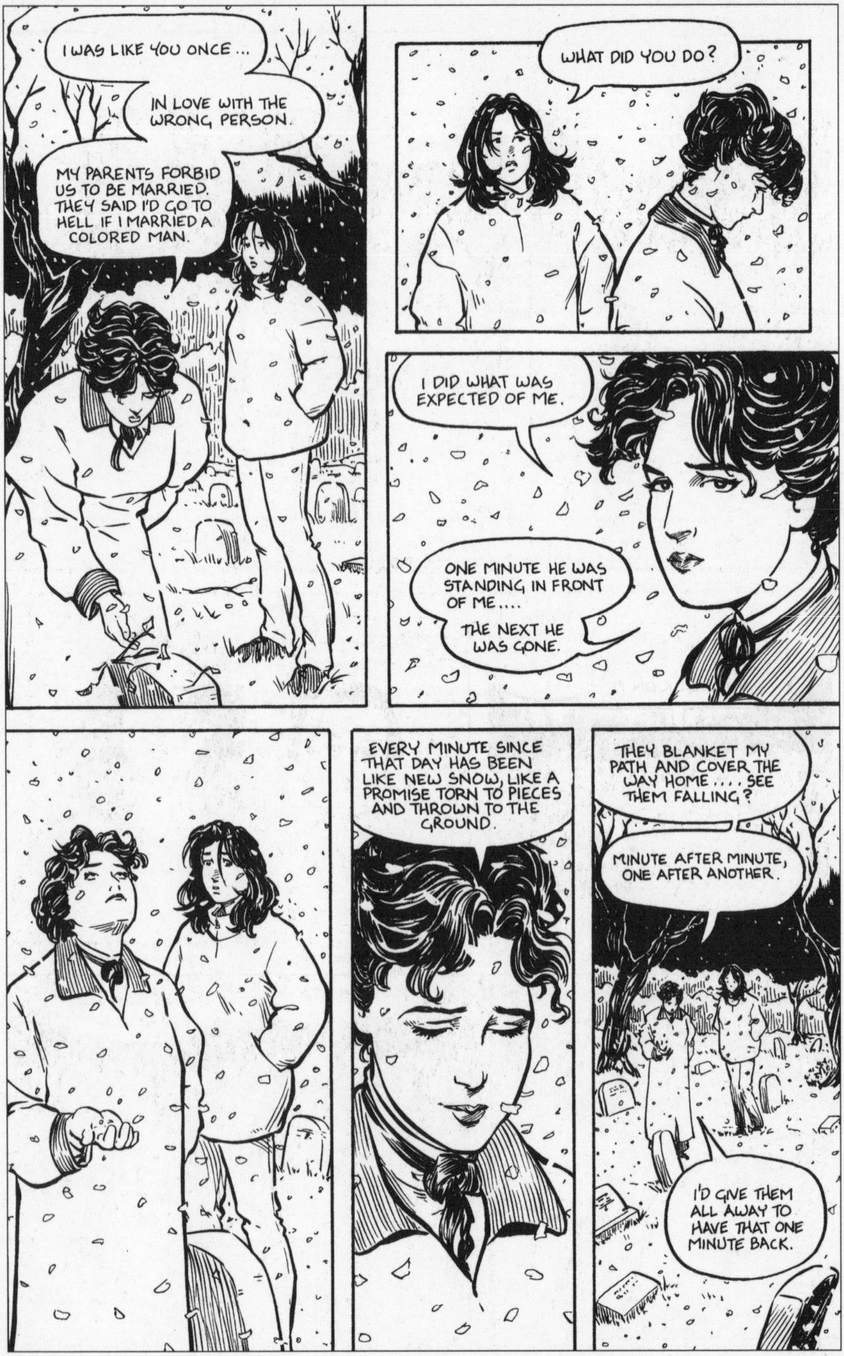
I WAS LIKE YOU ONCE...
IN LOVE WITH THE WRONG PERSON.
MY PARENTS FORBID US TO BE MARRIED. THEY SAID I'D GO TO HELL IF I MARRIED A COLORED MAN.
WHAT DID YOU DO?
I DID WHAT WAS EXPECTED OF ME.
ONE MINUTE HE WAS STANDING IN FRONT OF ME....
THE NEXT HE WAS GONE.
EVERY MINUTE SINCE THAT DAY HAS BEEN LIKE NEW SNOW, LIKE A PROMISE TORN TO PIECES AND THROWN TO THE GROUND.
THEY BLANKET MY PATH AND COVER THE WAY HOME.... SEE THEM FALLING?
MINUTE AFTER MINUTE, ONE AFTER ANOTHER.
I'D GIVE THEM ALL AWAY TO HAVE THAT ONE MINUTE BACK.

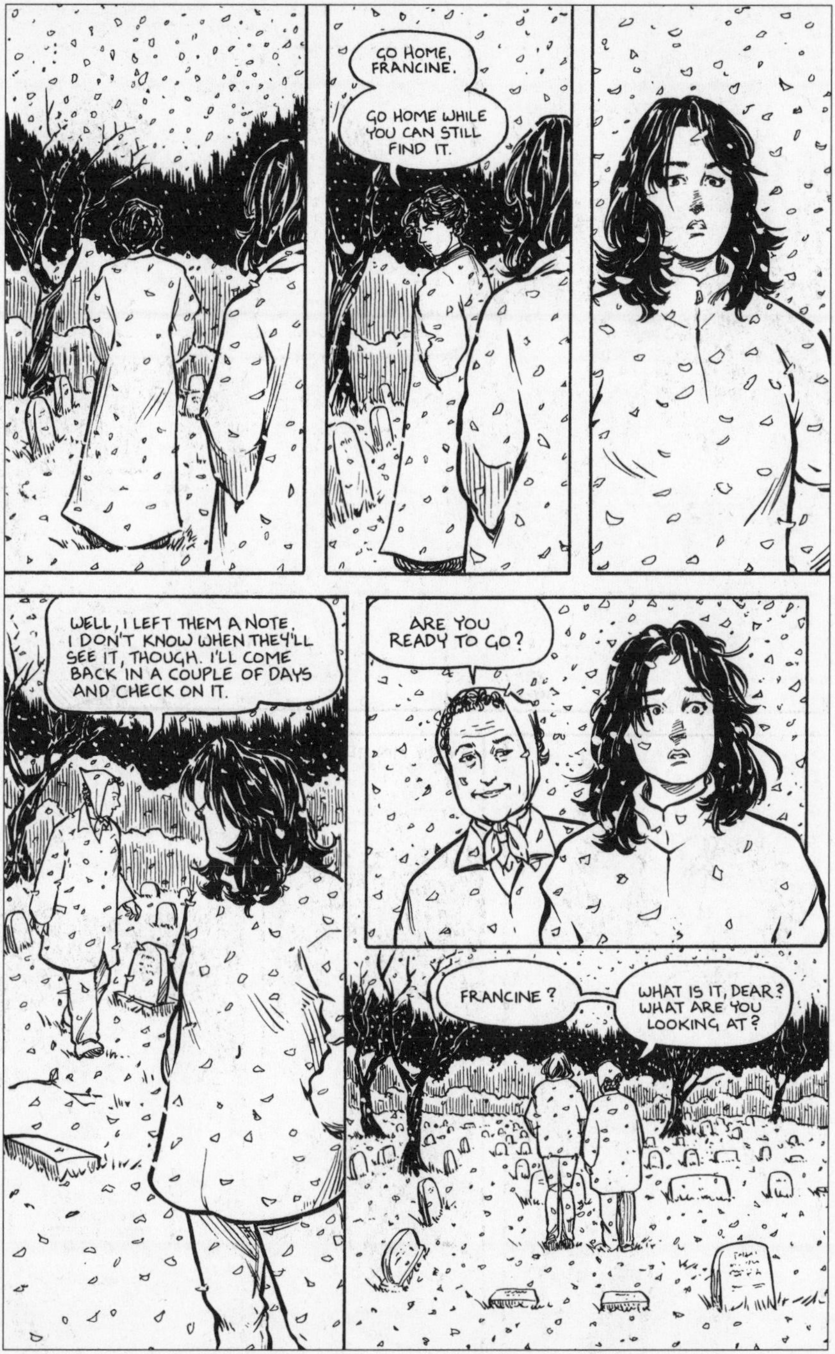
GO HOME, FRANCINE.
GO HOME WHILE YOU CAN STILL FIND IT.
WELL, I LEFT THEM A NOTE. I DON'T KNOW WHEN THEY'LL SEE IT, THOUGH. I'LL COME BACK IN A COUPLE OF DAYS AND CHECK ON IT.
ARE YOU READY TO GO?
FRANCINE?
WHAT IS IT, DEAR? WHAT ARE YOU LOOKING AT?

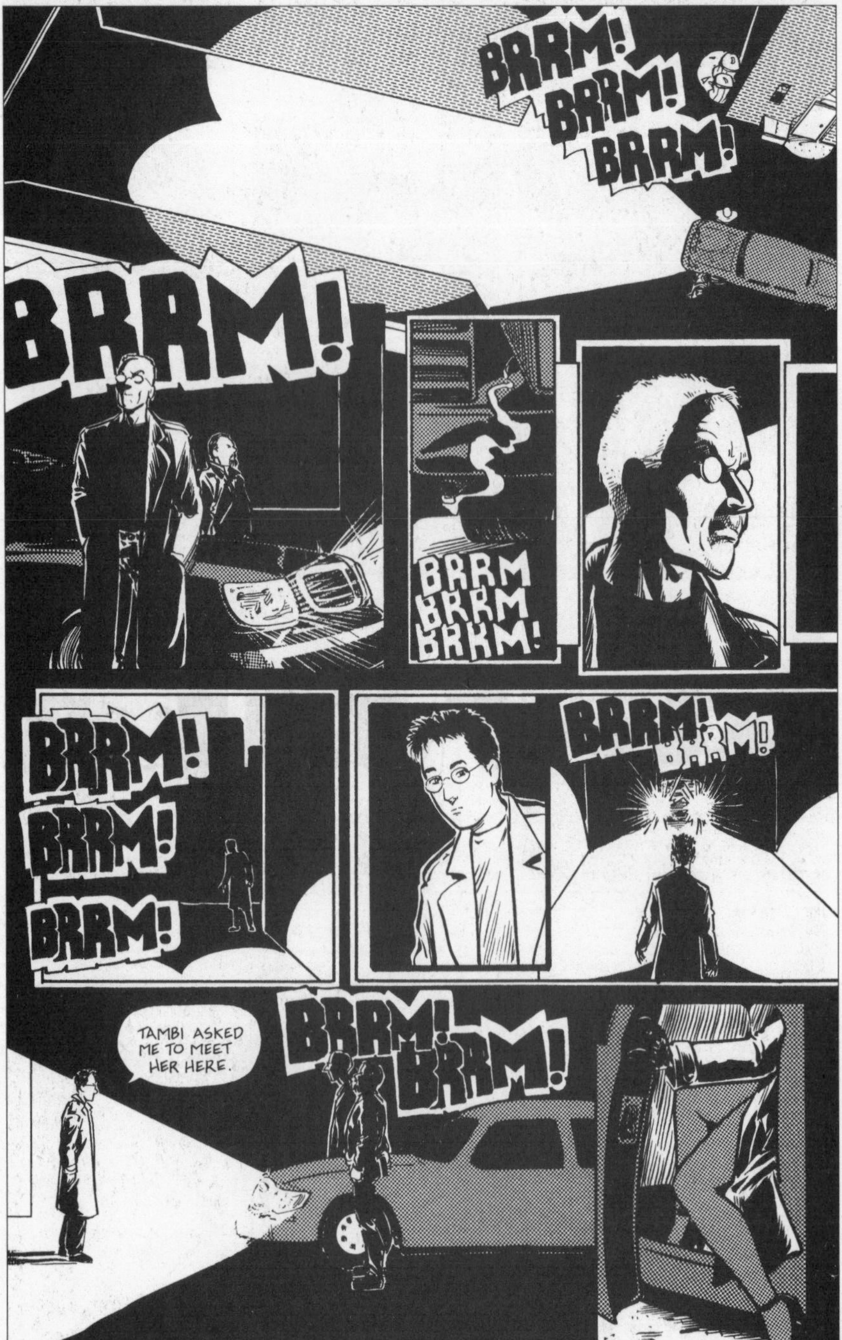
BRRM! BRRM! BRRM!
BRRM!
BRRM
BRRM
BRRM!
BRRM!
BRRM!
BRRM!
BRRM! BRRM!
TAMBI ASKED ME TO MEET HER HERE.
BRRM! BRRM!

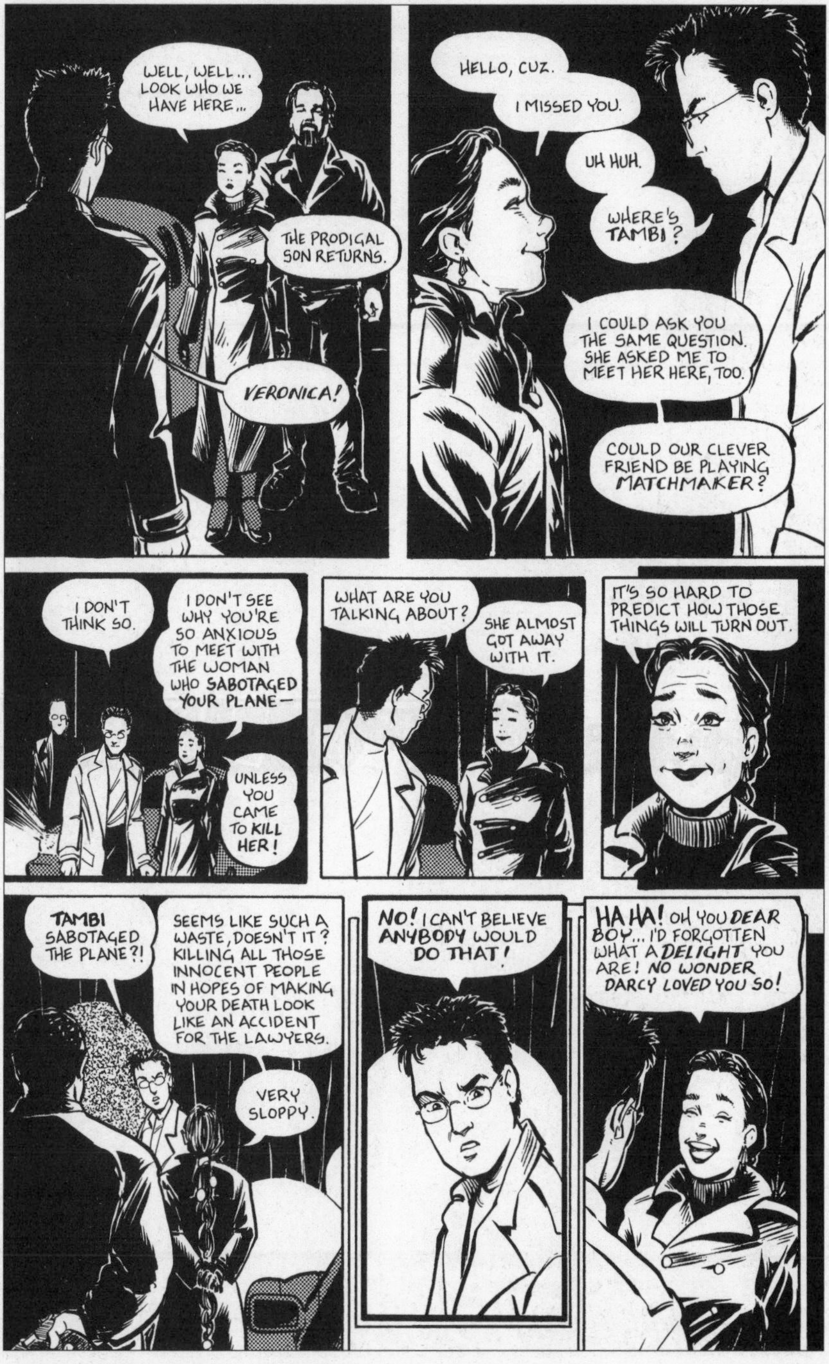
WELL, WELL... LOOK WHO WE HAVE HERE...
THE PRODIGAL SON RETURNS.
VERONICA!
HELLO, CUZ.
I MISSED YOU.
UH HUH.
WHERE'S TAMBI?
I COULD ASK YOU THE SAME QUESTION. SHE ASKED ME TO MEET HER HERE, TOO.
COULD OUR CLEVER FRIEND BE PLAYING MATCHMAKER?
I DON'T THINK SO.
I DON'T SEE WHY YOU'RE SO ANXIOUS TO MEET WITH THE WOMAN WHO SABOTAGED YOUR PLANE—
UNLESS YOU CAME TO KILL HER!
WHAT ARE YOU TALKING ABOUT?
SHE ALMOST GOT AWAY WITH IT.
IT'S SO HARD TO PREDICT HOW THOSE THINGS WILL TURN OUT.
TAMBI SABOTAGED THE PLANE?!
SEEMS LIKE SUCH A WASTE, DOESN'T IT? KILLING ALL THOSE INNOCENT PEOPLE IN HOPES OF MAKING YOUR DEATH LOOK LIKE AN ACCIDENT FOR THE LAWYERS.
VERY SLOPPY.
NO! I CAN'T BELIEVE ANYBODY WOULD DO THAT!
HA HA! OH YOU DEAR BOY... I'D FORGOTTEN WHAT A DELIGHT YOU ARE! NO WONDER DARCY LOVED YOU SO!

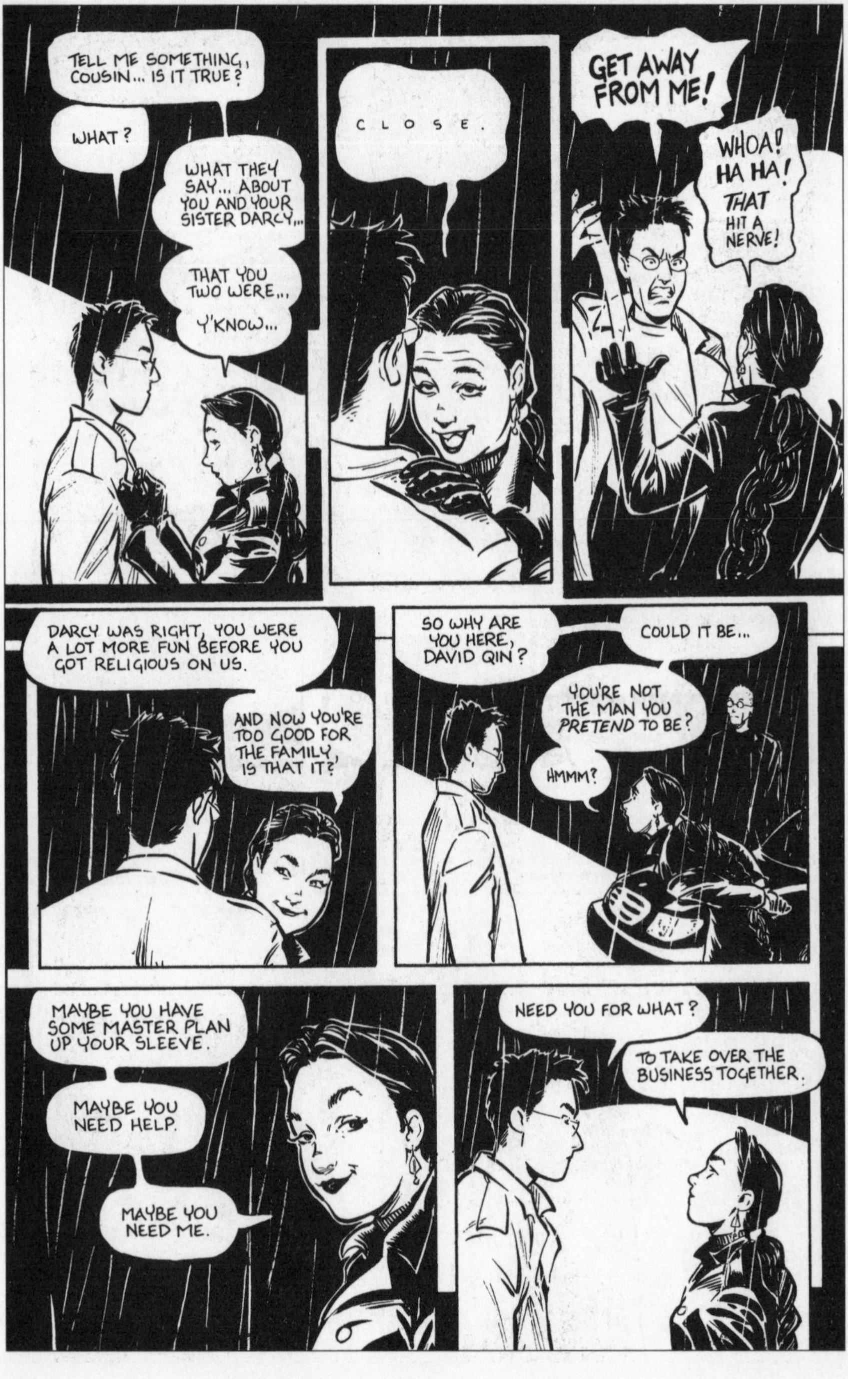
TELL ME SOMETHING, COUSIN... IS IT TRUE?
WHAT?
WHAT THEY SAY... ABOUT YOU AND YOUR SISTER DARCY...
THAT YOU TWO WERE...
Y'KNOW...
C L O S E.
GET AWAY FROM ME!
WHOA! HA HA! THAT HIT A NERVE!
DARCY WAS RIGHT, YOU WERE A LOT MORE FUN BEFORE YOU GOT RELIGIOUS ON US.
AND NOW YOU'RE TOO GOOD FOR THE FAMILY, IS THAT IT?
SO WHY ARE YOU HERE, DAVID QIN?
COULD IT BE...
YOU'RE NOT THE MAN YOU PRETEND TO BE?
HMMM?
MAYBE YOU HAVE SOME MASTER PLAN UP YOUR SLEEVE.
MAYBE YOU NEED HELP.
MAYBE YOU NEED ME.
NEED YOU FOR WHAT?
TO TAKE OVER THE BUSINESS TOGETHER.

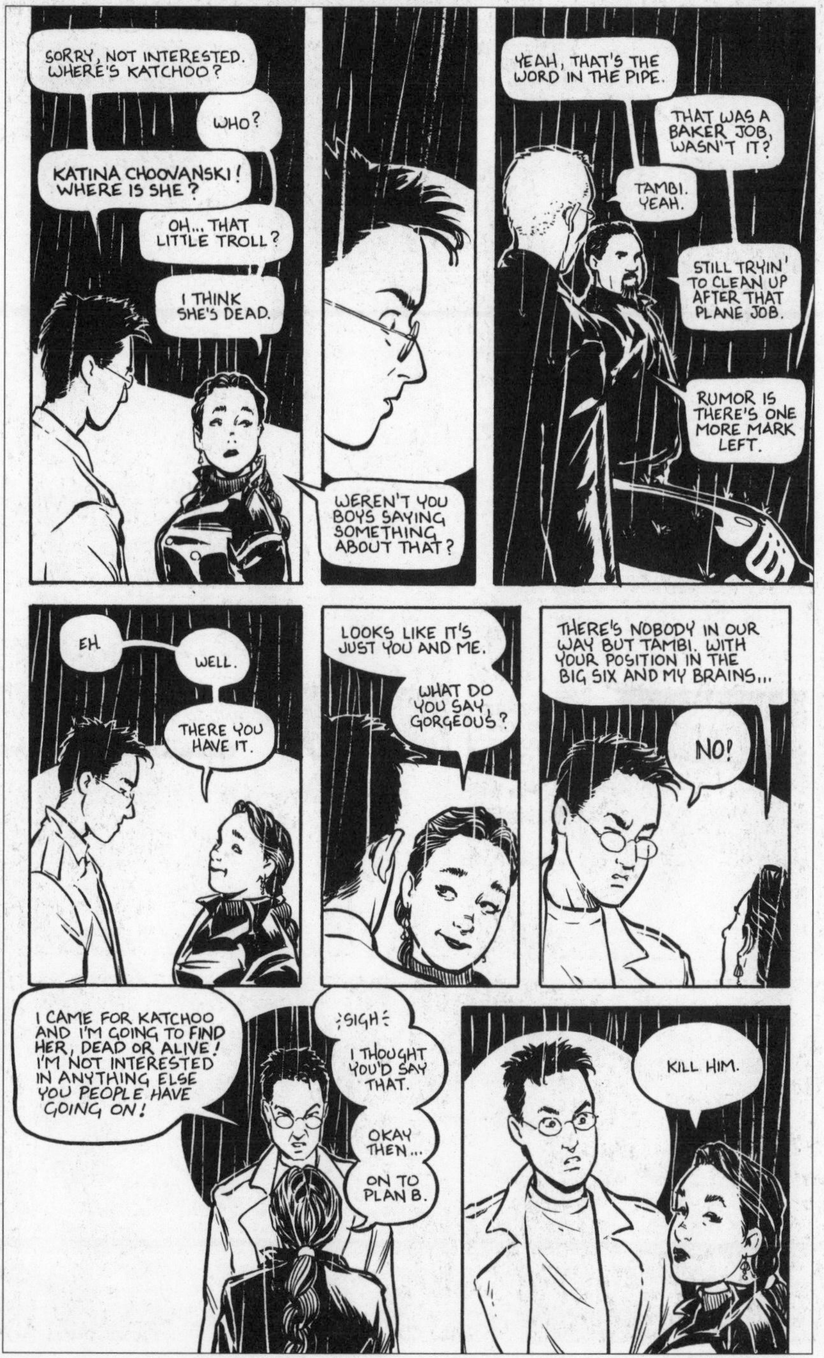
SORRY, NOT INTERESTED. WHERE'S KATCHOO?
WHO?
KATINA CHOOVANSKI! WHERE IS SHE?
OH... THAT LITTLE TROLL?
I THINK SHE'S DEAD.
WEREN'T YOU BOYS SAYING SOMETHING ABOUT THAT?
YEAH, THAT'S THE WORD IN THE PIPE.
THAT WAS A BAKER JOB, WASN'T IT?
TAMBI. YEAH.
STILL TRYIN' TO CLEAN UP AFTER THAT PLANE JOB.
RUMOR IS THERE'S ONE MORE MARK LEFT.
EH.
WELL.
THERE YOU HAVE IT.
LOOKS LIKE IT'S JUST YOU AND ME.
WHAT DO YOU SAY, GORGEOUS?
THERE'S NOBODY IN OUR WAY BUT TAMBI. WITH YOUR POSITION IN THE BIG SIX AND MY BRAINS...
NO!
I CAME FOR KATCHOO AND I'M GOING TO FIND HER, DEAD OR ALIVE! I'M NOT INTERESTED IN ANYTHING ELSE YOU PEOPLE HAVE GOING ON!
SIGH
I THOUGHT YOU'D SAY THAT.
OKAY THEN...
ON TO PLAN B.
KILL HIM.

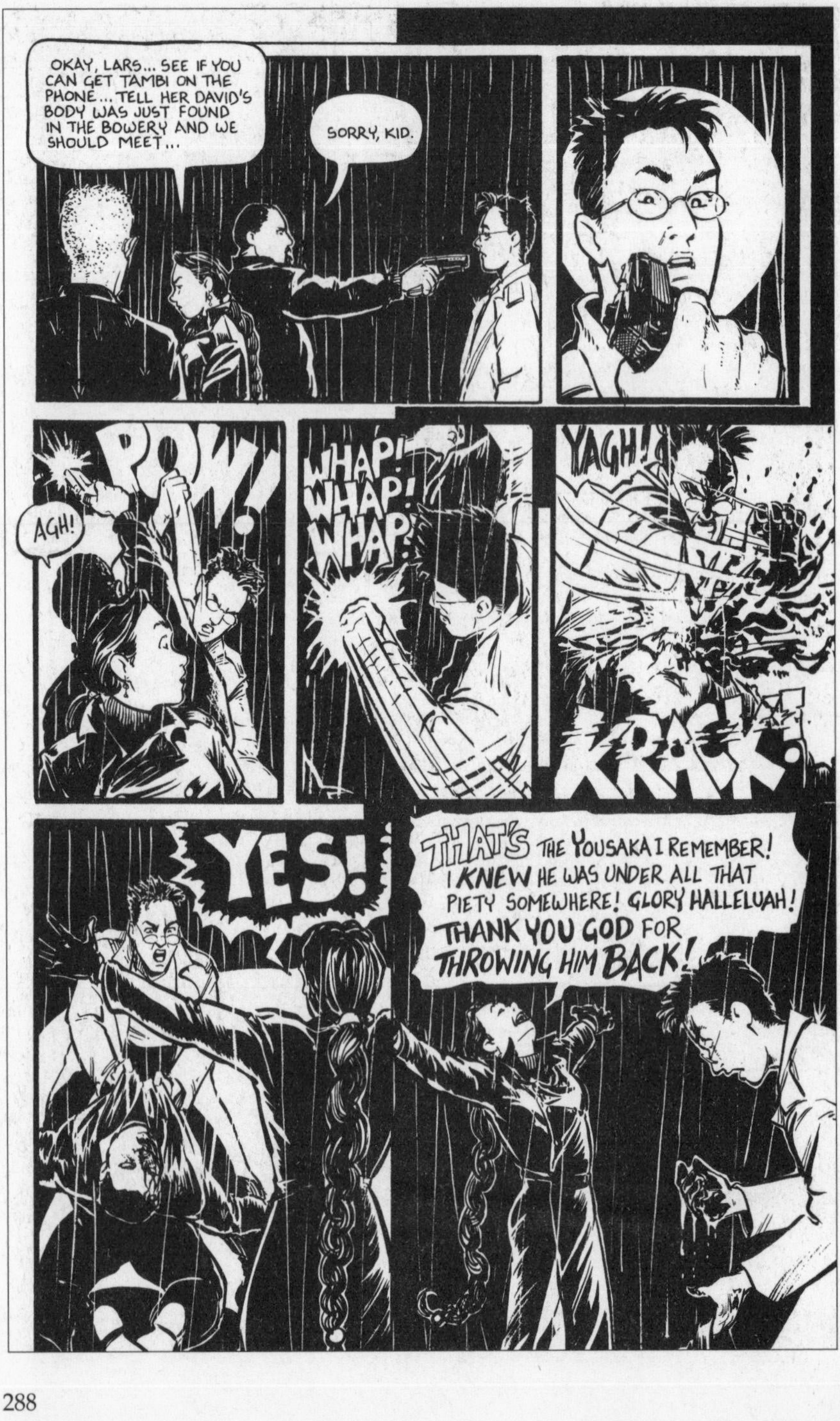

OKAY, LARS... SEE IF YOU CAN GET TAMBI ON THE PHONE... TELL HER DAVID'S BODY WAS JUST FOUND IN THE BOWERY AND WE SHOULD MEET...
SORRY, KID.
POW!
AGH!
WHAP! WHAP! WHAP!
YAGH!
KRACK!
YES!
THAT'S THE YOUSAKA I REMEMBER! I KNEW HE WAS UNDER ALL THAT PIETY SOMEWHERE! GLORY HALLELUAH! THANK YOU GOD FOR THROWING HIM BACK!

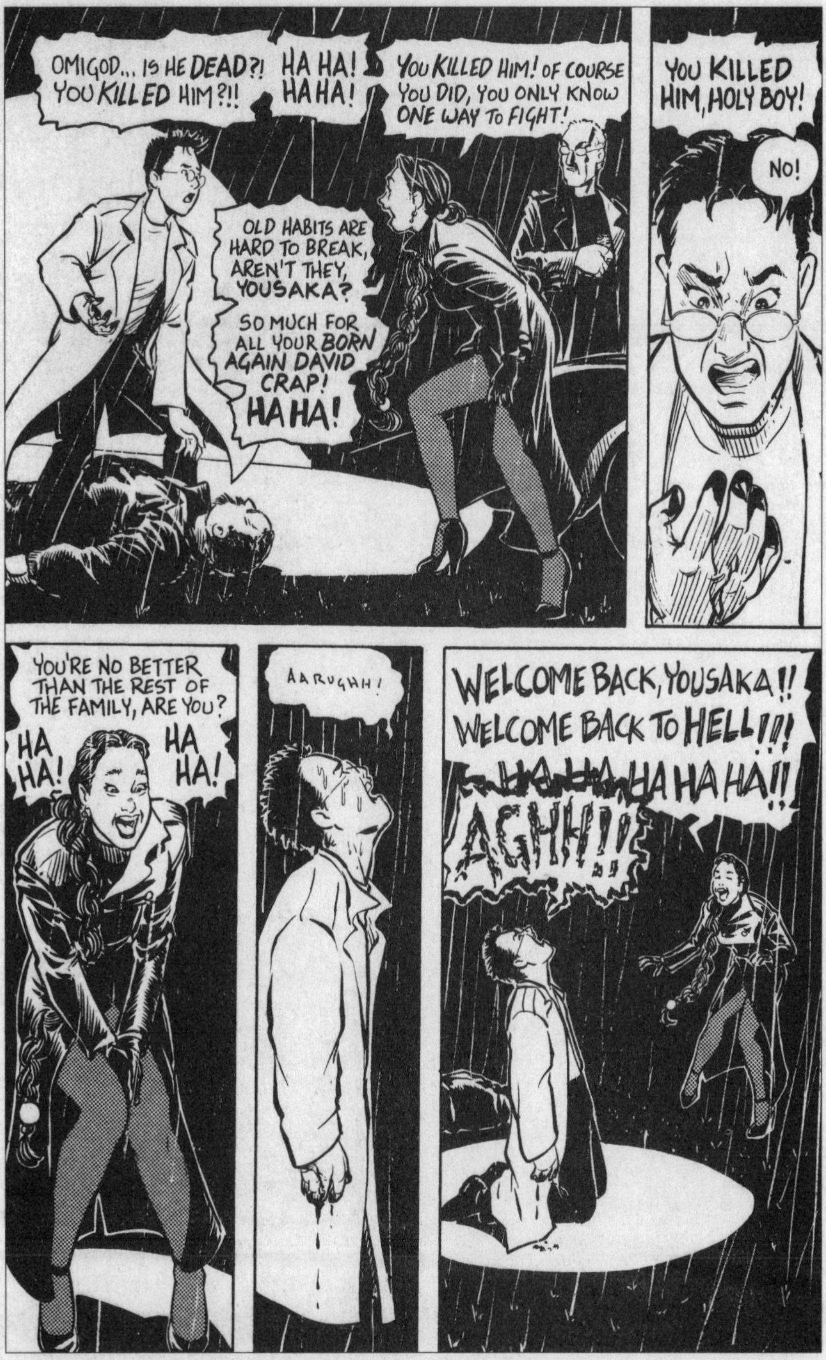
OMIGOD... IS HE DEAD?! YOU KILLED HIM?!!
HA HA! HA HA!
YOU KILLED HIM! OF COURSE YOU DID, YOU ONLY KNOW ONE WAY TO FIGHT!
OLD HABITS ARE HARD TO BREAK, AREN'T THEY, YOUSAKA?
SO MUCH FOR ALL YOUR BORN AGAIN DAVID CRAP! HA HA!
YOU KILLED HIM, HOLY BOY!
NO!
YOU'RE NO BETTER THAN THE REST OF THE FAMILY, ARE YOU?
HA HA! HA HA!
AARUGHH!
WELCOME BACK, YOUSAKA!! WELCOME BACK TO HELL!!!
HA HA HA HA HA HA!!
AGHH!!

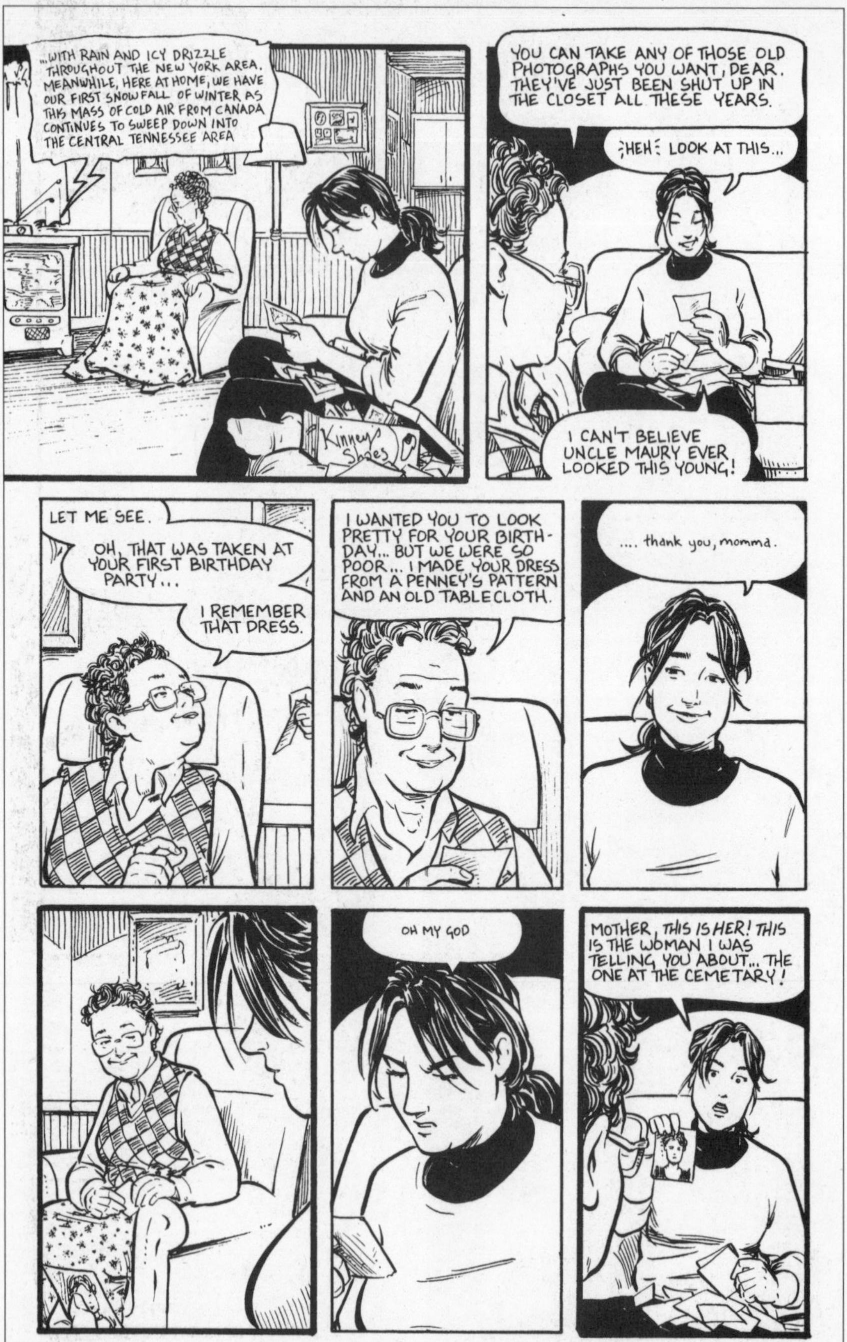
...WITH RAIN AND ICY DRIZZLE THROUGHOUT THE NEW YORK AREA. MEANWHILE, HERE AT HOME, WE HAVE OUR FIRST SNOWFALL OF WINTER AS THIS MASS OF COLD AIR FROM CANADA CONTINUES TO SWEEP DOWN INTO THE CENTRAL TENNESSEE AREA
Kinney's Shoes
YOU CAN TAKE ANY OF THOSE OLD PHOTOGRAPHS YOU WANT, DEAR. THEY'VE JUST BEEN SHUT UP IN THE CLOSET ALL THESE YEARS.
HEH LOOK AT THIS...
I CAN'T BELIEVE UNCLE MAURY EVER LOOKED THIS YOUNG!
LET ME SEE.
OH, THAT WAS TAKEN AT YOUR FIRST BIRTHDAY PARTY...
I REMEMBER THAT DRESS.
I WANTED YOU TO LOOK PRETTY FOR YOUR BIRTHDAY... BUT WE WERE SO POOR... I MADE YOUR DRESS FROM A PENNEY'S PATTERN AND AN OLD TABLECLOTH.
.... thank you, momma.
OH MY GOD
MOTHER, THIS IS HER! THIS IS THE WOMAN I WAS TELLING YOU ABOUT... THE ONE AT THE CEMETARY!

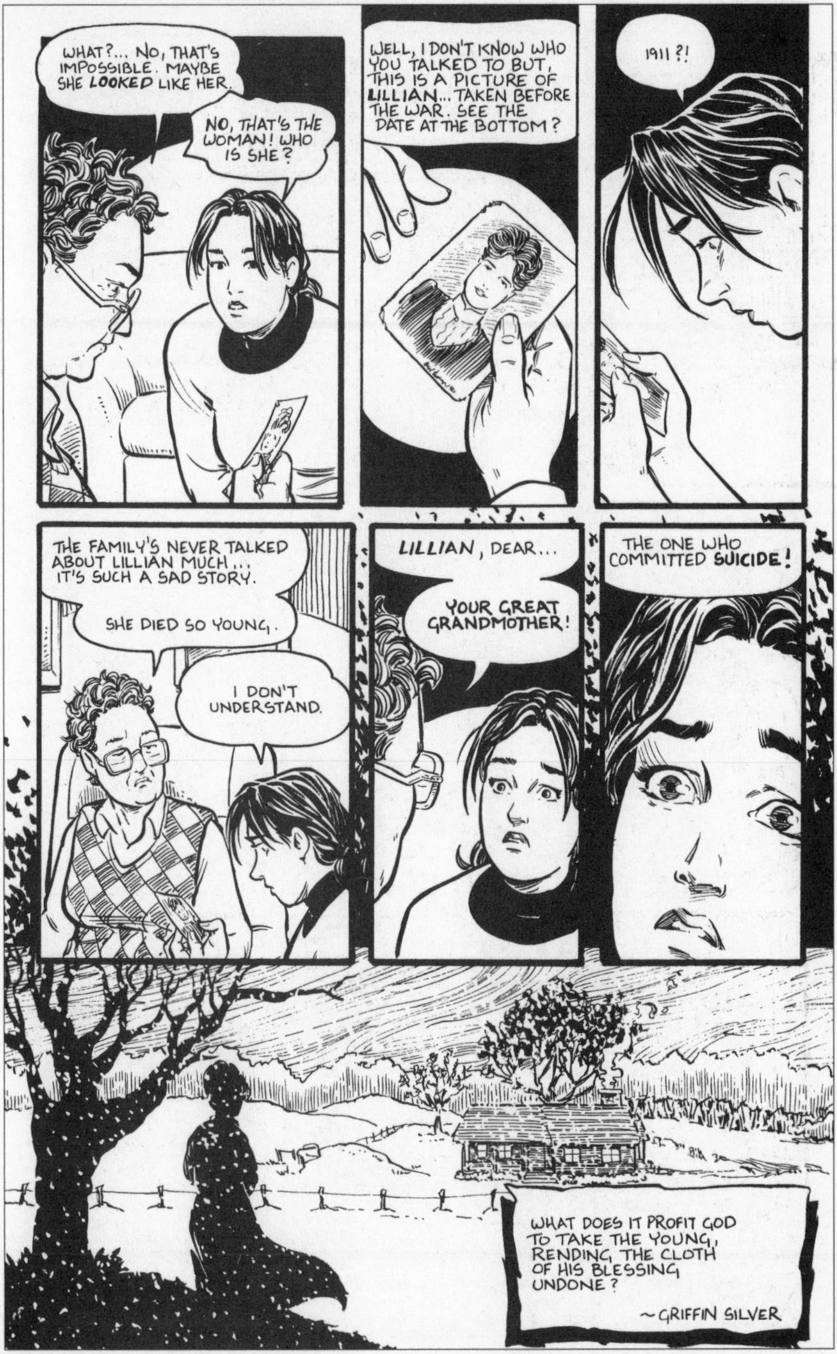
WHAT?... NO, THAT'S IMPOSSIBLE. MAYBE SHE **LOOKED** LIKE HER.
NO, THAT'S THE WOMAN! WHO IS SHE?
WELL, I DON'T KNOW WHO YOU TALKED TO BUT, THIS IS A PICTURE OF **LILLIAN**... TAKEN BEFORE THE WAR. SEE THE DATE AT THE BOTTOM?
1911?!
THE FAMILY'S NEVER TALKED ABOUT LILLIAN MUCH... IT'S SUCH A SAD STORY.
SHE DIED SO YOUNG.
I DON'T UNDERSTAND.
LILLIAN, DEAR...
YOUR GREAT GRANDMOTHER!
THE ONE WHO COMMITTED **SUICIDE**!
WHAT DOES IT PROFIT GOD TO TAKE THE YOUNG, RENDING THE CLOTH OF HIS BLESSING UNDONE?
~GRIFFIN SILVER

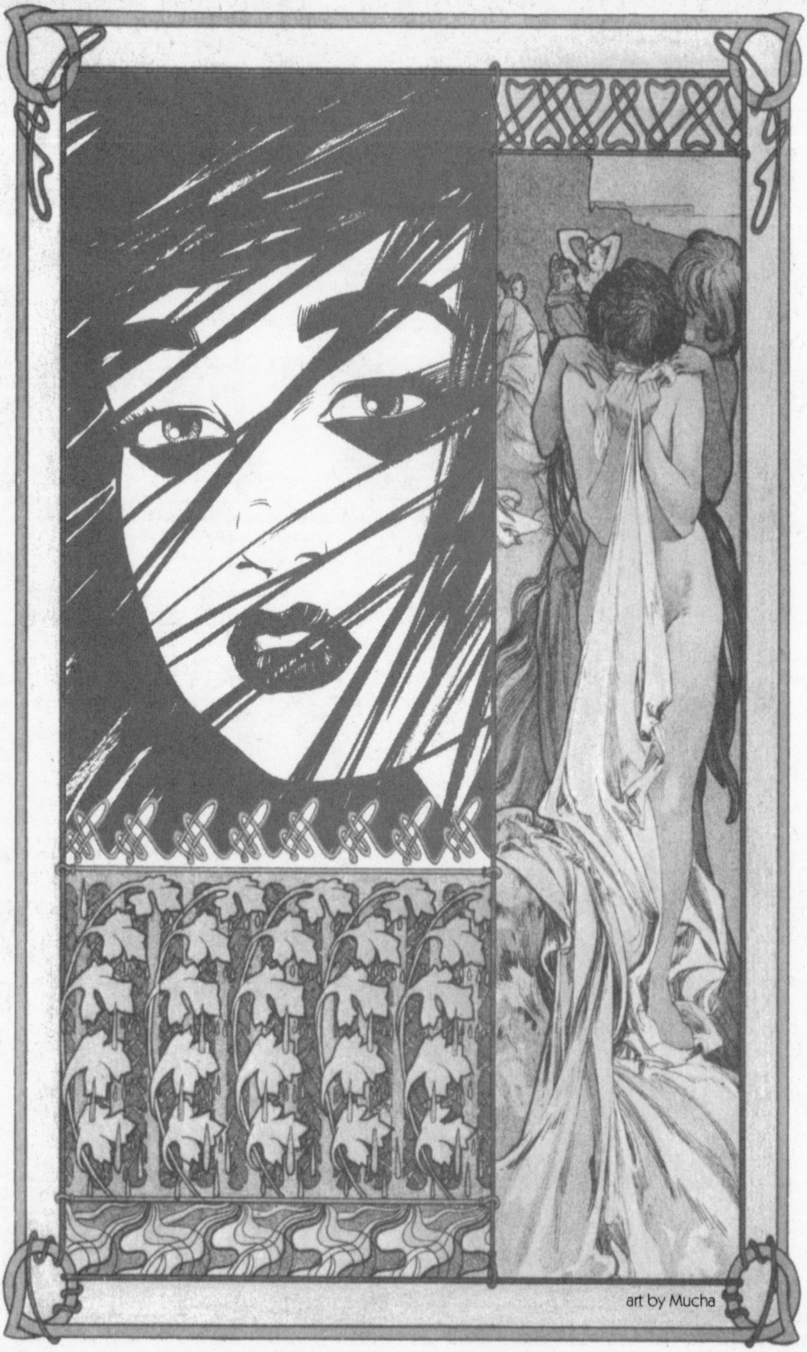
art by Mucha

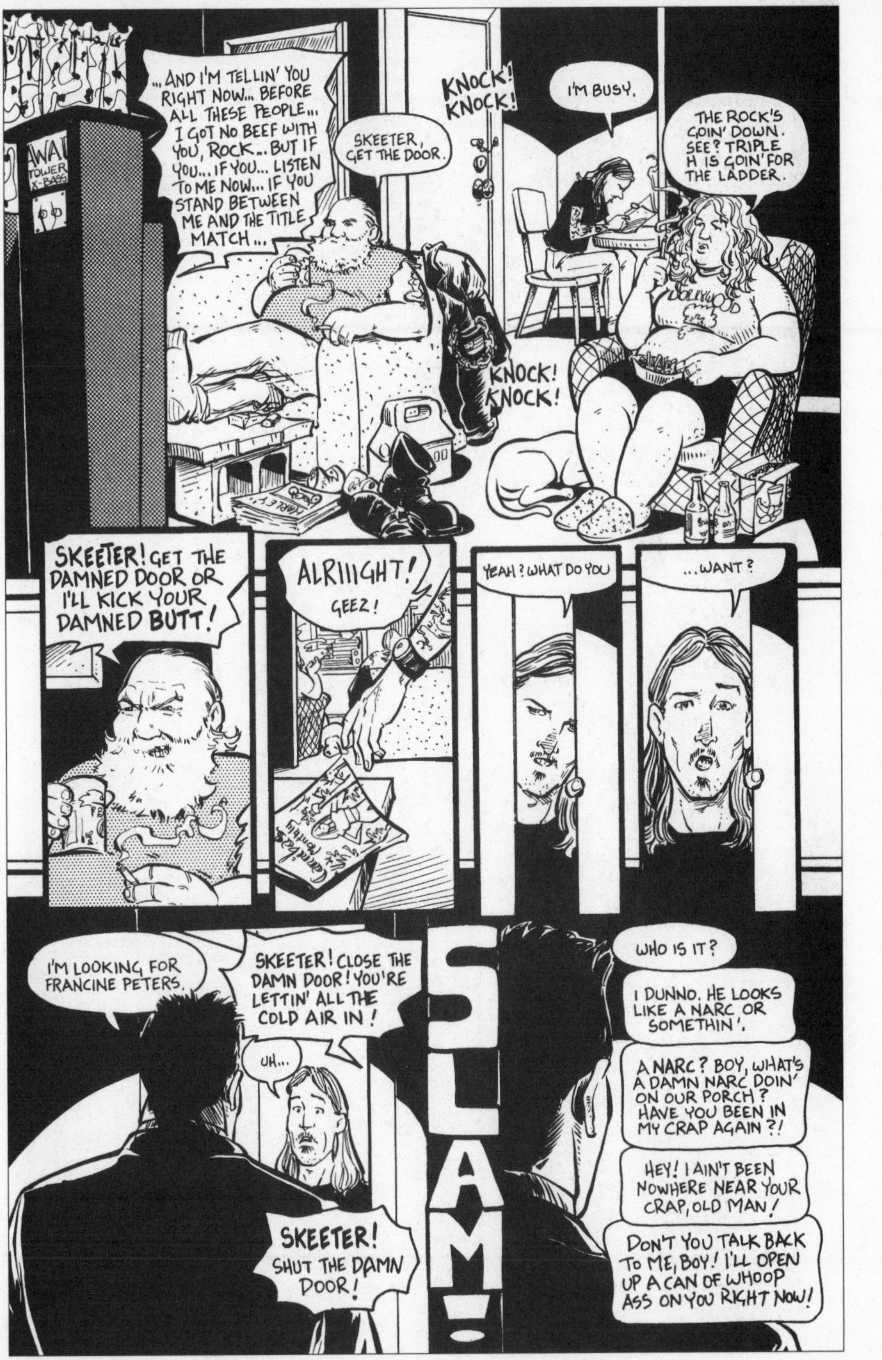

...AND I'M TELLIN' YOU RIGHT NOW... BEFORE ALL THESE PEOPLE... I GOT NO BEEF WITH YOU, ROCK... BUT IF YOU... IF YOU... LISTEN TO ME NOW... IF YOU STAND BETWEEN ME AND THE TITLE MATCH...
SKEETER, GET THE DOOR.
KNOCK! KNOCK!
I'M BUSY.
THE ROCK'S GOIN' DOWN. SEE? TRIPLE H IS GOIN' FOR THE LADDER.
KNOCK! KNOCK!
SKEETER! GET THE DAMNED DOOR OR I'LL KICK YOUR DAMNED BUTT!
ALRIIIGHT! GEEZ!
YEAH? WHAT DO YOU
...WANT?
I'M LOOKING FOR FRANCINE PETERS.
SKEETER! CLOSE THE DAMN DOOR! YOU'RE LETTIN' ALL THE COLD AIR IN!
UH...
SKEETER! SHUT THE DAMN DOOR!
SLAM!
WHO IS IT?
I DUNNO. HE LOOKS LIKE A NARC OR SOMETHIN'.
A NARC? BOY, WHAT'S A DAMN NARC DOIN' ON OUR PORCH? HAVE YOU BEEN IN MY CRAP AGAIN?!
HEY! I AIN'T BEEN NOWHERE NEAR YOUR CRAP, OLD MAN!
DON'T YOU TALK BACK TO ME, BOY! I'LL OPEN UP A CAN OF WHOOP ASS ON YOU RIGHT NOW!

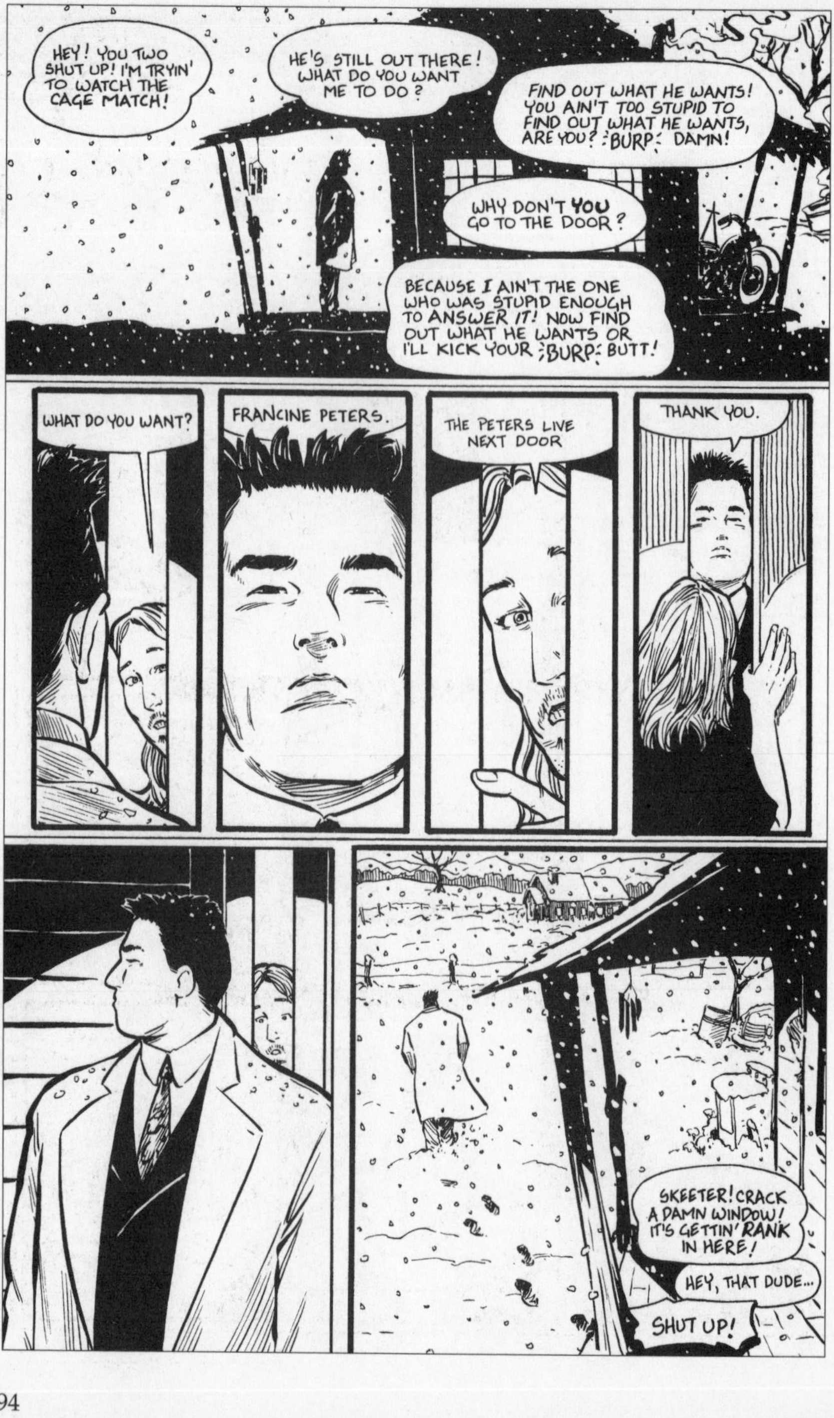
HEY! YOU TWO SHUT UP! I'M TRYIN' TO WATCH THE CAGE MATCH!
HE'S STILL OUT THERE! WHAT DO YOU WANT ME TO DO?
FIND OUT WHAT HE WANTS! YOU AIN'T TOO STUPID TO FIND OUT WHAT HE WANTS, ARE YOU? BURP DAMN!
WHY DON'T YOU GO TO THE DOOR?
BECAUSE I AIN'T THE ONE WHO WAS STUPID ENOUGH TO ANSWER IT! NOW FIND OUT WHAT HE WANTS OR I'LL KICK YOUR BURP BUTT!
WHAT DO YOU WANT?
FRANCINE PETERS.
THE PETERS LIVE NEXT DOOR
THANK YOU.
SKEETER! CRACK A DAMN WINDOW! IT'S GETTIN' RANK IN HERE!
HEY, THAT DUDE...
SHUT UP!

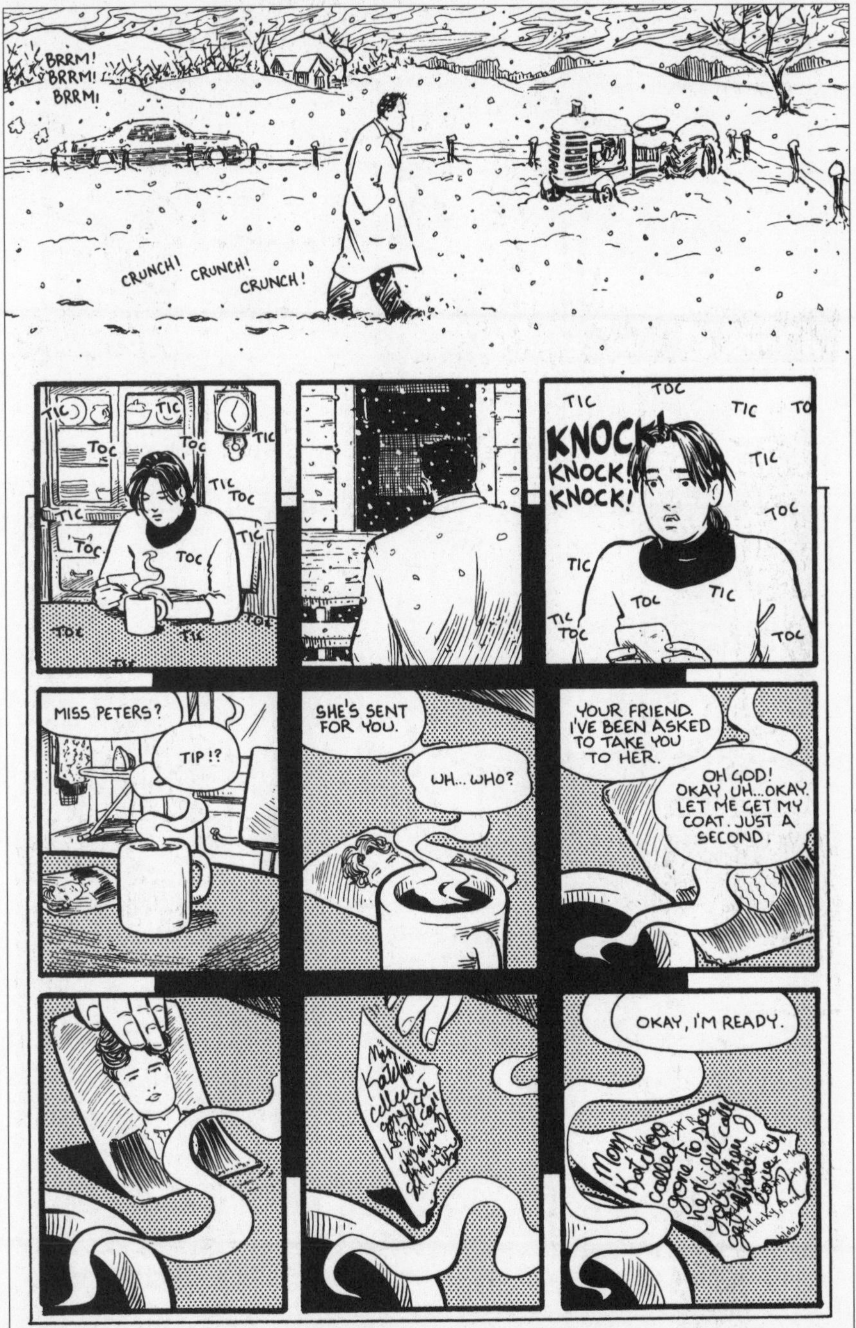
BRRM! BRRM! BRRM!
CRUNCH! CRUNCH! CRUNCH!
TIC TOC TIC TOC TIC TOC
KNOCK! KNOCK! KNOCK!
MISS PETERS?
TIP!?
SHE'S SENT FOR YOU.
WH... WHO?
YOUR FRIEND. I'VE BEEN ASKED TO TAKE YOU TO HER.
OH GOD! OKAY, UH... OKAY. LET ME GET MY COAT. JUST A SECOND.
OKAY, I'M READY.

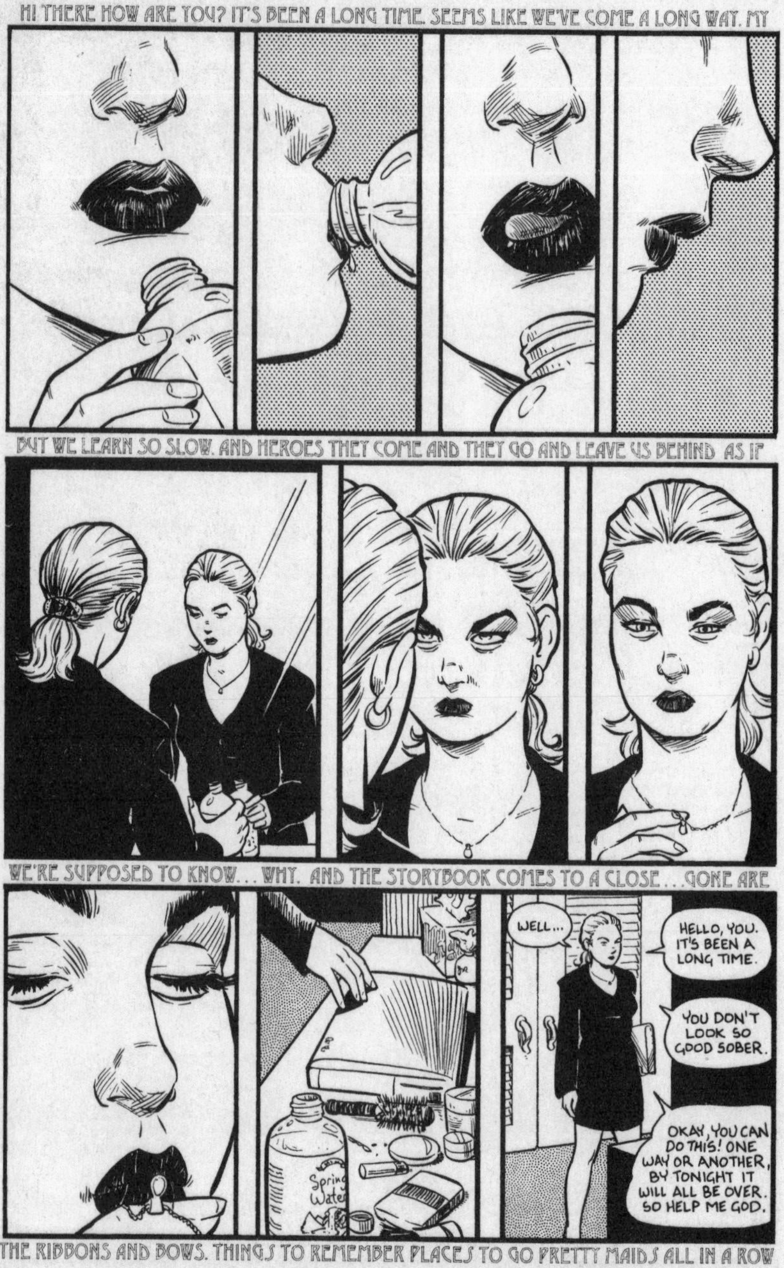
HI THERE HOW ARE YOU? IT'S BEEN A LONG TIME. SEEMS LIKE WE'VE COME A LONG WAY. MY
BUT WE LEARN SO SLOW. AND HEROES THEY COME AND THEY GO AND LEAVE US BEHIND AS IF
WE'RE SUPPOSED TO KNOW... WHY. AND THE STORYBOOK COMES TO A CLOSE... GONE ARE
Spring Water
WELL...
HELLO, YOU. IT'S BEEN A LONG TIME.
YOU DON'T LOOK SO GOOD SOBER.
OKAY, YOU CAN DO THIS! ONE WAY OR ANOTHER, BY TONIGHT IT WILL ALL BE OVER. SO HELP ME GOD.
THE RIBBONS AND BOWS. THINGS TO REMEMBER PLACES TO GO PRETTY MAIDS ALL IN A ROW

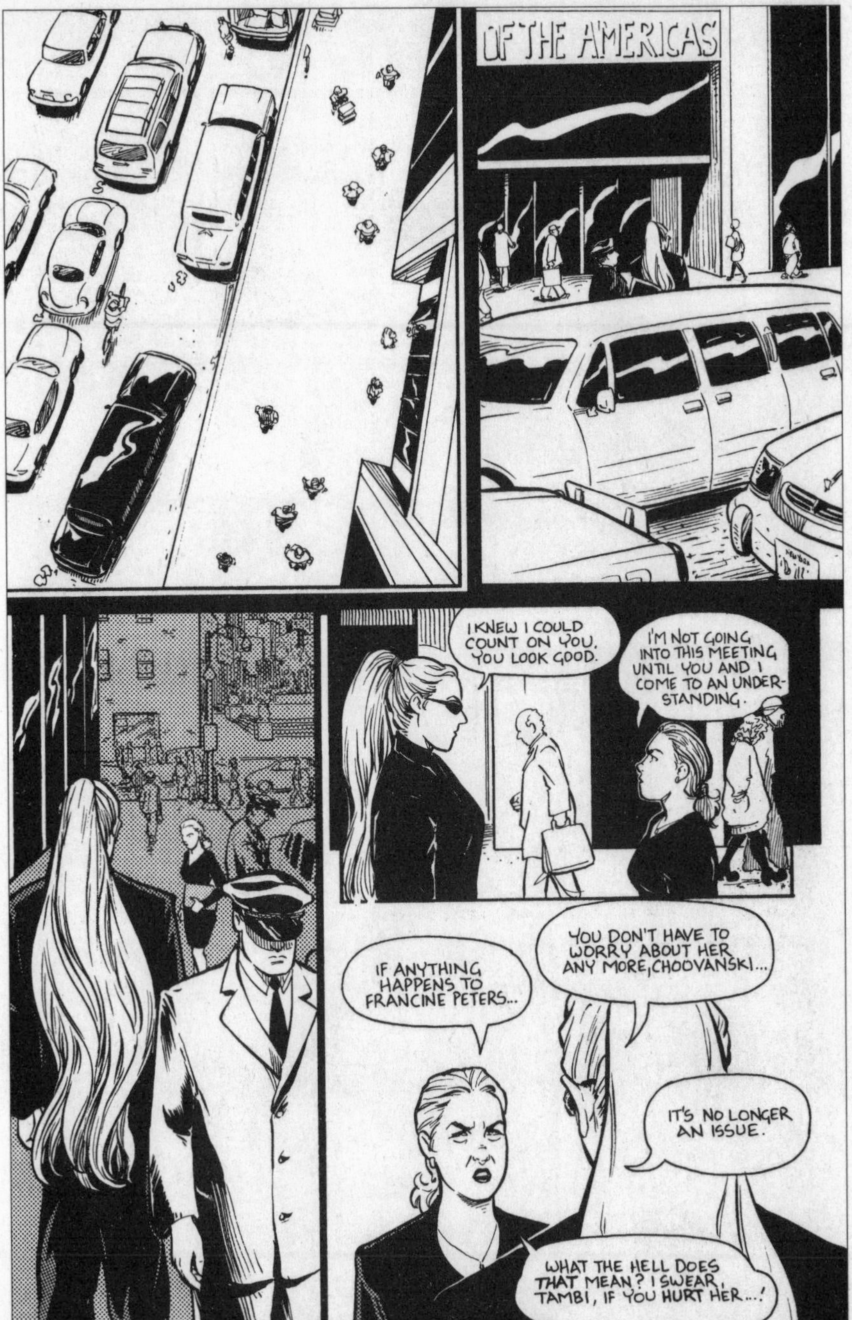
OF THE AMERICAS
I KNEW I COULD COUNT ON YOU. YOU LOOK GOOD.
I'M NOT GOING INTO THIS MEETING UNTIL YOU AND I COME TO AN UNDER-STANDING.
IF ANYTHING HAPPENS TO FRANCINE PETERS...
YOU DON'T HAVE TO WORRY ABOUT HER ANY MORE, CHOOVANSKI...
IT'S NO LONGER AN ISSUE.
WHAT THE HELL DOES THAT MEAN? I SWEAR, TAMBI, IF YOU HURT HER...!

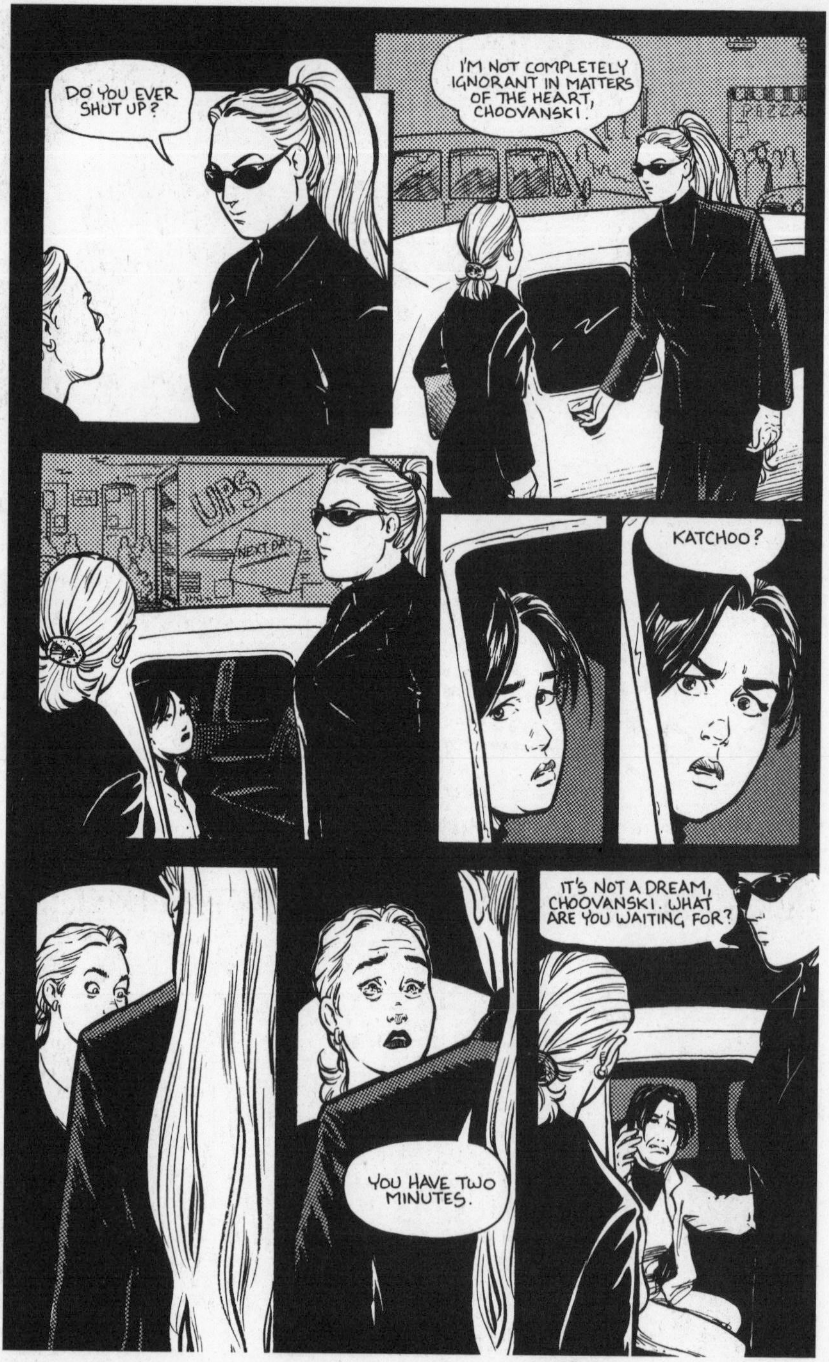
DO YOU EVER SHUT UP?
I'M NOT COMPLETELY IGNORANT IN MATTERS OF THE HEART, CHOOVANSKI.
UPS
NEXT DAY
PIZZA
KATCHOO?
YOU HAVE TWO MINUTES.
IT'S NOT A DREAM, CHOOVANSKI. WHAT ARE YOU WAITING FOR?

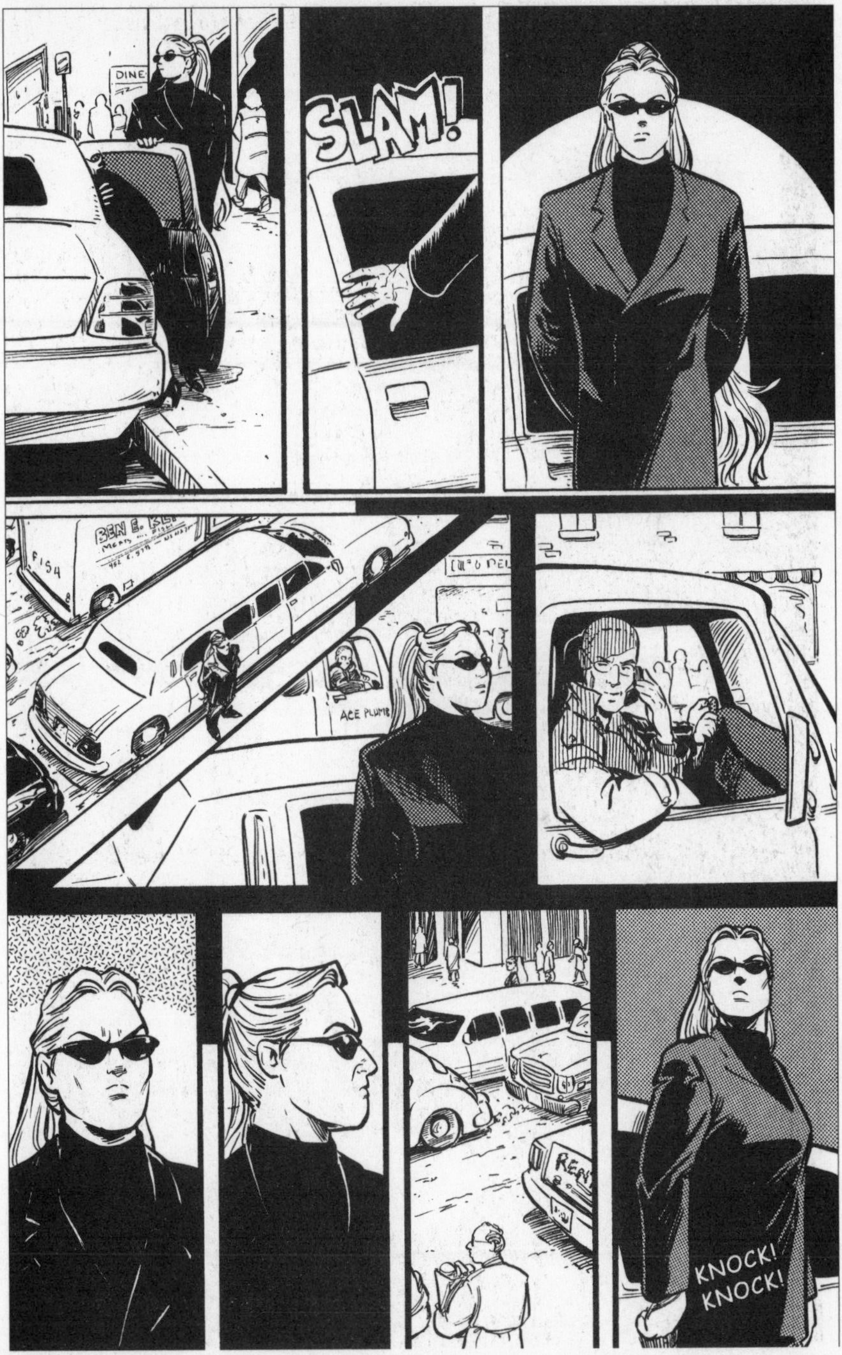
SLAM!
FISH
ACE PLUMB
KNOCK! KNOCK!

The long white limousine pulled slowly to the curb in front of the Bank Of The Americas building in Manhattan's lower east side at precisely two minutes before noon. The driver put the car into park and left the engine idling, waiting for a signal from the rear that his passengers were ready to get out, but no signal came. Five minutes passed. Ten. He would wait until hell froze over if that's what she wanted. Fifteen.

Francine watched her own reflection in the sunglasses of the amazon blonde who sat across from her in the back of the limo. With the exception of a curt introduction at the airport, Tambi had not spoken to her since her arrival this morning in the private jet that brought her from Nashville.

Introductions had not been necessary, Francine recognized her grim host on sight – Tambi Baker, the woman who worked for Darcy Parker's Packard-Yerr corporation. The woman who had arranged to pay for all of David's medical expenses after the plane crash. The woman Katchoo once called a killer. This was her, right? The same woman who had taken her and David by force to Darcy Parker's hotel room that awful night two years ago, then shot Katchoo?

"Aren't you supposed to be in jail?" Francine asked, as they walked to the waiting limousine.

Tambi looked at her, the face stoic behind the sunglasses.

"I mean, kidnapping me and David, shooting Katchoo... I thought you were in jail."

"You're thinking of someone else."

"Huh. She sure looked like you."

Francine thought she saw a slight twitch at the corner of the mouth but the face remained expressionless. Tambi held the door for her and Francine got in. Something was different about this woman, but too much time had passed since that night to be sure. Still, how many long haired, bleached-blonde, body builder killer babes could there be in the world?

Conversation had been useless after that. Francine's questions were met with stony silence. She resolved to be patient and go with it, suppressing the urge to roll down the window and scream for help because salvation might keep her from Katchoo.

"Wait here," Tambi said suddenly. In one quick move she was out of the car, closing the door firmly behind her. Francine turned around to see another limousine had pulled up to the curb behind them. It was difficult to see clearly through the dark tinted glass but Francine watched as a small, slender woman emerged and approached the waiting Tambi. They spoke a moment before Tambi reached over and opened the car door. Francine looked up at Tambi to see if this was her cue to get out, but Tambi seemed to be waiting on the other woman.

Turning her attention, Francine saw an elegant woman in an expensive dress and matching shoes. Her thick blonde hair was pulled back tight, her mouth striking in dark, rose colored lipstick that highlighted the delicate pale of her skin. Makeup failed to hide dark circles and heavy bags that seemed to anchor sad green eyes.

Francine's first thought was, Darcy Parker. Or at least, how she remembered Mrs. Parker. But, she was dead. Suicide. David's inheritance. And brunette. This blonde... who recognized her...

Francine's heart stopped. "Katchoo?" she said in disbelief.

Katchoo's face turned white, her mouth open in disbelief.

"You have two minutes," said Tambi.

Francine choked back tears and impulsively held her arms out to the soul mate she had not seen in over a year.

"It's not a dream, Choovanski. What are you waiting for?" Tambi said.

Katchoo blinked in disbelief. Stepping into the dream, Katchoo leaned over and fell into waiting arms that held her tight and wouldn't let go. The car door shut behind them, sealing them off from the outside world.

Francine sobbed uncontrollably into Katchoo's shoulder. "I thought I'd never see you again," she said.

Only then, when she heard the familiar southern drawl, and felt the soft crush of her friend's embrace, did Katchoo realize the dream was real. She tried to speak, to offer the apology she'd been waiting a year to deliver, but no words came. She could only close her eyes and hold on for dear life. The faint aroma of baby powder tickled her nose, making Katchoo smile. "I'm home" she whispered hoarsely.

No more words were spoken until a sharp knock came on the window.

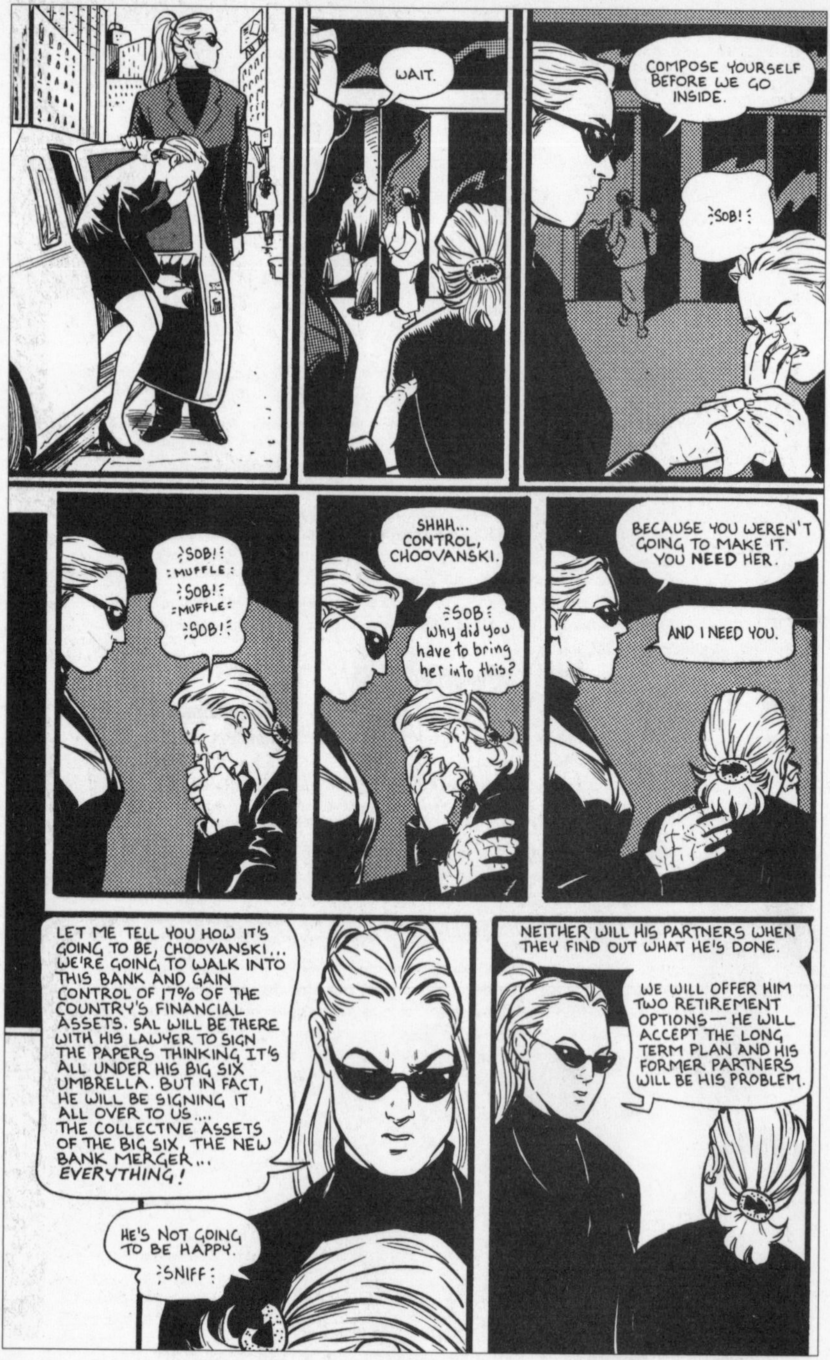
WAIT.
COMPOSE YOURSELF BEFORE WE GO INSIDE.
SOB!
SOB! MUFFLE SOB! MUFFLE SOB!
SHHH... CONTROL, CHOOVANSKI.
SOB why did you have to bring her into this?
BECAUSE YOU WEREN'T GOING TO MAKE IT. YOU NEED HER.
AND I NEED YOU.
LET ME TELL YOU HOW IT'S GOING TO BE, CHOOVANSKI... WE'RE GOING TO WALK INTO THIS BANK AND GAIN CONTROL OF 17% OF THE COUNTRY'S FINANCIAL ASSETS. SAL WILL BE THERE WITH HIS LAWYER TO SIGN THE PAPERS THINKING IT'S ALL UNDER HIS BIG SIX UMBRELLA. BUT IN FACT, HE WILL BE SIGNING IT ALL OVER TO US.... THE COLLECTIVE ASSETS OF THE BIG SIX, THE NEW BANK MERGER... EVERYTHING!
HE'S NOT GOING TO BE HAPPY.
SNIFF
NEITHER WILL HIS PARTNERS WHEN THEY FIND OUT WHAT HE'S DONE.
WE WILL OFFER HIM TWO RETIREMENT OPTIONS— HE WILL ACCEPT THE LONG TERM PLAN AND HIS FORMER PARTNERS WILL BE HIS PROBLEM.

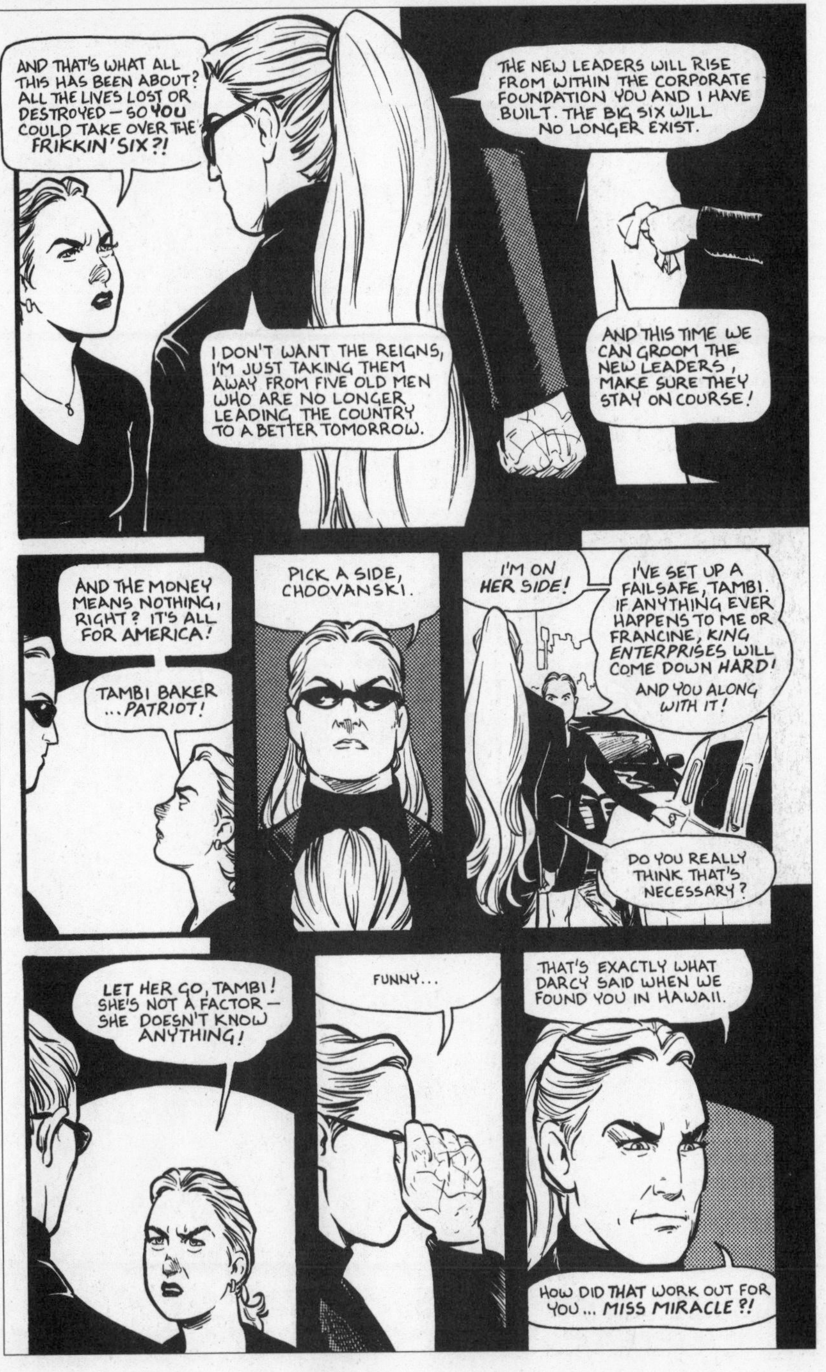
AND THAT'S WHAT ALL THIS HAS BEEN ABOUT? ALL THE LIVES LOST OR DESTROYED — SO YOU COULD TAKE OVER THE FRIKKIN' SIX?!
THE NEW LEADERS WILL RISE FROM WITHIN THE CORPORATE FOUNDATION YOU AND I HAVE BUILT. THE BIG SIX WILL NO LONGER EXIST.
I DON'T WANT THE REIGNS, I'M JUST TAKING THEM AWAY FROM FIVE OLD MEN WHO ARE NO LONGER LEADING THE COUNTRY TO A BETTER TOMORROW.
AND THIS TIME WE CAN GROOM THE NEW LEADERS, MAKE SURE THEY STAY ON COURSE!
AND THE MONEY MEANS NOTHING, RIGHT? IT'S ALL FOR AMERICA!
TAMBI BAKER ...PATRIOT!
PICK A SIDE, CHOOVANSKI.
I'M ON HER SIDE!
I'VE SET UP A FAILSAFE, TAMBI. IF ANYTHING EVER HAPPENS TO ME OR FRANCINE, KING ENTERPRISES WILL COME DOWN HARD!
AND YOU ALONG WITH IT!
DO YOU REALLY THINK THAT'S NECESSARY?
LET HER GO, TAMBI! SHE'S NOT A FACTOR — SHE DOESN'T KNOW ANYTHING!
FUNNY...
THAT'S EXACTLY WHAT DARCY SAID WHEN WE FOUND YOU IN HAWAII.
HOW DID THAT WORK OUT FOR YOU... MISS MIRACLE?!

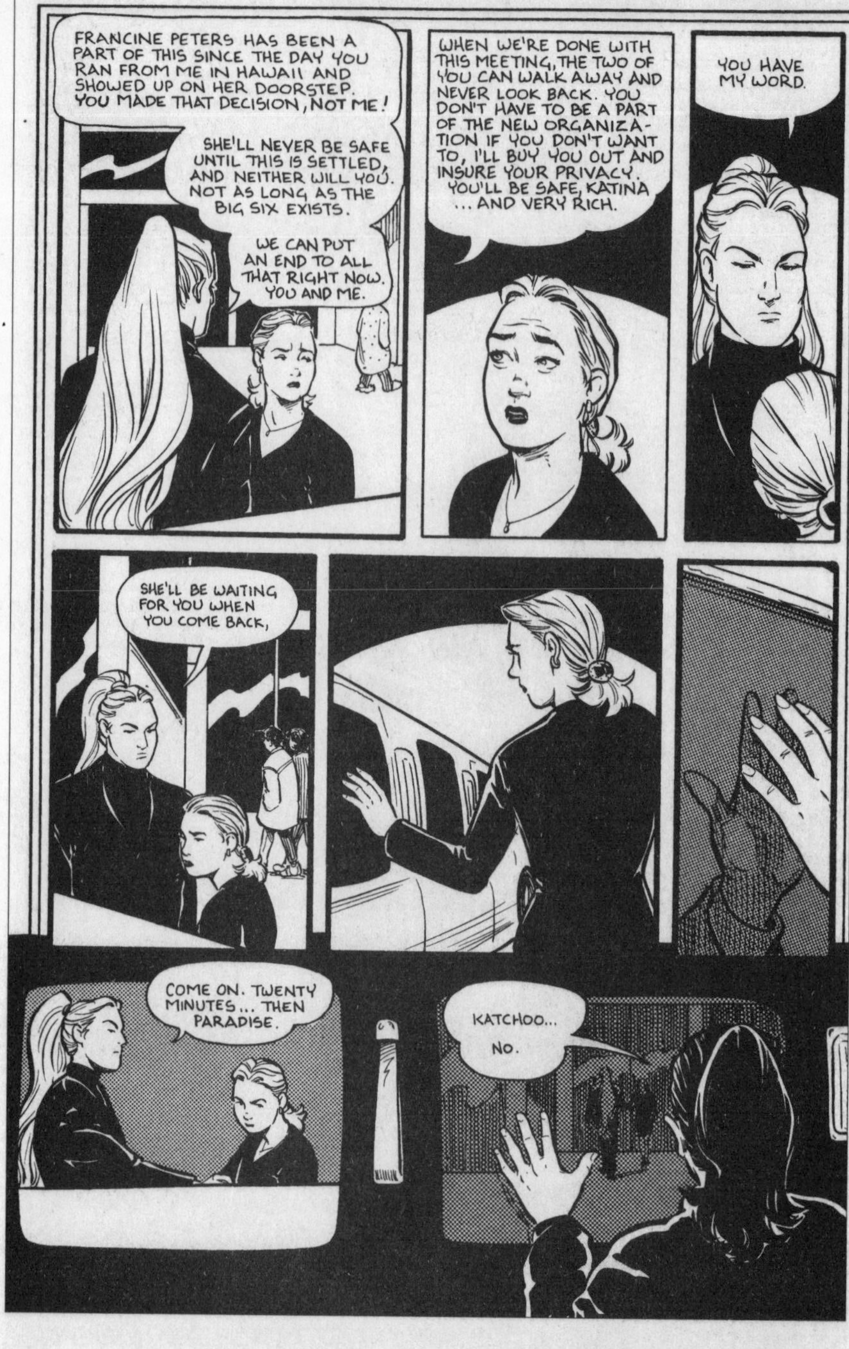
FRANCINE PETERS HAS BEEN A PART OF THIS SINCE THE DAY YOU RAN FROM ME IN HAWAII AND SHOWED UP ON HER DOORSTEP. YOU MADE THAT DECISION, NOT ME!
SHE'LL NEVER BE SAFE UNTIL THIS IS SETTLED, AND NEITHER WILL YOU. NOT AS LONG AS THE BIG SIX EXISTS.
WE CAN PUT AN END TO ALL THAT RIGHT NOW. YOU AND ME.
WHEN WE'RE DONE WITH THIS MEETING, THE TWO OF YOU CAN WALK AWAY AND NEVER LOOK BACK. YOU DON'T HAVE TO BE A PART OF THE NEW ORGANIZATION IF YOU DON'T WANT TO, I'LL BUY YOU OUT AND INSURE YOUR PRIVACY. YOU'LL BE SAFE, KATINA ... AND VERY RICH.
YOU HAVE MY WORD.
SHE'LL BE WAITING FOR YOU WHEN YOU COME BACK,
COME ON. TWENTY MINUTES ... THEN PARADISE.
KATCHOO... NO.

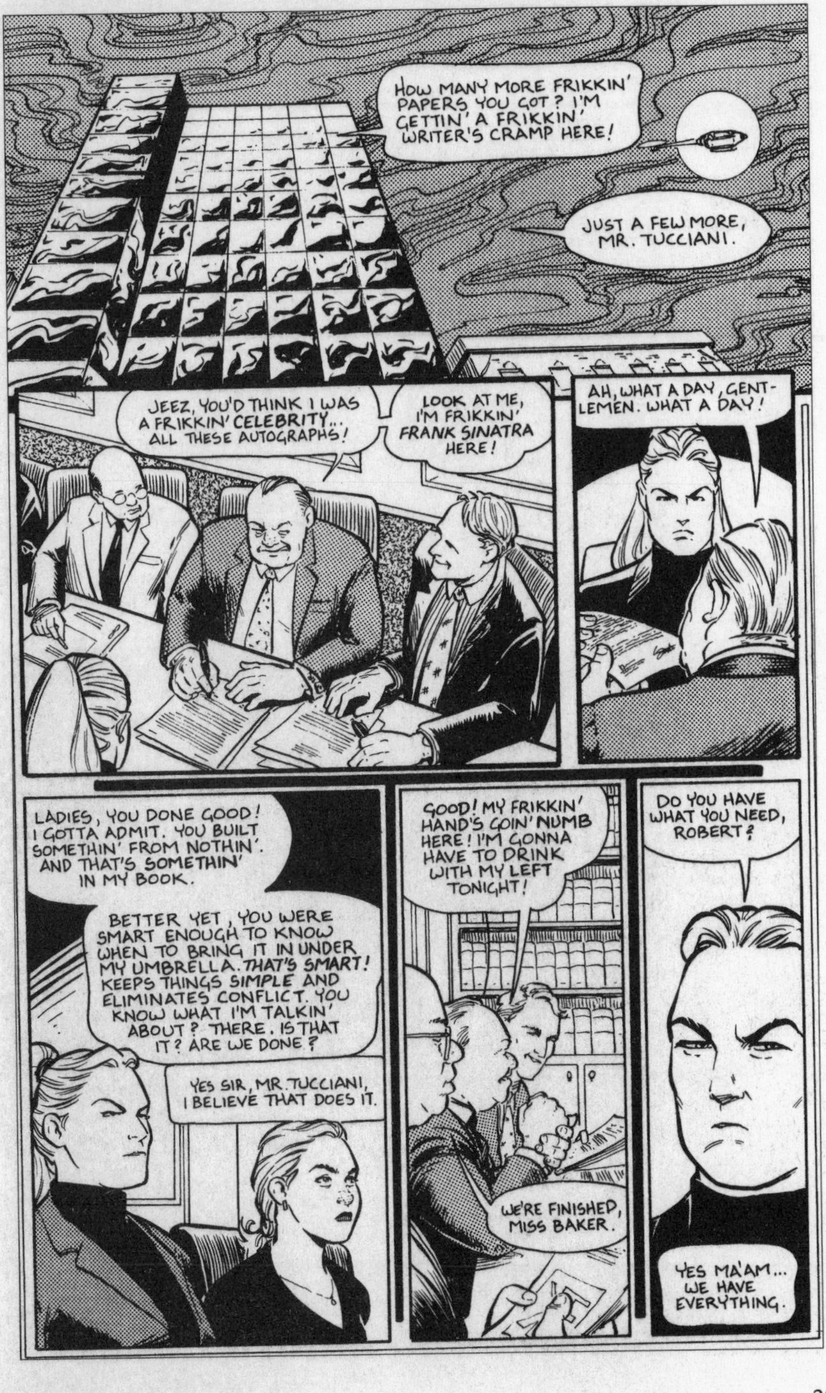
HOW MANY MORE FRIKKIN' PAPERS YOU GOT? I'M GETTIN' A FRIKKIN' WRITER'S CRAMP HERE!
JUST A FEW MORE, MR. TUCCIANI.
JEEZ, YOU'D THINK I WAS A FRIKKIN' CELEBRITY... ALL THESE AUTOGRAPHS!
LOOK AT ME, I'M FRIKKIN' FRANK SINATRA HERE!
AH, WHAT A DAY, GENTLEMEN. WHAT A DAY!
LADIES, YOU DONE GOOD! I GOTTA ADMIT. YOU BUILT SOMETHIN' FROM NOTHIN'. AND THAT'S SOMETHIN' IN MY BOOK.
BETTER YET, YOU WERE SMART ENOUGH TO KNOW WHEN TO BRING IT IN UNDER MY UMBRELLA. THAT'S SMART! KEEPS THINGS SIMPLE AND ELIMINATES CONFLICT. YOU KNOW WHAT I'M TALKIN' ABOUT? THERE. IS THAT IT? ARE WE DONE?
YES SIR, MR. TUCCIANI, I BELIEVE THAT DOES IT.
GOOD! MY FRIKKIN' HAND'S GOIN' NUMB HERE! I'M GONNA HAVE TO DRINK WITH MY LEFT TONIGHT!
WE'RE FINISHED, MISS BAKER.
DO YOU HAVE WHAT YOU NEED, ROBERT?
YES MA'AM... WE HAVE EVERYTHING.

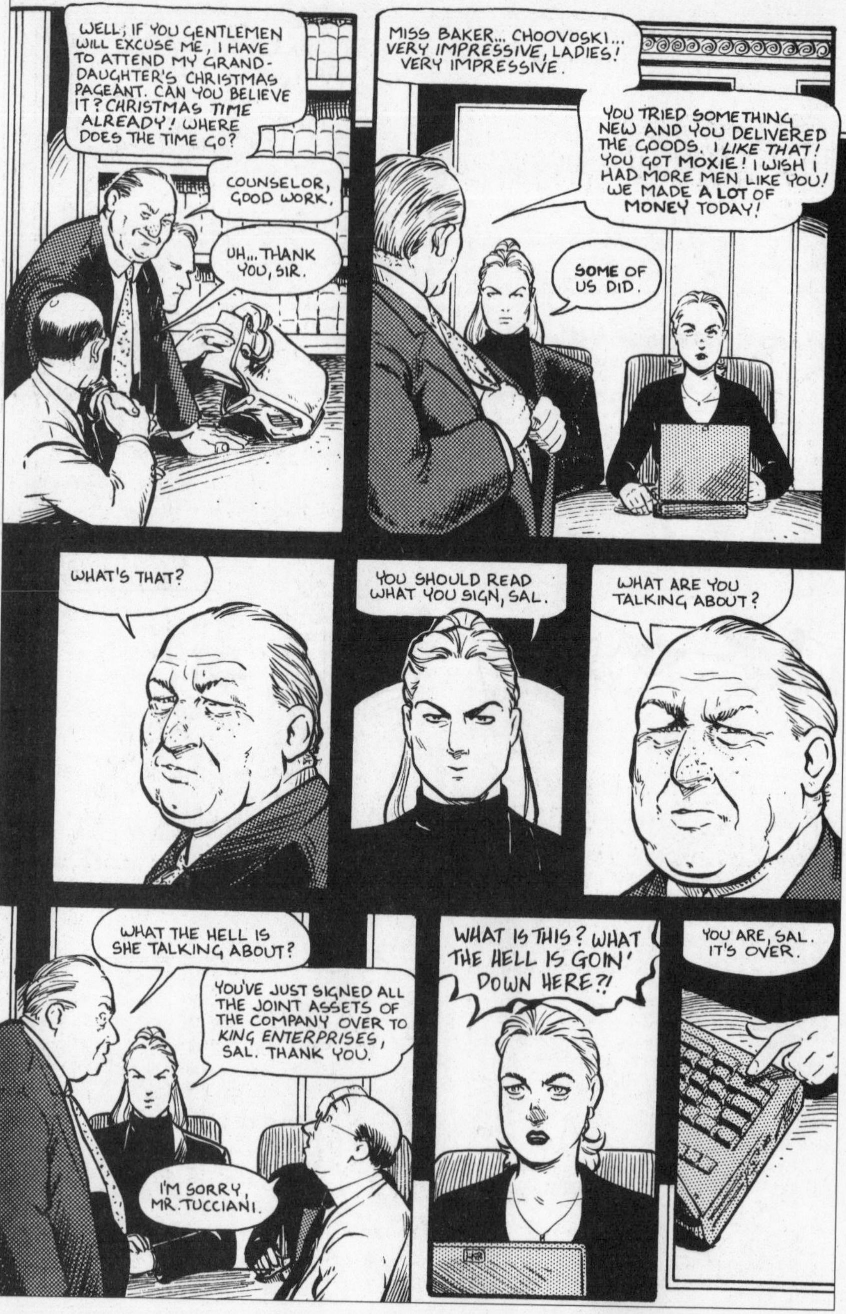

WELL, IF YOU GENTLEMEN WILL EXCUSE ME, I HAVE TO ATTEND MY GRAND-DAUGHTER'S CHRISTMAS PAGEANT. CAN YOU BELIEVE IT? CHRISTMAS TIME ALREADY! WHERE DOES THE TIME GO?
COUNSELOR, GOOD WORK.
UH... THANK YOU, SIR.
MISS BAKER... CHOOVOSKI... VERY IMPRESSIVE, LADIES! VERY IMPRESSIVE.
YOU TRIED SOMETHING NEW AND YOU DELIVERED THE GOODS. I LIKE THAT! YOU GOT MOXIE! I WISH I HAD MORE MEN LIKE YOU! WE MADE A LOT OF MONEY TODAY!
SOME OF US DID.
WHAT'S THAT?
YOU SHOULD READ WHAT YOU SIGN, SAL.
WHAT ARE YOU TALKING ABOUT?
WHAT THE HELL IS SHE TALKING ABOUT?
YOU'VE JUST SIGNED ALL THE JOINT ASSETS OF THE COMPANY OVER TO KING ENTERPRISES, SAL. THANK YOU.
I'M SORRY, MR. TUCCIANI.
WHAT IS THIS? WHAT THE HELL IS GOIN' DOWN HERE?!
YOU ARE, SAL. IT'S OVER.

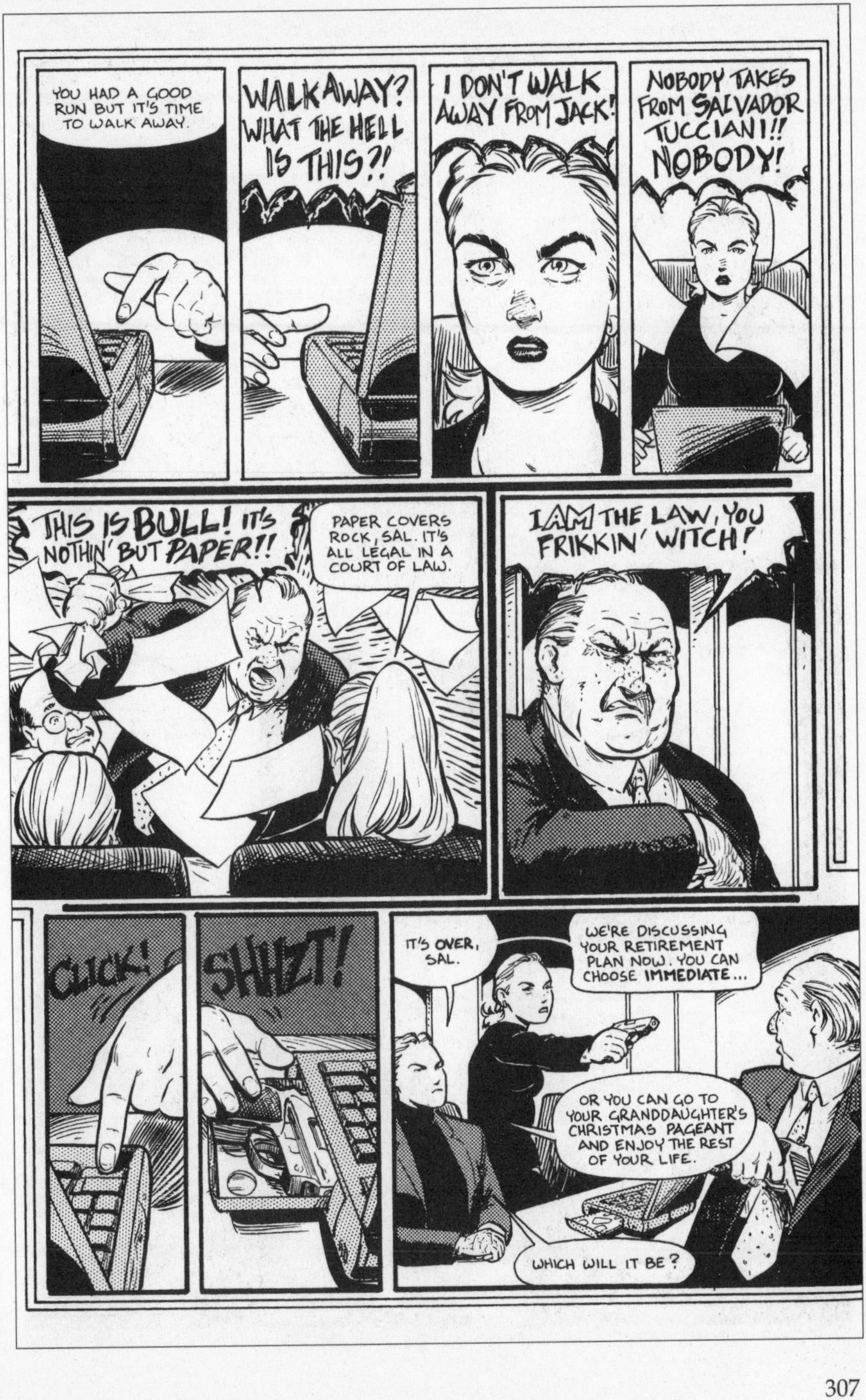
YOU HAD A GOOD RUN BUT IT'S TIME TO WALK AWAY.
WALKAWAY? WHAT THE HELL IS THIS?!
I DON'T WALK AWAY FROM JACK!
NOBODY TAKES FROM SALVADOR TUCCIANI!! NOBODY!
THIS IS BULL! IT'S NOTHIN' BUT PAPER!!
PAPER COVERS ROCK, SAL. IT'S ALL LEGAL IN A COURT OF LAW.
I AM THE LAW, YOU FRIKKIN' WITCH!
CLICK!
SHHZT!
IT'S OVER, SAL.
WE'RE DISCUSSING YOUR RETIREMENT PLAN NOW. YOU CAN CHOOSE IMMEDIATE...
OR YOU CAN GO TO YOUR GRANDDAUGHTER'S CHRISTMAS PAGEANT AND ENJOY THE REST OF YOUR LIFE.
WHICH WILL IT BE?

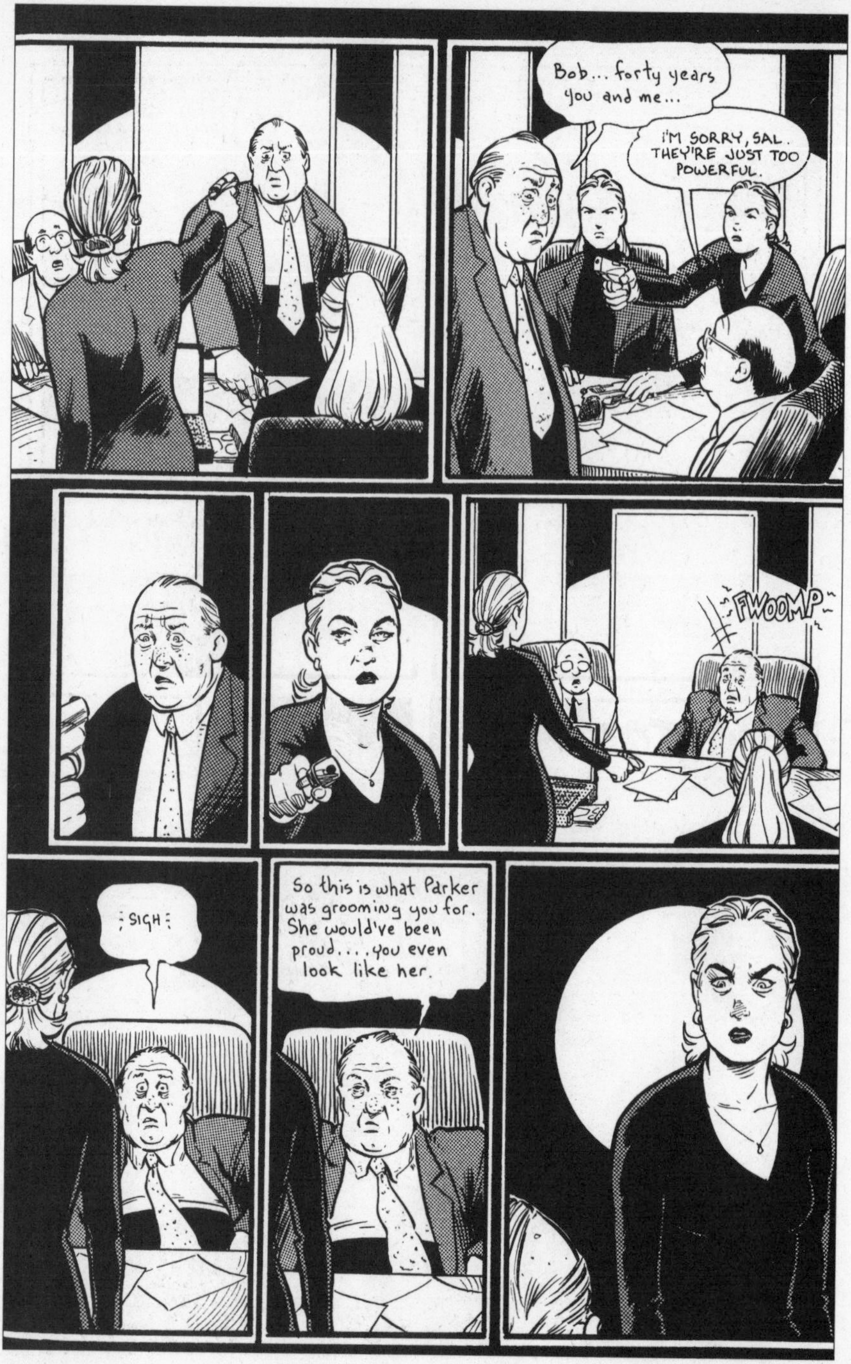
Bob... forty years you and me...
I'M SORRY, SAL. THEY'RE JUST TOO POWERFUL.
FWOOMP
SIGH
So this is what Parker was grooming you for. She would've been proud....you even look like her.

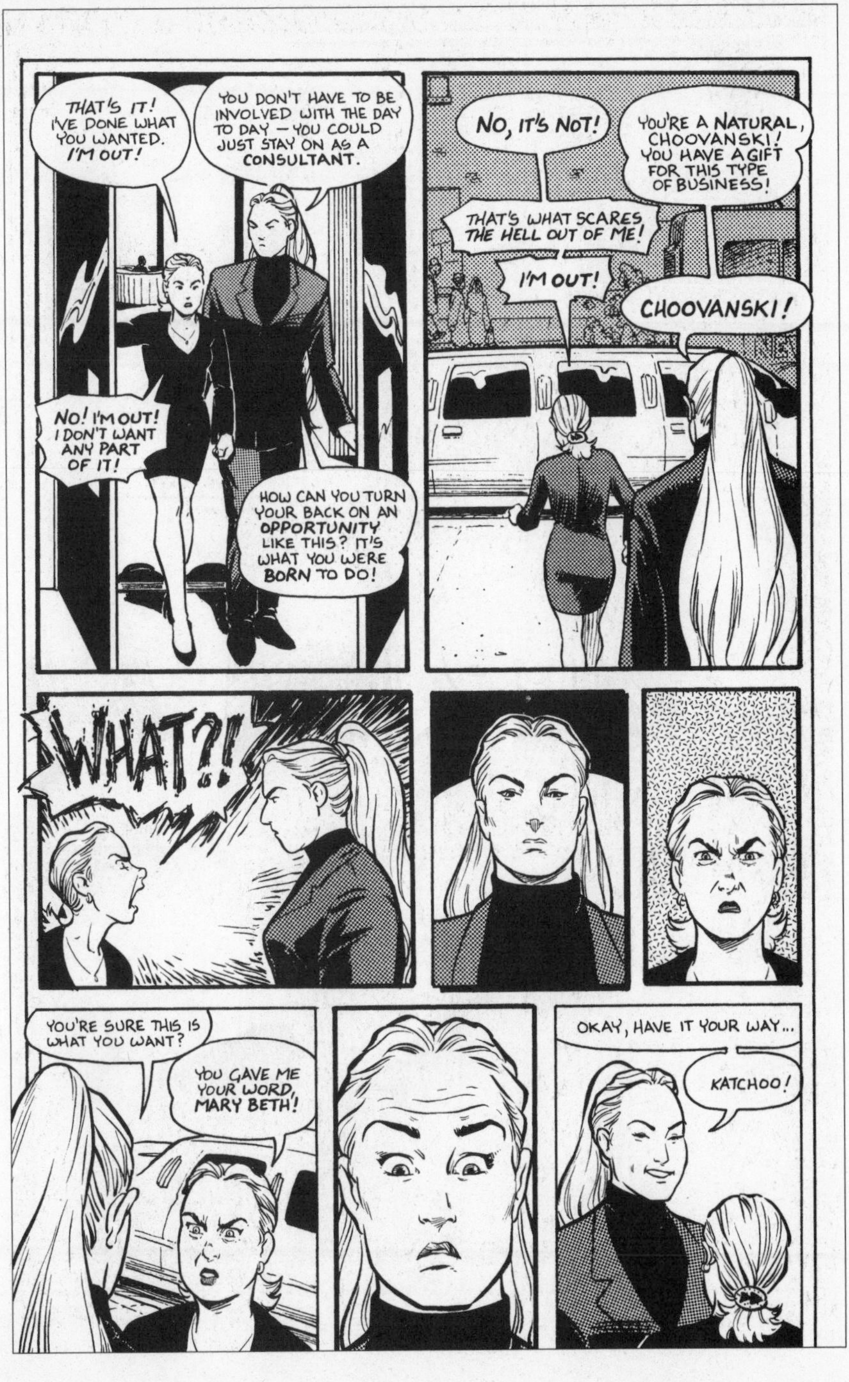
THAT'S IT! I'VE DONE WHAT YOU WANTED. I'M OUT!
YOU DON'T HAVE TO BE INVOLVED WITH THE DAY TO DAY — YOU COULD JUST STAY ON AS A CONSULTANT.
NO! I'M OUT! I DON'T WANT ANY PART OF IT!
HOW CAN YOU TURN YOUR BACK ON AN OPPORTUNITY LIKE THIS? IT'S WHAT YOU WERE BORN TO DO!
NO, IT'S NOT!
YOU'RE A NATURAL, CHOOVANSKI! YOU HAVE A GIFT FOR THIS TYPE OF BUSINESS!
THAT'S WHAT SCARES THE HELL OUT OF ME!
I'M OUT!
CHOOVANSKI!
WHAT?!
YOU'RE SURE THIS IS WHAT YOU WANT?
YOU GAVE ME YOUR WORD, MARY BETH!
OKAY, HAVE IT YOUR WAY...
KATCHOO!

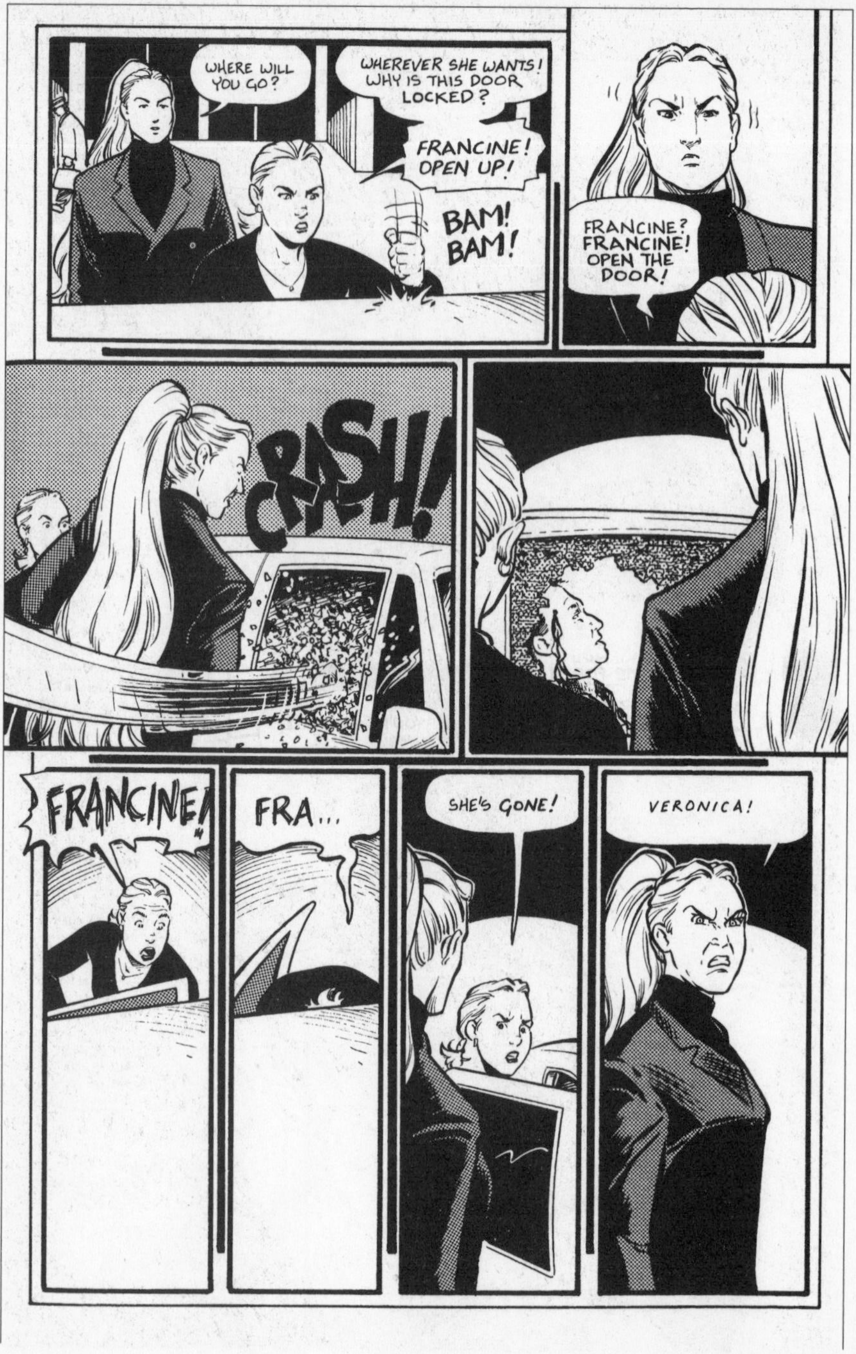
WHERE WILL YOU GO?
WHEREVER SHE WANTS! WHY IS THIS DOOR LOCKED?
FRANCINE! OPEN UP!
BAM! BAM!
FRANCINE? FRANCINE! OPEN THE DOOR!
CRASH!
FRANCINE!
FRA...
SHE'S GONE!
VERONICA!

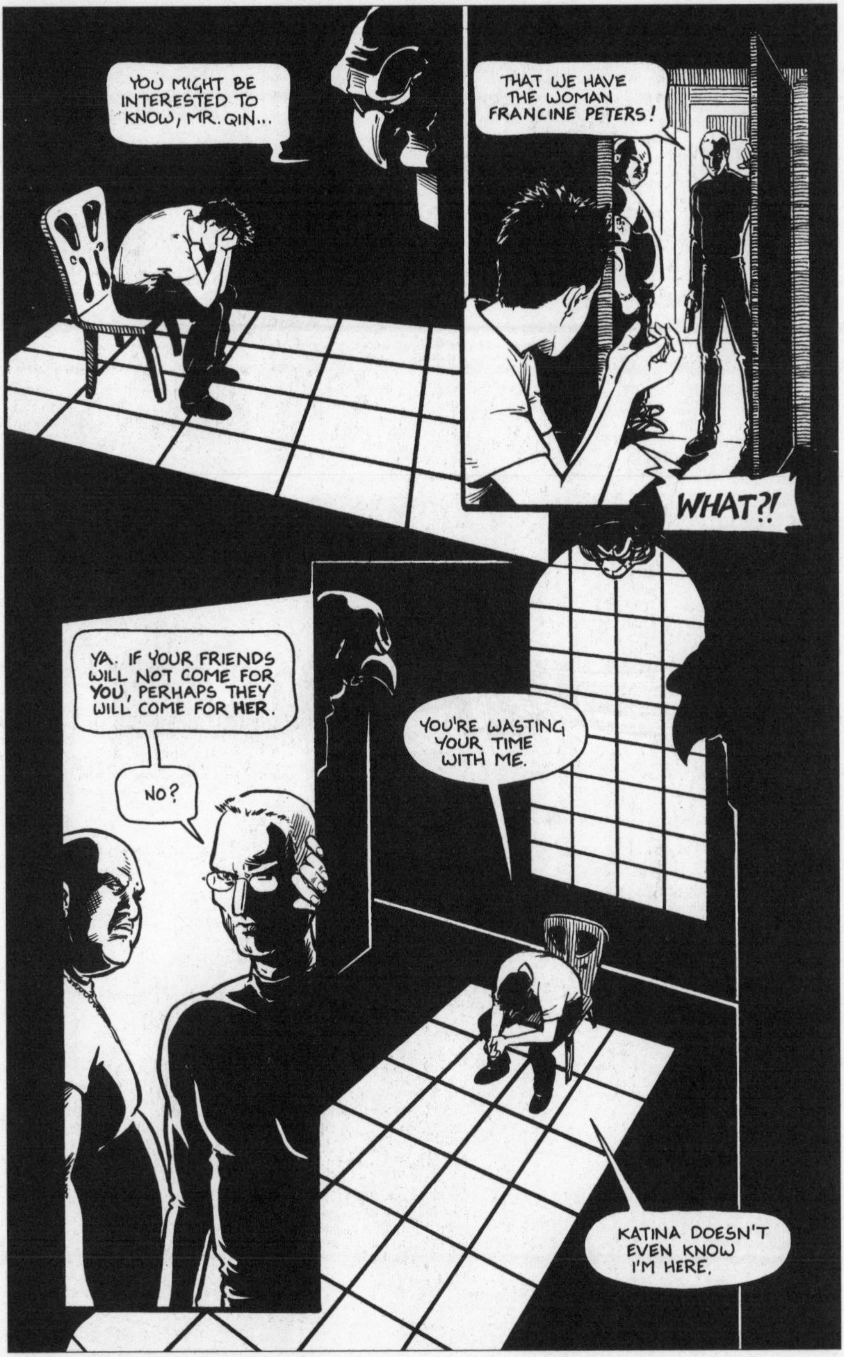
YOU MIGHT BE INTERESTED TO KNOW, MR. QIN...
THAT WE HAVE THE WOMAN FRANCINE PETERS!
WHAT?!
YA. IF YOUR FRIENDS WILL NOT COME FOR YOU, PERHAPS THEY WILL COME FOR HER.
NO?
YOU'RE WASTING YOUR TIME WITH ME.
KATINA DOESN'T EVEN KNOW I'M HERE.

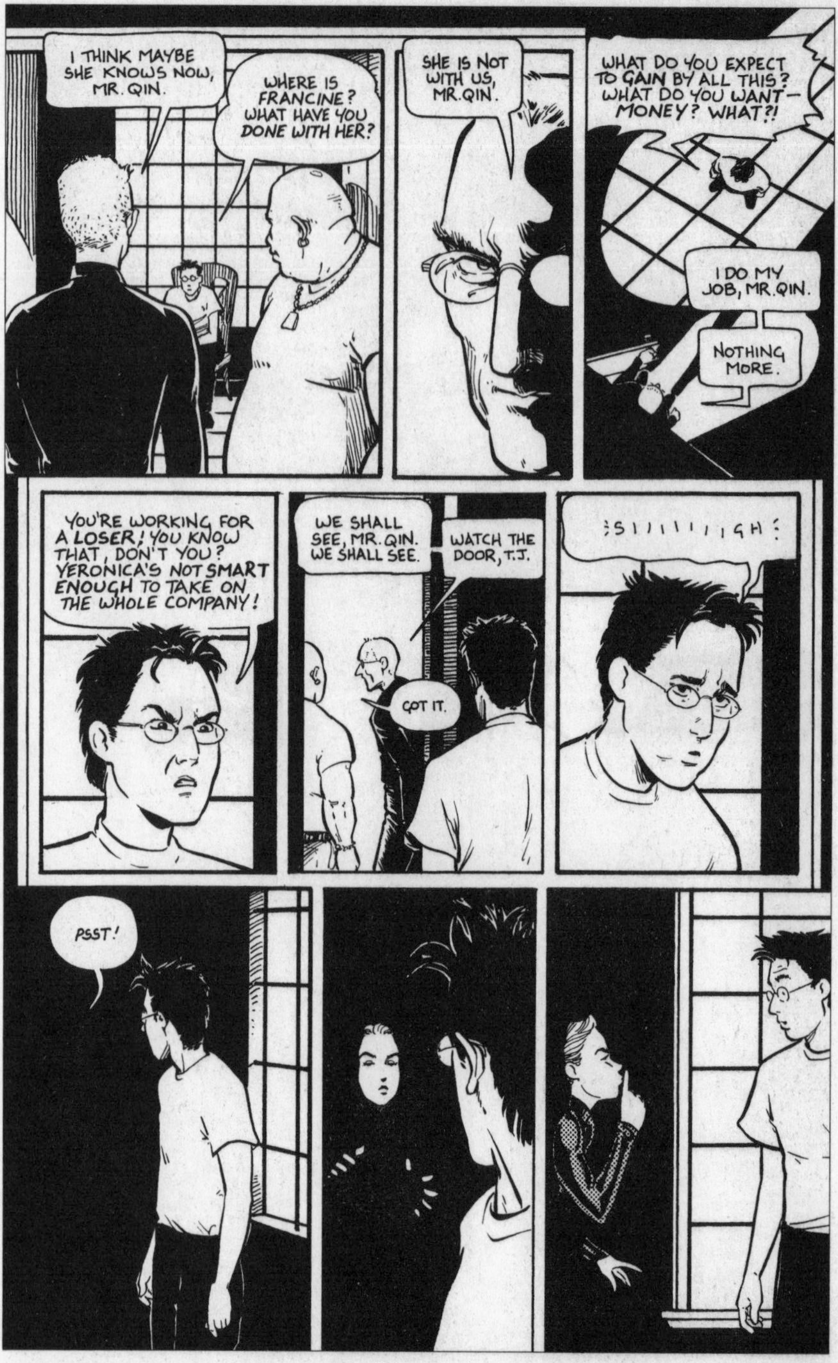
I THINK MAYBE SHE KNOWS NOW, MR. QIN.
WHERE IS FRANCINE? WHAT HAVE YOU DONE WITH HER?
SHE IS NOT WITH US, MR. QIN.
WHAT DO YOU EXPECT TO GAIN BY ALL THIS? WHAT DO YOU WANT— MONEY? WHAT?!
I DO MY JOB, MR. QIN.
NOTHING MORE.
YOU'RE WORKING FOR A LOSER! YOU KNOW THAT, DON'T YOU? VERONICA'S NOT SMART ENOUGH TO TAKE ON THE WHOLE COMPANY!
WE SHALL SEE, MR. QIN. WE SHALL SEE.
WATCH THE DOOR, T.J.
GOT IT.
SIIIIIIIGH
PSST!

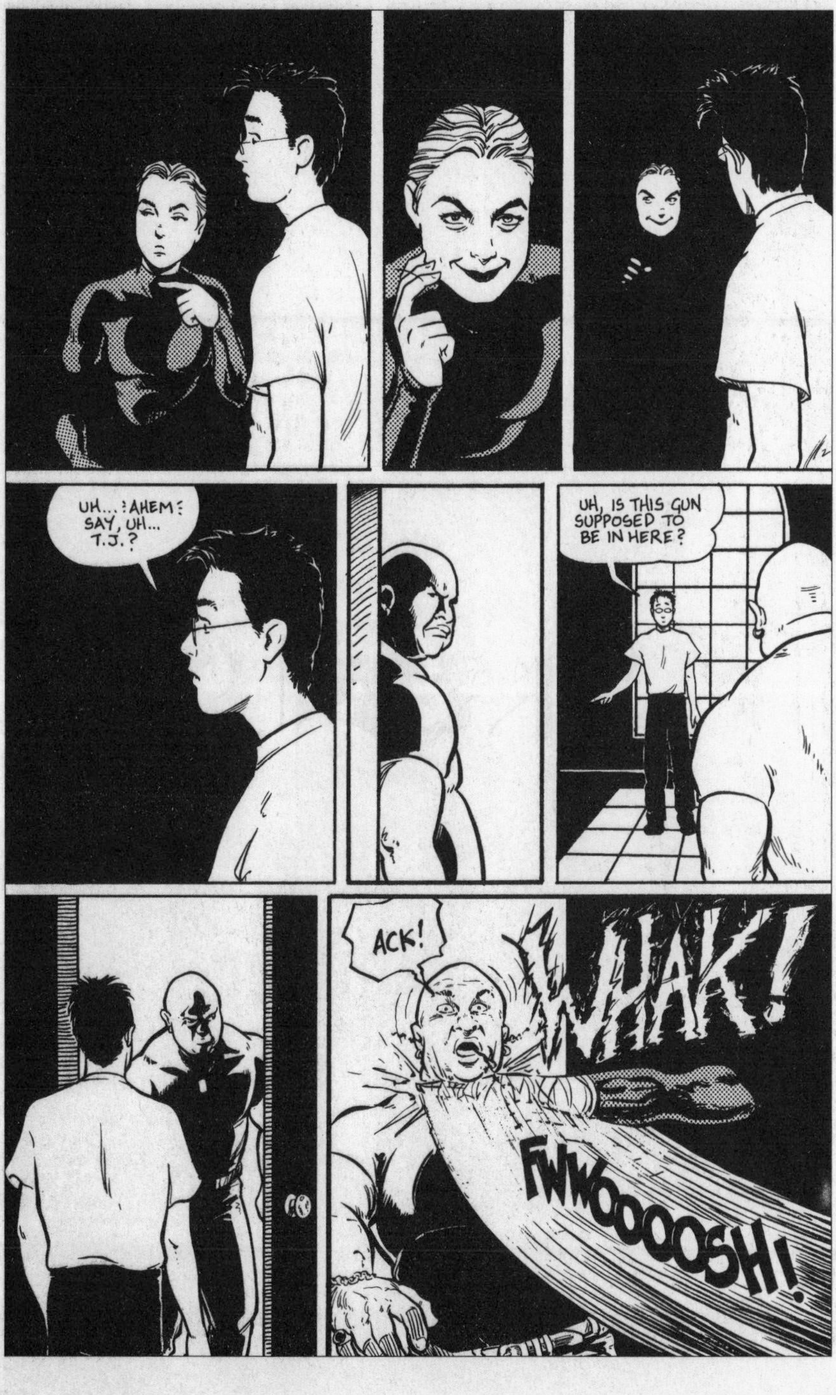
UH... AHEM SAY, UH... T.J.?
UH, IS THIS GUN SUPPOSED TO BE IN HERE?
ACK!
WHAK!
FWWOOOOOSH!

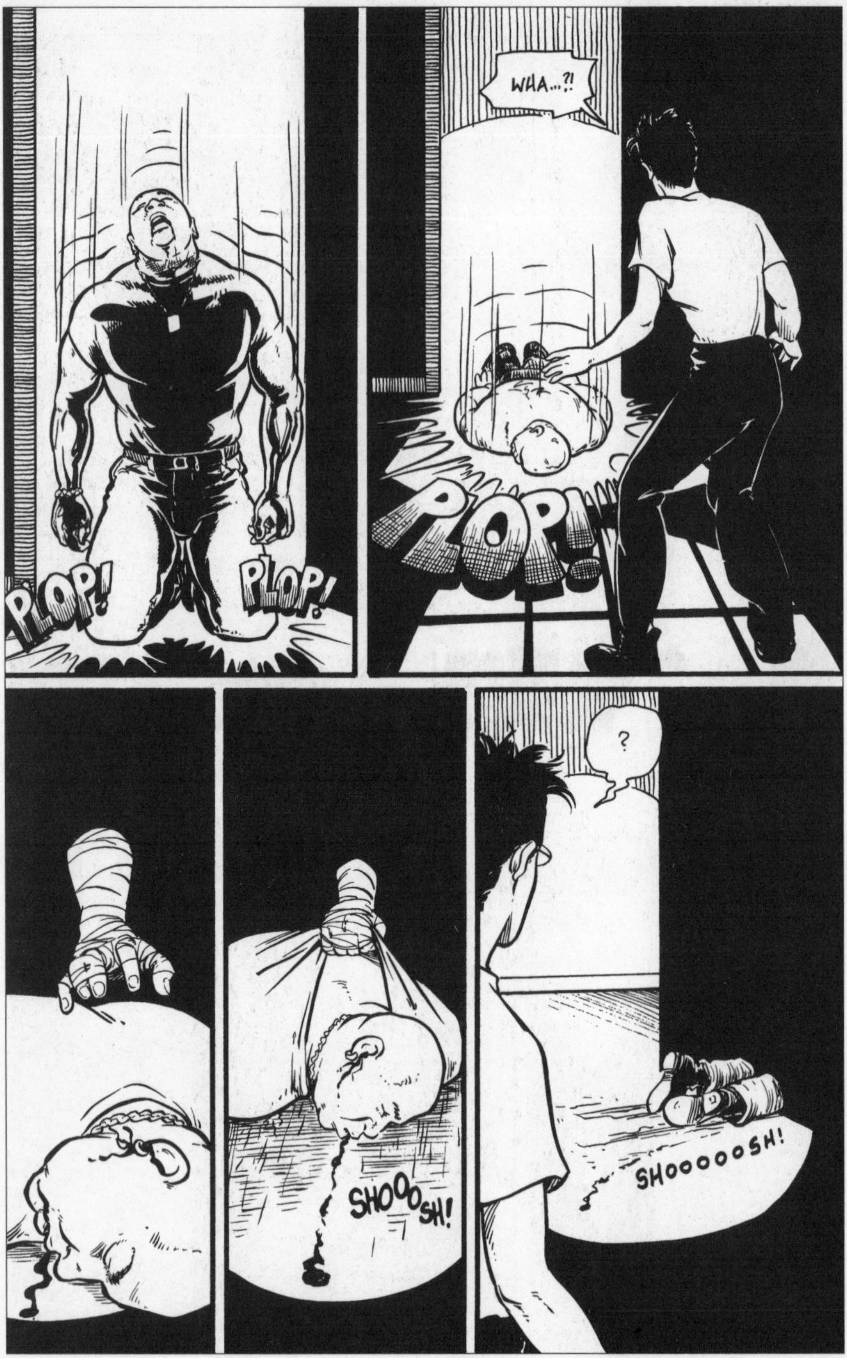
PLOP!
PLOP!
WHA...?!
PLOP!
?
SHOOOOSH!
SHOOOOOOSH!

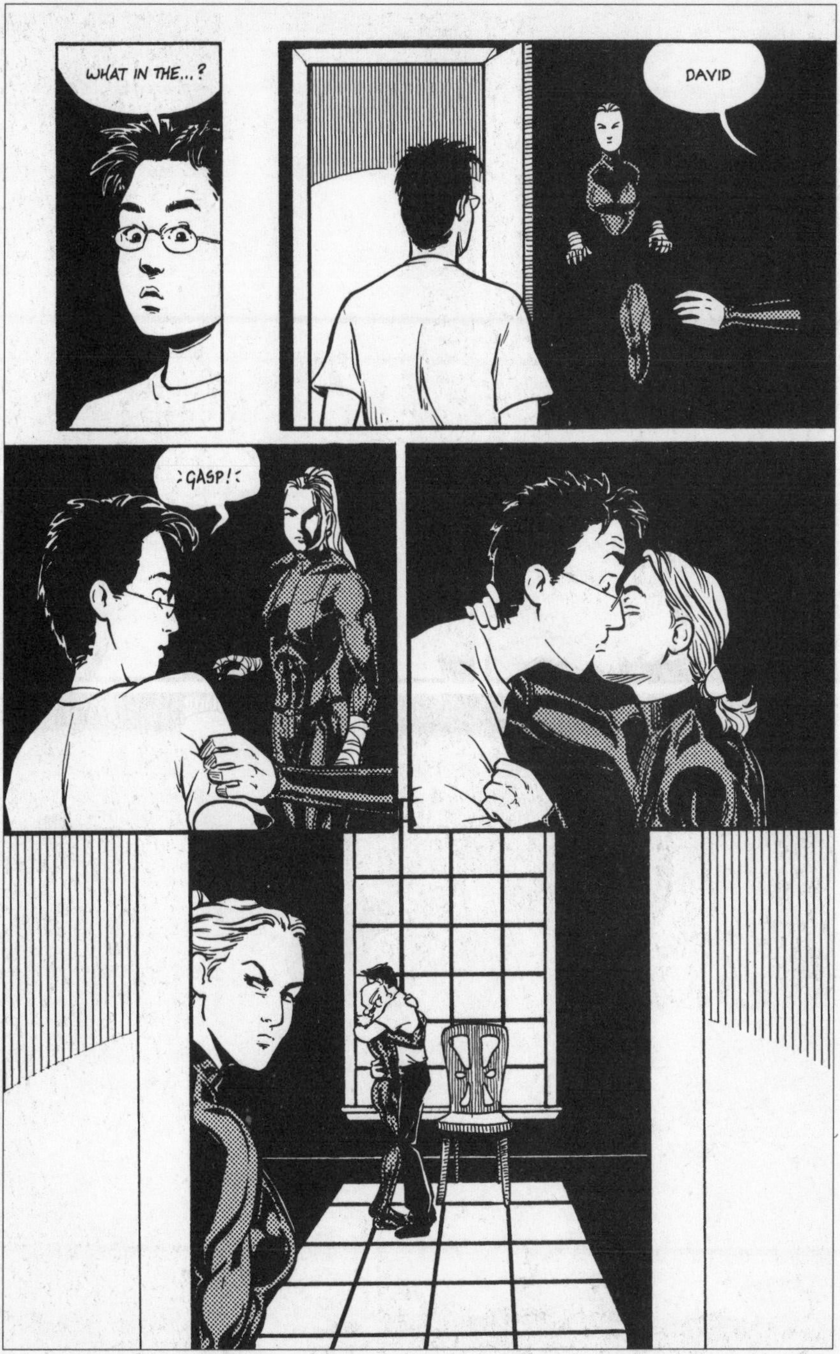
WHAT IN THE...?
DAVID
GASP!

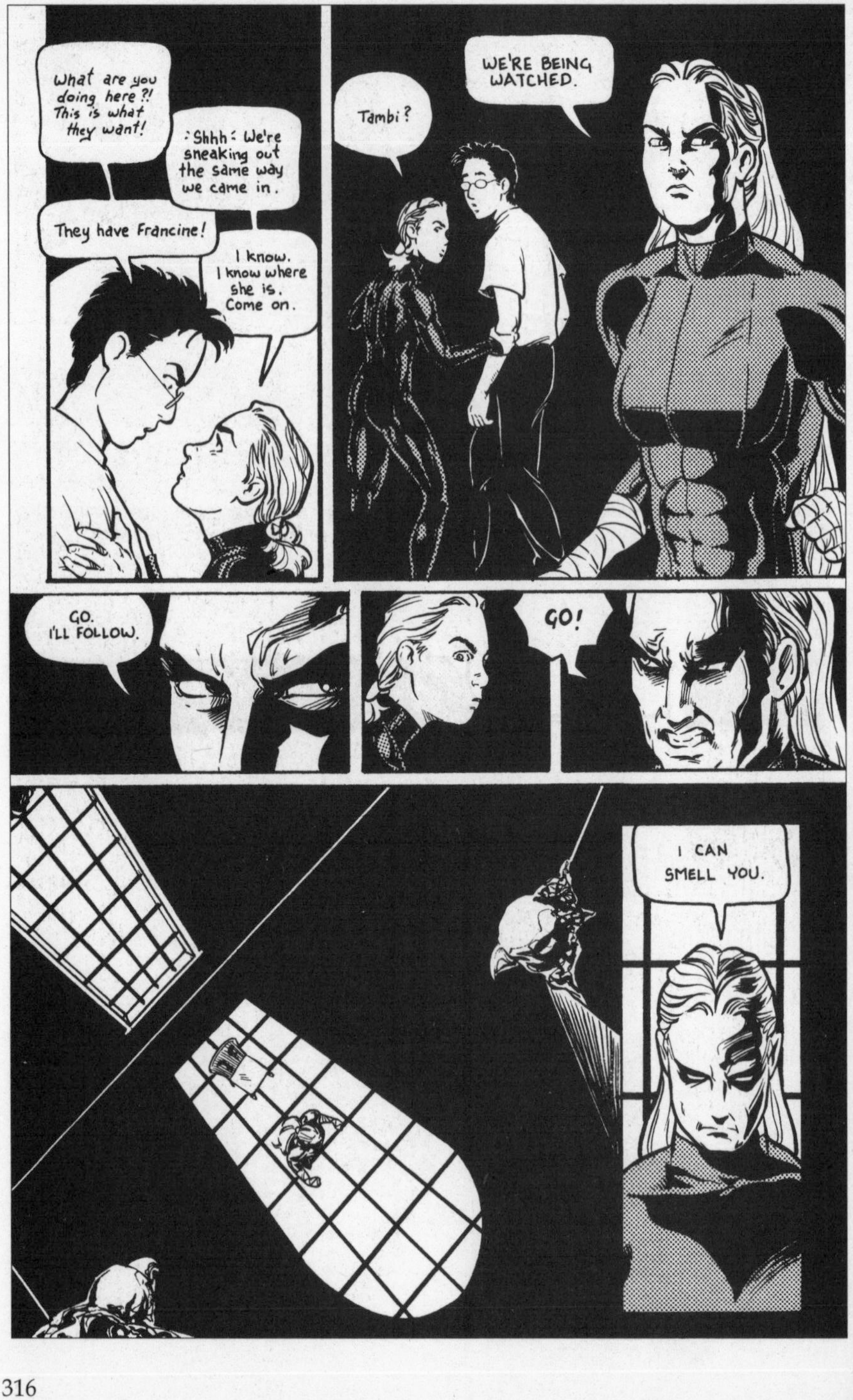
What are you doing here?! This is what they want!
:Shhh: We're sneaking out the same way we came in.
They have Francine!
I know. I know where she is. Come on.
Tambi?
WE'RE BEING WATCHED.
GO. I'LL FOLLOW.
GO!
I CAN SMELL YOU.

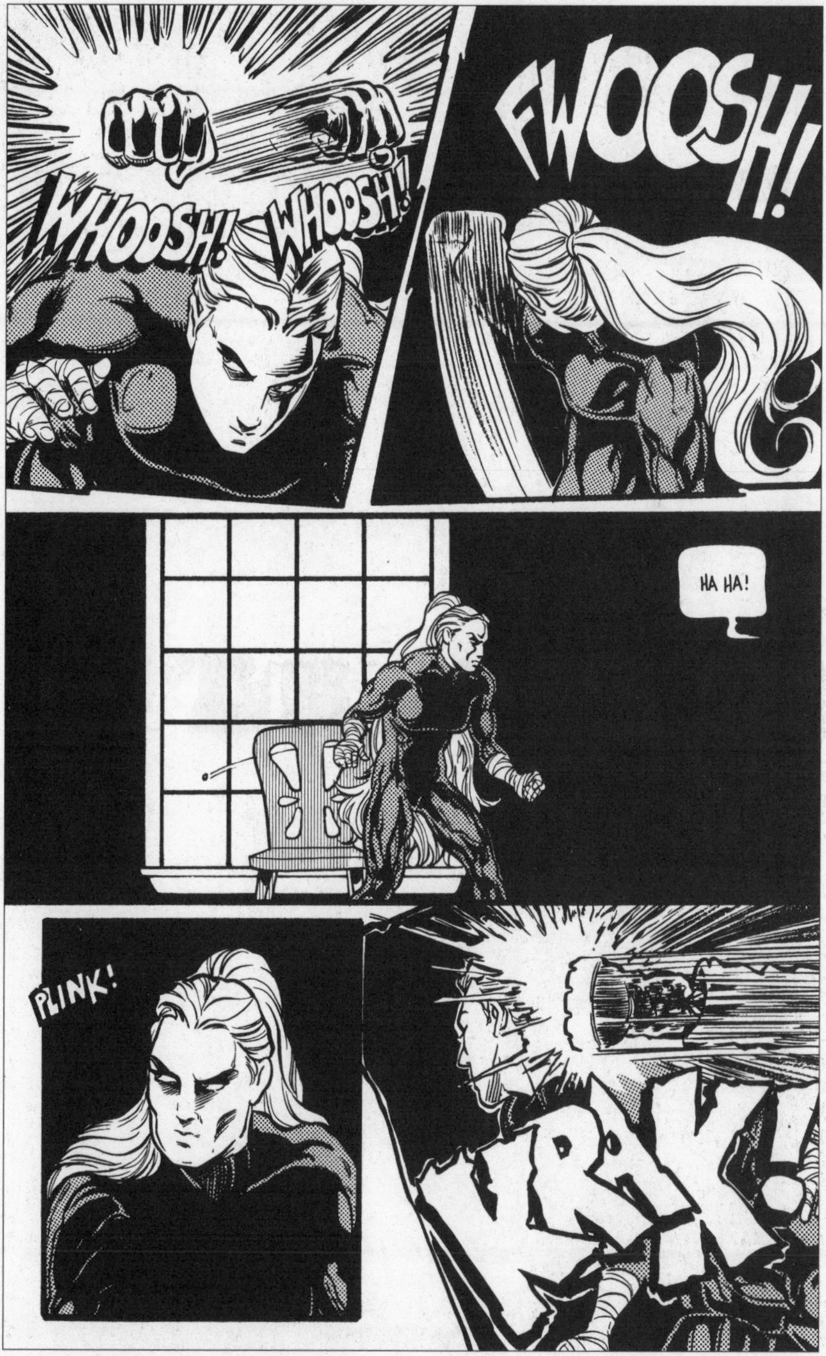
WHOOSH! WHOOSH!
FWOOSH!
HA HA!
PLINK!
KRAK!

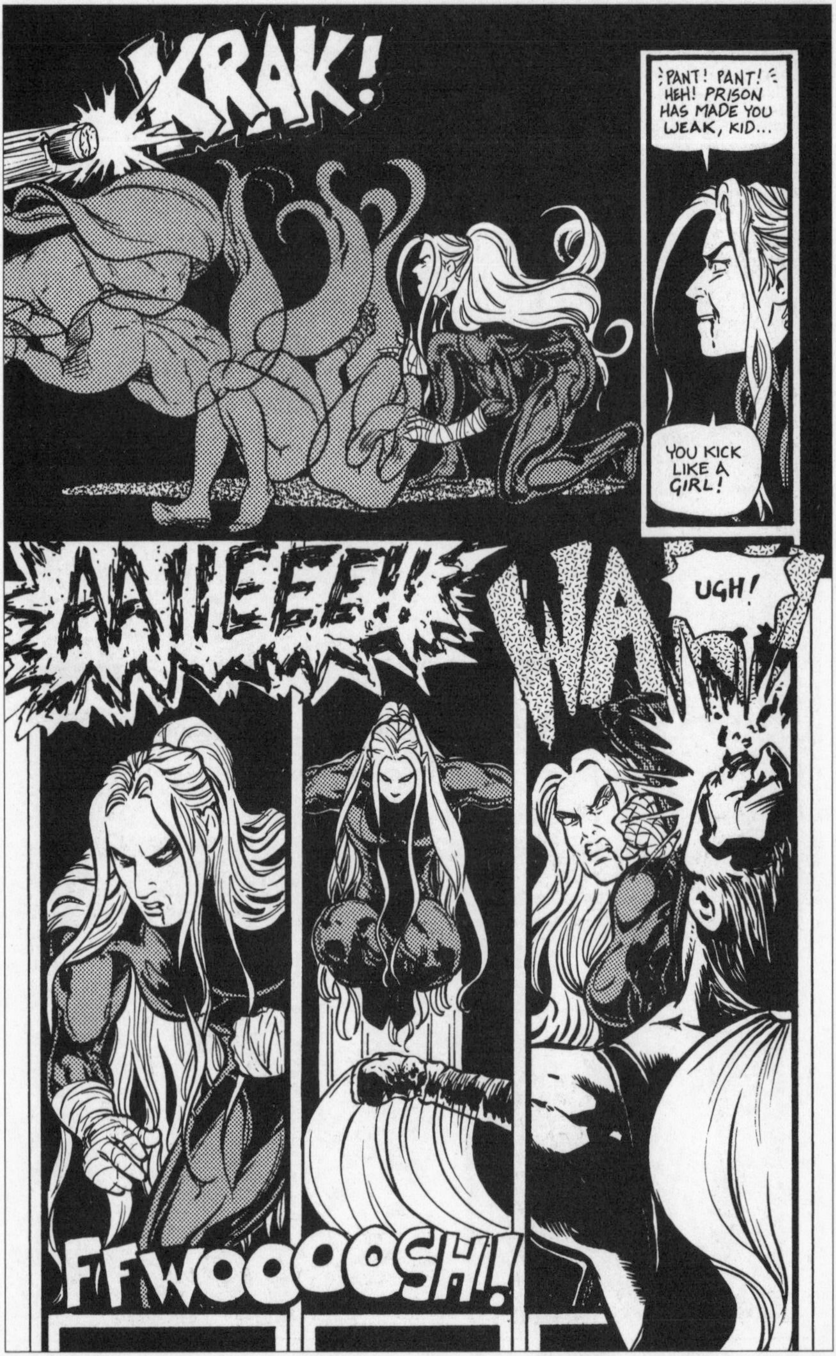
KRAK!
PANT! PANT! HEH! PRISON HAS MADE YOU WEAK, KID...
YOU KICK LIKE A GIRL!
AAIIEEE!!
WA
UGH!
FFWOOOOSH!

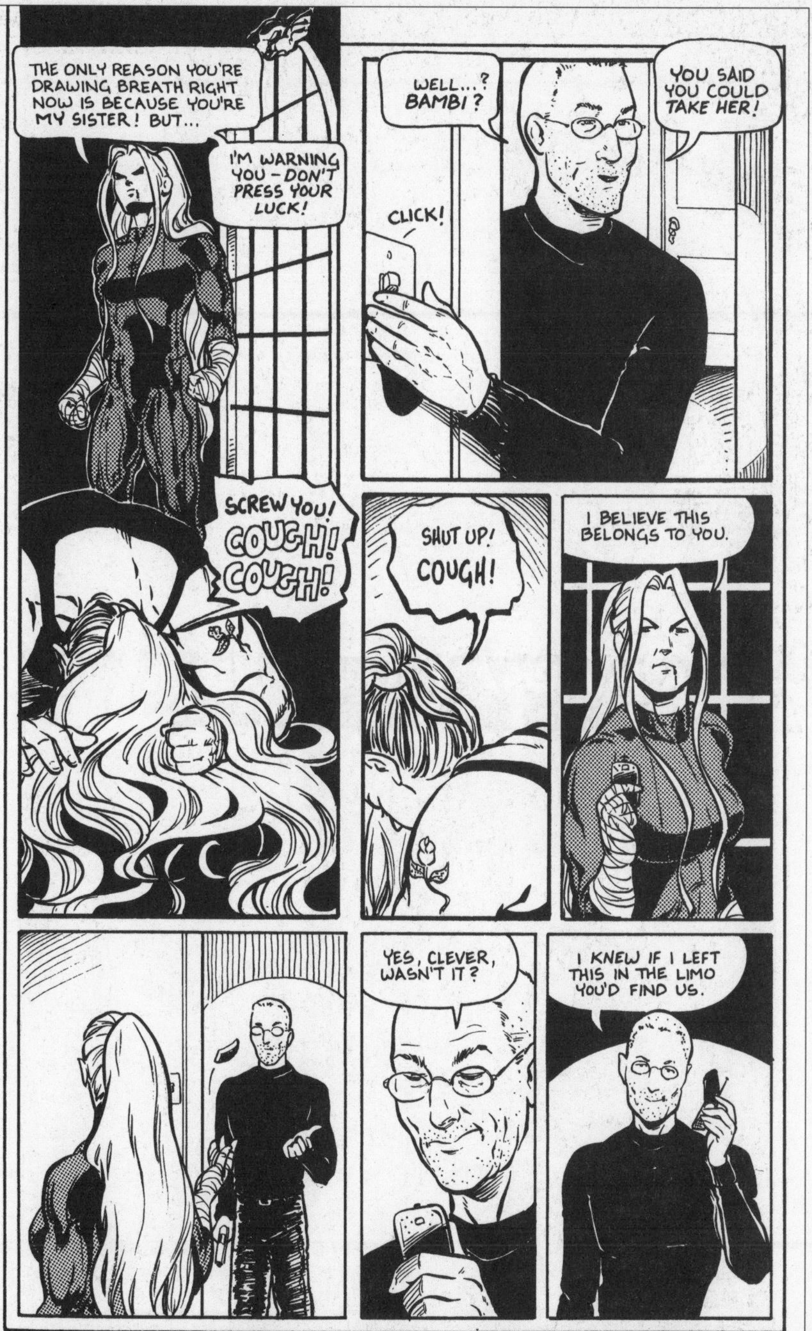
THE ONLY REASON YOU'RE DRAWING BREATH RIGHT NOW IS BECAUSE YOU'RE MY SISTER! BUT...
I'M WARNING YOU - DON'T PRESS YOUR LUCK!
WELL...? BAMBI?
YOU SAID YOU COULD TAKE HER!
CLICK!
SCREW YOU! COUGH! COUGH!
SHUT UP! COUGH!
I BELIEVE THIS BELONGS TO YOU.
YES, CLEVER, WASN'T IT?
I KNEW IF I LEFT THIS IN THE LIMO YOU'D FIND US.

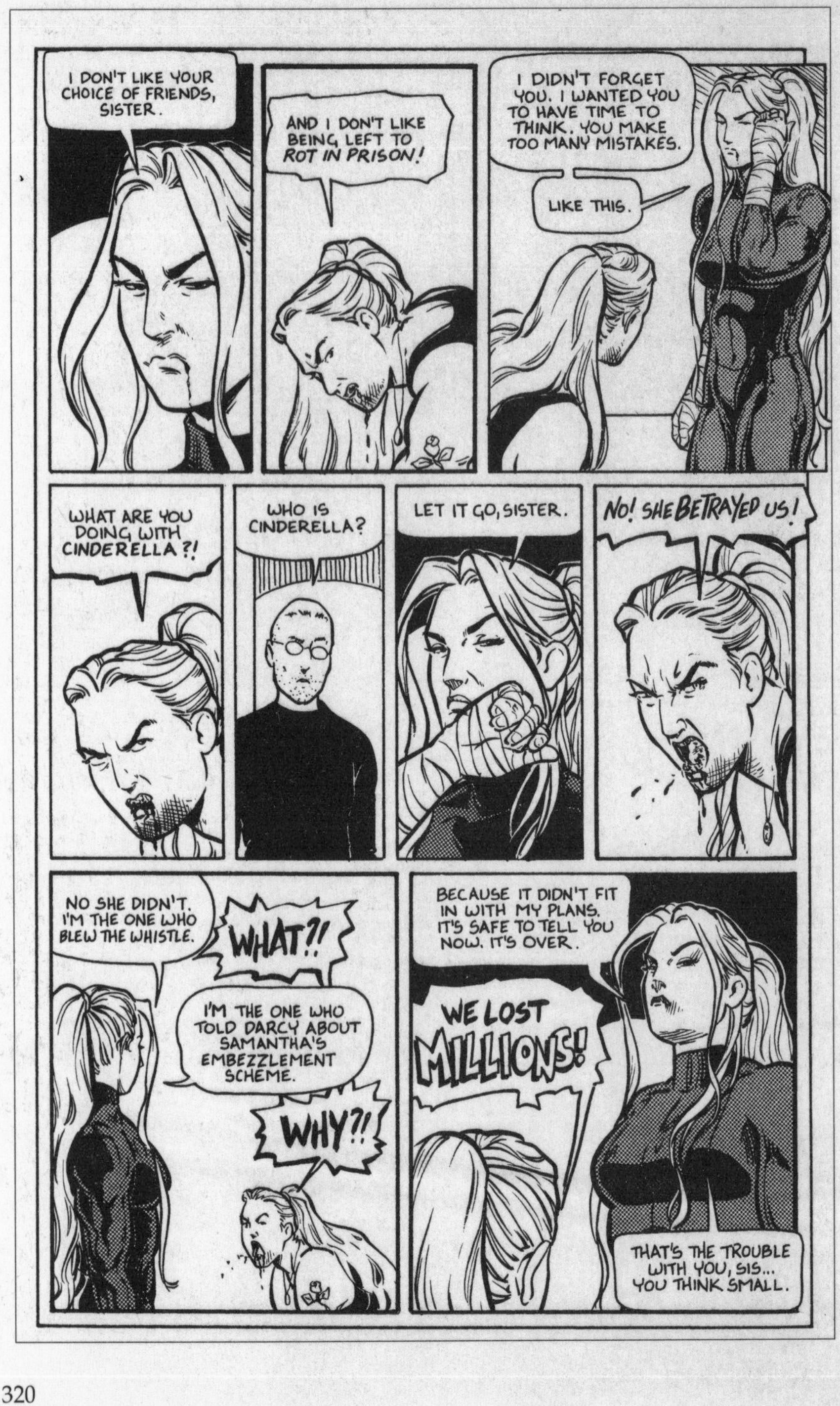
I DON'T LIKE YOUR CHOICE OF FRIENDS, SISTER.
AND I DON'T LIKE BEING LEFT TO ROT IN PRISON!
I DIDN'T FORGET YOU. I WANTED YOU TO HAVE TIME TO THINK. YOU MAKE TOO MANY MISTAKES.
LIKE THIS.
WHAT ARE YOU DOING WITH CINDERELLA?!
WHO IS CINDERELLA?
LET IT GO, SISTER.
NO! SHE BETRAYED US!
NO SHE DIDN'T. I'M THE ONE WHO BLEW THE WHISTLE.
WHAT?!
I'M THE ONE WHO TOLD DARCY ABOUT SAMANTHA'S EMBEZZLEMENT SCHEME.
WHY?!
BECAUSE IT DIDN'T FIT IN WITH MY PLANS. IT'S SAFE TO TELL YOU NOW. IT'S OVER.
WE LOST MILLIONS!
THAT'S THE TROUBLE WITH YOU, SIS... YOU THINK SMALL.

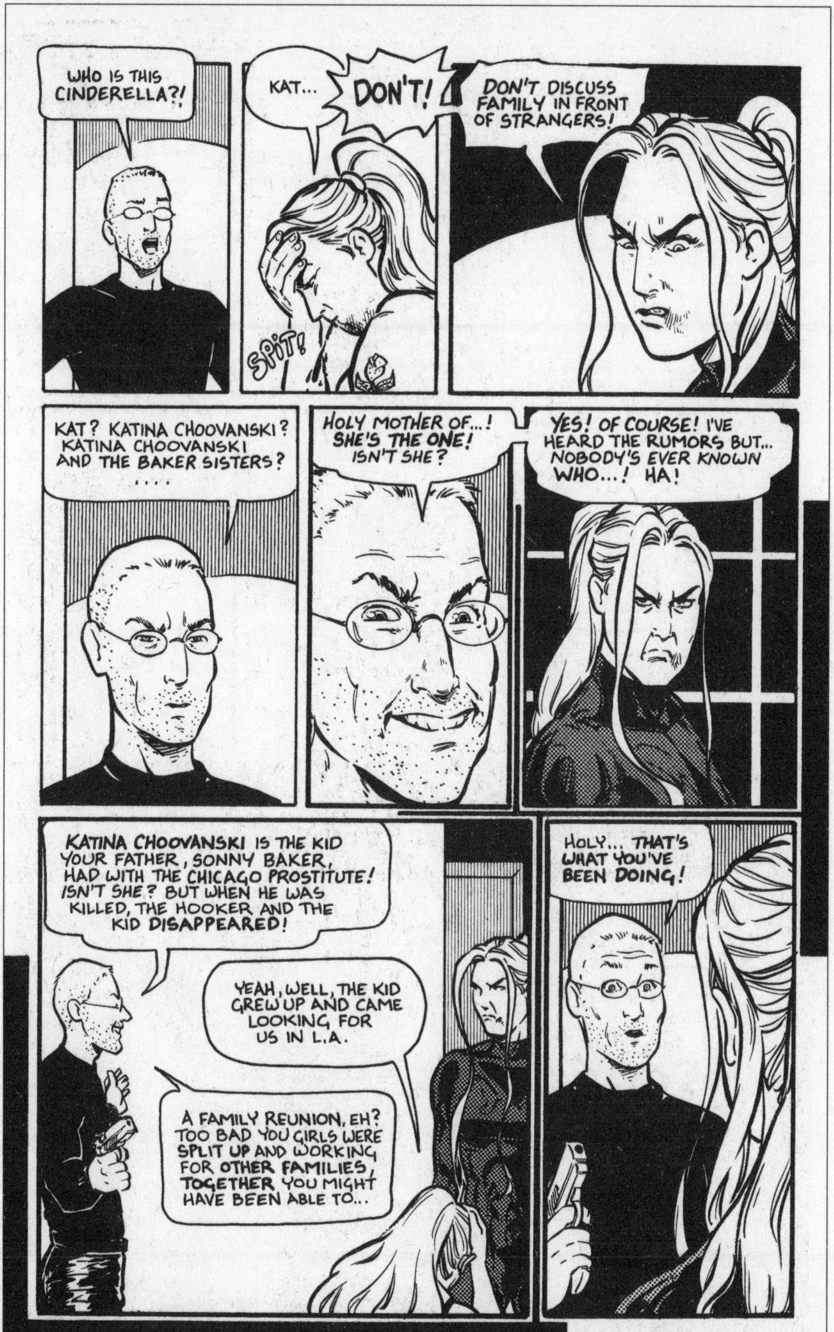
WHO IS THIS CINDERELLA?!
KAT...
DON'T!
DON'T DISCUSS FAMILY IN FRONT OF STRANGERS!
SPIT!
KAT? KATINA CHOOVANSKI? KATINA CHOOVANSKI AND THE BAKER SISTERS? ....
HOLY MOTHER OF...! SHE'S THE ONE! ISN'T SHE?
YES! OF COURSE! I'VE HEARD THE RUMORS BUT... NOBODY'S EVER KNOWN WHO...! HA!
KATINA CHOOVANSKI IS THE KID YOUR FATHER, SONNY BAKER, HAD WITH THE CHICAGO PROSTITUTE! ISN'T SHE? BUT WHEN HE WAS KILLED, THE HOOKER AND THE KID DISAPPEARED!
YEAH, WELL, THE KID GREW UP AND CAME LOOKING FOR US IN L.A.
A FAMILY REUNION, EH? TOO BAD YOU GIRLS WERE SPLIT UP AND WORKING FOR OTHER FAMILIES, TOGETHER YOU MIGHT HAVE BEEN ABLE TO...
HOLY... THAT'S WHAT YOU'VE BEEN DOING!

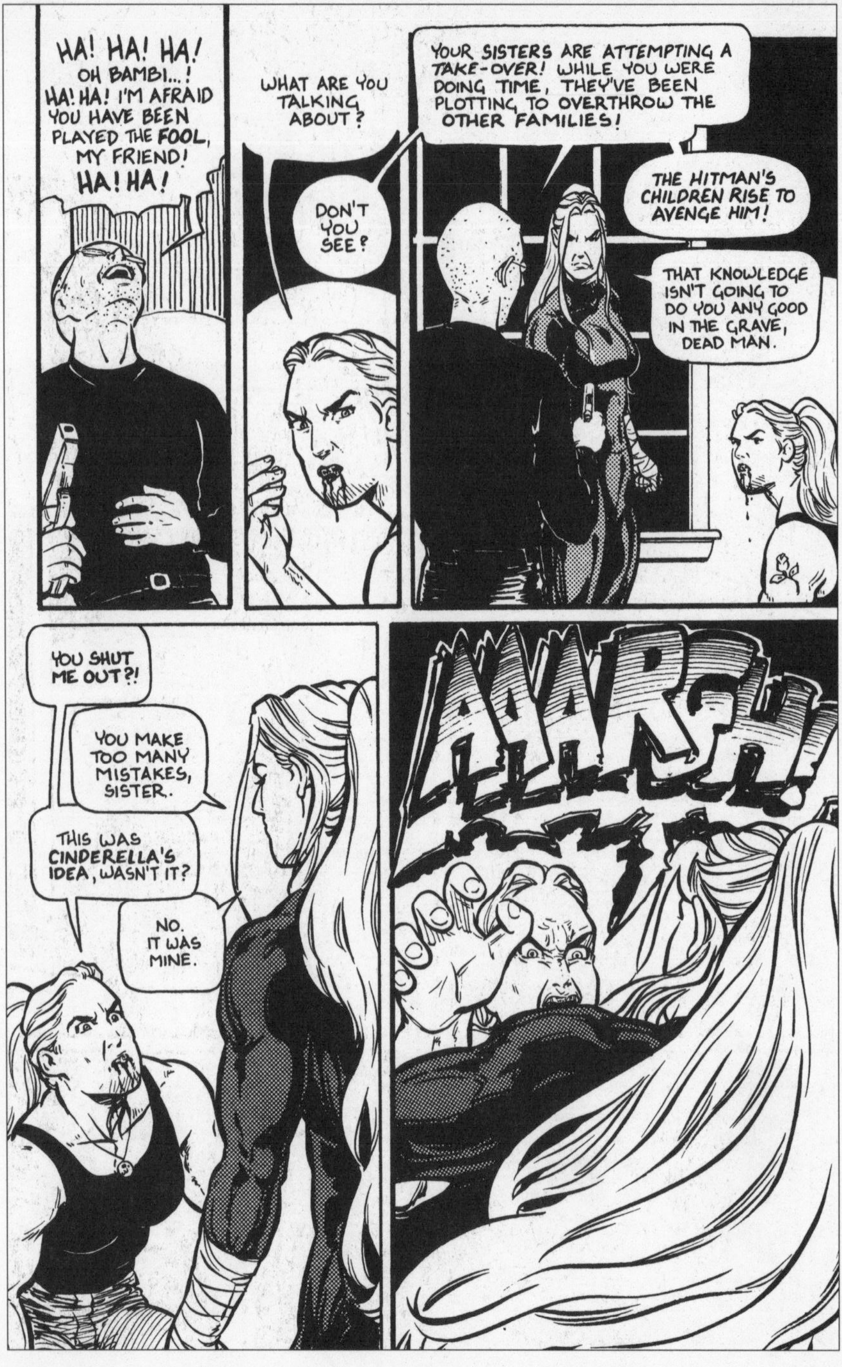
HA! HA! HA! OH BAMBI...! HA! HA! I'M AFRAID YOU HAVE BEEN PLAYED THE FOOL, MY FRIEND! HA! HA!
WHAT ARE YOU TALKING ABOUT?
DON'T YOU SEE?
YOUR SISTERS ARE ATTEMPTING A TAKE-OVER! WHILE YOU WERE DOING TIME, THEY'VE BEEN PLOTTING TO OVERTHROW THE OTHER FAMILIES!
THE HITMAN'S CHILDREN RISE TO AVENGE HIM!
THAT KNOWLEDGE ISN'T GOING TO DO YOU ANY GOOD IN THE GRAVE, DEAD MAN.
YOU SHUT ME OUT?!
YOU MAKE TOO MANY MISTAKES, SISTER.
THIS WAS CINDERELLA'S IDEA, WASN'T IT?
NO. IT WAS MINE.
AAARGH!

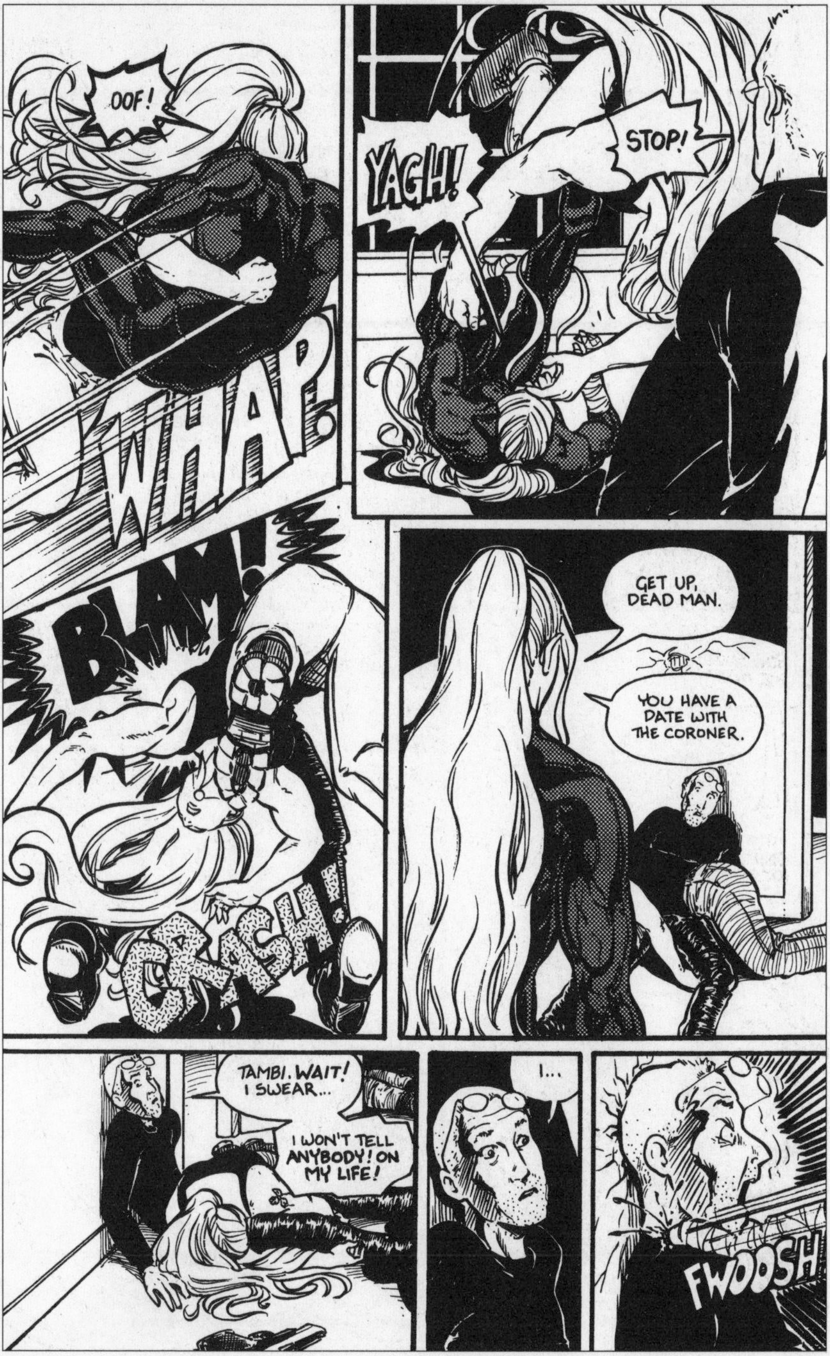
OOF!
YAGH!
STOP!
WHAP!
BLAM!
CRASH!
GET UP, DEAD MAN.
YOU HAVE A DATE WITH THE CORONER.
TAMBI. WAIT! I SWEAR...
I WON'T TELL ANYBODY! ON MY LIFE!
I...
FWOOSH

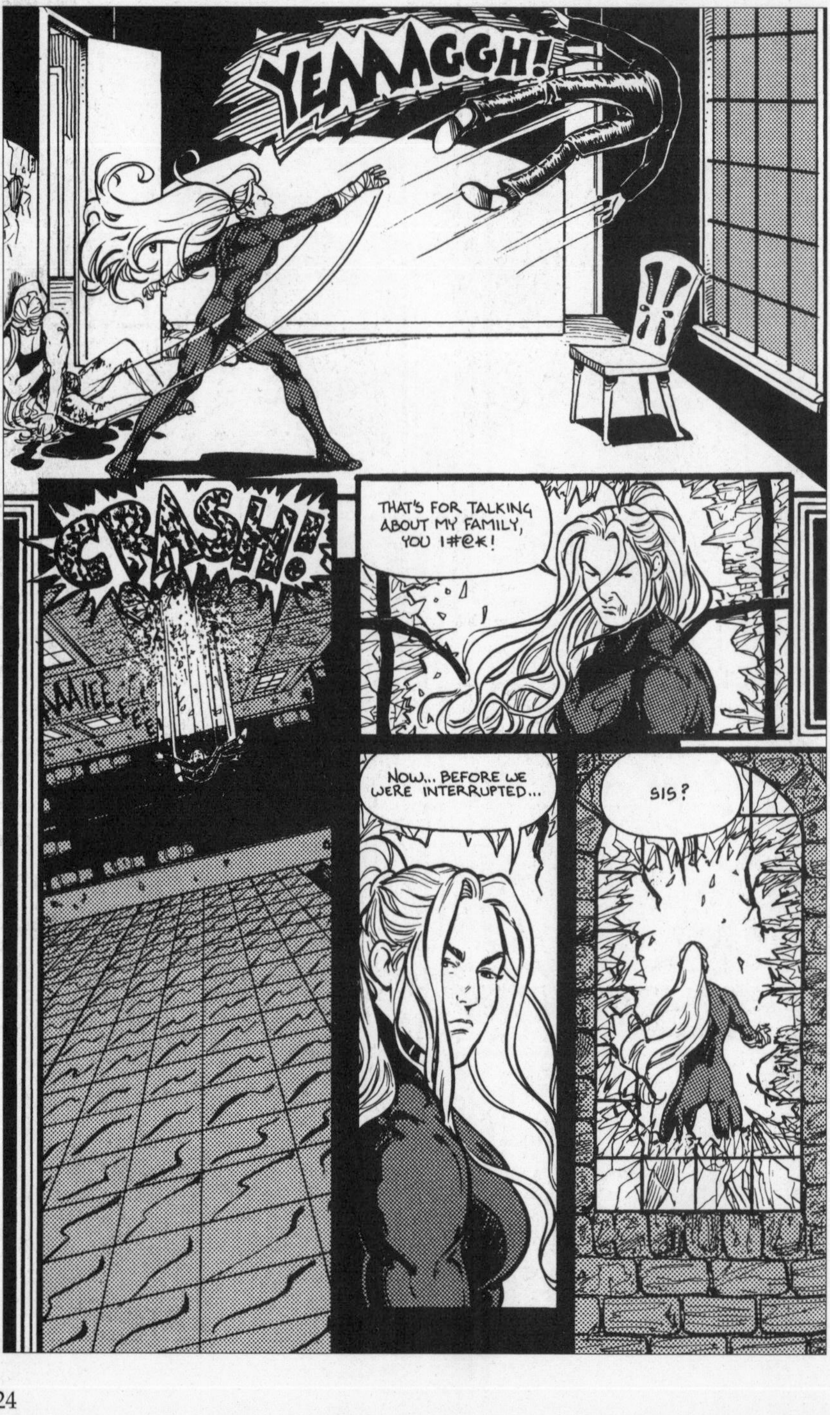
YEAAAGGH!
CRASH!
THAT'S FOR TALKING ABOUT MY FAMILY, YOU !#@*!
NOW... BEFORE WE WERE INTERRUPTED...
SIS?

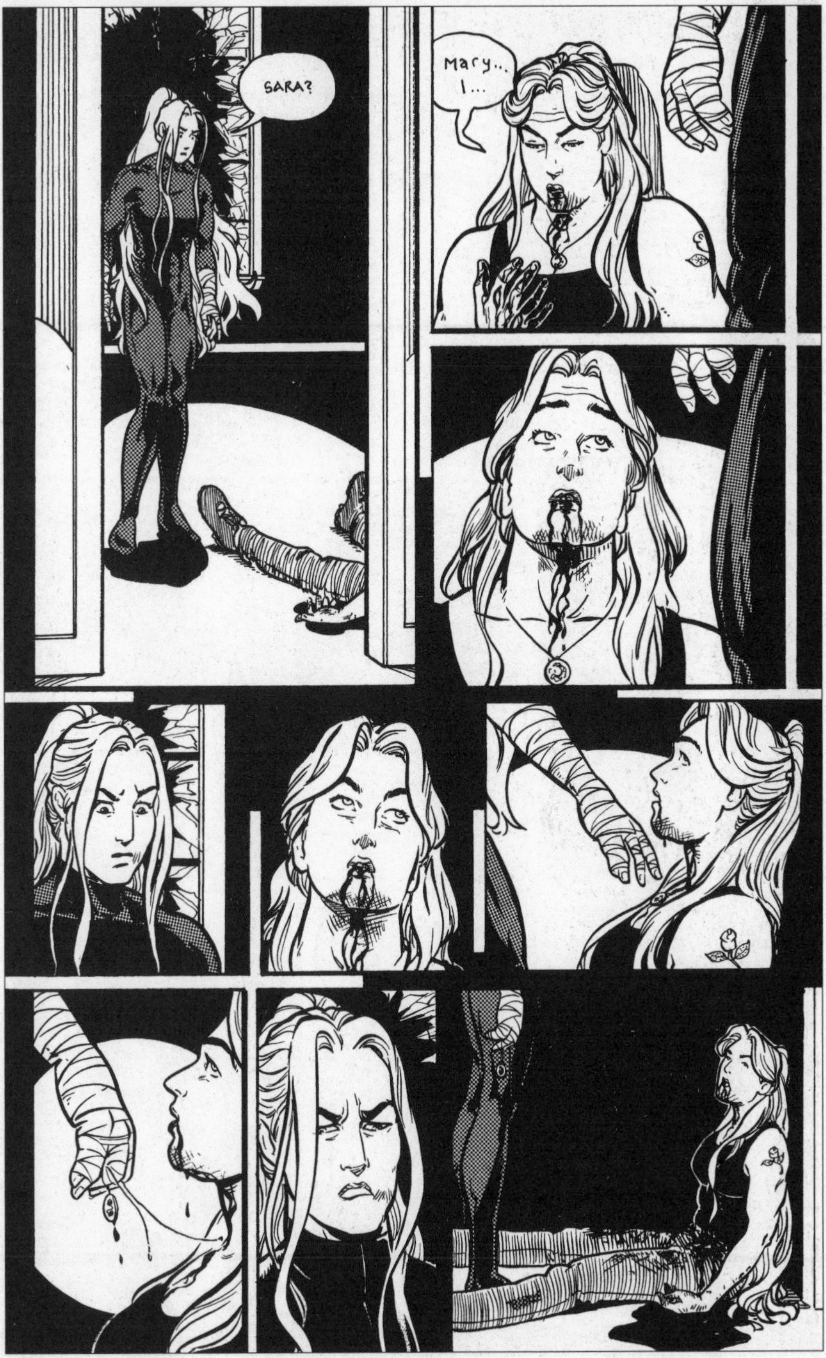
SARA?
Mary... I...

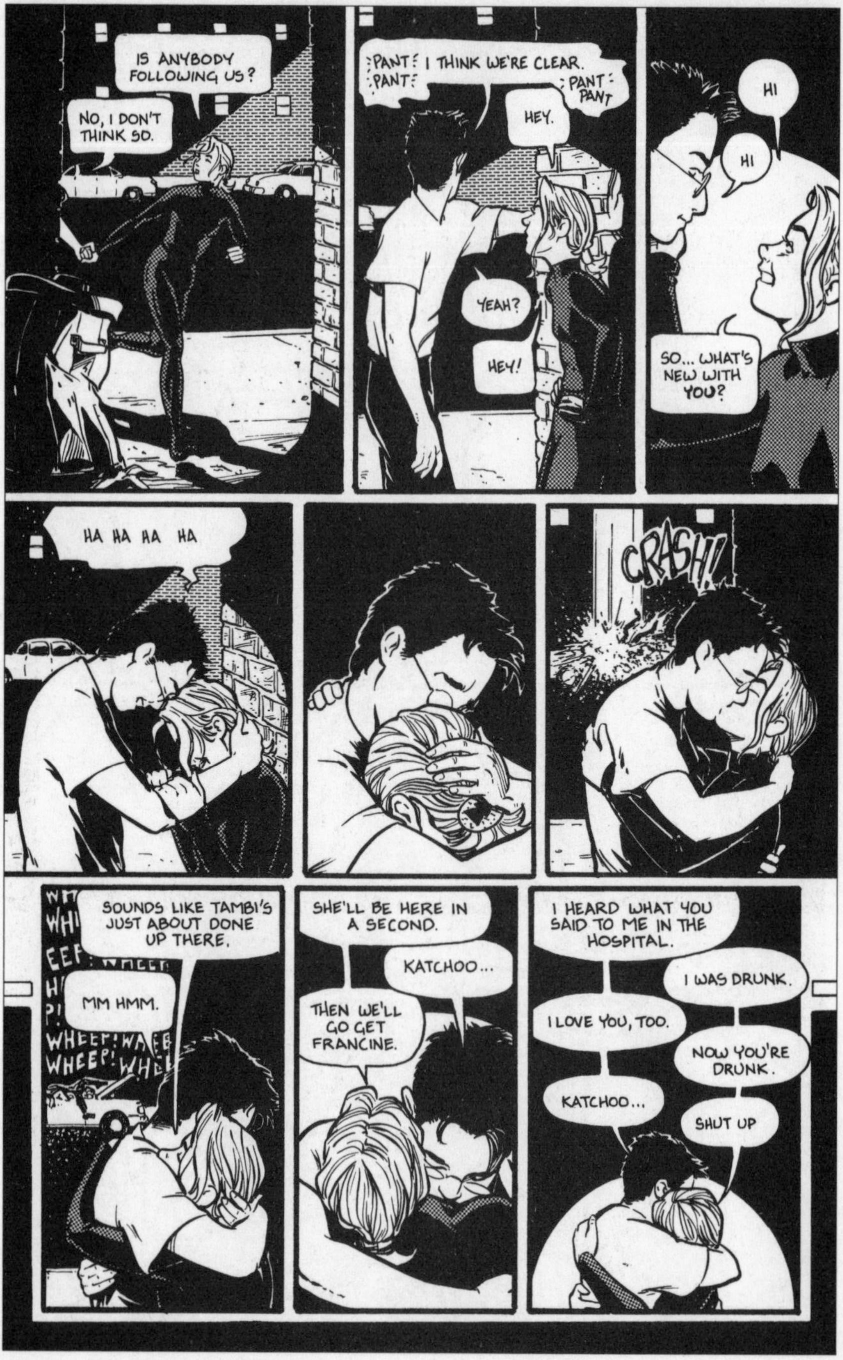
IS ANYBODY FOLLOWING US?
NO, I DON'T THINK SO.
PANT PANT
I THINK WE'RE CLEAR.
PANT PANT
HEY.
YEAH?
HEY!
HI
HI
SO... WHAT'S NEW WITH YOU?
HA HA HA HA
CRASH!
SOUNDS LIKE TAMBI'S JUST ABOUT DONE UP THERE.
MM HMM.
WHEEP! WHEEP!
SHE'LL BE HERE IN A SECOND.
KATCHOO...
THEN WE'LL GO GET FRANCINE.
I HEARD WHAT YOU SAID TO ME IN THE HOSPITAL.
I WAS DRUNK.
I LOVE YOU, TOO.
NOW YOU'RE DRUNK.
KATCHOO...
SHUT UP

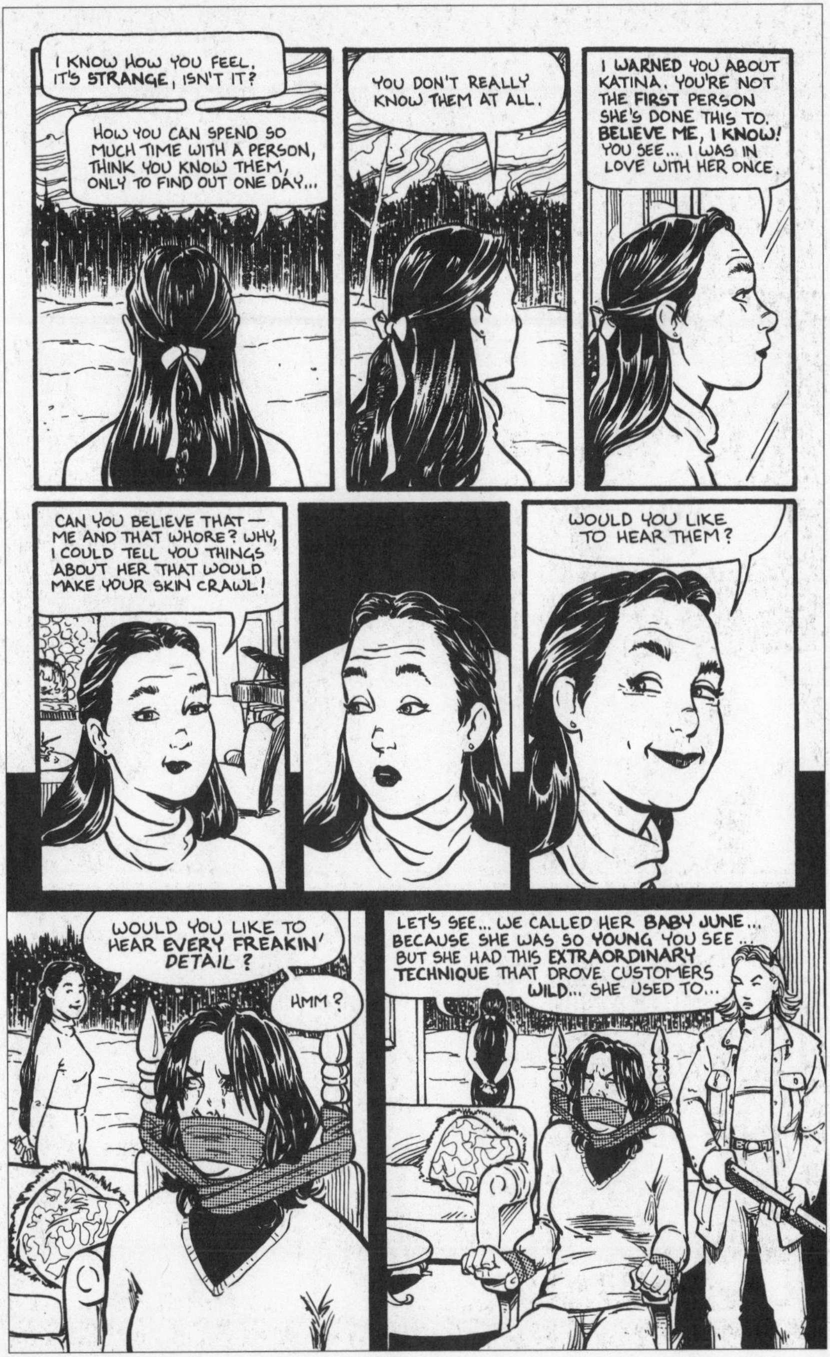
I KNOW HOW YOU FEEL. IT'S STRANGE, ISN'T IT?
HOW YOU CAN SPEND SO MUCH TIME WITH A PERSON, THINK YOU KNOW THEM, ONLY TO FIND OUT ONE DAY...
YOU DON'T REALLY KNOW THEM AT ALL.
I WARNED YOU ABOUT KATINA. YOU'RE NOT THE FIRST PERSON SHE'S DONE THIS TO. BELIEVE ME, I KNOW! YOU SEE... I WAS IN LOVE WITH HER ONCE.
CAN YOU BELIEVE THAT— ME AND THAT WHORE? WHY, I COULD TELL YOU THINGS ABOUT HER THAT WOULD MAKE YOUR SKIN CRAWL!
WOULD YOU LIKE TO HEAR THEM?
WOULD YOU LIKE TO HEAR EVERY FREAKIN' DETAIL?
HMM?
LET'S SEE... WE CALLED HER BABY JUNE... BECAUSE SHE WAS SO YOUNG YOU SEE... BUT SHE HAD THIS EXTRAORDINARY TECHNIQUE THAT DROVE CUSTOMERS WILD... SHE USED TO...

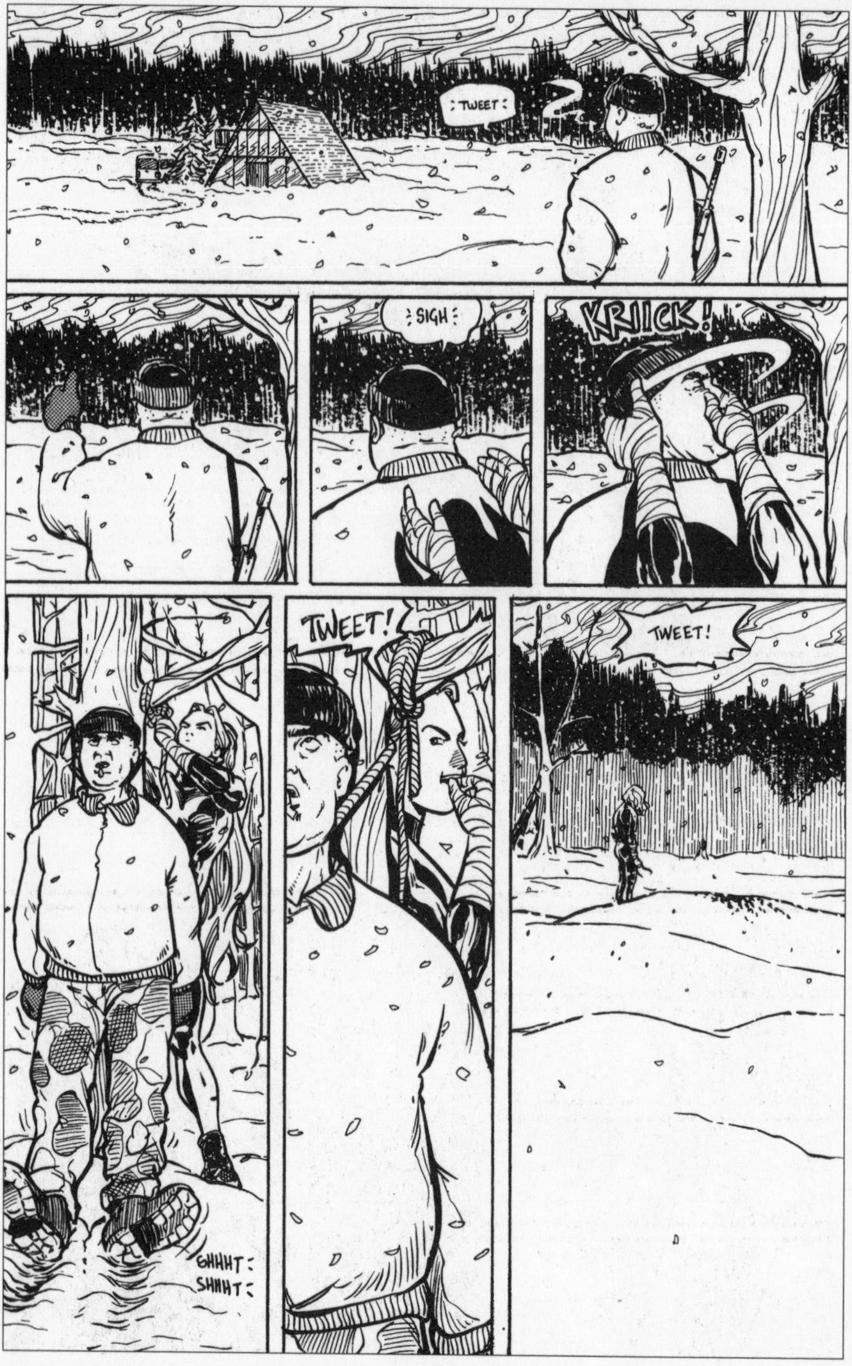
TWEET
SIGH
KRIICK!
SHHHT
SHHHT
TWEET!
TWEET!

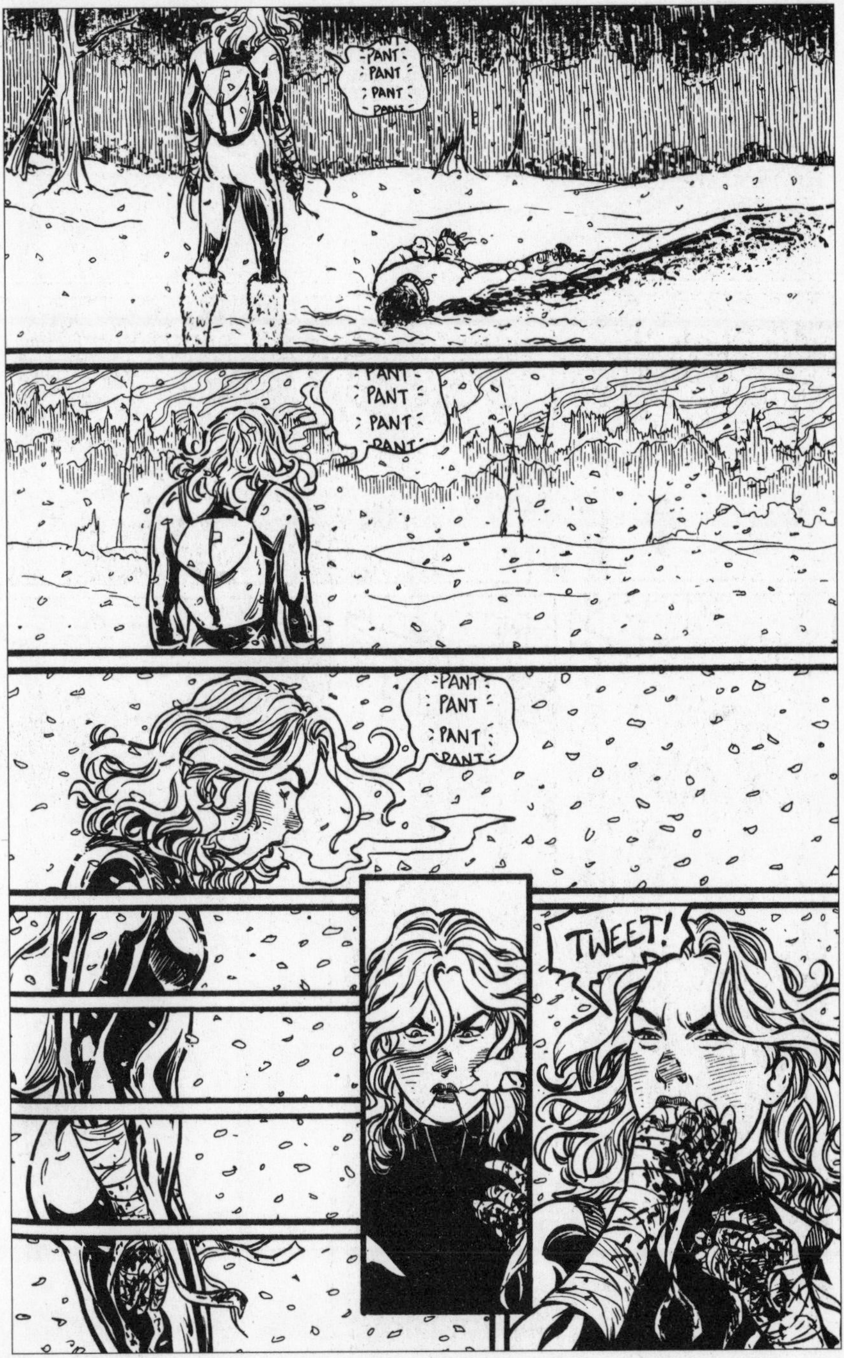
PANT PANT PANT
PANT PANT PANT
PANT PANT PANT
TWEET!

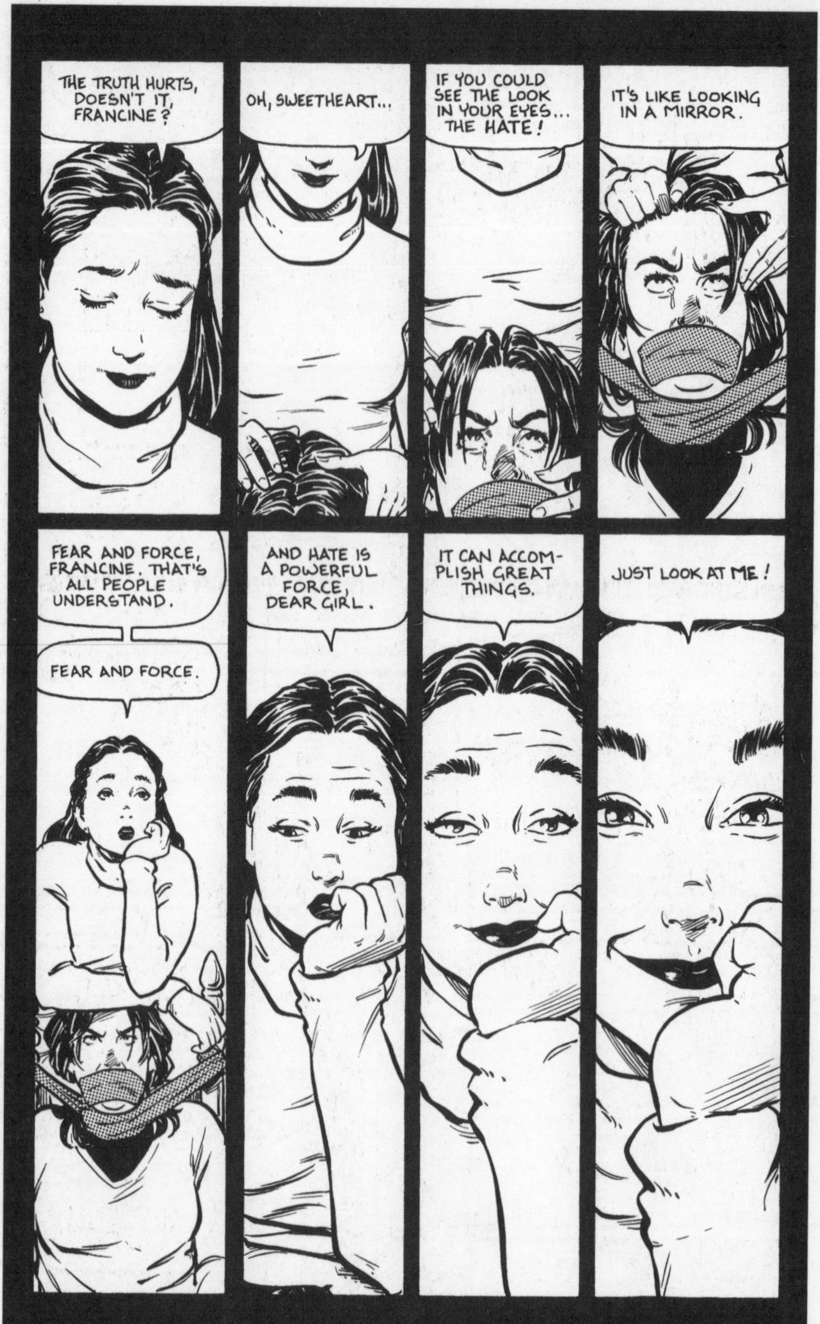
THE TRUTH HURTS, DOESN'T IT, FRANCINE?
OH, SWEETHEART...
IF YOU COULD SEE THE LOOK IN YOUR EYES... THE HATE!
IT'S LIKE LOOKING IN A MIRROR.
FEAR AND FORCE, FRANCINE. THAT'S ALL PEOPLE UNDERSTAND.
FEAR AND FORCE.
AND HATE IS A POWERFUL FORCE, DEAR GIRL.
IT CAN ACCOMPLISH GREAT THINGS.
JUST LOOK AT ME!

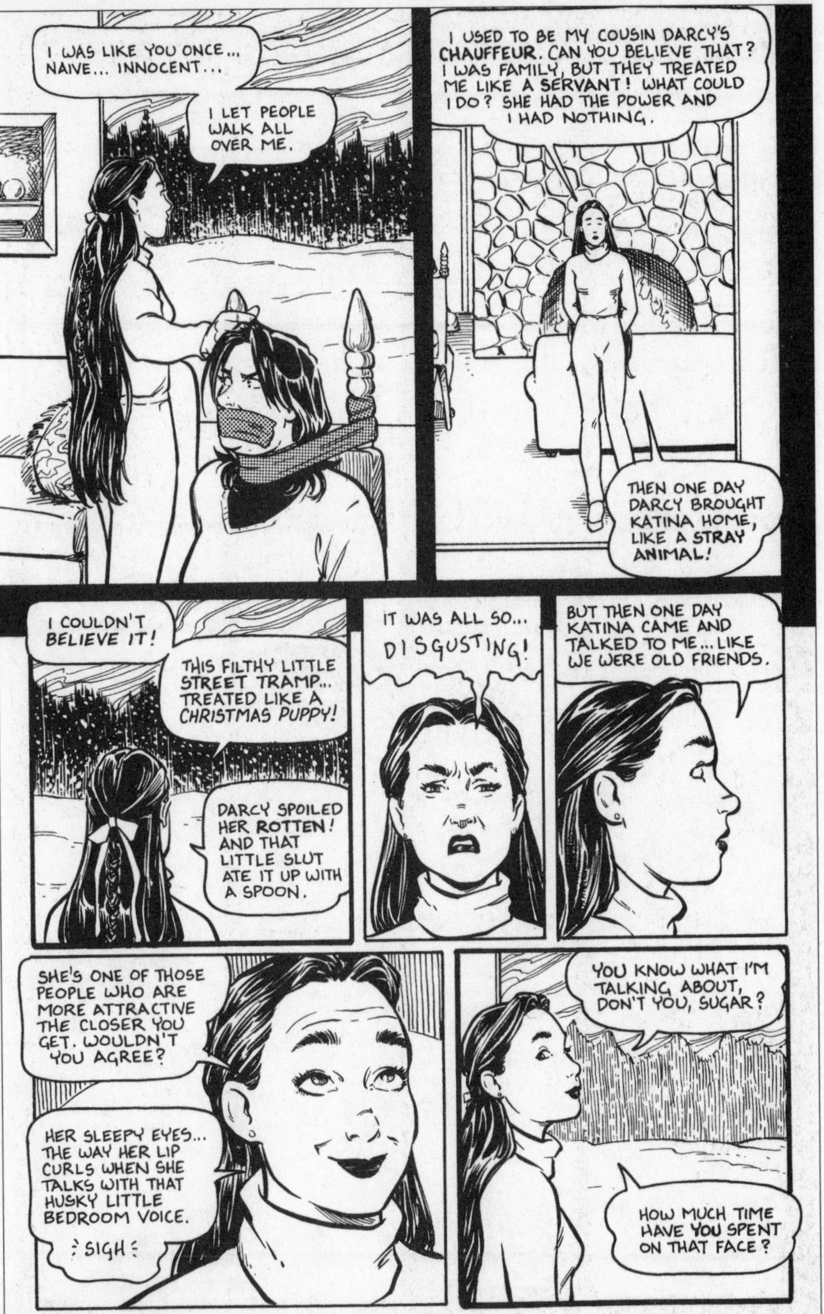
I WAS LIKE YOU ONCE... NAIVE... INNOCENT...
I LET PEOPLE WALK ALL OVER ME.
I USED TO BE MY COUSIN DARCY'S CHAUFFEUR. CAN YOU BELIEVE THAT? I WAS FAMILY, BUT THEY TREATED ME LIKE A SERVANT! WHAT COULD I DO? SHE HAD THE POWER AND I HAD NOTHING.
THEN ONE DAY DARCY BROUGHT KATINA HOME, LIKE A STRAY ANIMAL!
I COULDN'T BELIEVE IT!
THIS FILTHY LITTLE STREET TRAMP... TREATED LIKE A CHRISTMAS PUPPY!
DARCY SPOILED HER ROTTEN! AND THAT LITTLE SLUT ATE IT UP WITH A SPOON.
IT WAS ALL SO... DISGUSTING!
BUT THEN ONE DAY KATINA CAME AND TALKED TO ME... LIKE WE WERE OLD FRIENDS.
SHE'S ONE OF THOSE PEOPLE WHO ARE MORE ATTRACTIVE THE CLOSER YOU GET. WOULDN'T YOU AGREE?
HER SLEEPY EYES... THE WAY HER LIP CURLS WHEN SHE TALKS WITH THAT HUSKY LITTLE BEDROOM VOICE.
SIGH
YOU KNOW WHAT I'M TALKING ABOUT, DON'T YOU, SUGAR?
HOW MUCH TIME HAVE YOU SPENT ON THAT FACE?

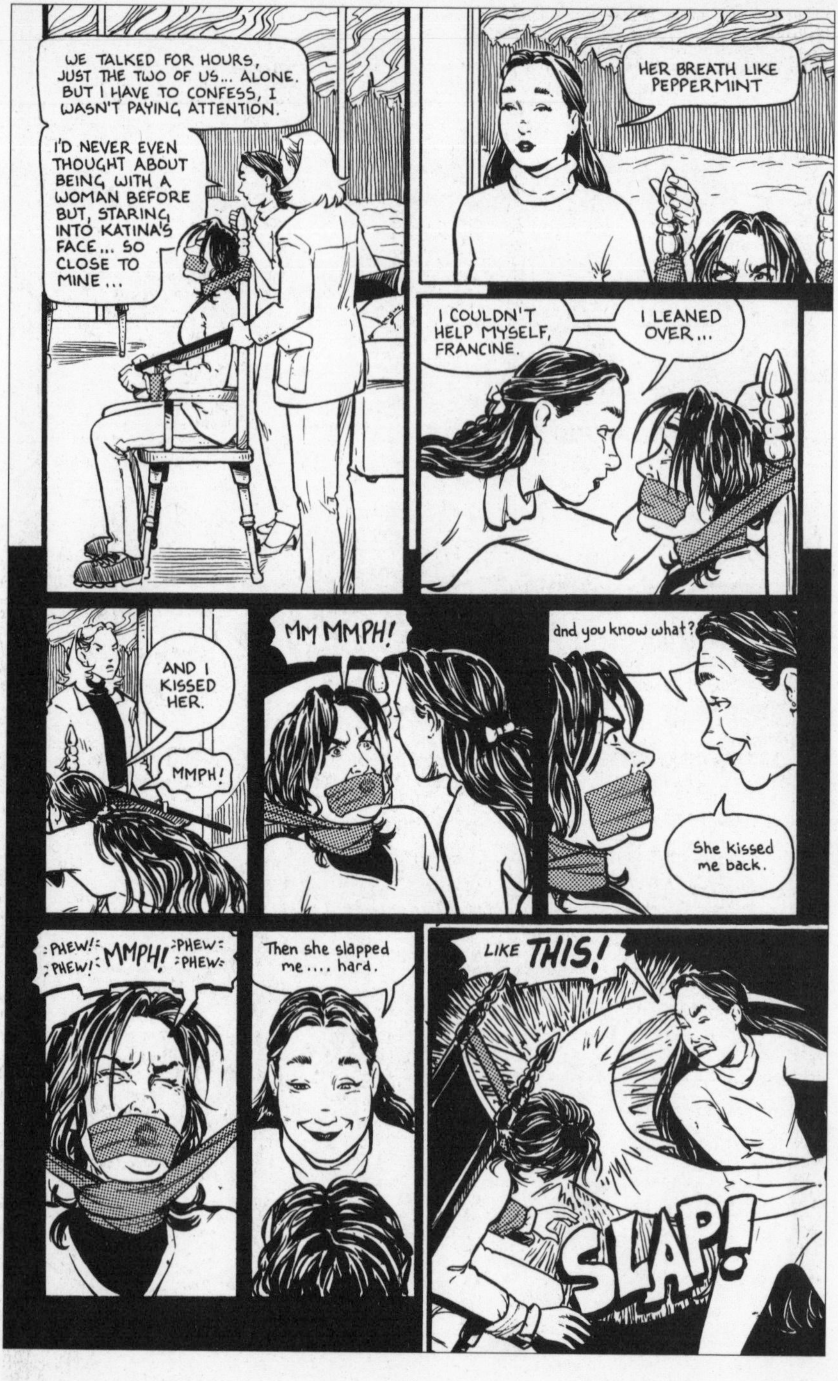

WE TALKED FOR HOURS, JUST THE TWO OF US... ALONE. BUT I HAVE TO CONFESS, I WASN'T PAYING ATTENTION.
I'D NEVER EVEN THOUGHT ABOUT BEING WITH A WOMAN BEFORE BUT, STARING INTO KATINA'S FACE... SO CLOSE TO MINE...
HER BREATH LIKE PEPPERMINT
I COULDN'T HELP MYSELF, FRANCINE.
I LEANED OVER...
AND I KISSED HER.
MMPH!
MM MMPH!
and you know what?
She kissed me back.
PHEW! PHEW! MMPH! PHEW PHEW
Then she slapped me.... hard.
LIKE THIS!
SLAP!

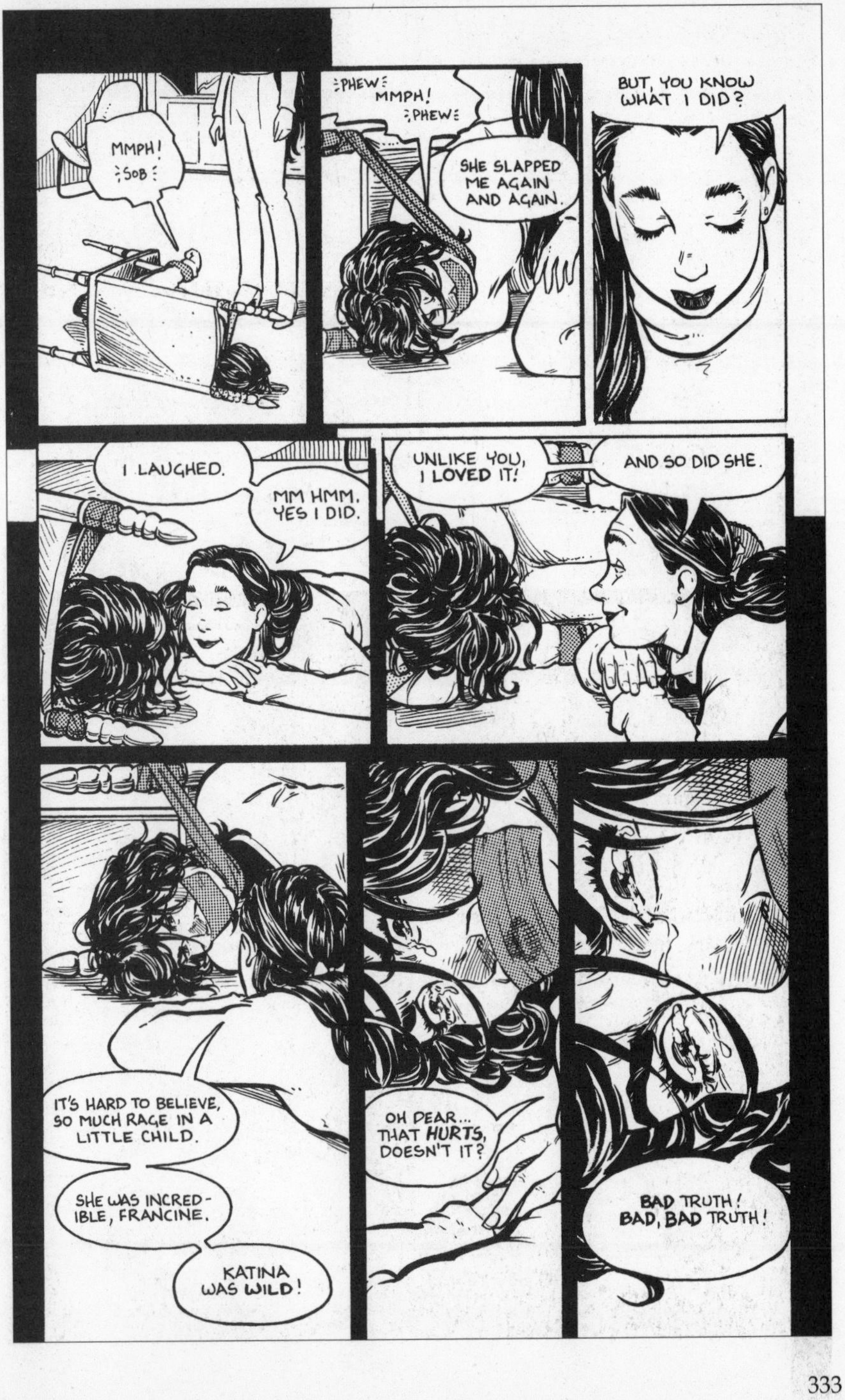
MMPH!
SOB
PHEW
MMPH!
PHEW
SHE SLAPPED ME AGAIN AND AGAIN.
BUT, YOU KNOW WHAT I DID?
I LAUGHED.
MM HMM. YES I DID.
UNLIKE YOU, I LOVED IT!
AND SO DID SHE.
IT'S HARD TO BELIEVE, SO MUCH RAGE IN A LITTLE CHILD.
SHE WAS INCRED-IBLE, FRANCINE.
KATINA WAS WILD!
OH DEAR... THAT HURTS, DOESN'T IT?
BAD TRUTH! BAD, BAD TRUTH!

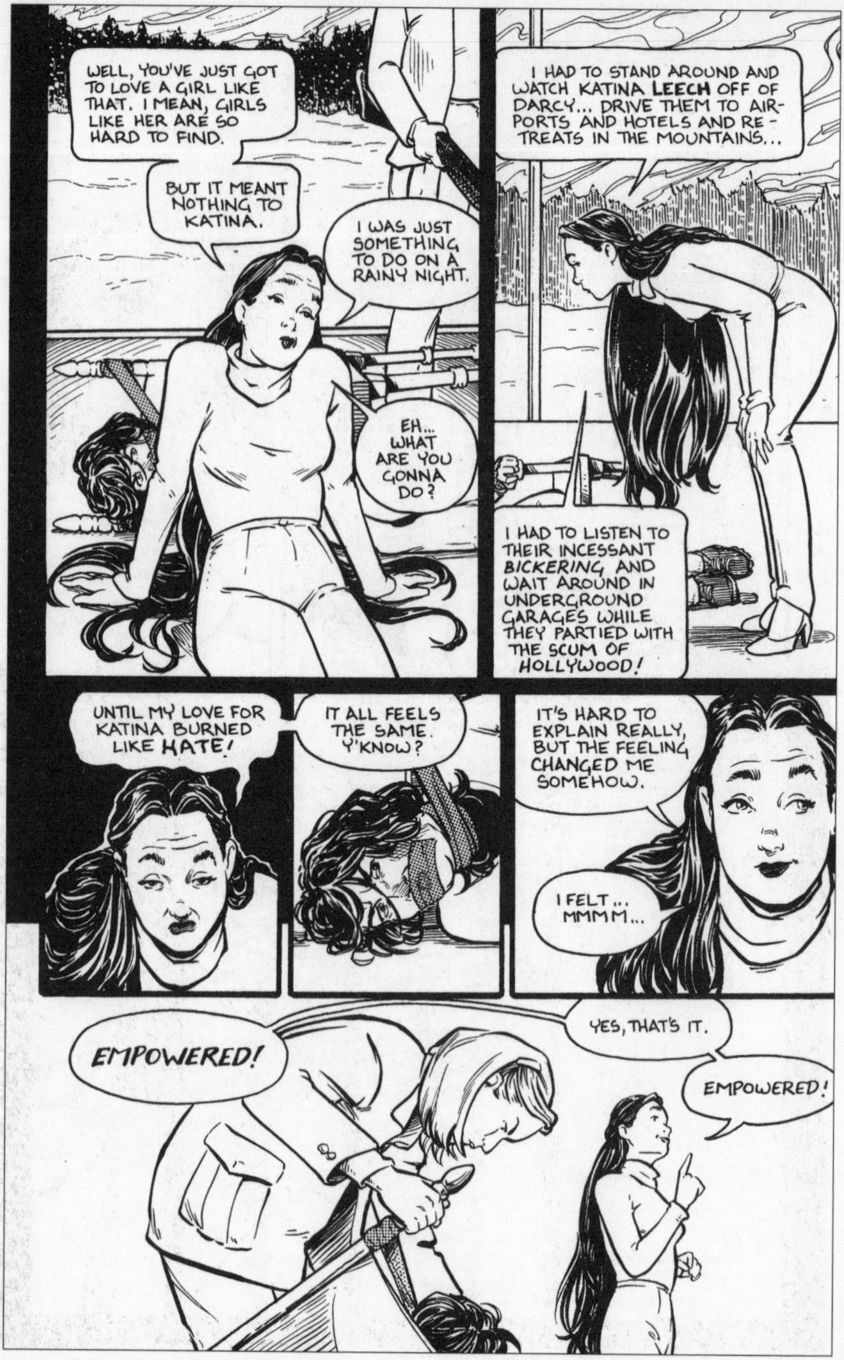

WELL, YOU'VE JUST GOT TO LOVE A GIRL LIKE THAT. I MEAN, GIRLS LIKE HER ARE SO HARD TO FIND.
BUT IT MEANT NOTHING TO KATINA.
I WAS JUST SOMETHING TO DO ON A RAINY NIGHT.
EH... WHAT ARE YOU GONNA DO?
I HAD TO STAND AROUND AND WATCH KATINA LEECH OFF OF DARCY... DRIVE THEM TO AIR-PORTS AND HOTELS AND RE-TREATS IN THE MOUNTAINS...
I HAD TO LISTEN TO THEIR INCESSANT BICKERING AND WAIT AROUND IN UNDERGROUND GARAGES WHILE THEY PARTIED WITH THE SCUM OF HOLLYWOOD!
UNTIL MY LOVE FOR KATINA BURNED LIKE HATE!
IT ALL FEELS THE SAME. Y'KNOW?
IT'S HARD TO EXPLAIN REALLY, BUT THE FEELING CHANGED ME SOMEHOW.
I FELT... MMMM...
EMPOWERED!
YES, THAT'S IT.
EMPOWERED!

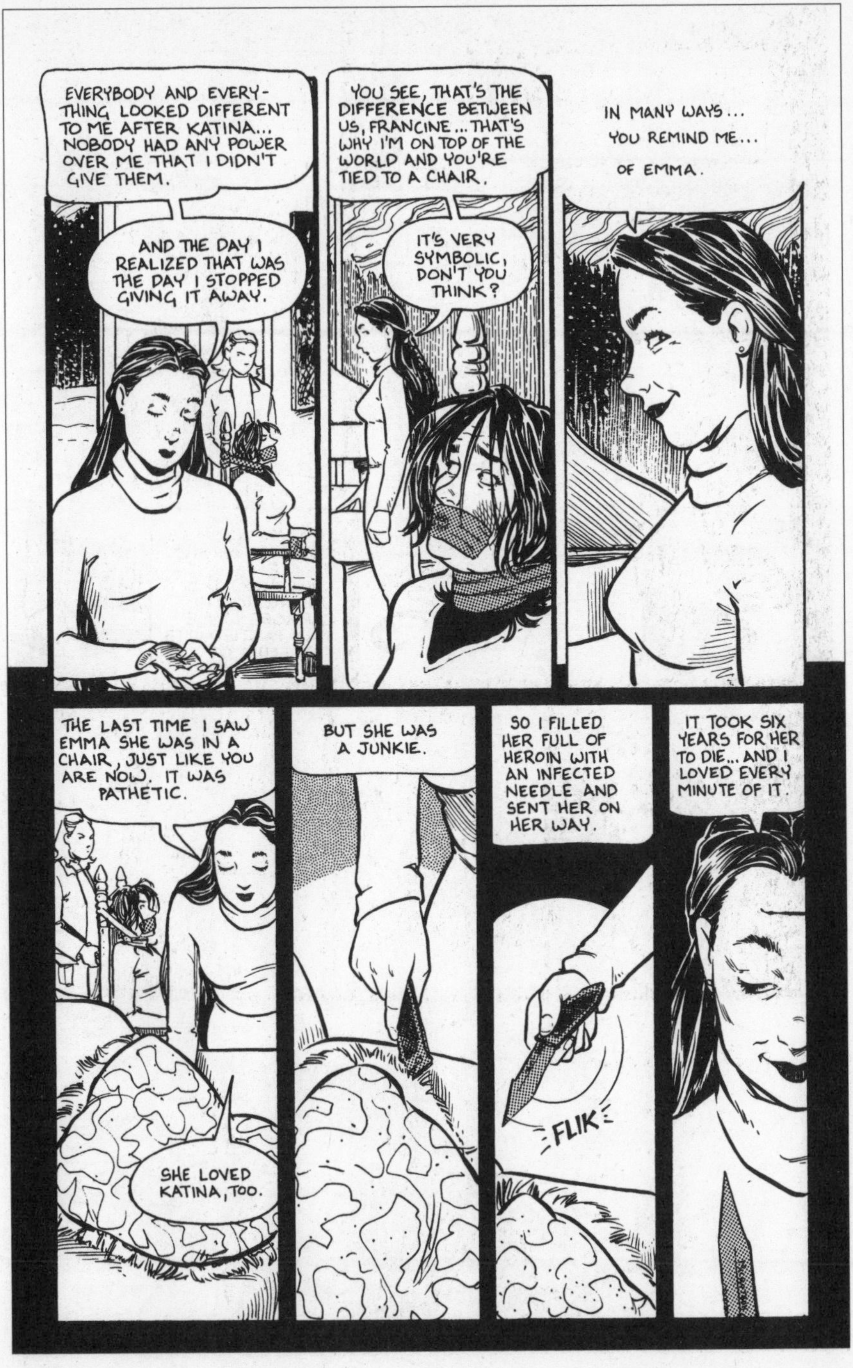
EVERYBODY AND EVERYTHING LOOKED DIFFERENT TO ME AFTER KATINA... NOBODY HAD ANY POWER OVER ME THAT I DIDN'T GIVE THEM.
AND THE DAY I REALIZED THAT WAS THE DAY I STOPPED GIVING IT AWAY.
YOU SEE, THAT'S THE DIFFERENCE BETWEEN US, FRANCINE... THAT'S WHY I'M ON TOP OF THE WORLD AND YOU'RE TIED TO A CHAIR.
IT'S VERY SYMBOLIC, DON'T YOU THINK?
IN MANY WAYS... YOU REMIND ME... OF EMMA.
THE LAST TIME I SAW EMMA SHE WAS IN A CHAIR, JUST LIKE YOU ARE NOW. IT WAS PATHETIC.
SHE LOVED KATINA, TOO.
BUT SHE WAS A JUNKIE.
SO I FILLED HER FULL OF HEROIN WITH AN INFECTED NEEDLE AND SENT HER ON HER WAY.
FLIK
IT TOOK SIX YEARS FOR HER TO DIE... AND I LOVED EVERY MINUTE OF IT.

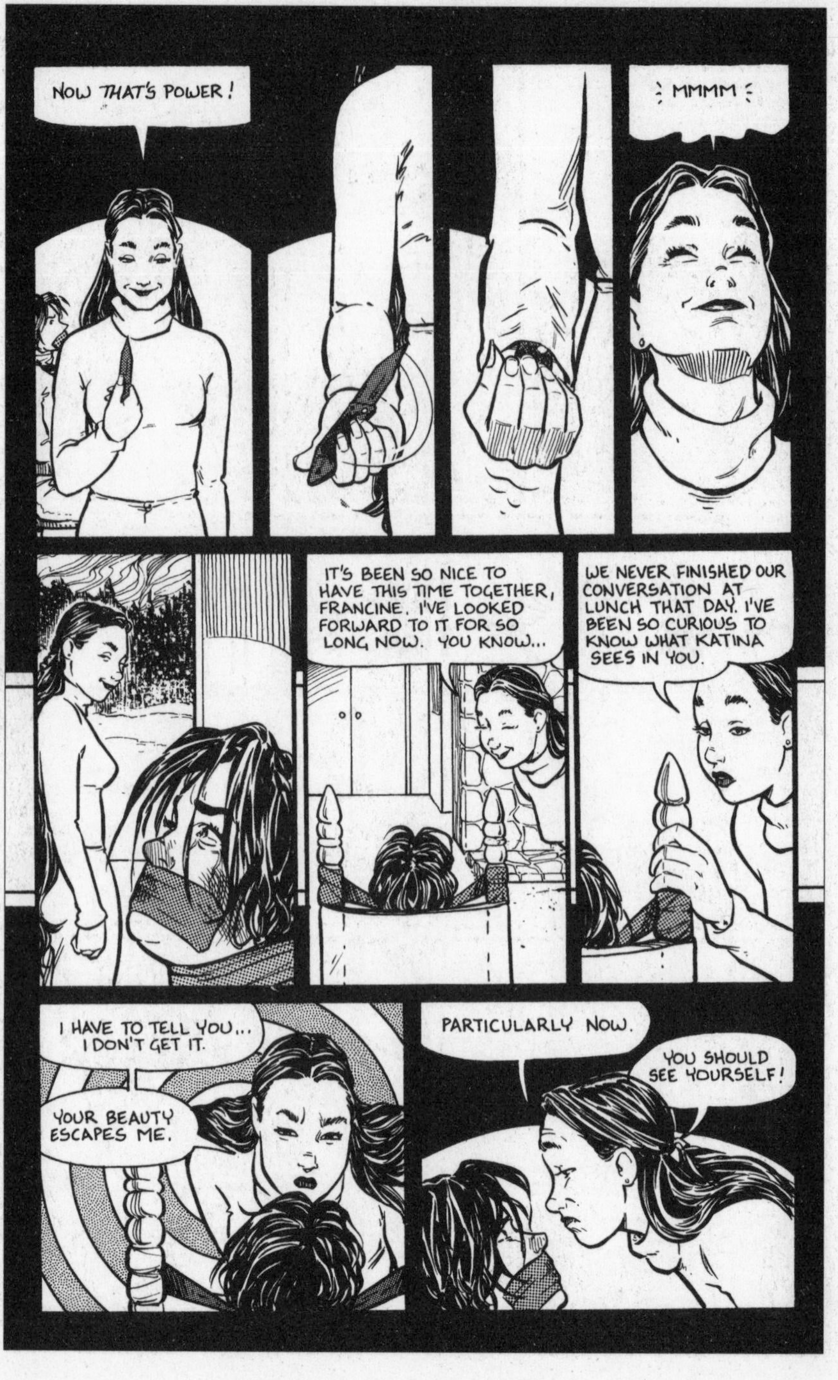
NOW THAT'S POWER!
MMMM
IT'S BEEN SO NICE TO HAVE THIS TIME TOGETHER, FRANCINE. I'VE LOOKED FORWARD TO IT FOR SO LONG NOW. YOU KNOW...
WE NEVER FINISHED OUR CONVERSATION AT LUNCH THAT DAY. I'VE BEEN SO CURIOUS TO KNOW WHAT KATINA SEES IN YOU.
I HAVE TO TELL YOU... I DON'T GET IT.
YOUR BEAUTY ESCAPES ME.
PARTICULARLY NOW.
YOU SHOULD SEE YOURSELF!

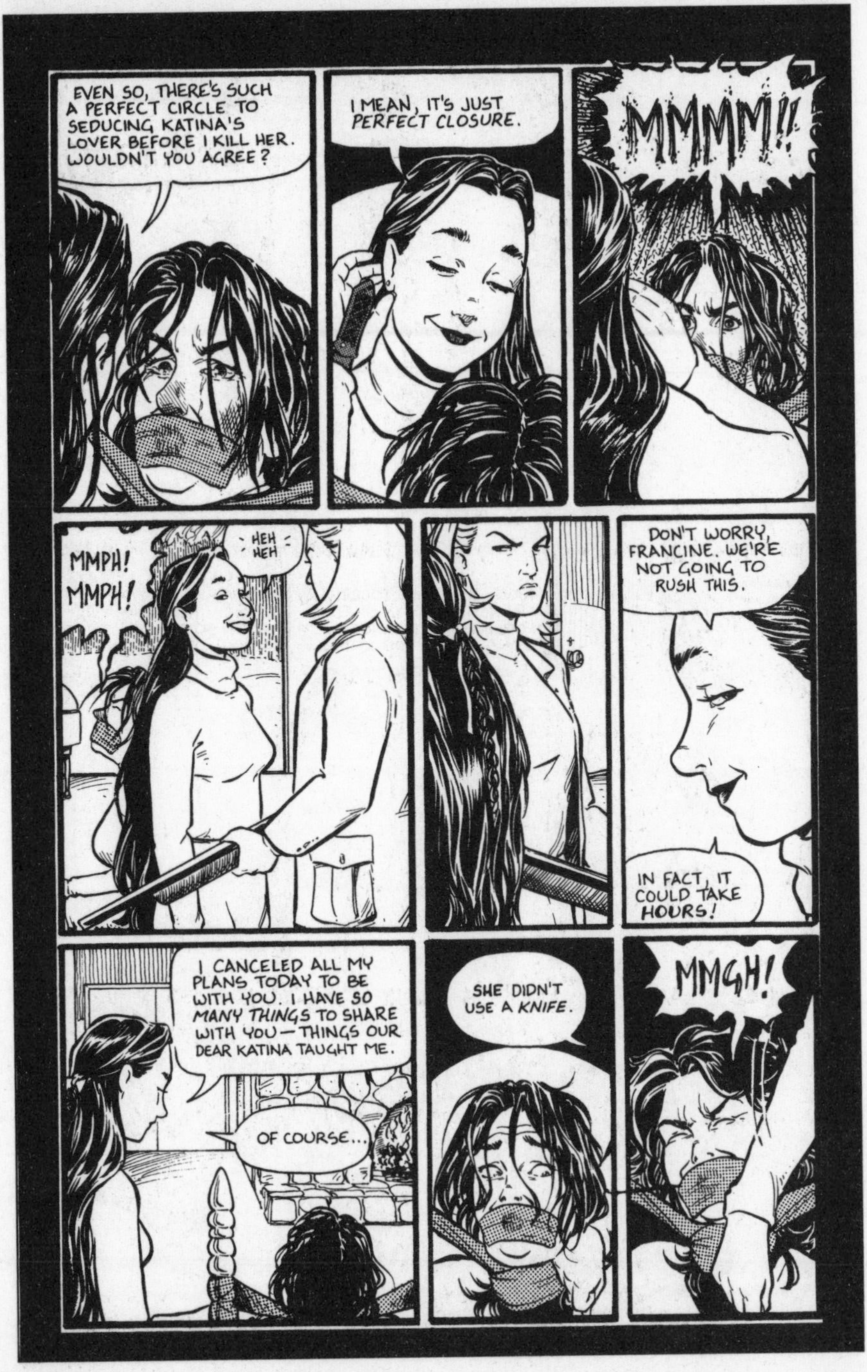
EVEN SO, THERE'S SUCH A PERFECT CIRCLE TO SEDUCING KATINA'S LOVER BEFORE I KILL HER. WOULDN'T YOU AGREE?
I MEAN, IT'S JUST PERFECT CLOSURE.
MMMM!!
MMPH! MMPH!
HEH HEH
DON'T WORRY, FRANCINE. WE'RE NOT GOING TO RUSH THIS.
IN FACT, IT COULD TAKE HOURS!
I CANCELED ALL MY PLANS TODAY TO BE WITH YOU. I HAVE SO MANY THINGS TO SHARE WITH YOU—THINGS OUR DEAR KATINA TAUGHT ME.
OF COURSE...
SHE DIDN'T USE A KNIFE.
MMGH!

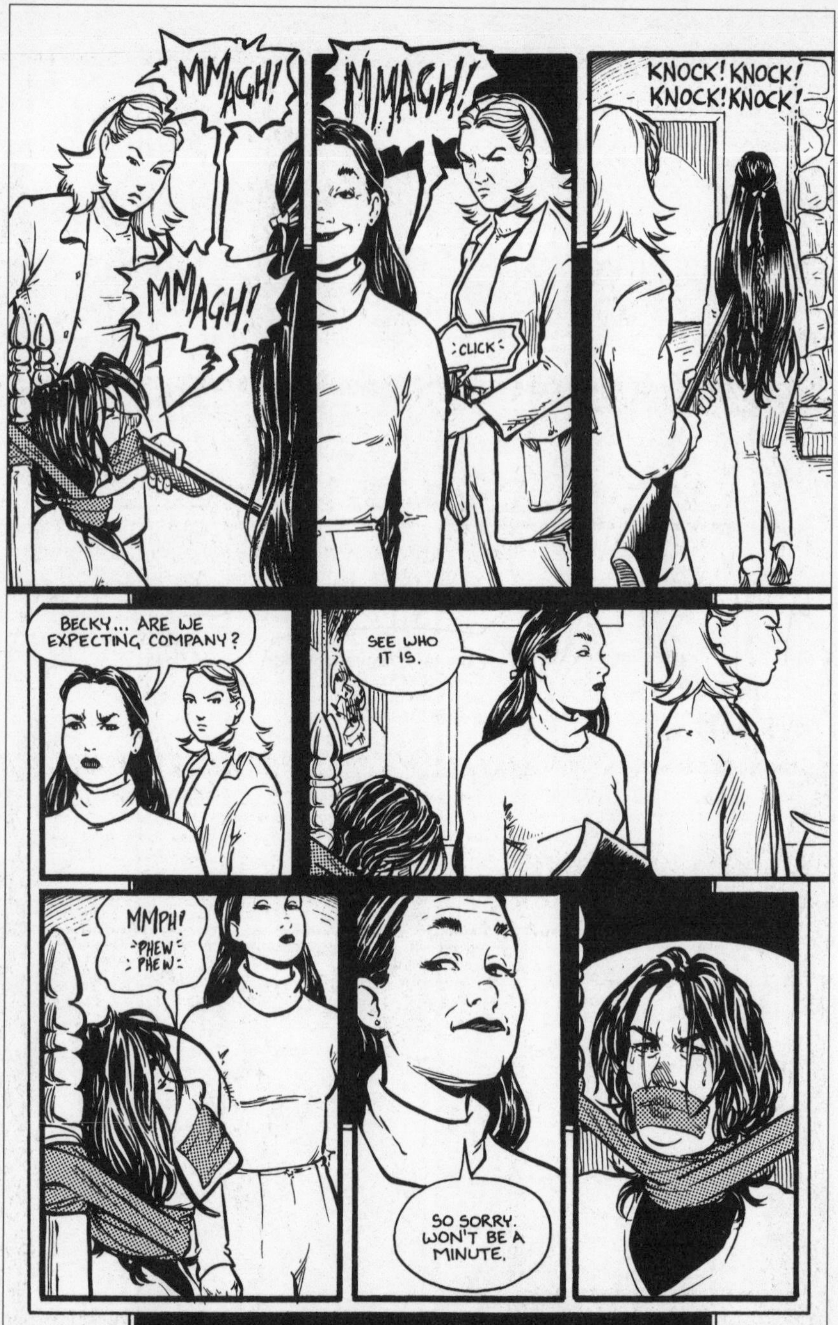
MMAGH!
MMAGH!
MMAGH!
CLICK
KNOCK! KNOCK!
KNOCK! KNOCK!
BECKY... ARE WE EXPECTING COMPANY?
SEE WHO IT IS.
MMPH!
PHEW
PHEW
SO SORRY. WON'T BE A MINUTE.

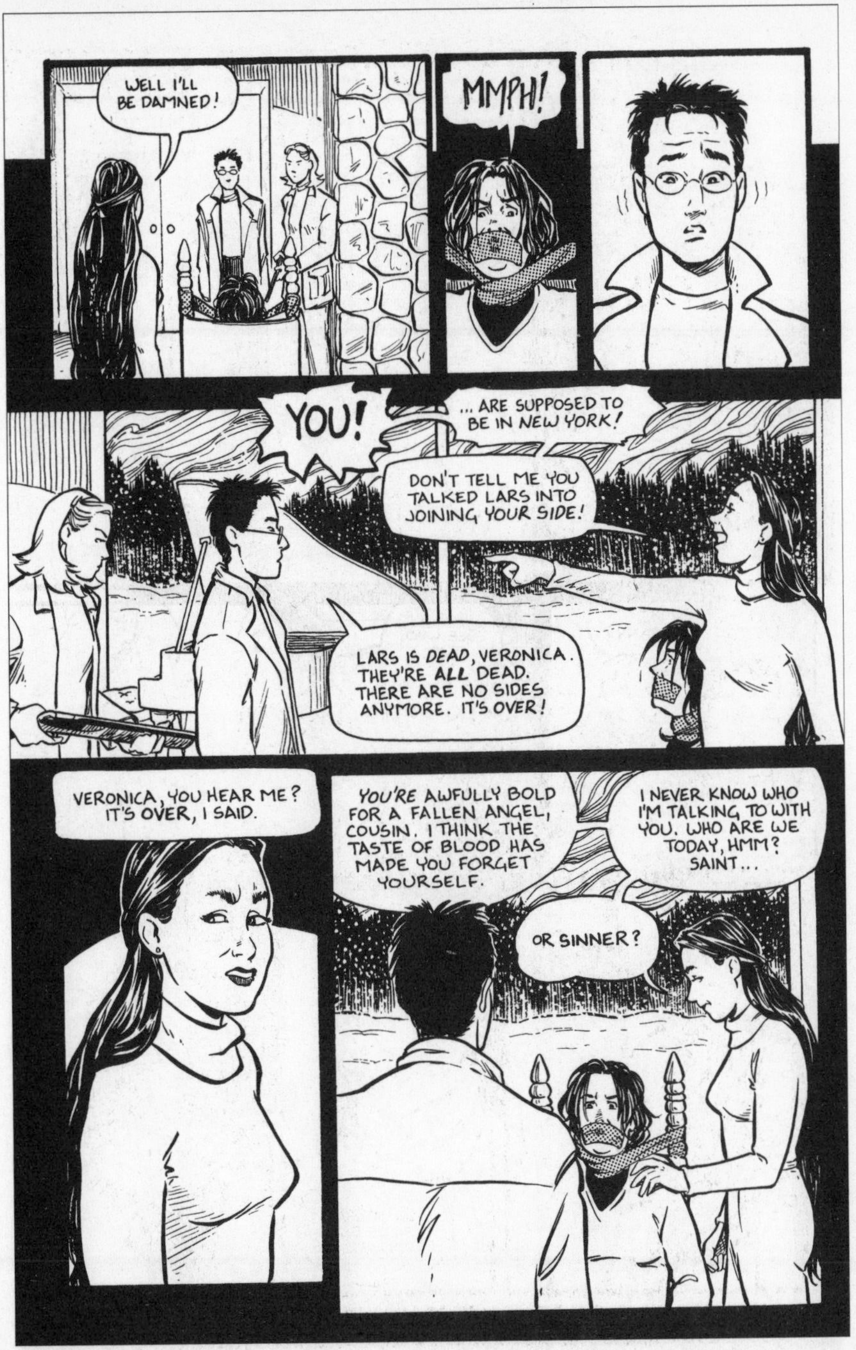
WELL I'LL BE DAMNED!
MMPH!
YOU!
... ARE SUPPOSED TO BE IN NEW YORK!
DON'T TELL ME YOU TALKED LARS INTO JOINING YOUR SIDE!
LARS IS DEAD, VERONICA. THEY'RE ALL DEAD. THERE ARE NO SIDES ANYMORE. IT'S OVER!
VERONICA, YOU HEAR ME? IT'S OVER, I SAID.
YOU'RE AWFULLY BOLD FOR A FALLEN ANGEL, COUSIN. I THINK THE TASTE OF BLOOD HAS MADE YOU FORGET YOURSELF.
I NEVER KNOW WHO I'M TALKING TO WITH YOU. WHO ARE WE TODAY, HMM? SAINT...
OR SINNER?

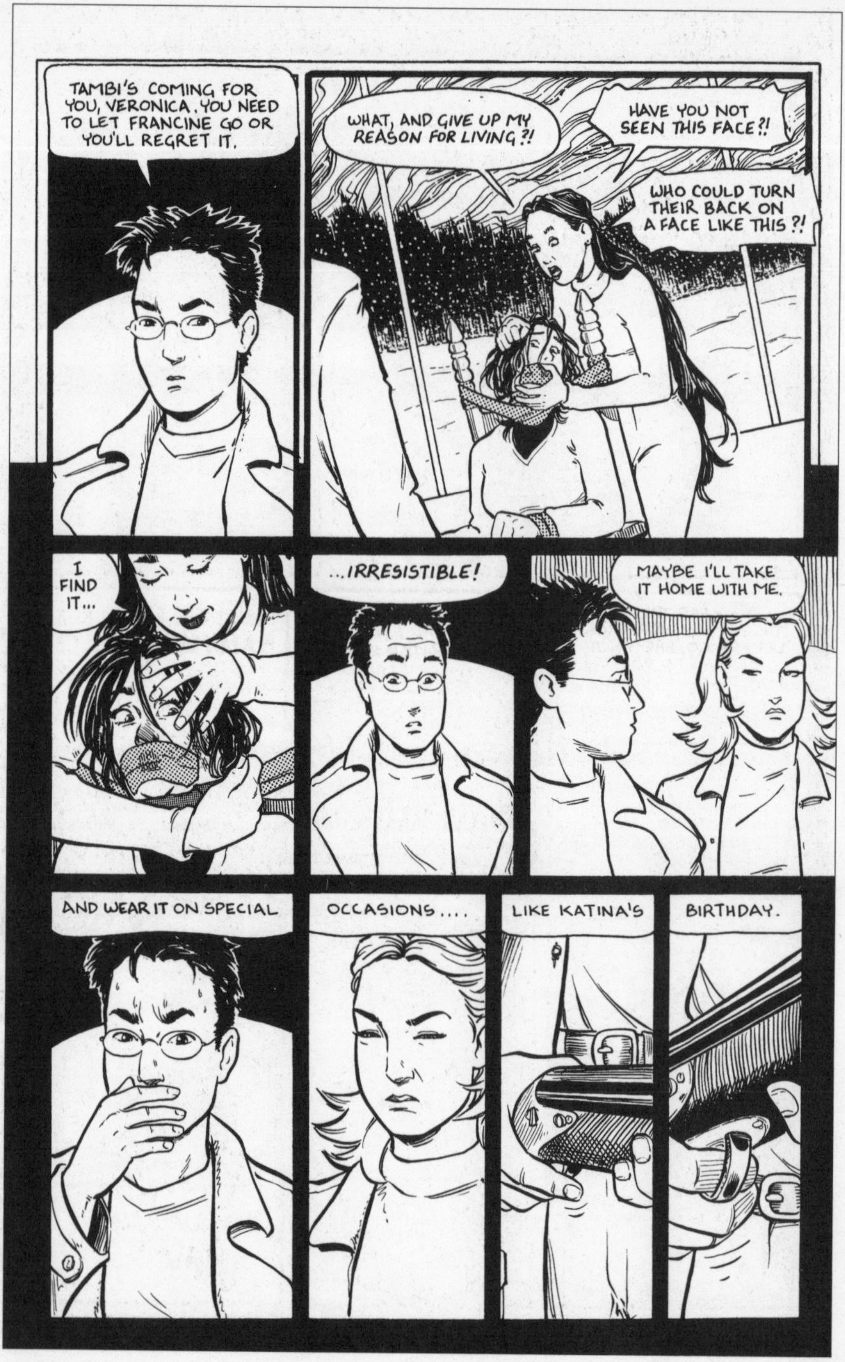
TAMBI'S COMING FOR YOU, VERONICA. YOU NEED TO LET FRANCINE GO OR YOU'LL REGRET IT.
WHAT, AND GIVE UP MY REASON FOR LIVING?!
HAVE YOU NOT SEEN THIS FACE?!
WHO COULD TURN THEIR BACK ON A FACE LIKE THIS?!
I FIND IT...
...IRRESISTIBLE!
MAYBE I'LL TAKE IT HOME WITH ME.
AND WEAR IT ON SPECIAL
OCCASIONS....
LIKE KATINA'S
BIRTHDAY.

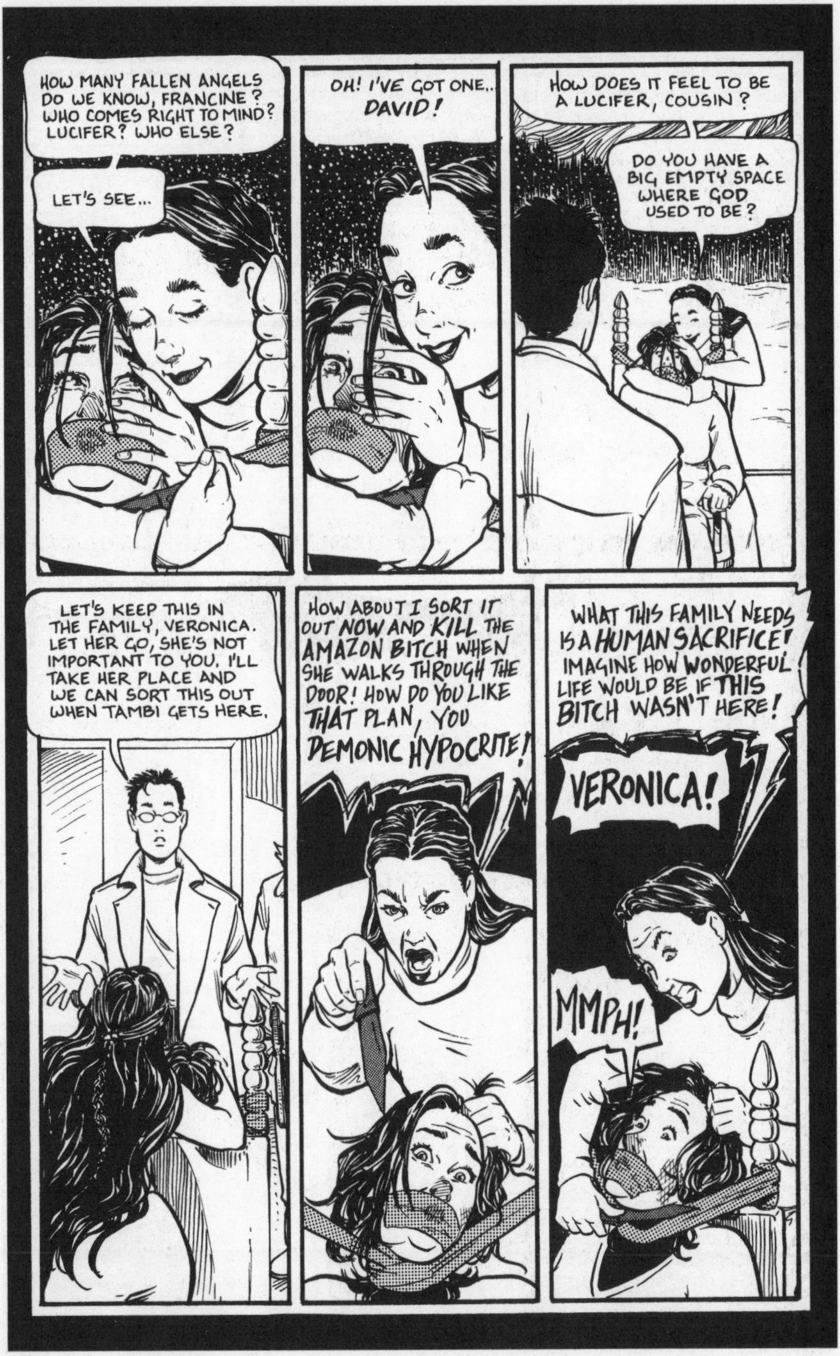

HOW MANY FALLEN ANGELS DO WE KNOW, FRANCINE? WHO COMES RIGHT TO MIND? LUCIFER? WHO ELSE?
LET'S SEE...
OH! I'VE GOT ONE.. DAVID!
HOW DOES IT FEEL TO BE A LUCIFER, COUSIN?
DO YOU HAVE A BIG EMPTY SPACE WHERE GOD USED TO BE?
LET'S KEEP THIS IN THE FAMILY, VERONICA. LET HER GO, SHE'S NOT IMPORTANT TO YOU. I'LL TAKE HER PLACE AND WE CAN SORT THIS OUT WHEN TAMBI GETS HERE.
HOW ABOUT I SORT IT OUT NOW AND KILL THE AMAZON BITCH WHEN SHE WALKS THROUGH THE DOOR! HOW DO YOU LIKE THAT PLAN, YOU DEMONIC HYPOCRITE!
WHAT THIS FAMILY NEEDS IS A HUMAN SACRIFICE! IMAGINE HOW WONDERFUL LIFE WOULD BE IF THIS BITCH WASN'T HERE!
VERONICA!
MMPH!

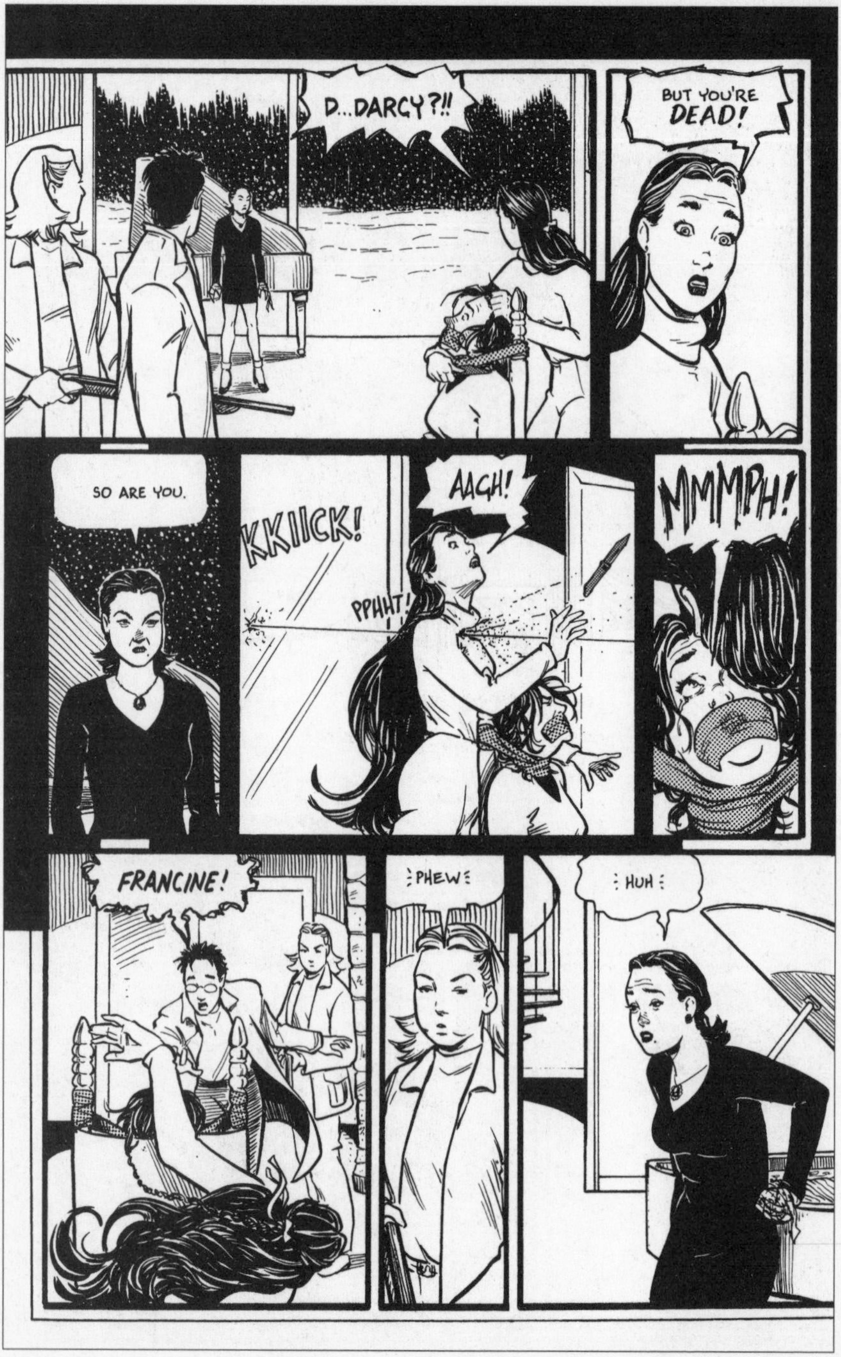
D...DARCY?!!
BUT YOU'RE DEAD!
SO ARE YOU.
KKIICK!
AAGH!
PPHHT!
MMMPH!
FRANCINE!
PHEW
HUH

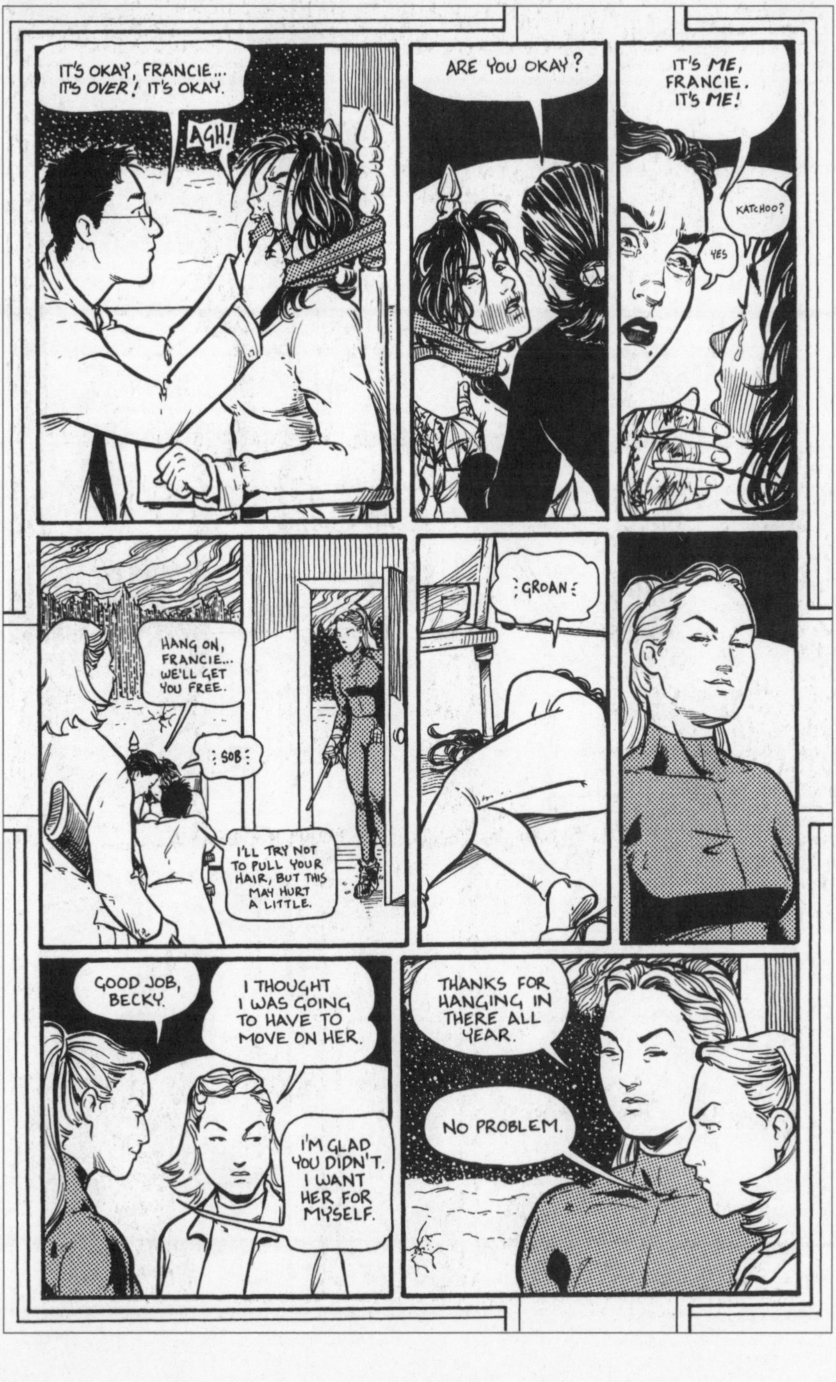

IT'S OKAY, FRANCIE... IT'S OVER! IT'S OKAY.
AGH!
ARE YOU OKAY?
IT'S ME, FRANCIE. IT'S ME!
KATCHOO?
YES
HANG ON, FRANCIE... WE'LL GET YOU FREE.
SOB
I'LL TRY NOT TO PULL YOUR HAIR, BUT THIS MAY HURT A LITTLE.
GROAN
GOOD JOB, BECKY.
I THOUGHT I WAS GOING TO HAVE TO MOVE ON HER.
I'M GLAD YOU DIDN'T. I WANT HER FOR MYSELF.
THANKS FOR HANGING IN THERE ALL YEAR.
NO PROBLEM.

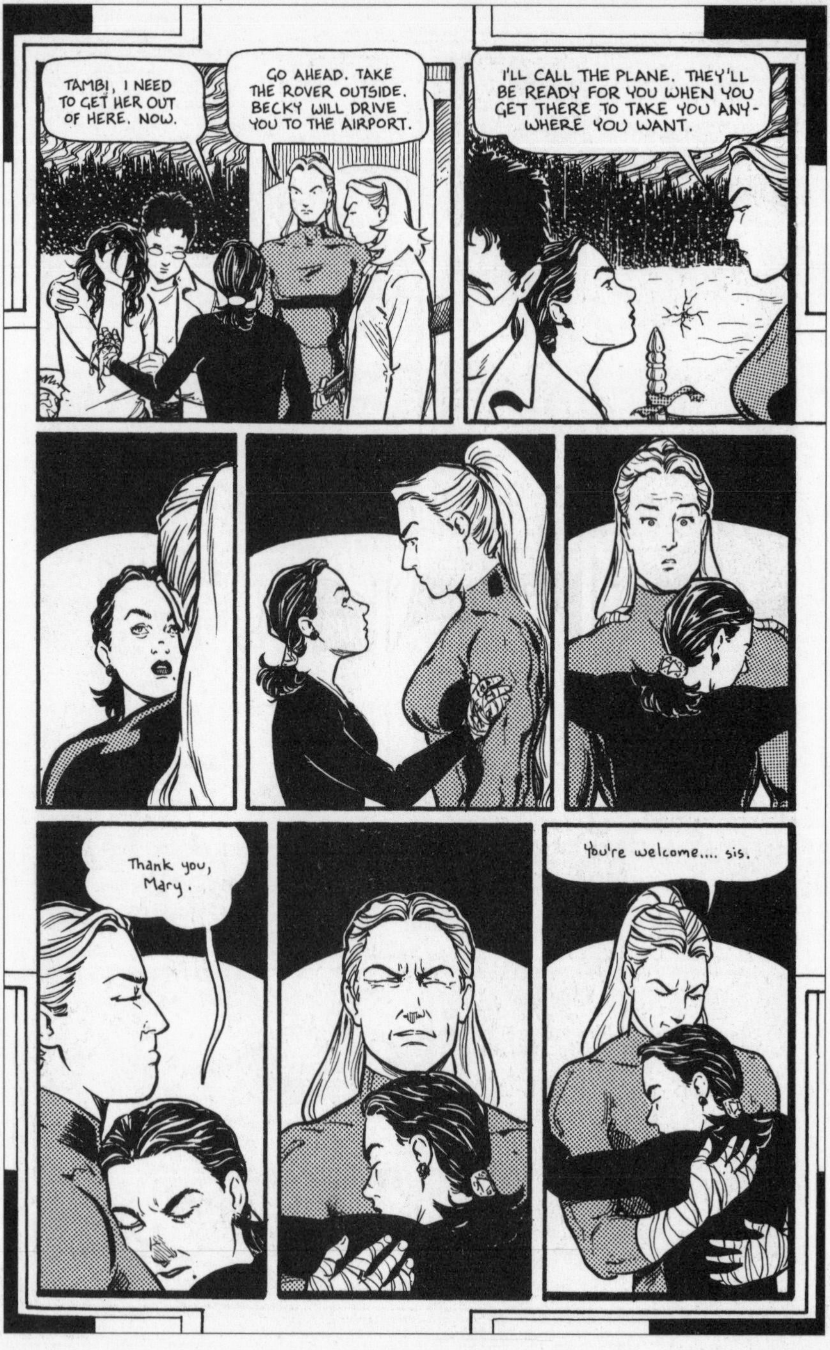
TAMBI, I NEED TO GET HER OUT OF HERE. NOW.
GO AHEAD. TAKE THE ROVER OUTSIDE. BECKY WILL DRIVE YOU TO THE AIRPORT.
I'LL CALL THE PLANE. THEY'LL BE READY FOR YOU WHEN YOU GET THERE TO TAKE YOU ANYWHERE YOU WANT.
Thank you, Mary.
You're welcome.... sis.

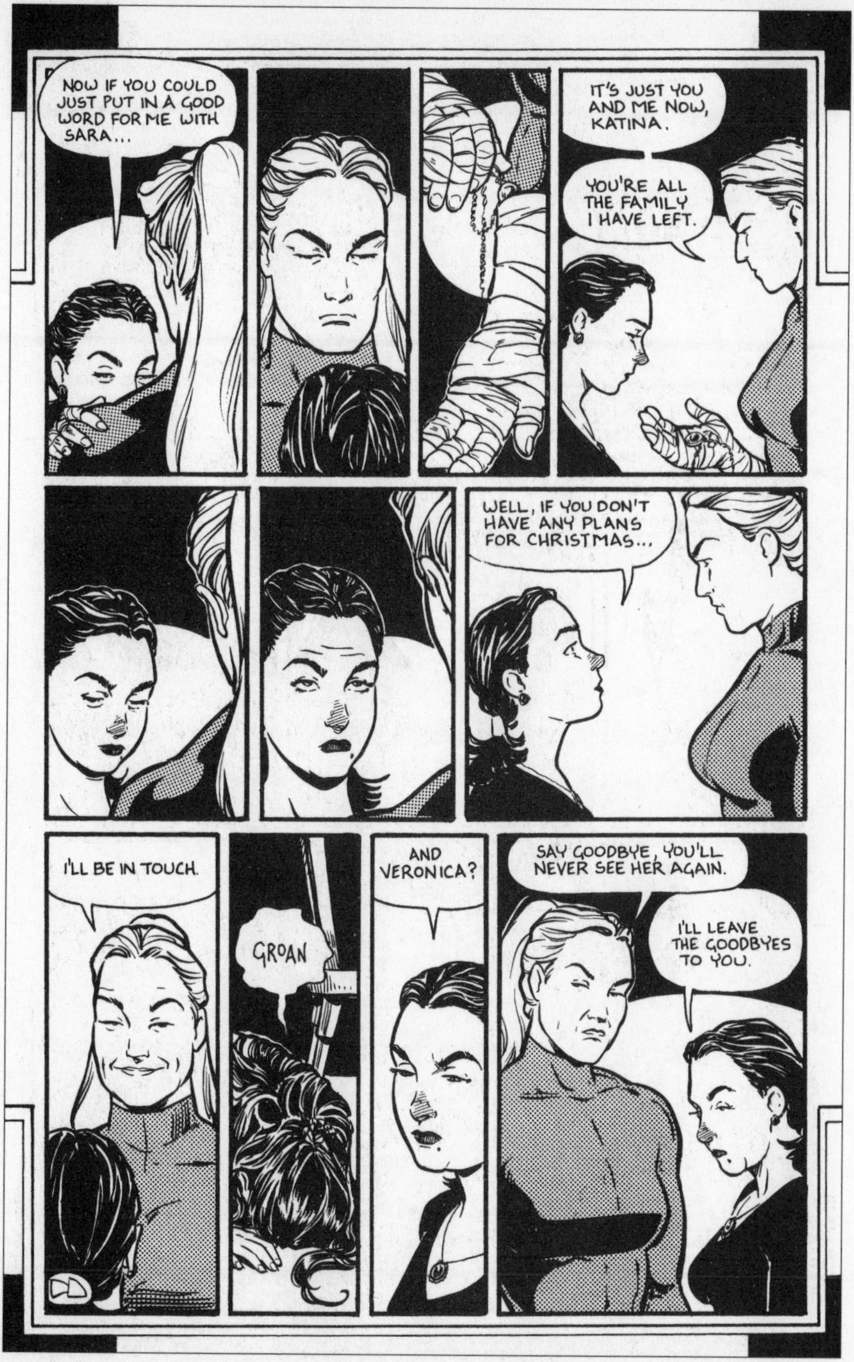
NOW IF YOU COULD JUST PUT IN A GOOD WORD FOR ME WITH SARA...
IT'S JUST YOU AND ME NOW, KATINA.
YOU'RE ALL THE FAMILY I HAVE LEFT.
WELL, IF YOU DON'T HAVE ANY PLANS FOR CHRISTMAS...
I'LL BE IN TOUCH.
GROAN
AND VERONICA?
SAY GOODBYE, YOU'LL NEVER SEE HER AGAIN.
I'LL LEAVE THE GOODBYES TO YOU.

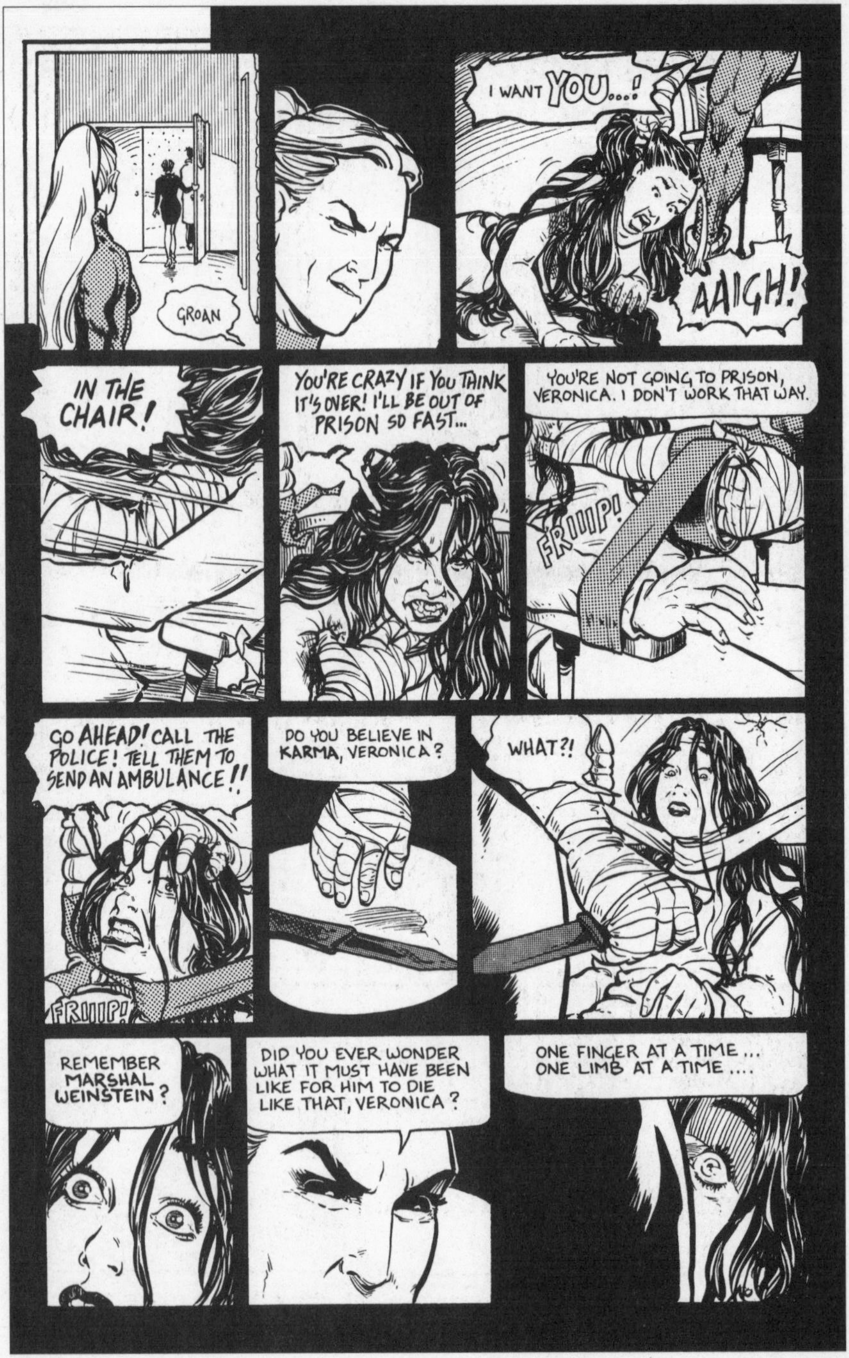
GROAN
I WANT YOU...!
AAIGH!
IN THE CHAIR!
YOU'RE CRAZY IF YOU THINK IT'S OVER! I'LL BE OUT OF PRISON SO FAST...
YOU'RE NOT GOING TO PRISON, VERONICA. I DON'T WORK THAT WAY.
FRIIIP!
GO AHEAD! CALL THE POLICE! TELL THEM TO SEND AN AMBULANCE!!
FRIIIP!
DO YOU BELIEVE IN KARMA, VERONICA?
WHAT?!
REMEMBER MARSHAL WEINSTEIN?
DID YOU EVER WONDER WHAT IT MUST HAVE BEEN LIKE FOR HIM TO DIE LIKE THAT, VERONICA?
ONE FINGER AT A TIME...
ONE LIMB AT A TIME....

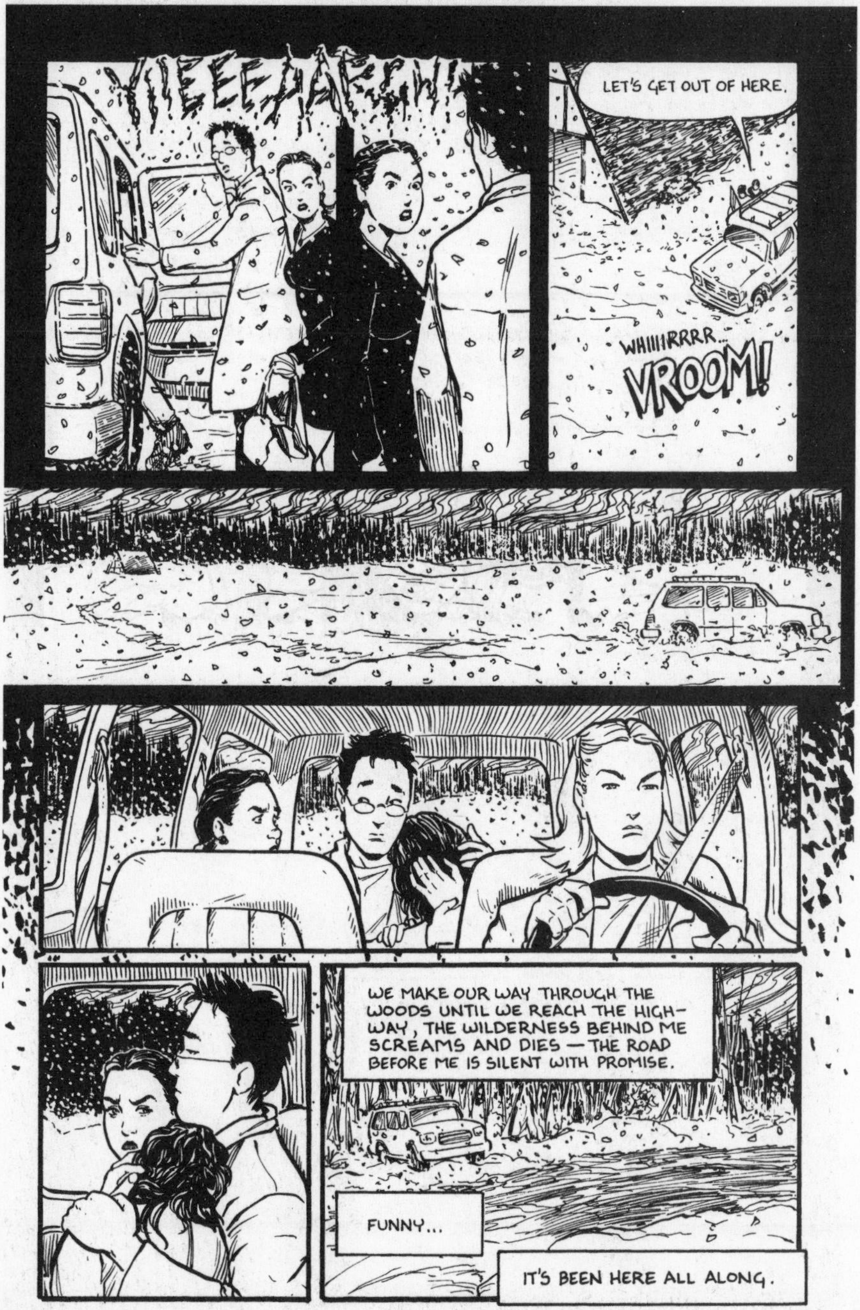
LET'S GET OUT OF HERE.
WHIIIIRRRR...
VROOM!
WE MAKE OUR WAY THROUGH THE WOODS UNTIL WE REACH THE HIGH-WAY, THE WILDERNESS BEHIND ME SCREAMS AND DIES — THE ROAD BEFORE ME IS SILENT WITH PROMISE.
FUNNY...
IT'S BEEN HERE ALL ALONG.

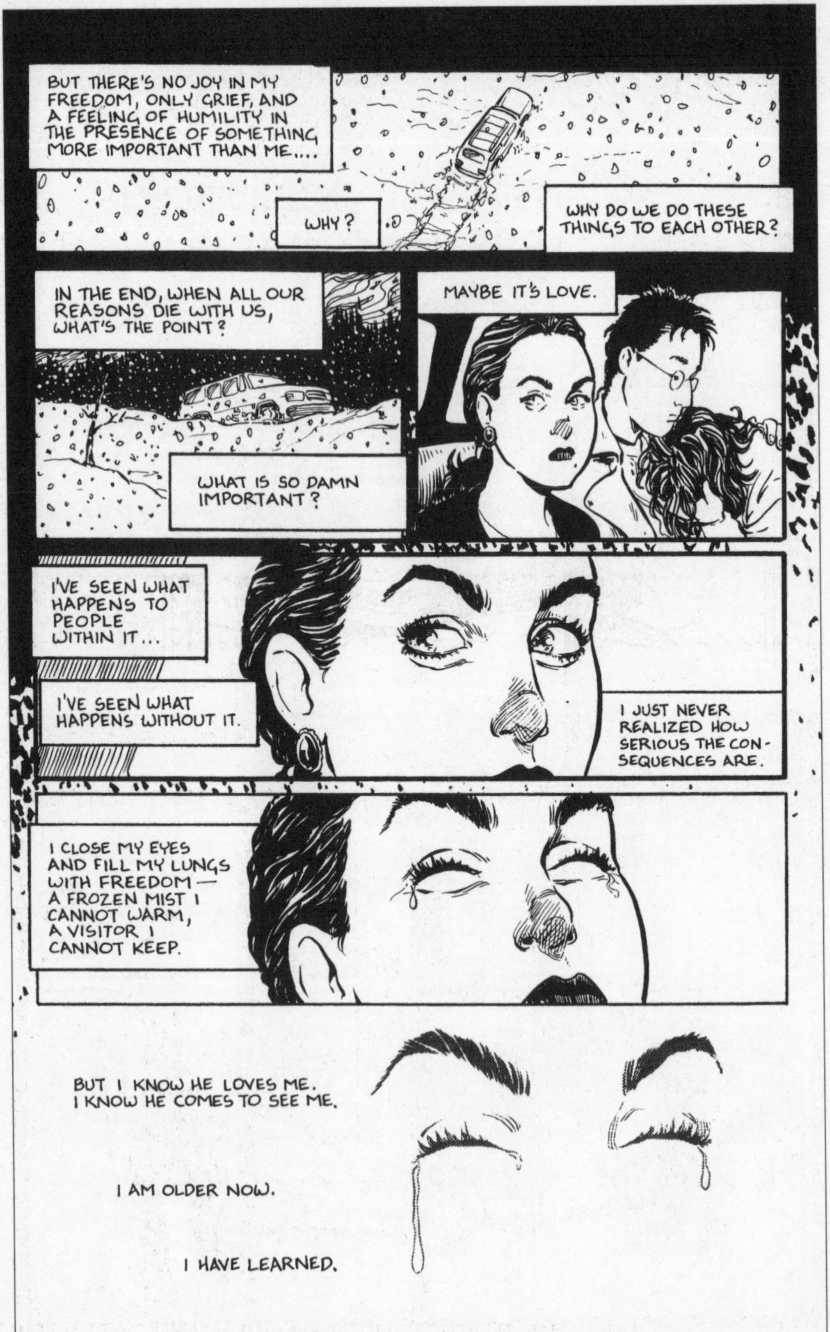
BUT THERE'S NO JOY IN MY FREEDOM, ONLY GRIEF, AND A FEELING OF HUMILITY IN THE PRESENCE OF SOMETHING MORE IMPORTANT THAN ME....
WHY?
WHY DO WE DO THESE THINGS TO EACH OTHER?
IN THE END, WHEN ALL OUR REASONS DIE WITH US, WHAT'S THE POINT?
WHAT IS SO DAMN IMPORTANT?
MAYBE IT'S LOVE.
I'VE SEEN WHAT HAPPENS TO PEOPLE WITHIN IT...
I'VE SEEN WHAT HAPPENS WITHOUT IT.
I JUST NEVER REALIZED HOW SERIOUS THE CON-SEQUENCES ARE.
I CLOSE MY EYES AND FILL MY LUNGS WITH FREEDOM— A FROZEN MIST I CANNOT WARM, A VISITOR I CANNOT KEEP.
BUT I KNOW HE LOVES ME. I KNOW HE COMES TO SEE ME.
I AM OLDER NOW.
I HAVE LEARNED.

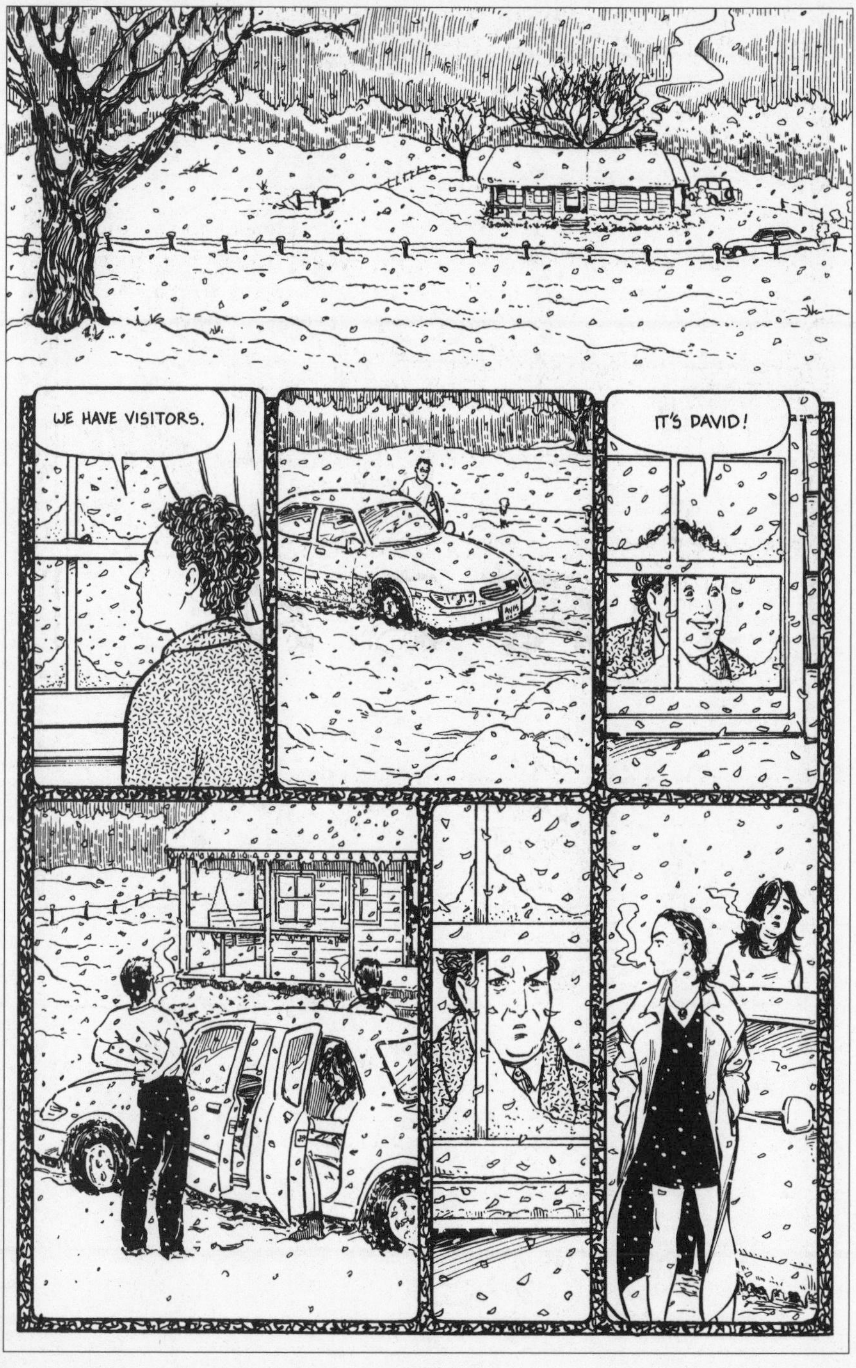
WE HAVE VISITORS.
IT'S DAVID!

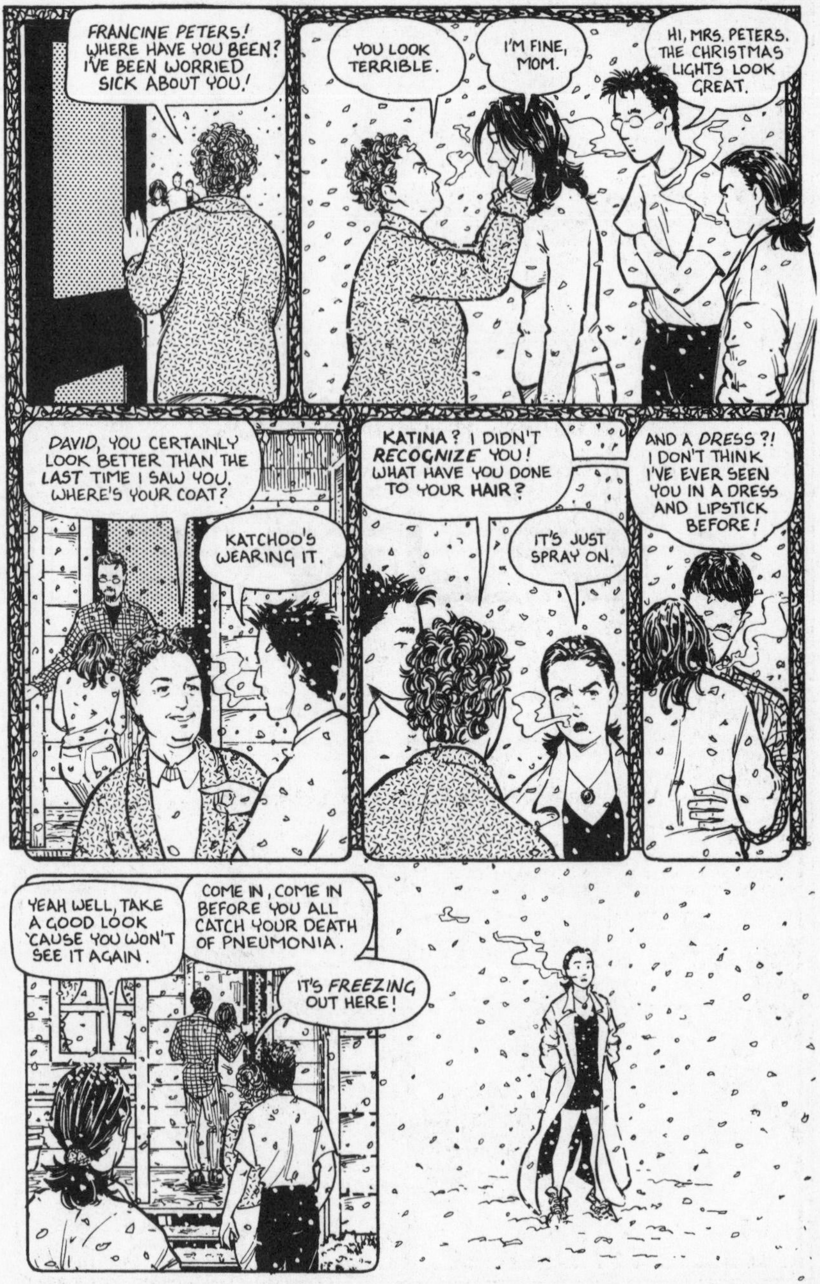
FRANCINE PETERS! WHERE HAVE YOU BEEN? I'VE BEEN WORRIED SICK ABOUT YOU!
YOU LOOK TERRIBLE.
I'M FINE, MOM.
HI, MRS. PETERS. THE CHRISTMAS LIGHTS LOOK GREAT.
DAVID, YOU CERTAINLY LOOK BETTER THAN THE LAST TIME I SAW YOU. WHERE'S YOUR COAT?
KATCHOO'S WEARING IT.
KATINA? I DIDN'T RECOGNIZE YOU! WHAT HAVE YOU DONE TO YOUR HAIR?
IT'S JUST SPRAY ON.
AND A DRESS?! I DON'T THINK I'VE EVER SEEN YOU IN A DRESS AND LIPSTICK BEFORE!
YEAH WELL, TAKE A GOOD LOOK 'CAUSE YOU WON'T SEE IT AGAIN.
COME IN, COME IN BEFORE YOU ALL CATCH YOUR DEATH OF PNEUMONIA.
IT'S FREEZING OUT HERE!

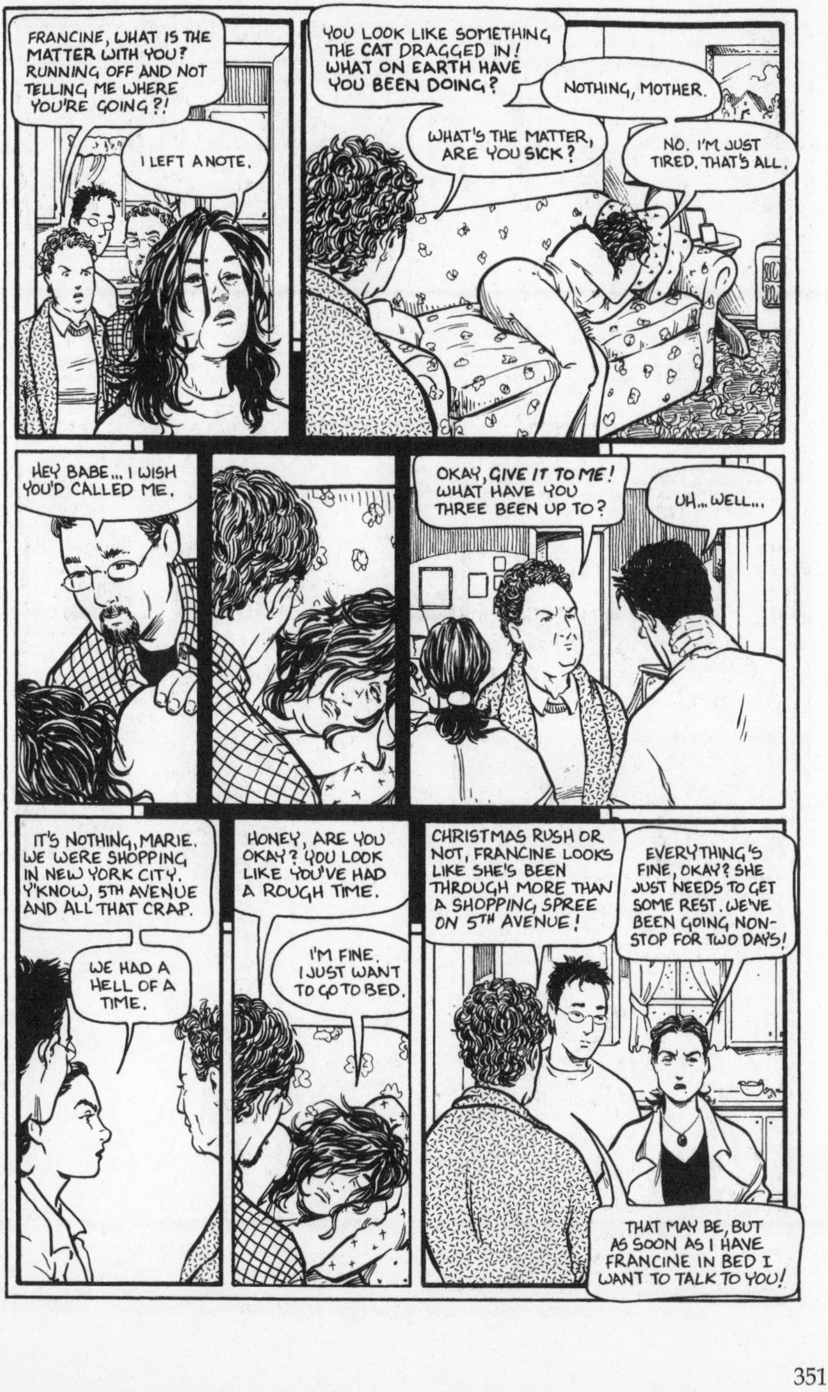
FRANCINE, WHAT IS THE MATTER WITH YOU? RUNNING OFF AND NOT TELLING ME WHERE YOU'RE GOING?!
I LEFT A NOTE.
YOU LOOK LIKE SOMETHING THE CAT DRAGGED IN! WHAT ON EARTH HAVE YOU BEEN DOING?
NOTHING, MOTHER.
WHAT'S THE MATTER, ARE YOU SICK?
NO. I'M JUST TIRED. THAT'S ALL.
HEY BABE... I WISH YOU'D CALLED ME.
OKAY, GIVE IT TO ME! WHAT HAVE YOU THREE BEEN UP TO?
UH... WELL...
IT'S NOTHING, MARIE. WE WERE SHOPPING IN NEW YORK CITY. Y'KNOW, 5TH AVENUE AND ALL THAT CRAP.
WE HAD A HELL OF A TIME.
HONEY, ARE YOU OKAY? YOU LOOK LIKE YOU'VE HAD A ROUGH TIME.
I'M FINE. I JUST WANT TO GO TO BED.
CHRISTMAS RUSH OR NOT, FRANCINE LOOKS LIKE SHE'S BEEN THROUGH MORE THAN A SHOPPING SPREE ON 5TH AVENUE!
EVERYTHING'S FINE, OKAY? SHE JUST NEEDS TO GET SOME REST. WE'VE BEEN GOING NON-STOP FOR TWO DAYS!
THAT MAY BE, BUT AS SOON AS I HAVE FRANCINE IN BED I WANT TO TALK TO YOU!

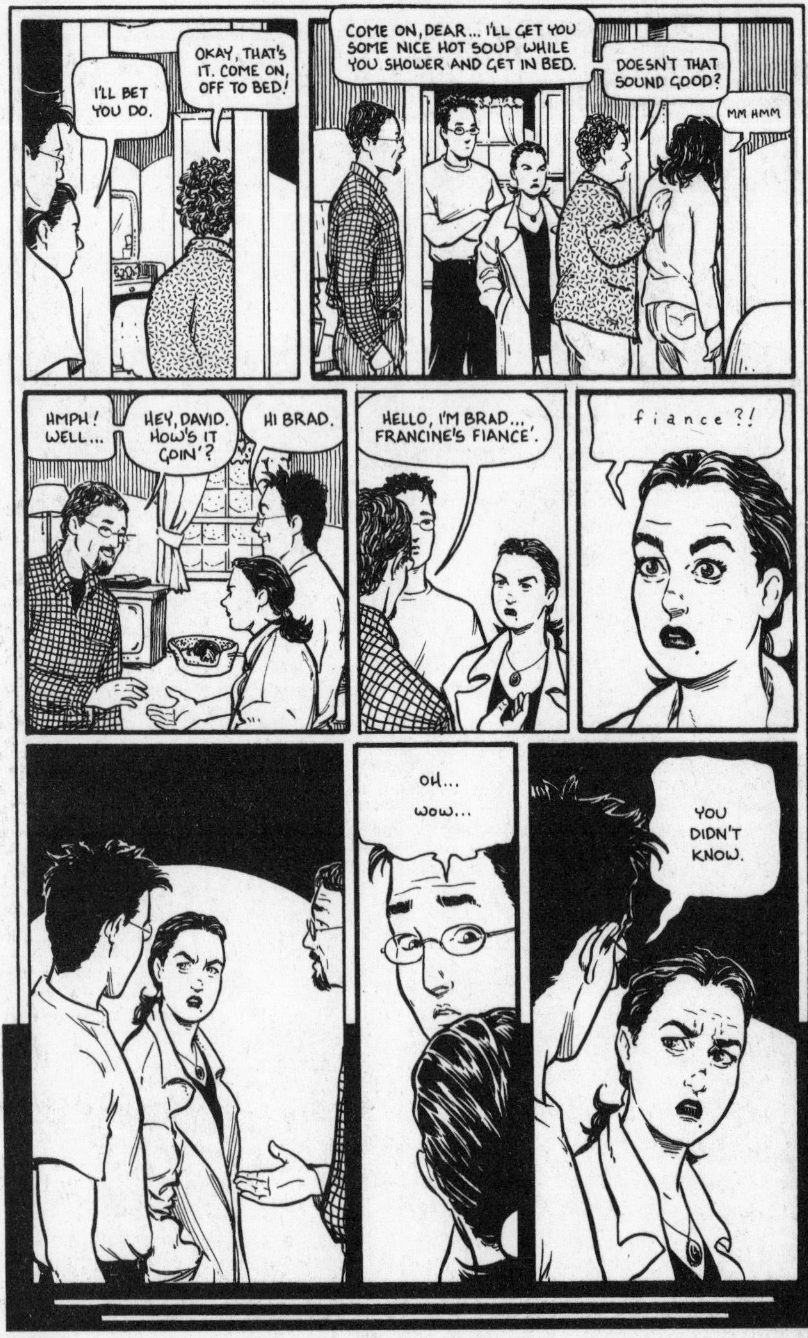
I'LL BET YOU DO.
OKAY, THAT'S IT. COME ON, OFF TO BED!
COME ON, DEAR... I'LL GET YOU SOME NICE HOT SOUP WHILE YOU SHOWER AND GET IN BED.
DOESN'T THAT SOUND GOOD?
MM HMM
HMPH! WELL...
HEY, DAVID. HOW'S IT GOIN'?
HI BRAD.
HELLO, I'M BRAD... FRANCINE'S FIANCE'.
f i a n c e ?!
OH...
WOW...
YOU DIDN'T KNOW.

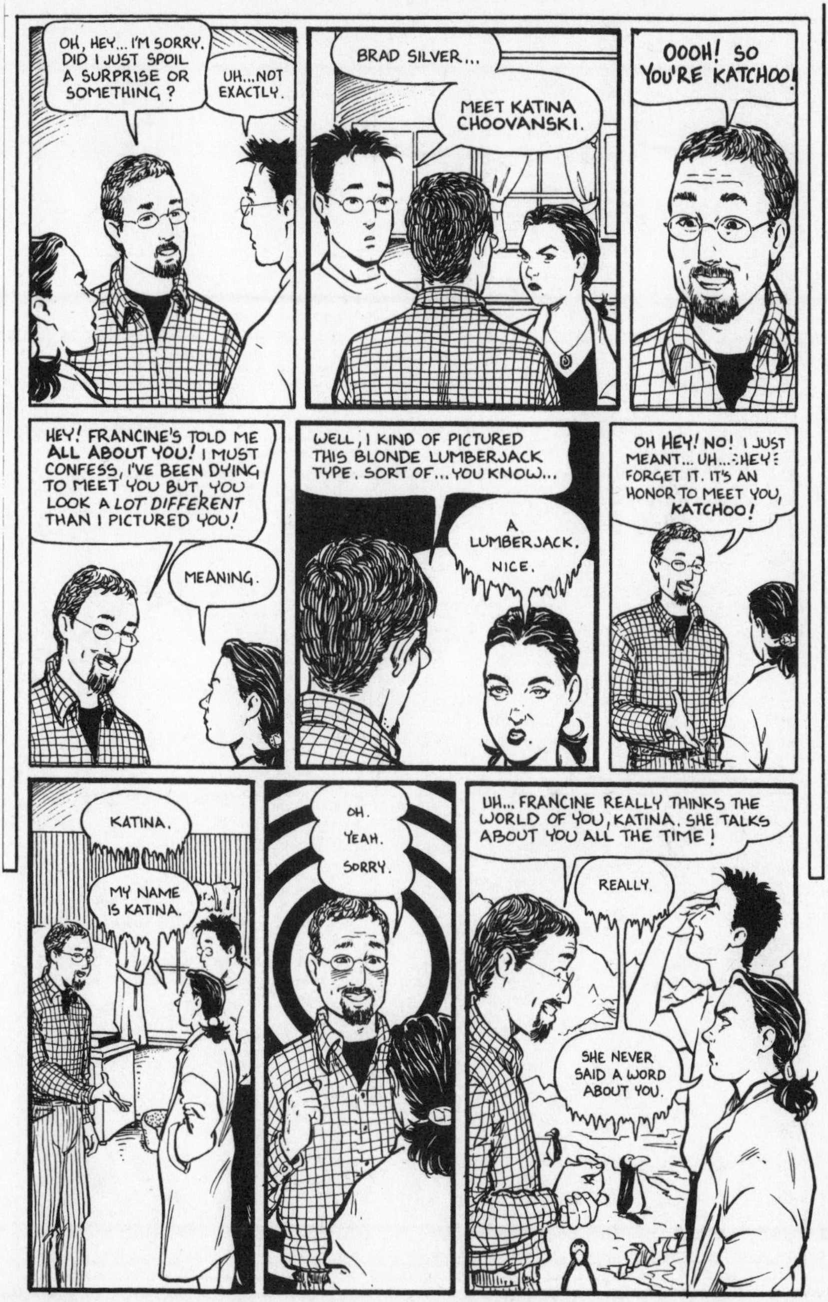

OH, HEY... I'M SORRY. DID I JUST SPOIL A SURPRISE OR SOMETHING?
UH...NOT EXACTLY.
BRAD SILVER...
MEET KATINA CHOOVANSKI.
OOOH! SO YOU'RE KATCHOO!
HEY! FRANCINE'S TOLD ME ALL ABOUT YOU! I MUST CONFESS, I'VE BEEN DYING TO MEET YOU BUT, YOU LOOK A LOT DIFFERENT THAN I PICTURED YOU!
MEANING.
WELL, I KIND OF PICTURED THIS BLONDE LUMBERJACK TYPE. SORT OF... YOU KNOW...
A LUMBERJACK. NICE.
OH HEY! NO! I JUST MEANT... UH... HEY! FORGET IT. IT'S AN HONOR TO MEET YOU, KATCHOO!
KATINA.
MY NAME IS KATINA.
OH.
YEAH.
SORRY.
UH... FRANCINE REALLY THINKS THE WORLD OF YOU, KATINA. SHE TALKS ABOUT YOU ALL THE TIME!
REALLY.
SHE NEVER SAID A WORD ABOUT YOU.

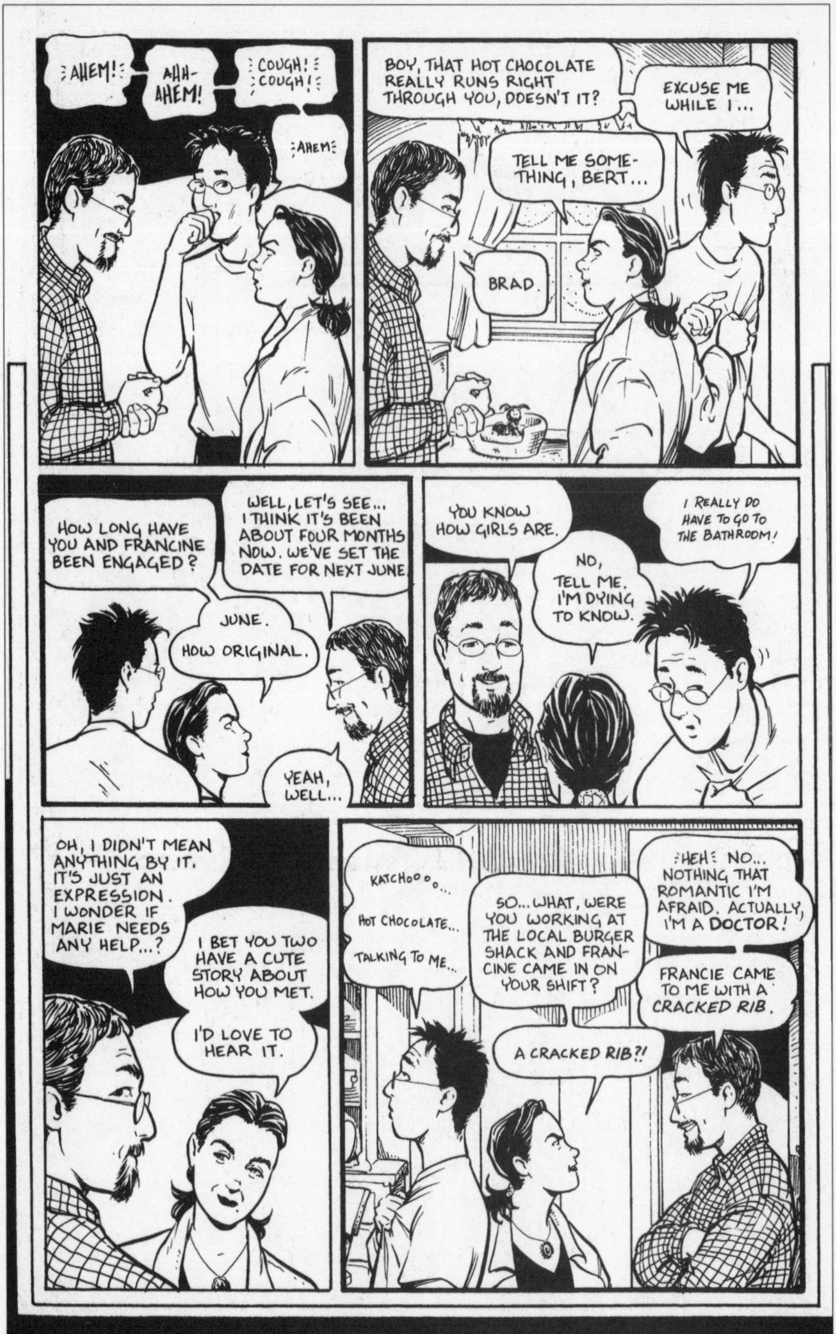
AHEM!
AHH-AHEM!
COUGH! COUGH!
AHEM
BOY, THAT HOT CHOCOLATE REALLY RUNS RIGHT THROUGH YOU, DOESN'T IT?
EXCUSE ME WHILE I...
TELL ME SOME-THING, BERT...
BRAD.
HOW LONG HAVE YOU AND FRANCINE BEEN ENGAGED?
WELL, LET'S SEE... I THINK IT'S BEEN ABOUT FOUR MONTHS NOW. WE'VE SET THE DATE FOR NEXT JUNE.
JUNE.
HOW ORIGINAL.
YEAH, WELL...
YOU KNOW HOW GIRLS ARE.
I REALLY DO HAVE TO GO TO THE BATHROOM!
NO, TELL ME. I'M DYING TO KNOW.
OH, I DIDN'T MEAN ANYTHING BY IT. IT'S JUST AN EXPRESSION. I WONDER IF MARIE NEEDS ANY HELP...?
I BET YOU TWO HAVE A CUTE STORY ABOUT HOW YOU MET.
I'D LOVE TO HEAR IT.
KATCHOOo o...
HOT CHOCOLATE...
TALKING TO ME...
SO... WHAT, WERE YOU WORKING AT THE LOCAL BURGER SHACK AND FRAN-CINE CAME IN ON YOUR SHIFT?
HEH NO... NOTHING THAT ROMANTIC I'M AFRAID. ACTUALLY, I'M A DOCTOR!
FRANCIE CAME TO ME WITH A CRACKED RIB.
A CRACKED RIB?!

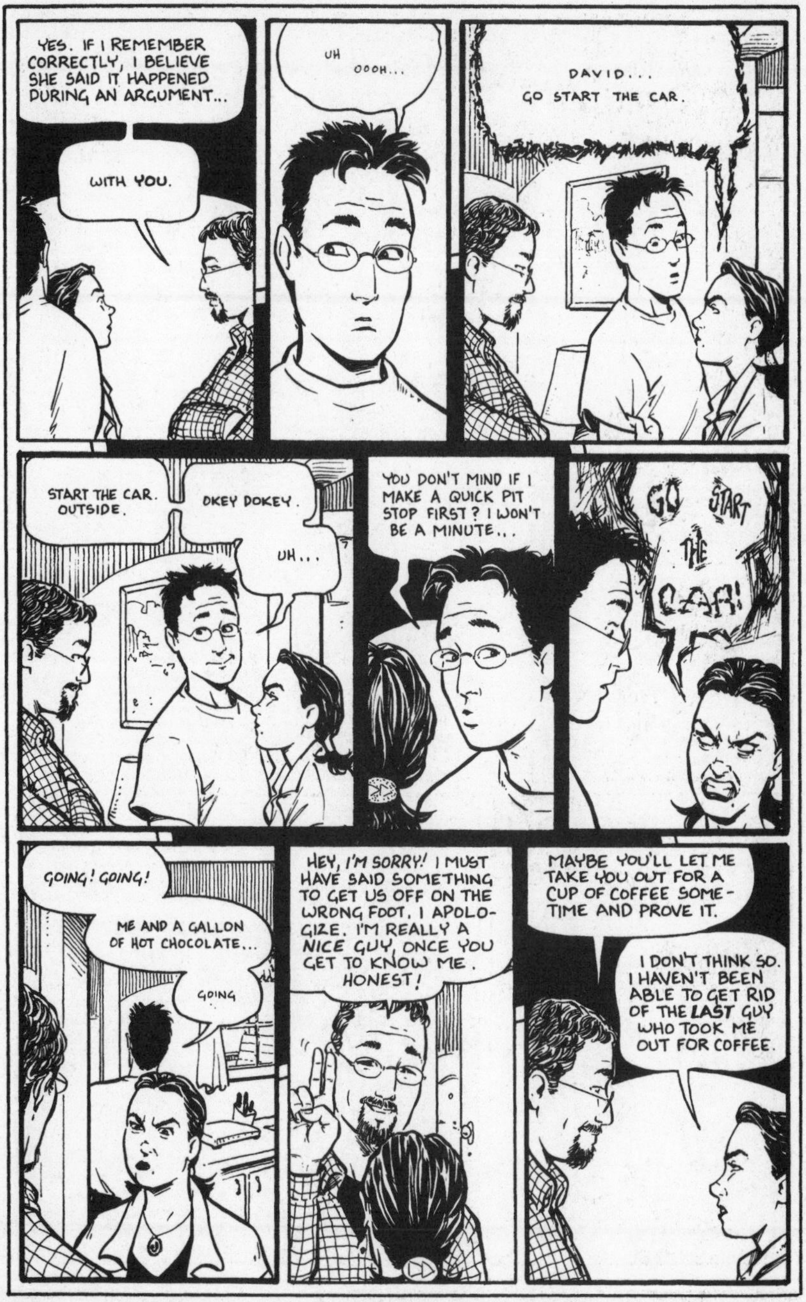
YES. IF I REMEMBER CORRECTLY, I BELIEVE SHE SAID IT HAPPENED DURING AN ARGUMENT...
WITH YOU.
UH
OOOH...
DAVID...
GO START THE CAR.
START THE CAR. OUTSIDE.
OKEY DOKEY.
UH...
YOU DON'T MIND IF I MAKE A QUICK PIT STOP FIRST? I WON'T BE A MINUTE...
GO START THE CAR!
GOING! GOING!
ME AND A GALLON OF HOT CHOCOLATE...
GOING
HEY, I'M SORRY! I MUST HAVE SAID SOMETHING TO GET US OFF ON THE WRONG FOOT. I APOLOGIZE. I'M REALLY A NICE GUY, ONCE YOU GET TO KNOW ME. HONEST!
MAYBE YOU'LL LET ME TAKE YOU OUT FOR A CUP OF COFFEE SOMETIME AND PROVE IT.
I DON'T THINK SO. I HAVEN'T BEEN ABLE TO GET RID OF THE LAST GUY WHO TOOK ME OUT FOR COFFEE.

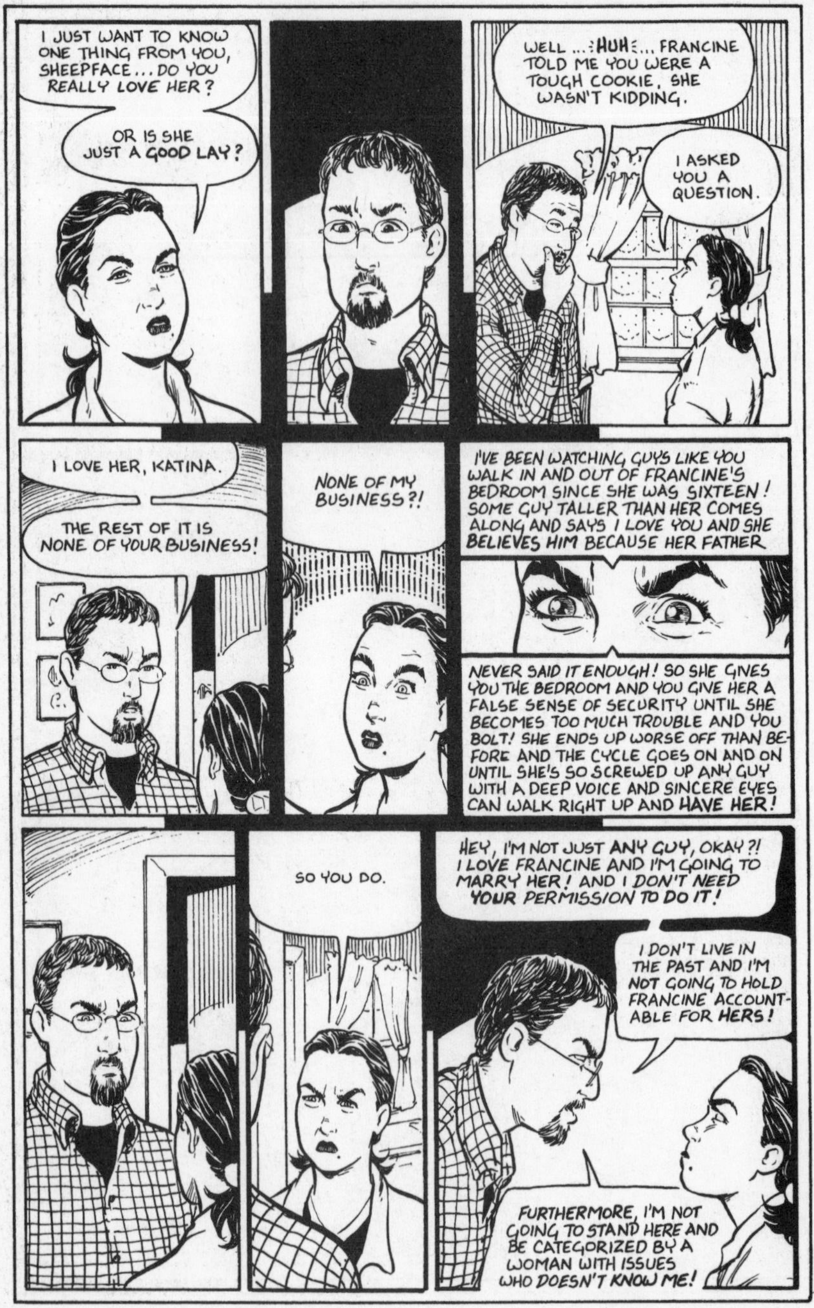
I JUST WANT TO KNOW ONE THING FROM YOU, SHEEPFACE... DO YOU REALLY LOVE HER?
OR IS SHE JUST A GOOD LAY?
WELL ... HUH ... FRANCINE TOLD ME YOU WERE A TOUGH COOKIE, SHE WASN'T KIDDING.
I ASKED YOU A QUESTION.
I LOVE HER, KATINA.
THE REST OF IT IS NONE OF YOUR BUSINESS!
NONE OF MY BUSINESS?!
I'VE BEEN WATCHING GUYS LIKE YOU WALK IN AND OUT OF FRANCINE'S BEDROOM SINCE SHE WAS SIXTEEN! SOME GUY TALLER THAN HER COMES ALONG AND SAYS I LOVE YOU AND SHE BELIEVES HIM BECAUSE HER FATHER
NEVER SAID IT ENOUGH! SO SHE GIVES YOU THE BEDROOM AND YOU GIVE HER A FALSE SENSE OF SECURITY UNTIL SHE BECOMES TOO MUCH TROUBLE AND YOU BOLT! SHE ENDS UP WORSE OFF THAN BEFORE AND THE CYCLE GOES ON AND ON UNTIL SHE'S SO SCREWED UP ANY GUY WITH A DEEP VOICE AND SINCERE EYES CAN WALK RIGHT UP AND HAVE HER!
SO YOU DO.
HEY, I'M NOT JUST ANY GUY, OKAY?! I LOVE FRANCINE AND I'M GOING TO MARRY HER! AND I DON'T NEED YOUR PERMISSION TO DO IT!
I DON'T LIVE IN THE PAST AND I'M NOT GOING TO HOLD FRANCINE ACCOUNTABLE FOR HERS!
FURTHERMORE, I'M NOT GOING TO STAND HERE AND BE CATEGORIZED BY A WOMAN WITH ISSUES WHO DOESN'T KNOW ME!

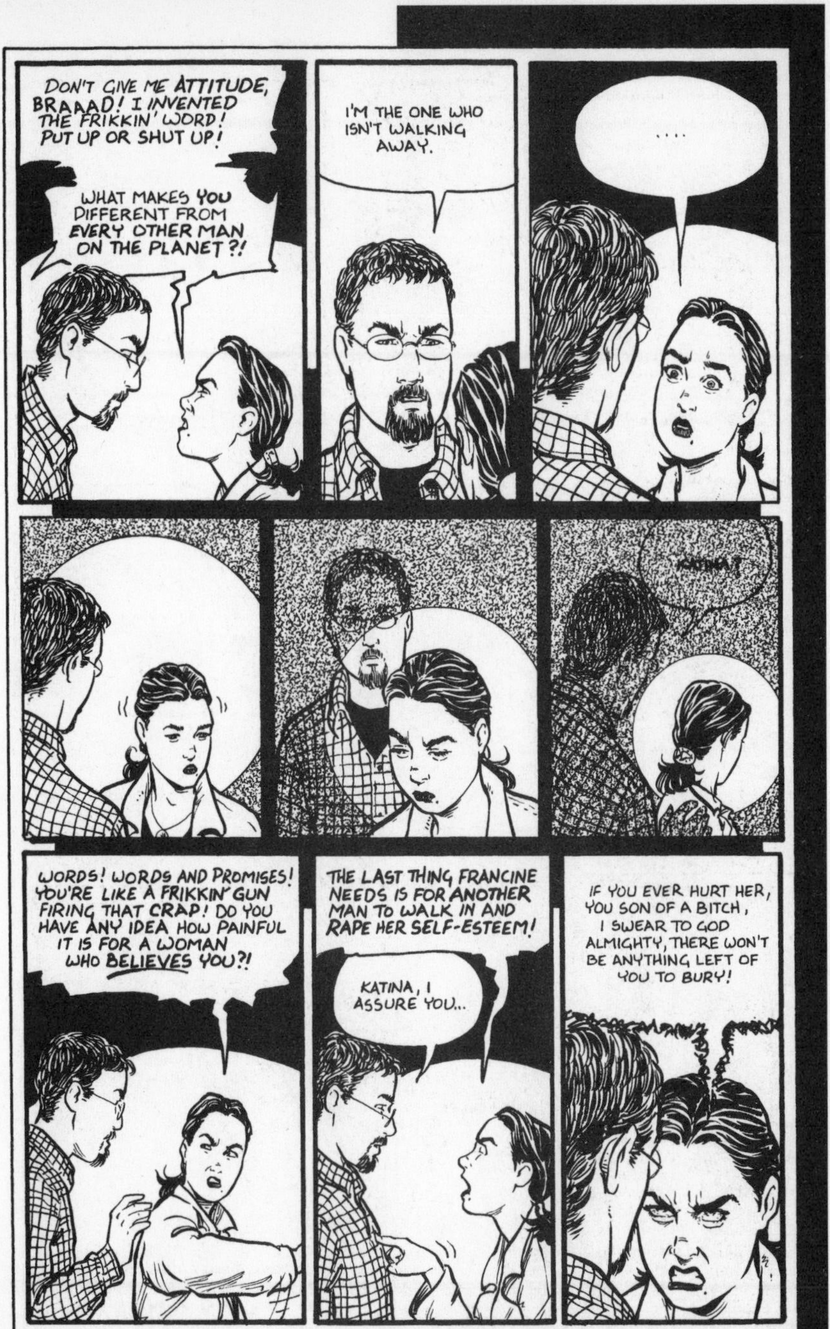
DON'T GIVE ME ATTITUDE, BRAAAD! I INVENTED THE FRIKKIN' WORD! PUT UP OR SHUT UP!
WHAT MAKES YOU DIFFERENT FROM EVERY OTHER MAN ON THE PLANET?!
I'M THE ONE WHO ISN'T WALKING AWAY.
....
KATINA?
WORDS! WORDS AND PROMISES! YOU'RE LIKE A FRIKKIN' GUN FIRING THAT CRAP! DO YOU HAVE ANY IDEA HOW PAINFUL IT IS FOR A WOMAN WHO BELIEVES YOU?!
THE LAST THING FRANCINE NEEDS IS FOR ANOTHER MAN TO WALK IN AND RAPE HER SELF-ESTEEM!
KATINA, I ASSURE YOU..
IF YOU EVER HURT HER, YOU SON OF A BITCH, I SWEAR TO GOD ALMIGHTY, THERE WON'T BE ANYTHING LEFT OF YOU TO BURY!

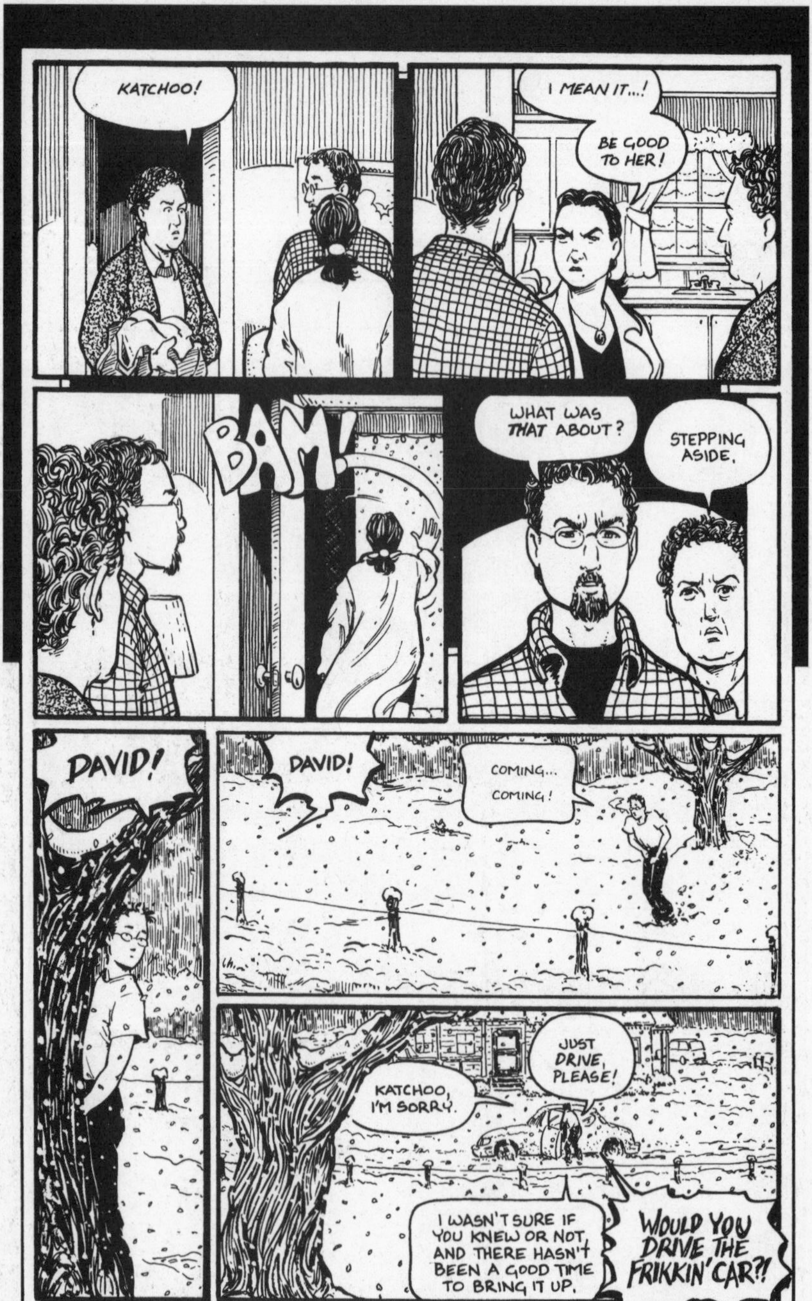
KATCHOO!
I MEAN IT...!
BE GOOD TO HER!
BAM!
WHAT WAS THAT ABOUT?
STEPPING ASIDE.
DAVID!
DAVID!
COMING... COMING!
KATCHOO, I'M SORRY.
JUST DRIVE, PLEASE!
I WASN'T SURE IF YOU KNEW OR NOT, AND THERE HASN'T BEEN A GOOD TIME TO BRING IT UP.
WOULD YOU DRIVE THE FRIKKIN' CAR?!

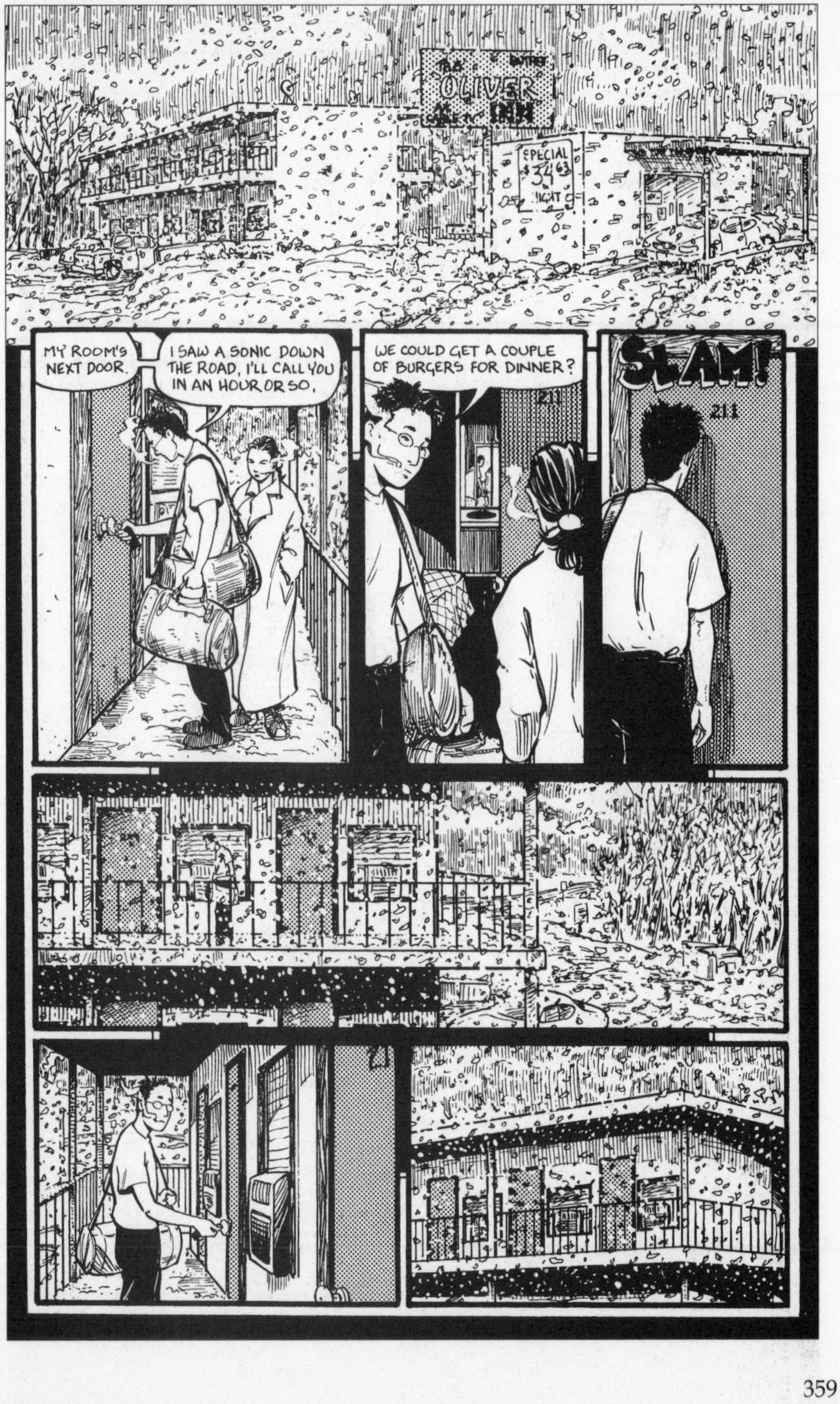
OLIVER
INN
SPECIAL
MY ROOM'S NEXT DOOR.
I SAW A SONIC DOWN THE ROAD, I'LL CALL YOU IN AN HOUR OR SO.
WE COULD GET A COUPLE OF BURGERS FOR DINNER?
211
SLAM!
211

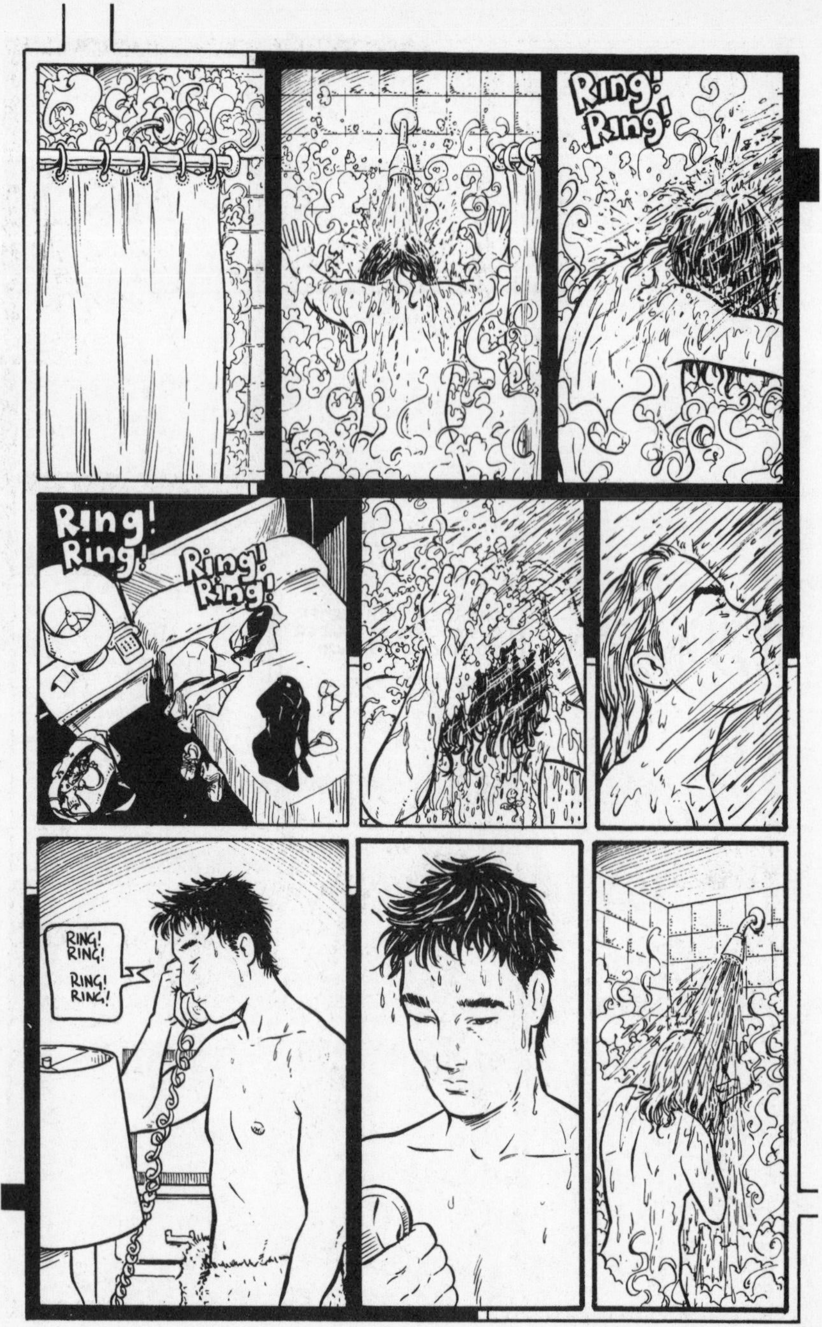
Ring! Ring!
Ring! Ring!
Ring! Ring!
RING! RING!
RING! RING!

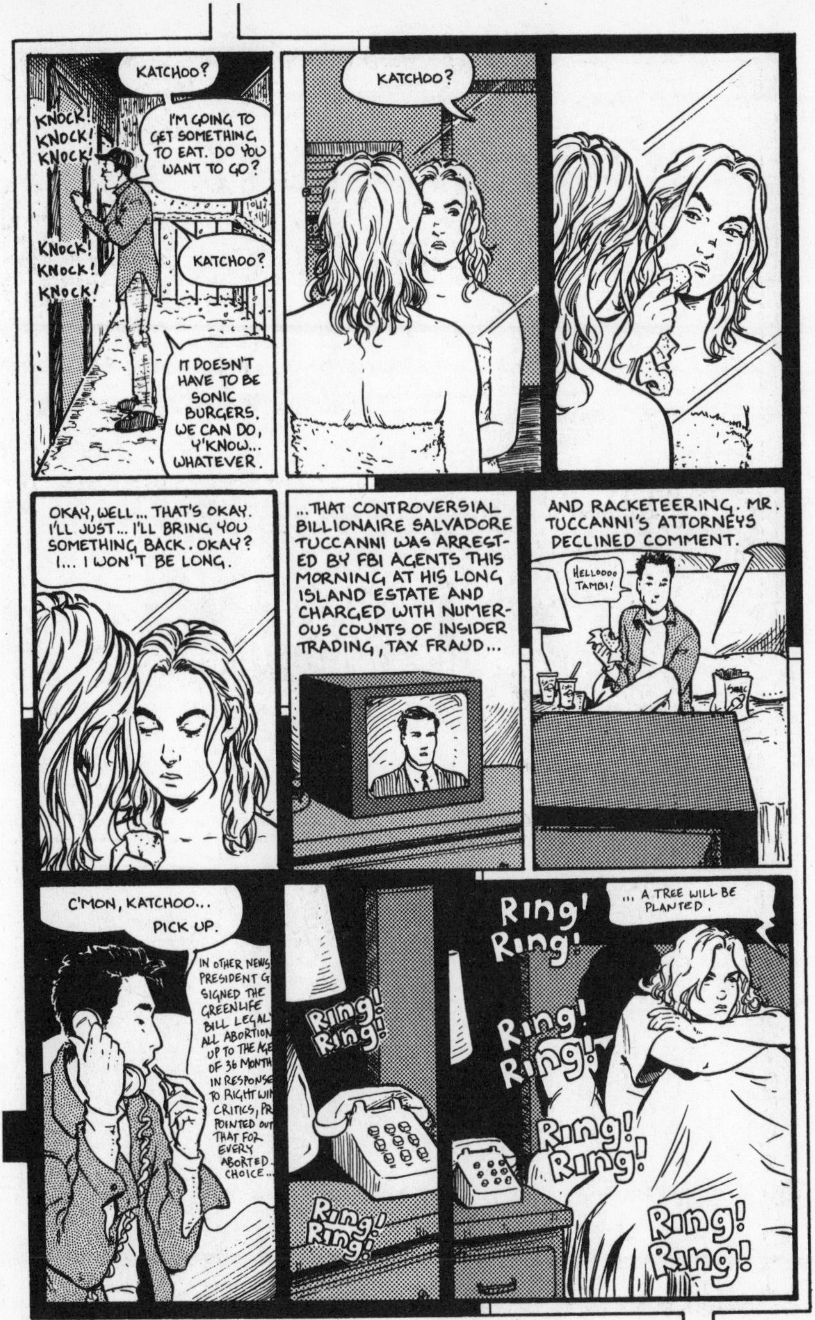
KATCHOO?
KNOCK! KNOCK! KNOCK!
I'M GOING TO GET SOMETHING TO EAT. DO YOU WANT TO GO?
KNOCK! KNOCK! KNOCK!
KATCHOO?
IT DOESN'T HAVE TO BE SONIC BURGERS. WE CAN DO, Y'KNOW... WHATEVER.
KATCHOO?
OKAY, WELL... THAT'S OKAY. I'LL JUST... I'LL BRING YOU SOMETHING BACK. OKAY? I... I WON'T BE LONG.
...THAT CONTROVERSIAL BILLIONAIRE SALVADORE TUCCANNI WAS ARRESTED BY FBI AGENTS THIS MORNING AT HIS LONG ISLAND ESTATE AND CHARGED WITH NUMEROUS COUNTS OF INSIDER TRADING, TAX FRAUD...
AND RACKETEERING. MR. TUCCANNI'S ATTORNEYS DECLINED COMMENT.
HELLOOOO TAMBI!
C'MON, KATCHOO... PICK UP.
IN OTHER NEWS PRESIDENT G SIGNED THE GREENLIFE BILL LEGAL ALL ABORTION UP TO THE AGE OF 36 MONTH IN RESPONSE TO RIGHT WI CRITICS, PR POINTED OUT THAT FOR EVERY ABORTED... CHOICE...
Ring! Ring!
Ring! Ring!
Ring! Ring!
... A TREE WILL BE PLANTED.
Ring! Ring!
Ring! Ring!
Ring! Ring!
Ring! Ring!

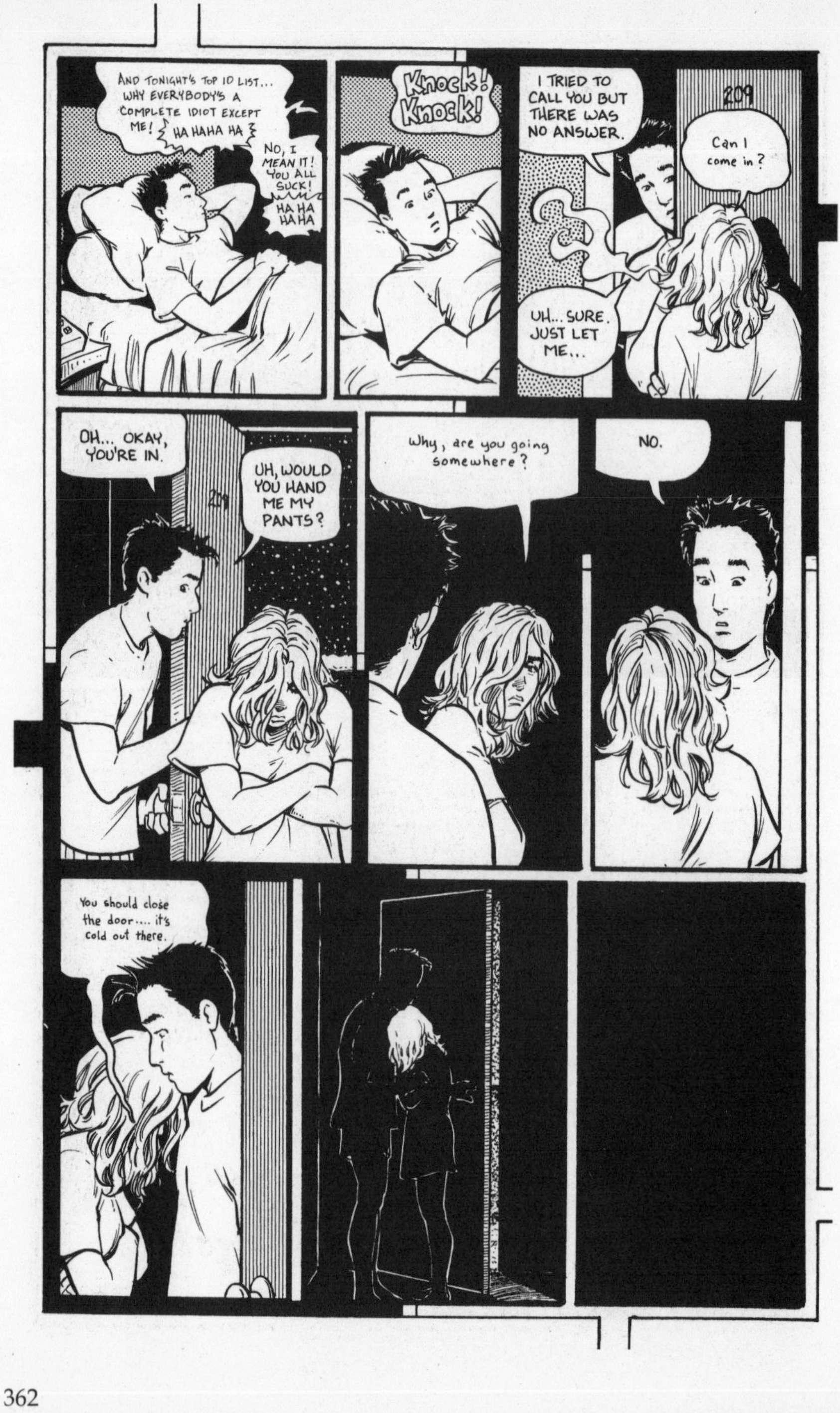
AND TONIGHT'S TOP 10 LIST... WHY EVERYBODY'S A COMPLETE IDIOT EXCEPT ME! HA HAHA HA
NO, I MEAN IT! YOU ALL SUCK! HA HA HAHA
Knock! Knock!
I TRIED TO CALL YOU BUT THERE WAS NO ANSWER.
209
Can I come in?
UH... SURE. JUST LET ME...
OH... OKAY, YOU'RE IN.
UH, WOULD YOU HAND ME MY PANTS?
Why, are you going somewhere?
NO.
You should close the door.... it's cold out there.

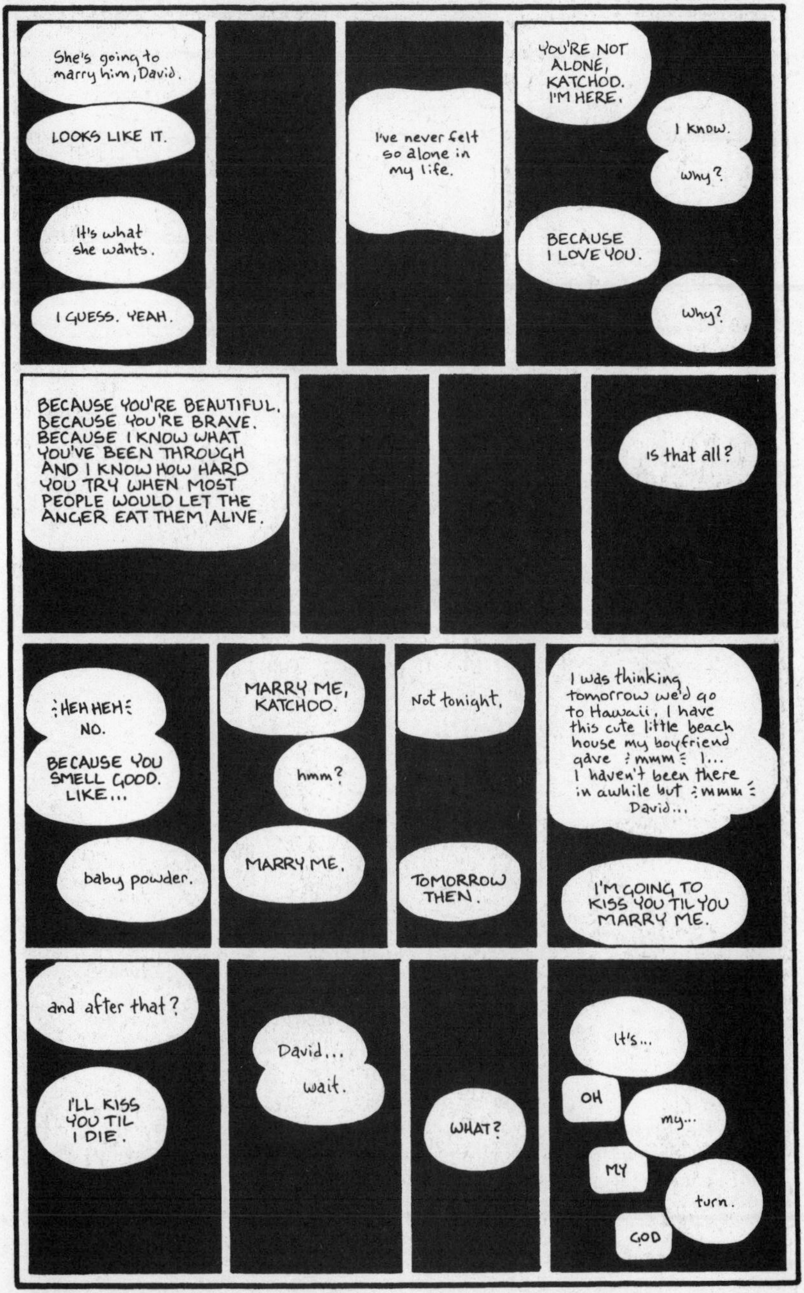

She's going to marry him, David.
LOOKS LIKE IT.
It's what she wants.
I GUESS. YEAH.
I've never felt so alone in my life.
YOU'RE NOT ALONE, KATCHOO. I'M HERE.
I know.
why?
BECAUSE I LOVE YOU.
Why?
BECAUSE YOU'RE BEAUTIFUL. BECAUSE YOU'RE BRAVE. BECAUSE I KNOW WHAT YOU'VE BEEN THROUGH AND I KNOW HOW HARD YOU TRY WHEN MOST PEOPLE WOULD LET THE ANGER EAT THEM ALIVE.
is that all?
:HEH HEH: NO.
BECAUSE YOU SMELL GOOD. LIKE...
baby powder.
MARRY ME, KATCHOO.
hmm?
MARRY ME.
Not tonight.
TOMORROW THEN.
I was thinking tomorrow we'd go to Hawaii. I have this cute little beach house my boyfriend gave :mmm: I... I haven't been there in awhile but :mmm: David...
I'M GOING TO KISS YOU TIL YOU MARRY ME.
and after that?
I'LL KISS YOU TIL I DIE.
David... wait.
WHAT?
It's...
OH
my...
MY
turn.
GOD

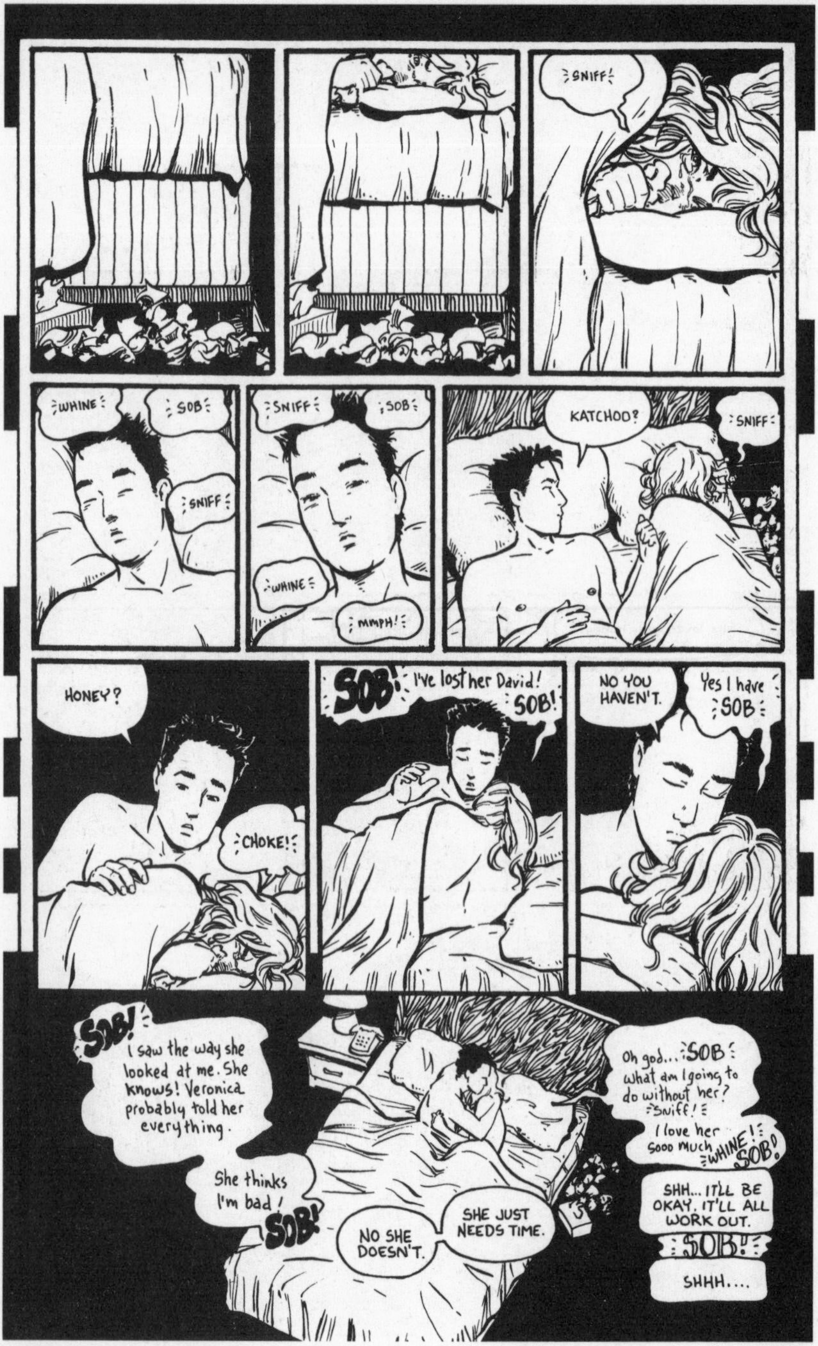
SNIFF
WHINE
SOB
SNIFF
SNIFF
SOB
WHINE
MMPH!
KATCHOO?
SNIFF
HONEY?
CHOKE!
SOB! I've lost her David! SOB!
NO YOU HAVEN'T.
Yes I have SOB
SOB! I saw the way she looked at me. She knows! Veronica probably told her everything.
She thinks I'm bad! SOB!
NO SHE DOESN'T.
SHE JUST NEEDS TIME.
Oh god... SOB what am I going to do without her? SNIFF! I love her sooo much WHINE! SOB!
SHH... IT'LL BE OKAY. IT'LL ALL WORK OUT.
SOB!
SHHH....

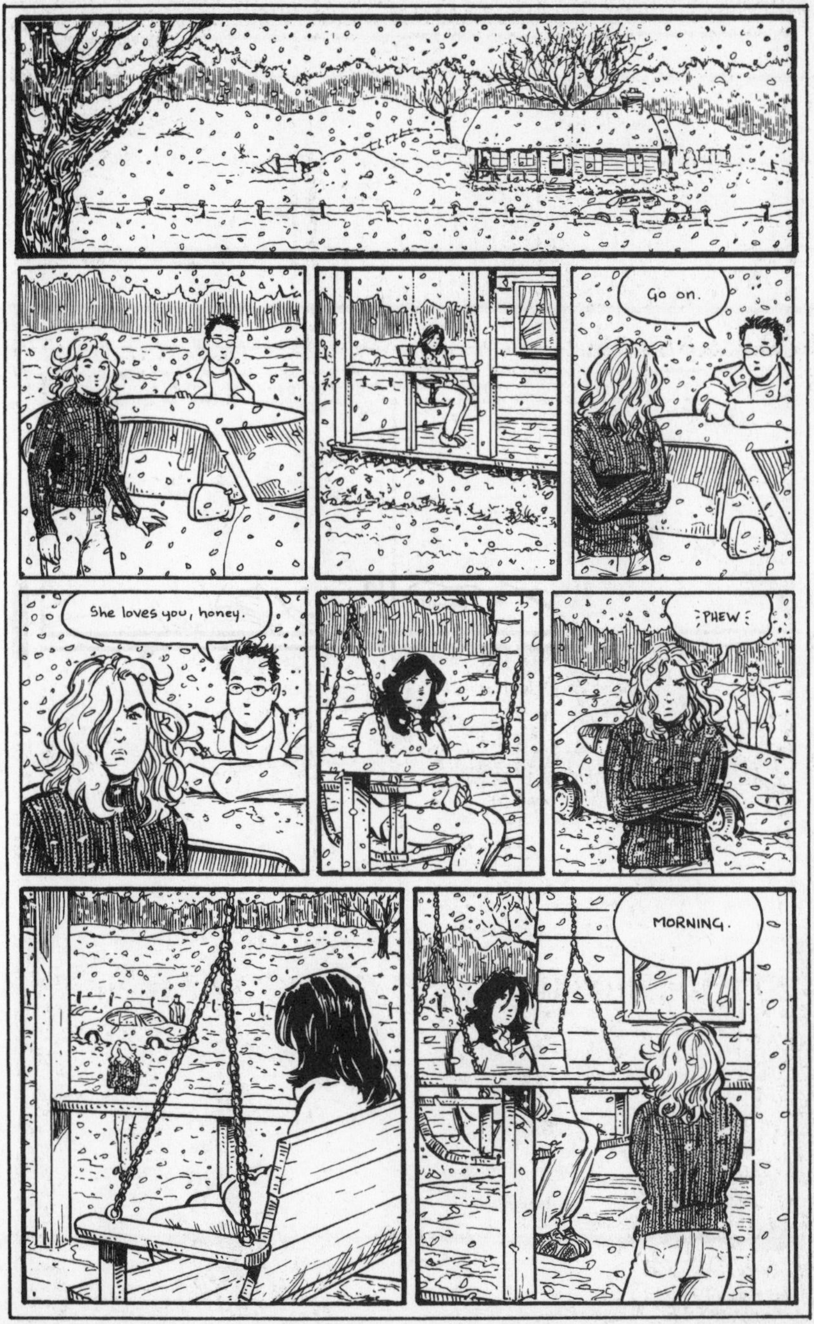
Go on.
She loves you, honey.
PHEW
MORNING.

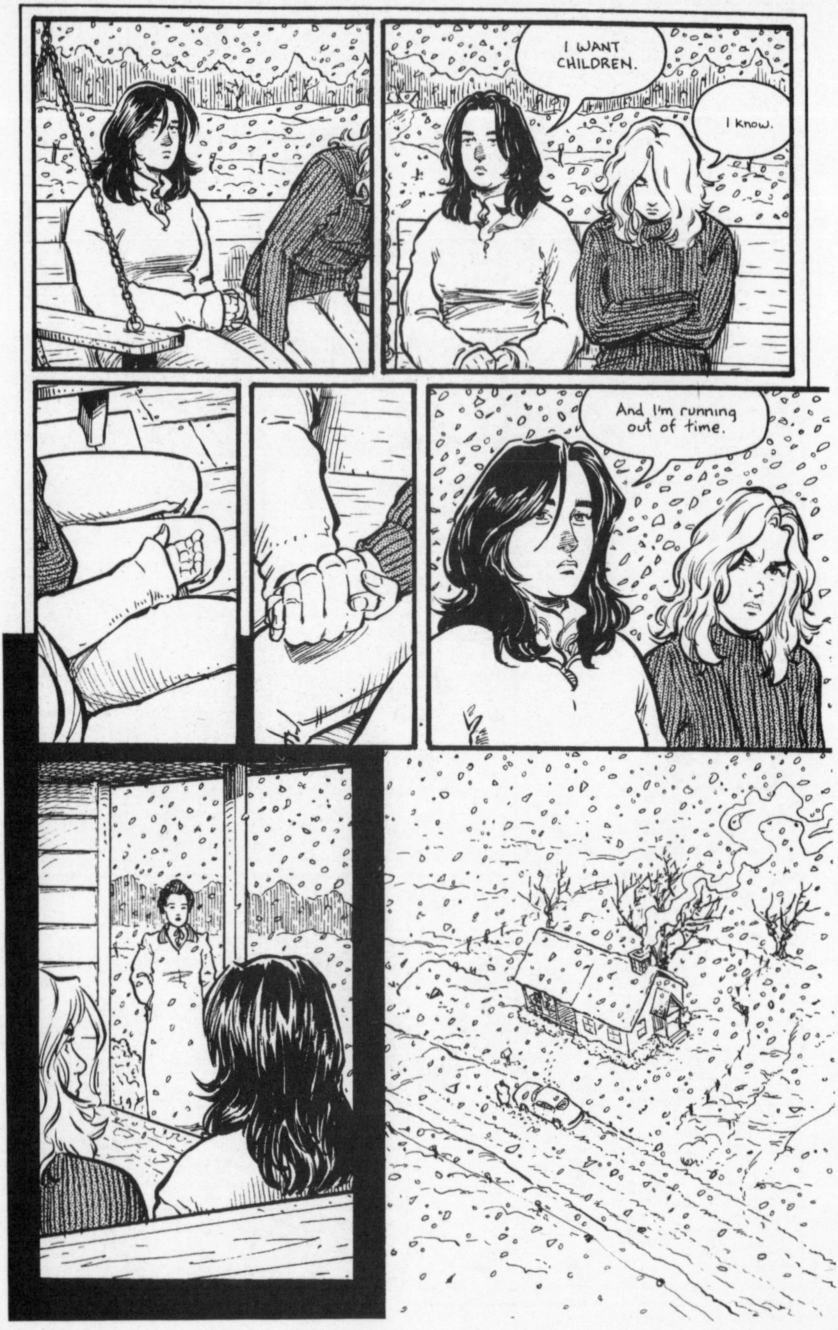
I WANT CHILDREN.
I know.
And I'm running out of time.

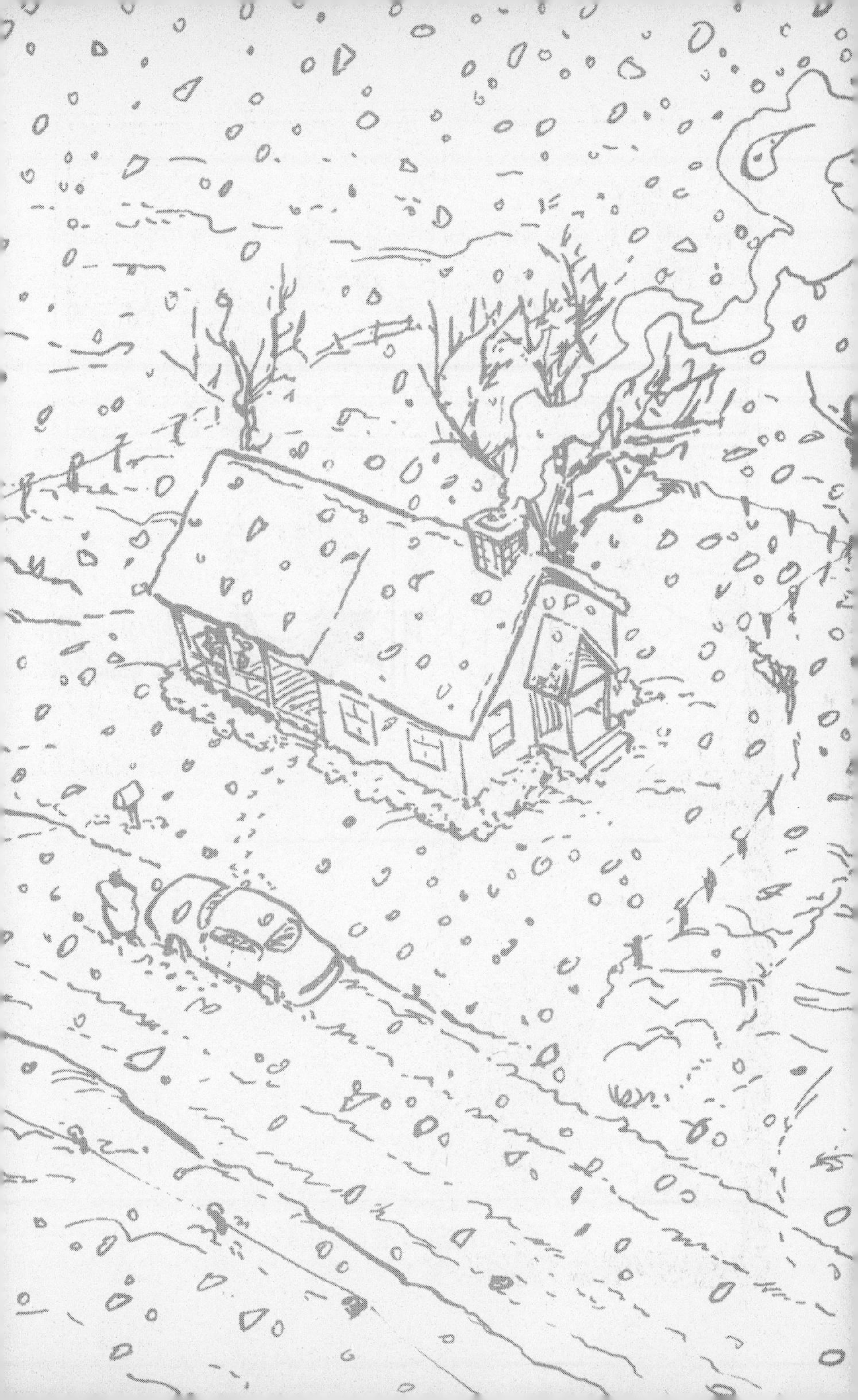

www.StrangersInParadise.com